The World's Largest Wetlands
Ecology and Conservation

During the past century, humans have destroyed approximately 50 percent of the world's wetlands. As wetlands shrink in area, their important functions decline too: there is reduced carbon storage, lower biological diversity, lower fish production, less available water during drought, higher flood levels in spring, and higher risk of water pollution. The world's largest wetlands have not been described, ranked, and compared previously. For the first time, an international team of scholars shares its understanding of the status, ecological dynamics, functions, and conservation needs of the world's largest wetlands.

LAUCHLAN H. FRASER was recently appointed the Canada Research Chair in Community and Ecosystem Ecology at Thompson Rivers University. He has published over 25 scholarly papers and is on the editorial boards of *Applied Vegetation Science* and the *Ohio Journal of Science*. Dr. Fraser's research group examines the processes that organize plant communities and the functional consequences of different emergent patterns on ecosystem functions. His laboratory focuses on ecosystems that are among those most affected by anthropogenic and natural disturbances, namely freshwater wetlands and temperate grasslands.

PAUL A. KEDDY holds the Edward G. Schlieder Endowed Chair for Environmental Studies. Over his career Dr. Keddy has published more than a hundred scholarly papers on plant ecology and wetlands, as well as serving organizations including The National Science Foundation (NSF), The Natural Sciences and Engineering Research Council (NSERC), the World Wide Fund for Nature, and The Nature Conservancy. He has been recognized by the Institute for Scientific Information as a Highly Cited Researcher in the field of Ecology and the Environment. His current research examines the environmental factors that control wetlands, and how these factors can be manipulated to maintain and restore biological diversity.

The World's Largest Wetlands

Ecology and Conservation

Edited by
LAUCHLAN H. FRASER
AND PAUL A. KEDDY

LIBRARY
FRANKLIN PIERCE UNIVERSITY
RINDGE, NH 03461

CAMBRIDGE
UNIVERSITY PRESS

CAMBRIDGE UNIVERSITY PRESS
Cambridge, New York, Melbourne, Madrid, Cape Town, Singapore, São Paulo, Delhi

Cambridge University Press
The Edinburgh Building, Cambridge CB2 8RU, UK

Published in the United States of America by Cambridge University Press, New York

www.cambridge.org
Information on this title: www.cambridge.org/9780521111362

© Cambridge University Press 2005

This publication is in copyright. Subject to statutory exception
and to the provisions of relevant collective licensing agreements,
no reproduction of any part may take place without the written
permission of Cambridge University Press.

First published 2005
This digitally printed version 2009

A catalogue record for this publication is available from the British Library

ISBN 978-0-521-83404-9 hardback
ISBN 978-0-521-11136-2 paperback

QH
541.5
.M3
W67
2005

Cambridge University Press has no responsibility for the persistence or accuracy of
URLs for external or third-party Internet websites referred to in this publication, and
does not guarantee that any content on such websites is, or will remain, accurate or
appropriate.

Contents

v

Contributors

Kenneth F. Abraham
Ontario Ministry of Naturnal Resources, Wildlife Research and Development Section, 300 Water Street, 3rd Floor North, Peterborough, Ontario, Canada K9J 8M5

Cleber J. R. Alho
UNIDERP (Universidade para o Desenvolvimento do Estado e para a Região do Pantanal), Campo Grande, MS, Brasil

Osman Ali
Institute of Environmental Studies, University of Khartoum, P. O. Box 321, Sudan

Mary T. K. Arroyo
Millennium Center for Advanced Studies in Ecology and Research on Biodiversity, Facultad de Ciencias, Universidad de Chile, Casilla 653, Santiago, Chile

Manuel Arroyo-Kalin
Department of Archaeology, University of Cambridge, Downing Street, Cambridge, CB2 3DZ, UK

Daniel Campbell
Department of Biological Sciences, Southeastern Louisiana University, Hammond, LA 70402, USA

Lauchlan H. Fraser
Department of Natural Resource Sciences, Thompson Rivers University, Kamloops, British Columbia, Canada V2C 5N3

James G. Gosselink
Department of Biological Sciences, Louisiana State University, Baton Rouge, LA 70803, USA

Linda A. Halsey
Department of Biological Sciences, University of Alberta, Edmonton, AB, Canada, T6G 2E9

Suzanne S. Hoeppner
Department of Biological Sciences, Southeastern Louisiana University, Hammond, LA 70402, USA

Wolfgang J. Junk
Max-Planck-Institute for Limnology, PB 165, 24306 Plön, Germany

Cathy J. Keddy
Ecologist, Ponchatoula, LA, USA

Paul A. Keddy
Department of Biological Sciences, Southeastern Louisiana University, Hammond, LA 70402, USA

Jacques Lemoalle
IRD, Montpellier, France

Maritza Mihoc
Departamento de Botánica, Facultad de Ciencias Naturales y Oceanográficas, Universidad de Concepción, Casilla 160-C, Concepción, Chile

Barbara J. Nicholson
Department of Biology, Central Connecticut State University, New Britain, CT 06050, USA

Maria T. F. Piedade
Instituto Nacional de Pesquisas da Amazonia (INPA), PB 478, 69.011-970 Manaus, AM, Brazil.

Patricio Pliscoff
Millennium Center for Advanced Studies in Ecology & Research on Biodiversity, Facultad de Ciencias, Universidad de Chile, Casilla 653, Santiago, Chile

Gary P. Shaffer
Department of Biological Sciences, Southeastern Louisiana University, Hammond, LA 70402, USA

Ayzik I. Solomeshch
Institute of Biology Ufa Scientific Center, Russian Academy of Science, 450054, October av. 69, Ufa, Russia

Irina Springuel
South Valley University, Aswan, 81528, Egypt

Arnold G. van der Valk
Department of Botany, Iowa State University, Ames, Iowa 50011, USA

Dale H. Vitt
Department of Plant Biology, Southern Illinois University, Carbondale, IL 62901–6509, USA

Preface

From the vast deltas of the Amazon and Volga, to the bogs of the arctic tundra, and the mosaic prairie potholes of North America, wetlands come in all shapes and sizes. Wetlands are the fragile interface between land and water. Human civilization has been inextricably linked to wetlands because of their economic and aesthetic value. Only recently has it been shown that wetlands perform very important functions in our environment. They have been described as "the kidneys of the landscape" because of their effect on hydrological and chemical cycles, and because they receive downstream wastes from both natural and human sources. They have been found to cleanse polluted waters, prevent floods, protect shorelines, and recharge groundwater aquifers. Wetlands are also referred to as "biological supermarkets" because of the numbers of species and the abundance of biomass they support. They play major roles in the landscape by providing habitat for a wide variety of flora and fauna. These generalizations apply whether one is describing the bottomland hardwoods of the Mississippi River valley, the Pantanal in South America, or the Sudd wetlands of the Upper Nile in Africa.

Approximately 50% of the world's wetlands have been lost. No country is isolated from the impacts of human overpopulation. Therefore we took a global perspective to ensure that the largest wetlands are understood and wisely managed. Little is known about some of the largest wetlands. The research that has been done is fragmented and published (if at all) in obscure journals. A global overview has never been presented in systematic and complete manner.

We brought together leading scientists from around the world to explore and discuss the world's largest wetlands in Quebec City, Canada at INTECOL 2000, The International Association of Ecology 6th International Wetland Symposium. This was not simply a descriptive assignment for each participant; the emphasis was on reviewing scientifically explored patterns and processes of each of the major wetlands of the world. We are most thankful to the contributors to this book who accepted our challenge and boldly wrote about these large wetlands.

Funding from a US Department of Agriculture, Cooperative State Research, Education, and Extension Service grant helped with the considerable costs associated with travel and accommodation for the INTECOL 2000 conference. The Society of Wetland Scientists and The Natural Sciences and Engineering Research Council of Canada also contributed financially to our first international symposium. We have many friends and colleagues to thank for their assistance during the development of this project. Michaelyn Broussard, Dan Campbell, and Cathy Keddy handled some of the administrative logistics. Cameron Carlyle, Larry Feinstein, Jason Karnezis, Tara Miletti, and Christian Picard read earlier drafts of the chapters for clarity. Clayton Rubec and Gene Turner helped organize the symposium in Quebec City. Ward Cooper, Alan Crowden, and Clare Georgy from Cambridge University Press provided much-appreciated assistance. We are very grateful to Mandy Kingsmill, our copy-editor, for her careful attention to detail.

1

Introduction: big is beautiful

P. A. KEDDY
Southeastern Louisiana University

L. H. FRASER
Thompson Rivers University

This book actually requires no introduction. The title says it all. You may there-fore safely turn to the chapters dealing with each wetland. If you are curious about the tale behind the title, and wish to read further here, the tale is largely the search for scientific and conservation priorities. To succeed at scientific research or conservation action, clear priorities must be set – there are always vastly more scientific questions, and vastly more conservation problems, than humans can solve. One way to prioritize is by size: if we can identify the big scientific problems or the big conservation issues, we can address them first. This may appear self-evident, but often it seems that it is not.

No two editors can restructure conservation bureaucracies or scientific com-munities. However, a clear snapshot of the state of global wetlands, could, we believe, have such an effect. By highlighting all the world's largest wetlands in one book – wetlands that range across ecosystem types, international boundaries, and styles of research – we aspire to nudge all areas of wetland ecology and con-servation biology back towards a common view and a common purpose. This pur-pose would include documenting the patterns in wetlands, unraveling the mech-anisms behind these patterns, describing functions that extend beyond the bor-ders of wetlands, predicting future consequences of human manipulation, and ensuring that the world's wetlands are protected and managed within a global context.

When we held our first symposium in Quebec City in 2000 (with start-up funds courtesy of the US Department of Agriculture (USDA) and the Society of Wetland Scientists), there was standing room only, suggesting that our fellow

The World's Largest Wetlands: Ecology and Conservation, eds. L. H. Fraser and P. A. Keddy.
Published by Cambridge University Press. © Cambridge University Press 2005.

professionals recognized the need for such an overview. Five years later, there is this book. We hope that it will further encourage and inspire those individuals who share our view, and that it will prove useful in guiding global conservation activities. Large wetlands deserve equivalent global status with frontier forests (Bryant *et al.* 1997) and biodiversity hotspots (Myers 1988, Myers *et al.* 2000).

This volume is not intended to be a book on the principles of wetland ecology. Such books already exist. They provide the context for this book on large wetlands. Some existing books focus on general principles, and explore how these recur in different types of wetlands (Keddy 2000). Some focus on a specified region, like North America, and address the major wetland types in turn (Mitsch & Gosselink 2000). Some global compendia strive for comprehensiveness (Whigham *et al.* 1992). Other books use a single issue, such as function, as a theme for exploring many habitats, including wetlands (de Groot 1992). All of these approaches have value. We do not intend to repeat them. Nor will we use this introduction to review wetland ecology; that is the purpose of the preceding books. In this volume we want to focus on size, function, and conservation significance.

Why size matters

Why does size matter? Schumacher (1973) entitled his now classic book *Small is Beautiful*. He was examining economic development, "economics as if people mattered." In the realm of ecology, we beg to differ with Schumacher's title; here *large* is beautiful. Most wetland functions (Table 1.1) increase with area. Some, such as oxygen production or fish production (Fig. 1.1), may be directly proportional to area. Another, such as carbon sequestration, will be a function of area times depth. Other functions have more-complex relationships – species richness ("biodiversity") generally increases with area as $c(area)^z$ where z is an exponent usually less than 3.0 and c is a constant (Fig. 1.2). Whatever the research and conservation goal, be it basic understanding of global carbon cycles or the design of global nature reserve systems, area therefore demands attention. Functions will then further vary locally with climate, biogeographic realm, topographic heterogeneity, substrate type, and season.

A provisional list of the world's largest wetlands was compiled in the late 1990s and was published in Keddy (2000). Then, as now, we have accepted credibly published estimates of area, recognizing that such published estimates include different kinds of assumptions, techniques, and accuracy. Although there is room for debate about what kinds of plant communities belong in the category of wetland, we suspect that problems of definition were not a serious source of error,

Table 1.1 *Functions that may be performed by natural environments including wetlands (from de Groot 1992).*

Regulation functions

1. Protection against harmful cosmic influences
2. Regulation of the local and global energy balance
3. Regulation of the chemical composition of the atmosphere
4. Regulation of the chemical composition of the oceans
5. Regulation of the local and global climate (including the hydrological cycle)
6. Regulation of runoff and flood prevention (watershed protection)
7. Water-catchment and groundwater recharge
8. Prevention of soil erosion and sediment control
9. Formation of topsoil and maintenance of soil fertility
10. Fixation of solar energy and biomass production
11. Storage and recycling of organic matter
12. Storage and recycling of nutrients
13. Storage and recycling of human waste
14. Regulation of biological control mechanisms
15. Maintenance of migration and nursery habitats
16. Maintenance of biological (and genetic) diversity

Carrier functions

Providing space and a suitable substrate for:

1. Human habitation and (indigenous) settlements
2. Cultivation (crop growing, animal husbandry, aquaculture)
3. Energy conversion
4. Recreation and tourism
5. Nature protection

Production functions

1. Oxygen
2. Water (for drinking, irrigation, industry, etc.)
3. Food and nutritious drinks
4. Genetic resources
5. Medicinal resources
6. Raw materials for clothing and household fabrics
7. Raw materials for building, construction, and industrial use
8. Biochemicals (other than fuel and medicines)
9. Fuel and energy
10. Fodder and fertilizer
11. Ornamental resources

Information functions

1. Aesthetic information
2. Spiritual and religious information
3. Historic information (heritage value)
4. Cultural and artistic inspiration
5. Scientific and educational information

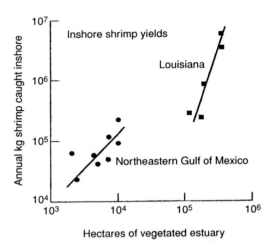

Figure 1.1 There is a linear relationship between the area of wetland in an estuary and the annual catch of inshore shrimp (from Turner 1977).

since there is general agreement among wetland ecologists as to what comprises wetlands (Keddy 2000, Mitsch & Gosselink 2000). One source of uncertainty is estimates of area in wetlands having networks of seasonally flooded channels (such as the Amazon) or having sets of isolated basins (such as the North American prairie potholes). A further difficulty might arise from inconsistencies in the inclusion of areas with heavy human disturbance, such as the vast areas of wetland protected by levees and converted to agriculture in the Mississippi River basin. Some authors may have left out heavily developed or urbanized areas along the borders of wetlands. We neither the resources nor the inclination to impose one standard method upon all participants; given the scale at which we are operating, and other possible sources of error, we suspect that such differences in opinion and methodology would not have a major impact upon the ranking used here. Such issues might, however, become more of a concern at small scales (that is wetlands under 50 000 km^2) where there are many more candidates to evaluate and relatively smaller differences among them. As with all scientific estimates, our estimates of area are certainly provisional and will be subject to eventual revision as better methodologies aries. Table 1.2 and Fig. 1.3 give the latest picture constructed from data in this book.

Two wetlands are in excess of 1 million km^2 in extent: the West Siberian Lowland and the Amazon basin. The West Siberian Lowland is a vast peatland that probably plays a significant role in regulating global climate, both in carbon sequestration and in controlling the flows of northern rivers into the Arctic Ocean. The Amazon River floodplain is a vast alluvial wetland with water-level fluctuations that regularly exceed 5 m in amplitude each year. This floodplain

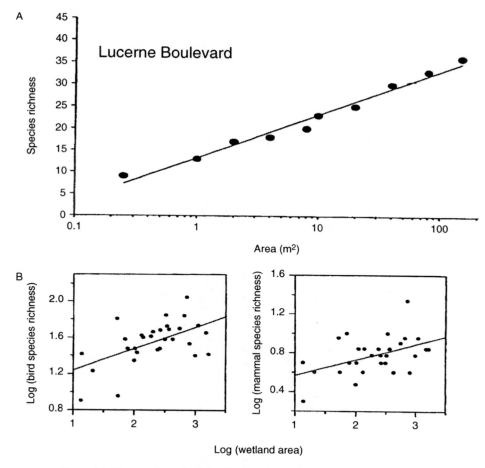

Figure 1.2 The number of species in a habitat increases with area. At the small scale, less than a hectare (A), there is a linear relationship between the number of plant species and log wetland area (Weiher 1999). At the larger scale, over hundreds of hectares (B), the log of the number species increases linearly with the log of area (Findlay & Houlahan 1997).

is one of the world's major repositories of biological diversity, particularly for fish and trees. Given the volume of sediment transported by the river, the delta may also be an important locale for carbon sequestration. These two wetlands comprise Chapters 2 and 3 of this book.

Of the remaining wetlands, seven are in the order of 100 000 to 400 000 km². (Hudson Bay Lowland, Congo River basin, Mackenzie River basin, Pantanal, Mississippi River basin, River Nile basin, Lake Chad basin). The most-heavily

Table 1.2 *The world's largest wetlands (areas rounded to the nearest 1 000 km^2).*

Rank	Continent	Wetland	Description	Area (km^2)	Source
1	Eurasia	West Siberian Lowland	Bogs, mires fens	2 745 000	Solomeshch, Chapter 2
2	South America	Amazon River basin	Floodplain forest and savanna, marshes, mangrove	1 738 000	Junk and Piedade, Chapter 3
3	North America	Hudson Bay Lowland	Bogs, fens, swamps, marshes	374 000	Abraham and Keddy, Chapter 4
4	Africa	Congo River basin	Swamps, riverine forest, wet prairie	189 000	Campbell, Chapter 5
5	North America	Mackenzie River basin	Bogs, fens, swamps, marshes	166 000	Vitt et al., Chapter 6
6	South America	Pantanal	Savannas, grasslands, riverine forest	138 000	Alho, Chapter 7
7	North America	Mississippi River basin	Bottomland hardwood forest, swamps, marshes	108 000	Shaffer et al., Chapter 8
8	Africa	Lake Chad basin	Grass and shrub savanna, marshes	106 000	Lemoalle, Chapter 9
9	Africa	River Nile basin	Swamps, marshes	92 000	Springuel and Ali, Chapter 10
10	North America	Prairie potholes	Marshes, meadows	63 000	van der Valk, Chapter 11
11	South America	Magellanic moorland	Bogs	44 000	Arroyo et al., Chapter 12

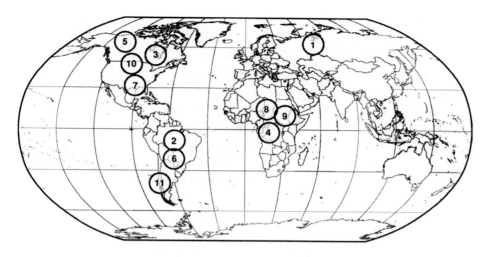

1	West Siberian Lowland	7	Mississippi River basin
2	Amazon River basin	8	Lake Chad basin
3	Hudson Bay Lowland	9	River Nile basin
4	Congo River basin	10	Prairie potholes
5	Mackenzie River basin	11	Magellanic moorland
6	Pantanal		

Figure 1.3 Locations of the world's largest wetlands. The numbers correspond to Table 1.2.

disturbed is probably the Mississippi River where >90% of the floodplain has been deforested and/or obstructed by levees; some might argue that until such areas are restored to wetland, they should be removed from the list. In Chapter 8 on the Mississippi, the prospects for restoration receive particular emphasis. The least well understood of these large wetlands appears to be the Congo River basin (Chapter 5), with most literature (except satellite reconnaissance) now several decades old and much of it inaccessible to those who cannot read French.

At smaller sizes, that is of the order of $50\,000\,km^2$, increasingly larger numbers of wetlands are candidates for consideration. We have included here the North American prairie potholes and the Magellanic moorland complex. We have excluded wetlands on the island of New Guinea (eastern Indonesia and Papua New Guinea) for lack of adequate data, although the maps of active alluvial plains in eastern Indonesia (Löffler 1982) and a map of poorly drained alluvial soils (Wood 1982) suggest that this area deserves further evaluation. Currently, the World Wild Fund for Nature (Olsen *et al.* 2001; World Wide Fund for Nature 2001) classifies this area as "Southern New Guinea freshwater swamp forests," with an area of $99\,900\,km^2$; taking an estimated half of this as wetland would yield an area of $50\,000\,km^2$.

One other big problem in this exercise was psychological rather than technical – the difficulty in finding people willing to contribute, particularly for areas in equatorial Africa and southeast Asia. We hope that this volume will encourage more prioritization for conservation planning for areas including the Congo and New Guinea. We suspect that part of our problem arose from the increasing emphasis upon reductionism in biology today, coupled – in ecology – with replacement of remaining field biologists by laboratory biologists. This may not only have reduced the pool of candidates from whom we could solicit contributions, but also seemed to have made some individuals, even those with established funding, unwilling to take the risk of presuming knowledge of any area larger than their own study sites. If anyone reading this book feels personally left out, or believes that we missed an important area, our apologies – we strongly encourage you to publish a scientific paper in an international journal using a similar format. Your contribution can then easily be included within future global compendia, maybe even within a future edition of this book. We encourage the publication of such work in international journals, because too often we found fine compendia that were out of print and/or otherwise inaccessible; in at least one case, the author had retired and had no forwarding address. Publications in scientific journals, in contrast, will always be available in most libraries.

We are left with the impression that too much activity in wetland conservation occurs at small scales, and that it is geographically localized within the densely industrialized areas of Western Europe and the eastern United States. The publications on the wetlands in the Netherlands, for example, vastly exceed those addressing the Congo or New Guinea. This was understandable back in the days of horse-drawn carriages and sailing ships. In the new global village – linked by airplanes, satellites, and computer networks – such imbalances are inexcusable. We hope that our book will help restore some balance and focus further attention upon large wetlands, their ecological functions, and their conservation.

Acknowledgements

We thank the US Department of Agriculture, the Society of Wetland Scientists, and The Natural Sciences and Engineering Research Council of Canada for contributing financially to our first international symposium. We also gratefully acknowledge the contributors to this book who have been willing to extend themselves to boldly write about large areas of wetlands. Michaelyn Broussard, Dan Campbell, Alan Crowden, Cathy Keddy, Clayton Rubec, and Gene Turner have further assisted us with the project at various stages in its development. All the contributors have gracefully handled reviews, requests for revisions, and changing deadlines. Finally, there are the hundreds of scientists and explorers, dating at least back to Wallace, who have explored isolated regions of the world, risking their lives and their health to provide the data that our contributors have been able to use.

References

Aselman, I. and Crutzen, P. J. (1989). Global distribution of natural freshwater wetlands and rice paddies, their net primary productivity, seasonality and possible methane emissions. *Journal of Atmospheric Chemistry*, **8**, 307–58.

Bryant, D., Nielsen, D., and Tangley, L. (1997). *The Last Frontier Forests: Ecosystems and Economies on the Edge*. Washington, DC: World Resources Institute.

Cowell, D. W., Wickware, G. M., and Sims, R. A. (1979). Ecological land classification of the Hudson Bay Lowland coastal zone, Ontario. In *Proceedings of the 2nd meeting of the Canadian Committee on Ecological Land Classification*. Ecology Land Series 7. Ottawa, Canada: Environment Canada, pp. 165–75.

de Groot, R. S. (1992). *Functions of Nature*. Groningen, the Netherlands: Wolters-Noordhoff.

Denny, P. (1985). Submerged and floating-leaved aquatic macrophytes. In *The Ecology and Management of African Wetland Vegetation*, ed. P. Denny. Dordrecht, the Netherlands: Junk.

Findlay, S. C. and Houlahan, J. (1997). Anthropogenic correlates of species richness in southeastern Ontario wetlands. *Conservation Biology*, **11**, 1–11.

Fremlin, G. (ed. in chief) (1974). *The National Atlas of Canada*, 4th edn., revised. Toronto, Canada: Macmillan.

Groombridge, B. (ed.) (1992). *Global Biodiversity. State of the Earth's Living Processes*. A report of the World Conservation Monitoring Centre. London: Chapman and Hall.

Hamilton, S. K., Sippel, S. J., and Melack, J. M. (1996). Inundation patterns in the Pantanal wetland of South America determined from passive microwave remote sensing. *Archiv für Hydrobiologie*, **137**(1), 1–23.

Hughes, R. H. and Hughes, J. S. (1992). *A Directory of African Wetlands*. Gland, Switzerland and Cambridge, UK: International Union for the Conservation of Nature and Natural Resources (IUCN).

Junk, W. J. (1992). Wetlands of tropical South America. In *Wetlands of the World*, vol. 1, eds. D. F. Whigham, D. Dykyjova and S. Hejny. Dordrecht, the Netherlands: Junk, pp. 679–739.

Keddy, P. A. (2000). *Wetland Ecology: Principles and Conservation*. Cambridge, UK: Cambridge University Press.

Leitch, J. A. (1989). Politicoeconomic overview of prairie potholes. In *Northern Prairie Weltands*, ed. A. van der Valk. Ames, IO: Iowa State University Press, pp. 2–14.

Llewellyn, D. W., Shaffer, G. P., Craig, N. J. et al. (1996). A decision-support system for prioritizing restoration sites on the Mississippi River Alluvial Plain. *Conservation Biology*, **10**(5), 1446–55.

Löffler, E. (1982). Landforms and landform development. In *Biogeography and Ecology of New Guinea*, ed. J. L. Gressitt. Monographiae Biologicae, 42. The Hague, the Netherlands: Junk.

Mitsch, W. J. and Gosselink, J. G. (2000). *Wetlands*, 3rd edn. New York: John Wiley.

Myers, N. (1988). Threatened biotas: "hotspots" in tropical forests. *Environmentalist*, **8**, 1–20.

Myers, N., Mittermeier, R. A., Mittermeier, C. G., da Fonseca, G. A. B., and Kent, J. (2000). Biodiversity hotspots for conservation priorities. *Nature*, **403**, 853–8.

Olsen, D. M., Dinerstein, E., Wikramanayake, E. D. et al. (2001). Terrestrial ecoregions of the world: a new map of life on Earth. *Bioscience*, **51**, 933–8.

Prance, G. T. and Schaller, G. B. (1982). Preliminary study of some vegetation types of the Pantanal, Mato Grosso, Brazil. *Brittonia*, **3**(2), 228–51.

Riley, J. L. (1982). Hudson Bay Lowland floristic inventory, wetlands catalogue and conservation strategy. *Naturaliste Canadien*, **109**, 543–55.

(2003). *Flora of the Hudson Bay Lowland and its Postglacial Origins*. Ottawa, Canada: National Research Council Press.

Schumacher, E. F. (1973). *Small is Beautiful: a Study of Economics as if People Mattered*. London: Blond and Briggs.

Thompson, K. and Hamilton, A. C. (1983). Peatlands and swamps of the African continent. In *Ecosystems of the World*, vol. 4B, *Mires: Swamp, Bog, Fen and Moor*, ed. A. J. P. Gore. Amsterdam, the Netherlands: Elsevier Science, pp. 331–73.

Turner, R. E. (1977). Intertidal vegetation and commercial yields of Penaeid shrimp. *Transactions of the American Fisheries Society*, **106**, 411–16.

Weiher, E. (1999). The combined effects of scale and productivity on species richness. *Journal of Ecology*, **87**, 1005–11.

Whigham, D. F., Dykyjova, D., and Hejny, S. (eds.) (1992). *Wetlands of the World*, vol. 1, *Africa, Australia, Canada and Greenland, Indian Subcontinent, Mediterranean, Mexico, New Guinea, United States. Handbook of Vegetation Sciences*. Dordrecht, the Netherlands: Junk.

Wood, A. W. (1982). The soils of New Guinea. In *Biogeography and Ecology of New Guinea*, ed. J. L. Gressitt. Monographiae Biologicae 42. The Hague, the Netherlands: Junk, pp. 73–83.

World Wide Fund for Nature (2001). http://www.worldwildlife.org/wildworld/profiles.

2

The West Siberian Lowland

A. I. SOLOMESHCH
Russian Academy of Sciences

Introduction

The West Siberian Lowland is a geographical region of Russia bordered by the Urals in the west and the Yenisey River in the east, the Kara Sea of the Arctic Ocean in the north and the Kazakh steppes in the south (Fig. 2.1). The region covers 2 745 000 km^2 stretching from 62–89° E to 53–73° N. The length from west to east is more than 2000 km and from south to north more than 2500 km. It is about seven times the size of Germany, five times the size of France, and approximately equal to the size of Argentina.

The Lowland represents 16% of the territory of Russia; it is the lowest and flattest part of the country and is tilted slightly towards the north. It is confined to Hercynian and West Siberian epiplatforms, which were regularly submerged by polar seas in its geological past. The relief of the Lowland is very flat, and is composed of quaternary sand, loam, and clay deposits. Altitudes range between 0 and 300 m above sea level with an average of 100 m. The climate is continental with winters lasting five to seven months. Mean monthly temperatures vary through a range of 40 °C, changing from +5 °C to +16 °C in July and from −20 °C to −25 °C in January. Annual precipitation varies from 390 to 600 mm. Permafrost covers one-third of the northern part of the region. The continuous permafrost on the Yamal and Gydan peninsulas, with a prevailing thickness of more than 500 m, declines southwards; it has a thickness of about 100 m at 67° N of northern latitude near the mouth of the Ob River.

The World's Largest Wetlands: Ecology and Conservation, eds. L. H. Fraser and P. A. Keddy.
Published by Cambridge University Press. © Cambridge University Press 2005.

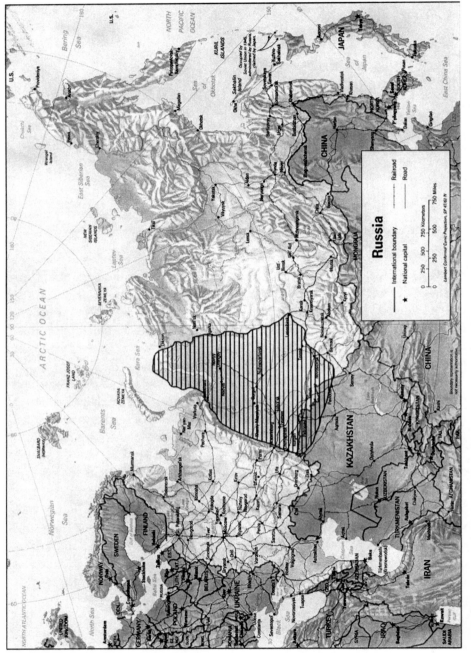

Figure 2.1 Location of the West Siberian Lowland.

The Lowland is drained by the Ob, Yenisey, Irtysh, Nadym, Pur, and Taz rivers, and their tributaries. The Ob and Yenisey are the largest rivers in northern Asia. Because of the flat relief, low drainage, and cold and humid continental climate, the Lowland is characterized by a great expanse of peatlands. At present, wetland ecosystems cover almost 50% of the territory of the West Siberian Lowland; they accumulate approximately 22.8 million tons (throughout this book, tons refers to metric tons) of carbon per year, making them an important component of the global carbon cycle. This region also plays an important role for freshwater accumulation as it contains more than 800 000 lakes. The West Siberian Lowland provides habitat for many plants and animals. Tundra, boreal forest, and temperate grassland biomes replace each other in the Lowland moving from north to south, and wetlands are a major proportion of each biome. Although the human population density is not high, natural wetlands are threatened by rapidly developing oil, gas, and forest industries.

The objective of this overview is to characterize the variety of the West Siberian wetlands, give examples of the most-typical and rare species of plants and animals, estimate their role in the global carbon cycle, and describe the anthropogenic impact and the measures that have been taken for biodiversity conservation in this region.

Natural zonation and mire zones of the West Siberian Lowland

Modern flora and vegetation of the West Siberian Lowland was established in the Tertiary period of the Cenozoic era. Ecosystems of dark-coniferous forests, typical of the modern vegetation in the middle and south taiga zones, are derived from the vegetation of late Pleistocene and early Holocene (Krylov 1961). They were dominated by *Pinis sibirica*, *Picea abies*, and *Abies sibirica*, which play an important role in the canopy of modern taiga forests. The flora of the Pleistocene forests was rich, and included the genera *Fagus*, *Carpinus*, *Quercus*, and *Tilia*. These genera became extinct during the glacial stages of the Pleistocene, with the exception of *Tilia cordata*, which remains in several relict locations. Floristic complexes and vegetation zones shifted several times northwards and southwards, reflecting glacial fluctuations during the Quaternary period. During these glaciations the tundra zone established and replaced forests on the northern part of the Lowland. Large-scale expansion of peatlands started in the early Holocene, 10 000 to 12 000 years ago. Vast areas previously covered by forest vegetation were replaced by wetlands throughout the West Siberian Lowland. This paludification, which accelerated around 9000 years ago, continues to the present day (Neishtadt 1977). Peatlands are common throughout the West Siberian Lowland but are especially abundant in the middle part, in the taiga zone. Estimations of the extent of the peatland area differ from author to author, depending on their methodological approach. According to the most-comprehensive West Siberian peatland vegetation surveys (Ivanov & Novikov 1976, Romanova 1985), peatlands cover approximately 787 000 km^2 and occupy from 30% to 50% of the area of the entire Lowland. In some regions, such as Surgutskoye Polesie and Vasjuganye, the percentage of peatlands reaches 70% to 75%.

Because of its great expanse and flat relief the vegetation cover of the Lowland has clear natural zonation. Tundra, boreal, and steppe geobotanical zones replace each other from north to south. According to Il'ina et al. (1985), these zones are divided into nine geobotanical subzones: arctic tundra, subarctic tundra, forest-tundra, northern taiga, middle taiga, southern taiga, hemiboreal forest, forest-steppe, and steppe (Fig. 2.2).

Six peatland zones have been recognized in the most-comprehensive survey of the West Siberian peatlands (Ivanov & Novikov 1976): polygonal mires, flat-palsa mires, high-palsa mires, raised string bogs, flat eutrophic and mesotrophic mires, and reed and sedge fens (Table 2.1). These zones, shown in Fig. 2.3, are closely related to the West Siberian geobotanical subdivisions.

The hydrographic structure of the West Siberian Lowland differs considerably from region to region. On the very northern part of the Lowland in the tundra zone, and in the very southern part in the steppe zone, peatlands are associated with rivers and develop in floodplains. In contrast, in the middle part of the Lowland in the taiga zone, the largest peatlands develop on uplands (Fig. 2.4), while the floodplains – because of their better drainage – have mineral soils supporting forest and meadow vegetation. This explains the large extent of the peatlands in the middle part of the Lowland.

The biodiversity of the West Siberian mires has been investigated by a number of researchers. The original data were summarized in several large-scale vegetation surveys (Gorodkov 1938, Pyavchenko 1955, Katz 1971, Ivanov & Novikov 1976, Liss & Berezina 1981, Botch & Masing 1983, Romanova 1985, Krivenko 1999, 2000, Botch 2000), and are used for the descriptions of mire zones given below.

Zone of polygonal mires

This region is located beyond the Arctic Circle on the Yamal, Gydan, and Taz peninsulas of the Kara Sea of the Arctic Ocean. It corresponds to the subzones of arctic and subarctic tundra. The region represents 13% of the West Siberian Lowland and occupies 357 000 km^2, about twice the size of Washington State. The region is covered by extensive tundra vegetation underlain by continuous permafrost, which is more than 500 m deep. The territory has traditionally been used for reindeer husbandry and polar-fox hunting.

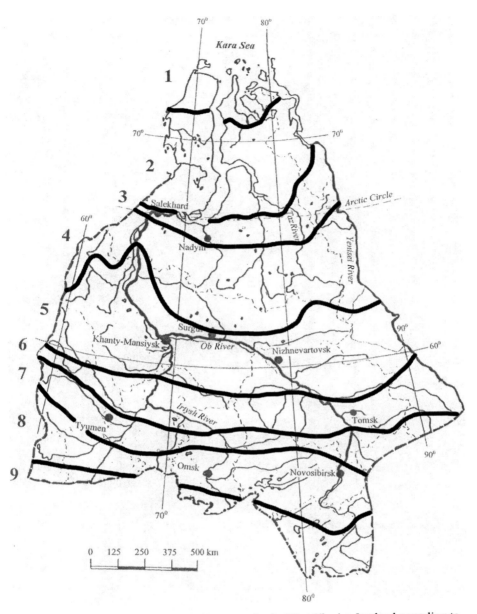

Figure 2.2 Zonation of vegetation cover in the West Siberian Lowland according to Il'ina *et al.* (1985). Tundra zone: 1, arctic tundra; 2, subarctic tundra; 3, forest-tundra. Boreal zone: 4, northern taiga; 5, middle taiga; 6, southern taiga; 7, hemiboreal forest. Steppe zone: 8, forest-steppe; 9, steppe.

Table 2.1 *General characteristics of mire zones of the West Siberian Lowland.*

Mire zones	Area (10³ km²)	% of the West Siberian Lowland	% mires in the zone[a]	Average altitude (m)	Average annual precipitation (mm)	Average annual runoff (mm)	Average annual evapotranspiration (mm)
Polygonal mires	357	13	20	40	480	250	230
Flat-palsa mires	220	8	40	50–80	550	260	290
High-palsa mires	165	6	25	60–100	600	280	320
Raised string bogs	1263	46	40	80–100	590	200	390
Flat eutrophic and mesotrophic mires	300	11	20	135–150	510	90	420
Reed and sedge fens and salt-water marshes	440	16	5	200	390	10	380
Total	2745	100					

[a] The percentage of mires depends on mire definition, and is probably underestimated. If we do not restrict their definition by certain peat depths, almost the whole area of the tundra zone with polygonal and palsa mires will be classified as wetland.

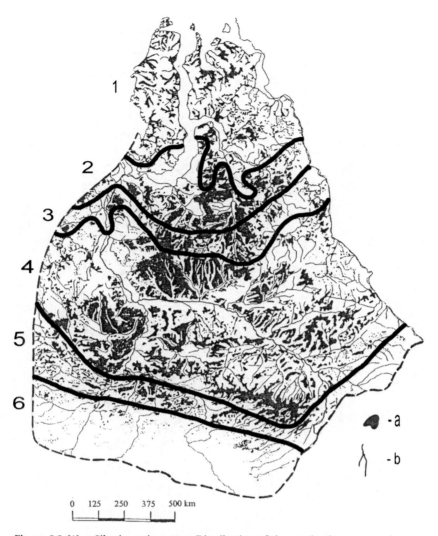

Figure 2.3 West Siberian mire zones. Distribution of the peatlands corresponds to Il'ina *et al.* (1985) and boundaries of mire zones to Ivanov and Novikov (1976). 1, zone of polygonal mires; 2, zone of flat-palsa mires; 3, zone of high-palsa mires; 4, zone of raised string bogs; 5, zone of flat eutrophic and mesotrophic mires; 6, zone of reed and sedge fens, and salt-water marshes. a, peatlands; b, rivers.

Vegetation

The region is characterized by long, cold, windy winters and by brief, relatively cold summers. The landscape is treeless because of the extreme cold, wind, and permafrost. Arctic and subarctic tundras represent zonal vegetation, and cover upland territory. Peatlands develop both on uplands and floodplains.

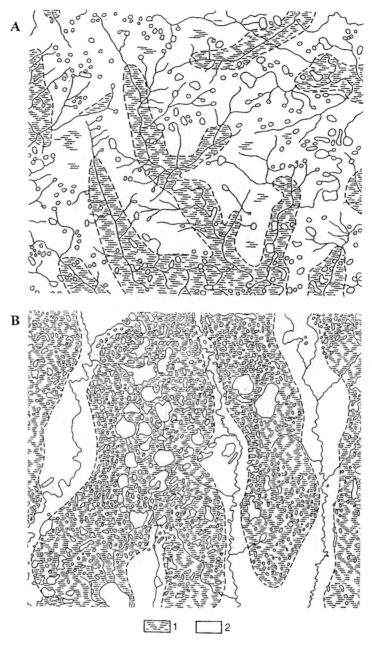

Figure 2.4 Hydrographic structure of the West Siberian Lowland (from Ivanov & Novikov 1976). A, the northern and southern parts of the Lowland (arctic, subarctic, southern forest-steppe, and steppe zones). Peatlands are mostly located in river floodplains. Uplands and watersheds are covered by zonal vegetation: tundras in the north and forest-steppes in the south. B, the middle part of the Lowland (taiga zone). The largest peatlands develop on uplands and watersheds, while floodplains – because of the better drainage by rivers – have mineral soil supporting forest and meadow vegetation. 1, peatlands; 2, lands with mesic soils.

Small patches of open boreal forests also occur in floodplains. Tundra vegetation is represented by a mosaic of arctic species of lichens, mosses, dwarf-shrubs, and herbs. The most-common dwarf-shrub and herbaceous species are: *Salix polaris*, *S. nummularia*, *Arctous alpina*, *Alopecurus alpinus*, *Armeria arctica*, *Cassiope tetragona*, *Carex concolor*, *C. ensifolia* ssp. *arctisibirica*, *Dryas octopetala*, *Dupontia fisheri*, *Minuartia arctica*, and *Polygonum viviparum*. The prevailing mosses are: *Aulacomnium turgidum*, *Dicranum elongatum*, *D. angustum*, *Hylocomium splendens* var. *alaskanum*, *Rhacomitrium lanuginosum*, and *Polytrichum juniperinum*. Lichens are represented by *Cladonia gracilis*, *C. rangiferina*, *C. macroceras*, *C. uncialis*, *Cetraria cucullata*, *C. islandica*, and *Thamnolia vermicularis* among others (Mel'tser 1985, Pristyazhnyuk 2001).

Wildlife

Plants and animals in this area are adapted to the extreme cold, general lack of shelter, and the thick layer of permafrost, living in an oppressive environment. The mat of mosses and lichens – with dwarf-shrubs, grasses, sedges, herbs, and berries – feed herds of reindeer *Rangifer tarandus*, and small rodents such as Siberian lemmings *Lemmus sibiricus* and collared lemming *Dicrostonyx torquatus*. Polar foxes *Alopex lagopus* and snowy owls *Nyctea scandiaca* survive almost exclusively on Siberian lemmings. Wetlands and tundras of the Yamal, Gydan, and Taz peninsulas, and the lower Ob River region, are very important as breeding areas for many waterfowl species wintering in Western Europe, southwest Asia, and Africa. Ducks are the most numerous migrating waterfowl.

Common animal species. Mammals: reindeer *Rangifer tarandus*, muskrat *Ondatra zibethica*, ermine *Mustela erminea*, red fox *Vulpes vulpes*, polar fox *Alopex lagopus*, wolf *Canis lupus*, elk *Alces alces*, mountain hare *Lepus timudus*. Birds: Eurasian wigeon *Anas penelope*, common teal *A. crecca*, mallard *A. platyrhynchos*, northern pintail *A. acuta*, garganey *A. querquedula*, northern shoveler *A. clypeata*, tufted duck *Aythya fuligula*, greater scaup *A. marila*, long-tailed duck *Clangula hyemalis*, black scoter *Melanitta nigra*, velvet scoter *M. fusca*, white-fronted goose *Anser albifrons*, bean goose *A. fabalis*, black-throated diver *Gavia arctica*, red-throated diver *G. stellata*. Fish: least cisco *Coreogonus sardinella*, peled *C. peled*, broad whitefish *C. nasus*, Siberian whitefish *C. lavaretus pidschian*, muscun *C. muscun*, inconnu *Stenodus leucichthys*, Siberian sturgeon *Acipenser baerii baerii*, sterlet *A. ruthenus*.

Rare and endangered animal species. Polar bear *Ursus maritimus*, walrus *Odobenus rosmarus*, red-breasted goose *Branta ruficollis*, lesser white-fronted goose *Anser erythropus*, Bewick's swan *Cygnus bewickii*, Siberian crane *Grus leucogeranus*, osprey *Pandion haliaetus*, white-tailed eagle *Haliaeetus albicilla*, golden eagle *Aquila chrysaetos*, peregrine falcon *Falco peregrinus*, gyrfalcon *F. rusticolus*, tugun *Coreogonus tugun*,

Arctic char *Salvelinus alpinus*, taimen *Hucho taimen*, Siberian sculpin *Cottus sibiricus* (Krivenko 2000).

Peatlands

Peatlands with deep peat deposits cover 16% to 25% of the landscape. The depth of peat varies from 0.1–0.4 m in the arctic subzone to 1.0–5.0 m in subarctic subzones, with a pH range of 3.0 to 5.5. They are 2000 to 3000 years old. The mires of this zone have been described by Andreev (1934), Gorodkov (1938, 1944), Katz (1939), Katz and Katz (1946, 1948), Pyavchenko (1955), Botch *et al.* (1971), Botch and Masing (1983), and Romanova (1985).

Two principal types of mires are typical of this region: homogenous and polygonal mires. Homogenous mires develop in river floodplains, around lakes, and in depressions on the watersheds. They have either a flat or a tussocky structure due to the occurrence of tussock-forming cottongrass and mosses. Polygonal mires cover flat depressions on watersheds and well-drained places in floodplains. The largest mire massifs of this zone are connected with river terraces and floodplain areas (Fig. 2.4). The polygons have diameters of 10 to 30 m. They are characterized by wet hollows dominated by grasses, sedges, and hypnoid mosses, surrounded by drier ridges (about 0.3 m high and 0.5 m wide) covered with *Sphagnum* and hypnoid mosses and dwarf-shrubs. Ridges are separated from each other by deep, wet cracks filled with water (Botch & Masing 1983). Cracks are of frost origin and have widths of 0.2 to 1.0 m and depths of 0.05 to 0.8 m (Ivanov & Novikov 1976). Polygons differ in their degree of frozenness and development of ice wedges. There are several morphological variants of polygonal mires: low-center ice-wedge polygons, high-center ice-wedge polygons, and frost-crack polygons, which correspond to different stages of their development.

The zone of polygonal mires is subdivided into three subzones: arctic, northern subarctic and southern subarctic. The arctic subzone of polygonal mires corresponds to the territory of arctic tundra, the northern subarctic subzone of polygonal mires to the northern and middle subarctic tundra, and the south subzone of polygonal mires corresponds to the southern part of the subarctic tundra (Aleksandrova 1971). All these subzones consist of mires of polygonal and homogenous types. Their dominant and most-constant species are given in Tables 2.2 to 2.4, prepared from data from several publications (e.g. Botch & Masing 1983, Romanova 1985). While mires of all subzones share many common species, they differ from each other in that there are some species present that are unique to each subzone. *Carex concolor*, *Drepanocladus uncinatus*, and *Calliergon sarmentosum* are very common. They dominate in all communities of the arctic and northern subarctic zones.

The floristic composition of ridges and flat tops of polygonal mires is shown in Table 2.2. *Rubus chamaemorus* grows in all subzones. Communities on ridges and flat tops of polygons of arctic and northern subarctic subzones are similar in that they contain *Carex concolor, Salix pulchra, Salix reptans, Aulacomnium palustre, A. turgidum, Sphagnum fimbriatum, Calliergon sarmentosum, Drepanocladus uncinatus,* and *Homalothecium nitens.* Ridge communities of the arctic subzone differ by having the presence of *Dupontia fischeri, Luzula wahlenbergii, Dicranum elongatum, Cladonia gracilis* ssp. *elongata,* and *Cetraria hiascens.* Ridges of both subarctic subzones are dominated by *Betula nana, Vaccinium vitis-idaea, Andromeda polifolia, Dicranum angustum,* and *Cladonia rangiferina.* Ridges of the northern subarctic subzone differ by the presence of *Carex rariflora, Arctagrostis latifolia, Dryas punctata,* and *Hylocomium splendens.* Communities of the southern subarctic subzone differ by having the presence of *Ledum decumbens, Cetraria cucullata, Sphagnum angustifolium, Polytrichum strictum, Sphagnum lenense,* and *S. nemorum.*

Sphagnum balticum is common in hollows and cracks of polygonal mires of all subzones. *Carex concolor, Calliergon sarmentosum,* and *Drepanocladus uncinatus* dominate in the first two subzones. Hollows and cracks of the arctic subzone are also dominated by *Arctophila fulva, Dupontia fischeri,* and *Eriophorum medium.* Sedges *Carex rariflora* and *C. rotundata* are common in both subarctic subzones. Hollows and cracks of the northern subarctic subzone differ by the presence of *Carex chordorrhiza,* while the same habitats of the southern subarctic subzone are characterized by the presence of *Eriophorum russeolum, Sphagnum lindbergii,* and *S. majus* (Table 2.3). If cracks and hollows become depressed because of termocarst processes, the species that once occupied them can move to polygons and ridges.

Homogenous mires typically develop in river floodplains and depressions in the watersheds. The peat thickness varies from 0.2 to 0.8 m, while pH varies from 3.5 to 5.0 (Botch & Masing 1983). Cotton grass *Eriophorum polystachyon* and hypnoid mosses *Calliergon sarmentosum, Drepanocladus uncinatus, D. exannulatus,* and *D. revolvens* grow in communities of all subzones of the polygonal mire zone (Table 2.4). *Carex concolor* is a dominant species of both arctic and northern subarctic subzones. Homogenous mires of the arctic subzone are dominated by *Eriophorum brachyantherum, E. medium, Arctophila fulva,* and *Dupontia fischeri.* Homogenous mires of subarctic subzones are characterized by a high abundance of *Betula nana* and *Sphagnum balticum.* The presence of *Carex aquatilis, C. rariflora, C. disperma, Menyanthes trifoliata, Comarum palustre,* and *Sphagnum squarrosum* is a distinctive feature of homogenous mires of the northern subarctic subzone. Homogenous mires of the southern subarctic subzone are more floristically rich and differ by having the presence of *Ledum decumbens, Andromeda polifolia, Vaccinium vitis-idaea, Empetrum nigrum, Oxycoccus palustris, Rubus chamaemorus, Eriophorum vaginatum,*

Table 2.2 *Floristic composition of ridges and flat tops of polygonal mires.*

	Arctic subzone	Northern subarctic subzone	Southern subarctic subzone
Peat deposits (m)	0.1–0.4	1.0–5.0	1.0–5.0
pH	4.5–5.5	3.0–4.0	3.0–4.0
Species			
Rubus chamaemorus	+	+	+
Dupontia fischeri	+	–	–
Luzula wahlenbergii	+	–	–
Dicranum elongatum	+	–	–
Cetraria hiascens	+	–	–
Cladonia gracilis ssp. elongata	+	–	–
Carex concolor	+	+	–
Salix pulchra	+	+	–
Salix reptans	+	+	–
Aulacomnium palustre	+	+	–
Aulacomnium turgidum	+	+	–
Sphagnum fimbriatum	+	+	–
Calliergon sarmentosum	+	+	–
Drepanocladus uncinatus	+	+	–
Homalothecium nitens	+	+	–
Carex rariflora	–	+	–
Arctagrostis latifolia	–	+	–
Dryas punctata	–	+	–
Hylocomium splendens	–	+	–
Betula nana	–	+	+
Vaccinium vitis-idaea	–	+	+
Andromeda polifolia	–	+	+
Dicranum angustum	–	+	+
Cladonia rangiferina	–	+	+
Ledum decumbens	–	–	+
Cetraria cucullata	–	–	+
Sphagnum angustifolium	–	–	+
Polytrichum strictum	–	–	+
Sphagnum lenense	–	–	+
Sphagnum nemorum	–	–	+

Carex limosa, C. rotundata, Sphagnum angustifolium, S. fimbriatum, S. warnstorfii, Cladonia alpestris, C. rangiferina, Cetraria islandica, and *C. cucullata.*

Zones of palsa mires

Palsa mires are typical of the southern tundra, forest-tundra, and northern taiga subzones, and develop in subarctic climate in discontinuous

Table 2.3 *Floristic composition of hollows and cracks of polygonal mires.*

Species	Arctic subzone	Northern subarctic subzone	Southern subarctic subzone
Sphagnum balticum	+	+	+
Arctophila fulva	+	−	−
Dupontia fischeri	+	−	−
Eriophorum medium	+	−	−
Carex concolor	+	+	−
Calliergon sarmentosum	+	+	−
Drepanocladus uncinatus	+	+	−
Carex chordorrhiza	−	+	−
Carex rariflora	−	+	+
Carex rotundata	−	+	+
Eriophorum russeolum	−	−	+
Sphagnum lindbergii	−	−	+
Sphagnum majus	−	−	+

permafrost conditions. The zone covers 385 000 km², which is about the size of Montana in the United States, and represents 14% of the West Siberian Lowland. Altitudes range from 50 to 100 m above sea level. The southern limit of this zone is near 64° N latitude, but it extends southerly to 62° N latitude in the Nadym and Taz river regions. The climate is humid with average annual precipitation of 550 to 600 mm and evapotranspiration of 290 to 320 mm. Peatlands cover 25% to 40% of the landscape. The territory has traditionally been used for reindeer breeding, hunting, and fishing.

Vegetation

Landscapes of this zone consist of open tundra forests, shrub tundra, peatlands, and thermokarst oligotrophic, distrophic, and mesotrophic lakes. Open forests represent zonal vegetation on watersheds. The overstory is dominated by *Larix sibirica, Picea obovata, Pinus sibirica,* and *Betula tortuosa.* Their ground layer is characterized by a thick cover of mosses, formed notably by *Pleurozium schreberi, Hylocomium splendens,* and *Aulacomnium turgidum;* the lichens *Cladonia rangiferina, C. arbuscula, C. alpestris, C. coccifera,* and *Cetraria nivalis;* and dwarf-shrubs, particularly *Betula nana, Salix pulchra, Ledum palustre, Chamaedaphne calyculata, Vaccinium uliginosum, Empetrum nigrum, Oxycoccus microcarpus,* and *Rubus chamaemorus.* Open forests form a mosaic with shrub tundras dominated by *Betula nana, Salix glauca, S. pulchra,* and *Duschekia fruticosa.* The vegetation of mesotrophic lakes consists of *Sparganium erectum, Potamogeton perfoliatus,* and *Polygonum amphibium.* Wet meadows are often dominated by *Arctophila fulva,* which occurs along rivers and lake banks.

Table 2.4 *Floristic composition of homogenous mires in the polygonal mire zone.*

Species	Arctic subzone	Northern subarctic subzone	Southern subarctic subzone
Eriophorum polystachyon	+	+	+
Calliergon sarmentosum	+	+	+
Drepanocladus uncinatus	+	+	+
Drepanocladus exannulatus	+	+	+
Drepanocladus revolvens	+	+	+
Eriophorum brachyantherum	+	−	−
Eriophorum medium	+	−	−
Arctophila fulva	+	−	−
Dupontia fischeri	+	−	−
Carex concolor	+	+	−
Carex aquatilis	−	+	−
Carex rariflora	−	+	−
Carex disperma	−	+	−
Menyanthes trifoliata	−	+	−
Comarum palustre	−	+	−
Sphagnum squarrosum	−	+	−
Betula nana	−	+	+
Sphagnum balticum	−	+	+
Ledum decumbens	−	−	+
Andromeda polifolia	−	−	+
Vaccinium vitis-idaea	−	−	+
Empetrum nigrum	−	−	+
Oxycoccus palustris	−	−	+
Rubus chamaemorus	−	−	+
Eriophorum vaginatum	−	−	+
Carex limosa	−	−	+
Carex rotundata	−	−	+
Sphagnum angustifolium	−	−	+
Sphagnum fimbriatum	−	−	+
Sphagnum warnstorfii	−	−	+
Cladonia alpestris	−	−	+
Cladonia rangiferina	−	−	+
Cetraria islandica	−	−	+
Cetraria cucullata	−	−	+

Wildlife

Diversity of wildlife is high due to a combination of tundra and taiga species. The ranges of many tundra species extend far to the south, while southern species also occur here especially in the Ob river valley, which carries warm water from the south. As a result, typical tundra bird species such as the black-bellied plover *Pluvialis squatarola*, dunlin *Calidris alpina*, and long-tailed duck *Clangula hyemalis*, co-occur here with southerly birds like the garganey *Anas querquedula*, greylag goose *Anser anser*, and little gull *Larus minuta*.

Common animal species. Mammals: reindeer *Rangifer tarandus*, muskrat *Ondatra zibethica*, otter *Lutra lutra*. Birds: northern pintail *Anas acuta*, common teal *A. crecca*, tufted duck *Aythya fuligula*, black scoter *Melanita nigra*, smew *Mergus albellus*, bean goose *Anser fabalis*, whooper swan *Cygnus cygnus*. Fish: broad whitefish *Coreogonus nasus*, Siberian whitefish *C. lavaretus pidschian*, peled *C. peled*, orfe *Leuciscus idus*, pike *Esox lucius*, burlot *Lota lota*, ruffe *Gymnocephalus cernua*, crucian carp *Carassius carassius*, spiny loach *Cobutus taenia*, bearded stone loach *Nemachilus barbatus*.

Rare and endangered animal species. West Siberian beaver *Castor fiber pohlei*, Siberian crane *Grus leucogeranus*, red-breasted goose *Branta ruficollis*, lesser white-fronted goose *Anser erythropus*, white-tailed eagle *Haliaeetus albicilla*, osprey *Pandion haliaetus*, golden eagle *Aquila chrysaetos*, peregrine falcon *Falco peregrinus*, river lamprey *Lampetra fluviatilis*, Siberian sturgeon *Acipenser baerii baerii*, lenok *Brachymystax lenok* (Krivenko 2000).

Peatlands

Peatlands cover an average of 25% to 40% of the territory of this zone, and about 70% of the watershed between the Nadym and Taz rivers (Ivanov & Novikov 1976). The peatlands of this zone have been described by Govorukhin (1933, 1947), Andreev (1934), Katz (1939), Gorodkov (1944), Pyavchenko (1955), Botch and Masing (1983), Ivanov and Novikov (1976), and Romanova (1985).

Palsas are frozen peat mounds, which consist of frozen mounds or ridges and wet hollows. Their height varies from 0.3 to 0.5 m in the north to 4 to 6 m and up to 8 m in the south. Peat depth varies from 1 to 2 m in the northern part of the region to 3 to 5 m in the southern part (Botch & Masing 1983). The average age of the peat is 5000 to 8000 years (Botch *et al.* 1995). The permafrost layer appears to be deeper under mounds in the southern part of the zone, and under hollows the permafrost layer can be non-existent. The origin of palsas is still uncertain. According to Govorukhin (1933, 1947), one of the most important factors in their formation is the accumulation of an abundant amount of water in the upper ground layer, which then freezes in winter.

Flat and high palsas are distinguished according to their height and size (Katz 1971). Flat palsas, which occur in the northern part of the palsa zone, have an average height of 0.5 to 1.0 m. The size of frozen mounds varies from several square meters to several hundred square meters. High palsas cover the southern part of the palsa zone, where the frozen mounds are 6 to 8 m in height, decreasing to 2 to 4 m northwards. High palsas may be steep or gently sloping, but are always steeper in comparison with flat palsas. The size of high-palsa mounds is greater than that of flat-palsa mounds. Wet hollows among frozen mounds have an elongated shape and are connected to each other, draining the territory. Melting water flows through them to lakes or rivers. Zones of flat-palsa and high-palsa mires cover 220 000 and 165 000 km^2, respectively. Russian scientists distinguish between flat- and high-palsa zones (Pyavchenko 1955, Katz 1971, Romanova 1985), but floristically they are rather similar. Their floristic composition is shown in Table 2.5.

Palsa vegetation consists of dwarf-shrubs, such as *Betula nana*, *Ledum palustre*, *Vaccinium uliginosum*, and *V. vitis-idaea*; cotton grass *Eriophorum vaginatum*; cloudberry *Rubus chamaemorus*; hypnoid and sphagnoid mosses *Sphagnum fuscum*, *S. lenense*, *S. magellanicum*, *S. angustifolium*, *Dicranum elongatum*, *D. congestum*, *D. undulatum*, and *Polytrichum strictum*; and lichens *Cetraria cucullata*, *C. nivalis*, *Cladonia arbuscula*, *C. mitis*, and *C. deformis*. High palsas are distinguished by the presence of the tree species *Pinus sylvestris*, *Larix sibirica*, *Betula pubescens*, and *Picea obovata*, which are only 3 to 5 m in height and dwarf-shrubs *Chamaedaphne calyculata* and *Empetrum nigrum*. Hollows are covered by sedges *Carex rotundata*, *C. chordorrhiza*, *C. rariflora*, cotton grasses *Eriophorum russeolum*, *E. polystachyon*, and mosses *Sphagnum lindbergii*, *S. majus*, *S. subsecundum*, *Drepanocladus revolvens*, *Calliergon* spp. In the southern part of the palsa-mire zone, *Menyanthes trifoliata*, *Comarum palustre*, and *Carex limosa* appear in hollows.

Zone of raised string bogs

The zone of raised string bogs corresponds to the boreal taiga zone and covers 1 263 000 km^2 in the central part of the West Siberian Lowland (about three times the size of Montana). It extends all the way from the Ural Mountains in the west to the Yenisey River in the east, between the latitudes of 55° and 64° N. It is characterized by flat relief about 80 to 100 m above sea level that rises to about 190 m in the Sibirskie Uvaly region. Average annual precipitation is 590 mm and evapotranspiration is 390 mm (Table 2.1). The climate and flat topography with its slow runoff provides very favourable conditions for paludification. The zone is drained by the Ob River – and its tributaries the Irtysh, Vakh, Ket, Konda, Severnaia Sosva, Malaia Sosva, and Tchulym. Almost all of the area, including watersheds and floodplains, is waterlogged. The hydrographic structure of this zone differs from the northern and southern parts of the West Siberian Lowland. The largest peatlands are most typical of the central flat parts of the watersheds where, together with forests, they comprise the zonal vegetation and cover vast territories (Fig. 2.4B). Mires with deep peat deposits cover 40%

Table 2.5 *Floristic composition of palsa mires.*

Species	Frozen mounds and ridges	Wet hollows
Betula nana	+	−
Ledum palustre	+	−
Rubus chamaemorus	+	−
Vaccinium uliginosum	+	−
Vaccinium vitis-idaea	+	−
Eriophorum vaginatum	+	−
Pinus sylvestris[a]	+	−
Larix sibirica[a]	+	−
Betula pubescens[a]	+	−
Picea obovata[a]	+	−
Empetrum nigrum[a]	+	−
Chamaedaphne calyculata[a]	+	−
Sphagnum lenense	+	−
Sphagnum apiculatum	+	−
Sphagnum warnstorfii	+	−
Sphagnum magellanicum	+	−
Sphagnum angustifolium	+	−
Sphagnum fuscum	+	−
Cetraria cucullata	+	−
Cetraria nivalis	+	−
Cladonia arbuscula	+	−
Cladonia mitis	+	−
Cladonia deformis	+	−
Dicranum elongatum	+	−
Dicranum congestum	+	−
Dicranum undulatum	+	−
Polytrichum strictum	+	−
Sphagnum balticum	+	+
Carex rotundata	−	+
Carex chordorrhiza	−	+
Carex rariflora	−	+
Carex limosa[a]	−	+
Eriophorum russeolum	−	+
Eriophorum polystachyon	−	+
Menyanthes trifoliata[a]	−	+
Comarum palustre[a]	−	+
Sphagnum lindbergii	−	+
Sphagnum majus	−	+
Sphagnum subsecundum	−	+
Drepanocladus revolvens	−	+
Calliergon spp.	−	+

[a]Plants that are more typical of the high-palsa zone.

to 70% of the landscape. Traditional activities include hunting, fishing, reindeer grazing, and berry gathering.

Vegetation

The zonal vegetation on uplands is boreal forests and raised string bogs. Forests are dominated by *Larix sibirica, Picea obovata, Pinus sibirica, Abies sibirica, Pinus sylvestris, Betula pubescens,* and *B. tortuosa.* The structure and composition of boreal forests changes from north to south and the zone is subdivided into northern, middle, and southern subzones. The layer of mosses and lichens is similar for all subzones. Common species of mosses include *Pleurozium schreberi, Hylocomium splendens, Dicranum polysetum, Ptilium crista-castrensis, Polytrichum commune, Sphagnum girgensohnii, S. nemoreum, S. magellanicum,* and *S. warnstorfii.* Common lichens are *Cladonia alpestris, C. arbuscula, C. rangiferina, Cetraria laevigata,* and *Peltigera aphtosa.* Forests of the northern subzone are rather open, with a canopy density of 40% to 50%. Larch *Larix sibirica,* which averages 10 to 12 m in height, forms the tree layer. Dwarf-shrubs *Ledum palustre, Vaccinium uluginosum, V. vitis-idaea,* and *Empetrum nigrum* form the ground layer. The middle taiga subzone is typified by dark-coniferous forests dominated by *Picea obovata* and *Pinus sibirica.* These forests are taller and more productive than forests of the northern taiga subzone, with an average height of 17 to 20 m, and an average canopy density of 60% to 70%. Prevailing species in the dwarf-shrub and herb layer are *Linnaea borealis, Maianthemum bifolium, Trientalis europaea, Vaccinium vitis-idaea,* and *V. myrtillus.* Forest productivity increases in the southern taiga subzone. *Abies sibirica, Picea obovata,* and *Pinus sibirica* form the tree layer – which has an average height of 25 to 30 m, a canopy density of 60% to 80%, and trunk diameter of 50 to 60 cm at the age of 120 to 150 years. Common species in the ground layer are *Oxalis acetosella, Gymnocarpium dryopteris, Lycopodium clavatum, Luzula pilosa, Maianthemum bifolium, Carex macroura, Calamagrostis obtusata, Aconitum septentrionale, Cacalia hastata, Aegopodium podagraria, Athyrium filix-femina, Actaea erythrocarpa, Filipendula ulmaria, Milium effusum, Pulmonaria obscura,* and *Equisetum sylvaticum.* The cover of mosses and lichens is much lower than in the middle and northern taiga subzones. Pine forests dominated by *Pinus sylvestris* develop on sandy soils with better drainage. Paludification is very common in all taiga subzones and all forest types (Lapshina 1985, 1987).

River floodplains are covered by wet and moist meadows, shrub communities, and forests. Wet meadows – dominated by *Carex aquatilis, C. acuta, C. caespitosa, Calamagrostis langsdorfii, Phalaroides arundinacea, Arctophila fulva, Equisetum fluviatilis, Eleocharis acicularis, E. palustris, Agrostis stolonifera, Beckmannia eruciformis, Poa palustris, P. pratensis, Achillea ptarmica, Lythrum salicaria, Veronica longifolia,* and *Thalictrum simplex* – develop on the lowest levels of the floodplains. More-elevated places are covered by woodlands – with *Salix viminalis, S. cinerea, S. alba, Rosa acicularis, R. cinnamomea, Swida alba, Ribes nigrum, Populus tremula,* and *Betula pendula* – with meadow species in the ground layer. Boreal forests develop on river terraces, and are similar to the forests on watersheds (Il'ina 1985, Taran 1993, 2001). Ecosystems of this zone have great potential for forestry, agriculture, and fisheries.

Wildlife

The fauna of the region is typical of the boreal zone. Many common species have high commercial value. Species of birds that breed in the tundra zone can be found here during their migration. Mass migrations of ducks and geese can be observed.

Common animal species. Mammals: brown bear *Ursus arctos,* elk *Alces alces,* wolf *Canis lupus,* red fox *Vulpes vulpes,* lynx *Felis lynx,* wolverine *Gulo gulo,* sable *Martes zibellina,* marten *Martes martes,* ermine *Mustela ermine,* least weasel *M. nivalis,* American mink *M. vison,* otter *Lutra lutra,* muskrat *Ondatra zibethica.* Birds: teal *Anas crecca,* pintail *A. acuta,* tufted duck *Aythya fuligula,* goldeneye *Bucephala clangula,* capercaillie *Tetrao urogallus,* black grouse *Lyrurus tetrix,* hazelhen *Bonasa bonasia,* willow grouse *Lagopus lagopus.* Fish: broad whitefish *Coregonus nasus,* peled *C. peled,* Siberian sturgeon *Acipenser baerii baerii,* sterlet *A. ruthenus,* inconnu *Stenodus leucichthys nelma,* pike *Esox lucius.*

Rare and endangered animal species. West Siberian beaver *Castor fiber pohlei,* black stork *Ciconia nigra,* Siberian crane *Grus leucogeranus,* white-tailed eagle *Haliaeetus albicilla,* osprey *Pandion haliaetus,* golden eagle *Aquila chrysaetos,* peregrine falcon *Falco peregrinus,* oystercatcher *Haematopus ostralegus,* slender-billed curlew *Numenius tenuirostris,* river lamprey *Lampetra fluviatilis,* Siberian sturgeon *Acipenser baerii baerii,* lenok *Brachymystax lenok* (Krivenko 2000).

Peatlands

This part of western Siberia is extremely paludified. Peatlands cover a vast area of the watersheds, which have very slow runoff because of their flat relief. They occupy 40% of this zone according to Ivanov and Novikov (1976), and up to 50% according to other authors (Romanova 1985). Their occurrence increases to about 70% on watersheds of the Ob, Irtysh, and Konda rivers and decreases to 5% to 10% in the western and eastern parts of the zone. The average peat depth is 2 to 5 m. These bogs are approximately 8000 years old. Raised string bogs are the most-common peatland type, and represent almost half of all western-Siberian mires. The West Siberian raised string bogs have been described by Bronzov (1930, 1936), Khramov and Valutsky (1977), Liss and Berezina (1981),

Botch and Masing (1983), Romanova (1985), Kustova (1987a, b), and Lapshina *et al.* (2000).

The largest peatland in western Siberia is the Vasyugan bog (55° 40′ to 57° 18′ N; 76° 04′ to 82° 30′ E), considered to be the largest peatland in the world. It extends about 500 km from west to east and 100 km from south to north, covering an area of 54 000 km^2 and containing 14.3×10^9 tons of peat (Katz & Neishtadt 1963, Khramov & Valutsky 1977, Lapshina *et al.* 2000). It is located on the watershed between the Ob and Irtysh rivers on the border of the Tomsk, Tyumen, Omsk, and Novosibirsk administrative districts (peatland 33 in Fig. 2.10), and consists of a mosaic of community types (Fig. 2.5). Other large peatland systems are the Nazym–Pim interfluvial area (61° 30′ N; 70° 40′ E) covering 20 250 km^2 of the watershed between the Nazym and Pim rivers, and the Salym–Yugan peatland system (60° 58′ N; 69° 43′ E) which covers 15 000 km^2 in the catchments of the Bolshoi Yugan, Bolshoi Salym, and Tukan rivers (Botch 2000, Krivenko 2000).

Large bogs have a convex cupola, with centers 3 to 6 m (up to 10 m) higher than their margins. The flat central parts of these bogs are treeless with dystrophic and oligotrophic lakes and wet hollows separated by drier, low peat ridges. The peat consists mainly of *Sphagnum fuscum*, *S. magellanicum*, and *S. angustifolium* on ridges; and *S. balticum*, *S. fallax*, *S. majus*, *S. lindbergii*, and *S. papillosum* in hollows. Other plants typical of ridges are dwarf-trees *Pinus sylvestris*, *P. sibirica*, *Betula nana*; shrubs *Chamaedaphne calyculata*, *Ledum palustre*; dwarf-shrubs *Vaccinium uliginosum*, *V. vitis-idaea*; and lichens *Cladonia alpestris*, *C. rangiferina*, *Cetraria islandica*. Hollows are covered by *Carex limosa*, *C. lasiocarpa*, *C. rostrata*, *Menyanthes trifoliata*, *Comarum palustre*, *Equisetum fluviatile*, *Drepanocladus*, and *Calliergon* spp. Plants such as *Andromeda polifolia*, *Eriophorum vaginatum*, and *Oxycoccus palustris* occur both on ridges and in hollows (Table 2.6). Gently sloping bog margins are covered with open woodlands dominated by Scots pine *Pinus sylvestris*; the shrubs, herbs, and mosses that occur in the ground layer are the same as those found on the bog ridges.

Flat eutrophic and mesotrophic mire zone

Flat eutrophic and mesotrophic mires develop in the hemiboreal subzone of western Siberia, which is transitional between the Siberian taiga and forest-steppe zones. It has the shape of a long strip oriented from west to east. The width of the zone from north to south is about 150 km. It covers about 300 000 km^2 (about the size of Arizona), and represents 11% of the West Siberian Lowland. The relief of the zone is flat, at 135 to 150 m above sea level. The climate

Figure 2.5 Fragment of the vegetation map of the Vasyugan bog (from Il'ina *et al.*
1985). Middle taiga units: 82, pine and birch–pine forests with *Sphagnum fuscum*,
S. magellanicum, and *Polytrichum commune* complex with dwarf-shrub bogs; 83, bogs
with *Sphagnum fuscum*, *Chamaedaphne calyculata*, *Pinus sylvestris* f. *litwinovii*, and *Pinus
sibirica* f. *turfosa* on strings in complex with mesoeutrophic mires in hollows with
Sphagnum balticum and *S. dusenii*; 84, pine–dwarf-shrub–sphagnum-dominated bogs
with *Pinus sylvestris* f. *uliginosa* and f. *litwinovii*, *Chamaedaphne calyculata*, and *Sphagnum
fuscum*. Southern taiga units: 88, dark-coniferous boreal forests with *Pinus sibirica*,
Picea obovata, *Abies sibirica*, *Pleurozium schreberi*, *Hylocomium splendens*, *Rhytidiadelphus
triquetrus*, *Maianthemum bifilium*, *Oxalis acetosella*, *Carex macroura*, *Aconitum
septentrionale*, and *Cacalia hastata*; 89, secondary dark-coniferous–birch forests with
Betula pendula, *Carex macroura*, and *Calamagrostis obtusata*. 90, secondary dark-
coniferous–aspen forests with *Populus tremula*, *Caragana arborescens*, *Aconitum
septentrionale*, *Crepis sibirica*, and *Calamagrostis obtusata*. 92, arable lands in the place of
boreal dark-coniferous forests. 101, dark-coniferous moist forests with *Pinus sibirica*,
Abies sibirica, *Hylocomium splendens*, and *Sphagnum squarrosum*, *S. wulfianum*, and *Carex
globularis*. 102, secondary birch–dark-coniferous moist forests with *Calamagrostis
langsdorfii* and *Equisetum sylvaticum*. 106, secondary birch–dark-coniferous moist
forests with *Calamagrostis canescens*, *Equisetum sylvaticum*, *Sphagnum angustifolium*, and
S. warnstorfii in complex with sphagnum- and sedge-dominated mires.

is continental, although for the first time as we move from north to south the
average annual temperature becomes slightly higher than 0 °C. The snow period
is about 180 days and the frost-free period 100 to 120 days; annual precipitation is 510 mm, annual runoff 90 mm, and annual evapotranspiration 420 mm
(Table 2.1). Approximately 20% of the zone is paludified.

Table 2.6 *Floristic composition of raised string bogs.*

Species	Ridges	Hollows
Pinus sylvestris	+	−
Pinus sibirica	+	−
Betula nana	+	−
Ledum palustre	+	−
Chamaedaphne calyculata	+	−
Rubus chamaemorus	+	−
Vaccinium uliginosum	+	−
Vaccinium vitis-idaea	+	−
Sphagnum fuscum	+	−
Sphagnum magellanicum	+	−
Sphagnum angustifolium	+	−
Polytrichum strictum	+	−
Cladonia rangiferina	+	−
Cladonia alpestris	+	−
Cetraria islandica	+	−
Oxycoccus palustris	+	+
Andromeda polifolia	+	+
Eriophorum vaginatum	+	+
Carex limosa	−	+
Carex lasiocarpa	−	+
Carex diandra	−	+
Carex rostrata	−	+
Rhynchospora alba	−	+
Scheuchzeria palustris	−	+
Drosera anglica	−	+
Menyanthes trifoliata	−	+
Comarum palustre	−	+
Equisetum fluviatile	−	+
Utricularia minor	−	+
Sphagnum balticum	−	+
Sphagnum fallax	−	+
Sphagnum majus	−	+
Sphagnum lindbergii	−	+
Sphagnum jensenii	−	+
Sphagnum papillosum	−	+
Calliergon stramineum	−	+
Drepanocladus sendtneri	−	+
Scorpidium scorpioides	−	+

Vegetation

The zonal vegetation is represented by aspen–birch forests dominated by *Betula pendula* and *Populus tremula*. Aspen and birch comprise the canopies of secondary forests in all other regions of Eurasia, and only here do they dominate in climax forests. The shrub layer includes *Rosa majalis*, *Sorbus sibirica*, and *Viburnum opulus* among others. Common plants in the ground layer are as follows: *Calamagrostis arundinacea*, *C. epigeios*, *Brachypodium pinnatum*, *Poa pratensis Carex macroura*, *Angelica sylvestris*, *Galium boreale*, *Geranium pseudosibiricum*, *Hieracium umbellatum*, *Rubus saxatilis*, *Sanguisorba officinalis*, *Trifolium lupinaster*, *Silene nutans*, *Vicia cracca*, and *V. sepium*. Both nemoral – *Aegopodium podagraria*, *Lathyrus vernus*, and *Pulmonaria dacica* – and boreal species – *Maianthemum bifolium*, *Vaccinium vitis-idaea*, and *V. myrtillus* – are typically present in the herb layer (Ermakov *et al.* 2000). Pine forests with *Pinus sylvestris* occur on sandy and loamy-sandy soils. They often have an admixture of boreal species in the ground layer including the mosses *Pleurozium schreberi*, *Dicranum polysetum*, and *Rhytidiadelphus triquetrus*. Forests on watersheds occur in a mosaic with grasslands. Floodplain terraces are covered by mesophytic and xero-mesophytic grasslands with *Festuca ovina*, *Elytrigia repens*, *Poa pratensis*, *Medicago falcata*, and *Lathyrus pratensis*. Floodplain forests are dominated by *Populus nigra*, *P. alba*, *P. tremula*, *Salix alba*, *S. viminalis*, and *Betula pendula*. Semi-aquatic meadows develop in the lowest floodplain levels. They are dominated by *Carex acuta*, *C. cespitosa*, *Calamagrostis canescens*, *Phragmites australis*, *Phalaroides arundinacea*, *Lythrum salicaria*, and *Galium uliginosum*.

Wildlife

The fauna of this mire zone is represented by a mixture of taiga and forest-steppe species along with both European and eastern-Siberian species. It has no endemic species, but plays an important role as a corridor along which species move seasonally from north to south and vice versa. A list of endangered animals of the area includes: mammals, West Siberian beaver *Castor fiber pohlei*; birds, Siberian crane *Grus leucogeranus* and tawny owl *Strix aluco*; fish, tugun *Coregonus tugun* (Krivenko 2000).

Peatlands

Peatlands cover, on average, 20% of the zone. The Barabinskaia lowland, located in the northeastern part of this zone, has the highest proportion of mires – 31.6% is paludified (Romanova 1985). The average depth of peat deposits varies from 1 to 3 m; they are 2000 to 7000 years old. The peatlands of this zone typically have a complex structure. They have been described by Kuzmina (1953), Ivanov and Novikov (1976), Botch and Masing (1983), and Romanova (1985).

Eutrophic sedge-moss fens and woody swamps, moistened from below by rich mineral groundwater, are very common. Characteristic species of sedge fens are *Carex cespitosa*, *C. juncella*, *C. chordorrhiza*, *C. diandra*, *C. lasiocarpa*, *C. omskiana*, *C. vesicaria*, *Comarum palustre*, *Equisetum fluviatile*, and *Menyanthes trifoliata*. Typical mosses are *Drepanocladus vernicosus*, *D. sendtneri*, *Tomenthypnum nitens*, and *Calliergon* spp. Eutrophic woody swamps are dominated by *Betula pubescens* in the overstory and by hygrophytes – such as *Calamagrostis langsdorffii*, *C. canescens*, *Filipendula ulmaria*, *Phragmites australis*, *Carex juncella*, and *C. cespitosa* – in the ground layer. They are a typical component of floodplains, but can also develop on uplands in place of the aspen–birch forests when they become paludified.

Oligotrophic and mesotrophic mires that are surrounded by eutrophic sedge-moss fens have a convex shape. Floristically, they are similar to the raised string bogs of the boreal regions. *Pinus sylvestris* and *Betula pubescens* typically dominate their tree layer, while *Ledum palustre* and *Chamaedaphne calyculata* dominate their shrub layer. Herbaceous and dwarf-shrub species – such as *Eriophorum vaginatum*, *Oxycoccus palustris*, *Rubus chamaemorus*, *Vaccinium vitis-idaea* – and mosses *Sphagnum fuscum*, *S. magellanicum*, and *S. angustifolium* form the ground layer. In this zone oligotrophic and mesotrophic mires represent relict vegetation, and cover not more than 5% to 10% of the whole peatland area.

In a typical mire complex, eutrophic sedge fens and woody swamps cover the peripheries and areas around mineral islands making up the greater mire matrix, while mesotrophic sedge-hypnum moss bogs and oligotrophic sedge-sphagnum moss bogs occur in central parts of mire complexes.

Reed and sedge-fen mire zone and salt-water marshes

Reed and sedge-fen mires are typical of the forest-steppe zone of the southern part of the West Siberian Lowland. The region covers 440 000 km^2 (about the size of California) and represents 16% of the West Siberian Lowland. It is located at the southern section of the West Siberian epiplatform. The relief is flat and consists of numerous blind depressions; the elevation varies from 120 to 280 m. The climate is continental with hot summers and periodic droughts. Average annual precipitation is 390 mm, annual runoff 10 mm, and evapotranspiration 380 mm. The winters last 150 to 170 days. The average July temperature is +18 to +20 °C, and the average January temperature is −16 to −21 °C. The river network is not dense and many rivers end in blind basins. Shallow lakes containing either fresh water or bitter-salt waters are very common. The groundwater table is typically close to the surface. The zonal soil types are chernozems which develop under steppe vegetation. The saline soils "solod" and "solonchak" are also common. The territory has traditionally been used for grazing and hunting.

Vegetation

Zonal vegetation types are grasslands (meadow-steppes) and aspen–birch forests. Characteristic plants of the zonal grasslands are *Stipa pennata, S. capillata, Helictotrichon schellianum, Festuca pseudovina, Koeleria cristata, Phleum phleoides, Poa angustifolia, Achillea nobilis, Adonis vernalis, Anemone sylvestris, Artemisia austriaca, A. dracunculus, A. latifolia, A. scoparia, A. sericea, Astragalus danicus, Carex praecox, C. supina, Eryngium planum, Filipendula vulgaris, Fragaria viridis, Galium verum, Inula salicina, Lathyrus tuberosus, Medicago falcata, Onobrychis sibirica, Plantago stepposa, Pulsatilla flavescens, Ranunculus polyanthemos, Seseli libanotis,* and *Vicia cracca.* Large grassland areas were ploughed during the 1950s and converted to arable land; their remnants are often found around birch–aspen groves. Halophytic grasslands are also very common (Korolyuk 1999) and have traditionally been used for grazing. The most-common halophytic species are *Aster tripolium, Artemisia laciniata, A. nitrosa, A. pontica, Atriplex littoralis, Cirsium esculentum, Galatella biflora, G. punctata, Glaux maritima, Glycyrrhiza uralensis, Hordeum brevisubulatum, Juncus gerardii, Limonium gmelinii, Petrosimonia litwinowii, Plantago cornuti, P. maxima, P. salsa, Puccinelia distans, P. tenuissima, Saussurea amara, Salicornia europaea, Suaeda corniculata,* and *S. prostrata.*

Forest vegetation is characterized by small groves of birch *Betula pendula* and aspen *Populus tremula.* Floristically they are similar to those groves of the hemiboreal zone. Pine forests with *Pinus sylvestris* are associated with sandy soils. The ground layer of the pine forests contains both forest species (*Vaccinium vitis-idaea, V. myrtillus, Calamagrostis arundinacea,* and *Carex macroura*) and steppe species (*Calamagrostis epigeios, Carex supine, Koeleria cristata, Artemisia commutata,* and *A. sericea*). Forests of this zone were intensively developed for agriculture. Secondary grasslands, which develop after clear-cutting, are similar to zonal grasslands but differ in that they have a high constancy of plants that typically occur in the forest ground layer such as the rhizome grasses – *Bromopsis inermis, Calamagrostis epigeios, Elytrigia repens,* and *Poa pratensis* – and other mesophyllous forest plants such as *Serratula coronata, Silene nutans, Solidago virgaurea, Galium boreale,* and *Hieracium umbellatum.*

Wildlife

Species typical of continental forest-steppe and steppe regions coexist here. Consequently, the diversity of fauna is rather high.

Common mammal species. Rodents: ground squirrels *Citellus rufescens, C. erythrogenus,* hamster *Cricetus cricetus,* jerboa *Allactaga saltator,* voles *Microtus oeconomus, Clethrionomys rutilus,* and steppe lemming *Eremiomys lagurus.* Other mammal species: wolf *Canis lupus,* corsac fox *Vulpes corsac,* ermine *Mustela erminea,* Siberian polecat *Mustela eversmanni*, roe deer *Capreolus capreolus*, badger *Meles meles*, hare *Lepus timidus*, and flying squirrel *Pteromys volans*. Birds: grey-headed green woodpecker *Picus canus*, jay *Garrulus glandarius*, Eurasian roller *Coracias garrulus*, swans *Cygnus cygnus, C. olor*, greylag goose *Anser anser*, ruddy shelduck *Casarca ferruginea*, common shelduck *Tadorna tadorna*, white-headed duck *Oxyura leucocephala*, grebes *Colymbus cristatus, C. auritus, C. nigricollis*, black tern *Chlidonias nigra*, marsh harrier *Circus aeruginosus*, short-eared owl *Asio flammeus*, common snipe *Gallinago gallinago*, greenshank *Tringa nebularia*, cormorant *Phalacrocorax carbo*, and white pelican *Pelecanus onocrotalus*. Amphibians: common newt *Triturus vulgaris* and frog *Rana terrestris*. Fish: pike *Esox lucius*, roach *Rutilus rutilus*, crucian carp *Carassius carassius*, dace *Leuciscus leuciscus*, river perch *Perca fluviatilis*, ruffe *Gymnocephalus cernuus*, lake minnow *Phoxinus percnurus*, and tench *Tinca tinca*.

Endangered species. Mammals: Russian desman *Desmana moschata*. Birds: black stork *Ciconia nigra*, white-tailed eagle *Haliaeetus albicilla*, osprey *Pandion haliaetus*, Dalmatian pelican *Pelecanus crispus*, ferruginous duck *Aythya nyroca*, oystercatcher *Haematopus ostralegus*, Asian dowitcher *Limnodromus semipalmatus*, great black-headed gull *Larus ichthyaetus*, Caspian tern *Sterna caspia*, and little tern *S. albifrons* (Krivenko 2000).

Peatlands

Peatlands cover about 5% of the region and are mostly associated with floodplain depressions. In the northern part of the region they also occur on uplands in depressions and around lakes. Mires are typically covered by reed (*Phragmites australis*), sedges (*Carex appropinquata, C. omskiana, C. cespitosa, C. riparia*, and *C. vesicaria*), grasses (*Scolochloa festucacea, Calamagrostis neglecta*), and herbs (*Caltha palustris, Comarum palustre, Scirpus lacustris*, and *Typha latifolia*). Mesotrophic and oligotrophic mires also occur in combination with reed and sedge fens as relicts of earlier periods. These relict peatlands, with *Pinus sylvestris* and *Betula pubescens* in the overstory and *Sphagnum* mosses in the ground layer, are rare and represent not more than 5% to 10% of peatlands of this area. They are approximately 5000 to 7000 years old and have peat depths from 1 to 3 m (Botch & Masing 1983, Romanova 1985).

Classes of ecological–floristic classification of the West Siberian Lowland

Syntaxonomic studies of the West Siberian vegetation using the Braun-Blanquet approach (Westhoff & van der Maarel 1973) began in the 1980s. This work is not complete, but the majority of classes of ecological–floristic classification have probably been revealed (Kustova 1987a, b, Taran 1993, 2001, Solomeshch *et al.* 1997, Korolyuk 1999, Ermakov *et al.* 2000). The list of classes shows the diversity of the West Siberian vegetation that exists across the Lowland. Classes of tundra, forest, steppe, and salt-marsh vegetation are restricted in their distribution to particular climatic zones; in contrast, classes of bog, fen, aquatic, and anthropogenic vegetation may be found in several or all zones.

Tundras

Class *Carici rupestris-Kobresietea bellardii* Ohba 1974: circumpolar arctic and alpine grasslands with *Carex* and dwarf-shrub species.

Class *Loiseleurio-Vaccinietea* Eggler 1952: circumpolar arctic and alpine dwarf-shrub heaths with mosses and lichens.

Bogs and fens

Class *Oxycocco-Sphagnetea* Br.-Bl. et Tx. ex Westhoff, Dijk et Passchier 1946: ombrotrophic bogs and wet heathlands on oligotrophic acid peats.

Class *Scheuchzerio-Caricetea fuscae* Tx. 1937: bog-pool and fen vegetation dominated by small sedges and bryophytes on mesotrophic acid peats.

Freshwater aquatic vegetation

Class *Lemnetea* Tx. 1955: communities of free-floating and submerged aquatic plants in relatively nutrient-rich fresh waters.

Class *Potametea* Klika in Klika & Novak 1941: communities of rooted aquatic plants with submerged and floating leaves in mesotrophic and eutrophic fresh waters.

Class *Phragmito-Magnocaricetea* Klika in Klika & Novak 1941: communities of rooted aquatic and semi-aquatic plants in fresh mesotrophic and eutrophic waters, swamps, marshes, and fens.

Semi-aquatic vegetation

Class *Isoëto-Nanojuncetea* Br.-Bl. et Tx. ex Westhoff, Dijk et Passchier 1946: pioneer, ephemeral vegetation on bare, periodically flooded ground.

Grasslands

Class *Molinio-Arrhenatheretea* Tx. 1937: anthropogenic mesophytic meadows and pastures on more or less fertile soils.

Class *Festuco-Brometea* Br.-Bl. et Tx. in Br.-Bl. 1949: xerothermic and semi-xerothermic steppe grasslands.

Salt-marsh and salt-steppe vegetation

Class *Thero-Salicornietea* (Pignatti 1953) Tx. in Tx. et Oberdorfer 1958: pioneer halophyte communities of annual succulents on wet sites.

Class *Puccinellio-Salicornietea* Topa 1939 incl. *Asteretea tripolium* Westhoff & Beeftink in Beeftink 1962: continental salt marshes with prevalence of perennial non-succulent herbaceous species.

Class *Festuco-Limonietea* Karpov & Mirkin 1985: salt-steppes on solonetz soils in eastern Europe and western Siberia.

Forests

Class *Vaccinio-Piceetea* Br.-Bl. in Br.-Bl., Siss. et Vlieger 1939: boreal coniferous forests on nutrient-poor acid soils.

Class *Querco-Fagetea* Br.-Bl. et Vlieger in Vlieger 1937: nemoral mixed broadleaved forests on nutrient-rich soils.

Class *Brachypodio pinnati–Betuletea pendulae* Ermakov, Korolyuk & Latchinsky 1991: hemiboreal birch–pine, pine, and mixed-grass forests on nutrient-rich soils in the temperate–continental sector of south Siberia.

Class *Pulsatillo-Pinetea* Oberdorfer 1992: thermophilous pine forests on sandy soils.

Class *Salicetea purpureae* Moor 1958: willow scrub and woodland on levees and river banks.

Class *Alnetea glutinosae* Br.-Bl. et Tx. 1943 em. Müller & Görs 1958: alder woodlands and swamps on eutrophic peats.

Moss vegetation

Class *Hypnetea cupressiformis* Ježek et Vondraček 1962: epiphytic moss vegetation on the bark of living trees.

Class *Lepidozio-Lophocoletea heterophyllae* von Hubschmann 1976: moss vegetation on rotten wood and bark.

Anthropogenic vegetation

Class *Stellarietea mediae* Tx., Lohm. et Preising ex Rochow 1951: weed vegetation of arable crops, gardens, and disturbed places dominated by annual plants.

Class *Artemisietae vulgaris* Tx., Lohm. et Preising ex Rochow 1951: ruderal vegetation dominated by biennial and perennial weeds.

Class *Galio-Urticetea* Passarge ex Kopecky 1969: perennial nitrophilous vegetation on relatively stable substrates.

Class *Epilobietea angustifolii* Tx. et Preising ex Rochow 1951: pioneer vegetation after forests clearings or burning.

Class *Bidentetea tripartitae* Tx., Lohm. et Preising ex Rochow 1951: pioneer nitrophilous annual vegetation on periodically flooded mud.

Class *Polygono arenastri-Poetea annuae* Rivas-Mart in ez 1975: vegetation of intensively trampled and/or grazed mesophytic habitats dominated by annual plants.

Class *Polygono-Artemisietea austriacae* Mirkin, Sakhapov & Solomeshch in Mirkin *et al.* 1986: short xerophytic vegetation of heavily trampled and grazed dry habitats in steppe zone of Eastern Europe and Siberia.

The list of classes shows close relationships between West Siberian and European vegetation. Among the 28 classes found here, only one is unique to western Siberia. The class *Brachypodio pinnati-Betuletea pendulae*, composed of hemiboreal birch–pine and mixed-grass forests, replaces the European broadleaved forests of the class *Querco-Fagetea* in the temperate–continental sector of southern Siberia (Ermakov *et al.* 2000). All the other classes are either circumpolar or widespread in Central and Eastern Europe.

Carbon pools and accumulation rates in the West Siberian peatlands

Peatland ecosystems are the main component of West Siberian landscapes. Because of their great extent and capacity to accumulate water and organic materials, they represent an enormous natural resource. The environmental functions of peatlands include freshwater storage, control of groundwater level, and the determination of natural and agricultural ecosystem productivity. Peatlands regulate climate, temperature, and precipitation; purify water; sequester carbon dioxide from the atmosphere; and generate oxygen. They foster biodiversity by providing habitat for many plants and animals. Peatlands have a socio-economic value; they are important to human welfare as a resource for fuels (peat, wood), fertilizers (e.g. sapropel), and activities such as hunting, fishing, collecting berries and mushrooms, balneology, recreation, and tourism. They provide opportunities for indigenous peoples to continue traditional economic activities and lifestyles.

The amount of fresh water in the peatlands of the taiga, hemiboreal, and forest-steppe zones of western Siberia has been estimated at 994 km^3 (Ivanov

& Novikov 1976). The actual amount of fresh water in West Siberian peatlands is much higher, because this estimate does not include water from mires of the arctic and forest-tundra zones. The present state of the Arctic Ocean and its influence on the global climate depend on outflow from Siberian rivers. The two largest north-Asian rivers are the Yenisey (4020 km) and Ob (3700 km). The Ob drains the major part of the lowland. The middle Ob flows northwest through the swampy forests of the southern and middle taiga zones, and is joined by the Chulym, Ket, and Irtysh rivers. The Ob estuary, when it enters the Kara Sea of the Arctic Ocean, is 800 km long and 60 to 80 km wide. The Yenisey, forming the eastern boundary of the West Siberian Lowland, enters the Kara Sea through a 400-km-long estuary. The freshwater discharge by the Ob and Yenisey averages 530 and 603 km^3 per year, respectively (Aagaard & Carmack 1989). The Mississippi River discharge, for comparison, is about 580 km^3 per year (Meade 1995). This freshwater flow contributes significantly to the stratification of the ocean near the surface, and supports sea-ice formation. Changes in the present freshwater balance would influence the extent of sea-ice cover. Thus, the West Siberian Lowland significantly influences the regulation of arctic climate and the global freshwater cycle.

The true environmental and socio-economic value of the West Siberian peatlands has never been explicitly evaluated. A detailed analysis of all ecosystem functions is beyond the scope of this chapter. Thus the emphasis of this chapter is on carbon accumulation because of the particular importance of this issue for large-scale environmental problems such as global warming and climate change; these problems are of great concern because of the effects of human activities on environmental dynamics.

Exploration of the West Siberian Lowland has been very difficult because of the climatic and topographic conditions. The first cursory estimation of total peat stocks in western Siberia was performed in the 1950s, when the West Siberian Peat Exploratory Expedition was established (Glavtorffond RSFSR 1956). Almost 20 years later the next evaluation was performed when more-detailed maps were available. The area of the West Siberian peatlands was estimated at 0.369 million km^2, and total peat deposits at 119.3 Pg (1 Pg = 10^{15} g). However, the lack of information on shallow peatlands (less than 0.5 to 0.7 m deep), with no commercial value and therefore not included in peat inventories, caused uncertainty in this estimate. Further uncertainty resulted from a deficiency in data on commercial peat depth and bulk density (Loginov & Khoroshev 1972, Markov & Khoroshev 1975).

One of the most-comprehensive, long-term studies of ecosystem productivity in the raised string bogs, which cover the largest area and are characterized by the deepest peat deposits, was conducted by Khramov and Valutsky (1977). They measured productivity separately for nearly a dozen different ecosystems that together represent a mosaic of vegetation of the Vasyugan bog, which is the largest in western Siberia, and probably in the world. It was shown that ecosystems at the bog margins were, as a rule, more productive than ecosystems in the bog center. Total above-ground biomass in open woodlands, typically dominated by *Pinus sylvestris* and *Ledum palustris*, varies from 1900 to 5800 g m^{-2} (19 to 58 tons ha^{-1}), with an annual accumulation rate from 200 to 400 g m^{-2} (2 to 4 tons ha^{-1}). From 70% to 85% of this biomass is concentrated in the tree layer. Treeless vegetation in the bog center – with *Sphagnum fuscum* on ridges and *Sphagnum papillosum* in hollows – is less productive, averaging 340 g m^{-2} (3.4 tons ha^{-1}) of dry above-ground biomass, 60% to 75% of which is accumulated in the moss layer. These results represent above-ground biomass but not the total carbon pool. Peat depth, age, and carbon emission rates have not been studied. Because the work of Khramov and Valutsky (1997) was restricted to raised string bogs, it may not be appropriate to extrapolate these results to other peatlands zones.

An improved estimate of area, carbon pools, and rates of carbon accumulation in peatlands of the former Soviet Union – including the West Siberian Lowland – was provided by Botch *et al.* (1995). Aerial photographs, small-scale vegetation maps, and expert assessments were used to improve estimates of the area of non-commercial peatlands with thin peat layers, which are especially common in northern areas. The total peatland area of the former Soviet Union was estimated at 1.65 million km^2 and the peat carbon pool at 215 Pg. The rate of carbon accumulation varied from 12 g m^{-2} per year in polygonal mires, to 31.4 g m^{-2} per year in raised string bogs, and up to 72 to 80 g m^{-2} per year in swamps, fens, and marshes. The total rate of carbon accumulation was 52 Tg per year (1 Tg = 10^{12} g). Unfortunately, all estimates were provided for the entire country; data for the West Siberian Lowland may not be directly taken from this, one of the most-recent and -comprehensive surveys, as they are combined with data from all other regions.

Carbon storage in the West Siberian peatlands on lands under the jurisdiction of the Russian Forestry Service was estimated at 51 Pg (Efremov *et al.* 1998). However, this estimate may not be considered final for several reasons. First, the estimate does not include arctic and non-commercial peat deposits. Secondly, only peatlands that were under the jurisdiction of the Russian Forestry Service were included. Thirdly, the authors pointed out that data from different agencies were inconsistent, and sparse forests that formed on peat soils and sometimes on thick peat deposits had not been surveyed for peat storage. The carbon-pool estimate by Efremov *et al.* (1998) is consistent with the estimate of total peat deposits of 119.3 Pg reported by Markov and Khoroshev (1975) because carbon content in peat deposits averages at 56% (see Table 2.7).

Another study conducted by scientists from the Russian State Hydrological Institute (St. Petersburg) estimated the total area of West Siberian mires at about 0.713 million km^2 and storage at 207.8 Pg of peat deposits (Novikov & Usova 2000). They also estimated the distribution of peat deposits according to peat type: moss peat represented 37%, transitional peat 13%, and fen peat 50%. Their estimate of the total peat storage was almost twice as high as that reported by Markov and Khoroshev (1975).

A study of carbon accumulation in the Salym-Yugan raised string bog, the second-largest bog sysytem in western Siberia, was based on 11 study sites (Turunen *et al.* 2001). Special attention was given to differences in peat dry bulk density depending on peat depth. The average long-term rate of carbon accumulation was estimated at 17.2 g m^{-2} per year, ranging from 12.1 to 23.7 g m^{-2} per year. Results obtained in one bog were extrapolated to all raised string bogs of Russia, including those in the European part of the country. The carbon pool was estimated, not for West Siberian peatlands but for all the raised string bogs of Russia, and was roughly half of the earlier estimate for the same type of peatlands (Botch *et al.* 1995). Regardless of which method was more accurate, the Turunen *et al.* (2001) estimate may not properly be extrapolated to all the West Siberian Lowland because it was obtained in only one bog system, and does not represent the variety of climatic zones and peatland types across West Siberia.

Another study of carbon accumulation rates in the raised string bogs of the southern taiga zone of western Siberia estimated the average rate of carbon accumulation at 41.2 g m^{-2} per year, with values ranging from 24.9 to 56.7 g m^{-2} per year (Bleuten & Lapshina 2001, Lapshina *et al.* 2001). This is more than twice the estimate published by Turunen *et al.* (2001).

Estimates of carbon accumulation rates, even when they are based on modern methodologies, are very inconsistent and may vary considerably – not only between peatland types, but even within one given peatland – depending upon the sample location. Such data based on locally restricted samples may not be appropriately extrapolated to a larger scale. In this chapter, in order to obtain estimates of the size of the carbon pool and accumulation rates for the West Siberian Lowland, values for peatland area and average depth of peat were applied according to Ivanov and Novikov (1976). Carbon content and peat accumulation rates were taken from Botch *et al.* (1995); because their data were based on expert assessment and were averaged across all vegetation zones and many study sites, we assume that they are more reliable for large-scale extrapolation.

According to this estimate, the West Siberian peatlands cover an area of 0.787 million km², contain 134.5 Pg of dry peat, a 76.4 Pg of carbon pool, and have an average carbon accumulation rate of 22.8 Tg per year (Table 2.7). The peatland area of 0.787 million km² is twice the size of commercial West Siberian peatlands reported by Markov and Khoroshev (1975), and half of all former-Soviet-Union peatlands. This result is similar to the estimate of the former-Soviet-Union peatland area by Botch et al. (1995), which was also roughly twice the area of commercial peatlands. At the same time, the total dry peat content of 134.5 Pg is only 13% higher than the value of 119.3 Pg for commercial peatlands, as reported by Markov and Khoroshev (1975). This low increase in dry peat content reflects that non-commercial peatlands with shallow peat deposits contribute only a small amount to dry peat content totals. The total carbon pool estimate of 76.4 Pg is comparable with the estimate of 51 Pg obtained for West Siberian peatlands on lands under the jurisdiction of the Russian Forestry Service (Efremov et al. 1998), as the latter estimate does not include all peatlands.

Northern peatlands are located almost totally in Russia, Fennoscandian countries, Canada, and Alaska; they have a total area of 3.46 million km², 270 to 455 Pg of carbon stored as peat, and an average carbon accumulation rate of 66 to 96 Tg per year (Gorham 1991, Turunen et al. 2002). Taking into account the range of these estimates, we conclude that the peatlands of the West Siberian Lowland represent 23% of boreal and subarctic peatlands, provide 17% to 28% of global carbon peat deposits, and 24% to 35% of global annual carbon accumulation rates. Therefore, they are perceived to be an important component of the global carbon cycle.

The rates of carbon accumulation in western Siberia during the Holocene were different depending on time and location. Peatland growth rates during the climate warm phases decreased in the south due to drier conditions, while they increased in the north because of more-favorable temperature and moisture conditions and the longer growing season. On the contrary, during the climate cooling phases, peatland growth rate increased in the south and decreased in the north. Recent data show that peat accumulation rates are higher in the forest-steppe and southern taiga zones – and lower in tundra, forest-tundra, and northern taiga zones (Vasiliev 2000, Lapshina et al. 2001).

Finally, in addition to the influence of their peatlands, West Siberian forests also play an important part in the global carbon cycle. Assessments of the organic carbon reserves in West Siberian forests range from 21.5 to 28.1 Pg (Aleksyev & Birdsey 1998, Shvidenko & Nilsson 1998), making the role of the West Siberian Lowland in the global carbon cycle even greater.

Table 2.7 *Carbon pool and accumulation rates in the West Siberian peatlands.*

Peatland type	Peatland area (10³ km²)	Average peat depth (m)	Volume of peat (10⁹ m³)	Dry bulk density (tons m³)	Weight of dry peat (Pg)	Carbon content (%)	Carbon pool (Pg)	Carbon pool distribution (%)	Rate of carbon accumulation (tons km² per year)	Carbon accumulation (Tg per year)
Polygonal mires	71	0.5	36	0.14	5.0	57	2.9	3.8	12.0	0.85
Flat-palsa mires	88	0.8	70	0.14	9.8	57	5.6	7.3	16.0	1.41
High-palsa mires	41	1.0	41	0.14	5.7	57	3.3	4.3	16.0	0.66
Raised string bogs	505	2.4	1212	0.08	96.0	56	54.3	71.1	31.4	15.86
Flat eutrophic and mesotrophic mires	60	1.7	103	0.14	14.4	57	8.2	10.7	38.1	2.29
Reed and sedge fens	22	1.2	26	0.14	3.6	57	2.1	2.8	79.8	1.76
Total	787		1488		134.5		76.4	100		22.83

Human impact on the West Siberian Lowland

The West Siberian Lowland comprises ten administrative subdivisions of the Russian Federation, and includes a narrow strip of northern Kazakhstan in the south. The population of the region in 2001 was around 21.35 million (Table 2.8). The average population density is 8.2 people per km^2, which is not high. The density is much lower in the north because the vast majority of people live in cities in the southern part of the Lowland. For example, the Yamal–Nenetsky autonomous district, representing the northern part of West Siberia and covering one-third of the entire Lowland, has only 0.65 people per km^2. Some areas, especially in the north, have never been highly populated or modified by people and remain comparatively untouched.

The recent intensive development of oil and gas industries has had a great impact on all West Siberian ecosystems, especially raised string bogs and palsa mires. The largest oil and gas deposits in Russia are located in boreal and sub-arctic zones of the West Siberian Lowland, and more specifically in the mid and lower Ob river basin. They have enormous economic importance for the Russian Federation. Intensive oil and gas exploration, extraction, and transportation of oil resources started in the mid 1960s. Unfortunately, arctic and boreal wetlands are highly vulnerable to oil spills. The negative environmental impact associated with oil development is mainly due to pollution of ponds with crude oil and the salt water and chemicals used in the oil-drilling process, habitat destruction and fragmentation, and burning of accompanying gas (Vasiliev 1998, Bleuten *et al.* 1999). Arctic wetlands on the Yamal, Gydan, and Taz peninsulas – and boreal raised string bogs – are very vulnerable to caterpillar-tracked vehicles, which destroy vegetation in the vicinity of oil-rigs and settlements.

In the southern taiga, where the majority of industrial plants are located, atmospheric and water pollution have strong negative effects on ecosystems. Data from 2001 on atmospheric emissions of pollutants, water pollution, and toxic waste formation are shown in Table 2.8. The major sources of toxic waste are metallurgical plants and fossil-fuel electrical power stations. The pollution of surface waters in this region with oil products and phenols is the highest in Russia. Water pollution originating from the upper and middle Ob River in the boreal zone also has a negative influence on aquatic ecosystems of the lower Ob River in the subarctic zone, and has damaged formerly famous fisheries in this region (Krivenko 1999, 2000). Along with oil and gas drilling, continued timber harvesting and man-made fires have become the main environmental threats in the southern taiga zone. Creating pastures in forests leads to fragmentation or complete destruction of forest ecosystems; hunting and poaching also decrease faunal diversity.

Table 2.8 *Population, and water and atmospheric pollution in the West Siberian Lowland.*[a]

Administrative districts[b]	Area (10³ km²)	Population (× 10⁶)	Atmospheric pollution (10³ tons)	Water pollution (10⁶ m³)	Formation of toxic waste (10³ tons)
Yamal-Nenetsky District	750.3	0.49	586.63 (0.1)[c]	33.2	249.3 (8.2)
Khanty-Mansijsky District	523.1	1.33	1725.97 (0.5)	33.3	1 307.8 (19.3)
Tyumensky Oblast'	161.8	1.40	68.64 (20.6)	78.6	16.1 (66.9)
Sverdlovsky Oblast'	194.8	4.66	1407.05 (86.8)	817.6	4 251.9 (95.5)
Chelyabinsky Oblast'	87.9	3.68	984.06 (80.3)	773.7	15 006.0 (57.8)
Kurgansky Oblast'	71.0	1.11	91.23 (59.2)	18.1	49.9 (15.3)
Omsky Oblast'	139.7	2.18	238.35 (89.1)	229.5	2 396.2 (16.5)
Tomsky Oblast'	316.9	1.07	254.60 (51.7)	19.2	299.9 (2.4)
Novosibirsky Oblast'	178.2	2.75	198.05 (80.3)	73.8	925.8 (77.3)
Altaysky Kray	169.1	2.68	255.16 (76.0)	34.3	683.9 (26.1)
Total	2592.8[d]	21.35	5809.74	2111.3	25 186.8

[a] Data compiled from the State Report on the Status of the Environment of the Russian Federation in 2001 (Gosudarstvennyi Komitet po Okhrane Okruzhaiuschchei Sredy 2001) available on http://www.eco-net.ru/index.php?id=814/

[b] Sverdlovsky, Chelyabinsky, and Kurgansky districts according to the territorial division of the Russian Federation belong to the Ural region, probably because of historical and economic reasons. They are included here, because of their location eastwards from the Ural Mountains in the West Siberian Lowland. The north-Kazakhstan territories along the southern border of the Lowland are not included because they do not correspond to any political subdivisions, and are not supported by statistical data. Kemerovskiy District is not included because it is located eastwards from the West Siberian Lowland on the northern foothills of the Altai Mountains.

[c] The percentage of atmospheric pollutants and toxic waste that was treated on site, is shown in parentheses.

[d] Differences in the estimations of total area of the West Siberian Lowland in Tables 2.1 and 2.8 are due to the fact that western Siberia has had no official standing as a political division.

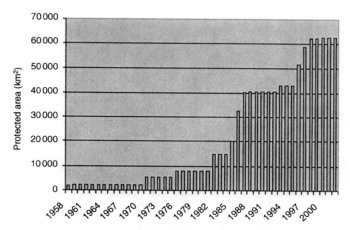

Figure 2.6 Establishment of nature-protected areas in the West Siberian Lowland. Only protected areas managed by federal government are included.

Rich in biodiversity, the forest-steppe and steppe regions of western Siberia have been altered by human activities for several centuries, and the landscapes of this zone have been changed markedly. Agricultural activities – such as ploughing floodplains to the edges of riverbanks, ploughing the runoff surfaces of watersheds, and overgrazing – have negative influences on wetlands. For the last 100 years, birch forests of this region have been intensively developed for agriculture by cutting or burning for conversion to arable lands, pastures, or hay meadows. Deforestation of the landscape strongly affects wetlands.

Conservation of the West Siberian wetlands

West Siberian wetlands provide habitats for many threatened species of flora and fauna. Due to anthropogenic impact, many West Siberian ecosystems have declined in extent and biodiversity, and have been evaluated as rare or endangered (Koropachinskiy 1996, Solomeshch *et al.* 1997). To reduce the loss of biodiversity and protect the most-vulnerable ecosystems from extinction a network of nature-protected areas was created. The first protected areas, the "Tyumensky" and "Kirzinsky" refuges, were established in 1958 in the heavily grazed forest-steppe zone. The network developed slowly over the following 20 years, and started to grow faster in the early 1980s (Fig. 2.6). Large nature reserves with areas up to 6000 to 8000 km^2 each were established in the middle and northern parts of the West Siberian Lowland that are threatened by rapidly developing oil and gas industries (Fig. 2.7, Table 2.9). The network consists of five main categories of protected areas that differ in size and degree of protection: Zapovednik, National Park, Nature Park, Zakaznik, and Nature Monument. This

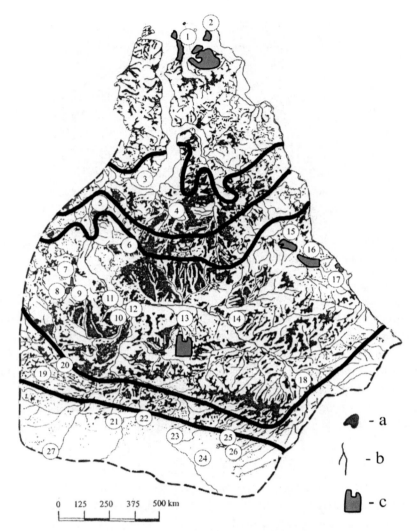

Figure 2.7 Nature-protected areas of the West Siberian Lowland. Numbers in circles are the protected areas shown in Table 2.9. Key: a, peatlands; b, rivers; c, nature-protected areas shown to scale. Thick black lines indicate boundaries of mire zones according to Fig. 2.3.

diversity of protected-area categories provides sufficient flexibility to enable compromise between conservation objectives and economic development. Each of these categories is defined by national environmental legislation.

Zapovednik [IUCN (International Union for the Conservation of Nature and Natural Resources) protected-area category Ia]. Strict nature reserve managed mainly for scientific research and monitoring. Zapovedniks ensure the highest

Table 2.9 *Protected areas of the West Siberian Lowland*[a]

N	Protected area	Type of protection	District of Russia[b]	Year of establishment	Area (km^2)
Zone of polygonal mires					
1	Gydansky	Zapovednik	1	1996	8781.7
2	Bolshoy Arctichesky	Zapovednik	2	1993	~800.0
Zone of flat-palsa mires					
3	Nizhne–Obsky	Zakaznik	1	1985	1280.0
4	Nadymskiy	Zakaznik	1	1986	5640.0
Zone of high-palsa mires					
5	Kunovatsky	Zakaznik	1	1985	2200.0
Zone of raised string bogs					
6	Numto	Nature Park	3	1997	7218.0
7	Malaya Sosva	Zapovednik	3	1976	2255.6
8	Verkhne–Kondinsky	Zakaznik	3	1971	2416.0
9	Kondinskie ozera	Nature Park	3	1998	360.1
10	Vaspukhol'sky	Zakaznik	3	1993	932.1
11	Yelizarovsky	Zakaznik	3	1982	766.0
12	Samarovsky Chugas	Nature Park	3	2000	7.5
13	Yugansky	Zapovednik	3	1982	6486.4
14	Sibirskie Uvaly	Nature Park	3	1998	2996.2
15	Verkhne–Tazovsky	Zapovednik	1	1986	6313.1
16	Yelogujsky	Zakaznik	4	1987	7476.0
17	Centralno–Sibirsky	Zapovednik	4	1985	~1800.0
18	Tomsky	Zakaznik	5	1988	500.0
Zone of flat eutrophic and mesotrophic mires					
19	Pripyshmenskie Bory	National Park	6	1993	490.5
20	Tjumensky	Zakaznik	7	1958	535.9
Zone of reed and sedge fens, and salt-water marshes					
21	Beloozersky	Zakaznik	7	1986	178.5
22	Bairovsky	Zakaznik	8	1959	570.0
23	Ptichia Gavan'	Nature Park	8	1994	1.0
24	Stepnoy	Zakaznik	8	1971	750.0
25	Kirzinsky	Zakaznik	9	1958	1198.1
26	Chanovsky	Zakaznik	9	1994	80.0
27	Kurgansky	Zakaznik	10	1985	318.5
Total					62351.2

[a] Data compiled from the State Report on the Status of the Environment of the Russian Federation in 2001 (Gosudarstvennyi Komitet po Okhrane Okruzhaiuschchei Sredy 2001) available on http://www.eco-net.ru/index.php?id=814/.

[b] Administrative districts of Russia: 1, Yamal–Nenetsky District; 2, Taimyrsky District; 3, Khanty–Mansijsky District; 4, Krasnoiarsky Kray; 5, Tomsky Oblast'; 6, Sverdlovsky Oblast'; 7, Tyumensky Oblast'; 8, Omsky Oblast'; 9, Novosibirsky Oblast'; 10, Kurgansky Oblast'; 11, Altaysky Kray.

degree of nature protection, and are staffed by both enforcement and scientific personnel. All economic activities are prohibited within their boundaries. Four Zapovedniks were established in western Siberia: Gydansky (8782 km^2), Verkhne-Tazovsky (6313 km^2), Yugansky (6486 km^2), and Malaya Sosva (2256 km^2). Two East Siberian Zapovedniks have small portions of their areas in the West Siberian Lowland: Centralno-Sibirsky ($\sim1800 \text{ km}^2$) and Bolshoy Arctichesky ($\sim800 \text{ km}^2$). Responsibility for protection of Zapovedniks has been assigned to the federal government, specifically to the Russian Ministry of Nature Protection, which financially supports the staff of the Zapovedniks and their activities.

National Park (IUCN category II). Protected area managed mainly for ecosystem protection and recreation. In comparison to Zapovedniks, National Parks have greater flexibility in their management. The purposes of National Parks include maintenance of natural and cultural heritages, scientific and conservation education, and recreation. Nature-protection objectives in National Parks have priority over recreational activities. National Parks always have certain areas with a regime of strict protection, which includes exclusion of tourists. These parks are also controlled by the federal government. Only one National Park, Pripyshmenskie Bory (490.5 km^2), has been established in the southern taiga zone of the West Siberian Lowland.

Nature Park (IUCN category II). Protected area similar to the National Park category, but nature-protection and recreation activities have equal priorities. Another difference is that the conservation regime in Nature Parks is under the jurisdiction of regional authorities who receive financial support from regional budgets. The Nature Park is a relatively new category of the Russian protected-area network. Five parks with a total area of $10\,582.8 \text{ km}^2$ have been established in western Siberia since 1994.

Zakaznik (IUCN category IV). A protected area managed mainly to meet the requirements of specific species. A significant part of their territories may be in agricultural or industrial use, but certain restrictions are applied to support sustainable existence or restoration of populations of target wildlife or plant species. These may be rare species, but more often they are game wildlife, medicinal plants, or berries. Zakazniks usually have two to three personnel for regulation enforcement. Zakazniks may be under the jurisdiction of the federal government or a regional authority. Fifteen federal Zakazniks with a total area of $24\,841.1 \text{ km}^2$ have been established in the West Siberian Lowland (Table 2.9). Information about the exact location, areal extent, date of establishment, and biodiversity of Zakazniks managed by regional authorities is less readily available; therefore, they are not included in Table 2.9. There are more than

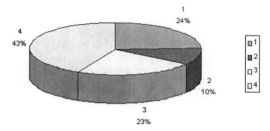

Figure 2.8 Structure of nature-protected areas in the West Siberian Lowland.
1, Zapovedniks; 2, Nature and National Parks; 3, Federal Zakazniks; 4, Regional
Zakazniks.

84 Zakazniks managed by regional authorities in western Siberia: 40 in Tyumensky Oblast' (29 294 km^2), 17 in Tomsky Oblast' ($\sim$14 000 km^2), 17 in Kurgansky
Oblast', 5 in Omsky Oblast', and at least 5 zakazniks in Novosibirsk Oblast' (3500
km^2). Zakazniks have also been established in West Siberian parts of Sverdlovsky
and Chelyabinsky Oblasts. In total they cover more than 46 800 km^2.

Nature Monument (IUCN category III). A protected area managed mainly for
conservation of specific natural features that are of outstanding or unique value
because of their rarity, representative or aesthetic qualities, or cultural significance. Usually they are comparatively small and often protect local populations
of rare species, nesting places of endangered birds, old trees, etc. Nature Monuments sometimes consist of wetlands. All West Siberian Nature Monuments are
under the jurisdiction of regional authorities, and information on their distribution and areal extent is not as available as for federal protected areas. For
this reason, wetlands designated as Nature Monuments are not included in this
survey.

Wetlands comprise a significant part of the West Siberian protected areas.
They are especially abundant in Gydansky and Yugansky zapovedniks, Numto
Nature Park, Nadymsky and Nizhne-Obsky zakazniks, and many others. The protected areas in total cover 109 151.2 km^2, and make up 3.98% of the West Siberian
Lowland. Zakaznics are the most-common type of protected area: Zakazniks
managed by regional authorities represent 43% and Zakazniks managed by
the federal government 23% of the protected-area network. Some 24% of the
protected area receives the greatest degree of protection as Zapovedniks, offering a high level of nature conservation. Nature and National Parks together
make up 10% of the protected area (Fig. 2.8). The actual extent of the protected area is even higher as our estimate does not include all Zakazniks
managed by regional authorities, and does not include Nature Monuments at
all.

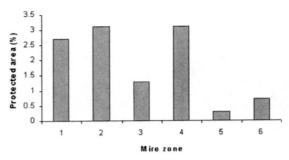

Figure 2.9 The proportion of protected area in each of the mire zones of the West Siberian Lowland. Mire zones 1 to 6 correspond to those shown in Fig. 2.3.

Although protected areas were established in all mire zones, and represent all types of West Siberian wetlands, they are very unevenly distributed. The vast majority of protected areas are located in the zone of raised string bogs. Zones of polygonal and palsa mires have a much smaller area that is protected. Zones of flat eutrophic and mesotrophic mires, and the zone of reed and sedge fens and salt-water marshes have the least amount of protected area (Fig. 2.7). The proportion of protected areas ranges from 0.3%–0.7% in the south to 1.3%–3.1% in more-northerly zones (Fig. 2.9). The disparity in the degree of protection across mire zones is probably due to the greater difficulty in establishing protected areas in the more densely populated forest-steppe and steppe zones that are more favorable for agriculture. Ecosystems of the forest-steppe and steppe zones need a higher level of protection (Korolyuk 1994, Koropachinskiy 1996), and greater emphasis should be given to these zones in future development of the nature-protected-area network.

Many West Siberian wetlands meet the criteria of the Ramsar Convention on wetlands and should be protected as Ramsar sites. Seven territories with a total area of 41 467.3 km^2 were designated as Wetlands of International Importance in 1994. Six years later, with the support of the international organization Wetlands International, another 34 wetlands with an estimated total area of 150 312.4 km^2 were proposed for inclusion on the Ramsar List (Krivenko 1999, 2000). Altogether they represent all types of wetlands, and could provide adequate conservation of West Siberian wetlands biodiversity (Fig. 2.10, Table 2.10). However, their designation as Wetlands of International Importance does not automatically mean that they will be protected. They have not yet been incorporated in Russian national environmental legislation. In order to achieve this, it is necessary to include Wetlands of International Importance as a specific category in the Federal Natural Protected Areas Law. Only after that may they be withdrawn from economic activities and staffed by personnel who could enforce the conservation.

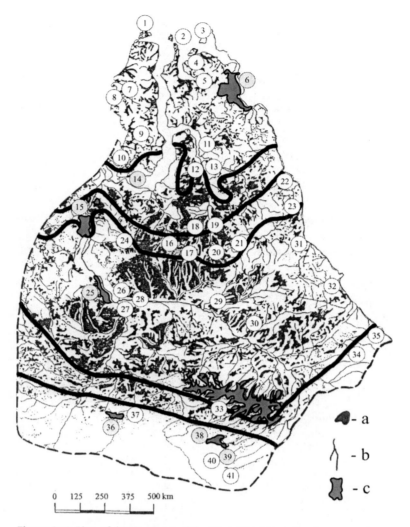

Figure 2.10 Plan of development of the West Siberian wetland conservation network. Numbers in circles are the wetlands shown in Table 2.10. Numbers in grey circles show wetlands designated as Wetlands of International Importance (Ramsar Sites) in 1994. Numbers in white circles show wetlands that were proposed for inclusion in the Ramsar List. Key: a, peatlands; b, rivers; c, wetland areas shown to scale. Thick lines indicate boundaries of mire zones shown in Fig. 2.3.

At present, only those parts of the Wetlands of International Importance that overlap with other nature-protected categories defined by current legislation (Zapovedniks, Zakazniks, etc.) are protected; these wetlands are denoted by super-script *d* in Table 2.10. Because of the absence of effective protection for Wetlands of International Importance, they are not included in the illustrations of the

Table 2.10 *Wetlands of International Importance in the West Siberian Lowland.*[a]

N	Protected area	Status[b]	District of Russia[c]	Area (km²)
Zone of polygonal mires				
1	Isle of Belyi and Malygin Strait	B	1	2 900.0
2	Kara Sea Islands north of the Gydan peninsula[d]	B	1	1 768.5
3	Sibiryakova Island[d]	B	2	835.0
4	Oleny Island and coast of Yuratskaya Bay[d]	B	1	3 400.0
5	Lakes northeast of Gydan peninsula	B	1	2 100.0
6	Brekhtovsky Islands in the Yenisey estuary	A	2	14 000.0
7	River catchments of western Yamal	B	1	6 500.0
8	Mordy-Yakha River catchment	B	1	2 500.0
9	Yuribey River valley	B	1	1 500.0
10	River catchments of South Yamal	B	1	6 900.0
11	Lower Messo River	B	1	2 900.0
12	Pur delta	B	1	300.0
13	Lower Taz River	B	1	3 500.0
Zone of flat-palsa mires				
14	Islands in Ob estuary Kara Sea[d]	A	1	1 280.0
Zone of high-palsa mires				
15	Lower Dvuobje[d]	A	1	5 400.0
16	Lake complex between the Pyaku-Pur and Nadym rivers	B	1	2 695.0
17	Yurto lakes in the watershed between the Veng-Pur and Ety-Pur rivers	B	1	1 375.0
18	Lake complex on the left bank of the Pur River[d]	B	1	300.0
19	Lake systems of the Bolshaya Yakha river catchment	B	1	300.0
20	A group of lakes in the Chaselka and Kharam-Pur interfluvial area	B	1	300.0
21	Chertovskaya lake system	B	1	500.0
22	Bolshaya, Konoshchelje, and Yenisey floodplain	B	4	~600.00

Table 2.10 (*cont.*)

N	Protected area	Status[b]	District of Russia[c]	Area (km²)
23	Upper and middle Nizhnyaya Bayikha River	B	4	506.00
Zone of raised string bogs				
24	Numto watershed[d]	B	3	1 073.9
25	Upper Dvuobje[d]	A	3	4 700.0
26	Nazym–Pim interfluvial area	B	3	20 250.0
27	Salym-Yugan peatland system	B	3	15 000.0
28	Middle Ob floodplain	B	3	5 500.0
29	Kolik–Egan and Sabun interfluvial area	B	3	12 885.0
30	Polta river catchment	B	5	500.0
31	Yelogui–Artyugina interfluvial area and left-bank floodplain of the middle Yenisey river	B	4	570.0
32	Vorogovo Islands	B	4	340.0
33	Bolshoe Vasyuganskoe peatland system	B	5, 8, 9	50 000.0
Zone of flat eutrophic and mesotrophic mires				
34	Lake Kosogol and adjacent Serezh River floodplain	B	4	100.0
35	Saratovskoye mire	B	4	94.0
Zone of reed and sedge fens, and salt-water marshes				
36	Tobol-Ishim forest-steppe	A	7	12 170.0
37	Bolshie Krutinskiye lakes	B	8	300.0
38	Chany lakes	A	9	3 648.5
39	Wetlands in the lower Bagan area	A	9	268.8
40	Karasuksko–Barlaiskaya lake system	B	9	20.0
41	Kulundinskiye lakes	B	11	2 000.0
Total area with status A				41 367.3
Total area with status B				150 312.4

[a] Data compiled from Krivenko (1999, 2000) and Botch (2000).

[b] Status: A, areas designated as Wetlands of International Importance in 1994; B, areas which met the criteria of the Ramsar Convention on wetlands and were nominated for designation as a Wetland of International Importance in 2000.

[c] Administrative districts of Russia are the same as in Table 2.9.

[d] Wetlands of International Importance, which are completely included or partly overlap with Zapovedniks, Zakazniks, or Nature Parks.

Table 2.11 *Biodiversity in three West Siberian zapovedniks.*[a]

No.	Zapovedniks	Area (km²)	Higher vascular plants	Mosses	Lichens	Fungi	Mammals	Birds	Reptiles	Amphibians	Fish
1	Malaya Sosva	2255.62	390	138	121	150	38	180	1	2	13
2	Verkhne-Tazovsky	6313.08	310	111	91	53	35	–	2	3	20
3	Yugansky	6486.36	320	109	161	139	36	204	2	4	10

[a] Data compiled from the website: Russian Nature Reserves on web, http://reserves.biodiversity.ru/.

current state of the nature-protected-area network shown in Figs. 2.8 and 2.9. Wetlands of International Importance should be considered as priorities for further development of the system of protected areas in western Siberia.

The biodiversity of West Siberian protected areas is not high (Table 2.11). The widely accepted concepts of "biodiversity hotspots" and "silver bullets," which are focused mainly on the diversity of endemic species (Mayers *et al.* 2000) and were developed to emphasize the importance of protecting tropical and subtropical regions, may not be appropriate for West Siberian wetlands. In terms of biodiversity protection, the real value of the West Siberian protected areas is probably the conservation of habitat for the largest populations of many rare and game wildlife species, and migrating birds in particular. Migrating species by definition are not endemic, as they migrate from one region to another. Another criterion for conservation of West Siberian wetlands is that they certainly have a key role in global cycles, especially those involving carbon sequestration and freshwater storage. The West Siberian Lowland provides a good example that the "biodiversity hotspots" strategy is not a universal approach (Kareiva & Marvier 2003) and that additional criteria should be applied for the development of a worldwide network of nature-protected areas.

The nature-protected-areas network in the West Siberian Lowland is in the process of development, and it is probably too early to measure results. The above calculations are not intended to provide final estimates of the effectiveness of nature protection, but rather to summarize the results achieved and to gain insights into future directions of conservation activities. The effectiveness of nature protection also depends on social processes. Because of the economic difficulties faced by the country, Russian protected areas currently experience a shortage of funding, which in some cases has diminished the effectiveness of their conservation. Nevertheless, in general, it has been possible to preserve these areas. The fast development of the protected-area network, support of this process at the federal government level, the ability of protected areas to conserve nature during unfavorable economic conditions, and the activities and financial support of international and non-governmental organizations allows an optimistic outlook that the West Siberian wetlands will be protected for future generations.

Acknowledgements

I thank Tom Rambo for help in translating the text; and Lauchlan Fraser, Paul Keddy, and Elena Lapshina for their thoughtful comments of the earlier drafts on the chapter. I am grateful to Michael Barbour and to the Department of

Environmental Horticulture at the University of California, Davis for providing support and the research environment.

References

Aagaard, K. and Carmack, E. C. (1989). The role of sea ice and other fresh water in the Arctic circulation. *Journal of Geophysical Research*, **94**(10), 14485–98.

Aleksandrova, V. D. (1971). Printsipy zonal'nogo delenia rastitel'nosti Arktiki [*Principles of zonal subdivision of Arctic vegetation*]. *Botanichesky Zhurnal*, **56**(1), 3–21.

Aleksyev, V. A. and Birdsey, R. A. (eds.) (1998). *Carbon Storage in Forests* and Peatlands of Russia. General/Technical Report NE-244. US Department of Agriculture, Forest Service, North-Eastern Forest Experiment Station. Radnor, PA: US Department of Agriculture, Forest Service.

Andreev, V. N. (1934). Kormovaya baza Yamal'skogo olenevodstva [*Forage basis of Yamal peninsula reindeer husbandry*]. *Sovetskoe Olenevodstvo*, **1**, 99–164.

Bleuten, W. and Lapshina, E. D. (eds.) (2001). *Carbon Storage and Atmospheric Exchange by West Siberian Peatlands*. Utrecht, the Netherlands: Blackwell.

Bleuten, W., Lapshina, E. D., Ivens, W., Shinkarenko, W. P., and Wiersma, E. (1999). Ecosystem recovery and natural degradation of spilled crude oil in peat bog ecosystems of West Siberia. *International Peat Journal*, **9**, 73–82.

Botch, M. S. (ed.) (2000). *Wetlands in Russia*, vol. 2, *Important Peatlands*. Wetlands International Global Series 2. Moscow: Pensoft Publisher.

Botch, M. S. and Masing, V. V. (1983). Mire ecosystems in the USSR. In *Ecosystems of the World*, vol. 4A, *Mires: Swamp, Bog, Fen and Moor*, ed. A. J. P. Gore. New York: Elsevier Science, pp. 95–152.

Botch, M. S., Gerasimenko, T. V., and Tolchel'nikov, Yu. S. (1971). Bolota Yamala [*Peatlands of the Yamal Peninsula*]. *Botanichesky Zhurnal*, **56**(10), 1421–35.

Botch, M. S., Kobak, K. I., Vinson, T. S., and Kolchugina, T. P. (1995). Carbon pools and accumulation in peatlands of the former Soviet Union. *Global Biogeochemical Cycles*, **9**(1), 37–46.

Bronzov, A. Y. (1930). Verkhovye bolota Narymskogo kraya (bassein reki Vasiugan) [*Bogs of the Narymski region (watershed of the Vasiugan River)*]. *Trudy Nauchno-Issledovatelskogo Torfyanogo Instituta*, **3**, 3–100.

Bronzov, A. Y. (1936). Gipnovye bolota na yuzhnoi okraine Zapadno-Sibirskoi ravninnoi taigi [*Hypnoid mires on the southern limit of the western Siberian plain taiga*]. *Pochvovedenie*, **2**, 224–45.

Efremov, S. P., Efremova, T. T., and Melentyeva, N. V. (1998). Carbon storage in peatland ecosystems. In *Carbon Storage in Forests and Peatlands of Russia*, eds. V. A. Alekseev and R. A. Birdseg. General/Technical Report NE-244. US Department of Agriculture, Forest Service, North-Eastern Forest Experiment Station. Radnor, PA: US Department of Agriculture, Forest Service, pp. 69–76.

Ermakov, N., Dring, J., and Rodwell, J. (2000). Classification of continental hemiboreal forests of North Asia. *Braun-Blanquetia*, **28**, 1–131.

Glavtorffond RSFSR (1956). *Torfianye mestorozhdenia Zapadnoi Sibiri* [*Peat Deposits in Western Siberia*]. Moscow: Glavtorffond RSFSR.

Gorham, E. (1991). Northern peatlands: role in the carbon cycle and probable responses to climate warming. *Ecological Applications*, **1**, 182–95.

Gorodkov, B. N. (1938). Rastitel'nost Arctiki i gornykh tundr S.S.S.R. [*Vegetation of arctic and mountain tundras*]. In *Rastitel'nost' S.S.S.R.* [*Vegetation of the USSR*], vol. 1. Moscow and Leningrad: Akademia Nauk S.S.S.R., pp. 297–354.

(1944). Tundry Ob–Yeniseiskogo vodorazdela [*Tundras of Ob–Yenisey watershed*]. *Sovetskaya Botanika*, **2**(5), 20–31.

Gosudarstvennyi Komitet po Okhrane Okruzhaiushchei Sredy (2001). *Gosudarstvennyi doklad o sostoianii okruzhaiushchei prirodnoi sredy Rossijskoi Federatsii v 2001 Godu* [*State Report on the Status of the Environment of the Russian Federation in 2001*]. Moscow: Gosudarstvennyi Komitet po Okhrane Okruzhaiushchei Sredy.

Govorukhin, V. S. (1933). Ocherk rastitel'nosti lesnykh pastbishch severnogo olenia v tundrakh Obsko–Tazovskogo poluostrova [*Outline of vegetation of reindeer woodland pastures in tundras of Ob–Taz rivers peninsula*]. *Zemlevedenie*, **34**(1), 68–92.

(1947). Bugristye bolota Severnoy Azii i poteplenie Arktiki (Zapadnaia Sibir', bassein reki Sev. Sos'va) [*Palsa mires of northern Asia and Arctic warming (western Siberia, Sev. Sos'va river watershed)*]. *Uchenye Zapiski Moskovskogo Oblastnogo Instituta*, **94**, 106–24.

Il'ina, I. S., Lapshina, E. I., Lavrenko, N. N., et al. (eds.) (1985). *Rastitel'nyi pokrov Zapadno-Sibirskoy ravniny* [*Vegetation Cover of the West Siberian Plain*]. Novosibirsk: Nauka, Sibirskoe otdelenie.

Ivanov, K. E. and Novikov, S. M. (eds.) (1976). *Bolota Zapadnoi Sibiri, ikh stroenie i gidrologicheski rezhim* [*Mires of West Siberia, their Structure and Hydrological Regime*]. Leningrad: Girdometeoizdat.

Kareiva, P. and Marvier, M. (2003). Conserving biodiversity coldspots. *American Scientist*, **91**, 344–51.

Katz, N. Y. (1939). Bolota nizoviev reki Obi [*Mires of the lower Ob river*]. In *Prezidentu Akademii Nauk SSSR akademiku V. L. Komarovu k 70-letiu so dnia rozhdenia*. Leningrad: Nauka, pp. 372–405.

(1971). *Bolota zemnogo shara* [*Mires of the World*]. Moscow: Nauka.

Katz, N. Y. and Katz, S. V. (1946). Istoria rastitel'nosti bolot Severa Sibiri kak pokazatel' izmenenia poslelednikovogo landshafta [*History of the northern Siberian mire vegetation as an indicator of changes in the post-glacial landscape*]. *Trudy Instituta Geografii*, **37**, 331–48.

(1948). Stratigrafia torfyanikov Priobskogo severa [*Stratigraphy of peatlands of the northern part of the Priobsky region*]. *Trudy Komissii po Izucheniyu Chetvertichnogo Perioda*, **7**(1), 15–54.

Katz, N. Y. and Neishtadt, M. I. (1963). Bolota [*Mires*]. In *Zapadnaia Sibir*. Moscow: Geografgiz, pp. 230–48.

Khramov, A. A. and Valutsky, V. I. (1977). *Lesnye i bolotnye fitotsenozy vostochnogo Vasiugania* [*Forest and Mire Phytocoenosises of eastern Vasiuganie*]. Novosibirsk: Nauka.

Korolyuk, A. Ju. (1994). Okhrana bioraznoobrazia rastitel'nosti stepnogo bioma Zapadnoy Sibiri [*Conservation of vegetation biodiversity of the steppe biome in Western Siberia*]. *Sibirsky Ekologichesky Zhurnal*, **1**(6), 589–94.

(1999). Phytosociological report from the saline habitats in SW Siberia and N Kasachstan. In *Halophyte Uses in Different Climates*, eds. H. Lieth and M. Moschenko. Leiden, the Netherlands: Backhuys Publishers, pp. 131–44.

Koropachinskiy, I. Yu. (ed.) (1996). *Zelyonaya Kniga Sibiri. Redkie i huzhdayushchiesya v okhrane rastitel'nye soobshchestva* [Green Book of Siberia. Rare and Endangered Plant Communities]. Novosibirsk: Nauka, Sibirskaya izdatel'skaya firma RAN.

Krivenko, V. G. (ed.) (1999). *Wetlands in Russia*, vol. 1, *Wetlands of International Importance*. AEME Publication 52. Moscow: Wetlands International.

(2000). *Wetlands in Russia*, vol. 3, *Wetlands Included in the Perspective List of Ramsar Sites*. Wetlands International Global Series 6. Moscow: Wetlands International.

Krylov, G. V. (1961). *Lesa Zapadnoi Sibiri* [Forests of Western Siberia]. Moscow: Izdatelstvo AN SSSR.

Kustova, N. V. (1987a). Sintaksonomia rastitel'nosti nadpoimennykh terras doliny nizhnego Irtysha. I. Associatsii oligotrofnykh sfagnovykh bolot klassov *Vaccinietea uliginosi, Oxycocco–Sphagnetea* [*Vegetation syntaxonomy of upper floodplain terraces of the lower Irtysh valley. Part I. Associations of oligotrophic bogs of the classes Vaccinietea uliginosi, Oxycocco–Sphagnetea*]. Deposited in VINITI All-Union Institute of Scientific and Technical Information 07.09.87, N 6558-B87, Moscow.

(1987b). Sintaksonomia rastitel'nosti nadpoimennykh terras doliny nizhnego Irtysha. II. Associatsii mesotrofnykh bolot klassa *Scheuchzerio-Caricetea fuscae* [*Vegetation syntaxonomy of upper floodplain terraces of the lower Irtysh valley. Part II. Associations of mesotrophic mires of the class Scheuchzerio-Caricetea fuscae*]. Deposited in VINITI All-Union Institute of Scientific and Technical Information 07.09.87, N 6559-B87, Moscow.

Kuzmina, M. S. (1953). Rastitelnost' Baraby [Vegetation of Baraba]. *Trudy Pochvennogo Instituta AN SSSR*, **36**, 106–171.

Lapshina, E. I. (1985). Srednetayezhnye elovo–kedrovye lesa i proizvodnye soobshchestva na ikh meste [*Middle taiga spruce–cedar forests and secondary forests in their place*]. In *Rastitel'nyi pokrov Zapadno-Sibirskoy ravniny* [*Vegetation Cover of the West Siberian Plain*], eds. I. S. Il'ina *et al.* Novosibirsk: Nauka, Sibirskoe otdelenie, pp. 72–90.

(1987). Rastitel'nost' basseina reki Taz v verkhnem techenii [*Vegetation of the upper part of the Taz river basin*]. In *Geobotanicheskie issledovania v Zapadnoy Sibiri* [*Geobotanical Investigations of Western Siberia*], ed. E. E., Milanovsky. Novosibirsk: Nauka, Sibirskoe otdelenie, pp. 47–70.

Lapshina, E. D., Korolyuk, A. Ju., Bleuten, W., Muldiyarov, E. Ya., and Valutsky, V. I. (2000). Struktura rastitel'nogo pokrova zapadnoy chasti Bol'shogo Vasyuganskogo bolota na primere klyuchevogo uchastka "Uzas" [*Structure of the vegetation cover of the western part of the great Vasyugan bog example from the key area "Uzas"*]. *Sibirsky Ecologichesky Zhurnal*, **7**(5), 563–76.

Lapshina, E. D., Pologova, N. N., and Muldiyarov, E. Ya. (2001). Pattern of development and carbon accumulation in homogenous *Sphagnum fuscum*-peat deposit on the south of West Siberia. In *West Siberian Peatlands and Carbon Cycle: Past and Present*. Novosibirsk: Nauka, pp. 101–4.

Liss, O. L. and Berezina, N. A. (1981). *Bolota Zapadnoy Sibiri* [*Mires of Western Siberia*]. Moscow: Izdatel'stvo Moskovskogo Universiteta.

Loginov, P. E. and Khoroshev, P. I. (1972). *Torfianye resursy Zapadno-Sibirskoy ravniny* [*Peat Resources of the West Siberian Lowland*]. Moscow: Geoltorfrazvedka.

Markov, V. D. and Khoroshev, P. I. (1975). K otsenke prognoznykh zapasov torfa in the USSR [*Estimation of peat resources in the USSR*]. *Torfianaia Promyshlennost*, **6**, 20–4.

Meade, R. H. (ed.) (1995). *Contaminants in the Mississippi River*. US Geological Survey, Circular 1133.

Mel'tser, L. I. (1985). Tundrovaya rastitel'nost' [*Tundra vegetation*]. In *Rastitel'nyi pokrov Zapadno-Sibirskoy ravniny* [*Vegetation Cover of the West Siberian Plain*], Ch. 3, eds. I. S. Il'ina. Novosibirsk: Nauka, Sibirskoe otdelenie, pp. 41–54.

Myers, N., Mittermeier, R. A., Mittermeier, C. G., da Fonseca, G. A. B., and Kent, J. (2000). Biodiversity hotspots for conservation priorities. *Nature*, **403**, 853–8.

Neishtadt, M. I. (1977). Vozniknovenie i skorost' razvitia processov zabolachivania [*Formation and speed of paludification processes*]. In *Nauchnye predposylki osvoenia bolot Zapadnoi Sibiri* [*Scientific Principles Regarding the Peatlands of Western Siberia*]. Moscow: Nauka, pp. 39–47.

Novikov, S. M. and Usova, L. I. (2000). New data on the peatland areas and peat storage in the territory of Russia. In *Dynamics of Mire Ecosystems of Northern Eurasia in Holocene: Materials of International Symposium, October 5–9, 1998, Petrozavodsk*, eds. G. A. Elina, O. L. Kuznetsov, and P. F. Shavelin. Petrozavodsk, Russia: Institute of Biology, Karelian Scientific Center RAS, pp. 49–52.

Pristyazhnyuk, S. A. (2001). Sravnitel'ny analiz napochvennykh lishainikovykh sinuziy v subarkticheskikh tundrakh poluostrova Yamal [*Comparative analysis of epigeous lichen synusias in the subarctic tundras of the Yamal peninsula*]. *Botanichesky Zhurnal (St. Petersburg)*, **86**(7), 15–25.

Pyavchenko, N. I. (1955). *Bugristye torfyaniki* [*Boggy Peatlands*]. Moscow: Academia Nauk S.S.S.R.

Romanova, E. A. (1985). Rastitel'nost' bolot [*Mire vegetation*]. In *Rastitel'nyi pokrov Zapadno-Sibirskoy ravniny* [*Vegetation Cover of the West Siberian Plain*], Ch. 8, ed. I. S. Il'ina. Novosibirsk: Nauka, Sibirskoe otdelenie, pp. 138–61.

Shvidenko, A. and Nilsson, S. (1998). *Phytomass, Increment, Mortality and Carbon Budget of Russian Forests*. Interim report IR-98-105. Laxenburg, Austria: International Institute for Applied System Analysis.

Solomeshch, A., Mirkin, B., Ermakov, N. *et al.* (1997). *Red Data Book of Plant Communities in the Former USSR*. Lancaster, UK: Lancaster University.

Taran, G. S. (1993). Sintaxonomichesky obzor lesnoy rastitel'nosti poimy Credney Obi [*Syntaxonomical survey of the forest vegetation of the middle Ob floodplain*]. *Sibirsky Biologichesky Zhurnal*, **6**, 85–91.

(2001). Assotsiatia Cypero-Limoselletum (Oberd. 1957) Korneck 1960 Isoeto-Nanojuncetea) v poime Sredney Obi [*Association Cypero-Limoselletum (Oberd. 1957) Korneck 1960 Isoeto-Nanojuncetea in the middle Ob floodplain*]. *Rstitel'nost' Rossii (St. Petersburg)*, **1**(1), 43–56.

Turunen, J., Pitkanen, A., Tahvanainen, T., and Tolonen, K. (2001). Carbon accumulation in West Siberian mires, Russia. *Global Biogeochemical Cycles*, **15**, 285–96.

Turunen, J., Tomppo, E., Tolonen, K., and Reinikainen, A. (2002). Estimating carbon accumulation rates of undrained mires in Finland: application to boreal and subarctic regions. *The Holocene*, **12**(1), 69–80.

Vasiliev, S. V. (1998). *Vozdeistvie neftegazodobyvaiushchei promyshlennosti na lesnye i bolotnye ecosistemy [Impact of Oil and Gas Industries on Forest and Swamp Ecosystems]*. Novosibirsk: Nauka.

(2000). Peat accumulation rates in western Siberia. In *Dynamics of Mire Ecosystems of Northern Eurasia in Holocene: Materials of International Symposium, October 5–9, 1998, Petrozavodsk*, eds. G. A. Elina, O. L. Kuznetsov, and Shavelin, P. F. Petrozavodsk, Russia: Institute of Biology, Karelian Scientific Center RAS, pp. 56–9.

Westhoff, V. and van der Maarel, E. (1978). The Braun–Blanquet approach. In *Classification of Plant Communities*, ed. R. H. Whittaker. The Hague, the Netherlands: Junk, pp. 287–399.

3

The Amazon River basin

W. J. JUNK

Max-Planck-Institute for Limnology

M. T. F. PIEDADE

Instituto Nacional de Pesquisas da Amazonia (INPA)

Introduction

Since the arrival of human beings about 12 000 years ago, wetlands have been favorite colonization areas because of their rich food resources. On Marajó Island at the mouth of the Amazon River and in its lower course, Amerindians built large chiefdoms on elevated places that provided protection against flooding (Roosevelt 1999). They sustainably managed the populations of manatees, river turtles, and other game animals and fish, as evidenced by the first Europeans arriving in Amazonia being deeply impressed by the large numbers of these animals. Acuña (1641) gave detailed information about the use of the aquatic resources of the Amazon River and emphasized the fertility of the floodplain. The vegetation cover was only marginally affected by the Amerindians because they did not raise domestic animals, which would have required deforestation for the preparation of pastures. They grew bananas, manioc, corn, vegetables, fruit trees, and medicinal plants in species-rich home gardens on the levees. In pre-Columbian times, the population density in the Amazon River floodplain was approximately 28 humans per km^2 in comparison with 1.2 humans per km^2 in the nutrient-poor uplands (mean, 14.6) (Denevan 1976).

After the arrival of the Europeans in 1500, the indigenous population decreased rapidly because of introduced diseases, wars, and slave raidings. Indigenous resource management for subsistence changed to export-oriented exploitation by Europeans, and in a few centuries the previously large populations of turtles and manatees – and later, caimans and otters – were depleted to

The World's Largest Wetlands: Ecology and Conservation, eds. L. H. Fraser and P. A. Keddy.
Published by Cambridge University Press. © Cambridge University Press 2005.

very low levels. During that period, the human population in the Amazonian floodplains was much lower than in pre-Columbian times.

The rubber boom, which started in the middle of the nineteenth century, led to an increase in the demand for timber for construction and fuel wood for an increasing number of steamboats. Cattle ranching – and since the beginning of the twentieth century also water-buffalo ranching – spread in the lower Amazon River floodplain; this development began to affect the floodplain forests. With the end of the rubber boom in the early 1910s, Amazonia fell back again into a period of abandonment. From 1940 to 1970, the planting of jute for fiber production increased deforestation on the levees along the lower Amazon River. The development, until the 1960s, of small-holder agriculture and cattle ranching on the Amazon floodplain near Manaus is described by Sternberg (1998). A summary of the development of central Amazonia since the late pre-Conquest time is given by Goulding et al. (1996) and Ohly (2000).

In 1960, the Brazilian government started to connect the isolated Amazon region to the southern part of the country by the construction of a highway to Belém at the mouth of the Amazon River. This development was accelerated in the 1970s by the construction of other highways through the Amazon basin and by the colonization of the areas along the roads by people from the south and northeast of the country. The construction of airports and hydroelectric power plants – and the establishment of large agro-industrial projects, mining projects, and a tax-free zone at Manaus – stimulated economic development (Kohlhepp 2001). In 2000, approximately 24 million people lived in the Amazon basin – about 21 million of them in the Brazilian part – and 68% of the Brazilian population lived in urban areas, with an increasing tendency toward urbanization (Becker 1995, IBGE 2002). The rural population concentrates along the roads and in the fertile floodplains of white-water rivers. Regional agricultural production is insufficient to supply large cities like Manaus with food, except for inland fishery. New development programs, such as the *Avança Brazil* Program, will further increase the population, stimulate agro-industrial development of the region, and accelerate deforestation (Laurance et al. 2001).

The new boom period has dramatically changed the relationship between humans and the environment. Despite the still-low population density, the impact of humans threatens the integrity of entire ecosystems. Large hydroelectric power plants, soybean and sugar-cane plantations, deforestation for cattle ranching, timber extraction, and mining activities increasingly affect streams, rivers, and wetlands and their biota both directly and indirectly. In 1999, 13.9% of the Brazilian part of Amazonia was deforested (INPE 2000), but selective logging has affected large parts of the rain forest (Nepstad et al. 1999), and forest destruction is accelerating (Laurance et al. 2001).

In the following paragraphs, we summarize current knowledge on the geology, geomorphology, paleoclimate, and recent climate of Amazonia; we also offer a preliminary classification of Amazonian wetlands based on hydrological and hydrogeochemical parameters. We present a general description of the state of knowledge of the ecology of wetlands and their role in the landscape. We also outline the threats to the wetland and discuss possibilities for sustainable management and protection. Many examples are from the Brazilian part of the Amazon basin because it covers 67.8% of the total area and because scientific research and economic development, with its associated problems, are more advanced there than in other areas. The general conclusions, however, are valid for the entire basin.

Geology, geomorphology, and hydrochemistry

The Amazon River transports about one-sixth of all fresh water that drains from the continents to the oceans (Milliman 1990). The large basin covers an area of about 7 million km^2 near the equator between 4° N and 19° S and 47° and 79° W. It is bordered in the west by the Andes and in the south and north by the archaic shields of central Brazil and the Guianas, respectively. The archaic shields are in part covered by leached and nutrient-poor sediments of different age and consistency; these sediments form flat plateaus ("*chapadas*"), from which the rivers fall in cascades into the central basin. The pre-Andean zone along the foothills of the Andes is covered by relatively young and nutrient-rich fluviatile sediments representing large paleo-floodplains of the Amazon River and its tributaries (Salo *et al.* 1986). These sediments are eroded by the rivers that drain the Andean zone and are deposited in large bordering floodplains down to the Amazon delta. The central part of the basin is covered by leached, nutrient-poor fluviatile and lacustrine sediments of Cretaceous/Tertiary origin (Fig. 3.1). More than 1 million km^2 of Amazonia lies less than 100 m above the present sea level. About two-thirds of the basin is covered by evergreen rain forest; on the central Brazilian and Guiana shields, different types of savanna vegetation ("*cerrado*") occur.

In contrast to East Africa – where large, deep, and old lakes are prominent features of the landscape – the Amazon basin is characterized by rivers, streams, and associated wetlands and floodplain lakes. Permanent lakes resulting from tectonic events are rare and small, and occur mostly in the periphery of the basin. Because of river dynamics, even large floodplain lakes undergo fast morphological changes. With an age of a few thousand years, they are ephemeral in geological and evolutionary terms.

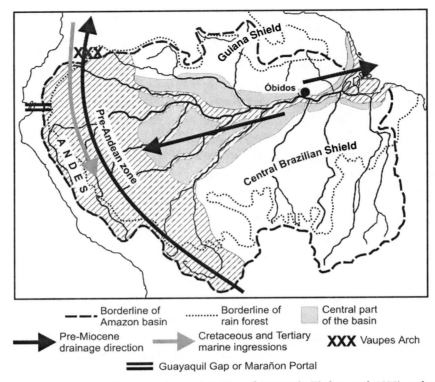

Figure 3.1 Major geochemical regions of Amazonia (Fittkau *et al.* 1975), and actual and paleo-drainage system.

An eye-catching characteristic of Amazonian streams and rivers is the water color (Fig. 3.2), which is often used in names such as Rio Claro ("clear river"), Rio Negro ("black river"), and Rio Branco ("white river"). Sioli (1950) discovered that different water colors pointed to differences in water quality. He related these differences to the geology, geomorphology, and biogeochemistry of the respective catchment areas. White-water rivers are turbid because of a high load of suspended solids. They are relatively rich in dissolved minerals (electrical conductance, 40 to 80 μS cm^{-1}) and have a near-neutral pH value. Sediments and dissolved minerals are derived from erosion in the Andes and the Andean foothills. Water and sediments are relatively fertile. Black-water rivers have dark, transparent water because of high amounts of dissolved humic substances. These substances are formed mainly in podzolic soils, which occur in small patches throughout the Amazon basin and occupy major areas in the catchment area of the Negro River (Klinge 1967). The water is acidic (pH 4 to 5) and low in dissolved minerals (electrical conductance, 7 to 15 μS cm^{-1}). Water and floodplain soils are of low fertility. Nutrients and unsuitable light conditions are limiting for

Figure 3.2 Black water and white water at the confluence of the Negro and Amazon rivers near Manaus.

aquatic primary production. Clear-water rivers drain areas where there is little erosion, mainly on the archaic shields and the flat central basin covered with latosols. Their water is transparent and can be greenish the pH value varies from acidic to neutral depending on the geology of the catchment area. The amounts of dissolved minerals are low to intermediate (electrical conductance, 4 to 40 μS cm^{-1}). The fertility of water and sediments is low to intermediate. A review of the chemical composition of Amazonian waters is given in Furch (1997), and also in Furch and Junk (1997). The differences in water quality have a strong impact on species composition and productivity, in both the water and in the floodplain soils.

Because of the flat relief of large parts of the area and pronounced seasonal variations in precipitation, drainage during the rainy season is insufficient and leads to periodic inundation of interfluvial depressions and the development of extended floodplains along streams and rivers. Floodplains along nutrient-rich, white-water rivers are locally called "*várzea;*" those along nutrient-poor, clear-water and black-water rivers are called "*igapó.*" Rough estimates indicate that about 20% to 25% of Amazonian soils are periodically inundated (Junk 1992). This points to the overwhelming importance of water and wetlands in the landscape.

Genesis and age of Amazonian wetlands

The Amazon basin is part of a very old depression that already existed in the Gondwana continent and then opened to the west. When South America separated from Africa, about 110 million years before present (BP), the basin was already closed in the west by the Early Andes. Rivers drained from Óbidos to the west into a depression along the eastern border of the Early Andes that opened to the Caribbean Sea (Fig. 3.1). Katzer (1903) proposed an additional opening to the Pacific (Marañon Portal or Guayaquil Gap) which probably closed during the Late Cretaceous period [73 million years ago (Ma)]. With the uplift of the Andes, the pre-Andean depression was subjected to varying degrees of marine ingression (Fig. 3.1) in the Late Cretaceous (83 to 67 Ma), the Early Tertiary (61 to 60 Ma), and the Late Tertiary (11.8 to 10 Ma) periods – as indicated by marine sediments. After interruption of marine ingressions, the depression was covered by rivers, lakes, and extended wetlands. Large freshwater lakes were formed in the Tertiary period (Lago Pozo in the Middle Eocene–Early Oligocene, 43 to 30 Ma; and Lago Pebas in the Late Tertiary, 20 to 11.8 Ma) and were filled with sediments of riverine origin from the Andes and the shields of central Brazil and the Guianas. In the Late Miocene (8 Ma), the connection to the Caribbean Sea was closed by the Vaupes Arch, the Amazon River opened its way to the Atlantic Ocean, and the modern Amazon drainage system of incised large valleys and floodplains in the soft sediments was formed (Lundberg et al. 1998).

Major geomorphological changes occurred during the Pleistocene glacial periods because of dramatic changes in sea level. The paleo-sea-level curve, which is essential for understanding the formation of the large Amazonian river-floodplains, is known in detail only for the very last period from 100 000 to 10 000 BP; however, it is partially known for the rest of the Pleistocene, going back to 2.4 million years BP (Fig. 3.3). At least three warm periods with sea-level stages either similar to, or 10 to 20 m higher than, those of today are believed to have occurred during the last 200 000 to 400 000 years. A lowering of the sea level by up to 130 m during glacial periods increased the slope and led to the deep incision of the rivers in central Amazonia. Seismic studies and sediment cores indicate the existence of a glacial paleo-floodplain that was about 20 m lower near Manaus (Müller et al. 1995), and about 65 m lower near Santarem (G. Irion, W. J. Junk, and J. A. S. N de Mello, unpublished data), than the recent floodplain. The rise in sea level during interglacial periods dammed the rivers in their valleys and accelerated sediment deposition. Sea-level fluctuations affected the river system at least 2500 km upstream of the Amazon mouth and in the areas north and south of the main river as far as the rims of the Guiana and Central Brazilian shields.

Most of the active floodplains along the lower reaches of the large Amazonian white-water rivers are the result of sediment deposition after the last glacial period, which had its maximum about 20 000 years BP and ended about 12 000 years BP. Some areas are remnants of Pleistocene várzeas of different ages

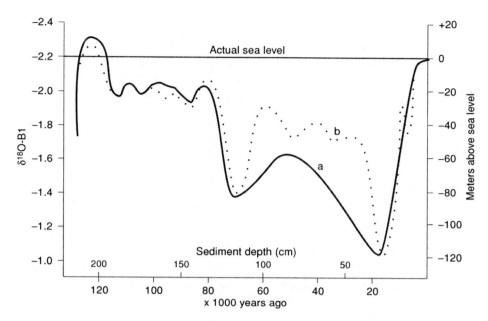

Figure 3.3 Curve *a*, the correlation of the $\delta^{18}O$ content of planktonic foraminifera in a sediment core from the Pacific and the course of the recent Quaternary sea-level fluctuations. The amplitudes of the sea-level fluctuations were calculated from the terraces on Barbados and New Guinea (Shackleton & Opdyke 1973). Curve *b* is from Johnson (1983), modified from data obtained on the Pacific West Coast of the United States.

locally called "*terra alta*" and might have formed, for instance, during the last high sea-level stage about 120 000 years BP (summarized in Irion *et al.* 1997).

Climate and hydrology

Today, the climate in the Amazon basin is hot and humid. The mean annual temperature in central Amazonia is 26.6 °C. During the warmest months (August to November), the average temperature ranges from 27.2 to 27.6 °C, and during the coldest months (January to April) it ranges from 25.9 to 26.1 °C. The diurnal temperature fluctuations are larger than the annual fluctuations and can exceed 10 °C. Minimum temperatures below 20 °C occur each year when cold, southern-polar air masses move northward and influence the weather in central Amazonia for 1 to 3 days in May, locally called "*friagem*." The relative air humidity remains high for the entire year, averaging 75.6% in September and 86.7% in April.

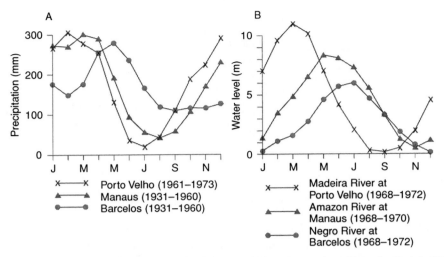

Figure 3.4 Monthly rainfall (A) and water-level fluctuations (B) in the Madeira River at Porto Velho, the Amazon River at Manaus, and the Negro River at Barcelos; these areas correspond to the southern, central, and northern parts of the basin (Junk 1994).

Precipitation is clearly periodic, with a rainy season in central Amazonia from December to April and a dry season from June to October. Annual rainfall varies from 1800 to 3000 mm in the center, up to 6000 mm near the Andes, and 1200 to 1800 mm at the borders. Evaporation exceeds precipitation during the dry season at the borders of the basin and even in the central part. The periodicity of rainfall leads to predictable, monomodal water-level fluctuations of the large rivers (Fig. 3.4) and the formation of extended floodplains along the river courses. In small streams, baseline discharge increases during the rainy season, but flood peaks depend on local rain events and are unpredictable (Fig. 3.5). Because of the slight declivity of the central basin and the plateaus on top of the Central Brazilian and the Guiana shields, drainage is insufficient, and large interfluvial wetlands are formed that are flooded during the rainy season and become mostly dry during the dry season. Most of these wetlands are temporarily connected by small streams and rivers to the Amazonian drainage system.

The impact of paleoclimatic changes on the flora and fauna of the Amazon basin is a controversial issue. Because of the position of the central part near the equator, changes have been less dramatic than in more-distant areas. Some authors postulate a decrease in temperature and precipitation during glacial periods that led to fractionation of the rain forest. Repeated genetic isolation of plant and animal species associated with patchy forest habitats during glacial periods would explain large species diversity and patchy species distribution in

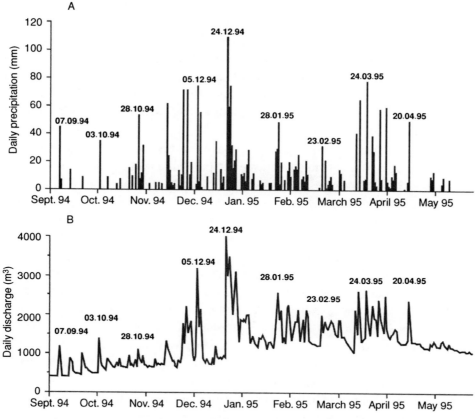

Figure 3.5 Daily precipitation (A) and discharge (B) of a low-order stream in Mato Grosso (Wantzen 1998b).

the recent rain forest (this is the "refuge theory," summarized in Haffer & Prance 2001). During the last ice age, a fall in temperature of about 5 °C and a decrease in rainfall by 30% to 50% is assumed (van der Hammen & Hooghiemstra 2000). Other authors contest this hypothesis and assume a slight drop in temperature, but permanently moist conditions and forest cover (summarized in Colinvaux *et al.* 2001).

The effects of a decrease in temperature and a reduction in precipitation on Amazonian wetlands have not yet been studied, but we assume that even smaller drought events seriously affected most interfluvial Amazonian wetlands since they depend on local rainfall surplus. For instance, many small interfluvial wetlands and even low-order streams dried out completely in Acre and Roraima during the extreme El Niño event in 1997–98 (W. J. Junk, personal observations). Large river-floodplains were less affected by paleoclimatic changes. Even assuming a 30% to 50% reduction in rainfall, bordering floodplains along the lower courses always existed because of the size of the rivers, their extended catchment areas, and a pronounced seasonal rainfall. The huge number of highly adapted endemic plant and animal species point to low extinction rates during glacial periods and support the very old age of the Amazonian river-floodplain systems. Flood-adapted species from these permanent river-floodplains were an important gene pool during moist periods for the recolonization of ephemeral interfluvial wetlands.

Climate changes during glacial periods probably increased with increasing distance from the equator. For instance, the Pantanal of Mato Grosso at the upper Paraguay River extends between 16° and 20° S about 2000 km south of the equator. Precipitation varies from 1600 mm per year in the north to 1200 mm per year in the south, with a pronounced dry period. This leads to much greater fire risk than in the Amazon River floodplain. It is assumed that during glacial periods the area was mostly dry, and that today's wetland conditions were only established about 2000 years ago (Ab'Saber 1988). Recent studies show that paleo-dune fields described by Klammer (1982) for large areas of the Pantanal of Mato Grosso are in fact paleo-levees of ancient rivers and cannot be used as arguments for the existence of a pronounced glacial dry period (Colinvaux et al. 2001). However, even a small decrease in precipitation can result in severe drought stress and profound changes in vegetation cover in the area, as shown by the current multi-annual dry periods (Nunes da Cunha & Junk 2004). Today, the total number of aquatic and palustric plant and animal species, and the number of endemic species, in the Pantanal is comparatively small and points to large extinction rates during severe dry periods. Wetland species of the Pantanal originate from the lower Paraguay River floodplain, the surrounding Cerrado, and from Amazonia.

The connection between the different Amazonian wetland systems is important because it allows many biological linkages. Many fish species, such as the "jaraqui" (*Semaprochilodus insignis, S. taeniurus*), the "matrincha" (*Brycon melanopterus*), and the large catfishes (*Brachyplatystoma flavicans, B. vaillanti, B. filamentosum*), participate in large spawning and feeding migrations up- and down-river and into the tributaries; they also use the bordering floodplains in different parts of the river system. Connectivity also increases the buffer capacity of the system against major, short-term natural or man-made catastrophes. Local extinction of species, for example by extreme droughts during El Niño events or by industrial pollution, can be compensated for by reimmigration from unaffected areas.

On the other hand, large-scale development projects can affect distant wetlands. The construction of large reservoirs for hydroelectric power generation, for instance Tucurui at the Tocantins River and Balbina at the Uatumã River, have changed the hydrological regime and affected the floodplains below the reservoirs; they also interrupted the migration routes of fish and other aquatic animals. Mercury release from gold mining in the upper Tapajós River catchment has led to increased mercury levels in fish in the downriver reaches and to subclinical mercury accumulation in fishermen in villages about 700 km downstream of the mining areas (Akagi *et al.* 1995).

State of knowledge, distribution, and classification of Amazonian wetlands

Wetlands are ecosystems at the interphase between terrestrial and aquatic systems. The concept of ecotones, first used by Clements (1905) to describe tension zones between plant communities, has now become scale independent and is also applied to large transition areas on a landscape scale. According to the definition of Hansen and di Castri (1992), wetlands around lakes or large river-floodplains are considered as ecotones. Other authors give them the status of specific ecosystems (Junk 1980, Odum 1981, Mitsch & Gosselink 2000) because periodic or permanently standing water, anoxic waterlogged soils, and in some wetland types the periodic change from terrestrial to aquatic or wetland conditions, provide specific environmental conditions that result in characteristic biogeochemical processes, specific adaptations of wetland organisms, and peculiarities in community structure and development.

The large variety of wetland ecosystems led to different definitions, summarized by Mitsch and Gosselink (2000). An internationally recognized definition is given in the first article of the Ramsar Convention, which describes wetlands as "areas of marsh, fen, peatland or water, whether natural or artificial, permanent or temporary, with water that is static or flowing, fresh, brackish or salt, including areas of marine water the depth of which at low tide does not exceed six meters" (Navid 1989). This definition encompasses coastal and shallow marine areas (including coral reefs), as well as river courses and temporary lakes or depressions in semi-arid zones (Hails 1996), and was adopted to embrace all the wetland habitats of migratory water birds.

Despite their large extent and economic importance, there is little information on many of the Amazonian wetlands. Numerous studies concentrate on the Amazon and lower Negro River floodplain (summarized in Sioli 1984, Junk 1997, Padoch *et al.* 1999, Junk *et al.* 2000a), some streams near Manaus (summarized in Wantzen & Junk 2000), and some pre-Andean headwater rivers and their wetlands (Salo *et al.* 1986, Salo 1990, Puhakka *et al.* 1992). The discharge from the Amazor river and its tributaries, and the amount of suspended and

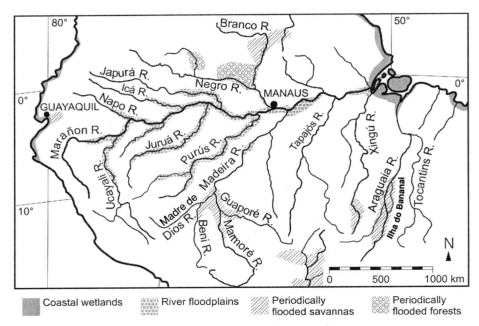

Figure 3.6 Distribution and classification of major Amazonian wetlands.

dissolved material in that discharge, have been measured (Meade *et al.* 1985, Mertes & Meade 1985, Richey *et al.* 1986, Meade 1994, Mertes 1994). Habitat conditions and fish fauna in the periodically flooded savannas of Rupununi have been described by Lowe-McConnell (1964); and descriptions of geo-ecology, biodiversity, fish fauna, conservation, and management of the flooded savannas of the Beni and Iténez rivers are given by Hanagarth (1993), Hanagarth & Szwagrzak (1998), Sarmiento (1998, 2000), and Herrera-MacBryde *et al.* (2000). A considerable amount of literature on fishery exists, but fishery statistics are of low quality (summarized in Soares & Junk 2000). Detailed information is spread among zoological, botanical, and limnological literature. Small wetland areas are mostly ignored, yet they represent a considerable portion of the total wetland area. The distribution of the major wetland types in tropical South America is given in Fig. 3.6.

The large and well-known wetland areas are officially recognized and listed in wetland inventories (Scott & Carbonell 1986, Diegues 1994, Finlayson & Spiers 1999). These inventories organize wetlands according to ecoregions and provide some information on ecology, status of integrity, and major threats. The advantage of this approach is that environmental, geographic, economic, and political variables can be compared. A major shortcoming, however, is the lack of a classification according to hydrological and hydrochemical parameters; such a classification would allow: (1) the application of general ecological theories and models; (2) a direct comparison between different wetlands of the same category and between ecoregions, countries, and continents; and (3) the prediction of the impact of human activities and the transfer of methods for sustainable management and protection.

As indicated by Navid's definition of wetlands, hydrology is of the utmost importance to their structures and functions and also to their classification. Wetlands with a fairly stable water level, such as peat bogs, contrast substantially with wetlands that have strongly fluctuating water levels, as indicated by the "flood-pulse concept," which describes the impact of periodic inundation and drought on wetland systems (Junk *et al.* 1989). Most Amazonian wetlands belong to the category of wetlands with strongly fluctuating water levels (the floodplain category).

The flood pulse leads to predictable or unpredictable oscillations of large areas between aquatic and terrestrial phases. Plants and animals have to adapt to these specific conditions. Predictability favors adaptation and increases nutrient-use efficiency. The mass transport of nutrients into and out of the floodplain in combination with nutrient sequestration by plants and animals influences soil and water fertility, which can control primary and secondary production. In nutrient-rich, white-water river-floodplains the nutrient input by dissolved and solid material during floods is high. Nutrient sequestering and nutrient transfer between terrestrial and aquatic phases by higher vegetation lead to nutrient accumulation and high productivity. An abundant and highly productive herbaceous plant community is characteristic of white-water river-floodplains (Fig. 3.7).

In nutrient-poor, black-water and clear-water river-floodplains and in areas flooded by rain water, the input of nutrients is low and nutrient losses by lixiviation during floods are hardly compensated for by the retention mechanisms of a highly adapted vegetation. High acidity in combination with low calcium content restrict the occurrence of bivalves and snails. Herbaceous plants are scarce (Fig. 3.8). Primary and secondary production is low, but species diversity can be high because of the low competitive strength of organisms as a result of nutrient limitation (Junk 1997).

Major Amazonian wetland categories are described according to hydrology, source of water, water quality, and vegetation cover by Klinge *et al.* (1990) and Junk (1992). A preliminary classification is given in Table 3.1. As with any ecological classification, this one is also artificial. For instance, sections along rivers in periodically inundated savannas behave like river-floodplains. Levees in predictably pulsing floodplains show characteristics of unpredictably pulsing systems because they are only flooded during very-high floods, which are

Figure 3.7 White-water floodplain lake at high water level, with luxurious floating vegetation in the foreground and flooded forest in the background.

unpredictable. Most categories are very large and certainly require further sub-classification. For instance, white-water river-floodplains cover an area of about 200 000 km^2 and have a large diversity of different subsystems; for example, new sediment bars with pioneer vegetation, low-lying mud flats with herbaceous vegetation, different types of backswamps and floodplain forests, connecting channels, and ria lakes and floodplain lakes with different levels of connectivity. Additional categories must be added when more information on different wetland types is available. The indicated areas of the categories are very-rough estimates. In the future, remote-sensing techniques will considerably improve the database.

Water and sediment storage and transport

During the rainy season, surface runoff is buffered by the wetlands, reducing flood amplitude of streams and rivers. The large differences in discharge between the dry and rainy season require intact riverine floodplains to increase the water-transport capacity of the main channel during floods. The floodplains act as a periodic sink for suspended material; after months, years,

Figure 3.8 Black-water floodplain lake with flooded forest. Note the lack of floating herbaceous vegetation.

decades, or even centuries, this material is remobilized and transported to the delta or into the ocean. Major changes in river-floodplains will lead to changes in sediment deposition and resuspension behavior and destabilize the floodplain with negative consequences for plants, animals, and humans.

All wetlands play a major role in the sponge potential of a landscape, i.e. the capacity to store water during wet periods, to release it slowly during low water levels in streams and rivers, and to help sustain soil moisture during dry periods (Brady & Riding 1996). Large wetlands in *cerrado* areas – such as Bananal Island at the Araguaia River; the Llanos dos Mojos between the rivers Madre de Dios, Beni, Mamoré, and Guaporé in Bolivia; and the savannas of Roraima and Rupununi – recycle large amounts of water into the atmosphere, increase air humidity on a regional scale, and reduce temperature oscillations. There are no data available yet on the impact of these wetlands on the regional climate, but the studies of Salati *et al.* (1979) show that more than 50% of the rain falling in

Table 3.1 *Preliminary classification of Amazonian wetlands.*

1. Wetland with a rather stable water level
    1.1 Isolated wetlands (peat bogs in the Andes; size unknown, but small)
    1.2 Wetlands connected to permanent lakes (wetlands along Andean lakes; size unknown, but small)
2. Wetlands with oscillating water level[a]
    2.1 Floodplains subjected to a predictable monomodal flood pulse
        2.1.1 Floodplains with a high flood amplitude (large river-floodplains along the Amazon River and its large tributaries)
            2.1.1.1 Floodplains of high fertility (white-water river-floodpalins, approx. 200 000 km²)
            2.1.1.2 Floodplains of intermediate fertility (clear-water river-floodplains, approx. 60 000 km²)
            2.1.1.3 Floodplains of low fertility (black-water river-floodplains, approx. 40 000 km²)
        2.1.2 Floodplains with a low flood amplitude (large interfluvial wetlands inundated mostly by rain water)
            2.1.2.1 Wetlands mostly covered by forest (areas at the upper Negro River, approx. 50 000 km²)
            2.1.2.2 Wetlands mostly covered by savanna (flooded savannas in Roraima and Rupununi, Llanos dos Mojos, Bananal savannas, approx. 250 000 km²)
    2.2 Wetlands subjected to a predictable polymodal flood pulse
        2.2.1 Marine and brackish water wetlands affected by the tide (approx. 13 000 km²)
        2.2.2 Freshwater wetlands indirectly affected by the tide (approx. 25 000 km²)
    2.3 Wetlands subjected to an unpredictable polymodal flood pulse
        2.3.1 Wetlands associated with small streams and rivers (approx. 1 000 000 km²)
        2.3.2 Wetlands in depressions fed by rain water (approx. 100 000 km²)
3. Man-made wetlands (needs further classification; size unknown, but small)

[a] Including river channels and permanent floodplain lakes.

central Amazonia derives from evapotranspiration. According to Ponce (1995), up to 90% of the water flowing into the Pantanal of Mato Grosso, situated in the upper Paraguay basin, is recycled into the atmosphere. Large-scale wetland destruction could reduce local rainfall and seriously change natural vegetation cover, and also threaten the export-oriented agro-industries in the *cerrado* belt.

Recent studies by Nepstad *et al.* (1999) have shown that during strong El Niño years, large areas of the forested part of the Amazon basin can become so dry that they are susceptible to wildfires. Intact wetlands increase soil and air humidity and act as a fire barrier. Wildfires in the forest move slowly with flames of up to only 1 m height and can be stopped by intact riverine wetlands with widths of some tens of meters.

Figure 3.9 Stream in the *cerrado* belt of Rondonia. A large, mobile sand load from the erosion of soybean plantations has covered the roots of the riparian forest and killed many trees. The formerly narrow and meandering stream has changed to a braided stream with unstable margins that become eroded during heavy rains.

Riparian wetlands have important filter functions in controlling the input of dissolved and solid substances from the watershed into streams and rivers. The water quality is of fundamental importance for the organisms living in and along the streams and also for the health, welfare, and economic development of the human population. Destruction of the streamside forest by soybean plantations in the *cerrado* belt in Rondonia has led to increased sediment input in the streams and a dramatic decrease in submerged aquatic macrophytes due to the large amounts of mobile, sandy bed load. Intact stretches of riverine forests have been destroyed by anoxic conditions in the rhizosphere because of high sediment deposition (Fig. 3.9).

Biogeochemical processes

Wetlands are known to be hotspots of biogeochemical processes. Primary production of herbaceous plants in the *várzea* reaches up to 100 tons dry weight per hectare per year and is much higher than in non-flooded grasslands. However, decomposition is also very high, and there is little long-term storage of organic carbon inside the floodplain. The carbon content of the Holocene sediments varies between 0.5% and 4%, with a mean of approximately 2%. A total amount of 6×10^7 tons C per year (<1 mm) is transported by the Amazon River to the Atlantic Ocean (Richey *et al.* 1980). Most of this material consists of poorly degradable organic carbon from the catchment area, but Junk (1985) estimates that 1.7×10^7 tons of particulate organic carbon might derive from the floodplains.

In the non-flooded "*terra firme*" forest, tree growth is reduced during El Niño years and 0.2 Pg C per year are released from undisturbed forests to the atmosphere (Prentice & Lloyd 1998, Tian *et al.* 1998). Tree growth in the *várzea* is increased by up to 150% during El Niño years because of a longer terrestrial phase and is responsible for up to 25% of the carbon released from *terra firme* forests (Schöngart 2003).

Amazonian wetlands are an important source of methane for the atmosphere, with methane arising from the degradation of organic material in anoxic soils and water. The amount of data on methane emission is still small, and the variation of the emission rates is large. Wassmann and Martius (1997) estimate the methane source strength of the Amazon *várzea* (180 000 km^2) as 1 to 9 Tg CH_4 per year, corresponding to 1% to 8% of the global source strength of wetlands. The contribution of other Amazonian wetlands is not known, but will certainly add to the total methane emission from the Amazon basin.

The *várzea* is also a hotspot of nitrogen turnover. Nitrogen fixation occurs in the water by nitrogen-fixing bacteria, algae, and some aquatic macrophytes; on land, fixation is mainly by leguminous herbaceous plants and trees. It is counteracted by strong denitrification in the moist soils when water levels decrease (Kern & Darwich 1997, Kern *et al.* 2002, Kreibich & Kern 2003).

According to Richey *et al.* (2001), the Amazonian rivers and wetlands are important CO_2 sources. The *várzea* is also a hotspot for the sulfur cycle because, during a high-water period, anoxia in deeper-water layers and in the sediments leads to H_2S formation, which can then in part enter the atmosphere.

Species richness

The Amazon basin is famous for its species richness. Biodiversity hotspots of global importance are described for the Andean region and the *cerrado* of central Brazil (Myers *et al.* 2000). However, databases for many groups of organisms are incomplete. Available estimates are based mostly on countries or continents and not on the Amazon catchment area (Groombridge 1992). Furthermore, all estimates given on major plant and animal groups – such as herbaceous plants, trees, and invertebrates – do not differentiate between terrestrial and aquatic or wetland species. Worldwide, wetland diversity has remained on the sidelines despite its large contribution to total biodiversity (Gopal & Junk 2000).

The numbers of animals that apparently prefer wetlands, such as amphibians, are misleading. Of the 3533 recognized frog species, 44% occur in tropical

America (Duellman 1988). More than 300 species from the Amazon lowland rain forest have been described, but many of them live on the forest floor or in the canopy; they reproduce in very small and ephemeral water bodies, such as pools or phytotelmes, or build foam nests and are not related to wetlands (Hödl 1990). In one of the very-few studies on wetland species, 15 sympatric species were described with synchronous breeding at the beginning of the rainy season in the floating vegetation of Lago Janauari, a floodplain lake near Manaus (Hödl 1977).

Even data on rather well-studied aquatic groups, such as fish, pose problems. Böhlke *et al.* (1978) estimated 5000 species of fish for South America, and an additional 500 to 600 species for Central America, and stated that the status of knowledge of the Amazonian fish fauna is comparable with that of the United States and Canada about 100 years ago. Schäfer (1998), extrapolating historical trends in the description of Characidae and Loricariidae, predicted more than 8000 species of fish in the Neotropics. Groombridge (1992) advanced an estimate that fish comprise 22 000 of the 43 000 to 46 500 species of vertebrates. Vari & Malabarba (1998) calculate that even if we allow for an eventual 50% increase in the number of recognized fish species world-wide – both freshwater and marine – to approximately 33 000 species, Neotropical freshwater fish (8000 species) would constitute approximately 24% of all fish worldwide. Available freshwater habitats represent less than 0.01% of the world's water, with the freshwater systems of the Neotropics encompassing 25% to 28% of that total, or in other words, 0.0025% to 0.0028% of the total water on Earth would harbor about one-eighth of all vertebrates. An estimated half of this biodiversity occurs in the Amazon basin. In the 1200-km-long reach of the lower Negro River, Goulding *et al.* (1988) collected more than 450 fish species and estimated that a total of more than 700 species occur there.

Much diversification of modern Neotropical fish fauna occurred during at least the roughly 70 million years from the Late Cretaceous to the Miocene. Earth history events from the Late Miocene to the Holocene had very little impact on taxonomic diversity. Great antiquity and static history of almost all modern lower taxa can be shown by fossil traces. For instance, over the course of the last 13.5 million years or longer, fish such as the "tambaqui" (*Colossoma macropomum*) persisted, apparently without changing its diet of fruits and seeds (Lundberg 1998, Lundberg *et al.* 1998). There are only few examples of allopatric speciation; one example is in Pleistocene Lago Valencia, which contains four endemic species (Mago-Leccia 1970). However, there are many cases of Late and post-Miocene local extirpation of modern groups; for example in Argentina, Chile, the Magdalena basin, the north coast of Venezuela, and the high Cuenca basin of Ecuador (Lundberg *et al.* 1998).

Gentry *et al.* (1997) estimate the presence of approximately 18 000 species of angiosperms in the Amazon basin, but no data exist on the percentage of aquatic or palustric species. Junk (1989) estimates approximately 1000 flood-resistant tree species, which is about ten times more than in bottomland hardwood forests of the southeastern United States. On 4 ha in the Amazon River floodplain at Mamirauá Sustainable Development Reserve near Tefé, 226 tree species with a diameter at breast height of >10 cm were found; most of the species were flood-plain specific (Wittmann *et al.* 2002). This number would increase considerably if smaller tree specimens were also be considered. Beta-diversity between river basins may be large. Kubitzki (1989) points to a high level of endemic floodplain tree species in the upper Negro River.

Species diversity of herbaceous plants is relatively low and varies considerably between wetland types. Junk & Piedade (1993) recorded only 388 herbaceous plant species (with the exception of epiphytes) from the Amazon floodplain near Manaus. Of this total, 330 are considered terrestrial, growing during the low-water season on exposed sediments. Many of them are ruderal plants and neophytes; 34 species are aquatic and 24 have an intermediate status. Submersed rooted plants are lacking in most large river-floodplains, and aquatic macrophytes are rare in black-water rivers. In comparison, 247 wetland species from the Pantanal of Mato Grosso have been recorded (Pott & Pott 2000). The differences in macrophyte communities are explained by physical and chemical factors, for example, current, transparency, hydrochemistry, and the extent of water-level fluctuations.

Species diversity of zooplankton, phytoplankton, and benthos is not exceptionally high. In 15 samples collected over a 2-year period from Castanho Lake, Uherkovich & Schmidt (1974) found 209 algal taxa, but only 18 were frequent in most samples. Most taxa were cosmopolites, and a small number were warm-stenotherme. Five Euglenophyta and one Chlorococcales and a larger unspecified number of Conjugatophyceae were cited as endemic species. In Camaleão Lake, 14 planktonic cladoceran species, 7 copepod species, and 175 rotifers were found (Koste & Robertson 1983, Koste *et al.* 1984, Reid 1989). In many floodplain lakes, benthos is absent during the high-water period because of anoxic conditions. The floating vegetation of the *várzea* lakes is a species-rich habitat for aquatic invertebrates, but taxonomic constraints do not allow a detailed evaluation.

Studies on Amazonian streams and connected wetlands are scarce (summarized in Wantzen & Junk 2000). According to Fittkau (1973, 1982), species richness of Plecoptera and Ephemeroptera might be lower in Amazonian streams, that of Odonata and decapod Crustacea larger, and that of Trichoptera and Chironomidae similar to that of temperate regions. He postulates that the large annual temperature fluctuation in temperate streams led to a diversification in life-history traits and the partitioning of food resources. Patrick (1966) links the rather low number of aquatic organisms of small body size (algae, protozoa, insects) in Peruvian streams near Tingo Maria in the foothills of the Andes to the limited number of available niches.

With slightly over 1000 species, the bird fauna of the Amazonian lowland rain forest is highly diverse (Stotz *et al.* 1996). For the entire Amazon River basin, however, this number is an underestimate because it excludes the adjacent savannas (*cerrados*), the Andes from 600 to 900 m upward, and the Tepuis at the Venezuelan border. According to Groombridge (1992), Columbia (1721), Peru (1705), Brazil (1573), Indonesia (1519), Ecuador (1435), Venezuela (1306), and Bolivia (1257) are the countries with the highest bird-species diversity worldwide (number of species is given in parentheses). All species-rich South American countries contribute to the large species pool of Amazonia. About 38% of the Amazonian lowland forest species are endemic, and 107 species (without migrating species) are described as using aquatic habitats (Stotz *et al.* 1996). The total number of bird species in the wetlands, however, is much higher. On one small island (approximately 100 km^2 at low water level) in the Amazon River near Manaus, 204 species were observed, 45 of which were non-migratory wetland birds. The occurrence of at least 21 long-distance northern migrants and 8 southern migrants points to the supra-regional importance of the Amazon River floodplain as a bird habitat (Petermann 1997). In total, migrating birds play a very small role in the Amazonian bird fauna.

More than 400 mammal species live in the Amazon basin, but most of them are terrestrial species. For example, several of the 124 bat species registered for the Brazilian section also occur in the wetlands, but only the fishing bat *Noctilio leporinus* and perhaps a few others are wetland specific. The entire known distribution area of the white uakari (*Cacajao calvus calvus*) and the black-headed squirrel monkey *Saimiri vanzolinii* is in the Mamirauá Sustainable Development Reserve near Tefé, which is situated entirely in the Amazon River floodplain. Two freshwater dolphins (*Inia geoffrensis*, *Sotalia fluviatilis*) and one manatee species (*Trichechus inunguis*) occur in the large Amazonian rivers and floodplain lakes. The capybara (*Hydrochaerus hydrochaeris*) occurs in all types of wetlands, except very small streams. The giant otter (*Pteronura brasiliensis*) and the river otter (*Lontra longicaudis*) colonize medium-sized rivers with clear water and adjacent wetlands. In flooded savannas, the swamp deer (*Blastocerus dichotomus*) occurs.

Fifteen turtle species from Amazonia have been described, with *Trachemys adintrix* being endemic (Vogt *et al.* 2001). The big river turtles (*Podocnemis expansa*,

P. unifilis) formerly formed large populations in Amazonian rivers and wet-lands, but have nearly become extinct. In addition, the caiman populations (*Melanosuchus niger, Caiman crocodilus, Paleosuchus palpebrosus, P. trigonatus*) have decreased considerably because they have been hunted for their skins.

Periodic long-term flooding represents a serious stress on terrestrial inverte-brates. Therefore, the number of soil-living species is smaller in floodplains than in *terra firme*. Four higher taxa are restricted to *terra firme*: Amblypygi, Palpigradi, Protura, and Ricinulei. The numbers of floodplain-specific species of spiders and termites seem to be low, and adaptations are only poorly developed. A total of 472 species of spiders were found near Manaus in a primary *terra firme* forest, 210 species in a black-water floodplain forest, and 130 species in a white-water floodplain forest (Höfer 1997). About 150 termite species from Brazilian Amazo-nia are known. Near Manaus, between 70 and 90 species (3 families) are generally found per hectare in *terra firme* forests, but only 12 and 11 species (2 families) are found in white-water and black-water floodplain forests, respectively.

In other groups, the number of floodplain-endemic species and the level of adaptation is high (Adis & Junk 2002). From 25 species of tiger beetles reported from the Manaus area, 14 species are exclusively found in *terra firme* habitats, 9 in the floodplains, and only 2 in both. Of 60 species of pseudoscorpions, 29 occurred in *terra firme* forests and 25 in floodplain forests, 2 species occurred in both forests and 2 were phoretic. From 110 morphospecies of millipedes (Diplopoda), 67% occurred in *terra firme*, 33% in floodplains, and only 10% were recorded in both areas. Floodplain-endemic species of ground beetles, soil-living mites (Acari), and springtails (Collembola) are also found.

In Africa and Asia, during the low-water season, floodplains provide water, food, and shelter for many ungulates from the uplands. Therefore, the flood-plains contribute considerably to the maintenance of the stability of the pop-ulations of these animals in the surrounding ecosystems. To what extent this holds true for Amazonian ungulates is not known.

Riverine wetlands represent forested corridors in the *cerrado* belts and favor migration of forest animals between isolated forest plots. The large-scale trans-formation of the *cerrado* into soybean plantations dramatically increased the importance of this corridor function of the riparian wetlands for the landscape-wide maintenance of biodiversity and genetic resources.

The refuge theory (Haffer 1982, Prance 1982 and many others) is used by many authors to explain the high terrestrial-species diversity in Amazonia. It postulates forest fragmentation during glacial periods because of reduced rain-fall, and speciation because of genetic isolation, as described in the earlier sec-tion on *Climate and hydrology*. However, the theory is not well-suited to explain wetland-species diversity because: (1) much diversification occurred in earlier time periods, as shown for fishes; and (2) interconnection of the wetlands allowed genetic exchange and/or recolonization during and after glacial periods.

Despite this interconnection, the few available data point to differences in species composition between wetland types, river reaches, and habitats. For instance, Goulding *et al.* (1988) found 35 endemic fish species in the middle Negro River. For 11 white-water species occurring near the mouth of the Negro River, they consider water chemical conditions as an ecological and biogeographical barrier. The large beta-diversity in floodplain tree species between black-water and white-water rivers is related to differences in the nutrient status. Kubitzki (1989) shows close relationships between floodplain forests of white-water rivers and non-flooded *terra firme* forests on latosols, and also between black-water rivers and oligotrophic woodlands of "*campina*" (forest) and "*caatinga*" (shrubland). Water-level fluctuations and hydrochemical differences influence the occurrence of aquatic macrophytes (Junk & Piedade 1993).

In the pre-Andean zone, lateral migration of the Amazon River and its tributaries led to the formation of a large and complex mosaic of active floodplains and paleo-floodplains, which led to the periodic isolation of plant and animal populations and accelerated speciation (Salo *et al.* 1986). Longitudinal gene flow along riverine wetlands, lateral gene flow between wetlands and uplands, isolation of aquatic populations by rapids and waterfalls along the edges of the Central Brazilian and the Guiana shields, and hydrochemical and geochemical barriers have led to complex distribution patterns that are only partly understood (Junk 2000).

Productivity of Amazonian wetlands and evaluation of their development potential

Considering the world-wide decrease in the availability of fertile soils for the extension of agriculture and husbandry, development planners are looking for alternatives and are focusing increasingly on wetlands. One of the principle statements of the workshop "*Wetland Soils*" held in Los Banos, the Philippines, in 1985 was that "the greatest potential for expansion of food-producing lands may be in wetland soils." It was also stated that "tropical South America probably has more wetland with high potential for development than any other continent." (IRRI 1985).

Amazonian black-water and clear-water wetlands have a low nutrient status because they are flooded by rain water or tributaries with low contents of dissolved and suspended material. Primary production in these areas is fairly low. The occasional large numbers of animals, admired by tourists during the low-water period, are not the expression of high productivity but the result of the concentration in remaining water bodies and high nutrient-use efficiency. Interference by humans will quickly lead to the collapse of these populations. Fast-growing, soft-wood pioneer tree species are mostly lacking in nutrient-poor floodplain systems, and tree growth is generally slow and does not allow for wood extraction on a major scale (Parolin & Ferreira 1998). Forested floodplains can be used by fisheries, and can also be used to produce ornamental fishes. Savanna floodplains have some potential for low-intensity cattle ranching. Ecotourism can become an additional economically important activity.

White-water river-floodplains receive nutrient-rich water and sediments from the Andes during floods. This annual input maintains the system at a high natural production level and indicates large economic potential for fishery, forestry, agriculture, and cattle or buffalo ranching. Estimates of land and labor productivity of different land-use systems in the *várzea* of the central Amazon River are given in Table 3.2. However, a detailed analysis shows that restrictions exist for the different management systems.

Inland fishery has the largest potential with the lowest negative environmental impact. Only one-third to one-half of the total potential of 900 000 tons per year is actually used (Bayley & Petrere 1989), and inland fishery will also in the future provide inexpensive animal protein for the Amazonian population. Sustainable management for fish production delivers high economic return, provides income for many people directly and indirectly involved in fishery activities, and protects the environment because high yields are related to an intact river-floodplain system. However, lack of adequate fishery statistics makes efficient management difficult.

In central Amazonia, conflicts for fishing rights between commercial fishermen and riverine people increasingly affect fishery (Soares & Junk 2000). Disappointing experience with the centralized management of natural resources in the *várzea* led the Brazilian Environmental Agency (IBAMA) to set up an experiment with decentralized and participatory administration of the fishery resources. It is based upon agreements between commercial fishermen and local communities to restrict fishing rights in certain lakes or rivers for the benefit of the local population, but to allow professional fishermen to use other lakes for commercial fishery (Fisher *et al.* 1992, IBAMA 1994, 1997, McGrath *et al.* 1994, Ruffino 1996, Isaac *et al.* 1998). This type of administration encourages the local population to manage the fishery resources in their lakes sustainably and invest in the protection of the floodplain forest that provides fruit as a food source for many valuable fish species. An extension of this concept for the multiple use of the *várzea* will make an important contribution to environmental protection because the local population is included in the management process and will directly benefit from protection measures (Junk 2000).

Table 3.2 *Comparison of land and labor productivity of different land-use systems in the várzea of the central Amazon River (Junk et al. 2000b).*

		Land productivity (US$ ha^{-1})	Labor productivity (US$ per man and per day)	Gross farm income (US$ per year)
Arable farming[a]				
Staple crop farm		424	2.32	1781
Vegetable farm				
Mixed farming	Low income	468	2.24	1639
	Medium income	883	4.59	3890
	High income	1130	7.62	6890
Vegetables				
Intensive	Tomato	1680	16.80	
	Cucumber	1300	12.20	
	Lettuce	3050	19.20	
Other field crops				
	Water melon	430	16.00	
	Jute	480	1.80	
	Rice *terra firma*[b]	100	4.20	
Animal farming[c]				
Cattle ranching				
Extensive	Beef	33.8	4.90	
	Cheese	30.6	5.56	
Intensive	Milk	59.7	6.97	
Water-buffalo ranching				
Extensive	Meat	32.9	11.25	
Forestry[d]				
Selective logging	Timber	9–13		
Forest culture	Timber, estimated	120		
Fishery[e]				
Actual		338		
Potential		675		

[a] Data based on Gutjahr (2000).

[b] Gutjahr (1996).

[c] Data based on Ohly and Hund (2000). One dam plus offspring.

[d] Data on selective logging: 0.5 t ha^{-1} per year, corresponding to 1 m^3 of timber (M. Worbes, personal communication). Commercial value of timber US$9–13 (Ayres *et al.* 1999). Estimated timber production in forest plantation 8 t ha^{-1} per year, corresponding to 16 m^3; price US$10 m^{-3}; estimated cost for plantation management, logging, and losses by logging: 25%.

[e] Theoretical production of comestible fish 90 g m^{-2} per year (Bayley 1983) with a market value of US$1 kg^{-1}; present use: 50% (Soares & Junk 2000). Costs for fishing effort: 25%.

The fishery industry is slowly increasing in Amazonia. Large water-level fluctuations and periodic heavy hypoxia make large river-floodplains unsuitable for
fish-culture stations. Isolated lakes in flooded savannas with little-fluctuating
water levels might offer some potential for fish culture.

Forestry has been reduced to the logging of a few floodplain species. Most
floodplain areas are already exploited by timber companies, and only a few areas
are still in a rather pristine state; for example, the Sustainable Development
Reserve of Mamirauá near Tefé. Several species have become seriously depleted
because of insufficient regrowth. "Sumauma" (*Ceiba pentandra*), one of the largest
trees and formerly very common in the *várzea*, became economically important
for the plywood industry about 20 years ago and was heavily exploited. Large
trees, and also young trees, are now rare. Considering the good nutrient status
of the *várzea* and the diameter-increment rates of economically important *várzea*
tree species – such as the "sumauma" – of 2 to 4 cm per year, forest polyculture
has to be considered an economically viable and ecologically recommendable
activity in the *várzea*.

Small-holder agriculture on a subsistence level has been successfully practiced in the *várzea* for centuries. It has its roots in pre-Columbian practices as
shown by the species-rich home gardens, which represent agroforestry systems of
indigenous origin. Small-holder agriculture is labor intensive and keeps a large
number of people in the floodplain who would otherwise migrate to the cities. It
efficiently uses the small-scale mosaic of soil conditions formed by erosion and
deposition processes in the floodplain. Weeds, diseases, and parasites can be better controlled without large-scale application of pesticides. The intensification
of production in small areas leads to higher incomes. Small-holder agriculture
affects small areas only because it is restricted to the levees near the main river
channels; these levees have a long growing season for crop plantation and allow
easy transport of products to the markets. Only 1% of the *várzea* near Manaus
is actually used (Gutjahr 1996). The total area suitable for this type of activity
may reach 3% to 5% of the entire *várzea*; however, most of it is already utilized
by cattle and water-buffalo ranchers. Agricultural production is highly seasonal;
super-saturation of the local markets hinders expansion of the production of
perishable products such as fruit and vegetables.

Large-scale crop plantations require large uniform areas to allow a high
degree of mechanization. Therefore, they do not fit in the small-scale mosaic
of habitats in the floodplain. In the 1970s, a large rice paddy plantation was
established in the floodplain of the Jarí River, a western tributary of the lower
Amazon. Multiple problems with weeds, parasites, soil fertility, and the labor
force resulted in the project being economically unviable (Fearnside 1988). In
recent years, soybean plantation in the *várzea* has been discussed. This would

require large-scale clearing of natural floodplain vegetation. Planting time would coincide with the low water levels of the dry season and harvest would occur at the beginning of the rainy season, which would require expensive irrigation of the plantations and then drying of the crop. Large-scale application of fertilizers and pesticides would seriously affect water quality and fish stocks. We consider such projects uneconomical and very detrimental to the *várzea*.

Dairy farming is a profitable and labor-intensive activity in the vicinity of urban centers. Farms are restricted to areas near river channels because farmers need quick access to the market throughout the year. Economically more important is large-scale cattle ranching for beef production. Stocking rates are low (1 to 1.2 animals per ha), but labor costs are also low because only a few herdsmen are required to take care of the animals. Cattle ranching is severely affected by the large water-level fluctuations. At low water, large pasture areas are available that cannot be adequately used by the cattle. With rising water levels the pasture area decreases, and at high water only the pastures on the levees are available. Therefore, large areas of floodplain forest on the levees are cleared to increase pasture area. During very-high floods, small herds are kept on floats or artificial earth mounds, while large herds are transferred to the uplands. Weight gain reaches 0.35 to 0.4 kg per animal per day during the period of high fodder availability (Ohly & Hund 2000). Near Manaus, artificial pastures have been planted on the levees using the flood-resistant African grass *Brachiaria humidicula*. Because of the destruction of the floodplain forest, large-scale cattle ranching is considered detrimental for the floodplain. Grasses and secondary vegetation on the levees are easily ignited during the dry period, and fire becomes an additional stress factor in a non-fire-adapted ecosystem.

In recent years, water-buffalo ranching has been spreading upstream from the lower Amazon. Water buffalos are better adapted to floodplain conditions and produce about twice as much meat per unit area as cattle because of a broader food spectrum and a higher stocking rate (Ohly & Hund 2000). Large herds have a strong negative impact on plant cover and habitat diversity. They destroy the dense vegetation that protects permanent floodplain lakes against sediment import from the river. Because of their habit of wallowing, the water buffalo stir up sediments in the shore regions of lakes. Mud particles are transported to deeper parts of the lakes and accelerate the filling-in process. After only a few years, permanent lakes, which are important refuges for the aquatic fauna and flora during the low-water period, are transformed into mud flats.

The sustainable development and protection of the *várzea* depends on the multiple use of its resources by fishery, labor-intensive small-holder agriculture combined with small-scale animal ranching, and forestry (Junk *et al.* 2000b). In spite of the relatively high fertility of the *várzea* soils and the annual input of nutrients by the floods, the *várzea* has no potential for large-scale export-oriented agro-industries. It would be a tragic and economically, ecologically, and socio-economically disastrous error to overestimate the agricultural potential of the *várzea*.

Threats

Many Amazonian wetlands are still in a fairly pristine condition. However, the rise in the human population and large development projects have led to increasing pressure. Governments still have the opportunity to select between various development options and scientists can provide recommendations for ecologically, economically, and socially acceptable alternatives. It has to be stressed that not every small wetland has to be protected to maintain the basic components of the landscape structure and function. An equilibrium has to be achieved between development planning and ecological considerations, including aspects of economic development, public health, quality of life, and environmental protection. This, however, requires cooperation between politicians, planners, scientists, and the local population in the decision-making and planning process.

Construction of hydroelectric power plants

The rise in the price of oil and the discussion on CO_2 emissions into the atmosphere make the use of hydroelectric energy increasingly attractive economically, despite many negative side-effects. The hydroelectric potential of rivers in the Brazilian Amazon region, with the exception of the main river, is estimated at 100 000 MW. The utilization of this potential would require the construction of 63 reservoirs, which would cover an area of about 100 000 km^2. All major tributaries of the Amazon River and their bordering floodplains would be affected, some of them very heavily, such as the Tocantins and Araguaia rivers with 27 reservoirs (Junk & de Mello 1987). To date, 5 reservoirs have been constructed in Amazonia: Balbina near Manaus at the Uatuma River (3147 km^2), Tucurui at the lower Tocantins River (2247 km^2), Curuá-Una near Santarém at the Curuá-Una River (100 km^2), Samuel near Porto Velho at the Jamarí River (465 km^2), and Coracy Nunes in Amapá (23 km^2). The shortage of energy in southern Brazil has accelerated the planning and construction of large reservoirs on the Xingú River (Fig. 3.10).

The multiple, negative side-effects related to the construction of large reservoirs are well known. Wetlands are affected mainly by the modification of the flood regime downriver and the interruption of the migration routes of aquatic animals. The composition of fish communities inside the reservoirs changes from

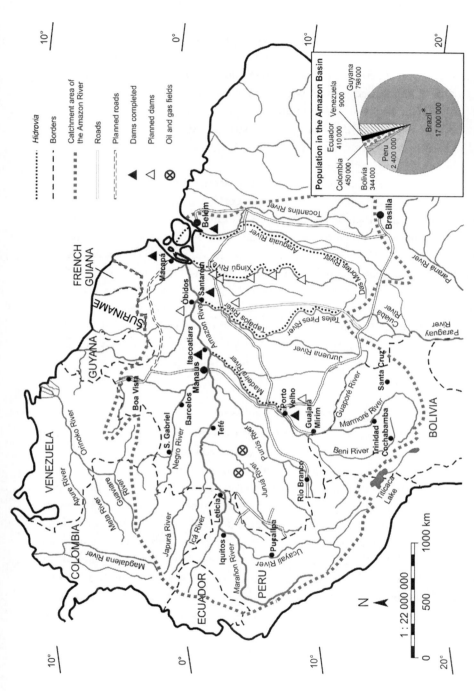

Figure 3.10 Geographical map with major rivers, countries participating in the Amazon basin, major highways, cities, planned and constructed dams, *hidrovias*, oil and gas fields (modified from Fearnside 1989), and population numbers (Comision Amazonica de Desarollo y Medio Ambiente 1992). *Since the drawing of the map, the Brazilian population has increased to approximately 21 million people.

lotic to lentic (Junk *et al.* 1981, Santos 1996, Santos & Oliveira 1999, Mérona *et al.* 2001). There are no data available about the impact of hydrological changes on the downriver floodplains. Shorter and smaller flood periods will considerably reduce the total floodplain area, the period of access to the floodplain for aquatic animals, and the connectivity of permanent floodplain lakes to the main channel. Former floodplain areas will become invaded by terrestrial species, and the area suitable for highly flood-resistant species will diminish. Productivity will decrease because part of the dissolved and suspended material will be retained inside the reservoirs, and the nutrient-transfer processes characteristic of the floodplains will be interrupted.

Not all technically feasible reservoirs are economically sound in the long run, when the ecological and sociological costs are taken into account. The construction of the Balbina reservoir at Uatumá River shows that short-term political arguments overruled ecological and even economic arguments (Fearnside 1989). The shortage of hydroelectric energy, due to low rainfall, affected economic development in southern Brazil in 2001 and led to the acceleration of the decision-making processes for the construction of new hydroelectric reservoirs. For instance, there are serious concerns on the part of non-government organizations about the inadequate elaboration of environmental-impact studies to determine suitable sites for reservoirs on the Araguaia River. Negative side-effects on the National Park and the Indigenous Reserve on Bananal Island could occur.

Construction of navigation channels ("hidrovias")

The production of large amounts of soybeans in the *cerrado* belt on the southern border of the Amazon basin led to the reconsideration of inexpensive shipping transport along the Amazonian rivers. *Hidrovias* have been constructed or are under construction on the Madeira River from Porto Velho to Itacoatiara (1056 km), on the Tapajós–Teles Pires rivers from Cachoeira Rasteira to Santarém (1043 km), the Tocantins–Araguaia rivers at Rio das Mortes (1516 km), on Marajó Island (Atuá and Anajás Rivers, 67 and 207 km, respectively; and a channel of 32 km), and on the Xingú River (Brito 2001) (Fig. 3.10). The construction of *hidrovias* includes straightening of sinuous stretches of the channels, dragging, removal of obstacles such as rocks, and the establishment of signals for ship traffic. In all cases, detailed environmental-impact analyses have not been undertaken.

The most-dramatic proposal for a *hidrovia* was the straightening and deepening of the upper Paraguay River inside the Pantanal of Mato Grosso, adjacent to the Amazon basin. It would have seriously affected one of the world's most impressive wetlands. In 2000, the Brazilian Government abandoned the plan, but private enterprises are still slowly continuing to construct harbors and other infrastructure.

Construction of dikes, drainage channels, and roads

Interfluvial wetlands are particularly sensitive to hydrological changes because the periodic flooding is shallow and often lasts only a few months. This favors drainage and flood-protection measures for implantation of conventional agriculture. Road construction on levees interrupts water flow and affects the hydrology of large areas because of the low declivity of the terrain. It is especially destructive in mangrove areas because it easily modifies the salinity levels that affect the growth and development of plants and animals.

Change in sediment load as a result of increased erosion and mining activities

Increasing deforestation of the Amazon basin and large agricultural projects lead to increased erosion and sediment import into streams, rivers, and related wetlands. Major impacts have already been observed in small, streamside wetlands and streams, where wetland vegetation and in-stream biodiversity has been strongly modified (Fig. 3.11) (Wantzen 1998b). The negative impact on wetlands can be reduced by the enforcement of the existing environmental legislation for the protection of streamside wetlands.

Sand and clay particles from tin-ore, diamond, and gold mining increase the sediment load in streams and rivers and reduce habitat and species diversity in the stream beds and connected wetlands. Mining residues (red mud) from bauxite mining were deposited in Lago Batatas, a floodplain lake at the lower Amazon, and significantly affected the environment (Bozelli et al. 2000).

Input of domestic waste water, agrochemicals, industrial wastes, and mining residues (mercury)

The population density in Amazonia is low and domestic wastewater input is in most cases quickly diluted and decomposed by the large water masses of the rivers. Even the waste water of a very large city like Manaus does not seriously affect the water quality of the Amazon River. There are no records of negative effects of agrochemicals on Amazonian waters and wetlands. The lixiviation of fertilizers can be shown only during a short period after the onset of heavy rains, but concentrations are quickly diluted (Wantzen 1997). There is no information on the effect of agrotoxic compounds on small streams and streamside wetlands in agro-industrial areas, but negative impacts are expected.

Mercury input from gold mining is a threat for large areas in Amazonia. Lacerda and Pfeiffer (1992) estimated a total release of between 1500 and 3000 tons in the Brazilian Amazon basin; today this may reach about 5000 tons in

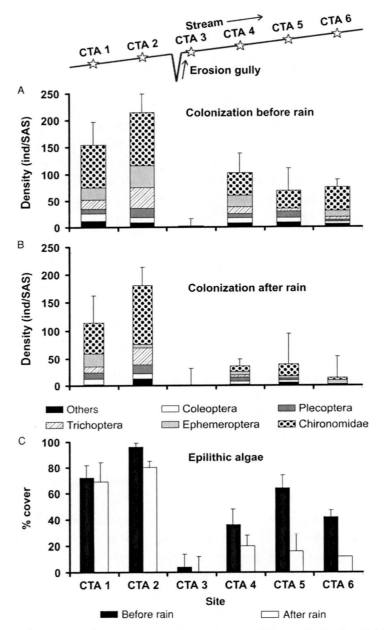

Figure 3.11 Results of colonization experiments using standardized artificial substrates for benthic invertebrates and glass slides for epilithic algae; ind/SAS., individuals per sample. Benthic colonization (A) before and (B) after a heavy rain event; (C) epilithic algal colonization (Wantzen 1998a).

the entire basin. The majority of the mercury is deposited in a low-toxicity metal-lic form in the sediments. However, there is a latent danger that this metallic mercury will become toxic through methylization, which is favored in acidic water with high concentrations of humic substances, and then slowly enter the food webs. In recent years, gold mining has decreased, but mining activities are still continuing. In central-Amazonian black-water rivers there is already a high natural mercury level (Forsberg et al. 1995, Fadini 1999), and additional release from gold mining can easily reach toxic levels (summarized in Nogueira & Junk 2000). In the Tapajós River, subclinical mercury levels were found in fishermen living 700 km downstream of the mining area (Akagi et al. 1995). However, recent studies contest the long-distance pollution effect of mercury from gold mining; they point to the importance of the increased input of natural mercury associ-ated with fine-particulate soil material because of deforestation and insufficient erosion control (Roulet et al. 1998a, b).

Large-scale land reclamation

Direct wetland destruction by agriculture and animal farming occurs in large wetlands, for example in the Amazon River floodplain. The most-threatened plant communities are the floodplain forests, which are easily destroyed and require one to two centuries to recover. Mangroves are heavily affected by the implantation of ponds for fish and shrimp culture, and also by deforestation and civil engineering (Lacerda 2002). Many small wetlands suffer from increased modification of the catchment area, which affects hydrology and sediment load; for example, large-scale modification of vegetation cover for agriculture and cattle ranching.

Changes in global climate

Predictions about the effects of changes in global climate on the Amazon basin are still speculative and vary considerably between areas. During the next century, a rise in the sea level of several tens of centimeters seems to be realistic. It will seriously affect coastal wetlands, mainly the mangroves.

The Amazon River floodplain along the lower river course will also be affected because the slope only reaches about 0.75 cm km^{-1}. The rising sea level will have a damming-back effect of the flood waters; this effect will probably be felt up to Santarém, about 700 km from the sea. Higher floods will affect human settlements and the floodplain forest on the levees. The effects on the entire system, however, will be small. Organisms living in the Amazon River floodplain are adapted to heavy perturbation by the annual floods. Furthermore, after the last glacial period, a rise in the sea level of about 1 cm per year over about

10 000 years was successfully overcome because even completely flooded areas in the lower reaches could be recolonized from intact refuges upstream.

The ecological buffer capacity of Amazonian interfluvial wetlands fed by rain water is much smaller. Initial data point to an increase in extreme climatic events, such as El Niño. Multi-annual severe droughts in shallowly flooded areas will lead to increased fire stress, which will reduce the area of highly adapted floodplain forest in favor of grasslands, and stress aquatic communities as shown for the Pantanal of Mato Grosso (Nunes da Cunha & Junk 2004).

Protection measures

The first step for environmental protection is a profound knowledge of the different wetland types, their extension, distribution, and threats. The previous sections have shown that our knowledge about Amazonian wetlands is insufficient despite considerable progress in studies on processes related to the Amazon River, its floodplain, and a few tributaries. Information on species diversity is fragmentary and in many cases does not allow any conclusions to be drawn. A detailed wetland classification based on large-scale inventories should provide the basis for the analysis of gaps of knowledge, for research programs, and for a national wetland policy including management and protection measures.

The close interaction between catchment areas, river courses, and connected wetlands leads to a strong dependence of the future of Amazonian wetlands on the economic development of the Amazon basin. Therefore, protection measures should include catchment-area management plans to control human impact on water discharge and the input of sediments, domestic and industrial waste water, and toxic substances into rivers and wetlands. In the past, this has in many cases not been done with the required intensity, as shown by the controversial discussion about the environmental impact of the Brazilian *Avança Brazil* Program with an investment volume of US$40 billion between 2000 and 2007. Scientists have severely criticized the government for not considering, or seriously underestimating, the negative side-effects on the environment, mainly degradation of 25% to 42% of the rain forest by the year 2020 (Becker 1999, Nepstad *et al.* 2000, Laurance *et al.* 2001). The impact on the wetlands of the affected areas has not been assessed.

Recommendations for protection measures also require a critical analysis of existing environmental legislation. As shown by Vieira (2000) for the Brazilian part of the basin, the large number and variety of wetlands in the vast and scarcely populated Amazon basin is not adequately covered by environmental legislation. In many cases, the lack of a clear delineation and definition of wetlands does not allow the formulation of adequate laws. For instance, the vegetation along streams and rivers is protected, the river bed being defined as the area covered by the peak flood level. This definition applies well for the protection of streams and small rivers, and associated narrow riverside wetlands including strips of non-flooded vegetation at their edges, but what about large river-floodplains that cover valleys that are tens of kilometers broad, where human population and agriculture concentrate on the highest levees along the river channels inside the floodplain? The first step towards more transparency should be the compilation and interpretation of existing, currently dispersed environmental laws into one volume to facilitate access to information by the population (Vieira 2000). The existing legislation should be improved and adapted according to recommendations based on a detailed wetland inventory and classification.

Environmental protection in general and wetland protection in particular will depend to a large extent on the implementation of the legislation, but controls are difficult. For instance, in areas used for agriculture and cattle ranching, destruction of riverine vegetation is a common practice, with negative impact on water quality and biodiversity. Poaching and the destruction of key habitats occur in most wetlands. The reason for the destructive behavior of the population is often a lack of understanding of basic ecology and its relationship to human welfare. Strong efforts are required to provide environmental education at all levels of the population.

The most-efficient way to increase acceptance of environmental legislation is the active participation of the local population in decentralized planning and management of natural resources (co-management). Community-based management has its roots in indigenous traditions and is still practiced by rural communities in Amazonian floodplains (Noda et al. 2000). Several forms of co-management are actually tested in Amazonia; examples include: co-management of fishery resources of the Amazon River floodplain (McGrath et al. 1994, 1999, Isaac et al. 1998); the establishment of extractive reserves ("reservas estrativistas") for the sustainable use of the rain forest; and the establishment of reserves for sustainable development, such as Mamirauá in the Amazon floodplain near Tefé (Mamiraua Management Plan 1996). Through the G-7 Pilot Program for Conservation of Brazilian Rain Forests, the local institutional capacity for environmental planning and protection has been strengthened. First steps have been made by passing responsibilities from federal and state level to municipal governments (Dillinger & Webb 1999). In these important efforts, which currently concentrate on the sustainable management and protection of tropical rain forests, water resources including wetlands should be included and become a specific, high-priority topic.

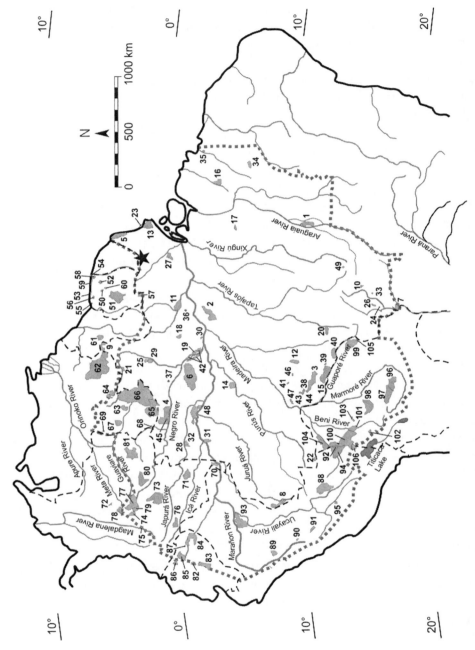

Figure 3.12 Protected areas in the Amazon region (CABS/CI 2000; SURAPA 2000). The Parque de Tumucumaque (3 800 000 ha), created in 2002 by the Brazilian Government in Amapá at the border of French Guiana, is indicated on the map by a star.

Table 3.3 *Total number and protected area of national parks,
biological and ecological stations, national reserves, wildlife refuges,
and sustainable development reserves in the Amazon region
sensu latu (about 7 000 000 km², Amazon Basin + Guianas +
Pre-Amazônia Maranhense + southern Venezuela extending into
the state of Bolívar) (CABS/CI 2000).*

Country	Number	Area (ha)
Bolivia	16	9 155 120
Brazil total	51	25 029 572[a]
Federal protected areas	33	17 469 153[a]
State protected areas	18	7 560 419
Colombia	12	5 869 849
Ecuador	6	2 145 513
French Guiana	No information	
Guyana	1	58 600
Peru	9	6 630 264
Suriname	8	1 870 900
Venezuela	8	8 640 050
Total number	111[a]	
Total protected area		59 399 868[a]

[a] Including 3 800 000 ha of Tumucumaque Park, established in 2002 in
Amapá, Brazil.

All countries participating in the Amazon basin have given the status of
National Parks, Biological Reserves, Reserves of Sustainable Development, and
other categories of protection to large areas. Approximately 8.5% of the Amazon
basin is protected (Fig. 3.12, Tables 3.3 and 3.5). Many of these reserves contain
important wetlands, for example: in Brazil, the Ecological Station of Anavilhanas
on the Negro River upstream of Manaus (3555 km²), the Sustainable Development
Reserve of Mamirauá in the Amazon River floodplain (11 240 km²), and the Jaú
National Park at Jaú River (22 720 km²); in Peru, the Manu Biosphere Reserve
(15 328 km²) and the National Park Pacaya-Samiria (20 800 km²); in Colombia, the
Natural National Parks La Paya (4420 km²) and Amacayacu (2930 km²); and in
Bolivia, the Beni River Biosphere Reserve (1350 km²), the National Reserve of Noel
Kempff Mercado (219 km²), and Rios Blanco y Negro (14 000 km²). Furthermore,
indigenous reserves provide some level of protection because indigenous land-
use systems hardly affect wetland integrity. However, often there are not enough
funds available to implement protection measures. The most-important threats
to protected areas are inadequate management, poaching, invasion by squatters,

Table 3.4 *List of protected areas in Amazonia, year of establishment, and size. Numbers indicate the position of the areas in Fig. 3.12.*

Brazil

		Year of establishment	Area (ha)
	National Park		
1	Araguaia	1959	562 312
2	Amazônia	1974	994 000
3	Pacaás Novos	1979	764 801
4	Pico da Neblina	1979	2 200 000
5	Cabo Orange	1980	619 000
6	Jaú	1980	2 272 000
7	Pantanal Matogrossense	1981	135 000
8	Serra do Divisor	1989	605 000
9	Monte Roraima	1989	116 000
10	Chapada dos Guimarães	1989	33 000
	Biological Reserve		
11	Rio Trombetas	1979	385 000
12	Jarú	1979	268 150
13	Lago Piratuba	1980	357 000
14	Abufari	1982	288 000
15	Guaporé	1982	600 000
16	Gurupi	1988	341 650

Brazil

		Year of establishment	Area (ha)
	Ecological Reserve		
39	Serra do Parecis	1990	38 950
40	Corumbiara	1990	585 031
41	Candeias	1990	8 985
42	Rio Negro	1995	436 042
	State Biological Reserve		
43	Traçadal	1990	22 540
44	Rio Ouro Preto	1990	46 438
45	Morro dos Seis Lagos	1990	36 900
	State Ecological Station		
46	Samuel	1989	20 865
47	Serra dos Três Irmãos	1990	99 813
	Sustainable Development Reserve		
48	Mamirauá	1990	1 124 000
	Amanã[a]	1997	2 326 000
	State Ecological Reserve		
49	Culuene	1989	3 000

No.	Name	Year	Area
17	Tapirapé	1989	103 000
18	Uatumã	1990	560 000
	Ecological Station		
19	Anavilhanas	1981	350 018
20	Iquê	1981	200 000
21	Maracá	1981	101 312
22	Rio Acre	1981	77 500
23	Maracá-Jipioca	1981	72 000
24	Taiamã	1981	11 200
25	Caracarai	1982	80 560
26	Serra das Araras	1982	28 700
27	Jari	1982	227 126
28	Juami-Japurá	1985	572 650
29	Niquiá	1985	286 600
	Ecological Reserve		
30	Sauim-Castanheiras	1982	109
31	Jutaí-Solimões	1983	284 285
32	Juami-Japurá	1983	173 180
	State Park		
33	Águas Quentes	1978	3 000
34	Mirador	1980	700 000
35	Baganca	1980	3 062
36	Nhamundá	1989	28 370
37	Serra do Araçá	1990	1 818 700
38	Guajará-Mirim	1990	258 813

Suriname

No.	Name	Year	Area
	Nature Reserve		
50	Brinckheuvel	1972	6 000
51	Central Suriname	1998	1 600 000
52	Copi	1986	28 000
53	Coppename Monding	1966	12 000
54	Galibi	1969	4 000
55	Hertenrits	1981	100
56	Peruvia	1986	31 000
57	Sipaliwini	1972	100 000
58	Wane Creek	1986	45 400
59	Wia-Wia	1961	36 000
	Nature Park		
60	Brownsberg	1969	8 400

Guyana

No.	Name	Year	Area
	National Park		
61	Kaietur	1929	58 600

Venezuela

No.	Name	Year	Area
	National Park		
62	Canaima	1962	3 000 000
63	Duida-Marahuaca	1978	210 000
64	Jaua-Sarisariñama	1978	330 000
65	Serranía de la Neblina	1978	1 360 000

(cont.)

Table 3.4 (*cont.*)

Venezuela

#		Year of establishment	Area (ha)
	National Park		
66	Parima-Tapirapecó	1991	3 420 000
67	Yapacana	1978	320 000
	Natural Monument		
68	Piedra del Cucuy		20
69	Cerro Autana		30

Colombia

#		Year of establishment	Area (ha)
	Natural National Park		
70	Amacayacu	1978	293 000
71	Cahuinarí	1987	575 500
72	Chingaza	1978	50 374
73	Chiribiquete	1989	1 280 000
74	Cordillera de los Picachos	1977	286 600
75	Cueva de los Guacharos	1960	9 000
76	La Paya	1984	442 000
77	Sierra de la Macarena	1948	630 000
78	Sumapaz	1977	154 000
79	Tinigua	1989	201 875
	Parque Nacional Caparí*	proposed	

Peru

#		Year of establishment	Area (ha)
	National Park		
88	Manu	1973	1 532 806
89	Rio Abiseo	1983	274 500
90	Tingo Maria	1965	18 000
91	Yanachaga-Chemillién	1986	122 000
92	Bahuaja-Sonene	1996/2000	1 091 416
	National Reserve		
93	Pacaya-Samiria	1982	2 080 000
	Tambopata	2000	262 315
	Reserved Zone		
94	Tambopata-Candamo	1977	1 216 627
	Historical Sanctuary		
95	Machu Picchu	1981	326 000

Bolivia

#		Year of establishment	Area (ha)
	National Park		
96	Amboró	1973	180 000
97	Carrasco	1988	622 600
98	Isiboro-Sécure	1965	1 200 000
99	Noel Kempff Mercado	1979	914 000

Natural National Reserve

No.	Name	Year	Area
80	Nukak	1989	855 000
81	Puinawai	1989	1 092 500

Ecuador

No.	Name	Year	Area
	National Park		
82	Cotopaxi	1975	33 400
83	Sangay	1975	517 700
84	Yasuni	1979	982 300
	Ecological Reserve		
85	Cayambe-Coca	1970	403 100
86	Cotocachi-Cayapas	1968	204 400
	Biological reserve		
87	Limoncocha	1985	4 613

Natural National Reserve

No.	Name	Year	Area
100	Madidi		1 571 500
101	Pilon Lajas	1977	400 000
102	Cotapata		58 620
	Biological Station		
103	Beni	1982	135 000
	National Reserve		
104	Manuripi Heath	1973	1 884 000
105	Neol Kempff Mercado	1988	21 900
106	Ulla Ulla	1990	150 000
	Rios Blanco y Negro[a]	1972	1 400 000
	Wildlife Refuge		
	El Dorado[a]	1988	180 000
	Estancias Elsner Espiritú[a]	1978	70 000
	Estancias Eslner San Rafael[a]	1978	20 000

[a] Not on the map (SURAPA 2000).

timber extraction, gold mining, road construction, reservoir construction, and fire. (CABS/CI 2000).

Scientific and political activities relevant to Amazonian wetlands

Research in Amazonia is hampered because of the small number of scientific institutions and scientists, the low amount of funds for research, and the difficult conditions for maintaining scientific infrastructure. Research projects are often set up by distinguished scientists, and then end or decline when the scientist moves away; alternatively, the projects may be set up as part of large research programs but then fail due to lack of financial support. For instance, cultivation of Amazonian fish species started in the 1920s with Rudolpho von Ihering at Museu Goeldi in Belém, but ended when he moved to northeast Brazil.

Therefore, scientific cooperation to stimulate and reinforce local research activities has always been of great importance for Amazonian institutions. This is well-exemplified at the National Amazon Research Institute (INPA), at Manaus, Brazil. The institute maintains close cooperation with large research institutions in southern Brazil, for example with the Universities of São Paulo and Piracicaba. In addition, long-term cooperation has been established with other institutions world-wide: in Germany, with the Max-Planck-Institute for Limnology, Plön for limnology and wetland ecology; in France, with ORSTOM (the French Institute of Scientific Research for Cooperative Development) for fishery; in the United States, with the University of Seattle for biogeochemical cycles (CAMREX Project) and the University of California for limnology. At the end of the 1980s, the project Amazônia I was financed by the International Atomic Energy Agency to introduce isotope studies in ecological research.

In the 1990s, a project on the co-management of fishery resources was established near Santarem (Project IARA) in cooperation with the Brazilian Environmental Agency (IBAMA) and the German Agency of Technical Cooperation (GTZ). At INPA, the SHIFT Program in cooperation with the German Ministry of Science and Technology (BMBF) and the Brazilian Research Council (CNPq) undertook studies on the sustainable use of wetland resources. In 1990, the International Pilot Program to Conserve the Brazilian Rain Forests (PPG-7) was created. As part of the PPG-7, in 2000, a project for the sustainable management of wetland resources was established in cooperation with IBAMA in Manaus (Project *Várzea*). In 1999, the Large-scale Biosphere–Atmosphere Experiment in Amazonia (LBA) was started by the Brazilian Government in cooperation with the United States (NASA) and the EC to study biogeochemical cycles in a basin-wide approach.

All countries participating in the Amazon basin have specific organizations to deal with aquatic resources. In Brazil, approximately 3 years ago, a National

Water Agency (ANA) was established; it is still developing an action plan. IBAMA is responsible for the development of environmental policy and the formulation and implementation of environmental legislation. The state governments have additional secretariats for the elaboration and implementation of regulations for the management and protection of the environment. Colombia published a national plan for wetland management (Ministerio del Medio Ambiente 2001); however, the drug war limits access and implementation in large areas of the country.

Cooperation between the countries participating in the Amazon basin is regulated by the *Tratado de Cooperação Amazônica*, signed in 1978. The treaty explicitly mentions cooperation in the use of waterways, management of natural resources, and science and technology.

Conclusions

About 20% to 25% of the Amazon River basin is covered by different types of wetlands, most of which are categorized as temporary wetlands with pronounced terrestrial and aquatic phases. Large river-floodplains and large interfluvial wetlands are subjected to a monomodal, predictable hydrological pulse according to dry and rainy seasons in the catchment area. Wetlands along streams and in small depressions are influenced by a polymodal, unpredictable pulse according to local rainfall, while coastal wetlands are influenced by a polymodal predictable pulse according to the tide.

Large Amazonian river-floodplains are old ecosystems that were, however, subjected to very-dynamic hydro-geomorphological processes; these processes affected the systems over time spans of years or even geological periods. The large species diversity and the high number of endemic species are attributed to large habitat diversity, the size of the area, and paleoclimatic stability that reduced extinction rates. Interfluvial wetlands probably suffered prolonged dry periods and high species extinction rates during glacial periods, but were recolonized during wet periods by the species pool of the connected large river-floodplains.

Wetlands fulfill multiple functions in the landscape, for example storage and transport of water and dissolved and solid substances, stabilization of local or regional climate, increase of habitat and species diversity, source or sink in biogeochemical cycles, and protein source (fish) and habitat for a considerable part of the human population. Some wetlands, such as the central Amazon River floodplain, are well-studied, but knowledge of many others is very restricted. A preliminary classification system based on hydrological and hydrochemical parameters has been proposed, but requires further specification.

Many Amazonian wetlands are of low nutrient status and show a low primary and secondary production. Their potential for agriculture, forestry, and animal ranching is low. Flooded savannas can be used for low-intensity cattle ranching. Ecotourism and fishing (game fishing) are recommendable as additional economic activities. The forest cover of forested wetlands of low nutrient status should be maintained because of slow tree growth. Only white-water river-floodplains (*várzeas*) have a sufficiently high nutrient status to allow exploitation of natural resources and to support agriculture and cattle ranching. Fishery has the greatest potential and creates the lowest environmental impact. Management of natural forests and forest plantations is recommendable because of rapid tree growth. Large-scale cattle and water-buffalo ranching has a negative impact on the environment because it requires the destruction of the floodplain forest to establish pastures on the levees, with negative side-effects on ecosystem stability, habitat and species diversity, and fishery. Ranches are not labor intensive and support only few people in the *várzea*.

Small-holder agriculture is best suited near urban centers that offer markets for the products. Flood-induced seasonality in production leads to periodic super-saturation of the markets with perishable products and limits the expansion of production. Large-scale crop plantations cannot be recommended because of the small-scale patchy habitat structure, resulting from sedimentation and erosion processes, which hinders mechanization. Lack of rain during the plantation period and excess rain during the harvesting period lead to additional costs. The destruction of natural habitats and the application of agrochemicals will negatively affect fish stocks and fishery.

Further threats to Amazonian wetlands include changes in hydrology and sediment input as a result of large-scale modification of the vegetation cover of the catchment areas and the wetlands by agro-industrial projects. The release of mercury by gold mining is decreasing; however, the total amount of about 5000 t of metallic mercury already released into the environment is a matter of concern. The construction of large hydroelectric reservoirs will affect major floodplain areas by changing the flood regime and interrupting migration routes of aquatic animals. Mangroves are threatened by the construction of shrimp culture ponds, pollution with domestic and industrial waste, and civil engineering. Road construction can have a serious impact on mangroves because of its interference with hydrology and subsequent changes in salinity. Changes in the global climate will seriously affect coastal wetlands because of the accompanying rise in sea level; the impact on the Amazon River floodplain will be felt up to 700 km upstream because of the small slope of the land, but the integrity of the system will not be seriously affected because it is well-adapted to flood-induced perturbations. Shallowly flooded interfluvial wetlands will suffer serious impacts from increasingly strong El Niño events and related drought and fire stress.

The improvement of wetland protection requires a detailed wetland inventory and classification. This is considered of fundamental importance for the sustainable development and protection of aquatic resources and should be of top priority in governmental politics because it is the basis for the improvement of existing environmental legislation and its rigorous implementation. Considering the close interactions between rivers, wetlands, and their catchment areas, every large development project requires a detailed environmental-impact analysis with special emphasis on the aquatic resources. There is also a need for the establishment of new laws for the protection of specific key wetland types to maintain wetland diversity and the associated functions in the long run. Environmental education, for example through an increasing number of projects for co-management of wetland resources, will increase acceptance of environmental legislation by the local population. Scientific infrastructure, human-capacity building, and research should be strengthened by national efforts and international cooperation. In addition to basic research on structure, function, and biodiversity, there is an urgent need for studies of the impact of human occupation of catchment areas on associated water bodies and wetlands, to provide a sound database for environmental-impact analyses.

References

Ab'Saber, A. N. (1988). O Pantanal Mato-Grossense e a teoria dos refugios. *Revista Brasileira de Geofísica*, **50**, 9–57.

Acuña, C. de (1641). New discovery of the great river of the Amazons. In *Expeditions into the Valley of the Amazons, 1539, 1540, 1639*, ed. C. R. Markham. London: The Hakluyt Society, pp. 47–142.

Adis, J. and Junk, W. J. (2002). Terrestrial invertebrates inhabiting lowland river floodplains of Central Amazonia and Central Europe: a review. *Freshwater Biology*, **47**, 711–31.

Akagi, H., Malm, O., Branches, F. *et al.* (1995). Human exposure to mercury due to gold mining in the Tapajós River Basin, Brazil: speciation of mercury in human hair, blood and urine. *Water, Air and Soil Pollution*, **80**, 85–94.

Ayres, J. M. C., Alves, A. R., Queiroz, H. L. de *et al.* (1999). Mamirauá: the conservation of biodiversity in an Amazonian flooded forest. In *Várzea: Diversity, Development, and Conservation of Amazonia's Whitewater Floodplains*, eds. C. Padoch, J. M. Ayres, M. Pinedo-Vasquez, and A. Henderson. Advances in Economic Botany 13. New York: The New York Botanical Garden Press, pp. 203–16.

Bayley, P. B. (1983). Central Amazon fish populations: biomass, and some dynamic characteristics. Ph.D. thesis, Dalhousie University, Halifax, Canada.

Bayley, P. B. and Petrere, M., Jr. (1989). Amazon fisheries: assessment methods, current status, and management options. *Canadian Journal of Fisheries and Aquatic Sciences* (Special Publication), **106**, 385–98.

Becker, B. K. (1995). Undoing myths: the Amazon – an urbanized forest. In *Brazilian Perspectives on Sustainable Development of the Amazon Region*, vol. 15, eds. M. Clüsener-Godt and I. Sachs. Paris: UNESCO. Carnforth, UK: Parthenon Publishing, pp. 53–89.

(1999). *Cenários de curto prazo para o desenvolvimento da Amazônia*. Brasília, Brazil: Ministério de Meio Ambiente/SCA.

Böhlke, J. E., Weitzman, S. H., and Menezes, N. A. (1978). Estado atual da sistemática dos peixes de água doce da América do Sul. *Acta Amazônica*, 8(4), 657–77.

Bozelli, R. L., Esteves, F. de A., and Roland, F. (2000). *Lago Batata: impacto e recuperação de um ecossistema Amazônico*. Rio de Janeiro, Brazil: Universidade Federal de Rio de Janeiro.

Brady, A. and Riding, T. (1996). *The Importance of Wetlands in Water Resource Management: a Literature Review*. NSW, Australia: Department of Land and Water Conservation.

Brito, M. (2001). Eixos amazônicos de integração e desenvolvimento: obras e empreendimentos. In *Biodiversidade na Amazônia Brasileira*, eds. A. Veríssimo, A. Moreira, D. Sawyer, I. dos Santos, and L. P. Pinto, Brasília, Brazil: Estação Liberdade & Instituto Socioambiental, pp. 321–6.

CABS/CI (Center for Applied Biodiversity Science/Conservation International) (2000). *Database on Amazonian Protected Areas*. Washington, DC: CABS and CI.

Clements, F. E. (1905). *Research Methods in Ecology*. Lincoln, NE: University Publishing Co.

Colinvaux, P. A., Irion, G., Räsänen, M. E., Bush, M. B. and Nunes de Mello, J. A. (2001). A paradigm to be discarded: geological and paleoecological data falsify the HAFFER & PRANCE refuge hypothesis of Amazonian speciation. *Amazoniana*, 16(3/4), 609–46.

Comision Amazonica de Desarollo y Medio Ambiente (1992). *Amazonia sin mitos*. New York: Banco Interamericano de Desarrollo, Programa de las Naciónes Unidas para el Desarrollo, Tratado deo Cooperacion Amazonica.

Denevan, W. M. (1976). The aboriginal population of Amazonia. In *The Native Population of the Americas*, ed. W. M. Denevan. Madison, WI: University of Wisconsin Press, pp. 205–34.

Diegues, A. C. S. (1994). *An Inventory of Brazilian Wetlands*. Gland, Switzerland: IUCN.

Dillinger, W. Z. and Webb, S. B. (1999). *Fiscal Management in Federal Democracies: Argentina and Brazil*. Policy Research Working Paper 2121. Washington, DC: World Bank.

Duellman, E. D. (1988). Patterns of species diversity in anuran amphibians in the American tropics. *Annales of the Missouri Botanical Garden*, **75**, 79–104.

Fadini, P. S. (1999). Comportamento biogeoquímico do mercúrio na bacia do Rio Negro. Ph.D. thesis, Universidade Estadual de Campinas, Campinas, Brazil.

Fearnside, P. M. (1988). Prospects for sustainable agricultural development in tropical forests. *ISI Atlas of Science, Animal and Plant Sciences*, 1(3–4), 251–6.

(1989). Brazil's Balbina Dam: environment versus the legacy of the pharaohs in Amazônia. *Environmental Management*, 13(4), 401–23.

Finlayson, C. M. and Spiers, A. G. (1999). *Global Review of Wetland Resources and Priorities for Wetland Inventory*, 2nd edn. Wageningen, the Netherlands: Wetlands International.

Fisher, C. F. A., Chagas, A. L. das G. A., and Dornelles, L. D. C. (1992). *Pesca de águas interiores*. Série de Estudos de Pesca 2. Brazil: IBAMA, Coleção Meio Ambiente.

Fittkau, E.-J. (1973). Artenmannigfaltigkeit amazonischer Lebensräume aus ökologischer Sicht. *Amazoniana*, 4(3), 321–40.

(1982). Struktur, Funktion und Diversität zentralamazonischer Ökosysteme. *Archiv für Hydrobiologie*, **95**, 29–45.

Fittkau, E. J., Irmler, U., Junk, W. J., Reiss, F., and Schmidt, G. W. (1975). Productivity, biomass and population dynamics in Amazonian water bodies. In *Tropical Ecological Systems. Trends in Terrestrial and Aquatic Research*, eds. F. B. Golley and E. Medina. New York: Springer Verlag, pp. 289–311.

Furch, K. (1997). Chemistry of várzea and igapó soils and nutrient inventory of their floodplain forests. In *The Central Amazon Floodplain: Ecology of a Pulsing System*, ed. W. J. Junk. Ecological Studies 126. Berlin, Germany: Springer Verlag, pp. 47–68.

Furch, K. and Junk, W. J. (1997). The chemical composition, food value and decomposition of herbaceous plants and leaf litter of the floodplain forest. In *The Central Amazon Floodplain: Ecology of a Pulsing System*, ed. W. J. Junk. Ecological Studies 126. Berlin, Germany: Springer Verlag, pp. 187–205.

Forsberg, B. R., Forsberg, M. C. S., Padovani, C. R., Sargentini, E., and Malm, O. (1995). High levels of mercury in fish and human hair from the Rio Negro basin (Brazilian Amazon): Natural background or anthropogenic contamination? In *Proceedings of the International Workshop on Environmental Mercury Pollution and its Health Effects in the Amazon River Basin, November, 1994, Rio de Janeiro, Brazil*, eds. H. Kato and W. C. Pfeiffer. Minamata, Japan: National Institute for Minamata Disease, pp. 33–40.

Gentry, A. H., Nelson, B. W., Herrera-MacBryde, O., Huber, O., and Villamil, B. (1997). Regional overview: South America. In *Centres of Plant Diversity. A Guide and Strategy for their Conservation*, vol. 3, *The Americas*, eds. S. Davis, V. H. Heywood, O. Berrera-MacBryde, J. Villa-Lobos, and A. C. Hamilton. Cambridge, UK: WWF and IUCN, pp. 269–307.

Gopal, B. and Junk, W. J. (2000). Biodiversity in wetlands: an introduction. In *Biodiversity in Wetlands: Assessment, Function and Conservation*, vol. 1, eds. B. Gopal, W. J. Junk, and J. A. Davis. Leiden, the Netherlands: Backhuys Publishers, pp. 1–10.

Goulding, M., Carvalho, M. L., and Ferreira, E. G. (1988). *Rio Negro: Rich Life in Poor Water*. The Hague, the Netherlands: SPB Academic Publishing.

Goulding, M., Smith, N. J. H., and Mahar, D. J. (1996). *Floods of Fortune: Ecology and Economy Along the Amazon*. New York: Columbia University Press.

Groombridge, B. (1992). *Global Biodiversity. Status of the Earth's Living Resources*. London: Chapman and Hall.

Gutjahr, E. (1996). Untersuchung zur Optimierung der Ackernutzung in den Überschwemmungsgebieten (Várzeas) des mittleren Amazonas. Ph.D. thesis, Verlag Dr. Kovac, Hamburg, Germany.

(2000). Prospects for arable farming in the floodplains of the Central Amazon. In *The Central Amazon Floodplain: Actual Use and Options for a Sustainable Management*, eds. W. J. Junk, J. J. Ohly, M. T. F. Piedade, and M. G. M Soares. Leiden, the Netherlands: Backhuys Publishers, pp. 141–70.

Haffer, J. (1982). General aspects of the refuge theory. In *Biological Diversification in the Tropics*, ed. G. T. Prance. New York: Columbia University Press, pp. 6–24.

Haffer, J. and Prance, G. T. (2001). Climatic forcing of evolution in Amazonia during the Cenozoic: on the refuge theory of biotic differentiation. *Amazoniana*, **16**(3/4), 579–608.

Hails, A. J. (1996). *Wetlands, Biodiversity and the Ramsar Convention. The Role of the Convention on Wetlands in the Conservation and Wise Use of Biodiversity*. Gland, Switzerland: Ramsar Convention Bureau. New Delhi, India: Ministry of Environment and Forests.

Hanagarth, W. (1993) *Acerca de la geolecologia de las sabanas del Beni en el Noreste de Bolivia*. La Paz, Bolivia: Instituto de Ecologia.

Hanagarth, W. and Szwagrzak, A. (1998). Geoecology and biodiversity: problems and perspectives for the management of the natural resources of Bolivia's forest and savanna ecosystems. In *Biodiversity: a Challenge for Development Research and Policy*, eds. E. Barthlott and M. Winiger. New York: Springer Verlag, pp. 289–312.

Hansen, A. J. and di Castri, F. (1992). *Landscape Boundaries: Consequences for Biotic Diversity and Ecological Flows*. Ecological Studies 92. Berlin, Germany: Springer Verlag.

Herrera-MacBryde, O., Dallmeier, F., MacBryde, B., Comiskey, J. A., and Miranda, C. (2000). *Biodiversity, Conservation, and Management in the Region of the Beni Biological Station Biosphere Reserve, Bolivia*. SI/MAB Series 4. Washington, DC: Smithsonian Institution.

Hödl, W. W. (1977). Call differences and calling site segregation in anuran species from Central Amazonian floating meadows. *Oecologia*, **28**, 351–63.

(1990). Reproductive diversity in Amazonian lowland frogs. *Fortschritte der Zoologie*, **38**, 41–60.

Höfer, H. (1997) The spider communities. In *The Central Amazon Floodplain: Ecology of a Pulsing System*, ed. W. J. Junk. Ecological Studies 126. Berlin, Germany: Springer Verlag, pp. 372–84.

IBAMA (Brazilian Environmental Agency) (1994). *Relatório preliminar sobre ordenamento pesqueiro para a bacia Amazônica*. Brasília, Brazil: Relatório Técnico, IBAMA.

(1997). *Administração participativa: um desafio à gestão ambiental*. Brasília, Brazil: Relatório Técnico, IBAMA.

IBGE (The Brazilian Institute for Geography and Statistics) (2002). Censo Demografico 2000.

http://www.ibge.gov.br.

INPE (2000). Monitoramento da floresta Amazônica Brazileira por satélite 1999–2000. http://www.inpe.br/Informacoes_Eventos/amz1999_2000/Prodes/index.htm.

Irion, G., Junk, W. J., and de Mello, J. A. S. N. (1997). The large central Amazonian river floodplains near Manaus: geological, climatological, hydrological, and geomorphological aspects. In *The Central Amazon Floodplain: Ecology of a Pulsing System*, ed. W. J. Junk. Ecological Studies 126. Berlin, Germany: Springer Verlag, pp. 23–46.

IRRI (International Rice Research Institute) (1985). Wetland soils, characterization, classification, and utilization. In *Proceedings of an IRRI Workshop, March 26–April 5, 1984, Los Baños, the Philipines* (under sponsorship of IRRI). Los Baños, the Philipines: International Rice Research Institute.

Isaac, V. J., Ruffino, M. L., and McGrath, D. (1998). In search of a new approach to fisheries management in the middle Amazon. In *Fishery Stock Assessment Model*, eds. T. J. Quinn II, F. Funk, J. Heifetz *et al.* Alaska Sea Grant College Program, AS-SG-98-01. Fairbanks, Alaska: University of Alaska, pp. 889–902.

Johnson, D. L. (1983). The Californian continental borderland: landbridges, watergaps and biotope dispersal. In *Quaternary Coastlines and Marine Archaeology*, eds. P. M. Masters and N. C. Flemming. London: Academic Press, pp. 481–527.

Junk, W. J. (1980). Áreas inundáveis: um desafio para limnologia. *Acta Amazonica*, 10(4), 775–95.

(1985). The Amazon floodplain: a sink or source of organic carbon? *Mitteilungen des Geologischen Palaeantologischen Institutes der Universität Hamburg*, 58, 267–83.

(1989). Flood tolerance and tree distribution in central Amazonian floodplains. In *Tropical Forests: Botanical Dynamics, Speciation and Diversity*, eds. L. B. Holm-Nielsen, I. C. Nielsen, and H. Balslev. New York: Academic Press, pp. 47–64.

(1992). Wetlands of tropical South America. In *Wetlands of the World*, vol. 1, eds. D. F. Whigham, D. Dykyjova and S. Hejny. Dordrecht, the Netherlands: Junk, pp. 679–739.

(1994). Ecology of the várzea, Floodplain of Amazonian white water rivers. In *The Amazon: Limnology and Landscape Ecology of a Mighty Tropical River and its Basin*, ed. H. Sioli. Dordrecht, the Netherlands: Junk, pp. 216–43.

(1997). *The Central Amazon Floodplain. Ecology of a Pulsing System*. Ecological Studies 126. Berlin, Germany: Springer Verlag.

(2000). Mechanisms for development and maintenance of biodiversity in Neotropical floodplains. In *Biodiversity in Wetlands*, eds. B. Gopal, W. J. Junk, and Davis. Leiden, the Netherlands: Backhuys Publishers, pp. 119–39.

Junk, W. J. and de Mello, J. A. S. N. (1987). Impactos ecológicos das represas hidrelétricas na bacia Amazônica Brasileira. *Tübinger Geographische Studien*, 95, 367–85.

Junk, W. J. and Piedade, M. T. F. (1993). Herbaceous plants of the Amazon floodplain near Manaus: species diversity and adaptations to the flood pulse. *Amazoniana*, 12(3/4), 467–84.

Junk, W. J., Robertson, B. A., Darwich, A. J., and Vieira, L. (1981). Investigações limnológicas e ictiológicas em Curuá-Una, a primeira represa hidrelétrica na Amazônia Central. *Acta Amazonica*, 11(4), 689–716.

Junk, W. J., Bayley, P. B., and Sparks, R. E. (1989). The flood pulse concept in river-floodplain systems. *Canadian Journal of Fisheries and Aquatic Sciences* (Special Publication), **106**, 110–27.

Junk, W. J., Ohly, J. J., Piedade, M. T. F., and Soares, M. G. M. (eds.) (2000a). *The Central Amazon Floodplain: Actual Use and Options for a Sustainable Management*. Leiden, The Netherlands: Backhuys Publishers.

  (2000b). Actual use and options for the sustainable management of the central Amazon floodplain: discussion and conclusions. In *The Central Amazon Floodplain: Actual Use and Options for a Sustainable Management*, eds. W. J. Junk, J. J. Ohly, M. T. F. Piedade, and M. G. M. Soares. Leiden, the Netherlands: Backhuys Publishers, pp. 535–79.

Katzer, F. (1903). *Grundzüge der Geologie des unteren Amazonas Gebietes*. Leipzig, Germany: Verlag Max Weg.

Kern, J. and A. Darwich, A. (1997). Nitrogen turnover in the várzea. In *The Central Amazon Floodplain: Ecology of a Pulsing System*, ed. W. J. Junk. Ecological Studies 126. Berlin, Germany: Springer Verlag, pp. 119–36.

Kern, J., Kreibich, H., and Darwich, A. (2002). Nitrogen dynamics on the Amazon floodplain in relation to the flood pulse of the Solimões River. In *The Ecohydrology of South American Rivers and Wetlands*, ed. M. E. McClain. Wallingford, UK: IAHS Press, pp. 35–47.

Klammer, G. (1982). Die Paläowüste des Pantanal von Mato Grosso und die pleistozäne Klimageschichte der Brasilianischen Randtropen. *Zeitschrift für Geomorphologie*, **26**(4), 393–416.

Klinge, H. (1967). Podzol soils: a source of blackwater rivers in Amazonia. *Atas do Simpósio Sobre a Biota Amazônica*, **3**, 117–25.

Klinge, H., Junk, W. J., and Revilla, J. C. (1990). Status and distribution of forested wetlands in tropical South America. *Forest Ecology and Management*, **33/34**, 81–101.

Kohlhepp, G. (2001). Amazonia 2000. *Amazoniana*, **16**(3/4), 363–95.

Koste, W. and Robertson, B. (1983). Taxonomic studies of the Rotifera (phylum Aschelminthes) from a Central Amazonian várzea lake, Lago Camaleão (Ilha de Marchantaria, Rio Solimões, Amazonas, Brazil). *Amazoniana*, **8**(2), 225–54.

Koste, W., Hardy, E., and Robertson, B. (1984). Further taxonomical studies of the Rotifera (phylum Aschelminthes) from a Central Amazonian várzea lake, Lago Camaleão (Ilha de Marchantaria, Rio Solimões, Amazonas, Brazil). *Amazoniana*, **8**(4), 555–76.

Kreibich, H. and Kern, J. (2003). Nitrogen fixation and denitrification in a floodplain forest near Manaus. *Hydrological Processes*, **17**, 1431–41.

Kubitzki, K. (1989). The ecogeographical differentiation of Amazonian inundation forests. *Plant Systematics and Evolution*, **163**, 285–304.

Lacerda, L. D. (2002). *Mangrove Ecosystems: Function and Management*. Berlin, Germany: Springer Verlag.

Lacerda, L. D. and Pfeiffer, W. (1992). Mercury from gold mining in the Amazon environment: an overview. *Química Nova*, **15**(2), 155–60.

Laurance, W. F., Cochrane, M. A., Bergen, S. *et al.* (2001). The future of the Brazilian Amazon. *Science*, **291**, 438–9.

Lowe-McConnell, R. H. (1964). The fishes of the Rupununi savanna district of British Guiana, South America. Part 1. Ecological groupings of fish species and effects of the seasonal cycle on the fish. *Journal of the Linnean Society of London (Zoology)*, 45(304), 103–44.

Lundberg, J. G. (1998). The temporal context for the diversification of Neotropical fishes. In *Phylogeny and Classification of Neotropical Fishes*, eds. L. R. Malabarba, R. E. Reis, R. P. Vari, Z. M. S. Lucena, and C. A. S. Lucena. Porto Alegre, Brazil: EDIPUCRS, pp. 49–68.

Lundberg, J. G., Marshall, L. G., Guerrero, J. *et al.* (1998). The stage for neotropical fish diversification. In *Phylogeny and Classification of Neotropical Fishes*, eds. L. R. Malabarba, R. E. Reis, R. P. Vari, Z. M. S. Lucena, and C. A. S. Lucena. Porto Alegre, Brazil: EDIPUCRS, pp. 13–48.

Mago-Leccia, F. (1970). *Lista de los pesces de Venezuela, incluyendo un estúdio preliminar sobre la ictiogeografia del pais*. Caracas: Ministerio de Agricultura y Cria, Oficina Nacional de Pesca.

Mamirauá Management Plan (1996). *Mamirauá Management Plan*. Brasília, Brazil: Sociedade Civil Mamirauá (SCM), National Council for Scientific and Technological Development (CNPq), Environmental Protection Institute of the State of Amazonas (IPAAM).

McGrath, D., Castro, F., and Futema, C. (1994). Reservas de lago e o manejo comunitário da pesca no Baixo Amazonas: uma avaliação preliminar. In *A Amazônia e a crise de modernização*, eds. M. A. D'Inaco and I. M. Silveira. Belém, Brazil: MPEG, pp. 389–402.

McGrath, D., Castro, F. de, Câmara, E., and Futemma, C. (1999). Community management of floodplain lakes and the sustainable development of Amazonian fisheries. In *Várzea: Diversity, Development, and Conservation of Amazonias's Whitewater Floodplains*, eds. C. Padoch, J. M. Ayres, M. Pinedo-Vasquez, and A. Henderson. Advances in Economic Botany 13. New York: The New York Botanical Garden Press, pp. 59–82.

Meade, R. H. (1994). Suspended sediments of the modern Amazon and Orinico rivers. *Quaternary International*, 21, 29–39.

Meade, R. H., Dunne, T., Richey, J. E., Santos, U. de M., and Salati, E. (1985). Storage and remobilization of suspended sediment in the lower Amazon river of Brazil. *Science*, 228, 488–90.

Mérona, B. de, Santos, G. M., and Almeida, R. G. (2001). Short term effects of Tucurui Dam (Amazonia, Brazil) on the trophic organization of fish communities. *Environmental Biology of Fishes*.

Mertes, L. A. K. (1994). Rates of floodplain sedimentation on the Central Amazon river. *Geology*, 22, 171–4.

Mertes, L. A. K. and Meade, R. H. (1985). *Particle Size of Sands Collected from the Bed of the Amazon River and its Tributaries in Brazil During 1982–84*. US Geological Survey Open File Report, pp. 85–333.

Milliman, J. D. (1990). River discharge of water and sediment to the oceans: variation in space and time. In *Facets of Modern Biogeochemistry*, eds. V. Ittekkot, S. Kempe, W. Michaelis, and A. Spitzy. Berlin, Germany: Springer Verlag, pp. 83–90.

Ministerio del Medio Ambiente (2001). *Política Nacional para humedales interiores de Colombia*. Bogotá, Colombia: Ministerio del Medio Ambiente.

Mitsch, W. J. and Gosselink, J. G. (2000). *Wetlands*, 3rd edn. New York: John Wiley.

Müller, J., Irion, G., de Mello, J. N., and Junk, W. J. (1995). Hydrological changes of the Amazon during the last glacial–interglacial cycle in Central Amazonia (Brazil). *Naturwissenschaften*, **82**, 232–5.

Myers, N., Mittermeier, R. A., Mittermeier, C. G., da Fonseca G. A. B., and Kent, J. (2000). Biodiversity hotspots for conservation priorities. *Nature*, **403**, 853–8.

Navid, D. (1989). The international law of migratory species: The Ramsar Convention. *Natural Resources Journal*, **29**, 1001–16.

Nepstad, D. C., Veríssimo, A., Alencar, A. *et al.* (1999). Large-scale impoverishment of Amazonian forests by logging and fire. *Nature*, **398**, 505–8.

Nepstad, D. C., Capobianco, J. P., Barros, A. C. *et al.* (2000). *Avança Brazil: Os custos ambientais para a Amazônia*. [*Avança Brazil: the Environmental Costs for Amazonia*]. Belém, Brazil. Gráfica e Editora Alves.

Noda, S. N., Noda, H., and Santos, H. P. dos (2000). Family farming systems in the floodplains of the state of Amazonas. In *The Central Amazon Floodplain: Actual Use and Options for a Sustainable Management*, eds. W. J. Junk, J. J. Ohly, M. T. F. Piedade, and M. G. M. Soares. Leiden, the Netherlands: Backhuys Publishers, pp. 215–42.

Nogueira, F. and Junk, W. J. (2000). Mercury from goldmining in Amazon wetlands: contamination sites, intoxication levels and dispersion pathways. In *The Central Amazon Floodplain: Actual Use and Options for a Sustainable Management*, eds. W. J. Junk, J. J. Ohly, M. T. F. Piedade, and M. G. M. Soares. Leiden, the Netherlands: Backhuys Publishers, pp. 477–503.

Nunes da Cunha, C. and Junk, W. J. (2004). Year-to-year changes in water level drive the invasion of *Vochysia divergens* in Pantanal grasslands. *Applied Vegetation Science*, **7**, 103–10.

Odum, E. P. (1981). Foreword. In *Wetlands of Bottomland Hardwood Forests*, eds. J. R. Clark and J. Benforado. Amsterdam, the Netherlands: Elsevier, pp. 8–10.

Ohly, J. J. (2000). Development of Central Amazonia in the modern era. In *The Central Amazon Floodplain: Actual Use and Options for a Sustainable Management*, eds. W. J. Junk, J. J. Ohly, M. T. F. Piedade, and M. G. M. Soares. Leiden, the Netherlands: Backhuys Publishers, pp. 27–73.

Ohly, J. J. and Hund, M. (2000). Floodplain animal husbandry in central Amazonia. In *The Central Amazon Floodplain: Actual Use and Options for a Sustainable Management*, eds. W. J. Junk, J. J. Ohly, M. T. F. Piedade, and M. G. M. Soares. Leiden, the Netherlands: Backhuys Publishers, pp. 313–43.

Padoch, C., Ayres, J. M., Pinedo-Vasquez, M., and Henderson, A. (eds.) (1999). *Várzea: Diversity, Development, and Conservation of Amazonia's Whitewater Floodplains*. Advances in Economic Botany 13. New York: The New York Botanical Garden Press.

Parolin, P. and Ferreira, L. V. (1998). Are there differences in specific wood gravities between trees in *várzea* and *igapó* (Central Amazonia)? *Ecotropica*, **4**, 25–32.

Patrick, R. (1966). The Catherwood Foundation Peruvian–Amazon Expedition I. Limnological observations and discussion of results. *Monographs of the Academy of Natural Sciences of Philadelphia*, **14**, 5–28.

Petermann, P. (1997). The birds. In *The Central Amazon Floodplain: Ecology of a Pulsing System*, ed. W. J. Junk. Ecological Studies 126. Berlin, Germany: Springer Verlag, pp. 419–54.

Ponce, V. M. (1995). *Impacto hidrológico e ambiental da hidrovia Paraná-Paraguai no Pantanal Matogrossense: um estudo de referência*. San Diego, CA: San Diego State University.

Pott, V. J. and Pott, A. (2000). *Plantas aquáticas do Pantanal*. Brasília, Brazil: Empresa Brasileira des Pesquisa Agropecuária (EMBRAPA).

Prance, G. T. (1982). *Biological Diversification in the Tropics*. New York: Columbia University Press.

Prentice, I. C. and Lloyd, J. (1998). C-quest in the Amazon Basin. *Nature*, **396**, 619–20.

Puhakka, M., Kalliola, R., Rajasilta, M., and Salo, J. (1992). River types, site evolution and successional vegetation patterns in Peruvian Amazonia. *Journal of Biogeography*, **19**, 651–65.

Reid, J. (1989). The distribution of the genus *Thermocyclops* (Copepoda, Cyclopoida) in the western hemisphere, with description of *T. parvus*, new species. *Hydrobiologia*, **175**, 149–74.

Richey, J. E., Brock, J. T., Naiman, R. J., Wissmar, R. C., and Stallard, R. F. (1980). Organic carbon: oxidation and transport in the Amazon River. *Science*, **207**, 1348–51.

Richey, J. E., Meade, R. H., Salati, E. *et al.* (1986). Water discharge and suspended sediment concentrations in the Amazon river. *Water Resources Research*, **22**, 756–64.

Richey, J. E., Krusche, A., Deegan L. *et al.* (2001). Land use changes and the biogeochemistry of river corridors in the Amazon. *Global Change Newsletter*, **45**, 19–23.

Roosevelt, A. C. (1999). Twelve thousand years of human–environment interaction in the Amazon Floodplain. In *Várzea: Diversity, Development, and Conservation of Amazonia's Whitewater Floodplains*, eds. C. Padoch, J. M. Ayres, M. Pinedo-Vasquez, and A. Henderson. Advances in Economic Botany 13. New York: The New York Botanical Garden Press, pp. 371–92.

Roulet, M., Lucotte, M., Canuel, R. *et al.* (1998a). Distribution and partition of total mercury in waters of the Tapajós River Basin, Brazilian Amazon. *Science of the Total Environment*, **223**, 203–11.

Roulet, M., Lucotte, M., Saint-Aubin, A. *et al.* (1998b). The geochemistry of mercury in central Amazonian soils developed on the Alter-do Chão formation of the lower Tapajós River Valley, Pará State, Brazil. *Science of the Total Environment*, **223**, 1–24.

Ruffino, M. L. (1996). Towards participatory fishery management on the lower Amazon. *EC Fisheries Cooperation Bulletin*, **9**(1), 15–18.

Salati, E., Dall'Olio, A., Matsui, E., and Bat, J. A. (1979). Recycling of water in the Amazon basin. An isotopic study. *Water Resources Research*, **15**(5), 1250–8.

Salo, J. (1990). External processes influencing origin and maintenance of inland water-land ecotones. In *The Ecology and Management of Aquatic-Terrestrial Ecotones*, eds. R. J. Naiman and H. Decamps. MAB Series 4. Paris, France: UNESCO Paris and The Parthenon Publishing Group, pp. 37–64.

Salo, J., Kalliola, R., Häkkinen, I. *et al.* (1986). River dynamics and the diversity of Amazon lowland forest. *Nature*, **322**, 254–8.

Santos, G. M. (1996). Impactos da hidreléctrica Samuel sobre as comunidades de peixes do Rio Jamari (Rondônia, Brazil). *Acta Amazônica*, **25**(3/4), 145–63.

Santos, G. M. and Oliveira, A. B., Jr. (1999). A pesca no reservatório da hidrelétrica de Balbina (Amazonas, Brazil). *Acta Amazônica*, **29**(1), 145–63.

Sarmiento, J. (1998). Ichthyology of Parque Nacional Noel Kempff Mercado. In *A Biological Assessment of Parque Nacional Noel Kempff Mercado, Bolivia*, eds. T. J. Killeen and T. Schulenberg. RAP Working Papers 10. Washington, DC: Conservation International, pp. 167–73, 356–67.

(2000). Observaciones preliminares sobre la composición e distribución de la ictiofauna de la Estación Biológica del Beni, Bolivia. In *Biodiversity, Conservation, and Management in the Region of the Beni Biological Station Biosphere Reserve, Bolivia*, eds. O. Herrera-MacBryde, F. Dallmeier, B. MacBryde, J. A. Comiskey, and C. Miranda. SI/MAB Series 4. Washington, DC: Smithsonian Institution, pp. 129–50.

Schäfer, S. A. (1998). Conflict and resolution: impact of new taxa on phylogenetic studies of the Neotropical Cascudinhos (Siluroidei: Loricariidae). In *Phylogeny and Classification of Neotropical Fishes*, eds. L. R. Malabarba, R. E. Reis, R. P. Vari, Z. M. S. Lucena, and C. A. S. Lucena. Porto Alegre, Brazil: EDIPUCRS, pp. 375–400.

Schöngart, J. (2003). Biomass increment, dynamics and modelling of the growth of white water floodplain forests. Ph.D. thesis, University of Göttingen, Germany.

Scott, D. A. and Carbonell, M. (1986). *Inventario de humedales de la región neotropical.* Cambridge, UK: IWRB and IUCN.

Shackleton, J. N. and Opdyke, N. D. (1973). Oxygen isotope and paleomagnetic stratigraphy of equatorial pacific core V28–V238: oxygen isotope temperatures and ice volumes on a 10^5 and 10^6 year scale. *Quaternary Research*, **3**, 39–55.

Sioli, H. (1950). Das Wasser im Amazonasgebiet. *Forschung und Fortschritt*, **26**, 274–80.

(1984). *The Amazon: Limnology and Landscape Ecology of a Mighty Tropical River and its Basin.* Monographiae Biologicae. Dordrecht, the Netherlands: Junk.

Soares, M. G. M. and Junk, W. J. (2000). Commercial fishery and fish culture of the state of Amazonas: status and perspectives. In *The Central Amazon Floodplain: Actual Use and Options for a Sustainable Management*, eds. W. J. Junk, J. J. Ohly, M. T. F. Piedade, and M. G. M. Soares. Leiden, the Netherlands: Backhuys Publishers, pp. 433–61.

Sternberg, H. O'. R. (1998). *A água e o homen na várzea do Careiro*, 2nd edn. Belém, Brazil: Museu Paraense Emílio Goeldi.

Stotz, D. F., Fitzpatrick, J. W., Parker T. E., III. and Moskovits, D. K. (1996). *Neotropical Birds. Ecology and Conservation.* Chicago, IL: University of Chicago Press.

SURAPA (Sub Network of Amazonian Protected Areas) (2000). CD-ROM.

Tian, H., Melillo, J. M., Kicklighter, D. W. *et al.* (1998). Effect of interannual climate variability on carbon storage in Amazonian ecosystems. *Nature*, **396**, 664–7.

Uherkovich, G. and Schmidt, G. W. (1974). Phytoplanktontaxa in dem zentralamazonischen Schwemmlandsee Lago do Castanho. *Amazoniana*, **5**, 243–83.

Van der Hammen, T. and Hooghiemstra, H. (2000). Neogene and Quaternary history of vegetation, climate, and plant diversity in Amazonia. *Quaternary Science Reviews*, **19**, 725–42.

Vari, R. P. and Malabarba, L. R. (1998). Neotropical ichthyology: an overview. In *Phylogeny and Classification of Neotropical Fishes*, eds. L. R. Malabarba, R. E. Reis, R. P. Vari, Z. M. S. Lucena, and C. A. S. Lucena. Porto Alegre, Brazil: EDIPUCRS, pp. 1–12.

Vieira, R. dos S. (2000). Legislation and the use of Amazonian floodplains. In *The Central Amazon Floodplain: Actual Use and Options for a Sustainable Management*, eds. W. J. Junk, J. J. Ohly, M. T. F. Piedade, and M. G. M. Soares. Leiden, the Netherlands: Backhuys Publishers, pp. 505–33.

Vogt, R. C., Moreira, G. M., and Duarte, A. C. de O. C. (2001). Biodiversidade de répteis do bioma floresta Amazônica e ações prioritárias para sua conservação. In *Biodiversidade na Amazônia Brasileira*, eds. A. Veríssimo, A. Moreira, D. Sawyer, I. dos Santos, and L. P. Pinto. Brasília, Brazil: Estação Liberdade & Instituto Socioambiental, pp. 89–96.

Wantzen, K. M. (1997). Einfluß anthropogen bedingter Versandung auf Habitatstruktur und Lebensgemeinschaften von Cerrado-Bächen in Mato Grosso, Brasilien. Ph.D. thesis, Universität Hamburg, Herbert Utz Verlag, Hamburg, Germany.

(1998a). Effects of siltation on benthic communities in clear water streams in Mato Grosso, Brazil. *Verhandlungen Internationale Vereinigung für Theoretische und Angewandte Limnologie*, **26**, 1155–9.

(1998b). *Abschätzung der Umweltwirkungen von anthropogen bedingter Bodenerosion auf Fließgewässer mittels Biomonitoring, Mato Grosso, Brasilien*. Eschborn, Germany: Deutsche Gesellschaft für Technische Zusammenarbiet GmbH (GTZ).

Wantzen, K. M. and Junk, W. J. (2000). The importance of stream-wetland-systems for biodiversity: a tropical perspective. In *Biodiversity in Wetlands*, eds. B. Gopal, W. J. Junk, and J. A. Davis, Leiden, the Netherlands: Backhuys Publishers, pp. 11–34.

Wassmann, R. and Martius, C. (1997). Methane emissions from the Amazon floodplains. In *The Central Amazon Floodplain: Ecology of a Pulsing System*, ed. W. J. Junk. Ecological Studies 126. Berlin, Germany: Springer Verlag, pp. 137–46.

Wittmann, F., Junk, W. J., and Anhuf, D. (2002). Tree species distribution and community structure of Central Amazonian *várzea* forests by remote-sensing techniques. *Journal of Tropical Ecology*, **18**(6), 805–20.

4

The Hudson Bay Lowland

K. F. ABRAHAM
Ontario Ministry of Natural Resources

C. J. KEDDY
Ecologist

Introduction

At the center of North America, lying south of Hudson Bay and west and south of James Bay (50° to 59° N, 76° to 96° W) is the world's third-largest wetland – the Hudson Bay Lowland (Zoltai 1973). This area is the size of Japan, larger than the United Kingdom or Germany but smaller than Zimbabwe, France, or Iraq.

The Lowland is located near the center of the former Laurentide Ice Sheet which formed during the late Wisconsin glaciation (Fig. 4.1) and is a legacy of that age (Zoltai 1973, Riley 2003). As the glacier receded, the depression left behind was inundated by melt waters which became the Tyrrell Sea (and later the modern Hudson Bay and James Bay). The Lowland has emerged over the last 7000 to 8000 years due to one of the continent's most-rapid rates of isostatic rebound (0.7 to 1.2 cm per year; Webber *et al.* 1970). At this rate, the Hudson Bay shoreline is moving northward 4 m per year. The maximum elevation, currently about 120 m above sea level, occurs at the Lowland's southern limit (Gray *et al.* 2001).

Stretching from Churchill to the Eastmain River (Fig. 4.2), the Hudson Bay Lowland covers 373 700 km², or 3.7% of Canada (ESWG 1995). Over 80% of the Lowland lies in northern Ontario. It is bounded inland by exposed bedrock of the Precambrian Shield (Hustich 1957). The oceanic connection of the Lowland led to relatively early exploration by Europeans involved in the fur trade (both

The World's Largest Wetlands: Ecology and Conservation, eds. L. H. Fraser and P. A. Keddy.
Published by Cambridge University Press. © Cambridge University Press 2005.

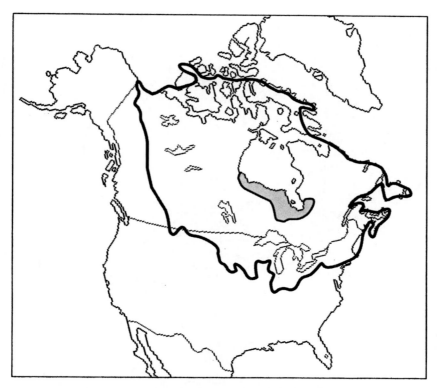

Figure 4.1 Location of the Hudson Bay Lowland (shaded) in relation to the Laurentide Ice Sheet (thick line) (after Riley 2003).

Fort Prince of Wales, near Churchill, and Moose Factory were occupied in the 1600s). The Lowland is currently sparsely inhabited and only minimally affected by industrial development.

Within North America, this area has the highest density and highest overall percentage surface cover of wetlands (Riley 1982, Pala & Boissoneau 1982, NWWG 1988). Recent physiographical classification subdivides the Hudson Bay Lowland ecozone into three ecoregions based on climate, landforms, vegetation, and ecological processes: Coastal Hudson Bay Lowland, Hudson Bay Lowland, and James Bay Lowland (ESWG 1995). Ecoregional climates vary from high subarctic along the coast to low subarctic to high boreal around southern James Bay. Wetlands are predominantly bogs, fens, and permafrost peatlands. Near the coast, well-drained beach ridges supporting spruce occur in parallel, alternating with wetlands. The Lowland includes approximately 1900 km of salt-water coastline located in the heart of the continent. This shoreline is dominated by marshes, tidal flats, and shallow water (ESWG 1995). Both Hudson and James bays receive freshwater run-off from the vast watershed to the south, making

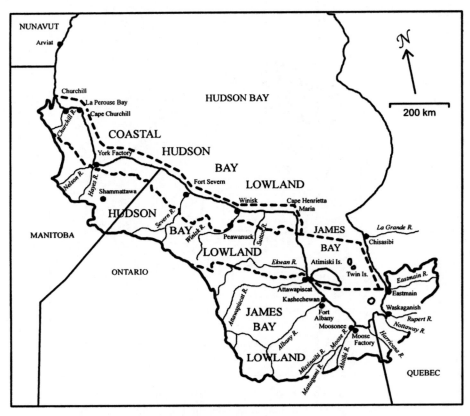

Figure 4.2 Ecoregions of the Hudson Bay Lowland and its regional setting.

the salinity only one-third that of normal oceanic water (Prinsenberg 1982). The bays are ice-covered for approximately eight months. Along the Ontario margin of Hudson Bay, 50% of the offshore waters may still be covered in ice in late July (Riley 2003).

The Lowland has attracted scientific study for many decades. The major period of investigation occurred in the 1970s and 1980s because of planned or predicted development of hydroelectric power resources and, to some extent, the potential for petroleum development. Both provincial and federal governments sought baseline information on the natural resources and ecological processes as a foundation for coordinated planning and future monitoring of impacts. The natural and human resources and the state of development of the Ontario portion of the Hudson Bay Lowland was documented as background for land-use planning (OMNR 1985). Before that, proceedings from two major scientific symposia on physical and biological processes, and human ecology of the Hudson Bay Lowland were published (*Proceedings of the Symposium on the Physical Environment of the Hudson Bay Lowland, March, 1973, University of Guelph, Guelph, Ontario* and *Scientific*

Studies on Hudson and James Bays, April 1981, University of Guelph, Guelph, Ontario; both published as special issues of *Naturaliste Canadien,* **109**(3/4). In addition to these proceedings, bibliographic compilations of published and unpublished literature have also been prepared (Haworth *et al.* 1978, Sims *et al.* 1979).

Zoltai (1973) provides a good introduction to the Hudson Bay Lowland. A recent comprehensive description and analysis of the flora has been published by Riley (2003). He includes a brief history of geological development, glacial history, and detailed interpretation of the postglacial origins of the vegetation. No other group of taxa in the Hudson Bay Lowland has received such intensive treatment.

Ecological processes

Ecological processes in the Lowland are governed by a combination of climate, hydrology, and geophysical history. Particularly important factors are the continuing isostatic rebound (influencing development of surface features at the interface of the sea and land, Glaser *et al.* 2004), the relative flatness (gradient of less than $1 \, \text{m} \, \text{km}^{-1}$, influencing hydrology, plant decay, and reworking of surface materials), cool temperatures (influencing the growing season and the persistence of permafrost, Brown 1973), and the prevailing influence of Hudson Bay on coastal and regional climate (Rouse 1991, Rouse & Bello 1985) and shoreline processes (Martini *et al.* 1980a, b). Wind also creates and modifies landscape features in the sandy areas near the coast (e.g. large dune formations near the Pen Islands, at Cape Churchill and Cape Henrietta Maria) and influences tree morphology through a combination of abrasion and the movement and deposition of snow (Scott *et al.* 1993).

Climate

The climate of the Hudson Bay Lowland is characterized by short, cool summers and cold winters. The ice of Hudson Bay and the contact of colder arctic air masses and warmer continental flows are important climatic influences. Gradients of temperature and precipitation exist from cooler and drier in the northwest (coastal Manitoba) to warmer and wetter in the southeast (southern James Bay) (synoptic data in Riley 2003). Table 4.1 summarizes the climatic variation among the three ecoregions of the Lowland.

Vegetation

Vegetation zones and/or forest regions of the Lowland have been described by various authors with minor variations – Hare (1954) describes: tundra, forest-tundra, subarctic woodland, and closed boreal; Coombs (1952) describes: forest-tundra, open boreal woodland, muskeg woodland, and main

Table 4.1 *Climatic variation within the Hudson Bay Lowland (ESWG 1995).*

		Mean temperature (°C)			Precipitation
Ecoregion	Climatic zone	Annual	Summer	Winter	(mm per year)
Coastal Hudson Bay Lowland	High subarctic	−4	10.5	−19	400–600
Hudson Bay Lowland	Low subarctic	−3.5	11	−18.5	<500–<700
James Bay Lowland	Humid high boreal	−2	11.5	−16	700–800

boreal forest; and Rowe (1972) identifies: forest-tundra ecotone and Hudson Bay Lowland open boreal. Riley (2003) identifies five floristic zones along a gradient from north to south, coastal to inland: maritime tundra (low arctic), peat plateau and woodland (high subarctic), peatland and woodland (low subarctic), southwest James Bay (low subarctic) and boreal peatland (high temperate). The Coastal Hudson Bay ecoregion has the southernmost zone of continuous tundra vegetation in North America. As the influence of Hudson Bay diminishes further inland (Rouse 1991), open spruce and tamarack forest patches are interspersed with large fen–bog complexes in the north (creating muskeg) (Zoltai 1973). In the south, a more-closed boreal forest occurs; this is especially developed in the Moose River basin, where the Hudson Bay Lowland borders the Precambrian Shield.

Wetlands

The four wetland regions represented in the Hudson Bay Lowland are shown in Fig. 4.3. Wetlands cover 76% to 100% of the Lowland (NWWG 1988) and over 90% is a saturated peatland plain (Riley 1989, 2003). Most of the Lowland is underlain by more than 30 cm of peat accumulation (Riley 1982). Peat depths in the coastal zone are less than 2 m (Dredge 1992); depths increase inland toward the limits of marine submergence where they may reach 4 m. This gradient in peat depth is primarily a result of age since emergence. This represents one of the greatest accumulations of peat in North America (Riley 1989).

Wetland types in Ontario were categorized by Riley (1982, 2003), following definitions of the National Wetlands Working Group (1988), as comprising 36% bog, 24% fen, 22% palsa–peat plateau, 13% swamp, and 5% marsh. The wetlands of the muskeg interior vary widely: from sedge, shrub, and treed fens in some areas, to open, shrub, and treed bogs in others; there are also areas of swamps and many shallow ponds and lakes, with emergent vegetation (Pala & Boissonneau

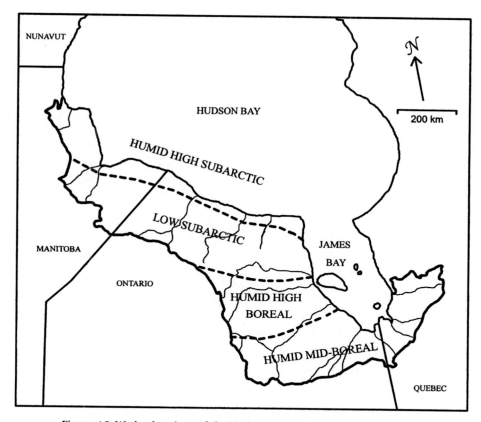

Figure 4.3 Wetland regions of the Hudson Bay Lowland.

1982). Natural fire frequency on the palsa fields or peat plateaus increases toward the northwest (Riley 2003).

The relative abundance of different types of wetlands in the Hudson Bay Lowland along a north–south corridor is shown in Fig. 4.4. Fens increase while swamps decrease northward along this gradient. Open bogs become less common in the subarctic regions. Both continuous and discontinuous permafrost, associated with peat plateaus, increase significantly north of the Attawapiskat River. Non-peat wetlands are most common in the high subarctic.

Wetlands are discussed further by region. Among regions, bogs have major similarities in species composition. The same is true for fens (NWWG 1988). Variation in species composition and the density and abundance of plants within vegetation types, within and among regions, is determined by the distribution of permafrost, wetland surface topography, and peat depth. To avoid duplication, details are provided under one region where a wetland type is common or in

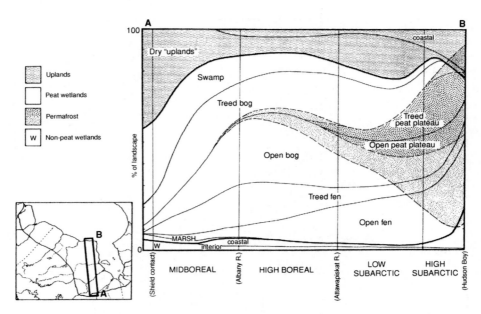

Figure 4.4 Vegetation change across the Hudson Bay Lowland from the southern boundary to the Hudson Bay coast (after Riley 1982).

which detailed studies have been carried out. Coastal wetlands for all regions are described following the regional discussions.

Humid midboreal wetland region

In this region, bogs, fens, and swamps are the most abundant wetlands (Fig. 4.4). Common types include domed bogs, flat bogs, northern ribbed fens, and horizontal fens (NWWG 1988). The following detailed wetland ecosystem descriptions are based on Jeglum and Cowell (1982).

Bog-pool moss mats – composed of *Sphagnum pulchrum*, *S. rubellum*, *S. tenellum*, and *S. majus* along with the liverwort *Gymnocolea inflata* and *Carex oligosperma* – form in small pools in ombrotrophic bogs. *Sphagnum* and graminoid bogs have a continuous cover of *Sphagnum* with less than 25% shrub cover. The major moss is *S. rubellum* and the graminoids include *Scirpus cespitosus*, *Carex limosa*, and *Rhynchospora alba*. In low-shrub bogs, ericaceous species (*Kalmia angustifolia*, *Ledum groenlandicum*), *Sphagnum fuscum*, *Cladina rangiferina*, and *Rubus chamaemorus* are characteristic. Low-shrub treed bogs are similar to the former, but have a higher cover of *Picea mariana*. Further discussion of the peatlands around southern James Bay can be found in Grondin and Ouzilleau (1980).

Five types of fen wetlands are identified: fen-pool moss mat, graminoid fen, low-shrub fen, tamarack treed fen, and cedar treed fen. The first type consists of floating moss mats (*Scorpidium scorpoides, Drepanocladus exannalatus*) on small fen pools. Common herbs include: *Menyanthes trifoliata, Carex limosa*, and *Rhynchospora alba*. In graminoid fens, *Carex interior, C. lasiocarpa, Equisetum fluviatile*, and *Scirpus cespitosus* are dominant. The shrubs *Betula glandulifera, Chamaedaphne calyculata, Myrica gale, Potentilla fruticosa*, and *Salix pedicularis* – as well as the mosses *Campylium stellatum* and *Sphagnum teres* – are typical of low-shrub fens. Fens with stunted, small tree-sized *Larix laricina* occur on the ridges of patterned fens and in large areas between river systems. Associated species include the shrub *Alnus rugosa* and the mosses *Calliergon stramineum, Hypnum lindbergii*, and *Sphagnum warnstortii*. In slightly drier conditions, *Thuja occidentalis* occurs on ridges with *Myrica gale, Carex exilis, Sphagnum angustifolium*, and *S. russowii*. Sims et al. (1982) further examine the soil and water characteristics of graminoid, low-shrub, graminoid-rich treed, and sphagnum-rich treed fens in the southern James Bay coastal area.

Swamps and marshes are prominent along the levees of rivers and streams, on the shores of large lakes, and on old beach ridges. Abundant marsh species include *Carex rostrata, Eleocharis palustris*, and *Potentilla palustris*. Thicket swamps are dominated by tall, clumped shrubs (*Alnus rugosa, Betula pumila, Cornus stolonifera, Salix planifolia*). Conifer swamps also occur, recognizable by the dominance of *Picea mariana*, and sometimes *P. glauca* and *Abies balsamea*. The most-common mosses are feather mosses – *Hylocomium splendens* on richer sites and *Pleurozium schreberi* on poorer sites. Conifer swamps cover large areas in the Moose River basin (Riley 2003).

Humid high boreal wetland region

Open bogs followed by treed bogs and treed fens are the most-abundant wetlands in this region (Fig. 4.4). Common types include flat bogs, plateau bogs, horizontal fens, and northern ribbed fens (NWWG 1988). Along streams or on the edges of bogs, swamps may occur. The region is affected by continuous and discontinuous permafrost (Riley 1982).

Flat bogs have featureless surfaces and occur in wide depressions. Trees typically occur only at the periphery of the bog. Dense shrubs (*Chamaedaphne calyculata, Kalmia angustifolia, Ledum groenlandicum*) with *Rubus chamaemorus* occur under the trees and in openings. *Smilax trifolia* is abundant. *Carex oligosperma, Sarracenia purpurea*, and *Andromeda glaucophylla* occur in small, wet depressions. Peat-plateau and palsa bogs are covered by fairly dense *Picea mariana* forests. They occur as small islands in fens. Sparse to dense low-shrub cover is similar to flat bogs and often occurs on hummocks formed by *Sphagnum* spp. Horizontal treed fens have an open canopy of *Larix laricina* and may have portions dominated by the shrubs *Chamaedaphne calyculata* and *Betula glandulifera*. The graminoids *Equisetum fluviatile* and *Scirpus hudsonianus* occur in both shrub and treed fens.

Low subarctic wetland region

In the low subarctic region, treed bogs are the most-common wetland (Fig. 4.4). Open bogs and open fens occupy roughly the same area, and treed fens are the next most frequent wetland. Plateau bogs become more prominent than in the boreal region. These wetlands occur as fen and peat-plateau bog complexes commonly made up of palsa bogs, northern ribbed fens, and horizontal fens (NWWG 1988). Details related to fens and palsa bogs reported here are from studies in the vicinity of Hawley Lake, about 70 km south-southeast of the Winisk River mouth (Sjörs 1961, Railton & Sparling 1973).

The vegetation of open fens, with pH in the range of 7.2 to 7.6, is composed largely of *Betula glandulosa*, *Andromeda polifolia*, *Myrica gale*, *Salix pedicellaris* var. *hypoglauca*, *Equisetum fluviatile*, *Carex chordorhiza*, *C. limosa* and the bryophytes *Scorpidium scorpioides*, *Drepanocladus intermedius*, and *Cinclidium stygium*. Treed fens with *Larix laricina* are similar to open fens in terms of shrub and herb cover, but the bryophytes *Sphagnum warnstorfianum* and *Tomentyprinum nitens* are noticeably abundant. Spring fens are found near brooks and lakes in small, sloping depressions. Characteristic species include: *Erigeron hyssopifolius*, *Primula mistassinica*, *Juncus albescens*, *J. alpinus*, *Eriophorum brachyantherum*, *Rubus acaulis*, and *Salix vestita*. Large ribbed fens are strongly patterned with *Sphagnum fuscum* hummocks a few feet high that are separated by broad, mud-bottomed depressions or "flarks." The ridges (strings), which cut across the fen at right angles to the direction of water movement, are typically covered by shrubs (*Betula glandulosa*, *Ledum groenlandicum*, *Chamaedaphne calyculata*) and mosses (*Sphagnum fuscum*, *S. magellanicum*). Flark vegetation is dominated by *Carex* spp. and *Eriophorum vaginatum* as well as *Drepanocladus* spp. and *Scorpidium* spp. (NWWG 1988). Elevation and the presence of permafrost determine species composition on the strings.

Palsa bogs may reach 1.5 km in diameter, but most are smaller. The largest are about 200 years old (Railton & Sparling 1973). Three main plant communities found on palsas are: lichens, dwarf-shrub and lichens, and *Picea mariana*. Lichen cover is composed of *Cladonia alpestris*, *C. rangiferina*, and *C. sylvatica*. Dwarf-shrub communities are characterized by *Andromeda glaucophylla*, *Vaccinium uliginosum*, *Kalmia polifolia*, *Ledum groenlandicum*, and *Vaccinium vitis-idaea*. *Polytrichum affine* (*strictum*) and *Cladonia* spp. are also abundant in the dwarf-shrub communities. Sparse *Picea mariana* communities also contain *Larix laricina*, *Vaccinium vitis-idaea*, *Cladonia alpestris* and *C. rangiferina*. Vegetation of the bog area between palsas is characterized by *Larix laricina*, *Chamaedaphne calyculata*, and *Sphagnum fuscum*.

Humid high subarctic wetland region

In the troughs between a series of parallel beach ridges associated with the Hudson Bay coast, which may extend inland many kilometers, subarctic meadow-marshes occur. They grade inland into fen systems and then to developing peat-plateau bogs (Riley 1982). Permafrost is more or less continuous in this region and it extends as a wedge under Hudson Bay. At Churchill it is up to 80 m thick (Riley 2003). Unfrozen fens, palsa bogs and peat-plateau bogs are typical, with the latter being most common (NWWG 1988; Fig. 4.4).

Peat-plateau bogs, raised about 1 m above the water table of the surrounding wetlands, may attain an area of several square kilometers (NWWG 1988). Peat plateaus are covered by a sparse spruce–lichen woodland with some shrubs (*Ledum decumbens* in open woodlands, *L. groenlandicum* in forested areas, also *Andromeda glaucophylla* and *Betula glandulosa*) and considerable lichen cover (*Cladonia mitis, C. stellaris, C. rangiferina, C. amaurocraea*). Fires, most common in the northwest, create open peat plateaus. Where a small area of permafrost thaws, the surface subsides, forming a collapse scar. *Sphagnum balticum* and *S. lindbergii* are typical of these scars in this region.

Coastal wetlands (all regions)

Coastal wetlands are broadest along the western James Bay coast. Along the shores of Hudson Bay, wetlands are more exposed and thus less diverse and narrower. Wetlands include offshore bottom vegetation (*Zostera marina*), tidal salt marshes, and supratidal meadow marshes (Riley 2003). In some areas, the intertidal/supratidal zone reaches over 8 km wide (Riley 1982). In addition, wetlands occur in association with beach–ridge complexes that may include – depending upon latitude and distance from the coast – tundra, lichen–woodlands, conifer forests, swamp, and treed bogs (Riley 2003).

Salt marshes are the most-common wetland type. They are dominated by *Puccinellia phryganodes, Scirpus maritimus, Eleocharis* spp., *Carex paleacea, C. glareosa, C. subspathacea, Hippuris vulgaris,* and *Senecio congestus.* Salt-marsh productivity has been estimated at 500 g m^{-2} per year by Glooschenko and Martini (1978). Inland, meadow marshes consist largely of *Festuca rubra, Hordeum jubatum, Potentilla anserina, Juncus balticus, Scirpus rufus, Deschampsia caespitosa, Calamagrostis stricta,* and *Dupontia fisheri* (Riley 2003). River-influenced brackish marshes occur along the James Bay coast near major rivers where the counterclockwise flow of currents results in salinities rarely exceeding 2 to 3 p.p.t. (Glooschenko 1980). These marshes are dominated by *Eleocharis palustris, Carex paleacea, Hippurus vulgaris,* and *Scirpus maritimus.* Vegetation in estuarine marshes, in river mouths, is largely composed of *Eleocharis palustris, E. acicularis, Sagittaria cuneata, Scirpus validus*, *S. americanus*, and numerous *Potamogeton*, *Carex*, *Juncus*, and *Equisetum* species (Glooschenko 1980).

Water resources and hydrology

The Lowland is drained by a dozen major and hundreds of minor rivers (Fig. 4.2). There are 1 primary, 13 secondary, and 30 tertiary watersheds in the Ontario portion of the Lowland alone – in which there are over 450 inland tributaries, over 305 coastal rivers and streams, and nearly 21 000 inland lakes. Peak river flows occur in May and lows historically occur in August. Spring floods may occur at elevations of up to 15 m above midsummer levels. Tidal influences in major rivers occur 15 to 20 km upstream, and average tidal fluctuations are 2 to 3 m (OMNR 1985).

Flora and fauna

The Lowland supports 816 native vascular plant species and 98 non-native species (Riley 2003). The flora is overwhelmingly transcontinental (81%), but reflects its low-arctic and subarctic position, and its relatively long distance from glacial refuges for most species. Non-native species are mostly confined to the villages and areas of highest human activity. Species of arctic affinity are concentrated along the coast and are most abundant at Cape Henrietta Maria (Fig. 4.2). Endemic species are rare due to the recent emergence and rapid migration of species into the region.

Approximately 300 bird species have been recorded in the Hudson Bay Lowland (Jehl & Smith 1970, Cadman et al. 1987, Wilson & McRae 1993, Chartier 1994). Migratory species predominate because of the inhospitable winter climate, and as would be expected in this wetland-dominated landscape, waterbirds are the most diverse and conspicuous. The coastal zone is particularly important to waterfowl (Ross 1982, 1983, Thomas & Prevett 1982). During spring migration, over 50% (several million birds) of the midcontinent population of lesser snow geese (*Anser caerulescens caerulescens*), 100 000 small Canada geese (*Branta canadensis hutchinsii*) (most of the tall-grass-prairie population), and most of the Atlantic brant (*Branta bernicla*) population (over 150 000) acquire critical reproductive nutrient reserves in Hudson Bay Lowland coastal marshes before moving to their arctic breeding grounds. In addition, over 500 000 lesser snow geese breed in several coastal colonies such as Cape Henrietta Maria and La Perouse Bay (Fig. 4.2) and over a million Canada geese (*Branta canadensis interior*) of the Eastern Prairie, Mississippi Valley, and Southern James Bay populations breed throughout the interior wetlands (Abraham et al. 1996, Canadian Wildlife Service Waterfowl Committee 2003). The region also provides critical breeding and staging resources for arctic and subarctic shorebirds (Morrison &

Harrington 1979, Morrison *et al.* 1991) including 10% to 20% of the eastern arctic red knot (*Calidris canutus*) population, and up to 30% (17 000) of the Hudsonian godwit (*Limosa haemastica*) population (R. K. Ross, personal communication 2004).

More than 50 species of terrestrial and marine mammals inhabit the Lowland (OMNR 1985). The signature mammal of the area is the polar bear (*Ursus maritimus*). Its southernmost population in the world, estimated at approximately 2400 (Kolenosky *et al.* 1991, Lunn *et al.* 1997b), occurs here. The woodland caribou (*Rangifer tarandus*), with a population of approximately 15 000 to 20 000, and wolverine (*Gulo gulo*) are two other important mammals of the Lowland. Ringed seals (*Phoca hispida*) and beluga whales (*Delphinapteras leucas*) frequent the larger river estuaries and near-shore areas during migration and molt; some may even winter in offshore leads and polynyas (Sergeant 1968, Lunn *et al.* 1997a). Small mammals are more typical of the boreal forest which harbors the southernmost populations of some arctic specialists like lemmings (Banfield 1974).

At least 35 species of fish have been recorded in the Lowland, including several of sport or commercial value (e.g. brook trout, lake trout, walleye, northern pike, and lake sturgeon) (OMNR 1985). The remoteness of the area's hundreds of rivers and tens of thousands of small lakes has precluded a comprehensive survey of fish-species occurrence.

Rare/endangered species

One species has probably become extinct in the Hudson Bay Lowland, two are considered threatened in Canada, and five are considered of special concern. The relatively young age of the Lowland means that evolution of species *in situ* has not had much time to occur. Riley (2003) documented only one endemic species of vascular plant (*Linus lewisii* var. *lepagei*, restricted to coastal Hudson and James bays); however, he found more than 30 species with disjunct populations (defined as occurring over 550 to 2100 km from the nearest regional populations).

Most birds are migratory and have broad distributions. Some arctic species reach their southern breeding limits in the Lowland, e.g. Pacific and red-throated loons (*Gavia pacifica*, *G. stellata*) and so they are uncommon to the region but not rare overall (Cadman *et al.* 1987). One species, the Eskimo curlew (*Numenius borealis*) historically occurred in migration (at least) but is now probably extinct (Environment Canada 2003a). Eskimo curlews were hunted extensively and were easy to kill because they traveled in large flocks. They have been protected under the Migratory Birds Convention in Canada and the United States since 1917, in Argentina as a shorebird since 1927, and under the Migratory Birds

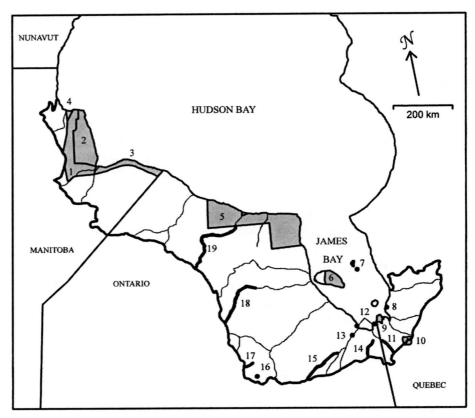

Figure 4.5 Protected areas of the Hudson Bay Lowland (areas described in Table 4.2). Wildlife Management Area/Sanctuary (1, 3, 7); National Park (2); Special Conservation Area (4); Provincial Park (5, 13, 14, 15, 17, 18, 19); Migratory Bird Sanctuary (6 9 12); Biodiversity Reserve (8, 9, 10); Aquatic Reserve (11); Provincial Conservation Reserve (16).

Convention between the United States and Mexico since 1936. Once one of the most-numerous birds in Canada, the Eskimo curlew population was less than 20 in 1978 and no nests have been found in over 110 years.

Ross's gull (*Rhodostethia rosea*), an arctic species with a circumpolar distribution, is threatened in Canada (COSEWIC 2003). The Churchill Special Conservation Area (Fig. 4.5) is one of its few breeding locations in Canada, where the maximum number of nests in any year has been five (Environment Canada 2003b). Ross's gull is protected under Canada's federal Species at Risk Act.

The short-eared owl (*Asio flammeus*), a species of special concern in Canada (COSEWIC 2003), breeds in coastal areas throughout the Hudson Bay Lowland. Reassessment is required before it can be considered for addition to Schedule 1 of the federal Species at Risk Act. Provincial legislation in most provinces makes it illegal to hunt, possess, or sell short-eared owls (Environment Canada 2003c).

Yellow rails (*Coturnicopus noveboracensis*) breed along the entire coast of the Hudson Bay Lowland. They are considered of special concern in Canada (COSEWIC 2003). Habitat loss in other parts of the breeding range, and particularly on the wintering grounds in the Gulf states, is the major threat. This species is protected under Canada's Species at Risk Act and under the Migratory Birds Convention Act (Environment Canada 2003d).

Most mammal species in the Lowland have broad North American distributions and few are considered rare. The Committee on the Status of Endangered Wildlife in Canada (COSEWIC 2003) considers the boreal population of woodland caribou threatened. Factors leading to the decline of this species include habitat destruction, intense hunting, disturbance by humans (roads, pipelines), and predation (by wolves, coyotes, and bears). Hunting is still permitted over much of its range and the level of hunting in the Hudson Bay Lowland is of concern. A provincial recovery team was formed in 2000 in Ontario. Woodland caribou are protected under the federal Species at Risk Act (Environment Canada 2003h).

Polar bears are identified as a species of special concern by COSEWIC (2003). Hunting, close to the maximum sustainable yield and regulated by provincial or territorial jurisdiction, is a major limiting factor. Other threats include ice fluctuations, availability of ringed seals, and bioaccumulation of toxic contaminants. Addition of this species to the Species at Risk Act of Canada requires a regulatory amendment. Polar bears are on Appendix II of the Convention on International Trade in Endangered Species (Environment Canada 2003f).

The western population of wolverine in Canada is listed as a species of Special Concern by COSEWIC (2003). Part of this population occurs throughout the entire mainland portion of the Hudson Bay Lowland, from the Albany River westward. Hunting of ungulates, the food of wolverines, by humans is a major cause of population decline. Since the status of this species was designated after the Species at Risk Act was proclaimed, a regulatory amendment is necessary to protect it by adding it to Schedule 1 (Environment Canada 2003g).

Other groups such as invertebrates are not as well-catalogued as birds and mammals so many other new species and the relative rarity of others remain to be documented. One exception is the monarch butterfly. There are three occurrences on the shore of James Bay for this species of Special Concern in Canada (COSEWIC 2003, Environment Canada 2003e). These sites, disjunct from the main range, are located near villages. The monarch butterfly is protected under the Canadian Species at Risk Act.

Conservation

Development and the human population

The Lowland remains essentially without roads. There are neither permanent nor winter roads from more-settled areas to the south. Only winter roads connect the more-isolated villages (e.g. one joins Moose Factory, Moosonee, Albany, Kashechewan, and Attawapiskat and another connects Fort Severn to Shammattawa, Fig. 4.2). There are permanent road networks only within and immediately around most villages. Two rail lines penetrate the Lowland, one reaching the Hudson Bay coast at Churchill and the other ending at Moosonee. Automobiles and trucks are imported by rail to Moosonee and Churchill and by barge or winter roads to villages further north.

The human population of approximately 10 000 is concentrated in only 11 villages, most located near the Hudson or James Bay coasts (average density is under 1 person per 30 km²). The predominantly Cree, Dene, and Métis people of these villages still rely heavily on traditional wildlife and fishery hunter–gatherer economies (Berkes *et al.* 1994, 1995), while developing other employment opportunities in government and other services. Churchill is a major regional transportation center, sea port, rail terminal, and tourist destination. Ecotourism based on the highly accessible polar bear population and the rich bird life is a mainstay of the local economy. Shammattawa, a small isolated Cree village, is linked by air only in the snow-free season and by a winter road to another small Cree village, Fort Severn. In Ontario, most of the population (70%) lives in seven coastal villages: Fort Severn, Peawanuck, Attawapiskat, Kashechewan, Fort Albany, Moosonee, and Moose Factory (OMNR 1985). A summer tourism industry focused on the Polar Bear Express train service originating in Cochrane, Ontario brings people from the south to the "arctic tidewater" at Moosonee and Moose Factory. Waskaganish and Eastmain are the easternmost settlements in the Hudson Bay Lowland. Traditional pursuits of hunting, trapping and fishing – as well as ecotourism – dominate the local economies.

Although resource-extraction industries such as forestry and mining exist in the Hudson Bay Lowland, these are nowhere dominant. However, climate change and increased demands for timber may make forestry more viable along the southern edge of the Hudson Bay Lowland (resulting in road development and landscape fragmentation). Recent discoveries and proposed development of diamond resources in Ontario (Macklem 2003) may change the economic picture of the Hudson Bay Lowland dramatically in the immediate future and have profound effects on ecological processes in development zones. Electricity in the remote villages is primarily produced by diesel generators, with fuel being barged or flown in. In the last five years, however, an electric-power transmission line has been extended along the coast from Moosonee northward and now services Kashechewan, Fort Albany, and Attawapiskat. The larger communities of Churchill and Moosonee–Moose Factory receive power from hydroelectric developments on the major rivers to the south (the Churchill–Nelson system and the Moose–Abitibi–Mattagami system, respectively).

Protected areas

The protected areas of the Lowland include a National Park, Biodiversity Reserves, an Aquatic Reserve, Provincial Parks, Ramsar sites, Wildlife Management Areas, Migratory Bird Sanctuaries, a Special Conservation Area and Areas of Natural and Scientific Interest (Fig. 4.5, Table 4.2).

The largest protected area of the Hudson Bay Lowland (25 633 km^2) comprises a National Park, two Wildlife Management Areas and a Special Conservation Area. The core area, Wapusk National Park (11 475 km^2), was established in 1996. It protects the world's largest concentration of polar bears and is mostly representative of wetlands in the Coastal Hudson Bay Lowland region (Fig. 4.2). Large expanses of peat-forming wetlands cover 85% of the park. Its flat landscape is broken by beach ridges. Water covers up to 50% of the land, as shallow lakes, meandering rivers, bogs, and fens (Parks Canada 2003a). Particularly significant are the northern range limits of wetland communities and plant species associated with the boreal forest (Parks Canada 2003b). The park also provides valuable habitat for 200 species of birds including the rare Ross's gull. Adjacent to the park are the Cape Churchill (8488 km^2) and Cape Tatnam (5312 km^2) Wildlife Management Areas (Manitoba Natural Resources 2001a). The first of these areas has open spruce habitat with tundra ponds, marshes, fens, and bogs. The area is important habitat for polar bears, beluga whales, and coastal caribou; it is known for wildlife viewing and research. Cape Tatnam highlights the striking transition from spruce forest to tundra. In addition to protecting polar bears, caribou, and geese, it is important for protecting shorebirds. The Churchill Special Conservation Area (358 km^2) was designated specifically to protect the nests of the Ross's gull (Manitoba Natural Resources 2001b).

Polar Bear Provincial Park (23 552 km^2) is the second-largest protected area in the Lowland (OMNR 2002a). Established as a park in 1970 and as a Ramsar site in 1987, it is significant because it protects plants and animals at the extremes of their ranges as well as the world's most-southerly example of high-subarctic tundra. It provides habitat for about 10% of the Hudson Bay Lowland population of snow geese. Poor surface drainage, climate, rainfall, periods of frost, permafrost, and flooding of rivers and streams in spring combine to create waterlogged conditions. Almost 75% of the area is covered by wet organic material or open water (Wetlands International 2003a). Extensive areas of peatlands are interspersed by flat-topped ridges. Non-forested peatlands (shrub or open bogs, fens, swamps) are the most-common wetland type, followed by

Table 4.2 *Protected areas of the Hudson Bay Lowland.*

Area[a]	Designation	Size[b] (km²)	IUCN Category	Year[b] established	Comments
Cape Churchill (1)	Wildlife Management Area	8 488	IV	1978	Adjacent to Wapusk NP
Wapusk (2)	National Park	11 475	II	1996	Includes IBA
Cape Tatnam (3)	Wildlife Management Area	5 312	IV	1973	Includes 2 IBA, 2 ASI
Churchill (4)	Special Conservation Area	358	IV	1988[c]	Created to protect Ross's gull nests
Polar Bear (5)	Wilderness Provincial Park	23 552	II	1970	Includes Ramsar wetland, 4 IBA
Akimiski Island (6)	Migratory Bird Sanctuary	3 180	IV	1941	Includes IBA
Twin Islands (7)	Wildlife Sanctuary	1 425	IV	1939	Part is IBA
Boatswain Bay (8)	Biodiversity Reserve	110	II	2003	Includes, MBS, IBA
Ministikawatin Peninsula (9)	Biodiversity Reserve	908	II	2003	Adjoins Hannah Bay MBS
Missisicabi Plain (10)	Biodiversity Reserve	678	II	2003	On southern boundary of Hudson Bay Lowland
North Harricana River (11)	Aquatic Reserve	254	II	2003	Corridor 1.5 to 4.5 km wide, 93 km long
Hannah Bay and Moose River (12)	Migratory Bird Sanctuaries	253	IV	1939 1958	Combined as Southern James Bay Ramsar wetland in 1987, 2 IBA
Tidewater (13)	Natural Environment Provincial Park	10	II	1970	4 islands in Moose River, 20 km from James Bay

Table 4.2 (*cont.*)

Area[a]	Designation	Size[b] (km²)	IUCN Category	Year[b] established	Comments
Kesagami (14)	Wilderness Provincial Park		II	1983	River corridor (75 km of Kesagami River in Hudson Bay Lowland)
Missinaibi River (15)	Waterway Provincial Park		II	1970	River corridor (150 km of Missinaibi River in Hudson Bay Lowland)
Jog Lake (16)	Conservation Reserve	428[d]	II	2003[d]	Near southern edge of Hudson Bay Lowland
Little Current River (17)	Waterway Provincial Park		II	1989	River corridor (50 km of river in Hudson Bay Lowland)
Otoskwin–Attawapiskat River (18)	Waterway Provincial Park		II	1989	River corridor (180 km of Attawapiskat River in Hudson Bay Lowland)
Winisk River (19)	Waterway Provincial Park		II	1969	River corridor (>300 km of river in Hudson Bay Lowland)

[a] Numbers correspond to areas mapped in Fig. 4.5.

[b] Based on UNEP World Conservation Monitoring Centre (2003) unless indicated.

[c] R. Romaniuk personal communication, 2004. Manitoba Conservation, Churchill.

[d] Canadian Legal Information Institute (2003).

ASI, Area of Special Interest; IBA, Important Bird Area (Bird Studies Canada 2003a): MBS, Migratory Bird Sanctuary; NP, National Park.

permanent shallow marine waters, sand, shingle or pebble shores, estuarine waters, intertidal mud flats, intertidal marshes, coastal brackish lagoons, permanent deltas, permanent flowing waters, permanent freshwater lakes, permanent freshwater marshes, tundra wetlands, shrub-dominated wetlands on inorganic soil, and forested peatlands. The largest of the kettle lakes and lakes formed by glacial erosion is 13 km by 5 km, with a depth of 3 m. The coastal areas are very flat, generally treeless, and extend over 8 km inland from the tidal flats. Tidal flats occur along most of the park's coast. The indigenous people are permitted to hunt, fish, and trap for subsistence and gather wild commodities for non-commercial purposes. Registered guests at two native-owned camps are the only non-native hunters of waterbirds, grouse, and snipe permitted in the park.

Protected areas associated with James Bay include two Biodiversity Reserves and several Migratory Bird Sanctuaries. In both the Boatswain Bay (110 km²) and Ministikawatin Peninsula (908 km²) Biodiversity Reserves (Table 4.2, Fig. 4.5), two-thirds of the ground cover is oligotrophic or minerotrophic peatland while the higher ground is covered by low-density *Picea mariana* and dry heaths (Environnement Québec 2003a, 2003b). The largest Migratory Bird Sanctuary occurs on Akimiski Island (3180 km²) while Twin Islands Wildlife Sanctuary covers 1425 km² (Industry Canada 2003). At the head of James Bay, two Migratory Bird Sanctuaries are combined to form the Southern James Bay Wetland of International Importance (253 km²; Wetlands International 2003b). Wetland types represented at this Ramsar site include (in decreasing order of abundance): intertidal mudflats (a few kilometers in width), permanent shallow marine waters, estuarine waters, intertidal marshes, permanent freshwater marshes/pools, shrub-dominated wetlands on inorganic soils, and forested peatlands.

Several protected areas occur inland on the Lowland. These include a Biodiversity Reserve, an Aquatic Reserve, a Natural Environment Provincial Park, a Conservation Reserve, five Waterway Corridors, and four Provincial Nature Reserves. Straddling the southern boundary of the Lowland in Québec is the Missisicabi Plain Biodiversity Reserve (Environnement Québec 2003c). Oligotrophic and minerotrophic peatlands cover about 75% of the reserve. The North Harricana River Aquatic Reserve protects a 93-km river corridor (riverbed and valley slopes) that varies in width from 1.5 to 4.5 km (Environnement Québec 2003d). One-third of the reserve is covered by peatlands.

In Ontario, Tidewater, a 10-km² Natural Environment Provincial Park, is located 20 km from James Bay in the Moose River estuary (OMNR 2003). The park consists of four islands. This IUCN Category-II area is managed to protect the landscapes and special features of the natural region it represents while providing opportunities for light recreation. Being near the tree line, the boreal forest is stunted and less dense than further south. The shoreline wetlands are influenced by tides varying by as much as 2.5 m between high and low tide.

Jog Lake Conservation Reserve – found at the southern limit of the Lowland – protects a large, circular, bog-rimmed lake. Drainage occurs in a radial pattern from the lake. Graminoid bogs, fens, and open and treed bogs cover most of the area (OMNR 1997). The protected waterway corridors in the Ontario portion of the Lowland total over 700 km in length and represent rivers draining into both James and Hudson bays (Table 4.2, OMNR 2004). The four small (4 to 50 ha) Nature Reserves (not listed in Table 4.2), designated in the Ontario portion of the Lowland between the Missinaibi and Mattagami rivers, are all Earth Science Areas of Natural and Scientific Interest (ANSI) (OMNR 2002b).

A further six Areas of Special Interest have been nominated in Manitoba that may be used in completing representation of provincial natural regions. Four of these areas are outside currently protected areas and would significantly increase representation of the Hudson Bay Lowland region (Manitoba Natural Resources 2003). Future protection designations of these areas will be determined by the interests of all parties involved in their management (Manitoba Industry, Economic Development and Mines 2003).

Although they do not have any inherent protection status, 23 Important Bird Areas vital to the long-term conservation of the world's birds have been identified along the coast of the Lowland (Bird Studies Canada 2003a, 2004). They range in size from 20 to 1673 km^2. Those occurring wholly or in part within larger protected areas such as the Churchill complex and Polar Bear Provincial Park total 6923 km^2. Important Bird Areas outside existing protected areas cover a total of 5602 km^2. Many marine and freshwater wetland habitats of the Coastal Hudson Bay Lowland region are represented in these areas. They are globally significant for congregatory species, waterfowl concentrations, shorebird concentrations, and migratory landbird concentrations. Only 13 areas – those within already designated protected areas – can be considered protected. Conservation plans are in preparation for each area.

Threats and priorities for conservation

The major threats to the ecological integrity of the Lowland in decreasing order of magnitude are: climate change (terrestrial warming and sea-level change), hydroelectric development and water export (dams, water diversion), unnatural increase in the abundance of light geese (coastal-marsh degradation), and diamond mining.

Although the exact impacts of climate change are uncertain, warming has been documented (Cohen *et al.* 1994, Gagnon & Gough 2001) and significant increases in mean temperatures will undoubtedly result in a retraction of permafrost, one of the most susceptible landscape features which reaches its southern limit here. The Lowland is at the interface of the boreal, subarctic, and arctic climate regimes, and the current position of the tree line is near the Lowland's northern edge. These transitional areas are predicted to exhibit some of the greatest ecological consequences of climate change (Maxwell 1992). Hudson Bay ice cover is a controlling factor of regional climate (Rouse 1991) and potential changes in sea ice as a result of warming (Gough & Wolfe 2001) suggest the area will become warmer. Consequent effects will include altered hydrological dynamics of the wetlands, which depend on high winter precipitation and spring runoff, and low evapotranspiration and shallow permafrost layers in the northern portions. Significant secondary drainage of surface wetlands is a possibility, as is permafrost collapse; Riley (2003) observed such collapse over the past 30 years. The Lowland and its peatlands are a significant carbon reservoir; regional climate warming may lead to increased methane emissions and loss of carbon to the atmosphere (Glooschenko et al. 1994, Roulet et al. 1994, Rouse et al. 1995). Permafrost collapse and increased precipitation could also negatively affect polar bear denning (Stirling et al. 1999; M. Obbard, personal communication 2004).

In addition to the terrestrial processes affected by climate warming, sea-level rise in James Bay and Hudson Bay over the next 100 years may inundate the relatively narrow zone of salt marshes and supratidal marshes, which are of extreme importance to the migratory fauna of the region and its people, who depend on them. If sea-level rise overcompensates for isostatic rebound (i.e. sea-level fall) (Gough 1998), it would also have a direct impact on most of the villages, particularly those on James Bay, that are located close to the coast at low elevations. Reduced ice cover and increased ice-free periods would limit the accumulation of fat and nutrient reserves by polar bears, which depend on the ice platform to hunt seals during the winter period in preparation for prolonged fasting while on land (Stirling & Derocher 1993, Stirling et al. 1999).

Hydroelectric dams, diversions, and water-export proposals present the second important threat to the environmental integrity of the Lowland. The natural flow of several large rivers that traverse the Lowland and carry fresh water to wetlands along the shores of Hudson and James Bays has been altered through the development of hydroelectric-power generating stations. This is important to the integrity of coastal as well as riverine wetlands because the volume of river flow and circulation of fresh water, particularly in James Bay, is important in maintaining nearshore salinity levels (Glooschenko 1980).

In Manitoba, flow from the Churchill River is diverted into the Nelson River for hydroelectric-power generation. Seven generating stations (built between 1952 and 1990) and three control structures regulate water flow to the Lowland via these two major rivers (Manitoba Hydro 2004a, b). Twelve new dams are proposed for this system (seven on the Nelson River, four on Burntwood River that links the Churchill and Nelson rivers, and one associated with the Churchill River)

(Manitoba Wildlands 2004a). An additional three were proposed for the Hayes River in the 1997 Manitoba Treaty Land Entitlement (Manitoba Wildlands 2004b).

In Ontario, the Moose River has 9 hydroelectric generating stations on its Abitibi and Mattagami tributaries (Fig. 4.2), which were constructed between 1911 and 1966 (Ontario Power Generation 2003). Southern demand for power may result in tapping the flow of other Lowland rivers. Of 18 new hydroelectric developments included in Ontario Hydro's (1990) demand–supply plan, 12 are in the Hudson Bay–James Bay region. Six new dams and 6 redevelopments of existing dams were proposed for the Moose, Abitibi, and Mattagami rivers. The plan called for development of these sites by 2016. The dozen projects would generate 1890 MW of electricity and flood at least 2299 ha of land. A large portion of Ontario's hydroelectric potential lies in other rivers flowing into James Bay (the Albany and the Attawapiskat) and into Hudson Bay (the Severn and the Winisk). While hydroelectric development of these rivers was not proposed in the plan, private-sector proposals may be considered.

In Québec, the first phase of the La Grande power-generating megaproject altered the flow in the La Grande River (Fig. 4.2) and affected water levels in numerous lakes 400 km inland. The next phase of this project, planned for 2007, will involve the diversion of substantial flow from the Rupert River, which enters James Bay at its southern extreme (Hydro Québec 2002). Flows in the Eastmain River, which enters James Bay near the Lowland's eastern boundary, will also be affected by this project.

A water-diversion scheme in the 1980s proposed to build a dyke across the mouth of James Bay, and reverse the flow of fresh water through rivers and a canal to the United States (Milko 1986); it was estimated that 61% of Hudson Bay's freshwater budget would be diverted, with major ecological implications to the region, particularly for migratory birds, marine mammals, and marine aquatic taxa (Rimmer 1991, 1992).

The third and most-recent threat to the integrity of the coastal wetlands of the Hudson Bay Lowland is unnaturally high population of light geese (greater snow geese, lesser snow geese, or Ross's geese) resulting from four decades of continuous and rapid growth (Abraham & Jefferies 1997). The vegetation cover of salt marshes and adjacent freshwater coastal marshes (Kotanen & Jefferies 1997, Jano et al. 1998, Jefferies & Rockwell 2002) is being destroyed through grazing by geese. This results in soil erosion and increased salinity levels (Jefferies 1997, Bird Studies Canada 2003b). Spin-off effects occur on a wide range of fauna as well (e.g. Milakovic et al. 2001, Rockwell et al. 2003, Milakovic & Jefferies 2003). The geese share their nesting habitat with many different species of birds. These include several major populations of Canada geese, half of the Atlantic brant population, and significant numbers of pintails, black ducks, green-winged teal, and mallards. Species such as the yellow rail, scaup, shoveler, and wigeon are now less common in areas overpopulated with light geese.

The primary factor contributing to this threat is land-use practices far to the south in the agricultural heartland of central North America (Jefferies *et al.* 2004). There are four main reasons for the population explosion (US House of Representatives 2003). First, agricultural areas in the United States and prairie Canada, which provide abundant food resources during migration and winter, have expanded. Currently there are about 900 000 ha of rice farms in Arkansas, Louisiana, and Texas. Further, millions of hectares of cereal-grain crops are being grown in the midwest United States. Secondly, several National Wildlife Refuges located along the flyway provide protection for thousands of migrating geese. Thirdly, harvest rates of geese have decreased considerably. Fourthly, because of the first three factors, mortality rates have declined and the number of breeding adults returning to nesting areas has greatly increased.

Wetland destruction by geese has occurred from the middle of James Bay (Akimiski Island) to north of Arviat, Nunavut on the west Hudson Bay coast beyond the Hudson Bay Lowland (Fig. 4.2; Abraham & Jefferies 1997). They have destroyed, for the foreseeable future, one-third of the approximately 55 000 ha of salt-marsh habitat along the coast of Hudson and James bays (US House of Representatives 2003). Another third is nearly devastated, and the geese have moved on to feed on the remaining third. In some places along the Lowland coast, heavy grazing has extended 10 km inland (Batt 1997).

Enclosure experiments are being conducted that indicate it may take at least 15 years for vegetation to begin to regrow in the absence of goose foraging. With goose populations increasing at the rate of 5% per year, the Arctic Goose Habitat Working Group recommended reducing the midcontinent population of light geese by 50% (of its size in the late 1990s) by 2005. This is to be accomplished by increasing harvesting through extending the season, increasing limits, and altering the permitted harvesting methods (Batt 1997).

The mining of diamonds on a large scale in the interior of the Lowland (e.g. west of Attawapiskat) is the fourth significant threat to the Lowland. It could have a significant effect on ecological functions in local areas. The infrastructure needed to extract and process ore to recover diamonds will probably include some form of road building to the interior, necessitating many stream and river crossings, enhanced air transportation facilities, hydroelectric transmission corridors through the interior to supply power for the mining operations, or perhaps fuel transportation systems from the James Bay coast (B. Mighton, personal communication 2004). It will also require taking water for ore processing, and mine wastes and tailings deposition and storage. Currently all of these infrastructure features are essentially absent outside the villages. The effects and their mitigation will depend on the scale of the operation, the degree of pre-construction planning undertaken, and the development of thoughtful solutions to problems not formerly encountered in the Lowland.

As the World Wildlife Fund (2003) recently pointed out, there are outstanding opportunities to protect intact habitats and species in the Hudson Bay Lowland in advance of widespread development and to buffer them against the effects of climate change and pollution from toxic chemicals. The general priorities for conservation of the region include: renewed and increased inventory of resources, which has waned since the 1980s; coordinated federal and provincial implementation of environmental screening and assessment of major industrial and power developments (including specific attention to cumulative-effects prediction); enhanced local planning and capacity-building among the villages; and enhancement of the value placed on the region's intrinsic features and the essentially undisturbed nature of this vast and unique wilderness area.

More specifically, the following actions are important for protecting wetlands in the Hudson Bay Lowland. The Areas of Special Interest identified as candidates to complete natural heritage representation in Manitoba need to be evaluated and assigned official status. Protection standards should be raised for Wildlife Management Areas and Migratory Bird Sanctuaries. Conservation plans for all Important Bird Areas are required to seek official recognition and protection status within current planning frameworks. A regulatory amendment to Schedule 1 of the Canadian Species at Risk Act is required to protect short-eared owls, polar bears, and wolverines in the Hudson Bay Lowland. Effective management programs are needed to reduce the light geese populations that are destroying coastal wetlands.

Acknowledgements

This is contribution 15-03 of the Wildlife Research and Development Section, Ontario Ministry of Natural Resources. We thank Paul Keddy and Lauchlan Fraser for the invitation to participate in the symposium and for their patience throughout the writing period.

References

Abraham, K. F. and Jefferies, R. L. (1997). High goose populations: causes, impacts and implications. In *Arctic Ecosystems in Peril: Report of the Arctic Goose Habitat Working Group*, ed. B. D. J. Batt. Arctic Goose Joint Venture Special Publication. Washington, DC: US Fish and Wildlife Service. Ottawa, Canada: Canadian Wildlife Service, pp. 7–72.

Abraham, K. F., Jefferies, R. L., Rockwell, R. F., and MacInnes, C. D. (1996). Why are there so many white geese in North America? In *Proceedings of the 7th*

International Waterfowl Symposium, February 4–6, 1996, Memphis Tennessee, ed. J. Ratti. Memphis, TN: Ducks Unlimited, pp. 79–92.

Banfield, A. W. F. (1974). *The Mammals of Canada*. Toronto, Canada: University of Toronto Press (reprinted 1977).

Batt, B. D. J. (ed.) (1997). *Arctic Ecosystems in Peril: Report of the Arctic Goose Habitat Working Group*. Arctic Goose Joint Venture Special Publication. Washington, DC: US Fish and Wildlife Service. Ottawa, Canada: Canadian Wildlife Service.

Berkes, F., George, P. J., Preston, R. J., Hughes, A., Turner, J., and Cummins, B. D. (1994). Wildlife harvesting and sustainable regional native economy in the Hudson and James Bay Lowland, Ontario. *Arctic*, **47**, 350–60.

Berkes, F., Hughes, A., George, P. J., Preston, R. J., Cummins, B. D., and Turner, J. (1995). The persistence of aboriginal land use: fish and wildlife harvest areas in the Hudson and James Bay Lowland, Ontario. *Arctic*, **48**, 81–93.

Bird Studies Canada (2003a). Important Bird Area criteria. http://www.bsc-eoc.org/birdmap_e.htm (accessed December, 2003).

  (2003b). Churchill and vicinity IBA site summary. http://www.bsc-eoc.org/iba/site.jsp?siteID=MB003 (accessed December, 2003).

  (2004). Important Bird Areas searchable database. http://www.bsc-eoc/iba/IBSites.html (accessed February, 2004).

Brown, R. J. E. (1973). Permafrost: distribution and relation to environmental factors in the Hudson Bay Lowland. In *Proceedings of the Symposium on the Physical Environment of the Hudson Bay Lowland, March 30–31, 1973, Guelph Ontario: University of Guelph*, pp. 35–68.

Cadman, M. D., Eagles, P. J., and Helleiner, F. M. (1987). *Atlas of Breeding Birds of Ontario*. Waterloo, Ontario: University of Waterloo Press.

Canadian Legal Information Institute (2003). Ontario Regulation 682/94 Exemption – Ontario Ministry of Natural Resources – MNR-61. http://www.canlii.org/on/regu/cron/20030812/o.reg.682-94/whole.html (accessed February, 2004).

Canadian Wildlife Service Waterfowl Committee (2003). *Population Status of Migratory Game Birds in Canada* (and Regulation *Proposals for Overabundant Species*) – *November 2003*. CWS Migratory Birds Regulatory Report 10. Ottawa, Ontario: Canadian Wildlife Service.

Chartier, B. (1994). *A Birder's Guide to Churchill*. ABA/Lane Birdfinding Guide Series. Colorado Springs, CO: ABA.

Cohen, S. J., Agnew, T. A., Headley, A., Louie, P. Y. T., Reycraft, J., and Skinner, W. (1994). *Climate Variability and Implications for the Future of the Hudson Bay Bioregion*. Hudson Bay Programme, Canadian Arctic Resources Committee, Ottawa, Ontario, and the Municipality of Sanikiluaq.

Coombs, D. B. (1952). A comparison of the northern limits of distribution of some vascular plant species in southern Ontario. *Canadian Field-Naturalist*, **109**, 63–90 (cited in Riley 2003).

COSEWIC (Committee on the Status of Endangered Wildlife in Canada) (2003). *COSEWIC Assessment Results, November 2003*. Ottawa, Canada: COSEWIC.

Dredge, L. A. (1992). *Field Guide to the Churchill Region Manitoba: Glaciations, Sea Level Changes, Permafrost Landforms, and Archeology of the Churchill and Gillam Areas.* Geological Survey of Canada, Miscellaneous Report 53.

Environment Canada (2003a). Species at risk: Eskimo curlew. http://www.speciesatrisk.gc.ca/search/speciesDetails_e.cfm?SpeciesID=21 (accessed February, 2004).

(2003b). Species at risk: Ross's gull. http://www.speciesatrisk.gc.ca/search/speciesDetails_e.cfm?SpeciesID=59 (accessed February, 2004).

(2003c). Species at risk: short-eared owl. http://www.speciesatrisk.gc.ca/search/speciesDetails_e.cfm?SpeciesID=60 (accessed February, 2004).

(2003d). Species at risk: yellow rail. http://www.speciesatrisk.gc.ca/search/speciesDetails_e.cfm?SpeciesID=574 (accessed February, 2004).

(2003e). Species at risk: monarch. http://www.speciesatrisk.gc.ca/search/speciesDetails_e.cfm?SpeciesID=294 (accessed February, 2004).

(2003f). Species at risk: polar bear. http://www.speciesatrisk.gc.ca/search/speciesDetails_e.cfm?SpeciesID=167 (accessed February, 2004).

(2003g). Species at risk: wolverine (western population). http://www.speciesatrisk.gc.ca/search/speciesDetails_e.cfm?SpeciesID=172 (accessed February, 2004).

(2003h). Species at risk: woodland caribou. http://www.speciesatrisk.gc.ca/search/speciesDetails_e.cfm?SpeciesID=636 (accessed February, 2004).

Environnement Québec (2003a). Boatswain Bay Biodiversity Reserve. http://www.menv.gouv.qc.ca/biodiversite/reserves-bio/boatswain/note-en.pdf (accessed January, 2004).

(2003b). Ministikawatin Peninsula Biodiversity Reserve. http://www.menv.gouv.qc.ca/biodiversite/reserves-bio/ministikawatin/note-en.pdf (accessed January, 2004).

(2003c). Missisicabi Plain Biodiversity Reserve. http://www.menv.gouv.qc.ca/biodiversite/reserves-bio/missisicabi/note-en.pdf (accessed January, 2004).

(2003d). North Harricana River Aquatic Reserve. http://www.menv.gouv.qc.ca/biodiversite/aquatique/harricana-nord/note-en.pdf (accessed February, 2004).

ESWG (Ecological Stratification Working Group) (1995). *A National Ecological Framework for Canada.* Ottawa/Hull; Canada: Agriculture and Agri-Food Canada and Environment Canada (report and national map at 1:7 500 000 scale).

Gagnon, A. S. and Gough, W. A. (2001). Hydroclimatic trends in the Hudson Bay region, Canada. *Canadian Water Resources Journal*, **27**, 245–62.

Glaser, P. H., Hansen, B. C. S., Siegel, D. I., Reeve, A. S., and Morin, P. J. (2004). Rates, pathways and drivers for peatland development in the Hudson Bay lowlands, northern Ontario, Canada. *Journal of Ecology*, **92**, 1036–53.

Glooschenko, W. A. (1980). Coastal ecosystems of the James/Hudson Bay area of Ontario, Canada. *Zeitschrift fur Geomorphologie NF Suppl.*, **34**, 214–24.

Glooschenko, W. A. and Martini, I. P. (1978). Hudson Bay lowlands baseline study. In *Coastal Zone '78, Proceedings of the Symposium on Technical, Environmental, Socioeconomic and Regulatory Aspects of Coastal Zone Management, March 14–16, 1978, San Francisco, California*. San Francisco, CA: ASCE, pp. 663–79.

Glooschenko, W. A., Roulet, N. T., Barrie, L. A., Schiff, H. I., and McAdie, H. G. (1994). Northern Wetlands Study (NOWES): an overview. *Journal of Geophysical Research*, **99**, 1423–8.

Gough, W. A. (1998). Projections of sea-level change in Hudson and James Bays, Canada, due to global warming. *Arctic and Alpine Research*, **30**, 84–8.

Gough, W. A. and Wolfe, E. (2001). Climate change scenarios for Hudson Bay, Canada, from general circulation models. *Arctic*, **54**, 142–8.

Gray, T., Whelan Enns, G., Zinger, N., Kavanagh, K., and Sims, M. (2001). Southern Hudson Bay taiga (NA0616). World Wildlife Fund. http://www.worldwildlife.org/wildworld/profiles/terrestrial/na/na0616_full.html (accessed December, 2003).

Grondin, P. and Ouzilleau, J. (1980). Les tourbières du sud de la jamésie, Québec. *Géographie Physique et Quarternaire*, **34**, 267–99.

Hare, F. K. (1954). The boreal conifer zone. *Geographical Studies*, **1**, 4–18.

Haworth, S. E., Cowell, D. W., and Sims, R. A. (1978). *Bibliography of Published and Unpublished Literature on the Hudson Bay Lowland*. Canadian Forestry Service, Information Report O-X-215.

Hustich, I. (1957). On the phytogeography of the subarctic Hudson Bay lowland. *Acta Geographica*, **16**, 1–46.

Hydro Québec (2002). Eastmain-1-A Powerhouse and Rupert Diversion. http://www.hydroquebec.competition/eastmain1a/en/pdf/rens_preliminaire.pdf (accessed December, 2003).

Industry Canada (Canada's Digital Collections) (2003). Akimiski Island, Hannah Bay & Boatswain Bay. http://collections.ic.gc.ca/sanctuaries/nwt/.akimiski/.htm (accessed December, 2003).

Jano, A P., Jefferies, R. L., and Rockwell, R. F. (1998). The detection of change by multi-temporal analysis of LANDSAT data: the effects of goose foraging. *Journal of Ecology*, **86**, 93–100.

Jefferies, R. L. (1997). Long-term damage to sub-arctic ecosystems by geese: ecological indicators and measures of ecosystem dysfunction. In *Disturbance and Recovery of Arctic Terrestrial Ecosystems*, ed. R. M. M. Crawford. NATO, ASI Series 25. Dordrecht, the Netherlands: Kluwer, pp. 151–65.

Jefferies, R. L. and Rockwell, R. F. (2002). Foraging geese, vegetation loss and soil degradation in an Arctic salt marsh. *Applied Vegetation Science*, **5**, 7–16.

Jefferies, R. L., Henry, H., and Abraham, K. F. (2004). Agricultural nutrient subsidies to migratory geese and ecological change to arctic coastal habitats. In *Food Webs at the Landscape Level*, eds. G. A. Polis, M. E. Power, and G. R. Huxel. Chicago, IL: University of Chicago Press, pp. 268–83.

Jeglum, J. K. and Cowell, D. W. (1982). Wetland ecosystems near Kinoje Lakes, southern interior Hudson Bay lowland. *Naturaliste Canadien*, **109**, 621–35.

Jehl, J. R., Jr. and Smith, B. A. (1970). *Birds of the Churchill Region, Manitoba*. Manitoba Museum of Man and Nature, Special Publication 1.

Kolenosky, G. B., Abraham, K. F., and Greenwood, C. J. (1991). *Polar Bears of Southern Hudson Bay*. Ontario Ministry of Natural Resources, Final Report. Maple, Ontario.

Kotanen, P. M. and Jefferies, R. L. (1997). Long-term destruction of wetland vegetation by Lesser Snow Geese. *Ecoscience*, **4**, 179–82.

Lunn, N. J., Stirling, I., and Nowicki, S. N. (1997a). Distribution and abundance of ringed (*Phoca hispida*) and bearded seals (*Erignathus barbatus*) in western Hudson Bay. *Canadian Journal of Fisheries and Aquatic Sciences*, **54**, 914–21.

Lunn, N. J., Stirling, I., Andriashek, D., and Kolenosky, G. B. (1997b). Re-estimating the size of the polar bear population in western Hudson Bay. *Arctic*, **50**, 234–40.

Macklem, K. (2003). Diamonds with an edge. *MacLeans Magazine*, September 8, 52–5.

Manitoba Hydro (2004a) History of Manitoba Hydro in 1970s.
http://www.hydro.mb.ca/about_us/history/hep_1970.html (accessed February, 2004).

(2004b) Generating station descriptions.
http://www.hydro.mb.ca/our_facilities/generating_stations.shtml (accessed February, 2004).

Manitoba Industry, Economic Development and Mines (2003). Manitoba's protected areas initiative: mining sector consultation process.
http://www.gov.mb.ca/itm/mrd/geo/exp-sup/min-pai.html (accessed December, 2003).

Manitoba Natural Resources (2001a). Wildlife management areas: Northeastern Region.
http://www.gov.mb.ca/conservation/wildlife/managing/wma_northeastern.html (accessed December, 2003).

(2001b). Wildlife management areas: Northeastern Region.
http://www.gov.mb.ca/conservation/wildlife/managing/special_conservation.html (accessed December, 2003).

(2003). Current areas of special interest in Manitoba.
http://www.gov.mb.ca/conservation/pai/images/maps/asi-map.pdf (accessed January, 2004).

Manitoba Wildlands (2004a). Map showing existing and proposed hydro projects based on Northern Manitoba–Northwestern Ontario First Nations Meeting on Energy Related Issues, Thunder Bay, Ontario, September 9, 2003.
http://www.manitobawildlands.org/maps/mb_gen_stations.jpg (accessed February, 2004).

(2004b). Map showing existing and proposed hydro projects based on 1997 Manitoba Treaty Land Entitlement.
http://www.manitobawildlands.org/maps/mb_dams_tle.jpg (accessed February, 2004).

Martini, I. P., Cowell, P. D., and Wickware, G. M. (1980a). Geomorphology of southern James Bay: a low energy emergent coast. In *The Coastline of Canada*, ed. S. B. McCann. Geological Survey of Canada Paper 80-10, pp. 293–301.

Martini, I. P., Morrison, R. I. G., Glooschenko, W. A., and Protz, R. (1980b). Coastal studies in James Bay, Ontario. *Geoscience Canada*, **7**, 11–21.

Maxwell, B. (1992). Arctic climate: potential for change under global warming. In *Arctic Ecosystems in a Changing Climate*, eds. F. S. Chapin, R. L. Jefferies, J. F. Reynolds, G. R. Shaver, and J. Svoboda. Toronto, Canada: Academic Press, pp. 11–34.

Milakovic, B. and Jefferies, R. L. (2003). The effects of goose herbivory and loss of vegetation on ground beetle and spider assemblages in an arctic supratidal marsh. *Ecoscience*, **10**, 57–65.

Milakovic, B., Carleton, T. J., and Jefferies, R. L. (2001). Changes in midge (Diptera: Chironomidae) populations of sub-arctic supratidal vernal ponds in response to goose foraging. *Ecoscience*, **8**, 58–67.

Milko, R. J. (1986). Potential ecological effects of the proposed GRAND Canal diversion project on Hudson and James Bays. *Arctic*, **39**, 316–26.

Morrison, R. I. G. and Harrington, B. A. (1979). Critical shorebird resources in James Bay and eastern North America. In *Transactions of the 44th North American Wildlife and Natural Resources Conference, 1979*. Washington, DC: Wildlife Management Institute, pp. 498–507.

Morrison, R. I. G., Butler, R. W., Dickson, H. L., Bourget, A., Hicklin, P. W., and Goossen, J. P. (1991). *Potential Western Hemisphere Shorebird Reserve Network Sites for Migrant Shorebirds in Canada*. Environment Canada, Canadian Wildlife Service, Technical Report Series 144.

NWWG (National Wetlands Working Group) (1988). *Wetlands of Canada*. Canadian Wildlife Service, Environment Canada, Ecological Land Classification Series 23.

Ontario Hydro (1990). *Providing the Balance of Power. Ontario Hydro's Plan to Serve Customers' Electricity Needs, Demand/Supply Plan Report*. Toronto, Canada: Ontario Hydro.

OMNR (Ontario Ministry of Natural Resources) (1985). *Moosonee District: Background Information*. Toronto, Canada: OMNR.

(1997). News release and fact sheets (February, 1997). Jog Lake Conservation reserve. http://www.mnr.gov.on.ca/MNR/csb/feb27fs97.html (accessed December, 2003).

(2002a). Polar bear (updated November, 2002). http://www.ontarioparks.com/english/pola.html (accessed December, 2003).

(2002b). Protected areas in Northeastern Ontario. http://www.ontarioparks.com/english/northeastmap.html (accessed December, 2003).

(2003). Tidewater (updated June, 2003). http://www.ontarioparks.com/english/tidew.html (accessed December, 2003).

(2004). Your parks (updated January, 2004). http://www.ontarioparks.com/english/yourparks.html (accessed March, 2004).

Ontario Power Generation (2003). Station profiles (updated May, 2003). http://www.opg.com/ops/H_locations.asp (accessed December, 2003).

Pala, S. and Boissonneau, A., (1982). Wetland classification maps for the Hudson Bay lowland. *Naturaliste Canadien*, **109**, 653–9.

Parks Canada (2003a). Wapusk National Park of Canada (updated November, 2003). http://www.parkscanada.pch.gc.ca/pn-np/mb/wapusk/natcul/natcul1a_E.asp (accessed February, 2004).

(2003b). Wapusk National Park of Canada (updated November, 2003). http://www.parkscanada.pch.gc.ca/pn-np/mb/wapusk/natcul/natcul1d_E.asp (accessed February, 2004).

Prinsenberg, S. J. (1982). Present and future circulation and salinity in James Bay. *Naturaliste Canadien*, **109**, 827–41.

Railton, J. B. and Sparling, J. H. (1973). Preliminary studies on the ecology of palsa mounds in northern Ontario. *Canadian Journal of Botany*, **51**, 1037–44.

Riley, J. L. (1982). Hudson Bay Lowland floristic inventory, wetlands catalogue and conservation strategy. *Naturaliste Canadien*, **109**, 543–55.

(1989). *Peat and Peatland Resources of Northeastern Ontario*. Ontario Geological Survey, Miscellaneous Paper 144.

(2003). *Flora of the Hudson Bay Lowland and its Postglacial Origins*. Ottawa, Canada: National Research Council Research Press.

Rimmer, C. (1991). The significance of James Bay to migratory birds. *Northeast Indian Quarterly*, Winter, 35–42.

(1992). James Bay: birds at risk. *American Birds*, **46**, 216–9.

Rockwell, R. F., Witte, C. R., Jefferies, R. L., and Weatherhead, P. J. (2003). Response of nesting Savannah Sparrows to 25 years of habitat change in a Snow Goose colony. *Ecoscience*, **10**, 33–7.

Ross, R. K. (1982). Duck distribution along the James and Hudson Bay coasts of Ontario. *Naturaliste Canadien*, **109**, 927–32.

(1983). An estimate of the Black Scoter, *Melanitta nigra*, population moulting in James and Hudson bays. *Canadian Field-Naturalist*, **97**, 147–50.

Roulet, N., Jano, A., Kelly, C. *et al.* (1994). Role of the Hudson Bay lowland as a source of atmospheric methane. *Journal of Geophysical Research*, **99**, 1439–54.

Rouse, W. R. (1991). Impacts of Hudson Bay on the terrestrial climate of the Hudson Bay lowlands. *Arctic and Alpine Research*, **23**, 24–30.

Rouse, W. R. and Bello, R. L. (1985). Impact of Hudson Bay on the energy balance in the Hudson Bay lowlands and the potential for climatic modification. *Atmosphere and Ocean*, **23**, 375–92.

Rouse, W. R., Holland, S., and Moore, T. R. (1995). Variability in methane emissions from wetlands at northern tree line near Churchill, Manitoba, Canada. *Arctic and Alpine Research*, **27**, 146–56.

Rowe, J. S. (1972). *Forest Regions of Canada*. Canadian Forestry Service Publication 1300.

Scott, P. A., Hansell, R. I. C., and Erickson, W. R. (1993). Influences of wind and snow on northern treeline environments at Churchill, Manitoba, Canada. *Arctic*, **46**, 316–23.

Sergeant, D. E. (1968). Marine life of Hudson Bay. In *Science, History and Hudson Bay*, Ch. 5, eds. C. S. Beals and D. A. Shenstone. Ottawa, Canada: Department of Energy, Mines and Resources, pp. 388–96.

Sims, R. A., Riley, J. L., and Jeglum, J. K. (1979). *Vegetation, Flora and Vegetational Ecology of the Hudson Bay Lowland: a Literature Review and Annotated Bibliography.* Canadian Forestry Service, Information Report O-X-297.

Sims, R. A., Cowell, D. W., and Wickware, G. M. (1982). Classification of fens near southern James Bay, Ontario, using vegetational physiognomy. *Canadian Journal of Botany*, **60**, 2608–23.

Sjörs, H. (1961). *Forest and Peatland at Hawley Lake, Northern Ontario.* Contributions to Botany, 1959. National Museum of Canada Bulletin 171. Ottawa, Canada: National Museum of Canada.

Stirling, I. and Derocher, A. E. (1993). Possible impacts of climatic warming on polar bears. *Arctic*, **46**, 240–5.

Stirling, I., Lunn, N. J., and Iacozza, J. (1999). Long-term trends in the population ecology of polar bears in western Hudson Bay in relation to climatic change. *Arctic*, **52**, 294–306.

Thomas, V. G. and Prevett, J. P. (1982). The roles of the James and Hudson Bay lowland in the annual cycle of geese. *Naturaliste Canadien*, **109**, 913–25.

UNEP World Conservation Monitoring Centre (2003). Protected areas database for Canada.
http://sea.unep-wcmc.org/wdbpa/ (accessed February, 2004).

US House of Representatives (2003). Background information.
http://www.house.gov/resources/106cong/fisheries/99apr15/990415background.htm (accessed December, 2003).

Webber, P. J., Richardson, J. W., and Andrews, J. T. (1970). Post-glacial uplift and substrate age at Cape Henrietta Maria, southeastern Hudson Bay, Canada. *Canadian Journal of Earth Sciences*, **7**, 317–28.

Wetlands International (2003a). A directory of wetlands of international importance: Canada 4CA018 – Polar Bear Provincial Park.
http://www.wetlands.org/RDB/Ramsar_Dir/Canada/CA018D02.htm (accessed December, 2003).

(2003b). A directory of wetlands of international importance: Canada 4CA025 – Southern James Bay (Moose River and Hannah Bay).
http://www.wetlands.org/RDB/Ramsar_Dir/Canada/CA025D02.htm (accessed December, 2003).

Wilson, N. C. and McRae, D. (1993). *Seasonal and Geographical Distribution of Birds for Selected Sites in Ontario's Hudson Bay Lowland.* Ontario Ministry of Natural Resources Report.

World Wildlife Fund (2003). The *Nature Audit. Setting Canada's Conservation Agenda for the 21st Century.* Report 1–2003. Toronto, Ontario: World Wildlife Fund.

Zoltai, S. C. (1973). Vegetation, surficial deposits and permafrost relationships in the Hudson Bay lowland. In *Proceedings of the Symposium on the Physical Environment of the Hudson Bay Lowland, March 30–31, 1973.* Guelph, Canada: University of Guelph, pp. 17–34.

5

The Congo River basin

D. CAMPBELL
Southeastern Louisiana University

The Congo River has the second greatest discharge of any river in the world after the Amazon. It drains 3.7 million km^2 of the African continent. Through its middle course from Boyoma Falls near Kisangani to Malebo Pool at Kinshasa/Brazzaville, the river drops only 115 m over 1740 km as it crosses the *cuvette centrale congolaise*, a vast, shallow depression along the equator in the heart of Africa (Hughes & Hughes 1992). Throughout the *cuvette centrale*, great swamps extend behind the river's levees and along the banks of the numerous tributaries that drain it (Fig. 5.1). These swamps and other wetlands are estimated to cover at least 69 000 km^2 in the Congo and 120 000 km^2 in the Democratic Republic of Congo (D. R. Congo, formerly Zaire; Hughes & Hughes 1992), for a total of *c*. 190 000 km. To put these swamps in perspective, they are larger than the states of Louisiana and Mississippi put together or over four times the size of Switzerland. This makes them the fourth- to fifth-largest area of wetlands in the world.

In contrast with their striking size, these swamps are poorly studied and understood. Older reviews of African wetland ecology hardly mention them (Thompson & Hamilton 1983, Denny 1985). Most of the primary research on the swamps themselves dates from the colonial era and is found in obscure publications in France and Belgium. In recent years, scientists in the Congo, and to a lesser extent the D. R. Congo, have been conducting research in African tropical rain forests, but with apparently little emphasis on swamps.[1]

---

[1] Several bibliographies exist on science and conservation of central African rain forests in general: Job (1994), Institut Royal des Sciences Naturelles de Belgique and Centre d'Echange

---

The World's Largest Wetlands: Ecology and Conservation, eds. L. H. Fraser and P. A. Keddy.
Published by Cambridge University Press. © Cambridge University Press 2005.

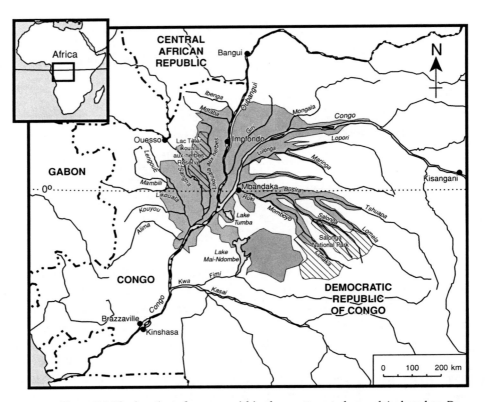

Figure 5.1 The location of swamps within the *cuvette centrale congolaise* based on De Grandi *et al.* (2000b). Areas with a mosaic of swamp and *terra firme* forest are also included. Protected areas are hatched: they include the Salonga National Park in D. R. Congo, which is one of the largest national parks in the world, and the Lac Télé/Likouala-aux-herbes Community Reserve in the Congo.

The Congo basin has had a dark, turbulent history since pre-colonial times (Hochschild 1998, Bobb 1999). The resultant political instability, social unrest, and poor infrastructure may account in part for the scientific inattention. Another great obstacle is the difficult terrain in these swamps. It is easy to understand why they have remained so unexplored. Modern-day explorers recently crossed the Congo basin on foot to the Atlantic Ocean; taking over 15 months to document and bring attention to the unexplored rain forests of this region before they are cleared or lumbered (Quammen & Nichols 2000, 2001a, 2001b). Even so, their progress was so poor in the swamps because of bad terrain that they had to skirt around them. Another telling image of our knowledge of these

d'Informations de la République Démocratique du Congo (1998–2002), Wilkie *et al.* (2001b), Royal Museum for Central Africa (Undated).

swamps is the "Mokele-Mbembe," a 9-m-long sauropod dinosaur reputed to live in the swamps around Lake Télé in northern Congo (Agnagna 1983). The vast, unexplored nature of these swamps gives credence to the suggestion that such a creature might exist beyond the spiritual realm.

Location

Remote sensing has led to the greatest recent advances in our knowledge of the swamps of the *cuvette centrale congolaise*. Previously, vegetation maps only roughly delimited the area of swamps in the region (White 1983). Within the last decade, remote sensing has provided an accurate picture of forest cover in the region. Early efforts failed to distinguish between swamp forests and lowland rain forest because of the resemblance of the two (Mayaux *et al.* 1997a, 1997b, Laporte *et al.* 1998). Recent advances using combinations of satellite imagery have succeeded in identifying swamp forests (De Grandi *et al.* 2000a, Mayaux & Malingreau 2000, Mayaux *et al.* 2000) and can even distinguish between periodically flooded and permanently flooded swamps (De Grandi *et al.* 2000b, Mayaux *et al.* 2002). Although they have yet to be ground-truthed, and the actual area of swamp has not been published, these maps provide a revolutionary glimpse of the extent and location of swamps in central Africa.

The swamps and wetlands of the *cuvette centrale* occur within a vast matrix of lowland rain forest, and both habitats often intermix in a mosaic (Fig. 5.1; De Grandi *et al.* 2000b). To the northwest from the Congo River, wetlands extend in an almost contiguous block to a rather abrupt limit in northern Congo and D. R. Congo. Several river systems slowly drain this area, many of which anastomose near their confluences with the Congo River. Southwest of the Congo River, swamps extend far upstream along rivers but form less of a continuous block and are most often separated from adjacent river systems by terraces of lowland tropical forest. Extensive swamps also occur adjacent to two large shallow lakes south of the Congo River, Lake Tumba, and Lake Mai-Ndombe.

Environmental history

The tropical forests of central Africa, including these swamps, have greatly changed their distribution and extent over recent millennia. They have repeatedly undergone episodes of expansion and contraction since the Middle Pleistocene epoch, around 1.05 Ma (Dupont *et al.* 2001). The underlying climate change was induced by glaciation cycles in higher latitudes. During glacial maxima, central Africa became cooler and more arid (Preuss 1990, Jahns 1996, Maley 1996, Dupont *et al.* 2001), and the tropical forests of the central basin retreated towards the highlands of east and west equatorial Africa. These repeated climate shifts may also be responsible for the relatively low proportion of endemic species in the central parts of the Congo basin as compared with the Cameroon highlands to the west and the Albertine Rift highlands in eastern D. R. Congo, Rwanda, Burundi, and Uganda to the east – which are biodiversity hotspots (Diamond & Hamilton 1980, Kingdon 1989, Sayer *et al.* 1992, Linder 2001, de Klerk *et al.* 2002). However, there is some evidence for a lowland refugium in the central basin during arid glacial periods, based on the present-day distribution of plants and primates (Ndjele 1988, Kingdon 1989, Colyn *et al.* 1991). Swamps appear to have persisted in the lowlands of the *cuvette centrale* through these arid phases but to a greatly reduced extent.

Climate and hydrology

The climate of the *cuvette centrale congolaise* and its hydrology have been well studied. The region has a wet tropical climate and a permanent Atlantic monsoon (Leroux 1983). Mean annual temperatures are 25 to 27 °C, and there is little seasonal change (Bernard 1945, Leroux 1983). Annual rainfall is high; it exceeds 1600 mm throughout the basin and exceeds 2000 mm in the central region over the Momboyo and Busira rivers (Bernard 1945, Bultot 1971, Leroux 1983). Rainfall tends to have a bimodal seasonal pattern throughout the central basin with two wet seasons and two dry seasons, but their timing alternates and their extent changes on either side of the equator (Bultot 1971, Leroux 1983). Annual evaporation is also high as a result of evapotranspiration from the forest cover and direct evaporation from water bodies and swamps. Evaporation is of the order of 1050 mm, which leaves between 600 and 900 mm of water to drain as annual runoff (Bultot 1971).

The hydrological system of the *cuvette centrale congolaise* is complex; it is comprised of the Congo River, the numerous tributaries, and these extensive swamps. The rivers have an extremely low gradient; they drop 3 cm km^{-1} on average in the central basin. Water flows between watersheds during high-water periods and flow can even reverse within water courses (Laraque *et al.* 1998a, 1998b). Furthermore, the pattern of river discharge differs across the *cuvette centrale*. North of the equator, tributaries such as the Oubangui and the Giri show unimodal patterns of discharge with peaks in October and November (Rosenqvist & Birkett 2002), while other tributaries such as the Sangha or the Likouala show bimodal patterns with a lesser peak in May (Laraque *et al.* 1998a, 2001). Southern-hemisphere tributaries have bimodal discharge patterns as they cross the central Congo basin with a peak from November to January and a lesser peak in March to May (Rosenqvist & Birkett 2002). The Congo River itself shows a strong bimodal pattern as a result of the alternating patterns and timing of discharge from either side of the equator.

A major consequence of the bimodal discharge is the low amplitude of water-level fluctuations in the *cuvette centrale congolaise* relative to other tropical river systems. For instance, the Congo River at Mbandaka has an average annual amplitude of 1.8 m; contrast this with up to 15 m at Manaus on the Rio Negro in the Amazon basin (Marlier 1973). Water-level fluctuations are, however, greater along tributaries toward the edges of the *cuvette*. In 1996 for example, the difference between high- and low-water stages on the Congo River at Mbandaka was of the order of 2.5 m, while on the Oubangui near the mouth of the Giri River, it was 5.5 m (Rosenqvist & Birkett 2002).

Soils and water quality

The soils underlying these swamps vary from mineral to organic depending on the deposition of alluvium from rivers, the progression of river meanders across the floodplains, and the accumulation of organic matter, mineral to organic soils underlie these swamps (Evrard 1968). Coarser mineral material accumulates near rivers to forms levees, while finer materials are deposited away from the rivers. However, river meanders shift across the floodplain with time and rework these sediments, thereby creating diverse sediment deposits across floodplains. In the D. R. Congo for instance, wide and active alluvial plains form along the Congo River, the Oubangui, and the Giri (Evrard 1968). Their soils range in texture from coarse sands to clays, often with high organic matter. Along tributaries to the south of the Congo, sands dominate. In backwater areas that remain waterlogged, organic matter accumulates, forming extensive muck and peat deposits. These peat deposits are variable in depth, typically around 1 m deep, but can extend to 17 m (Evrard 1968). Organic deposits are acidic (pH 3.9 to 5.2) with high carbon:nitrogen ratios (C:N = 10) and low exchangeable mineral cations.

Swamps and lakes, as well as the rivers that drain predominantly swamp watersheds, have tea-colored waters with high dissolved organic matter content. Their "black waters" are strongly acidic (pH 3.5 to 5.2), with low conductivity (10 to 140 μS cm^{-1}) and very low mineral content (<1 mg l^{-1}) (Marlier 1958, Dubois 1959, Berg 1961, Matthes 1964, Moukoulou *et al.* 1993, Laraque *et al.* 1998a, 1998b). Where rivers first enter the *cuvette centrale*, their waters have higher pH and mineral content and lower dissolved organic matter content (Probst *et al.* 1992, Moukoulo *et al.* 1993, Laraque *et al.* 1998a). Smaller tributaries mix with waters from swamps and soon become acidified, especially during high-water periods

(Berg 1961). However, the Congo, and major rivers such as the Oubangui, have higher pH and mineral content (Berg 1961, Moukoulou *et al.* 1993).

Vegetation

The botany of these swamp forests is poorly explored (Ndjele 1988, Hughes & Hughes 1992). The swamps are thought to harbour a diverse flora, although they are somewhat poorer in species numbers relative to other African rain forests (Evrard 1968, White 1983). Trees are mostly evergreen and many have adaptations to withstand the prolonged flooding, including stilt roots and pneumatophores (Evrard 1968). The canopies of mature communities are commonly 30 m tall, with emergents reaching 45 m. Lianas and epiphytes are common.

The vegetation of these swamps has only been characterized broadly. The best studies are those of Lebrun and Gilbert (1954) and Evrard (1968), who provide phytosociological syntheses of swamp plant communities in the D. R. Congo, but even they considered their studies to be preliminary. There has been little published work on the swamp vegetation since that time, and no equivalent is available for the Congo, although the swamp vegetation there is similar (Hughes & Hughes 1992).

According to Lebrun & Gilbert (1954), three main ecological factors control the forest vegetation: the water-level variation, including water depth and hydroperiod; the degree of alluvial deposition; and the intensity of dry-season drainage. They identify four general classes of wetland forest in the central basin: (1) pioneer riparian associations; (2) riverine forests; (3) permanently flooded swamp forests; and (4) periodically flooded forest (Table 5.1). The pioneer riparian associations are variable. They occur along rivers and shores, usually in high-energy environments with periodically fast-flowing waters and large water-level fluctuations. The numerous aerial roots and pneumatophores in these pioneer riparian associations help to trap sediments and form land. The second general vegetation class is the riverine forests. They occur in slightly higher, more-stable situations along rivers where flow still occurs, such as on river levees. These riverine forests often flood, but they will drain periodically during low-water periods. Swamp forests form the third major class of vegetation and dominate the *cuvette centrale congolaise*. They occur in stagnant, permanently flooded depressions. The swamp forests are variable in terms of dominant species, ground cover, and canopy height. Finally, there are the periodically inundated forests, which occur higher in the floodplain and are only periodically flooded during high waters. These forests grade slowly into upland *terra firme* forests through extensive transitional areas because of the flatness of the land.

Table 5.1 *Broad vegetation types in swamps of the central Congo basin (from Lebrun & Gilbert 1954, Evrard 1968, and Fay et al. 1989).*

Vegetation type	Landscape position	Hydrology	Substrate	Physiography	Dominant species
Pioneer riparian forests	Along rivers, lakes, and other water bodies; on bars of sand or muck in large rivers; in alluvial deposits of large valleys.	Flooded to wet, often high-energy environments with strong variation in water levels (2–5 m).	Coarser sediments with active deposition. Rapid land-building zones.	Evergreen heliophytic shrubs and small trees with tangled root systems and/or pneumatophores. Several vegetation associations are present. Canopy is 2–5 m tall, but taller in stands of *Raphia sese* (to 15 m) and *Uapaca heudelotii* (10–12 m).	*Alchornea cordifolia, Bridelia spp., Ficus asperifolia, Harungana robynsii, Macaranga lancifolia, Memecylon spp., Parinarium congensis, Raphia spp., Sakersia laurentii, Sesbania sesban, Uapaca heudelotii.*
Riverine forests	Alluvium-depositing river shores; along large islands; in minor flooded valleys.	High water-level variation. Mostly flooded with one or two drained periods per year.	Silt to clay soils; moderate land-building ability.	Multi-layered, mostly evergreen forest, with a 20–25 m canopy. Many epiphytes and lianas. Usually sparse herbaceous layer.	*Cleistopholis patens, Elaeis guineensis Ficus mucuso, Lannea welwitschii, Mimusops warneckei, Octoknema affinis, Oxystigma buchholzii, Pseudospondias microcarpa, Spondianthus preussii var. glaber.*
Permanently flooded swamp forest	Permanently flooded depressional areas in floodplain.	Soils remain saturated. Lacks a drained period.	Peaty to muck soils, but not mineral in nature. Land building by organic matter accumulation only.	Many types of forest. Canopy is often 30–35 m tall with taller emergents. Many canopy gaps occur. Herbaceous layer is important. Many monocots are present. Stilt roots are common, others have pneumatophores.	*Acioa dewevrei, Afromomum angustifolium, Alstonia congensis, Beilschmiedia corbisieri, Bertinia heudelotiana, Coelocaryon botryoides, Diospyros spp., Entandrophragma palustre, Eriocoelum microspermum, Erismadelphus exsul, Garcinia spp., Guibourtia demeusei, Kaoue germainii, Klainedoxa spp., Lasiomorpha senegalensis, Lophira alata, Macaranga spp., Manilkara spp., Mitragyna ciliata, M. stipulosa, Pandanus candelabrum, Raphia spp., Symphonia globulifera, Syzygium guineense var. palustre, Trichilia spp., Uapaca guineensis, Uapaca heudelotii, Xylopia rubescens.*
Periodically flooded forests	Upper floodplain.	Regularly flooded during high water (once or twice per year). Well drained during low-water periods.	Sandy to fine-textured soils. Poor land building ability due to low sediment inputs (some fine matter only).	Relatively low density of trees, but numerous lianas. Canopy reaches 20–25 m with taller emergents. Few herbs. Few monocots.	*Didelotia unifoliolata, Diospyros spp., Garcinia spp., Guibourtia demeusei, Monopetalanthus pteridophyllum, Mitragyna stipulosa, Oubanguia africana, Pachystela longepedicellata, Parinari congensis, Scytopetalum pierreanum, Uapaca spp.*

Non-forested wetlands also occur in the central Congo basin. Wide expanses of wet prairie ocuppy permanently inundated habitats along rivers, such as the lower Likouala, the Likouala-aux-herbes, and the Giri (Hughes & Hughes 1992; De Grandi *et al.* 2000b). Such prairies are dominated by the grasses *Echinochloa pyrimidalis*, *Leersia hexandra*, *Oryza barthii*, and *Vossia cuspidata*, and by large sedges (Hughes & Hughes 1992). These plants root in the mud, but also can form floating rafts along river channels. Along the western edge of the *cuvette centrale congolaise*, patches of open, peaty, boggy steppe and savanna occur; these form a mosaic with swamp forest (Hughes & Hughes 1992). Some of these patches may dry out seasonally and even burn. They include the "*esobes*" near Lake Tumba (Bouillenne *et al.* 1955, Deuse 1960) and the "*bais*" of northern Congo.

Wildlife

The Congo River basin as a whole has the second-most-diverse fish fauna in the world after the Amazon (Welcomme 1979), and this richness is evident within the *cuvette centrale congolaise* (Hughes & Hughes 1992). Several species provide locally important fishery. Diverse aquatic habitats are present: from large rivers to forest streams; from calm oxbows to great shallow lakes; and from open wet prairie to permanent forested swamp (Matthes 1964). During the high-water season, aquatic habitats expand by over 85 000 km^2 as the swamps flood (Hughes & Hughes 1992). With the exception of a few pelagic and benthic species of large rivers and lakes, fish species migrate toward wet prairies and swamps at the start of the flooded seasons in September and October, and to a lesser extent in May to June (Matthes 1964). They enter the swamps and marshes to breed as the waters rise. The fry then use these areas as nursery habitat until the waters recede. Some fish species remain in the permanently flooded swamps all year round, especially those in the families Protopteridae, Clariidae, and Anabantidae (Matthes 1964); they have specialized organs that allow them to breathe air in hypoxic waters.

The herpetofauna of the Congo basin is rich (LeBreton 1998), but it is not well documented in the *cuvette centrale congolaise* (Hughes & Hughes 1992). Many snakes and turtles and three species of crocodile inhabit these swamps, including the endemic African dwarf crocodile *Osteolaemus tetraspis* (Hughes & Hughes 1992, Riley & Huchzermeyer 1999). Mammals have received the greatest research interest, especially the large mammals and primates. According to Hughes and Hughes (1992), large mammals include forest elephant (*Loxodonta africana cyclotis*), hippopotamus (*Hippopotamus amphibius*) along waterways, duikers (*Cephalophus* spp.), dwarf antelope (*Neotragus batesi*), waterbuck (*Kobus ellipsiprymnus*), water chevrotain (*Hyemoschus aquaticus*), forest buffalo (*Syncerus caffer nanus*), bushbuck (*Tragelaphus scriptus, T. spekei*), giant forest hog (*Hylochoerus meinertzhageni*), pangolin (*Manis gigantea, M. tetradactyla*), blotched genet (*Genetta tigrina*), golden cat (*Felis aurata*), and leopard (*Panthera pardus*). Many species of monkeys are found throughout the swamps (*Allenopithecus nigroviridis, Cercocebus* spp., *Cercopithecus* spp., *Colobus* spp., *Miopithecus talapoin*) (Hughes & Hughes 1992). Chimpanzees (*Pan troglodytes*) are found throughout the region, but bonobos (*Pan paniscus*), the rarest of the great apes, are only found south of the Congo River. Bonobos are endemic here and threatened, but populations remain in remote areas such as Salonga National Park (Van Krunkelsven *et al.* 2000, Van Krunkelsven 2001). In contrast, western lowland gorillas (*Gorilla gorilla gorilla*) are only found north of the Congo River, where healthy populations remain in the swamps (Fay *et al.* 1989, Blake *et al.* 1995). Unlike other gorilla populations, they use swamp habitats year-round, especially those habitats with abundant *Raphia* palms.

Human populations

Human populations in the *cuvette centrale congolaise* are low (mostly <25 persons per km^2; Singh *et al.* 1999), and areas dominated by swamp are far more sparsely populated (Hughes & Hughes 1992). Populations are largely restricted to riverside communities as a result of the poor quality of the land for agriculture (Hughes & Hughes 1992). Mbandaka and Impfondo (Fig. 5.1) are the only cities, the remaining communities being smaller towns and villages. Most are Bantu-speaking peoples, although pygmies and related groups are also present (Colchester *et al.* 1998). Pygmies have traditionally led a hunter–gatherer existence in the forests and swamps while maintaining associations with Bantu in riverside communities; however, the traditional pygmy lifestyle is at risk. No data are available for population growth within the *cuvette centrale* itself, but the population of the entire Congo basin (Congo and D. R. Congo, and parts of Central African Republic, Gabon, Cameroon, and Angola) is growing rapidly at a compounded annualized rate of 3.3% since 1960, doubling every 22 years (Singh *et al.* 1999). This is amongst the highest rates of population growth in Africa.

Conservation concerns

The region remains one of the last great regions of wilderness on Earth (Myers *et al.* 2000). The rate of deforestation in tropical Africa – in terms of forest area lost per year – is modest compared with Latin America and southeast Asia (Achard *et al.* 2002), although the high population growth in the region will increase this pressure. The swamps themselves have not experienced much deforestation and remain in a relatively pristine condition (Hughes & Hughes 1992). They are unsuitable for agriculture, although in a number of sites adjacent to the banks of large rivers – where flooding is distinctly seasonal – there are extensive local clearings for rice production (Hughes & Hughes 1992).

Forests in the region are increasingly exploited to satisfy the demand for timber exports. The logging industry has concentrated on a few species in upland habitats (Plouvier 1998, Wilkie *et al.* 2001c). Desirable species are sparsely distributed in the forests, so logging is only practiced on a selective basis. In upland logging concessions in northern Congo, only one tree per 6.6 ha was removed, with an overall reduction of the canopy of less than 7% (Wilkie *et al.* 2001c). This low level of disturbance is not unlike that of natural treefalls. However, it is unclear to what extent swamps and periodically flooded forests are exploited since they pose serious access problems for logging equipment, at least seasonally. Among the dominant trees in these swamps, several species are of potential commercial interest, including *Lophira alata* (azobé), *Mitragyna stipulosa* and *M. ciliata* (abura), *Guibourtia demeusei* (bubinga), *Dyospiros* spp. (African ebony), *Alstonia congensis*, *Symphonia globulifera*, *Uapaca* spp., and *Berlinia* spp. (Chudnoff 1984). In upland habitats, companies do not practice any sustainable forestry practices and simply move on once a logging concession is depleted (Plouvier 1998). Therefore, once the upland forests have been high-graded of desirable species, swamps and periodically flooded forests may become attractive to logging companies, despite access problems.

The biggest impact of logging is not deforestation, but defaunation (Plouvier 1998, Wilkie *et al.* 2000, 2001c, Fa *et al.* 2002). The logging-road network greatly increases the ability of hunters to enter the forests and hunt. What was once a three- to four-day trip for a hunter on foot is now a single-day event on logging roads with vehicles (Wilkie *et al.* 2001c). Some 24 species, mostly monkeys and small ungulates, have been recorded as bushmeat in northern Congo (Wilkie *et al.* 2001c). Logging camps and the fast-growing urban centers provide a ready market for bushmeat, where it is an important protein source (Trefon 1998, Wilkie *et al.* 2001c). The extraction rate of bushmeat is 2.4 times that of the production rate in the central Congo (Fa *et al.* 2002). These pressures are unsustainable, and commercial hunters eventually deplete logging concessions and adjacent lands. It is unclear to what extent different habitats, such as periodically flooded forests and permanent swamps, escape these hunting pressures. Gorillas in swamp habitats are now more common at greater distances from roads (Blake *et al.* 1995).

Future construction of dams and hydroelectric development pose threats to African fresh waters in general (Welcomme 2003), including tributaries that feed the *cuvette centrale congolaise* (Chapman & Chapman 2003). Besides blocking fish movement, the main impact of dams to wetlands is to prevent the regular inundation of floodplains downstream (Welcomme 2003), which would disrupt the hydroperiods and the distribution of sediments and nutrients in these swamps.

Other resource-extraction activities may have future consequences on swamp habitats. The Congo basin in general has great potential for mining (Moody 1998), but little information is available on the prospects in the central basin. This is not the case for oil and gas. The outlook for oil and gas in the central Congo basin is promising (Lawrence & Mbungu-Makazu 1988). Oil and gas exploration and exploitation may have a significant impact on swamp communities in the coming years.

Recent civil war in the D. R. Congo and the Congo has had serious environmental consequences in the central Congo basin. In the short term, civil war may limit the exploitation of timber and mineral resources in this region; however, the availability of automatic weapons over the past decade has dramatically escalated the hunting of wildlife, including apes, in part to feed guerrilla armies (Dudley et al. 2002). The poaching of elephants for ivory has also increased in regions of conflict as a consequence of the weaponry and lawlessness (Van Krunkelsven et al. 2000, Vogel 2000, Dudley et al. 2002). Over the longer term, even once the fighting is over, lasting political instability may impede the sustainable exploitation of resources in the central basin and the efforts to conserve its biodiversity (Dudley et al. 2002).

Several national parks and reserves with swamp habitats have been established in the central Congo basin. In the D. R. Congo, Salonga National Park was created in 1970 in the central basin (Fig. 5.1) (UNEP World Conservation Monitoring Centre 2001). At 36 000 km^2 in size, it remains one of the largest parks in the world and is a World Heritage Site. It is mostly *terra firme* forest, but wide stretches of swamp habitat occur in the park along the Salonga and Luilaka rivers. In the Congo, the Lac Télé/Likouala-aux-herbes Community Reserve was established in 1998 and covers 4389 km^2, almost exclusively wetland habitat (Frazier 2002). It is designated as a RAMSAR Wetland of International Importance (Frazier 2002).

Although these parks exist on paper, in practice they fall far below any conservation ideal. Protected areas in the Congo basin are severely under-financed and neglected (Wilkie et al. 2001a). Salonga National Park was in the front line during the recent civil war (Vogel 2000). Gangs of poachers with automatic weapons controlled the rivers and hunted bonobos and elephants (Van Krunkelsven 2001). Logging and the clearing of land along access roads also remain a problem in the Salonga (UNEP World Conservation Monitoring Centre 2001). The situation in the Congo is perhaps more stable; yet bushmeat hunting and the illegal burning of floodplains remain serious problems in the Lac Télé/Likouala-aux-herbes Reserve (Wildlife Conservation Society 2001).

Concluding remarks

The swamps of the central Congo basin are vast and relatively pristine wetlands in the heart of the African tropical rain forest. However, the numerous references cited in this review are misleading and lie in striking contrast to the paucity of primary research from these swamps. They remain largely unexplored. Our lack of knowledge will remain a handicap for the long-term management of these swamps. Rapid population growth, underdevelopment, and regional conflict will place increasing pressure on the integrity of these swamps over the coming decades. Considering their vast extent; their rich biodiversity; their importance to local economies for supporting fisheries, hunting, and logging; and the threats they face, they deserve far-more attention from the scientific community.

From another perspective, these swamps present a great opportunity. They remain relatively undisturbed, so it is not too late to develop sound plans for their management and conservation. From this perspective, there are two opportunities. As a result of their vast size and relatively contiguous extent, they form a vast nucleus for the conservation of lowland tropical forests in central Africa. Secondly, by their very nature, they are not easily accessible to humans, and as such, they may escape the land clearance occuring in surrounding *terra firme* forests. Conservation planning efforts should build upon these strengths. The Congolese governments, in cooperation with each other and the international community, should place these strengths at the center of planning efforts for the management and conservation of lowland tropical forests in the Congo basin.

Acknowledgements

This chapter would not have been possible without support from the Schleider Chair for Environmental Studies at Southeastern Louisiana University.

References

Achard, F., Eva, H. D., Stibig, H.-J. *et al.* (2002). Determination of deforestation rates of the world's humid tropical forests. *Science*, **297**, 999–1002.

Agnagna, M. (1983). Results of the first Congolese Mokele-Mbembe expedition. *Cryptozoology*, **2**, 103–12.

Berg, A. (1961). *Rôle écologique des eaux de la Cuvette congolaise sur la croissance de la jacinthe d'eau [Eichhornia crassipes (Mart.) Solms].* Académie Royale des Sciences d'Outre-mer, Classe des sciences naturelles et médicales, Mémoire in-8°, Nouvelle série 12, pp. 1–120.

Bernard, É. (1945). *Le climat écologique de la cuvette centrale congolaise.* Bruxelles, Belgium: Institut National pour l'Etude Agronomique du Congo Belge.

Blake, S., Rogers, E., Fay, M. J., Ngangoué, M., and Ebeké, G. (1995). Swamp gorillas in northern Congo. *African Journal of Ecology,* **33**, 285–90.

Bobb, F. S. (1999). *Historical Dictionary of Democratic Republic of the Congo (Zaire).* Lanham, MD: The Scarecrow Press.

Bouillenne, R., Moureau, J., and Deuse, P. (1955). *Esquisse écologique des faciès forestiers et marécageux des bords du lac Tumba (Domaine de l'I.R.S.A.C., Mabali, Congo belge).* Académie Royale des Sciences coloniales, Classe des sciences naturelles et médicales, Mémoires in-8°, Nouvelle série 3, pp. 1–120.

Bultot, F. (1971). *Atlas climatique du bassin congolais,* vol. 2, *Les composantes du bilan d'eau.* Bruxelles, Belgium: Institut National pour l'Etude Agronomique au Congo.

Chapman, L. J. and Chapman, C. A. (2003). Fishes of the African rain forests: emerging and potential threats to a little-known fauna. In *Conservation, Ecology, and Management of African Fresh Waters,* eds. T. L. Crissman, L. J. Chapman, C. A. Chapman, and L. S. Kaufman. Gainesville, FL: University Press of Florida, pp. 176–209.

Chudnoff, M. (1984). *Tropical Timbers of the World.* Madison: US Department of Agriculture, Forest Service. http://128.104.77.230/TechSheets/tropicalwood.html (accessed February 2005).

Colchester, M., Jackson, D., and Kendrick, J. (1998). Forest peoples of the Congo basin: past exploitation, present threats and future prospects. In *The Congo Basin, Human and Natural Resources,* eds. C. Beselink and P. Sips. Amsterdam, the Netherlands: Netherlands Committee for IUCN, pp. 53–63.

Colyn, M., Gauthier-Hyon, A., and Verheyen, W. (1991). A re-appraisal of palaeoecological history in Central Africa: evidence for a major fluvial refuge in the Zaire basin. *Journal of Biogeography,* **18**, 403–7.

De Grandi, G. F., Mayaux, P., Malingreau, J.-P. (2000a). New perspectives on global ecosystems from wide-area radar mosaics: flooded forest mapping in the tropics. *International Journal of Remote Sensing,* **21**, 1235–49.

De Grandi, G. F., Mayaux, P., Rauste, Y. *et al.* (2000b). The Global Rain Forest Mapping Project JERS-1 radar mosaic of tropical Africa: development and product characterization aspects. *IEEE Transactions on Geoscience and Remote Sensing,* **38**, 2218–33.

de Klerk, H. M., Crowe, T. M., Fjeldså, J., and Burgess, N. D. (2002). Patterns of species richness and narrow endemism of terrestrial bird species in the Afrotropical region. *Journal of Zoology,* **256**, 327–42.

Denny, P. (ed.) (1985). *The Ecology and Management of African Wetland Vegetation: a Botanical Account of African Swamps and Shallow Waterbodies.* Dordrecht, the Netherlands: Junk.

Deuse, P. (1960). *Etude écologique et phytosociologique de la végétation des Esobe de la région est du lac Tumba (Congo belge)*. Académie Royale des Sciences d'Outre-Mer, Classe des sciences naturelles et médicales, Mémoires in-8°, Nouvelle série 11, pp. 1–44.

Diamond, A. W. and Hamilton, A. C. (1980). The distribution of forest passerine birds and Quaternary climatic change in tropical Africa. *Journal of Zoology, London*, **191**, 379–402.

Dubois, T. (1959). Note sur le chimie des eaux du Lac Tumba. *Académie Royale des Sciences d'Outre-Mer, Bulletin des Séances*, **6**, 1321–34.

Dudley, J. P., Ginsberg, J. R., Plumptre, A. J., Hart, J. A., and Campos, L. C. (2002). Effects of war and civil strife on wildlife and wildlife habitats. *Conservation Biology*, **16**, 319–29.

Dupont, L. M., Donner, B., Schneider, R., and Wefer, G. (2001). Mid-Pleistocene environmental change in tropical Africa began as early as 1.05 Ma. *Geology*, **29**, 195–8.

Evrard, C. (1968). *Recherches écologiques sur le peuplement forestier des sols hydromorphes de la cuvette centrale congolaise*. Série scientifique 110. Bruxelles, Belgium: Institut National pour l'Etude Agronomique au Congo.

Fa, J. E., Peres, C. A., and Meeuwig, J. (2002). Bushmeat exploitation in tropical forests: an intercontinental comparison. *Conservation Biology*, **16**, 232–7.

Fay, J. M., Agnagna, M., Moore, J., and Oko, R. (1989). Gorillas (*Gorilla gorilla gorilla*) in the Likouala swamp forests of north central Congo: preliminary data on populations and ecology. *International Journal of Primatology*, **10**, 477–86.

Frazier, S. (ed.) (2002). A Directory of Wetlands of International Importance. Ramsar Convention Bureau and Wetlands International. http://www.wetlands.org/RDB/Ramsar_Dir/1_Introduction/Introduction.htm#title (accessed February, 2005).

Hochschild, A. (1998). *King Leopold's Ghost: a Story of Greed, Terror, and Heroism in Colonial Africa*. Boston, MA: Houghton Mifflin.

Hughes, R. H. and Hughes, J. S. (1992). *A Directory of African Wetlands*. Gland Switzerland and Cambridge, UK: International Union for the Conservation of Nature and Natural Resources (IUCN).

Institut Royal des Sciences Naturelles de Belgique and Centre d'Echange d'Informations de la République Démocratique du Congo (1998–2002). Etat de la diversité biologique en République Démocratique du Congo: Bibliographie. http://bch-cbd.naturalsciences.be/congodr/cdr-fra/contribution/monographie/biblio.htm (accessed February, 2005).

Jahns, S. (1996). Vegetation history and climate changes in West Equatorial Africa during the late Pleistocene and Holocene, based on a marine pollen diagram from the Congo fan. *Vegetation History and Archaeobotany*, **5**, 207–13.

Job, D. A. (1994). Global climate change, natural resources management and biodiversity conservation in the Congo Basin: preliminary literature review. http://carpe.umd.edu/products/PDF_files/Biblio-Job.pdf (accessed February, 2005).

Kingdon, J. (1989). *Island Africa: the Evolution of Africa's Rare Animals and Plants*. Princeton, NJ: Princeton University Press.

Laporte, N. T., Goetz, S. J., Justice, C. O., and Heinicke, M. (1998). A new land cover map of central Africa derived from multi-resolution, multi-temporal AVHRR data. *International Journal of Remote Sensing*, **19**, 3537–50.

Laraque, A., Mietton, M., Olivry, J. C., and Pandi, A. (1998a). Influences des couvertures lithologiques et végétales sur les régimes et la qualité des eaux des affluents congolais du fleuve Congo. *Revue des Sciences de l'Eau*, **11**, 209–24.

Laraque, A., Poyaud, B., Rocchia, R. *et al.* (1998b). Origin and function of a closed depression in equatorial humid zones: the Lake Télé in North Congo. *Journal of Hydrology*, **207**, 236–53.

Laraque, A., Mahé, G., Orange, D., and Marieu, B. (2001). Spatiotemporal variations in hydrological regimes within Central Africa during the XXth century. *Journal of Hydrology*, **245**, 104–17.

Lawrence, S. R. and Mbungu-Makazu, M. (1988). Zaire's central basin: prospectivity outlook. *Oil and Gas Journal*, **86**, 105–8.

LeBreton, M. (1998). A brief overview of the herpetofauna of the Congo Basin region. In *The Congo Basin, Human and Natural Resources*, eds. C. Beselink and P. Sips. Amsterdam, the Netherlands: Netherlands Committee for IUCN, pp. 31–41.

Lebrun, L. and Gilbert, G. (1954). *Une classification écologique des forêts du Congo*. INEAC Série 63. Bruxelles, Belgium: Institut National pour l'Etude Agronomique au Congo.

Leroux, M. (1983). *Le climat de l'Afrique tropicale*. Paris: Editions Champions.

Linder, H. P. (2001). Plant diversity and endemism in sub-Saharan tropical Africa. *Journal of Biogeography*, **28**, 169–82.

Maley, J. (1996). The African rain forest – main characteristics of changes in vegetation and climate from the Upper Cretaceous to the Quaternary. *Proceedings of the Royal Society of Edinburgh*, **104B**, 31–73.

Marlier, G. (1958). Recherches hydrobiologiques au lac Tumba. *Hydrobiologia*, **10**, 352–85.

(1973). Limnology of the Congo and Amazon rivers. In *Tropical Forest Systems in Africa and South America: a Comparative Review*, eds. B. J. Meggers, E. S. Ayensu, and W. D. Duckworth. Washington, DC: Smithsonian Institution, pp. 223–8.

Matthes, H. (1964). *Les poissons du Lac Tumba et de la région d'Ikela: études systématique, écologique et zoogéographique*. Tervuren, Belgium: Musée Royal de l'Afrique Centrale.

Mayaux, P. and Malingreau, J.-P. (2000). Le couvert forestier d'Afrique centrale: un nouvel état des lieux. *Bulletin des Séances de l'Académie Royale des Sciences d'Outre-Mer*, **46**, 475–86.

Mayaux, P., Janodet, E., Blair-Myers, C. M., and Legeay-Janvier, P. (1997a). *Vegetation Map of Central Africa at 1:5 000 000*. TREES Series D, no. 1. Ispra, Italy: Space Applications Institute, Joint Research Centre, European Commission.

Mayaux, P., Richards, T., and Janodet, E. A. (1997b). A vegetation map of Central Africa derived from satellite imagery. *Journal of Biogeography*, **26**, 353–66.

Mayaux, P., De Grandi, G., and Malingreau, J.-P. (2000). Central Africa forest cover revisited: a multisatellite analysis. *Remote Sensing of Environment*, **71**, 183–96.

Mayaux, P., De Grandi, G. F., Rauste, Y., Simard, M., and Saatchi, S. (2002). Large-scale vegetation maps derived from the combined L-band GRFM and C-band CAMP wide area radar mosaics of Central Africa. *International Journal of Remote Sensing,* **23**, 1261–82.

Moody, R. (1998). *The Congo Basin.* The Netherlands: IUCN (World Conservation Union).

Moukolo, N., Laraque, A., Olivry, J. C., and Bricquet, J. P. (1993). Transport en solution et en suspension par le fleuve Congo (Zaïre) et ses principaux affluents de la rive droite. *Hydrological Sciences,* **38**, 133–45.

Myers, N., Mittermeier, R. A., Mittermeier, C. G., Da Fonseca, G. A. B., and Kent, J. (2000). Biodiversity hotspots for conservation priorities. *Nature,* **403**, 853–8.

Ndjele, M. (1988). Principales distributions obtenues par l'analyse factorielle des éléments phytogéographiques présumés endémiques dans la flore du Zaïre. *Monographs in Systematic Botany from the Missouri Botanical Garden,* **25**, 631–8.

Plouvier, D. (1998). The situation of tropical moist forests and forest management in Central Africa and markets for African timber. In *The Congo Basin, Human and Natural Resources,* eds. C. Beselink and P. Sips. Amsterdam, the Netherlands: Netherlands Committee for IUCN, pp. 100–9.

Preuss, J. (1990). L'évolution des paysages du basin intérieur du Zaire pendant les quarantes dernières millénaires. In *Paysages quaternaires de l'Afrique Centrale Atlantique,* eds. R. Lanfranchi and D. Schwartz. Paris: Editions de l'ORSTOM, pp. 260–70.

Probst, J. L., Nkounkou, R. R., Krempp, G. *et al.* (1992). Dissolved major elements exported by the Congo and the Ubangui rivers during the period 1987–1989. *Journal of Hydrology,* **135**, 237–57.

Quammen, D. and Nichols, M. (2000). Megatransect: across 1,200 miles of untamed Africa on foot. *National Geographic,* **198**(4), 2–29.

(2001a). Megatransect II: the green abyss. *National Geographic,* **199**(3), 2–37.

(2001b). Megatransect III: end of the line. *National Geographic,* **200**(2), 74–103.

Riley, J. and Huchzermeyer, F. W. (1999). African dwarf crocodiles in the Likouala Swamp forests of the Congo basin: habitat, density, and nesting. *Copeia,* **2**, 313–20.

Rosenqvist, Å. and Birkett, C. M. (2002). Evaluation of JERS-1 SAR mosaics for hydrological applications in the Congo River basin. *International Journal of Remote Sensing,* **23**, 1283–1302.

Royal Museum for Central Africa (Undated). Publications. http://www.africamuseum.be/publications (accessed February, 2005).

Sayer, J. A., Harcourt, C. S., and Collins, N. M. (1992). *The Conservation Atlas of Tropical Forests: Africa.* Basingstoke, UK: Macmillan.

Singh, A., Dieye, A., and Finco, M. (1999). Assessing environmental conditions of major river basins in Africa as surrogates for watershed health. *Ecosystem Health,* **5**, 264–74.

Thompson, K. and Hamilton, A. C. (1983). Peatlands and swamps of the African continent. In *Ecosystems of the World, vol. 4B: Mires: Swamp, Bog, Fen and Moor,* ed. A. J. P. Gore. Amsterdam, the Netherlands: Elsevier Science, pp. 331–73.

Trefon, T. (1998). Urban threats to biodiversity in the Congo basin. In *The Congo Basin, Human and Natural Resources*, eds. C. Beselink and P. Sips. Amsterdam, the Netherlands: Netherlands Committee for IUCN, pp. 89–99.

UNEP World Conservation Monitoring Centre (2001). Salonga National Park. http://www.unep-wcmc.org/protected_areas/data/wh/salonga.html (accessed February, 2005).

Van Krunkelsven, E. (2001). Density estimation of bonobos (*Pan paniscus*) in Salonga National Park, Congo. *Biological Conservation*, **99**, 387–91.

Van Krunkelsven, E., Bila-Isia, I., and Draulans, D. (2000). A survey of bonobos and other large mammals in the Salonga National Park, Democratic Republic of Congo. *Oryx*, **34**, 180–7.

Vogel, G. (2000). Conflict in Congo threatens bonobos and rare gorillas. *Science*, **287**, 2386–7.

Welcomme, R. L. (1979). *Fisheries Ecology of Floodplain Rivers*. London: Longman.
    (2003). River fisheries in Africa: their past, present, and future. In *Conservation, Ecology, and Management of African Fresh Waters*, eds. T. L. Crissman, L. J. Chapman, C. A. Chapman, and L. S. Kaufman. Gainesville, FL: University Press of Florida, pp. 145–75.

White, F. (1983). *The Vegetation of Africa: a Descriptive Memoir to Accompany the UNESCO/AETFAT/UNSO Vegetation Map of Africa*. Paris: UNESCO.

Wildlife Conservation Society (2001). Lac Télé Reserve conservation and management. http://www.wcs-congo.org/lacres.htm (accessed October, 2003).

Wilkie, D., Shaw, E., Rotberg, F., Morelli, G., and Auzel, P. (2000). Roads, development, and conservation in the Congo basin. *Conservation Biology*, **14**, 1614–22.

Wilkie, D. S., Carpenter, J. F., and Zhang, Q. (2001a). The under-financing of protected areas in the Congo Basin: so many parks and so little willingness-to-pay. *Biodiversity and Conservation*, **10**, 691–709.

Wilkie, D. S., Hakizumwami, E., Gami, N., and Difara, B. (2001b). Beyond boundaries: regional overview of transboundary natural resource management in Central Africa. In *Beyond Boundaries: Transboundary Natural Resource Management in Central Africa*. Washington, DC: Biodiversity Support Program. http://www.worldwildlife.org/bsp/publications/africa/125/125/titlepage.HTML (accessed February, 2005).

Wilkie, D. S., Sidle, J. G., Boundzanga, G. C., Auzel, P., and Blake, S. (2001c). Defaunation, not deforestation: commercial logging and market hunting in northern Congo. In *The Cutting Edge: Conserving Wildlife in Logged Tropical Forest*, eds. R. A. Fimbel, A. A. Grajal, and J. G. Robinson. New York: Columbia University Press, pp. 375–99.

6

The Mackenzie River basin

D. H. VITT
Southern Illinois University

L. A. HALSEY
University of Alberta

B. J. NICHOLSON
Central Connecticut State University

Introduction

In Canada, wetlands are defined as ". . . land that is saturated with water long enough to promote wetland or aquatic processes as indicated by poorly drained soils, hydrophytic vegetation, and various kinds of biological activity which are adapted to a wet environment." (National Wetlands Working Group 1988). The environmental processes that control wetland development form hydrological, chemical, and biotic gradients and commonly have strong cross-correlations. These interrelated gradients have been divided into five nodes that define Canada's wetland classes, of which three classes are non-peat-forming wetlands generally having <40 cm of accumulated organics and two classes are peatlands with >40 cm of accumulated organics. Non-peat-forming wetlands are subdivided into: (1) shallow open waters, (2) marshes, or (3) swamps; whereas peatlands can be subdivided into: (1) fens or (2) bogs (Fig. 6.1).

Non-peat-forming wetlands have a poorly developed bryophyte layer, which results from strong seasonal water-level fluctuations and high vascular plant production (Campbell *et al.* 2000). Peat accumulation is limited however, as decomposition rates are high. This situation is in contrast to the swamps and marshes found in more-temperate regions of the globe where peat accumulation can occur.

The World's Largest Wetlands: Ecology and Conservation, eds. L. H. Fraser and P. A. Keddy.
Published by Cambridge University Press. © Cambridge University Press 2005.

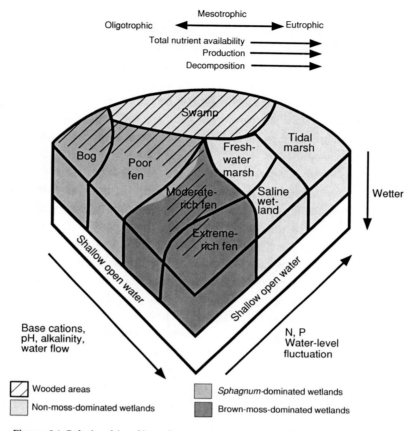

Figure 6.1 Relationship of bog, fen, marsh, swamp, and shallow open-water wetland classes to major chemical, biotic, and hydrological gradients. Fens and marshes are subdivided into several wetland forms in order to illustrate the pattern of variability of these classes. Saline wetlands may be either fens or marshes (modified from Zoltai & Vitt 1995).

Peatlands differ from non-peat-forming wetlands by a combination of inter-related hydrological, chemical, and biotic factors that results in a decrease in decomposition relative to plant production and therefore allows for the accumulation of peat. The stabilization of seasonal water levels and restriction of water flow through a wetland allows the establishment and development of a bryophyte layer. The stabilization of regional water tables appears to have been an important component of the successional change from prairie marshes to boreal fens in the western interior of Canada over the past 10 000 years (Zoltai & Vitt 1990).

The establishment of a bryophyte layer results in the accumulation and maintenance of nutrients in a non-available form which reduces vascular plant production. Stabilized water levels, anaerobic conditions, and decreased nutrient
availability lead to a substantial decrease in decomposition rates; this results
in the development of peat-accumulating ecosystems. Biotic (*Sphagnum* presence) and chemical (decomposition processes) factors lead to acidification and
oligotrophication. Canadian peatlands are classified into geogenous fens and
ombrogenous bogs, each with distinctive indicator species, acidity, alkalinity,
and base-cation content (Fig. 6.1).

Fens are geogenous ecosystems that are affected by mineral soil waters
(ground and/or surface) that may be relatively rich in mineral elements. In the
Mackenzie River Basin, most fens are bicarbonate dominated, with calcium as
the major cation. Fens can be classified into three types based on hydrology:
soligenous and largely influenced by flowing surface water; topogenous and
largely influenced by stagnant groundwater; or limnogenous and largely influenced by associated lakes and ponds. All three fen types have water levels at
or near the surface. Soligenous fens commonly have discrete patterns of open
pools (flarks) alternating with elongated shrubby to wooded ridges (strings) oriented perpendicular to the direction of surface-water flow. These patterned fens
may be either acidic or basic. Topogenous, limnogenous, and some soligenous
fens are non-patterned. Fens can be open and dominated by *Carex*, *Scirpus*, and
Eriophorum; shrubby and dominated by *Salix* and *Betula*; or wooded to forested
and dominated by some combination of *Picea mariana*, *Larix laricina*, *Betula*, and
Salix.

Originally based on criteria derived from vegetation, fens were subdivided
on the basis of the number of indicator species present. Poor fens are poor in
indicator species, while extreme-rich fens are rich in indicator species; moderate-
rich fens are intermediate. This gradient of indicator species correlates with a
chemical gradient (Sjörs 1952). Poor fens are acid (pH 4.5 to 5.5), poor in base
cations, and have no or little alkalinity. They are dominated by oligotrophic and
mesotrophic species of *Sphagnum*. Moderate-rich fens have slightly acid to neutral
pH (5.5 to 7.0) and low to moderate alkalinity with a ground layer dominated by
brown mosses – namely *Drepanocladus*, *Brachythecium mildeanum*, and *Calliergonella
cuspidata* – and low abundance of mesotrophic species of *Sphagnum*. Extreme-
rich fens have basic pH (above 7.0), high concentrations of base cations, and
high alkalinity. They are characterized by species of *Drepanocladus*, *Scorpidium
scorpioides*, and *Campylium stellatum* and may also have marl deposits.

Bogs are ombrogenous peatlands that receive their water only from precipitation and have low water flow. The water table is generally 40 to 60 cm below
the surface. Bogs are acidic ecosystems with pH below 4.5; they are poor in

base cations, and have little or no alkalinity. Bogs are dominated by: oligo-trophic species of *Sphagnum*, i.e. *S. fuscum*, *S. magellanicum*, and *S. angustifolium*; the feather mosses *Pleurozium schreberi* and *Hylocomium splendens*; and lichens of the genera *Cladonia* and *Cladina*. They may be open, wooded, or forested with trees almost exclusively limited to *Picea mariana*. Bogs occur as plateaus in con-tinental regions and as domes in more-humid regions. Comparing the surface-water temperatures of bogs and fens, bogs have the lowest temperatures (Vitt *et al.* 1995); this is a result of minimal water flow, relatively low water table, and higher insulating capacity due to the low thermal conductivity of *Sphagnum*. Permafrost consequently, is generally restricted to bogs at its southern limit, where the permafrost forms peat plateaus and palsas (Vitt *et al.* 1994), with the percentage of permafrost cover related to mean annual temperature (Halsey *et al.* 1995).

Wetlands represent a valuable economic and environmental resource capable of serving many purposes, including the supply of raw material for horticultural peat products, sorbents, energy generation, forestry, and industrial chemical pro-duction, in addition to acting as areas for consumptive and non-consumptive recreation. Wetlands in Canada have been used for sewage treatment and water filtration, as well as for agricultural water supply and as areas for land reclama-tion. Some wetlands can play a role in commercial fisheries, aquaculture, and wild-rice harvesting. Wetlands act as flow stabilizers and attenuaters, and buffer against wave-induced erosion along coastlines. Wetland ecosystems have impor-tant economic and environmental resource capabilities; these two factors can generate conflicts when development is being considered. In addition to these conflicts, wetlands provide essential habitat for rare, threatened, and endangered species; they are diverse habitats that often have a higher biodiversity than sur-rounding uplands (Shay 1981). Although visible waterfowl and large and small mammal populations are often cited as reasons for wetland protection, wetland invertebrate biodiversity can be extremely high and also in need of protection. One recent study documents 2181 species of arthropods in a small fen area in western Canada (Finnamore 1994).

The Mackenzie River Basin Wetland Complex (MRBWC), especially bogs, pro-vides critical habitat for caribou (Bradshaw *et al.* 1995, Anderson 1999) and sus-tains populations of moose, black bear, and deer. Although wetlands are often viewed as wastelands, their crucial role in the environment requires responsible management to safeguard the endowment for present and future generations. Stewardship must balance and integrate environmental and economic decisions, in addition to restoring already damaged or degraded wetlands through coopera-tive initiatives between provincial, federal, and international government bodies; public interest groups; and aboriginal peoples.

Understanding the type and distribution of wetlands in a region and the relationship of those wetlands to regional and local climatic and physiographical parameters provides the first step towards developing responsible management strategies. This chapter will examine the type and distribution of wetlands in one of the largest and most-diverse northern wetland complexes in the world: the Mackenzie River Basin Wetland Complex.

Distribution

The MRBWC is located almost exclusively within the Mackenzie River Basin of northern Canada. The vast majority of wetlands within the complex are peatlands and thus the MRBWC is defined here as a large, nearly contiguous area that contains ≥30% peatland cover (Fig. 6.2). While we have detailed inventories on peatland distribution by type for south of 60° N latitude and east of 120° W longitude (Vitt *et al.* 1996, D. H. Vitt and L. A. Halsey unpublished data), for the remainder of the MRBWC peatland distributions have been largely determined from other sources. These sources include soil surveys, terrain inventory maps, and biophysical reports – with summaries available (Maynard 1988, Tarnocai *et al.* 1999). We estimate that the MRBWC supports roughly $166\,300 \pm 10\,200$ km^2 of peatlands, with a 10% error estimate assigned to distributions from north of 60° N latitude and west of 120° W longitude. Thus, the MRBWC represents one of the largest northern wetland complexes in the world.

The MRBWC spans a latitudinal gradient of approximately 1125 km, greater than any other global peatland complex, including the largest: the Vasyugan Peatland Mosiac of western Siberia (see Botch & Masing 1983). Due to its extensive latitudinal gradient the MRBWC supports a wide variety of peat landform types, and different peat landforms are characteristically found in different parts of the basin.

Wetland landform types: bogs

Bogs develop in areas of restricted surface-water flow and are found along drainage divides within the MRBWC, in stagnation zones created in association with surface-water-flow obstructions, and within basins. The presence or absence of patterned ground, forest cover, permafrost, and internal lawns subdivides bog types.

Polygonal, open permafrost bogs

Polygonal, open permafrost bogs have no tree cover, though individuals of *Picea mariana* may occur as low, wind-blasted krumholz. Polygonal, open

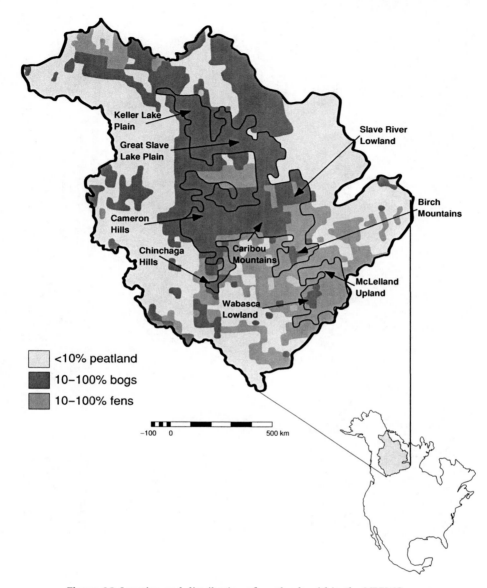

Figure 6.2 Location and distribution of peatlands within the MRBWC.

permafrost bogs are elevated above the surrounding non-permafrost peatland by about 1 m, and as such are similar to wooded permafrost bogs. Unlike wooded permafrost bogs, these peat landforms are characterized by a series of criss-crossed trenches that support a wedge of nearly pure ice that extends down-wards for several meters. Trenches form a polygon surface pattern (Fig. 6.3A) typical of other types of patterned ground associated with permafrost.

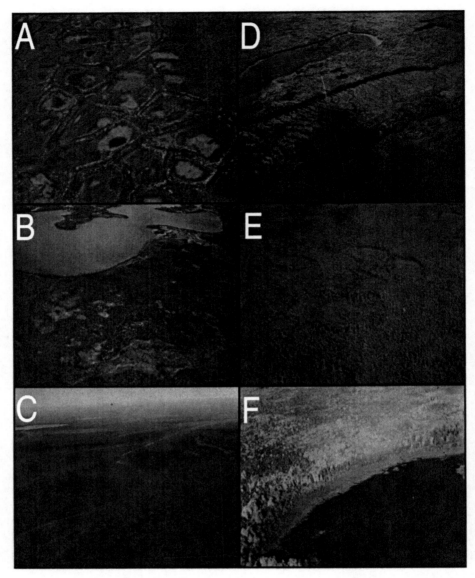

Figure 6.3 Aerial views of wetlands from the MRBWC. (A) Aerial view of a polygonal, open permafrost bog from 65° N and 123° W within the northern part of the MRBWC. Photo by S. Zoltai. (B) Aerial view of wooded permafrost bog with non-patterned open fens (collapse scars) from 58° N and 113° W within the central part of the MRBWC. Photo by D. Vitt. (C) Aerial view of non-permafrost bogs with internal lawns occurring as islands within non-patterned treed, shrubby, and open fens from 56° N and 113° W within the southern part of the MRBWC. Photo by D. Vitt. (D) Aerial view of a wooded non-permafrost bog without internal lawns in the background and patterned fen in the foreground from 57° N and 111° W within the southern part of the MRBWC. Photo by D. Vitt. (E) Aerial view of a non-patterned wooded fen with internal lawns from 56° N and 113° W within the southern part of the MRBWC. Photo by L. Halsey. (F) Aerial view of a non-peat-accumulating wetland from 56° N and 113° W within the southern part of the MRBWC. Photo by L. Halsey.

Polygonal, open permafrost bogs are restricted in their distribution to the northern part of the MRBWC. As such they are found on the Great Slave and Keller Lake Plain (Zoltai & Tarnocai 1975).

Non-patterned, open permafrost bogs (veneer bogs) with or without collapse scars

Non-patterned, open permafrost bogs have a scanty tree cover (generally <6%) and may contain circular to irregularly shaped collapse scars that have a sharp boundary with the surrounding bog and do not contain permafrost. Unlike all other peat landforms, non-patterned, open permafrost bogs are found on low-angle slopes, and are characterized by thin (0.3 to 1.5 m) accumulations of peat. This peat landform can grade laterally into wooded permafrost bogs that support thicker peat accumulations ($\geq$1.5 m) in areas with a minimal slope. The effect of bog slope topography is demonstrated by the presence of distinctive patterns of parallel lineations (runnels) oriented downslope. Tree height in the runnels is generally greater than between runnels, and vascular plant species are more diverse (Mills et al. 1978).

Non-patterned, open permafrost bogs are found in the central part of the MRBWC – within the Cameron Hills, Caribou Mountains, and Slave River Lowland (Vitt et al. 1996) – and extend northwards. Veneer bogs can be the dominant peat landform type in the northern part of the MRBWC where the mineral substrate is undulating to ridged (Zoltai & Pettapiece 1973).

Wooded permafrost bogs (peat plateaus) with or without collapse scars

Wooded permafrost bogs have a relatively flat, raised surface that is elevated 1 to 2 m above the surrounding non-permafrost fen (Fig. 6.3B). These wooded bog landforms are elevated above the surrounding landscape due to the presence of permafrost and can occur within small, isolated basins, or as extensive networks that span hundreds of square kilometers within broad low-lands. As with all other bog landforms within the MRBWC, trees are restricted to *Picea mariana* (Vitt et al. 1994); for wooded permafrost bogs, forest cover generally ranges from 6% to 70%.

Wooded permafrost bogs may or may not support collapse scars. Collapse scars are treeless, internal depressions that are typically 100 cm lower than the surrounding bog surface and they are not underlain by permafrost. Collapse scars vary from isolated, circular areas to irregular, elongated, interconnected drainage channels (Fig. 6.3B). While permafrost is not present in collapse scars, the collapse scar is always surrounded by permafrost. The term "collapse scar" suggests generation by the process of thermokarst (Zoltai 1971), and stratigraphic evidence has documented collapse-scar formation from local permafrost degradation (Zoltai 1993). However, not all collapse scars appear to have "collapsed."

Some collapse scars, particularly those connected to a channel, show no evidence of a previously drier (permafrost) surface (Chatwin 1981, Vitt *et al.* 1994, Kuhry 1998). Thus, collapse scars may also represent areas that permafrost has encroached.

Wooded permafrost bogs extend across the entire MRBWC and represent the dominant peat landform present within the Mackenzie River Basin. They are uncommon in the southern part of the wetland complex, but become the dominant peat landform in the central part of the basin, within the Cameron Hills and Caribou Mountains (Vitt *et al.* 1996).

Wooded non-permafrost bogs with internal lawns

These bogs are characterized by a heterogeneous surface comprised of a uniformly wooded component (forest cover between 6% and 70%) interspersed with open, wet lawns that often contain partially buried stands of dead trees. Wooded non-permafrost bogs with internal lawns generally occur as islands within larger fen complexes (Fig. 6.3C), or as peninsulas protruding into larger fens. Open, wet lawns are typically 40 to 60 cm below the surrounding wooded part of the bog and are termed internal lawns. Internal lawns may occur in extensive patterns radiating from the bog island center; or in indistinct, non-radiating patterns. In many cases internal lawn margins are surrounded by a stand of taller trees that are typically only a few trees thick. In addition, internal lawns may be associated with small, densely forested areas (cover $\geq 70\%$) that are elevated above the surrounding wooded non-permafrost bog by about 0.5 m.

Stratigraphic analyses of internal lawns within wooded non-permafrost bogs in the southeastern part of the MRBWC reveal an uppermost layer of about 30 to 50 cm of wet, oligotrophic species of *Sphagnum*. This wet *Sphagnum* is underlain by a thin layer of sedges, followed by a thin layer dominated by feather mosses, wood and/or black spruce needles, and roots. Below this layer is a thick layer of a variety of more-decomposed macrofossils, all indicate a habitat of dry wooded bog (Vitt *et al.* 1994). Such stratigraphy indicates that substantial changes occurred from a relatively dry, wooded bog habitat to a wet open lawn condition, and that this change was rapid, without transitional phases. Such changes are consistent with thermal subsidence of permafrost peatlands and suggest that internal lawns represent areas of permafrost degradation. Unlike collapse scars, which are surrounded by wooded permafrost bog, internal lawns are currently not surrounded by permafrost, and demarcate a former localized permafrost landform that was surrounded by wooded non-permafrost bog. Dendrochronologic control on internal-lawn formation suggests that degradation began roughly 100 years ago, generated by warming since the Little Ice Age, and continues to the present day (Vitt *et al.* 1994, Halsey *et al.* 1995).

Extensive probing of wooded non-permafrost bogs with internal lawns suggests that permafrost is absent, with the exception of its occasional presence
in small, densely forested areas associated with internal lawns. Small, densely
forested areas represent relict areas of localized permafrost that has not yet
melted (Halsey *et al.* 1995, Beilman *et al.* 2001).

Wooded non-permafrost bogs without internal lawns

Bogs that do not contain internal lawns are uniformly wooded and generally occur as islands within larger fen complexes (Fig. 6.3D), or as peninsulas
protruding into large fens. Wooded non-permafrost bogs without internal lawns
can also be confined to small basins in hummocky terrain. These peat landforms
have a flat to slightly domed surface, but do not have the characteristic forested
crest and associated radiating forest pattern typical of more-temperate climates
(Heinselman 1963, 1970, Glaser & Janssens 1986).

Extensive stratigraphic examination of these bogs documents their formation through the processes of acidification and oligotrophication (Zoltai *et al.*
1988, Nicholson & Vitt 1990, Kuhry 1994). In no case has evidence of permafrost
been found, either through extensive probing of individual sites or through
stratigraphic analyses. Thin layers of seasonal frost can be present well into the
summer, especially below hummocks.

Bogs without internal lawns are restricted to the southern part of the MRBWC.
They occur frequently within the Wabasca Lowland and McLelland Upland where
they represent more than 5% of the land cover, and up to half of the peatlands
(Vitt *et al.* 1996). Bogs without internal lawns decrease in frequency northwards,
with their northern extent defined by the flanks of the Cameron Hills and
Caribou Mountains (Vitt *et al.* 1996).

Wetland landform types: fens

Vegetative patterns that result from the presence of surface-water flow
allow for the distinction of fens from bogs. Fens have been subdivided on the
basis of patterning, forest cover, and internal lawns. Fens are found throughout
the MRBWC, and dominate the landscape in the southern part of the complex
and in part of the Slave River Lowland.

Patterned fens

Patterned fens have a heterogeneous surface, characterized by open, wet
flarks and drier, shrubby to wooded strings and margins (Fig. 6.3D). Strings are
oriented perpendicular to the direction of water flow, and form sinuous ribs
on gently sloping terrain and nets on more-level terrain where water flow is

multi-directional and results in the development of flow interference patterns. Patterned fens in the MRBWC are typically rich and are concentrated in the southeastern part of the complex (Vitt et al. 1996).

Non-patterned open fens

This fen type is characterized by <6% tree or shrub cover (Fig. 6.3B) and are found throughout the MRBWC. They can be distinguished from non-patterned, open permafrost bogs by the presence of a water table at or near the surface that allows for hydrological connectivity of surface and/or ground-water. In the northern part of the wetland complex non-patterned open fens are commonly poor (Nicholson et al. 1996), and are associated with drainage from wooded and open permafrost bogs. In the south they can be either poor or rich depending on the nature of their dominant water source, and occur as small, isolated basins and as flat, featureless fens that slope gently in the direction of drainage.

Non-patterned shrubby fens

Non-patterned shrubby fens are recognized by the presence of ≥6% shrub and <6% tree cover, and are also found throughout the MRBWC. Shrubby fens can be either poor or rich and are commonly found in the southern part of the wetland complex (Vitt et al. 1996), either within small, isolated basins, or as flat, featureless fens that slope gently in the direction of drainage (Fig. 6.3C). They are also common in the central part of the Slave River Lowland where they cover extensive tracts of land.

Non-patterned wooded fens with internal lawns

This wetland type is composed of a heterogeneous mixture of wooded and open areas (Fig. 6.3E). The wooded component of the peatland has a forest cover of ≥6%, composed of some combination of *Picea mariana* and *Larix laricina*. Non-patterned wooded fens are distinguished from wooded non-permafrost bogs by the presence of *Larix laricina* although this species may represent only a small component of the forest canopy (<1%). Open areas are wet lawns that often contain partially buried stands of dead trees and are termed internal lawns. In wooded fens, internal lawns are typically found along the perimeter of larger peatland complexes, and form indistinct, non-radiating patterns. In many cases internal lawn margins are surrounded by a stand of taller trees that are typically only a few trees thick. In addition, internal lawns may be associated with small, densely forested areas (forest cover ≥70%) that are elevated about 1 m above the surrounding non-patterned wooded fen.

Stratigraphic analyses of internal lawns within non-patterned wooded fens in the southeastern part of the MRBWC reveal a woody layer at a depth of 20 to 40 cm. In some cases, plants usually found under drier conditions, such as *Pleurozium schreberi* or *Tomenthypnum nitens*, have been found in this woody debris layer. Such stratigraphy indicates that substantial changes occurred from a relatively dry habitat to a wet open lawn condition – and that this change was rapid, without transitional phases. As with internal lawns found in wooded bogs, such changes are consistent with thermal subsidence of permafrost peatland and suggest that internal lawns represent areas of permafrost degradation. Extensive probing of non-patterned wooded fens with internal lawns suggests that permafrost is absent – with the exception of its occasional presence in small, densely forested areas associated with internal lawns. Small, densely forested areas represent relict areas of localized permafrost that have not yet melted (Halsey *et al.* 1995, Beilman *et al.* 2001).

Non-patterned wooded fens with internal lawns are restricted to the southern part of the MRBWC, particularly on the Wabasca Lowland, and are almost always rich. They extend as far north as the southern flanks of the Cameron Hills and Caribou Mountains.

Non-patterned wooded fens without internal lawns

Non-patterned wooded fens without internal lawns are composed of a homogeneous wooded peatland surface with a forest cover of $\geq 6\%$ (Fig. 6.3C). The forest canopy is composed of some combination of *Picea mariana* and *Larix laricina*, though the amount of larch present may be small ($<1\%$). It is the presence of larch that distinguishes this wetland type from wooded non-permafrost bogs in addition to hydrological differences. Non-patterned wooded fens without internal lawns are present throughout the MRBWC and may be poor, moderate-rich, or extreme-rich. They are most common in the southern part of the complex where they are the most-frequent wetland type.

Wetland landform types: non-peat-accumulating wetlands

Non-peat-accumulating wetlands are present in the MRBWC, although they comprise a small component of the total wetlands. Non-peat-accumulating wetlands are subdivided on the basis of forest and shrub cover.

Wooded swamps

Both coniferous and deciduous swamps are present within the MRBWC and, as such, wooded swamps are vegetatively quite diverse. Wooded swamps are defined by the presence of $\geq 6\%$ forest cover and by their landscape position. The association of wooded swamps with fluctuating water tables places them most frequently along floodplains, stream terraces, and peatland margins (Fig. 6.3F). As with other non-peat-accumulating wetland types, wooded swamps are found throughout the MRBWC.

Shrubby swamps

This wetland type supports a shrub cover of $\geq 6\%$ and can be distinguished from non-patterned shrubby fens by wetland location and shrub height. Shrubby swamps commonly occur in the landscape where water tables fluctuate seasonally – such as along floodplains and stream terraces – and at peatland margins (Fig. 6.3F). This wetland type is defined as non-peat-accumulating, and generally has <40 cm of accumulated organics. Peat depth in conjunction with water-table fluctuation favors shrub species that are generally taller (>2 m) while shrubby fens support species ≤ 2 m in height (see Cottrell 1995).

Marshes

Marshes are distinguished from other wetland forms by a lack of tree or shrub cover, and differ from non-patterned open fens in their landscape positions, hydrology, and groundcover (Fig. 6.3F). Unlike non-patterned open fens, marshes require frequent flooding and are associated with fluctuating water levels and relatively high water flows. As such they are always associated with standing water, which can be present in a transitory fashion. Marshes are typified by a paucity of bryophytes, and have high concentrations of nitrogen and phosphorus that lead to abundant vascular plant production. Peat accumulation is limited, however, by high decomposition rates. On the landscape they are most-commonly found along floodplains and lake margins. Marshes are present throughout the MRBWC.

Shallow open waters

Shallow open waters are non-peat-forming wetlands that are characterized by aquatic processes confined to less than 2 m depth at midsummer. These wetlands have submergent to floating vegetation and form a transition to truly aquatic ecosystems (Fig. 6.3F). The chemistry of this wetland class is variable and does not distinguish it from the other wetland classes; however, floristic composition may possibly be dependent on chemical conditions. This wetland class is found throughout the MRBWC.

Distributional controls

Studies that examined the spatial distribution of wetlands in other regions have demonstrated that climatic parameters are the dominant factors influencing type (Damman 1979, Glaser & Janssens 1986, Halsey *et al.* 1997), with physiographical controls such as substrate texture and topography also being important (Almquist-Jacobson & Foster 1995, Halsey *et al.* 1997, 1998). The MRBWC is defined as a nearly contiguous area of ≥30% peatland across the landscape. Differences in wetland-landform type and extent within the MRBWC should also be controlled by climatic and physiographical parameters. To elucidate how the allogenic factors of climate and physiography control wetland type and distribution a quantified wetland data set was related to climatic and physiographical parameters for part of the MRBWC and the surrounding area.

Maps of the wetland complex were created at 1:250 000 scale for the southeastern part of the wetland complex (south of 60° N and between 110° W and 120° W) following the methods of Halsey *et al.* (1997). Due to the presence of northern uplands in this area, the range of climatic variability present within the MRBWC is generally found, and hence the full range of peatland types and landforms are found, with the exception of polygonal, open permafrost bogs. Wetland distribution and extent was also determined as far south as 51° N (south of the southern peatland limit) to maximize variability and to define the controls on peatland distribution.

Wetland extent was digitized in ARC/INFO (geographic information software), with spatial information summarized into 0.25°-latitude and 0.5°-longitude grids. Climatic and physiographical data were also assembled for each of the grids from a number of sources. Mean annual temperatures and thermal seasonal aridity indices (TSAIs; total yearly precipitation/average mean May to October temperatures) were generated by a linear model using all available climate stations, excluding cities for the period 1951–80 (Environment Canada 1982). For mean annual temperature, $r^2 \geq 0.98$; while for TSAI, $r^2 \geq 0.72$. Climate values were generated from these models for each 0.25°-latitude and 0.5°-longitude grid. Physiographical parameters were gathered from a number of sources (see Vitt *et al.* 1996 for list of sources) and included dominant topography, mineral soil texture, and bedrock geology. Topography was coded on a five-point scale with level topography assigned a value of 1 and inclined assigned a value of 5. Mineral soil texture was subdivided on a six-point scale, with sediment of low hydraulic conductivity (clay) assigned a value of 1 and sediment of high hydraulic conductivity (sand and gravel) assigned a value of 6. Bedrock

Table 6.1 *Summary of DCCA of wetland data to climatic and physiographical controls.*

Axis	1	2	3	4
Eigen value	0.486	0.293	0.120	0.710
Length of gradient	2.069	3.625	2.069	2.392
Species–environment correlation	0.844	0.697	0.685	0.398
Cumulative percentage variance of species data explained	26.7	42.8	49.4	53.3

was classified on a four-point scale by pH; acidic, granitic bedrock was assigned a value of 1 and highly calcareous limestone and dolomite assigned a value of 4.

A hybrid detrended canonical correspondance analysis (DCCA) (ter Braak 1997) – composed of both a detrended correspondance analysis (DCA) to ordinate wetland data and a DCCA component that related the ordinated wetland data to environmental data – is used to examine how environmental factors are associated with ordinated wetland distribution. The DCCA explains over half of the variance in the wetland data set on the first four axes, with an 84% and 70% correlation between the wetland and environmental variables for the first and second axes, respectively (Table 6.1).

The first axis of the DCA is essentially the variance in the wetland data set created by the difference in the distribution between permafrost and non-permafrost peat landforms (Fig. 6.4). In the central and northern parts of the MRBWC, permafrost is prevalent and is dominated by open and wooded permafrost bogs associated with non-patterned open fens that are wet and poor. In the southern part of the MRBWC wooded non-permafrost bogs and non-patterned wooded fen with and without internal lawns are dominant.

Modeled mean annual temperature is the most important and significant environmental variable correlated to the first axis (Table 6.2). Mean annual temperatures have been correlated to permafrost distribution (Vitt *et al.* 1994, Halsey *et al.* 1995, Beilman *et al.* 2001), with permafrost cover increasing in bogs as mean annual temperature decreases. The texture of the underlying surficial sediments also explains a significant amount of the variation on the first axis (Table 6.2). Peatlands that occur in areas of the wetland complex with low mean annual temperatures contain higher amounts of permafrost when the mineral substrate is fine grained (clay loam to loam). In areas of the wetland complex that have relatively low mean annual temperatures but are dominated by soils with higher hydraulic conductivity (sandy loam, sand, and gravel), fens dominate. As fens

Table 6.2 *Statistics for variables used in the DCCA of wetland data to climatic and physiographical controls.*

Variable	Interset correlation		Canonical coefficient		T-value	
	Axis 1	Axis 2	Axis 1	Axis 2	Axis 1	Axis 2
Mean annual temperature	**0.75***	**0.57***	**0.54***	**0.26***	12.7	6.0
TSAI	−0.20	−0.35*	0.08	0.01	1.8	1.8
Texture	**−0.38***	−0.32*	**0.16***	0.08	3.5	1.7
Topography	0.02	0.08	−0.02	0.02	−0.5	0.6
Salts	−0.09	**0.40***	**0.15***	**−0.18***	−3.7	4.5

Asterisks indicate significance at $p = 0.005$. Absolute *t*-values >2.1 are used to indicate important canonical coefficients (ter Braak 1997). Bold values indicate variables with significant correlation and canonical coefficients.

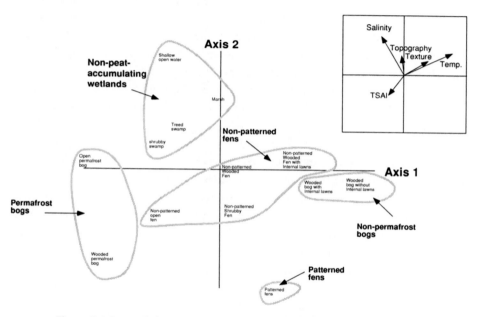

Figure 6.4 Detrended correspondance ordination of wetland landform types overlain by significant and important allogenic variables from the DCCA.

dominate, these peatlands do not tend to support expansive areas of permafrost peatland. The dominance of fens versus bogs in areas of the Slave River Lowland is a good example of the association between peat landform type and substrate texture. The area between Lake Athabasca and Great Slave Lake supports numerous dune fields (Craig 1965, David 1977) that are composed of soils with high hydraulic conductivity. Areas of the Slave River Lowland that are dominated by fens are typically associated with aeolian deposits, while bog-dominated areas are underlain by finer-grained glaciolacustrine sediments deposited by Glacial Lake McConnell (see Craig 1965) and have lower hydraulic conductivity.

The second axis of the DCA represents variation in the wetland data set created by the hydrology of wetland ecosystems. Wetlands with stable water tables (peatlands) are found at one end of the second axis (Fig. 6.4). Peatlands are further subdivided along the second axis on the basis of surface-water flow. Peatlands with relatively high rates of surface-water flow (soligenous, patterned fens), are followed by peatlands with relatively low rates of surface-water flow (limnogenous and topogenous, non-patterned fens) and bogs (peatlands with virtually no surface-water flow). This peatland surface-water-flow gradient is followed by wetlands that have fluctuating water tables (non-peat-accumulating wetlands) (Fig. 6.4).

Modeled mean annual temperature is again the most-important and significant environmental variable correlated to the second axis (Table 6.2). Temperature is a controlling factor in the wetland hydroperiod that ultimately governs water-table fluctuation. In addition to temperature, TSAI is also significantly correlated to the second axis, but does not have a significant canonical coefficient. This is due to the fact that variation in the wetland data set explained by TSAI is also explained by other environmental variable(s), most probably temperature.

The presence or absence of salts within the underlying surficial sediments is also a significant variable in explaining the variation in the wetland data set for the second axis of the DCA. Areas with relatively low mean annual temperatures that contain salts in the underlying surficial sediments have a much higher cover of non-peat-accumulating wetlands than do areas with equivalent mean annual temperatures and no salts in the underlying surficial sediments. For example, along the east-central part of the MRBWC, saline discharge (mainly NaCl) from springs originating from evaporite strata of Middle Devonian age (Bayrock 1972) limits peatlands (Vitt et al. 1996). In this area it is the presence of saline discharge that determines the boundary of the MRBWC.

Also significant in explaining the variation in the wetland data set for the second axis, but not having a significant canonical coefficient, was the texture of the underlying surficial sediment. When the texture of the underlying mineral soil is fine grained and hydraulic conductivity is low, peatlands with small amounts of surface-water flow, i.e. bogs, and non-patterned (limnogenous and topogenous) fens, are more abundant. In areas where the underlying mineral soil has a higher conductivity, peatlands with large amounts of surface-water flow (i.e. patterned [soligenous] fens) occur. Patterned fens are frequently found in the southeastern part of the MRBWC where glaciofluvial and aeolian deposits are common (Vitt *et al.* 1996).

Bryophyte flora

Peatland bryophytes are closely linked to such local environmental gradients as surface-water chemistry, hydrology, and shade (Vitt & Slack 1975, 1984, Vitt *et al.* 1975, 1990, Horton *et al.* 1979, Andrus *et al.* 1983, Gignac & Vitt 1990, Vitt & Chee 1990). Most ecological studies of peatlands have been confined to small geographical areas, thus very little is known about the effects of regional environmental variables such as climate on species distributions, although species are known to have geographic limits that are climatically controlled (Vitt & Andrus 1977, Andrus 1980, Janssens 1983). Certainly climate has affected development and distribution of peat landforms within the MRBWC and is well known to have affected distributions in other areas (Sjörs 1948, Eurola 1962, Moore & Bellamy 1974, Damman 1977, 1979, Halsey *et al.* 1995, 1997, 1998). Thus, in a large geographic peatland complex such as the MRBWC bryophyte species will differ as a result of both variations in local environmental factors and regional climatic gradients.

Nicholson *et al.* (1996) examined the bryophyte-species cover of 82 peatland stands within the Mackenzie River Basin. All stands were located within 50 km of a permanent weather station from which biotemperature (sum of positive mean monthly temperatures divided by 12), length of growing season (number of days having mean temperature above about 2 °C), thermal seasonal precipitation (rainfall occurring during growing season), yearly aridity index (annual precipitation falling as rain divided by the annual mean temperature plus 10), TSAI (precipitation during the growing season divided by the annual temperature plus 10), mean annual temperature, and total precipitation. In addition to climatic variables, the water table; conductivity; pH; and elemental concentrations of Ca, Mg, Na, and K were determined.

A TWINSPAN analysis (Hill 1979) of the 82 peatland stands identified 7 stand groups (Fig. 6.5). These 7 stand groups include: (1) widespread open to shrubby poor fens; (2) central to northern permafrost bogs with collapse scars and non-permafrost bogs with internal lawns; (3) southern treed bogs without internal lawns; (4) widespread permafrost bogs without collapse scars and non-permafrost bogs without internal lawns; (5) southern treed poor fens; (6) widespread moderate-rich fens; (7) widespread extreme-rich fens. Each stand group was characterized by a suite of dominant species (Fig. 6.5).

When species from the 82 stands are related to local and regional environmental variables with a DCCA (ter Braak 1997), local environmental variables are

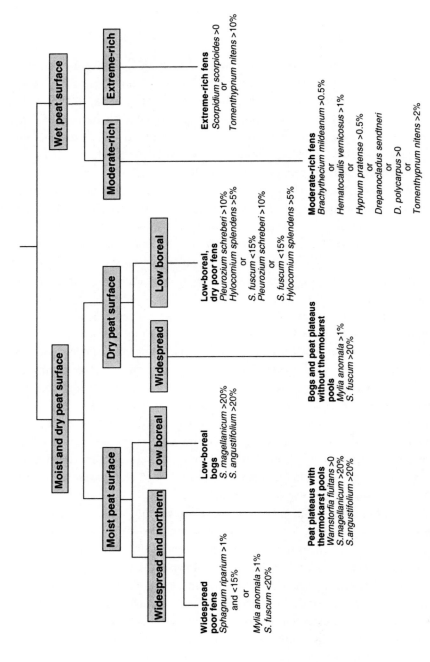

Figure 6.5 TWINSPAN-derived bryophyte vegetation groups. Bryophyte groups are identified by peatland type and indicator species for each group and their abundances are given.

found to explain most of the variation in species (Nicholson *et al.* 1996). Regional climatic variables were also found to explain a significant amount of variation on the first axis, however correlations were lower (Nicholson *et al.* 1996). A similar pattern occurs on the second axis with local environmental variables explaining most of the variation, with lower but significant correlation between regional climatic variables. Thus, while local environmental variables exert the dominant control on bryophyte flora of large, northern wetland complexes, regional climatic variables also play an important role (Nicholson *et al.* 1996).

Development

Timing of deglaciation and drainage of proglacial lakes limits peatland initiation in much of the Mackenzie River Basin, with the exception of the northwestern part that remained unglaciated during Late Wisconsinan time (Catto 1996, Duk-Rodkin & Lemmen 2000). There are no full-glacial peat deposits known from the unglaciated foothills and plains of the northwestern Mackenzie River Basin, though *Sphagnum* spores are consistently reported from lake sediments collected to the west (Halsey *et al.* 2000). In addition, submerged full-glacial peat deposits have been documented off the coast of Alaska (Elias *et al.* 1997). Within the basin, full-glacial records in the unglaciated area have concentrated on exposed river sections where glaciolacustrine sediments were deposited due to ice impoundment (see Lemmen *et al.* 1994, Catto 1996). Thus, while no deposits are known, it is possible that full-glacial peatlands were present in the extreme-northwestern part of the Mackenzie River Basin.

Peat accumulation is known to have initiated during the Late Wisconsinan in the northwestern part of the basin (ca. 12 500 BP), and basal radiocarbon dates become progressively younger to the southeast (Fig. 6.6). Peatland initiation extended southwards along the southern foothills of the Rocky Mountains and northern uplands of Alberta in the Early Holocene (Halsey *et al.* 1998). With a decrease in summer insolation, and an increase in precipitation around 8000 to 9000 years BP (Kutzbach & Guetter 1986), peatlands began to initiate throughout most of the western part of the Mackenzie River Basin, and expanded eastward in the Middle Holocene (Halsey *et al.* 1998). For areas south of 60° N latitude peatland initiation was restricted to the Late Holocene for southeastern lowlands (Peace–Wapiti River drainage basin), or to areas with saline mineral soils (Halsey *et al.* 1998). While saline soils are found north of 60° N latitude, where peatland initiation occurred at some point after 6000 years BP, details of initiation are not known. Thus, although the MRBWC did begin to accumulate peat in the northern and central part of the basin in the Early Holocene, much of the complex did not initiate until during and after the Middle Holocene.

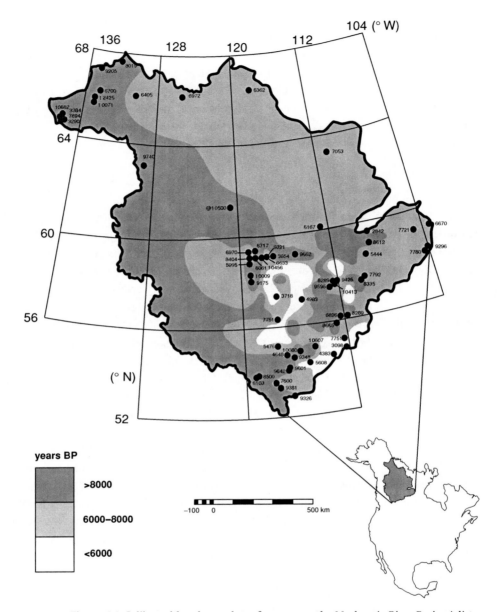

Figure 6.6 Calibrated basal peat dates from across the Mackenzie River Basin. A list of dates and sources is presented in Table 6.3. Dates were contoured in Macgridzo (Rockware 1991), except for south of 60° N and between 110° and 120° W latitude which represents a peatland initiation model from Halsey *et al.* (1998).

Table 6.3 *Basal radiocarbon dates from within the Mackenzie River Basin.*

Latitude (° N)	Longitude (° W)	Lab.	Depth	Date	Calibrated mean	Reference
67.41	132.05	BGS-148	150–152	7200 ± 60	8 019	Zoltai & Tarnocai 1975
67.16	135.14	BGS-159	Unknown	8190 ± 60	9 205	Zoltai & Tarnocai 1975
66.13	130.52	BGS-146	270–273	5600 ± 70	6 405	Zoltai & Tarnocai 1975
66.10	134.18	BGS-140	265–268	5910 ± 60	6 700	Zoltai & Tarnocai 1975
66.06	117.58	GSC-1783	113–117	5600 ± 140	6 362	Nichols 1975
65.59	135.03	BGS-144	Unknown	10470 ± 80	12 425	Zoltai & Tarnocai 1975
65.50	129.05	I-3735	Unknown	6120 ± 120	6 972	Mackay & Mathews 1973
65.34	135.30	GSC-2341	300	8980 ± 90	10 071	Hughes *et al.* 1981
64.52	138.19	GSC-310	162	9620 ± 150	10 882	Dyck *et al.* 1966
64.38	138.24	GSC-415	162	6840 ± 150	7 694	Lowden & Blake 1968
64.36	138.22	GSC-469	126	3180 ± 130	3 384	Lowden & Blake 1968
64.36	138.20	GSC-416	140	3100 ± 130	3 290	Lowden & Blake 1968
63.04	110.47	GSC-1840	157–159	6170 ± 130	>7 053	Nichols 1975
63.01	129.05	GSC-3097	230	8640 ± 160	9 740	MacDonald 1983
61.28	120.55	WAT-405	315	9400 ± ?	~10 500	Chatwin 1983
60.03	112.54	AECV-994C	112–115	5400 ± 110	6 167	S. C. Zoltai unpublished
59.36	108.35	S-1558	300	2690 ± 70	2 842	Rutherford *et al.* 1984

(cont.)

Table 6.3 (*cont.*)

Latitute (° N)	Longitude (° W)	Lab.	Depth	Date	Calibrated mean	Reference
59.16	118.41	AECV-979C	151–156	7870 ± 120	8 717	Zoltai 1993
59.12	117.30	WIS-281	50–52	3410 ± 55	3 654	Bender *et al.* 1969
59.10	103.06	S-1746	300	5850 ± 70	6 670	Schreiner 1983
59.08	104.53	S-1560	120	6855 ± 110	7 721	Schreiner 1983
59.07	118.37	AECV-983C	375–384	9170 ± 170	10 456	Zoltai 1993
59.07	118.09	AECV-986C	254–262	5840 ± 100	6 633	Zoltai 1993
59.06	117.41	AECV-1425C	236–238	8400 ± 100	9 321	Kuhry unpublished
59.02	108.52	S-2055	175	7755 ± 135	8 612	Schreiner 1983
59.01	118.47	BGS-354	128	5200 ± 100	5 999	Reid 1977
59.00	115.15	S-116	335	8600 ± 100	9 662	McCallum & Whittenberg 1962
58.39	119.05	WAT-3005	261–266	8820 ± 160	9 175	Bauer 2002
58.32	119.08	AECV-992C	188–197	7230 ± 120	8 061	Zoltai 1993
58.31	109.24	S-1659	Unknown	4685 ± 70	5 444	Schreiner 1983
58.25	119.29	AECV-987C	266–273	6110 ± 120	6 970	Zoltai 1993
58.18	119.17	AECV-991C	184–190	7620 ± 120	8 404	Zoltai 1993
58.18	119.22	BGS-2114	310–314	9365 ± 115	10 009	Bauer 2002
58.16	103.52	GSC-3211	190–194	6960 ± 80	7 780	Blake 1986
58.12	103.42	S-1332	Unknown	8335 ± 160	9 296	Schreiner 1983
57.43	109.28	AECV-1176C	230–240	7570 ± 150	8 335	P. Kuhry unpublished
57.42	112.22	AECV-1723C	133–140	8460 ± 150	9 425	Halsey *et al.* 1998
57.42	112.22	AECV-1722C	149–156	7510 ± 110	8 289	P. Kuhry unpublished
57.40	109.28	S-1487	Unknown	6960 ± 95	7 792	Schreiner 1983
57.28	117.11	WIS-283	115–120	3450 ± 60	3 718	Bender *et al.* 1969
57.26	112.57	AECV-1720C	113–128	9170 ± 110	10 413	P. Kuhry unpublished
57.26	112.57	AECV-1646C	113–128	8550 ± 110	9 595	Kuhry 1994

Table 6.3 (*cont.*)

Latitute (°N)	Longitude (°W)	Lab.	Depth	Date	Calibrated mean	Reference
57.02	115.08	AECV-1215C	261–267	4380 ± 110	4 983	Halsey et al. 1998
56.17	117.20	WIS-274	171–173	6880 ± 85	7 751	Bender et al. 1968
56.12	111.31	AECV-182C	192–200	7510 ± 110	8 289	Zoltai et al. 1988
56.11	112.09	BGS-786	416–421	5960 ± 160	6 828	Zoltai & Vitt 1990
55.54	112.04	AECV-261C	390–400	7740 ± 110	8 665	Nicholson & Vitt 1990
55.03	117.00	AECV-926C	220–230	4740 ± 100	5 476	Zoltai & Vitt 1990
55.01	114.09	AECV-1027C	385–400	9240 ± 140	10 607	Kuhry & Vitt 1996
54.58	112.00	BGS-780	288–294	6900 ± 240	7 751	Zoltai et al. 1988
54.45	115.52	BGS-778	548–554	8940 ± 240	10 080	Zoltai et al. 1988
54.42	116.00	GSC-500	410	8320 ± 260	9 348	Lowden et al. 1968
54.37	112.09	BGS-784	236–241	2900 ± 160	3 098	Zoltai et al. 1988
54.34	116.48	GSC-674	320	4150 ± 140	4 648	Lowden & Blake 1968
54.30	113.10	AECV-1094C	440–459	3900 ± 320	4 383	Halsey et al. 1998
54.22	115.06	GSC-752	180	4850 ± 130	5 608	Lowden & Blake 1968
54.13	116.55	GSC-673	270	8530 ± 170	9 601	Lowden & Blake 1968
54.10	116.54	GSC-525	310	8560 ± 170	9 642	Lowden Blake 1968
53.49	119.09	S-1277	238–244	5320 ± 95	6 103	Rutherford et al. 1979
53.49	119.09	S-1279	533–549	7705 ± 75	8 500	Rutherford et al. 1979
53.35	118.01	Beta-135662	350	6750 ± 40	7 600	Yu et al. 2003
53.20	117.28	BGS-775	502–510	8400 ± 270	9 381	Zoltai & Vitt 1990
52.51	116.28	BGS-772	352–357	8600 ± 250	9 626	Zoltai 1989

Once peatlands were established, surface isolation, oligotrophication, and acidification allowed for the establishment of *Sphagnum*. In areas where peat accumulation from *Sphagnum* was more rapid than the surrounding peatland, bogs developed. In the Mackenzie River Basin, the timing of *Sphagnum* establishment ranges from about 100 to 5400 years after peatland initiation (Fig. 6.7). The lag between *Sphagnum* establishment and peatland initiation is less for substrates of low hydraulic conductivity (clay to loam) than for high hydraulic conductivity (sandy loam to gravel). This is probably a function of the stronger hydraulic gradient present in soils of higher hydraulic conductivity, and hence stronger and more-persistent groundwater-to-surface connectivity.

Peatlands on substrates of relatively low hydraulic conductivity have a fairly persistent, 2000-year time lag prior to *Sphagnum* establishment (Fig. 6.7). This establishment pattern is similar to other areas of continental western Canada with similar substrates (see Kuhry *et al.* 1993). Peatlands on substrates of relatively high hydraulic conductivity are far-more variable in the time lag required for *Sphagnum* establishment (Fig. 6.7), due to the higher variability in the amount of peat accumulation required for surface isolation from groundwater connectivity.

In addition to surface isolation by peat accumulation, the development of permafrost and associated positive elevation change from volume expansion of frozen water can also lead to surface isolation and concomitant *Sphagnum* establishment. Permafrost initiated in the MRBWC after 5000 years BP in the north (Zoltai 1995), after 3000 years BP the central part (Zoltai 1993), and in the Little Ice Age in the southernmost extremity (Vitt *et al.* 1994). While permafrost is no longer forming in the southern part of the MRBWC (Vitt *et al.* 1994, Halsey *et al.* 1995), it continues to develop in the central and northern parts of the wetland complex as peatland surfaces are raised above the water table through peat accumulation. Thus, *Sphagnum* establishment and bog formation can continue to occur in conjunction with permafrost formation on substrates of low conductivity in the central and northern parts of the MRBWC, but not in the south. In the southern part of the MRBWC new areas of *Sphagnum* establishment and bog formation can only occur in areas paludified within the last 2000 years on substrates of low hydraulic conductivity. This 2000-year time interval is consistent with the pattern of *Sphagnum* establishment found within the basin (Fig. 6.7). On substrates of relatively high hydraulic conductivity, *Sphagnum* establishment and bog formation can continue throughout the basin on older peatlands due to the variable nature of groundwater connectivity.

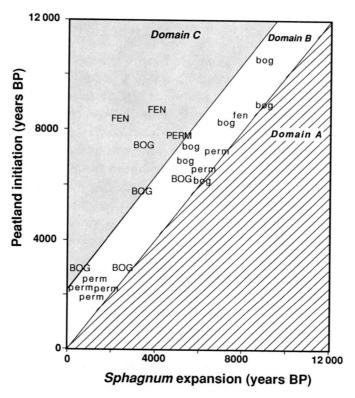

Figure 6.7 Relationship between time of peatland initiation and *Sphagnum* establishment. Sites identified in upper-case letters developed on substrates of relatively high hydraulic conductivity, while sites identified in lower-case letters developed on substrates of relatively low hydraulic conductivity (domain B). Sites are: bog, wooded non-permafrost bog; perm, open or wooded permafrost bog; fen, patterned and non-patterned fens. The hatched part of the graph (domain A) identifies a temporal zone that can not occur, as *Sphagnum* peat mosses can not expand if peatlands are not present. The shaded part of the graph (domain C) identifies a temporal zone where *Sphagnum* can only expand if sites are situated on sediments of relatively high hydraulic conductivity or if surface isolation occurs from permafrost formation. Radiocarbon dates were corrected from data obtained from Nichols (1975), Zoltai and Tarnocai (1975), Reid (1977), Zoltai *et al.* (1988), Nicholson and Vitt (1990), Zoltai and Vitt (1990), Zoltai (1993), Kuhry (1994), Kuhry and Vitt (1996), Bauer (2002), P. Kuhry (unpublished data), and S. C. Zoltai (unpublished data).

Carbon storage

In continental western Canada, peat accumulation and long-term carbon storage is generally limited to peatlands, with marshes and swamps accumulating relatively little to no carbon (Campbell *et al.* 2000, Vitt *et al.* 2000a). Western Canada contains roughly one-third of North American peatland carbon storage (Halsey *et al.* 2000), and as such contains more carbon than any other terrestrial ecosystem in North America. This vast carbon store is mainly partitioned between peatlands of the MRBWC and the Hudson Bay Lowland.

Peatland type and depth control carbon storage in the MRBWC. Analyses of different peatland types in western Canada indicate that ashless carbon densities differ between peatland types. Two groups can be statistically recognized: (1) open fens, and non-permafrost and permafrost bogs with a mean ashless carbon density of $0.049 \pm 0.004 \, \mathrm{g\,C\,cm^{-3}}$; and (2) wooded and shrubby fens with a mean ashless carbon density of $0.055 \pm 0.003 \, \mathrm{g\,C\,cm^{-3}}$ (Vitt *et al.* 2000a).

Peatland depths differ across the Mackenzie River Basin. In the southern part of the Mackenzie River Basin mean peat depths are greater than 220 cm, while in the high boreal to subarctic regions mean peat depths are around 200 cm excluding the southern low subarctic where mean peat depths are under 150 cm (Fig. 6.8). Mean peat depth across the entire basin is 222 cm, similar to Gorham's estimate of mean peat depth for Canadian peatlands of 220 cm (Gorham 1991).

Peatland depths differ due to different ages of initiation and different carbon accumulation rates in different peatland types. In the MRBWC, peatlands are generally oldest in the central and southwestern part of the wetland complex; here, the peatlands initiated prior to 8000 years BP and hence have had a longer time interval over which to accumulate peat. Peatlands in the mid- and high-boreal regions are dominated by non-permafrost systems, while in the low and high subarctic permafrost peatlands dominate. Non-permafrost peatlands are known to have statistically higher long-term carbon accumulation rates than permafrost peatlands both within the MRBWC (Robinson & Moore 1999, 2000), and in other regions of the world (e.g. Botch *et al.* 1995). Thus, in the southern part of the MRBWC, peatlands are deepest, as they have been accumulating peat for a relatively long time at a higher long-term rate. In contrast, peatlands in the central and northern parts of the wetland complex, while in some cases as old, have had lower long-term accumulation rates due to the development of permafrost in the later part of the Holocene. The relatively shallow average peat depths between $60°$ and $61°$ N latitude correspond to an area of saline discharge (see Bayrock 1972). Salts are known to limit bryophyte growth (Vitt *et al.* 1993), and peatland initiation and distribution (Halsey *et al.* 1997, 1998), hence the shallow mean peat depths in this region are probably realistic.

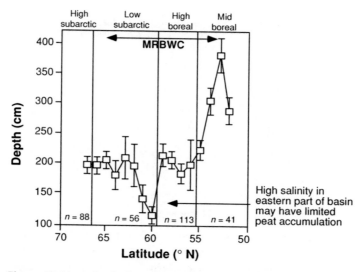

Figure 6.8 Mean depth distributions along a latitudinal gradient within the Mackenzie River Basin. Error bars represent the standard error of the mean. Depths were taken from peat depths extracted from: McCallum and Wittenberg (1962), Dyck *et al.* (1966), Bender *et al.* (1968, 1969), Lowden and Blake (1968), Mackay and Mathews (1973), Nichols (1975), Zoltai and Tarnocai (1975), Reid (1977), Rutherford *et al.* (1979, 1984), Hughes *et al.* (1981), Chatwin (1983), MacDonald (1983), Schreiner (1983), Zoltai *et al.* (1988), Zoltai (1989, 1993), Zoltai and Vitt (1990), Kuhry (1994), Kuhry and Vitt (1996), Halsey *et al.* (1998), Bauer (2002), P. Kuhry (unpublished data), Z. Yu (unpublished data), S. C. Zoltai (unpublished data).

Carbon storage in the MRBWC is estimated as 15.7 ± 2.6 Pg and represents about 7% of the 220 Pg of carbon currently present in peatlands of North America (see Halsey *et al.* 2000). The majority of this carbon is found within two different parts of the wetland complex, the Great Slave Lake Plain in the north and the central uplands of the Cameron Hills and Caribou Mountains (Fig. 6.9).

In 2002, Turetsky *et al.* published the first regional-scale assessment of peatland carbon storage from the western boreal under current disturbance regimes. This area includes the southern half of the MRBWC and may be fairly representative of disturbance in the MRBWC. They concluded that under the current disturbance regime, carbon uptake in continental peatlands is reduced by 85% when compared with a no-disturbance scenario. They estimated that across the western-Canadian boreal forest, about 13% of the peatlands are affected by recent disturbance. They also concluded that a 17% increase in the area burned annually and in the intensity of organic matter combustion would convert these peatlands into a regional net source of carbon to the atmosphere.

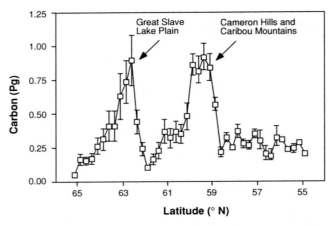

Figure 6.9 Distribution of carbon stored in peatlands of the MRBWC along a latitudinal gradient in 0.25°-latitude increments. Errors are generated by combining error estimates for distribution, standard error of mean depth and carbon density.

Currently, carbon is lost to the atmosphere in these continental peatlands through a variety of disturbance parameters. First, carbon has been lost from historical fires where, based on long-term peat stratigraphies, about 0.25% of the peatland area has burned annually. Secondly, carbon losses from current fires have a combined direct and indirect effect of releasing 6282 Gg C per year to the atmosphere. Thirdly, peat extraction, reservoir flooding, and oil-sands mining all result in small carbon fluxes to the atmosphere (each less than 150 Gg C per year). Currently, nitrogen deposition from Alberta's oil-sands mining (and in the MRBWC) have increased *Sphagnum* production over 3-fold, but peat accumulation rates have not increased in the areas affected by high nitrogen emissions (Vitt *et al.* 2003). Fourthly, permafrost melt (Vitt *et al.* 2000b) enhances the carbon sink (about 100 Gg C per year). Overall, carbon emissions from disturbed peatlands across western Canada total 6462 Gg C per year and reduce the regional carbon accumulation by 85% when compared with the no-disturbance scenario. Turetsky *et al.* (2002) concluded that natural and anthropogenic disturbances have a substantial influence on peatland carbon storage. The assessment presented in Turetsky *et al.* (2002) suggests that peatlands accumulate 24.5 g C m^{-2} per year during periods of no disturbance. However, under contemporary levels of disturbance and development across this boreal region, average carbon accumulation rates are reduced to 3.6 g C m^{-2} per year. Changing disturbance regimes must be more-carefully incorporated into carbon estimates if a true understanding of carbon balances is to be achieved. Fire and permafrost melt are both controlled by climate and will be important, interconnected processes in the future.

Summary

The MRBWC represents one of the largest northern wetland complexes in the world. The wetland complex supports approximately 166 300 km^2 of peatland across a latitudinal gradient of approximately 1125 km. Due to its extensive latitudinal gradient, the MRBWC supports a wide variety of peat landforms types, and different peat landforms are characteristically found in different parts of the basin. In the northern and central part of the wetland complex permafrost bogs dominate with patterned ground being restricted to the far north while fens dominate in the south and along part of the Slave River Lowland. Evidence of degraded permafrost in the form of internal lawns is also found in the southern part of the MRBWC. Non-peat-accumulating wetlands are found throughout the wetland complex although cover values are generally low.

A hybrid DCCA indicates that wetland distribution within the wetland complex is largely controlled by allogenic factors of climate and physiography. The first canonical axis represents the variance in wetland distribution occurring along a north-to-south gradient with mean annual temperature being most-strongly correlated to this gradient. Substrate texture is also significant with bogs developing on substrates of low hydraulic conductivity while fens tend to be associated with substrates of high hydraulic conductivity. The second canonical axis represents variation in the wetland data set created by the hydrology of wetland ecosystems. Peatlands with stable water tables are on one end and non-peat-accumulating wetlands and fluctuating water tables are on the opposite end of the axis. Mean annual temperature is again the most-important explanatory variable with the presence or absence of salinity also significant in explaining the second axis. As with wetland types, wetland flora – specifically bryophyte distributions – are also controlled by climatic factors.

Peat accumulation is known to have initiated during the Late Wisconsinan in the northwestern part of the Mackenzie River Basin (*c.* 12 500 BP), and basal radiocarbon dates become progressively younger to the southeast. Once peatlands were established, surface isolation, oligotrophication, and acidification allowed for the establishment of *Sphagnum*. In areas where peat accumulation from *Sphagnum* was more rapid than the surrounding peatland, bogs develop. Within the Mackenzie River Basin, the timing of *Sphagnum* establishment ranges from about 100 to 5400 years after peatland initiation. With the establishment of *Sphagnum*, thermal conductivity of the peat changes and permafrost develops. Permafrost initiated in the MRBWC after 5000 years BP in the north, after 3000 years BP in the central part, and in the Little Ice Age in the southernmost extremity.

Carbon storage in the MRBWC is estimated as 15.7 ± 2.6 Pg and represents about 7% of the 220 Pg of carbon currently present in peatlands of North America (see Halsey *et al.* 2000). Carbon storage in any part of the wetland complex is a function of peat depth and cover. As age is not necessarily correlated with depth, older peatlands do not always contain more carbon. The majority of carbon within the MRBWC is found in two different parts of the wetland complex, the Great Slave Lake Plain in the north and the central uplands of the Cameron Hills and Caribou Mountains.

Wetlands found within the MRBWC reflect a common thread found throughout northern wetlands, that is one of diversity and complexity. Clearly, northern wetlands are not all the same, nor did they all appear on the northern landscape at the same time. Wetland distribution, flora, and development are controlled primarily by climate – specifically mean annual temperature; however, physiographical factors related to substrate type and chemistry (salinity) have also played an important role in their evolution. Hence, future climatic change as well as natural and anthropogenic disturbances, especially fire, will have an impact on the type, distribution, and extent of this large, northern wetland complex.

References

Almquist-Jacobson, H. and Foster, D. R. (1995). Towards an integrated model for raised bog development: theory and field evidence. *Ecology*, **76**, 2503–16.

Anderson, R. B. (1999). Peatland habitat use and selection by woodland caribou (*Rangifer tarandus caribou*) in Northern Alberta. M.Sc. thesis, University of Alberta, Edmonton, Alberta, Canada.

Andrus, R. E. (1980). Sphagnaceae (peat moss family) of New York State. In *Contributions to a Flora of New York State*, vol. 3, ed. R. S. Mitchell. New York State Museum Bulletin 442.

Andrus, R. E., Wagner, D. J., and Titus, J. E. (1983). Vertical zonation of *Sphagnum* mosses along hummock–hollow gradients. *Canadian Journal of Botany*, **94**, 416–26.

Bauer, I. (2002). Internal and external controls over Holocene peatland development in Boreal Western Canada. Ph.D. dissertation, University of Alberta, Edmonton, Alberta, Canada.

Bayrock, L. A. (1972). *Surficial Geology, Peace Point and Fitzgerald (part)*. Alberta Research Council map. Edmonton, Canada: Alberta Research Council.

Beilman, D. W., Vitt, D. H., and Halsey, L. A. (2001). Localized permafrost peatlands in western Canada: definition, distributions, and degradation. *Arctic, Antarctic and Alpine Research*, **33**, 70–7.

Bender, M. M., Bryson, R. A., and Baerreis, D. A. (1968). University of Wisconsin radiocarbon dates, V. *Radiocarbon*, **10**, 473–8.

(1969). University of Wisconsin Radiocarbon dates, VI. *Radiocarbon*, **11**, 228–35.

Blake, W., Jr. (1986). *Geological Survey of Canada Radiocarbon Dates, XXV.* Geological Survey of Canada Paper 85-7.

Botch, M. S. and Masing, V. V. (1983). Mire ecosystems in the U.S.S.R. In *Ecosystems of the World*, vol. 4B, *Mires: Swamp, Bog, Fen and Moor*, ed. A. J. P. Gore. Amsterdam, the Netherlands: Elsevier Science, pp. 95–152.

Botch, M. S., Kobak, K. I., Vinson, T. S., and Kolchugina, T. P. (1995). Carbon pools and accumulation in peatlands of the former Soviet Union. *Global Biochemical Cycles*, **9**, 37–46.

Bradshaw, C. J. A., Hebert, D. M., Rippin, A. B., and Boutin, S. (1995). Winter peatland habitat selection by woodland caribou in northeastern Alberta. *Canadian Journal of Zoology*, **73**, 1567–74.

Campbell, C., Vitt, D. H., Halsey, L. A., Campbell, I., Thormann, M. N., and Bayley, S. E. (2000). *Net Primary Production and Standing Biomass in Wetlands in Boreal Canada*. NOR-X Report 369, Canadian Forest Service.

Catto, N. R. (1996). Richardson Mountains, Yukon–Northwest Territories: the northern portal of the postulated 'ice-free corridor'. *Quaternary International*, **32**, 3–19.

Chatwin, S. C. (1981). Permafrost aggradation and degradation in a sub-arctic peatland. M.Sc. thesis, University of Alberta, Edmonton, Alberta, Canada.

(1983). Holocene temperatures in the upper Mackenzie Valley determined by oxygen isotope analysis of peat cellulose. In *Proceedings of the Fourth International Conference on Permafrost, July 18–22, 1983, Fairbanks, Alaska*. Washington, DC: National Academy Press, pp. 127–30.

Cottrell, T. R. (1995). Willow colonization of Rocky Mountain mires. *Canadian Journal of Forest Research*, **25**, 215–22.

Craig, B. G. (1965). *Glacial Lake McConnell, and the Surficial Geology of Parts of Slave River and Redstone River Map-Areas, District of Mackenzie*. Geological Survey of Canada Bulletin 122.

Damman, A. W. H. (1977). Geographical changes in the vegetation pattern of raised bogs in the Bay of Fundy region of Maine and New Brunswick. *Vegetatio*, **35**, 137–51.

(1979). Geographic patterns in peatland development in eastern North America. In *Symposium on Classification of Peat and Peatlands, September 17–21, 1979, Hyytiala, Finland*, eds. E. Kivinen, L. Heikurainen, and P. Pakarinen. Jyväskylä, Finland: The International Peat Society, pp. 42–57.

David, P. (1977). *Sand Dune Occurrences of Canada: a Theme and Resource Inventory Study of Eolian Landforms of Canada*. Indian and Northern Affairs, National Parks Branch Contract 74-230.

Duk-Rodkin, A. and Lemmen, D. S. (2000). Glacial history of the Mackenzie region. In *The Physical Environment of the Mackenzie Valley, Northwest Territories: a Base Line for the Assessment of Environmental Change*, eds. L. D. Dyke and G. R. Brooks. Geological Survey of Canada Bulletin 547, pp. 18–27.

Dyke, W., Lowden, J. A., Fyles, J. G., and Blake, W., Jr. (1966). *Geological Survey of Canada Radiocarbon Dates, V*. Geological Survey of Canada Paper 66-48.

Elias, S. A., Short, S. K., and Birks, H. H. (1997). Late Wisconsin environments of the Bering Land Bridge. *Palaeogeography, Palaeoclimatology, Palaeoecology*, **136**, 293– 308.

Environment Canada (1982). *Canadian Climate Normals 1951–1980*, vols. 2 and 3. Ottawa, Canada: Atmospheric Environment Service.

Eurola, S. (1962). Über die regionale Einteilung der südfinnischen Moore. *Vanamo*, **33**, 1–243.

Finnamore, A. T. (1994). Hymenoptera of the Wagner Natural Area, a boreal spring fen in central Alberta. *Memoirs of the Entomological Society of Canada*, **169**, 181–200.

Gignac, L. D. and Vitt, D. H. (1990). Habitat limitations of *Sphagnum* along climatic, chemical, and physical gradients. *Bryologist*, **93**, 7–22.

Glaser, P. H. and Janssens, J. A. (1986). Raised bogs in eastern North America: transitions in landforms and gross stratigraphy. *Canadian Journal of Botany*, **64**, 395–415.

Gorham, E. (1991). Northern peatlands: role in the carbon cycle and probable responses to climatic warming. *Ecological Applications*, **1**, 182–95.

Halsey, L. A., Vitt, D. H., and Zoltai, S. C. (1995). Disequilibrium response of permafrost in boreal continental western Canada to climatic change. *Climatic Change*, **30**, 57–73.

(1997). Climatic and physiographic controls on wetland type and distribution in Manitoba, Canada. *Wetlands*, **17**, 243–62.

Halsey, L. A., Vitt, D. H., and Bauer, I. E. (1998). Peatland initiation during the Holocene in continental western Canada. *Climatic Change*, **40**, 315–42.

Halsey, L. A., Vitt, D. H., and Gignac, L. D. (2000). *Sphagnum*-dominated peatlands in North America since the last glacial maximum: their occurrence and extent. *Bryologist*, **103**, 334–52.

Heinselman, M. L. (1963). Forest sites, bog processes, and peatland types in the glacial Lake Agassiz area, Minnesota. *Ecological Monographs*, **33**, 327–74.

(1970). Landscape evolution and peatland types, and the Lake Agassiz Peatlands Natural Area, Minnesota. *Ecological Monographs*, **40**, 235–61.

Hill, M. O. (1979). *TWINSPAN. A Fortran Program for Arranging Multivariate Data in an Ordered Two-Way Table by Classification of Individuals and Attributes*. Ithaca, NY: Cornell University.

Horton, D. G., Vitt, D. H., and Slack, N. G. (1979). Habitats of circumboreal-subarctic Sphagna. I. A quantitative analysis and review of species in the Caribou Mountains, northern Alberta. *Canadian Journal of Botany*, **57**, 2283–317.

Hughes, O., Harrington, C. R., Janssens, J. A. *et al.* (1981). Upper Pleistocene stratigraphy, paleoecology, and archaeology of the northern Yukon interior, Eastern Beringia. I. Bonnet Plume Basin. *Arctic*, **34**, 29–365.

Janssens, J. A. (1983). Past and extant distributions of *Drepanocladus* in North America, with notes on the differentiation of fossil fragments. *Journal of the Hattori Botanical Laboratory*, **54**, 251–98.

Kuhry, P. (1994). The role of fire in the development of *Sphagnum* dominated peatlands in western boreal Canada. *Journal of Ecology*, **82**, 899–910.

(1998). Late Holocene permafrost dynamics in two subarctic peatlands of the Hudson Bay Lowlands (Manitoba), Canada. *Eurasian Soil Science*, **31**, 529–34.

Kuhry, P. and Vitt, D. H. (1996). Fossil carbon/nitrogen ratios as a measure of peat decomposition. *Ecology*, **77**, 271–5.

Kuhry, P., Nicholson, B. J., Gignac, L. D., Vitt, D. H., and Bayley, S. E. (1993). Development of *Sphagnum*-dominated peatlands in boreal continental Canada. *Canadian Journal of Botany*, **71**, 10–22.

Kutzbach, J. E. and Guetter, P. J. (1986). The influence of changing orbital parameters and surface boundary conditions on climate simulations for the past 18,000 years. *Journal of Atmospheric Sciences*, **43**, 1726–59.

Lemmen, D. S., Duk-Rodkin, A., and Bednarski, J. M. (1994). Late glacial drainage systems along the northwest margin of the Laurentide Ice Sheet. *Quaternary Science Reviews*, **13**, 805–28.

Lowden, J. A., and Blake, W., Jr. (1968). *Geological Survey of Canada Radiocarbon Dates, VII*. Geological Survey of Canada Paper 68-2B, pp. 207–45.

MacDonald, G. M. (1983). Holocene vegetation history of the upper Natla River area, Northwest Territories, Canada. *Arctic and Alpine Research*, **15**, 169–80.

Mackay, J. R. and Mathews, W. H. (1973). Geomorphology and Quaternary history of the Mackenzie River valley near Fort Good Hope, N.W.T., Canada. *Canadian Journal of Earth Sciences*, **10**, 26–41.

Maynard, D. E. (1988). *Peatland Inventory of British Columbia*. Mineral Resources Division, British Columbia Geological Survey Branch.

McCallum, K. J. and Wittenberg, J. (1962). University of Saskatchewan radiocarbon dates, III. *Radiocarbon*, **4**, 71–80.

Mills, G. F., Veldhuis, H., and Eilers, R. G. (1978). *A Guide to Biophysical Land Classification, Knee Lake, 53M*. Technical Report 78–2. Manitoba Department of Renewable Resources and Transportation Services.

Moore, P. D. and Bellamy, D. J. (1974). *Peatlands*. New York: Springer Verlag.

National Wetlands Working Group (1988). *Wetlands of Canada*. Ecological Land Classification Series 24. Ottawa, Canada: Sustainable Development Branch, Environment Canada Montreal, Canada: Polyscience Publications Inc.

Nichols, H. (1975). *Palynological and Paleoclimatic Study of the Late Quaternary Displacement of the Boreal Forest–Tundra Ecotone in Keewatin and Mackenzie, N. W. T. Canada*. Institute of Arctic and Alpine Research Occasional Paper 15.

Nicholson, B. J. and Vitt, D. H. (1990). The paleoecology of a peatland complex in continental western Canada. *Canadian Journal of Botany*, **68**, 121–38.

Nicholson, B. J., Gignac, L. D., and Bayley, S. E. (1996). Peatland distribution along a north–south transect in the Mackenzie River Basin in relation to climatic and environmental gradients. *Vegetatio*, **126**, 119–33.

Reid, D. E. (1977). *Permafrost in Peat Landforms in Northwestern Alberta*. Biological Report Series 37. Canadian Arctic Gas Study, Ltd.

200 Vitt, D. H., Halsey, L. A., and Nicholson, B. J.

Robinson, S. D. and Moore, T. R. (1999). Carbon and peat accumulation over the past 1200 years in a landscape with discontinuous permafrost, northwestern Canada. *Global Biochemical Cycles*, **13**, 591–602.

(2000). The influence of permafrost and fire upon carbon accumulation in High Boreal Peatlands, Northwest Territories, Canada. *Arctic, Antarctic, and Alpine Research*, **32**, 155–6.

Rockware (1991). *Macgridzo: the Contour Mapping Program for the Macintosh, Version 3.3*. Wheat Ridge, CO: Rockware.

Rutherford, A. A., Wittenberg, J., and Wilmeth, R. (1979). University of Saskatchewan radiocarbon dates, VII. *Radiocarbon*, **21**, 241–292.

Rutherford, A. A., Wittenberg, J., and Gordon, B. C. (1984). University of Saskatchewan radiocarbon dates, X. *Radiocarbon*, **26**, 241–292.

Schreiner, B. T. (1983). Lake Agassiz in Saskatchewan. In *Glacial Lake Agassiz*, eds. J. T. Teller and L. Clayton. Geological Association of Canada Special Paper 26, pp. 74–96.

Shay, J. (1981). Wetland protection in the 80's. In *Proceedings of the Ontario Wetland Conference, September 18–19, 1981, Toronto, Canada*, ed. A. Champagne. Toronto, Canada: Federation of Ontario Naturalists, pp. 19–25.

Sjörs, H. (1948). Myrvegetation I Bergslagen. Summary: mire vege in Bergslagen, Sweden. *Acta Phytogeographica Suecica*, **21**, 1–299.

(1952). On the relation between vegetation and electrolytes in north Swedish mire waters. *Oikos*, **2**, 242–58.

Tarnocai, C., Kettles, I. M., and Lacelle, B. (1999). *Peatlands of Canada*. Geological Survey of Canada Open File 3834.

Ter Braak, C. J. F. (1997). *CANOCA: A FORTRAN Program of Canonical, Community Ordination by (Partial) (Detrended) (Canonical) Correspondence Analysis, Principal Components and Redundancy Analysis (Version 3.1.5)*. Wageningen, the Netherlands: Agricultural Mathematics Group.

Turetsky, M., Wieder, K., Halsey, L. A., and Vitt, D. H. (2002). Current disturbance and the diminishing peatland carbon sink. *Geophysical Research Letters*, 10.1029/2001GLO14000, June 12, 2002.

Vitt, D. H. and Andrus, R. E. (1977). The genus *Sphagnum* in Alberta. *Canadian Journal of Botany*, **55**, 331–57.

Vitt, D. H. and Chee, W.-L. (1990). The relationships of vegetation to surface water chemistry and peat chemistry in fens of Alberta, Canada. *Vegetatio*, **89**, 87–106.

Vitt, D. H. and Slack, N. G. (1975). An analysis of the vegetation of *Sphagnum*-dominated kettle-hole bogs in relation to environmental gradients. *Canadian Journal of Botany*, **53**, 332–59.

(1984). Niche diversification of *Sphagnum* relative to environmental factors in northern Minnesota peatlands. *Canadian Journal of Botany*, **62**, 1409–30.

Vitt, D. H., Achuff, P., and Andrus, R. E. (1975). The vegetation and chemical properties of patterned fens in the Swan Hills, north central Alberta. *Canadian Journal of Botany*, **53**, 2776–95.

Vitt, D. H., Horton, D. G., Slack, N. G. and Malmer, N. (1990). *Sphagnum* dominated peatlands of the hyperoceanic British Columbia coast: patterns in surface water chemistry and vegetation. *Canadian Journal of Forest Research*, **20**, 696–711.

Vitt, D. H., Van Wirdum, G., Zoltai, S. C., and Halsey, L. A. (1993). Habitat requirements of *Scorpidium scorpioides* and fen development in continental Canada. *Bryologist*, **96**, 106–11.

Vitt, D. H., Halsey, L. A., and Zoltai, S. C. (1994). The bog landforms of continental western Canada relative to climate and permafrost patterns. *Arctic and Alpine Research*, **26**, 1–13.

Vitt, D. H., Bayley, S. E., and Jin, T-L. (1995). Seasonal variation in water chemistry over a bog-rich fen gradient in continental western Canada. *Canadian Journal of Fisheries and Aquatic Sciences*, **52**, 587–606.

Vitt, D. H., Halsey, L. A., Thormann, M. N., and Martin, T. (1996). *Peatland Inventory of Alberta. Phase 1: Overview of Peatland Resources in the Natural Regions and Subregions of the Province*. Alberta Peat Task Force. Edmonton, Canada: NCE-SFMN, University of Alberta.

Vitt, D. H., Halsey, L. A., Bauer, I. E., and Campbell, C. (2000a). Spatial and temporal trends in carbon storage of peatlands of continental western Canada through the Holocene. *Canadian Journal of Earth Sciences*, **37**, 683–93.

Vitt, D. H., Halsey, L. A., and Zoltai, S. C. (2000b). The changing landscape of Canada's western boreal forest: the current dynamics of permafrost. *Canadian Journal of Forest Research*, **30**, 283–7.

Vitt, D. H., Halsey, L. A., Wieder, K., and Turetsky, M. (2003). Response of *Sphagnum fuscum* to nitrogen deposition: a case study of ombrogenous peatlands in Alberta, Canada. *Bryologist*, **106**, 235–45.

Yu, Z., Vitt, D. H., Campbell, I. D., and Apps, M. J. (2003). Understanding Holocene peat accumulation pattern of continental fens in western Canada. *Canadian Journal of Botany*, **81**, 267–82.

Zoltai, S. C. (1971). *Southern Limit of Permafrost Features in Peat Landforms, Manitoba and Saskatchewan*. Geological Association of Canada Special Paper 9, pp. 305–10.

(1989). Late Quaternary volcanic ash in the peatlands of central Alberta. *Canadian Journal of Earth Sciences*, **26**, 207–14.

(1993). Cyclic development of permafrost in the peatlands of northwestern Alberta, Canada. *Arctic and Alpine Research*, **25**, 240–6.

(1995). Permafrost distribution in peatlands of west-central Canada during the Holocene warm period 6000 years BP. *Géographie Physique et Quaternaire*, **49**, 45–54.

Zoltai, S. C. and Pettapiece, W. W. (1973). *Terrain, Vegetation, and Permafrost Relationships in the Northern Part of the Mackenzie Valley and Northern Yukon*. Environmental–Social Committee, Northern Pipelines. Task Force on Northern Oil Development, Report 73-4.

Zoltai, S. C. and Tarnocai, C. (1975). Perennially frozen peatlands in the western Arctic and Subarctic of Canada. *Canadian Journal of Earth Sciences*, **12**, 28–43.

Zoltai, S. C. and Vitt, D. H. (1990). Holocene climatic change and the distribution of peatlands in the western interior of Canada. *Quaternary Research*, **33**, 231–40.

(1995). Canadian wetlands: environmental gradients and classification. *Vegetatio*, **118**, 131–7.

Zoltai, S. C., Tarnocai, C., Mills, G. F., and Veldhuis, H. (1988). Wetlands of subarctic Canada. In *Wetlands of Canada*, ed. National Wetlands Working Group. Ecological Land Classification Series 24. Ottawa, Canada: Sustainable Development Branch, Environment Canada. Montreal, Canada: Polyscience Publications Inc.

7

The Pantanal

C. J. R. ALHO

Universidade para o Desenvolvimento do Estado e para a Região do Pantanal
(UNIDERP)

The Pantanal is a savanna wetland which, because of its wildlife, is recognized as one of the most important freshwater systems in the world. It is fed by tributaries of the upper Paraguay River in the center of South America, mainly in Brazil. The north–south gradient in flood level creates a range of major habitats in a complex mosaic with annual seasonality. The rivers and streams are lined with gallery forests, and other arboreal habitats exist in the more-elevated areas. The remainder is either grasslands or seasonally flooded grasslands. The flora and fauna are related to the Cerrado biome of central Brazil, with the Amazonian influence contributing great species diversity. The vegetation is composed of 1863 phanerogam plant species listed for the floodplain and 3400 for the whole basin. The complex vegetation cover and the seasonal productivity support a diverse and abundant fauna. Many endangered species occur here, including the jaguar (*Panthera onca*). Waterfowl are exceptionally abundant during the dry season. Deforestation of dense savanna and strips of forest has increased dramatically, with subsequent erosion. Another threat is unsustainable agricultural and cattle-ranching practices, which convert the natural vegetation into pastures and soybean plantations, especially on the surrounding plateaus. Fires caused by humans are severe and have become part of the annual cycle for ranch owners. Despite the natural exuberance, the lack of infrastructure and poor utilization of touristic potential constitute the main obstacles to carrying out sustainable conservation.

The World's Largest Wetlands: Ecology and Conservation, eds. L. H. Fraser and P. A. Keddy.
Published by Cambridge University Press. © Cambridge University Press 2005.

Figure 7.1 The Pantanal's location in the South American continent, emphasizing its place within central-Brazil's major biome (Cerrado). There is a portion of floodplain entering Bolivia to the north, mainly west of the city of Cáceres, and a strip touching Paraguay to the south, mainly north of the city of Porto Murtinho, along the Paraguay River.

Introduction

The Pantanal biome is a wetland region located in the center of South America, in western Brazil's upper Paraguay River basin (latitude 15° 30′ to 22° 30′ S and longitude 54° 45′ to 58° 30′ W). The greater upper Paraguay basin is an area of 496 000 km² (363 442 km² in Brazil), within which the land ranging 200 to 1200 m above sea level is considered as highland or plateau and the flatland between 80 and 150 m is the floodplain, called The Pantanal, which occupies an area of 138 183 km², representing about 38% of the basin (ANA 2004) (Fig. 7.1). The upland consists of elevated plateaus and mountains to the north and east with elevations ranging from 250 to 1200 m. It is important to distinguish both regions (the Pantanal and the uplands) forming the upper Paraguay basin – in geographical, ecological, and economic terms – so as to understand their hydrology and their highly differentiated human use.

The importance of the Pantanal has been widely stressed, both nationally (designated a National Heritage Site by the Brazilian Constitution) as well as internationally (recognized as a Wetland Ecosystem of Extreme Importance for Biodiversity Conservation by the Ramsar Convention and credited by UNESCO as a Biosphere Reserve, where the Pantanal National Park is the core area of that reserve; IBAMA 2004, UNESCO 2004).

Rivers

The floodplain is mainly formed by the tributaries from the left margin of the Paraguay River, 74% of the Pantanal is in Brazil and 26% in Bolivia and Paraguay (Fig. 7.2). The streams and rivers on these highlands are most prevalent where rainfall is abundant in the wet season. In the plateaus small brooks flow into small rivers, which flow into large ones. The large rivers are shaped largely by terrain, velocity of the water, levels of dissolved oxygen, nutrient loads, temperature, and type of riverbed. These major rivers feeding the Pantanal are (from north to south): Paraguay, Bento Gomes, Cuiabá, São Lourenço–Itiquira, Taquari, Negro, Aquidauana–Miranda, Nabileque, and Apa. The Paraguay River joins the Paraná River in southern Brazil and they flow into the La Plata River. The tributaries of the Paraguay are slow moving when they meet the flatland and have coves with adjacent flood land. They periodically overflow their banks. The maze of fluctuating water levels, nutrients, and wildlife forms a dynamic ecosystem. The flooding occupies about 80% of the whole Pantanal. In contrast, during the dry season the water returns to the riverbeds and most of the flooded areas stay dry.

Greater and longer floods are found along the Paraguay River, between Porto Conceição and Porto Murtinho, reaching depths of 1 to 1.5 m. They can last for about six months, while on the floodplain where the water spreads into the shape of a fan the submersion is about 0.5 m. In these places the duration of the flood varies according to the region, with maximum durations recorded of 70 days (Paraguay and Jauru), 43 days (Cuiabá, Aquidauana–Miranda), and 19 to 29 days (Taquari and São Lourenço). In the floodplain that receives waters from the Negro and Taboco rivers the flood reaches 1.2 m and lasts about 90 days (PCBAP 1997).

The slow flow of the rivers when they reach the floodplain results in the current's speed decreasing and most of the suspended sediment being lost. Dissolved oxygen concentrations drop drastically, followed by accumulation of dissolved carbon dioxide and decreased pH (Hamilton *et al.* 1995).

Where the river water makes contact with the floodplain, depletion of dissolved oxygen, oversaturation of carbon dioxide and methane, loss of suspended

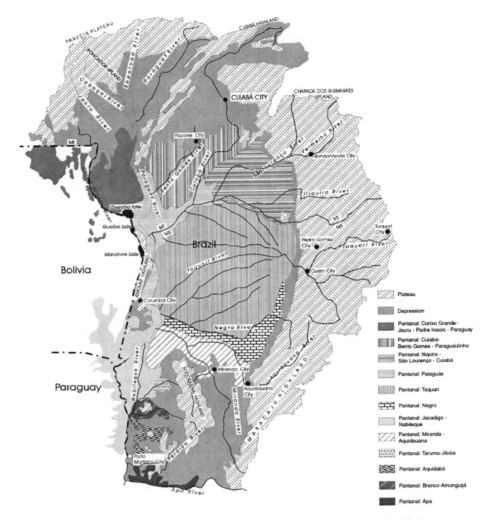

Figure 7.2 Map of the upper Paraguay basin showing the Pantanal with its subregions that are potentially affected by the water level of the Paraguay River and the surrounding uplands. Most of the flooding area is within Brazil, with lesser areas to the west of the Paraguay River in Bolivia and Paraguay.

sediments, and reduced export of nitrogen and phosphorous result. Oxygen depletion and associated chemical changes are most marked when river water first contacts the floodplain; in 1995, the water remained anoxic throughout the river channel for six weeks, causing massive fish mortality. Most chemical weathering of minerals seems to take place in the upland drainage basins rather than on the floodplains, and most major solutes display conservative mixing in the river-floodplain system (Hamilton *et al.* 1997).

Geomorphology

The Pantanal is a geographic depression where sediments have accumulated since the Quaternary period (forming the latter part of the Cenozoic era, beginning about 1 000 000 years ago and including the Holocene and Pleistocene epochs). The Pantanal is a sedimentary basin, a mosaic of alluvial fans of Pleistocene origin; it is periodically flooded and is surrounded by highlands. The relief of the upper Paraguay basin is marked by contrasts between the low, flat floodplain and the surrounding non-flooded area of plateaus and depressions (PCBAP 1997).

The limits of the upper Paraguay River basin include areas of Precambrian lithology (500 to 600 Ma) which support two packages of rocky material with Cretaceous and Tertiary cover.

The geological characteristics include elevations named Xingu Complex and Rio Apa Complex, representing the Brazilian Crystalline Complex, whose substrate reflects the different geological events. The plains are sediments deposited during the Quaternary period, which are markedly sandy, with restricted areas of clay and organic deposits. The relief of the whole upper Paraguay basin can be classified in three units: (1) the floodplain which is the Pantanal; (2) the adjacent residual elevations plus the depressions; and (3) the highlands.

In the Taquari subregion, nine relief units were identified using remote sensing applied to geomorphological mapping (Florenzano 1998). These units were grouped into three categories according to their morphogenesis: structural/denudational forms (scarps); denudational forms (pediments, tables, hills, and residual relief); and depositional forms (floodplains and Pantanal – the latter divided into low-, medium-, and high-moisture areas).

There are different identified morpho-structures forming the uplands which are responsible for soil type and, in consequence, different vegetation cover – varying from open Cerrado (savanna) to seasonal forests – and of course different human uses such as mining, agriculture, cattle ranching, and tourism.

These structures have produced the following highlands: Planalto dos Parecis, Chapada dos Guimarães, and others known as Províncias Serrana or Serra de Cuiabá (north); Taquari-Itiquira, Caiapônia, Maracaju-Campo Grande, Bodoquena, and São Domingos (east); Urucum-Amolar and other elevations (west); and Rio Apa (south) (PCBAP 1997). The watershed on the highlands feeds different basins, according to the direction of the elevations. Water to the extreme north (Parecis and Cuiabá elevations) flows into the Amazon basin; to the east (Bodoquena, Maracaju, and São Jerônimo) it flows into the Araguaia and the Paraná basins.

The uplands, including the mountains, tables, hills, plateaus, depressions, and other forms of relief are described below (Fig. 7.2).

1. North – in the west–east direction:
   - Chapada dos Parecis. A plateau with altitude of 700 m with most of its length outside the upper Paraguay basin.
   - Planalto do Jauru. A plateau located at the extreme north of the Pantanal, reaching 700 m in height.
   - Serra de Santa Bárbara. Precambrian mountains reaching 500 to 900 m in altitude, with cliffs.
   - Depressão do Jauru. A depression ranging from 150 to 200 m in altitude.
   - Planalto do Rio Branco. A hilly plateau connecting the Parecis with the Paraguay, Jauru, and Rio Branco valleys.
   - Província Serrana. A large mountain range, 400 km long and 40 km wide, located above the Depressão Cuiabana and extending from south-southwest to north-northeast. The Serra das Araras can reach 500 to 800 m in height and the depressions are at a height of 300 to 450 m.
   - Planalto de Tapirapuã–Tangará. Located near the Parecis, this plateau (450 to 500 m) is crossed by the Sepotuba River.
   - Depressão Alto Paraguay This depression touches the northern portion of Província Serrana.
   - Depressão Cuiabana. This depression starts in the region of Poconé and Santo Antônio do Leverger, south of the city of Cuiabá, and goes up to the springs of the Cuiabá and Manso rivers. The altitudes range from 150 to 450 m, being more elevated in the north. This region has been drastically eroded since the Cretaceous period, and has a smooth surface.
   - Chapada dos Guimarães. This beautiful plateau is part of the morpho-structure of the Paraná basin. The soils are red latosols with more-recent erosive processes and altitudes reaching 850 m, frequently in the form of cliffs.
   - Planalto do Casca. This is similar to Chapada dos Guimarães, but lower (45 to 650 m).
   - Arruda-Mutum. A plateau located near the Depressão Cuiabana, north of Cuiabá and west of Chapada dos Guimarães. Altitudes range from 400 to 500 m with a strong rugged surface.
2. East – in the north–south direction:
   - Planalto dos Alcantilados. A hilly plateau with cliffs.
   - Depressão de Rondonópolis. This depression, part of the morpho-structure of the Paraná basin with altitudes range from 300 to 500 m, is located near the source of the São Lourenço river.

- Chapada do rio Correntes. This is a plateau, reaching 800 m with cliffs.
- Depressão do São Jerônimo–Aquidauana. A depression going north to south, surrounding the Pantanal.
- Planalto do Taquari. A plateau located on the eastern edge of the Pantanal.
- Chapada das Emas. A plateau reaching 800 m, presenting cliffs, where the upper part of the Taquari River is located.
- Chapada de São Gabriel–Coxim–Campo Grande. A plateau with altitudes higher than 700 m.

3. South – in the east–west direction:
- Planalto de Maracaju–Campo Grande. Altitudes vary from 300 to 600 m, with hilly and rugged surfaces.
- Depressão do Miranda. A depression situated on the eastern side of Planalto da Bodoquena and to the west of the Apa River complex. A valley opened by the Miranda River.
- Planalto da Bodoquena. This is a set of mountains oriented north–south, with altitudes ranging from 400 to 650 m. An intense rugged surface. Limestone rocks with caves.
- Bonito highlands. Situated between the Planalto da Bodoquena and the Depressão do Miranda.
- Planalto do Amonguijá–Depressão do Apa. This is a set of small hills up to 350 m in altitude, surrounded by hilly depressions.

4. West – in the north–south direction:
- Amolar. Mountains situated to the north of Corumbá city, forming the boundary with Bolivia and shaping the Paraguay River. Amolar mountain complex and Urucum formation.
- Urucum. The Urucum elevation is rich in iron and manganese. It occurs near Corumbá city at heights ranging from 300 to 1000 m. Hills are isolated and located in lowland areas.

Wetland characteristics

The word Pantanal in Portuguese means "big swamp," and refers to a large tract of wet and spongy land, although technically the region is not a true swamp. Water chemistry, frequency and degree of flooding, soil types, and other factors define the nature of each kind of wetland and the vegetation it supports. Swamps are wetlands dominated by flood-tolerant trees or shrubs. Wetlands often represent a temporal and spatial transition from open water to dry land, and some plant species can bridge the transition between aquatic and terrestrial conditions.

As a wetland, the Pantanal is an ecosystem characterized by constant or recurrent shallow flooding near the surface of the substrate, due to the low drainage capacity of its river system. The vast plain inundated for a large part of the year – plus the presence of relevant physical, chemical, and principally biological characteristics – allow the Pantanal to qualify technically as well as politically as a true wetland. Common diagnostic features of wetlands are hydric soil and hydrophytic vegetation. Endemic flora and fauna of the Pantanal are good indicators of this wetland. These features are present except where specific human intervention has disrupted nature, which in the case of the Pantanal is not always obvious.

The water retained on its plain determines the cycle and shape of the environment as a typical wetland. The landscape is marked by contrasts between the seasonally flooded plains and the surrounding highland, which is not flooded, including patches of savanna and forest near inundated shallow areas.

Thus, three major factors characterize the Pantanal wetland: water, substrate, and biota. The hydrological regimes in the Pantanal are complex and varied. The substrate is a result of geomorphological and climatic evolutions that support recurrent and sustained saturation. A representative biota arises from species of flora and fauna specifically adapted to the local flooding cycles. Then, indicators (i.e. endemic flora and fauna) for the three factors (water, substrate, and biota) can be easily identified.

Ecological processes

Hydrological and climatic cycles

In recent times, ecological processes have depended upon the hydrological and climatic cycles rather than the physical system formed during geological evolution.

The Paraguay River and its tributaries (Cuiabá, São Lourenço, Bento Gomes, Itiquira, Taquari, Negro, and Miranda–Aquidauana) drain into the Pantanal's flat land. The Paraguay River is 2550 km long and has its headwaters in the Serra de Tapirapuã, in the state of Mato Grosso in Brazil: it runs southward between highlands to the west and the Brazilian plateau on the east. The plain is flooded by tributaries on the left bank of the Paraguay River and by the Paraguay itself, which encircles the plain on the western side forming an asymmetric drainage area between its two margins. The basin is mainly on the left bank, in Brazilian territory. In rainy years, such as 1984 and 1995, the width of the Paraguay River expands to 20 km.

The Paraguay basin consists of a series of huge alluvial plains drained by a complex network of rivers interspersed with marshes and a complex mosaic of habitats, including forests. Although most of the Paraguay basin is located on the plateaus, its central portion is depressed and flat, with slow drainage, which allows for seasonal flooding in the Pantanal.

The altitude in the floodplain varies from 80 to 150 m above sea level and the topographical gradients are weak, with the slope ranging from 0.3 to 0.5 m km^{-1} east–west and 0.03 to 0.15 m km^{-1} north–south (Franco & Pinheiro 1982). The river slope in the highlands is about 0.6 m km^{-1}, while on the plain it is 0.1 to 0.3 m km^{-1}. A digital model for treatment of topographic maps of the subregion of Nhecolândia has shown that at altitudes lower than 100 m, the floodplain flattens, while at altitudes above 100 m the terrain slopes more, going east towards Maracaju uplands (Fernandes et al. 1996). When the floodplain reaches the plateau, the altitude suddenly changes to 150 to 400 m. This gentle slope on the plain hinders drainage of the tributaries on the left margin of the Paraguay River, which come from springs on the Brazilian plateaus.

The rain fall in the rainy season, with most rain falling between November and March but with variations between the northern and southern regions, varies annually from 1200 to 1300 mm across the region and in some years can reach 2000 mm. Rainfall is more intensive in the northern uplands than in the south. The relationships between slope, soil, water, vegetation cover, and fauna are significant in differentiating the Pantanal plains – with an average altitude of 80 to 150 m – from their surrounding plateaus with altitudes varying from 200 to 1200 m. The Pantanal is located in a climatically dry area. Annual rainfall in the highlands is generally above 1200 mm, which produces a rapid response in the drainage basin. The reduced runoff on the plains results in flooding of the region. Depressions retain water volume, forming small temporary lakes and ponds or flooding the permanent ones. During low-water times the retained water volume does not return to the riverbed to be drained, but remains where it is and evaporates or infiltrates the soil.

The rainfall level on the plains is 800 to 1200 mm and potential evaporation is 1300 to 1600 mm; the hydric balance is therefore negative. The Pantanal is considered an enormous evaporation "window." The retention of water on the plains reaches 30% to 60%, transforming the Pantanal into a wetland. In the north flooding occurs from March to April, while in the south it occurs from July to August.

In addition to the annual variation in rainy and dry seasons, there are periodic floods and droughts recorded in the literature (Cadavid-Garcia & Castro 1986). The levels of the Paraguay River are influenced by several different factors on micro and macro scales. The variation in the river level depends mainly upon the regional climatic (precipitation) characteristics. The level of a river is an indicator of two important features: (1) drainage and (2) the size of its riverbed, including the adjacent inundated area.

Dynamics of inundation

Annual and pluri-annual flooding determines the ecosystem structure and function of the Pantanal. It is fundamental to know how the system works in order to understand the landscape units and the magnitude and abundance of the biodiversity, conservation measures can then be applied appropriately.

A study using a scanning multi-channel microwave radiometer to reveal flood patterns in the Pantanal showed maximum flooding occurring as early as February in the northern subregions and as late as June in the south, as a result of the delayed drainage of the region (Hamilton et al. 1996). An area of 131 000 km² was inundated annually during nine years of observation, between 1979 and 1987. Monthly estimates of the total area inundated range from 11 000 to 110 000 km².

The distinct annual tides of the rivers, causing the wet and dry seasons, result in hydrological seasonality with productivity of feeding and breeding grounds for wildlife subject to biochemical cycles (Junk 1992, Vinson & Hawkis 1998, Wantzen & Junk 2000). The habitats change as a function of the water discharge carrying nutrients and sediments; the water deposits inorganic and organic matter that enriches the microhabitats and favors the proliferation of microorganisms, invertebrates, fish, and so on.

At the same time, plants are well adapted to occupy the available spaces and, during the wet season, aquatic species reproduce rapidly. The trees interact with the environment through their roots. The organic matter – dead or alive – is rapidly altered, favoring the proliferation of invertebrates and the migration of fish from the river to the flooded areas.

The areas in the shady interior of the gallery forests produce less algae and biomass of floating plants than the sunny areas, but they receive more dead leaves, branches, and dead trunks, which play a crucial role in the energy balance of the system (Wantzen & Junk 2000). Dead trees are generally sources of diversity and abundance for invertebrates.

The hydrology is important in assessing the viability and environmental impact of development projects that modify the natural tides. The hydrology of the Pantanal rivers is unregulated. Flooding is seasonal, but it also varies throughout the plain because of the gentle gradients. The flood period tends to be delayed after the rains on the uplands because of the slow passage of flood waters through the floodplains. Most of the area is flooded by the overflow from the rivers, but some specific areas flood with local rainfall.

During the high water level, the flow moves slowly through depressions, locally known as "*corixos*," or along shallow water paths, "*vazantes*." The depth of the water close to the river channels is less than 6 m and is nearly 2 m on the floodplains (Hamilton *et al.* 1995).

After receiving the contribution from its tributaries in Brazilian territory, the Paraguay River at Ladário (Corumbá) presents two flood cycles. The first is influenced by the rivers Aquidauana, Miranda, Negro, and Taquari, with floods in February and March. The second is influenced by the discharge of the upper Paraguay River from April to June (Silva 1991).

The Paraguay River flows from north to south along the western side of the Pantanal, receiving water from its tributaries, *corixos*, and *vazantes*. The slope of the Paraguay River along the floodplains is 2.5 cm km^{-1} (EDIBAP 1979). The Paraguay River slopes gently beyond the city of Cáceres, going from 6.3 cm km^{-1} to 1.0 cm km^{-1} near the Apa River (Carvalho 1984). After peak rainfall on the plateaus, the discharge of the Paraguay River supplies water to the nearby flood-plain in such a way that the flood wave is delayed four to five months after the peak rainfall in the southern part. Thus, the changes in the water-level show that there is a delay of about four months before the water-level peak passes through the Pantanal from north to south and reaches Corumbá. At the time that the water level reaches its maximum at Corumbá, the dry season has already begun in the north (Heckman 1996). At the city of Corumbá, the annual discharge of the river is 1260 m^3 s^{-1}, where the river carries 80% of the total outflow from the region (EDIBAP 1979). However, Hamilton *et al.* (1997) found a figure of 2500 m^3 s^{-1}, a much higher discharge than previously reported.

The available information on hydrology shows that there is a difference between the north and the south concerning the flooding pattern, and that the fluctuation of flooding is higher in the north. Therefore, the physical and chemical conditions of the waters in the southern Pantanal are more stable than those in the north, since the north is drier during the dry season.

The peak discharge of the tributaries occurs earlier than that of the Paraguay River; the subsequent rising of the Paraguay River dams the flow of the tributaries. The peak in riparian land flooding occurs about four months later than the peak rainfall, and flooding is caused by river overflow rather than by local rainfall (Hamilton *et al.* 1996).

A study conducted on the dynamics of floodplain inundation in the alluvial fan of the Taquari River (Hamilton *et al.* 1998) has shown pronounced seasonal flooding, with its peak in February, demonstrating interannual variability in the maximum and minimum area inundated. The inflow of river water from the uplands to the Taquari subregion peaks one to two months later than the rainfall peak. Thus, local flooding may be the result of riparian land inflow and local rain. After March the water deficit is due to water loss from evaporation and evapotranspiration of the flooded region.

As the rise of the Paraguay River occurs some months after the rainy season, because of the delay of the flood wave, so too does the maximum flooding in the Taquari subregion. It can be observed approximately three months after the Taquari River discharge since the waters of the Paraguay River envelop the waters of the Taquari River at that time, flooding the region. The Taquari floodplains dry out after September and the seasonally flooded grasslands appear.

The flooding, therefore, is mainly controlled by the water level of the Paraguay River, which determines the flooding pattern. At these high water levels, waters from the Paraguay River penetrate into the floodplain adjacent to the tributaries, such as the Taquari River, and temporary reversal of flow may occur in some smaller channels. This reversed flow of water through channeled floodplain paths or *corixos* in the Pantanal is well known. Traces of the water's origin can be determined (major ions in diluted floodplain waters) in order to identify water from the Taquari and Paraguay rivers (Hamilton *et al.* 1998).

Historical records of the level of the Paraguay River at Ladário (a neighborhood of the city of Corumbá, in the state of Mato Grosso do Sul), showed the maximum flood levels reaching about 4 m from 1900 to 1960, but only 2 m from 1960 to 1972. During this period (1960–72) people occupied a large portion of the non-flooded area for diverse uses. However, since 1973 the levels have risen again to around 5 m.

Daily records on the level of the Paraguay River at Ladário, analyzed from January, 1900 to June, 1995, have shown the following results. (1) Significant variability was detected between years (that is, there is a permanent annual variability. (2) Significant variability exists at intervals of two to five years, not stationary; that is, a transient variability was observed within the period interval. (3) Significant variability occurs at intervals from ten to eleven years, not plainly stationary; that is, a persistent variability within a ten-year interval (Sá *et al.* 1998).

An additional study on periodicities, tendencies, and prediction based on dynamic spectral analysis conducted at the same place (Ladário) for the same period of time (1900–95) showed that the river flow is not stationary. Besides the annual variability there are other variations in the level of the river. The variation at intervals of two to four years may be associated with the El Niño phenomenon (Nordemann 1998).

The location of the Pantanal in a tropical area (latitudes 16° to 22° S), 1500 km from the Brazilian Atlantic coast, leads to some of the highest temperatures in the Brazilian territory. In addition, the region is in a depression where the attitude of the Paraguay River valley varies between 70 and 140 m above sea level. Over a long period (30 years) the average mean temperature varies from 19.9 °C (July) to 27.4 °C (December). The extreme range of temperatures may go beyond 40 °C, reaching 40 to 44 °C (August to November), while minimum temperatures may fall below 10 °C (usually only on two or three days from April to August) due to polar cold fronts passing through the basin. In some years, this episodic and rapid passage of anticyclone fronts may lower the temperature in the floodplain to 1 to 4 °C.

The air humidity is greater than 75% from December to March and greater than 80% from February to March, falling during the dry season (August to October) to 62%. The combination of monthly temperature and rain allows the area to be classified as Aw type (savanna climate), following the Koppens climate classification.

Annual changes and life cycles

As a wetland ecosystem, the Pantanal is characterized by an indistinct and ever-changing boundary between water and land. A variety of habitats are present, offering clear seasonality in food production and other ecological resources, and so a great number of animals can thrive with minimal competition. The ever-changing patterns of floating vegetation, annual plants, solid ground, and open water provide ample niches for a wide range of plants and animals.

Opportunistic plant species can rapidly respond to the water regimen, occupying an available space. This is the case for *Pontederia cordata* and *P. lanceolata*, which are able to grow as soon as their rhizomes feed on the water of a new flood season. Grasses that appear dead during high water suddenly grow, occupying all the space available, during the dry season. Dormant seeds "wake up" and germinate, covering the ground of dry lagoons. Some temporal species, such as *Momordica charantia*, alternate with bamboo species in covering the ground of the gallery forest. A large part of the area is flooded only during the height of the rainy season, and much non-flooded higher ground is interspersed throughout the region.

The higher ground (where there are patches of savanna and "cordilheira" of woodland) is only a couple of meters above average water level. The *cordilheiras* are the higher parts of ancient dunes (Klammer 1982) presently covered with forested savanna or semi-deciduous forest. Along rivers, the gallery forest is covered by vines such as "cipó-de-arraia" *Cissus spinosa* and "uvinha" *Cissus sicyoides*. They are more or less vigorous depending on the flooding pattern.

Flooding is the most important ecological phenomenon in the Pantanal. Every year many parts of the Pantanal change from terrestrial into aquatic habitats. From May to October the land dries out and grasslands and scattered pools appear. The most striking aspect of the Pantanal is its curious combination of mesic and xeric vegetation growing side by side. The reasons for this mixture are the topography and the seasonal climate. Hence, the patches of forest experience severe drought during the six-month dry season. The mixture of permanent and temporary flooded habitats, and gallery forests or patches of woodland, contribute to the richness of the vegetation and the productivity of the system which, in turn, support the exuberant abundance of fauna.

Several case studies carried out throughout the Pantanal support the relationship between flooding patterns and nutrient and life cycles with different emphases on: (1) seasonal succession of aquatic macrophyte vegetation communities (Prado *et al.* 1994); (2) arboreal communities (Schessl 1997, Cunha 1998, Cunha & Junk 2000); (3) structure and dynamics of young trees (Almeida 1998); (4) production of fruits by the palm *Bactris glaucescens* (Ferreira 2000); (5) aquatic habitats, limnology, water chemistry, primary production, and morphological patterns (Kretzchmar *et al.* 1993, Silva & Esteves 1993, 1995, Heckman 1994, 1997, Hardoim & Heckman 1996).

Annual life cycles: plants

The dry–wet cycle affects pond dynamics, the ecological succession of aquatic plants, and community composition and structure in the Pantanal (Pott *et al.* 1996). Pott *et al.* recorded 18 species during the dry season, with *Pistia stratiotes* having the highest absolute and relative frequency – followed by *Salvinia auriculata, Oxycaryum cubense, Eichhornia azurea*, and *Hydrocleys nymphoides*. During the wet season, with enlarged ponds, 38 species were found with highest absolute and relative frequencies of *Oxycaryum cubense, Eichhornia azurea, Ludwigia sedoides, Salvinia auriculata, Utricularia gibba, Hydrocleys nymphoides*, and *Luziola subintegra*.

In flooded areas of the Paiaguás subregion, the plant community in arboreal pockets of savanna changes, determining defined landscape characteristics (Pott & Adamoli 1996). In areas that flood rarely or never the grass "capim-carona" *Elyonurus muticus* dominates, followed by the "lixeira" tree *Curatella americana*. In forest pockets under moderate flooding "cambará" *Vochysia divergens* is dominant, in many cases transforming the landscape into continuous and homogeneous forest, locally named "cambarazal." In areas with much flooding the "canjiqueira" *Byrsonima orbygniana* is dominant, also forming homogeneous units named "canjiqueiral."

Ecological processes such as the flood pattern, however, are not the only factors affecting biodiversity. The seasonal change between the aquatic and terrestrial phases, resulting in rapid nutrient cycling, allows high productivity in a region generally considered to be poor in nutrients.

In conclusion, the annual rise and fall of the waters has a significant influence on plant species richness, diversity, and distribution patterns. It also results in: (1) adaptation to a wide range of flooding habitats and (2) decreased local habitat diversity and maintenance of landscape diversity and heterogeneity.

Annual life cycles: fish

Three distinct phases can be distinguished in the fish life cycle in relation to the water regime in the Pantanal (PRODEAGRO, 1997).

1. Flood season: a period of continuous rain with flooding of the plains, occurring from October to April. First, in the "*piracema*" type of migration the fish schools move upstream at the beginning of the rainy season. Later, migratory fish leave the riverbed and move into the adjacent flooding areas searching for food. Reproduction occurs at the beginning of the rainy season when a schooling behavior known as "*rodada*" is observed. Therefore, the *rodada* occurs at the end of the migratory trip known as *piracema*.
2. Drainage season: a period coinciding with the end of the rainy season from April to May. Fish disperse from flooded areas to the riverbed and permanent ponds or lagoons. This fish movement is known as "*lufada*." During this period fish are pursued and caught by natural predators.
3. Dry season: running from June to October. Fish start organizing schools for reproductive migration (*piracema*). Sedentary species face low levels of dissolved oxygen in the shallow water and some stay dormant in the mud during the dry season. Thus, the flood cycle is a crucial for migration and successful reproduction.

There are published data supporting the influence of flood pattern and habitat diversity on fish life cycles (Resende & Palmeira 1996), and seasonal changes in fish diets (Wantzen *et al.* 2000).

Annual life cycles: waterfowl

Most waterfowl species exhibit synchronized reproduction, where huge colonies of birds – such as wood stork (*Mycteria americana*), egrets (snowy egret *Egretta thula*, great white egret *Casmerodius albus*, and the capped heron *Pilherodius pileatus*), and others (such as the spoonbill *Ajaia ajaja*) – concentrate in nesting sites in the gallery forest during the dry season; to take advantage of the seasonal resources available. The breeding colonies are formed by hundreds of nesting birds following a pattern of species breeding at the same site or in designated trees. There is a strong relationship between nesting behavior exhibited by the bird species and seasonal variation of the water level. The birds take advantage of concentrations of fish and invertebrates in ponds. The concentration of birds in colonies allows concentration of nutrients due to dropping feces, prey, and hatchlings on the ground; this, in turn, attracts predators such as caimans, anacondas, wild foxes, and others. As a result the shallow water of the dry season presents locally high turbidity, elevated levels of nitrogen and phosphate forms, as well as modified dissolved oxygen levels.

Two waves of breeding species have been recognized in the same trees: a white colony and a black colony. In the subregion of Barão de Melgaço, during the dry season, in the period of July to October, the white colony is established in a few selected trees of the Cuiabá River gallery forest, in the Porto da Fazenda, close to ponds and flooded areas; 600 nests are concentrated in a single nesting site. This white colony is mainly composed of hatchlings of the wood stork *Mycteria americana*, followed in lower numbers by hatchlings of the egrets *Ardea alba* and *Egretta thula*, and finally by hatchlings of the spoonbill (*Platalea ajaja*). The black colony is composed of the cormorant *Phalacrocorax brasilianus*, followed by the anhinga *Anhinga anhinga*, and the white-necked heron *Ardea cocoi*.

Colonial reproduction is successful in having many pairs of eyes to remain vigilant to the frequent presence of predators. The principal flying predators are: the crested caracara hawk *Caracara* = *Polyborus plancus*, the great black hawk *Buteogallus urubitinga*, and the black vulture *Coragyps atratus*. Both female and male storks incubate and take care of the hatchlings. They feed the young about six times a day during the first three weeks. The parents catch prey in shallow waters (15 to 50 cm deep): mainly fish, molluscs, crustaceans, amphibians, reptiles, and insects. The colonial nesting site is active every year and the young storks born there return three to four years later, as adults, to reproduce in the same nesting site.

High densities of black-bellied tree duck *Dendrocygna autumnalis*, white-faced tree duck *Dendrocygna viduata*, the Brazilian duck *Amazonetta brasiliensis*, and the muscovy duck *Cairina moschata* are observed. Other common birds are the southern screamer *Chauna torquata* and macaws, including the hyacinth macaw *Anodorhynchus hyacinthinus*.

The Center for Study of Migratory Birds (Centro de Estudos, Marcação e Anilhamento de Aves; CEMAVE), a branch of IBAMA (the Brazilian Institute for the Environment and Renewable Natural Resources), has developed a study on *Jabiru mycteria* named *Projeto Tuiuiú* (Antas 1992, Antas & Nascimento 1996, Oliveira 1997). The study shows that there is a clear linkage between the flooding regimen of the Pantanal and the availability of food for the adult jabirus to raise their young. The birds need low water, especially in lagoons and ponds, in order to obtain the food they catch with their specialized beak. The preferred food is "mussum" fish (*Symbranchus marmoratus*), which can stay dormant and encapsulated in the mud throughout the dry season, to swim again when the water arises in the rainy season. The jabiru is a specialist in detecting and catching the dormant fish in the muddy bed of the drying pond. They also catch snails (*Pomacea* spp.).

Jabirus are not present in the Pantanal during the flooding season. They migrate to higher grounds and to still-unknown sites. Unusual rain and flooding occurred during the nesting season (dry season) of 1992. In the Nhecolândia subregion the hatching success, from 70 nests monitored by *Projeto Tuiuiú* in July, was zero; that is, no young were seen that year. On the Taquari River, an area of 600 km along the river was surveyed and 62 nests monitored in the same year; only one chick was born. Apparently, the incubating behavior of the parents depends upon the availability of food for the birds, which depends upon the flooding regimen. Reproductive success varies with the flooding schedule.

In 1995 (September to October), while I was conducting fieldwork in three sites (Cáceres subregion, the Ecological Reserve of Taiamã, and Porto Murtinho subregion), I observed a successful nesting season for jabirus. Dozens of nests were seen with three young in each nest and no abnormal flooding was reported for that season. The young jabirus are ready to leave the nests in October to November, coinciding with the period of the lowest water.

Projeto Tuiuiú also reports that different flooding patterns have different impacts on nesting activities. For example, the unusual flooding in July to August 1992 in the Taquari area suggests that reproductive activities in that area occurred later than those in the Aquidauana and Miranda regions. The production of young was normal in the Aquidauana–Miranda area and no chicks were born in the Taquari area, due to the abnormal local flooding in that subregion. The study reports that the stork *Mycteria americana* also exhibited nest-abandonment behavior due to flooding cycles at Rio Vermelho. The preferred trees for jabiru nests are: "piúva" *Tabebuia ochracea*, 55%; "manduvi" *Sterculia striata*, 31%; dead trees, 12%; "para-tudo" *Tabebuia insignis*, 1% and others, 1%.

CEMAVE and the CWS (Canadian Wildlife Service) have developed a project on migratory birds of the Pantanal in order to identify possible inter-American routes as well as to determine regional bird movement. The preliminary unpublished report points out that during the dry season, from May to October, the migrant birds from North America fly over the Pantanal and the resident aquatic birds are more visible, being concentrated in retained waters in ponds and depressions. It is evident that the seasonal change in the region is a key factor affecting migrants and resident birds, and other ecological interactions (Keast & Morton 1980).

Annual life cycles: hyacinth macaw

From a study of 76 macaw nests (Guedes 1993), it was observed that the hyacinth macaw (*Anodorhynchus hyacinthinus*) feeds upon the seeds of two palm trees (the "acuri" *Scheelea phalerata* and the "bocaiúva" *Acrocomia totai*) to get their major food supply. The "acuri" produces fruits all year round while the "bocaiúva" is more seasonal. Some individuals also eat the sprouts of the palms.

A high percentage of the macaw's nests (95%) are found in the "manduvi" tree (*Sterculia striata*), also abundant in the Pantanal gallery forests, and only 5% of the nests are found in the "angico-branco" tree (*Pittecelobium edwaldii*). Holes available in old "manduvi" trees are also a limiting factor for the species, since they constitute important reproductive niches.

The same "manduvi" trees are also selected by other species, which implies competition for nesting niches. Besides the hyacinth macaw, the red-and-green macaw (*Ara chloroptera*) and the colored forest falcon (*Micrastur semitorquatus*) compete for the same niches. Wild ducks (*Cairina moschata* and *Dendrocygna autumnalis*) also nest in those tree holes. Bees (*Apis mellifera*) and the bat falcon (*Falco rufigularis*) also use the tree cavities.

Annual life cycles: capybara

Studies on capybaras show that the use of habitats varies seasonally (Alho *et al.* 1989). The jaguar is identified as one important capybara predator (Schaller & Vasconcellos 1978a). During the dry season, capybaras spend the night in the forest; in the early morning they leave the forest to graze on the grassland. During the rainy season, the capybaras also spend the night in the forest, but in the morning usually emerge and go directly to the water or to grazing areas. The use of aquatic vegetation and forest vegetation in their diet at that time increases significantly, since few grazing areas remain above water level.

Many aspects of the behavior and ecology of the capybara are affected by seasonal fluctuations in the amount of available food. Some preferred food items that are richer in protein tend to be more seasonal than poorer-quality food items. There is a period of the year, from June until November, when the standing crop on lower areas susceptible to flooding is abundant and is consumed by capybaras. During the remainder of the year the presence of these food items is very scarce. Thus, the times of food abundance and scarcity are dictated by the flooding pattern.

Group sizes and social structure influence capybara social behavior. As soon as male sub-adults begin to reach sexual maturity, the dominant males exclude them from the social groups. The group size increases from the beginning (rainy season) to the middle of the year (dry season). During the floods the groups subdivide and are largely confined to the forest patches, while in the dry season more animals are observed feeding on the pasture of the grassland. During the latter period, there are young in the group.

Capybara groups have larger home ranges and core areas during the dry season than during the rainy season, a change associated with a reduction in grassland area due to flooding.

Annual life cycles: marsh deer

The marsh deer *Blastocerus dichotomus* is the largest deer in South America, with males reaching a height of up to 115 cm. It occurs over a wide area: northern Argentina, Paraguay, Bolivia, southeast Peru, and Brazil (Amazonia, the Cerrado, part of Southern Brazil, and the Pantanal). It is listed as an endangered species but it occurs at high population densities in the Pantanal (Schaller & Vasconcellos 1978b, Tomás 1993).

All vegetation communities in which marsh deer have been observed (Tomás 1993) are frequently flooded during the wet season (most habitats are formed by aquatic plants). These floristic communities occupy about 18% of the open habitats and 12.8% of the whole Nhecolândia ranch during the flood season, while the marshland – totally flooded – is completely occupied by aquatic vegetation (floating mats of *Eichhornea*, *Nymphaea*, *Reussia*, and other plants). The vegetation type most used by marsh deer is *Andropogon* grassland and other open areas dominated by *Pontederia*, *Scleria*, *Nymphaea*, *Eleocharis*, *Thalia*, *Axonopus*, *Oryza*, *Nymphoides*, and *Luziola* communities. Marsh deer select about 35 plant species, mainly aquatic plants. *Pontederia cordata* (including both flowers and leaves), *Thalia geniculata* (mainly flowers), *Nymphaea* spp., *Aeschynomene sensitiva*, *A. fluminensis*, *Discolobium pulchellum*, *Reussia* spp., *Leersia hexandra*, and others are frequently eaten by marsh deer. Tomás (1993) provides a list of those plants.

According to Tomás (1993), the ecological density (the density in suitable habitats such as marshlands) is 3.12 deer per km^2. In other areas the estimated density is 0.73 deer per km^2. Other estimates range from 0.09 deer per km^2 (low flooding habitats) to 0.38 deer per km^2 (highly inundated habitats) for dry season surveys. Seasonal flooding causes significant variation in the population distribution and density. During the dry season, deer prefer the boundary between the flooded areas and the drained range of the marshland. During the flood season the animals are dispersed.

The birth season extends over at least four months. Schaller and Vasconcellos (1978b) found in May a female with a full-term fetus, which had been killed by a jaguar, and in September they found a few females that were still heavily pregnant. Females usually have fawns with them but in some years, fawn crops are small. Yearling males are difficult to distinguish from females at a glance. Yearling numbers are seen as indicators of reproductive failure or high mortality due to diseases prevalent in the local cattle of the Pantanal.

Annual life cycles: jaguar

Due to direct pressure on the jaguar (*Panthera onca*) and because of habitat degradation, the species is now rare or extinct in several places. In some regions of the Pantanal, such as at the Ecological Reserve of Taiamã, the jaguar still occurs in high densities. I have had the chance to see jaguars in the area on three different occasions while working in the reserve.

Because jaguars learn to prey upon cattle and horses, the ranchers kill them. Humans are also reducing the panthers' territories, and ranchers kill them as well.

Schaller and Crawshaw (1980) studied the movement patterns of the jaguar in the Pantanal and found that one individual can have a home range of 30 km^2. The jaguar lives in gallery forests and other forest habitats but it also ranges in open areas. The Pantanal jaguar can swim very well and is highly adapted to the flooding pattern.

Annual life cycles: small mammals

Lacher and Alho (1989) describe the microhabitat use among small mammals in the Pantanal. The major habitats surveyed were seasonally inundated grasslands or "*campos*," permanent lagoons, savanna shrublands or "*cerrado*," and patches of semi-deciduous subtropical forest. The plant species composition is a mixture of central Brazilian *cerrado* and *chaco*, with some Amazonian species as well. Flooding during the rainy season is extensive, and in some areas only patches of forest remain above water. The campo habitat is mixed grassland composed of drier areas where the dominant species is the grass *Elionurus candidus*. Seasonally inundated areas are dominated by species of *Andropogon*, and marshy temporary ponds are dominated by *Axonopus pursuii*, *Mesosetum loliiforme*, and *Panicum laxum*. The grassland habitats are floristically rich, containing 42 species of grasses and sedges (Pott & Pott 1994). Another habitat surveyed is the small patches of gallery forests ("*capões de mata*"). The forest edge generally has dense patches of the bromeliad *Bromelia balansae*. "Acuri" palms (*Scheelea phalerata*) occur in patches in the forest, especially along margins. The *cerrado* site is "*campo cerrado*," a mix of grassland and savanna. The shady area also contains a field of *Andropogon*, a few forest patches, and some marshy areas. The "*caronal*" habitat was located in an extensive field of the grass "capim-carona" *Elionurus*. A substantial part of the census and assessment-line stations for mammals also falls within semi-deciduous subtropical forest. Four microhabitats were defined:

(1) the *campo* microhabitat contained solely grasslands; (2) the *cerrado* microhabitat contained all savanna woodlands; (3) the transition microhabitat contained *Bromelia*-dominated forest edge and small, wooded islands; and (4) the forest microhabitat was a non-*cerrado* semi-deciduous forest.

Three families of small mammals were surveyed (Cricetidae, Echimyidae, and Didelphidae). The rodent *Oryzomys fornesi* is the most abundant species, present at three of the four habitats. *Oryzomys subflavus* is abundant and *Thrichomys apereoides* is the only rodent species present in all four microhabitats. Small mammals have a preference for microhabitats dominated by the grass *Elionurus candidus* (78% of the captures), while fewer animals were captured in *Andropogon* (21%) and marsh-lands (1.6%) grasses. The wild rodent *Oryzomys subflavus* is more microhabitat specialist, preferring *cerrado* microhabitat. Most *Thricomys apereoides* and *Clyomys laticeps* were captured in the transition forest microhabitat. In fact, *Clyomys* was never captured in the forest and *Thricomys* was very rare in the forest, making the two echimyed species microhabitat specialists in the transition zone.

In conclusion, the two oryzomyine rodents (*Oryzomys fornesi* and *O. subflavus*) were more generalized in their use of microhabitats than were two echimyid species (*Clyomys laticeps* and *Thrichomys apereoides*). *Oryzomys fornesi* is a broad habitat generalist in the Nhecolândia subregion. *Oryzomys subflavus* selects the *cerrado* microhabitat. Both *Clyomys* and *Thricomys* were restricted to their transition microhabitat. Although both species overlap in the same microhabitat, competition is avoided since *Thricomys* is scansorial while *Clyomys* is fossorial.

Studies on small mammals in the Pantanal and Cerrado biomes (Lacher *et al.* 1986, Lacher & Alho 1989, Mares & Ernest, 1994) show that different species exhibit distinctive patterns of population increase and reproductive activity, with fluctuations between the dry and wet seasons, depending upon availability of ecological resources (food, reproductive nichs, and space).

Biodiversity

Brazilian natural ecosystems harbor about 70% of the known species of plants and animals on Earth (Mittermeyer *et al.* 1997, MMA 1998). The plant diversity is the highest in the world with 55 000 species representing 22% of the Earth's total. In the country there are 1622 species of birds (191 endemic species); 468 species of reptile (172 endemic); 3000 species of freshwater fish, and an estimated number of insects ranging from 1 to 15 million species. However, with this magnitude of species diversity the threats are also enormous. Brazil has 70 mammal species listed as endangered, 103 birds, and less than 8% of the Atlantic forest remains. The Cerrado biome of central Brazil has lost about 50% of its original area. The Pantanal has 1863 species of phanerogam plants, 263 species of fish, 85 species of reptile, 35 species of amphibian, 463 bird species, and 132 mammal species (Alho *et al.* 2002, 2003, Tubeis & Tomás 2003a, 2003b).

Subregions and habitats

Traditionally, the Pantanal is subdivided into distinct subregions (Fig. 7.2). There are different classifications according to different authors (classification of PCBAP, IBGE [the Brazilian Institute for Geography and Statistics], and others). Silva and Abdon (1998) delimited and quantified the Pantanal plain in Brazil, on a 1:250 000 scale, into 11 subregions: Pantanal de Cáceres (9.01%), Pantanal de Poconé (11.63%), Pantanal de Barão de Melgaço (13.15%), Pantanal de Paraguay (5.9%), Pantanal de Paiaguás (19.6%), Pantanal de Nhecolândia (19.48%), Pantanal de Abobral (2.05%), Pantanal de Aquidauana (3.62%), Pantanal de Miranda (3.17%), Pantanal de Nabileque (9.61%), and Pantanal de Porto Murtinho (2.78%). The criteria used for the delimitation were related to flooding, relief, soil, and vegetation. Flooding pattern and relief were considered the most-important components in identifying each subregion.

Some subregions, such as the Cáceres subregion, are subject to more-intense flooding that lasts for six months per year. In the subregions of Paiaguás and Nhecolândia the flood period lasts for three to four months. The Paraguay subregion has a long period of flooding, lasting up to six months, with the presence of permanent and temporary ponds. In the subregion of Poconé flooding lasts three to five months, while in Barão de Melgaço it lasts three to four months.

The region is formed by a complex mosaic of different kinds of habitats, strongly dependent on seasonal flooding. Due to the predominance of aquatic surroundings some formations receive local names such as *mata de galeria* (gallery forest); *cerrado* or *capão de cerrado* (savanna vegetation or patch of savanna); *cerradão* and *cordilheira* (denser savanna and patch of woodland); *baía* (a permanent or temporary pond or lake), *vazante* (a drainage channel between *baías* or depressed inundated areas, *corixo* (a creak or other small course of water), and *salina* (saline pond or lake with saline water, saltier than freshwater ponds).

Using the results of remote sensing and field work, Silva *et al.* (1998a) identified 14 dominant and floristically distinct phytophysiognomies in the Nabileque and Miranda subregions. The methodology allowed identification of structurally differentiated plant cover, corresponding to the strata of arboreal, scrub, and herbaceous vegetation. These habitats are known by the name of the dominant plant species such as the parkland habitat "*paratudal*" dominated by *Tabebuia aurea*; the palm savanna habitat "*carandazal*" dominated by *Copernicia alba*; the scrub habitat "*canjiqueiral*" dominated by *Byrsonima orbygniana*; the thorn scrub habitat "*espinheiral*" dominated by *Byttneria filipes, Bauhinia bauhinioides*, and *Cissus spinosa*. Other habitats were also identified such as gallery forest, semi-deciduous forest, forest island or patch of forest, seral stage of gallery forest, swamps, scrub grassland, flooded grassland, and others.

Another study using remote sensing presents the contribution of the normalized difference vegetation index (NDVI) and the fraction images derived from the linear mixing model for monitoring the dynamics of the land cover in the Pantanal region (Shimabukuro *et al.* 1998). These authors analyzed the land cover for the image dates (December 22, 1992 [dry season] to March 12, 1993 [rainy season]), and detected changes that occurred during the period of image acquisition. The results indicate an increase in vegetation cover during the dry season.

Similarly, Hernandez Filho *et al.* (1998) conducted a study on the Taquari basin of the Pantanal to map phytophysiognomy and land use using TM (thematic mapper)/Landsat and HRV (high-resolution visible)/Spot images. The following vegetation types were considered: *cerrado* (savanna); *cerradão* (denser *cerrado* or woodland), *cerrado* and *mata aluvial* (savanna plus alluvial forest), *mata aluvial* (alluvial forest), *formação alterada* (disturbed formation), *pastos implantados* (cultivated pasture), *culturas agrícolas implantadas* (field crops), and *corpos dágua* (water bodies). Although the paper focuses on criteria to discriminate vegetation cover, it also contributes to mapping the region.

Flora

The Pantanal is influenced by the great savanna biome of central Brazil – the Cerrado. Some specialists consider the Pantanal as a seasonally flooded extension of the Cerrado. The present landscape arrangement and natural ecosystems are the result of three factors: (1) geological changes occurring since the Quaternary period, which probably influenced the drainage patterns of the region; (2) the pronounced differences in annual cycles of wet and dry seasons plus exceptional periods of long flooding or droughts causing retraction or expansion of the Pantanal – thus, a phenomena related to greater or lesser primary productivity and ecological succession; (3) areas related to human intervention such as pastures, artificial ponds, or introduced trees near the ranch houses.

The Pantanal is influenced by the major Brazilian biomes: (1) Amazonia and its savanna ecotone provinces in the northwestern portion; (2) the Cerrado covering the plateaus in which rivers that drain into the Pantanal lie, notably in the eastern portion; (3) the extension of the Atlantic forest and its ecotone in the south-southeastern area; (4) the Chaco, which touches the region on its western limit.

In some forested habitats such as gallery forest, as well as in other humid forested habitats, Amazonian species occur. In non-flooded mesic habitats Chaco species occur. In other savanna arboreal habitats Cerrado species typical of central Brazil occur. Thus, the degree of endemism is very low. The natural habitats, including the forests, are especially high in productivity and species diversity for plants and animals because of deposits of rich alluvial soil and nutrients from floods.

Pott and Pott (1994) made a list of Pantanal plants, as a result of a 10-year period of field work; the list provides information on identification, distribution, and use of 1700 species. Later, this list was increased to 1863 Phanerogam species from the floodplains, collected, classified, and based on the herbarium of the CPAP-EMBRAPA (Pantanal Research Center for Agriculture and Cattle Husbandry), at Corumbá.

Prance and Schaller (1982) conducted a classic study in the region of the Serra do Amolar and Paraguay River, in the state of Mato Grosso do Sul, on the phytophysiognomies of the Pantanal. The *cerrado* habitat is dominated by the following species: *Caryocar brasiliense*, *Qualea parviflora*, *Qualea grandiflora*, *Tabebuia caraiba*, *Diptychandra glabra*, and *Hymenaea stigonocarpa*. In the semi-deciduous forest the dominant species are: *Acosmium cardenasii*, *Caesalpinia floribunda*, Nyctaginaceae, *Acacia paniculata*, *Rollinia* spp., *Talisia esculent*, and *Tabebuia ochracea*. The predominant herbaceous vegetation species of the flooded areas include: *Pontederia cordata*, *Eichhornia crassipes*, *Ceratopteris pterioides*, *Salvinia auriculata*, *Victoria amazonica*, *Echinodorus paniculatus*, *Thalia geniculata*, *Cyperus giganteus*, and *Typha domingensis*. The scrubby species in wet areas include: *Combretum laxum*, *Cupania castaneaefolia*, *Eugenia* spp. *Sphinctanthus microphyllus*, and *Xylosma benthamii*. Species occuring on alluvial areas include: *Cassia grandis*, *Aeschynonene fluminensis*, *A. sensitiva*, *Croton glandulosus*, and *Mabea fistulifera*. In sandy soil, *Couepia uiti* occurs. The following genera are found in gallery forest: *Ficus*, *Inga*, *Guarea*, *Pithecellobium*, *Pterocarpusi*, *Rheedia*, *Coccoloba*, and *Triplaris*. The representative species of the xeric vegetation are *Cereus peruvianus*, *C. bonplandii*, *Opuntia stenarthra*, and *Pereskia saccharosa*.

One of the most-important publications on the Pantanal is the PCBAP (Plano de Conservação da Bacia do Alto Paraguai [Plan for Conservation of the Upper Paraguay basin]), describing the physical and biotic environments of the Pantanal (PCBAP 1997). The PCBAP surveyed 3400 species of superior plants occurring in the upper Paraguay River basin and half of this number are considered to occur in the Pantanal. Apparently, the floristic survey of the wetland area is considered satisfactory but the recording of species occurrence on the plateaus is still incomplete.

The phytophysiognomic units of the Pantanal are characterized by their phytosociological and ecological arrangements, forming well-defined landscape units going from inundated floating plants, seasonal flooding fields, gallery forests, scrub and semi-deciduous forests, and different kinds of *cerrado* savanna.

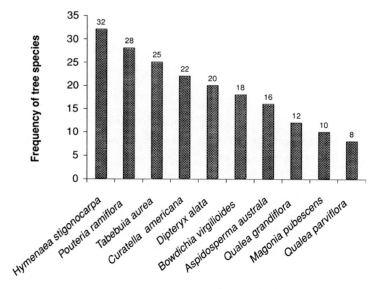

Figure 7.3 Occurrence of the 10 most-frequent tree species in cerrado habitat of the Barão de Melgaço subregion surveyed in 12 samples (quadrats of 10 m × 10 m for each sample) according to M. Conceição in Alho *et al.* (1998).

Cerrado: – *Arboreal savanna*

It is important to distinguish the "cerrado" in the general sense (*sensu lato*) when we consider the vegetation of central Brazil from "*cerrado*" in the restricted sense (*sensu stricto*), when we refer to a special kind of Brazilian savanna landscape. Here we are referring to the second case, as a certain type of habitat (*cerrado*, restricted sense) within a cerrado (general sense). The *cerrado* (savanna shrubland) habitat is formed by twisted trees, 5 to 10 m in height, and herbaceous vegetation. The *cerrado* trees are well-adapted to facing fire during the dry season. According to the study of Abdon *et al.* (1998) *Hymenaea stigonocarpa*, *Tabebuia aurea*, and *Caryocar brasiliense* comprise the superior stratum of dense *cerrado* with the trees reaching 12 m in height. The middle stratum, at 7 m, is represented by *Sapium haematospermum*, *Tabebuia aurea*, *Curatella americana*, and *Sclerolobium aureum*. The average diameter at breast height (DBH) is 17.4 cm and the average tree density is 1033 trees per ha.

Alho *et al.* (1998) identified the following species for "cerrado": *Alibertia sessilis*, *Andira cuyabensis*, *Aspidosperma australe*, *Bowdichia virgilioides*, *Byrsonima orbygniana*, *Caryocar brasiliense*, *Casearia sylvestris*, *Curatella americana*, *Dipteryx alata*, *Fagara hassleriana*, *Hymenaea stigonocarpa*, *Magonia pubescens*, *Mouriri elliptica*, *Pouteria ramiflora*, *Qualea grandiflora*, *Q. parviflora*, *Sapium haematospermum*, *Sclerolobium aureum*, *Simarouba versicolor*, *Tabebuia aurea*, and *Tocoyena formosa* (Fig. 7.3).

Salis *et al.* (1996) observed that this habitat is made up of small trees, with an average diameter of 9 cm and few reaching more than 6 m in height. The species *Qualea parviflora* and *Curatella americana* are the most frequent, about 50% of the occurrence, and *Caraipa savannatum* and *Qualea parviflora* are the main trees.

Cerradão

This denser *cerrado* or woodland habitat varies in structure according to local edaphic factors and the presence of water. In the Pantanal some *cerradão* habitats look like true forests, with a high density of less-twisted trees and trees with smoother bark. The canopy may range from 8 to 15 m in height. The *cerradão* occurs in non-flooded areas, generally in elevated soil 1 to 2 m high, forming what is called a *cordilheira*, i.e. a strip of dense vegetation or woodland. The dominant trees are *Eschwelera nana*, *Sclerolobium paniculatum*, and *Vochysia haenkeana*. The PCBAP recognizes some "*cerradão*" habitats with aspects of forest when trees like *Pterodon emarginatus* attain 20 m in height, associated with tree species such as *Terminalia argentata*, *Anadenanthera peregrina*, *Dipteryx alata*, *Magonia pubescens*, and *Guandua* spp.

Abdon *et al.* (1998) identified 30 tree species of *cerradão* that are consistent with the indicator species pointed out by other authors. These species are: *Acrocomia aculeata*, *Agonandra brasiliensis*, *Alchornia discolor*, *Alibertia sessilis*, *Aspidosperma tomentosum*, *Astronium fraxinifolium*, *Bowdichia virgilioides*, *Buchenavia tomentosa*, *Byrsonima coccolobifolia*, *Caryocar brasiliense*, *Casearia decandra*, *Copaifera martii*, *Cordia glabrata*, *Curatella americana*, *Diospyrus hispida*, *Dipteryx alata*, *Eugenia aurata*, *Fagara hassleriana*, *Hymenaea stigonocarpa*, *Luehea paniculata*, *Magonia pubescens*, *Mouriri elliptica*, *Ocotea suaveolens*, *Protium heptaphyllum*, *Rourea induta*, *Sclerolobium aureum*, *Swartzia jorori*, *Tabebuia aurea*, *Tocoyena formosa*, and *Vatairea macrocarpa*.

This habitat, in the Cáceres subregion, has about 1610 plants per hectare. There are about 35 species and the most important are: *Callistene major*, *Byrsonima crassifolia*, *Magonia pubescens*, *Anadenanthera colubrina*, and *Diptychandra aurantiaca*.

Some *cordilheiras* of *cerradão* occurring in the subregion of Barão de Melgaço include *Tabebuia impetiginosa*, *Hymenaea stignocarpa*, *Callisthene fasciculata*, *Magonia pubescens*, *Qualea parviflora*, *Hymenaea courbaril*, *Platimenea reticulata*, and *Guadua* spp. (Alho *et al.* 1998).

In the *cerradão* the average DBH for trees is 18.4 cm and the average tree density is 1320 trees per ha (Abdon *et al.* 1998). There are two strata: the highest reaches 16 m, and includes *Tabebuia aurea*, *Cordia glabrata*, *Luehea paniculata*, *Caryocar brasiliense*, *Hymenaea stigonocarpa*, *Dipteryx alata*, *Buchenavia tomentosa*, and *Ocotea suaveolens*; the median stratum attains 8 m of height and includes *Casearia decandra*, *Cordia glabrata*, *Aspidosperma tomentosum*, *Protium heptaphyllum*, *Caryocar brasiliense*, *Ocotea suaveolens*, *Astronium fraxinifolium*, *Magonia pubescens*, *Tabebuia*

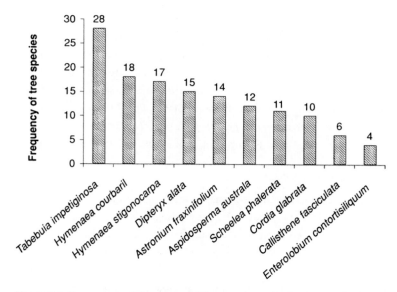

Figure 7.4 Occurrence of the ten most-frequent tree species in *cerradão* habitat of Barão de Melgaço subregion surveyed in eight samples (quadrats of 10 m × 10 m for each sample) according to M. Conceição in Alho *et al.* (1998).

aurea, and *Dipteryx alata*. In the *cerradão* the palm species *Scheelea phalerata* may or not may occur (Fig. 7.4).

Open savanna

The open savanna habitat is an intermediary formation or transition between savanna and grassland. The trees are sparse, with heights of 3 to 7 m and occasionally 10 m. The common trees, according to the study of Abdon *et al.* (1998) are: *Hymenaea stignocarpa*, *Vatairea macrocarpa*, *Caryocar brasiliense*, *Byrsonima orbygniana*, *Mouriri elliptica*, *Curatella americana*, *Pouteria ramiflora* and *Tabebuia roseo-alba*. The average DBH is 12.4 cm and the average tree density is 900 trees per ha.

In the Barão de Melgaço subregion the patches of *cerrado* are 5 to 10 m in height and include the following trees: *Byrsonima crassifolia*, *Dipteryx alata*, *Curatella americana*, *Hymenaea stigonocarpa*, *Vochysia divergens*, *Astronium frasini-folium*, *Genipa americana*, *Acrocomia aculeata*, *Dilodendron bipinnatum*, and *Ouractea spectabilis* (Alho *et al.* 1998).

This cerrado habitat may present a greater density where the trees may reach heights of 12 m and the upper stratum is represented by the following trees: *Hymenaea stigonocarpa*, *Tabebuia aurea*, and *Caryocar brasiliense* (Abdon *et al.* 1998). The middle stratum reaches a height of 7 m and is represented by *Sapium haematospermum, Tabebuia aurea, Curatella americana,* and *Sclerolobium aureum.* The tree density in this habitat is 1033 trees per ha and the DBH is 17.4 cm.

Some authors give the name "*savana parque*" to the more-or-less homogeneous units locally known as "*canjiqueiral*" and "*paratudal.*" The *canjiqueiral* is dominated by *Byrsonima orbygniana* but other species are present, such as *Qualea grandiflora, Hymenaea stigonocarpa,* and *Byrsonima coccolobifolia.* The *paratudal* is dominated by *Tabebuia aurea* – with *Byrsonima orbygniana, Tabebuia heptaphylla, Erythroxylum anguifugum, Inga edulis,* and *Fagara hassleriana* also occurring (Salis *et al.* 1996).

Grassland with patches of savanna

This is also called dirty savanna and the patches are called "*murundus.*" The patches of trees are located in more-elevated areas forming small islands in the field with trees such as *Buchenavia tomentosa, Stryphnodendron obovatum, Vochysia cinnamomea, Ocotea suaveolens, Pouteria ramiflora, Qualea parviflora,* and *Rourea induta* (Abdon *et al.* 1998). The grasses include *Axonopus purpusii, Elyonurus muticus, Mesosetum* spp., *Paspalum* spp., *Panicum* spp., and many other species of herbaceous vegetation. The predominant grass species in the open field are: *Paspalum hydrophilum, Paspalum pantanalis, Leersia hexandra, Panicum laxum,* and *Sorghastrum setosum.*

In drier areas the patches of *cerrado* 5 to 10 m high are composed of the following trees (Alho *et al.* 1998): *Hymenaea stigonocarpa, Pouteria ramiflora, Astronium fraximifolium, Magonia pubens, Diospira hispida, Qualea grandiflora, Plathymenia reticulata, Tabebuia aurea,* and *Dipteryx alata.* In some of these *cerrado* patches the palms *Scheelea phalerata* and *Bactris glaucescens* – and ground-cover vegetation such as *Bauhinia pentandra, Aechmea distichantha, Bromelia balansae, Cereus peruvianus* and *Guadua* spp. – occur.

Drainage-channel grassland with patches of gallery-forest habitat often surrounds seasonal or permanent ponds. Herbaceous vegetation such as the grasses *Andropogon hypogynus* and *Reimarochloa brasiliensis,* as well as seasonal aquatic plants like *Licania parviflora,* are typical. Patches of savanna vegetation with *Tabebuia* spp. and *Scheelea* spp. (Abdon *et al.* 1998) are often nearby.

The aquatic vegetation and shrub habitat varies according to the type of pond or flooded area. In shallow waters floating species such as *Oxycaryum cubense, Eichhornia azurea, Nymphaea amazonum, Hydrocleys nymphoides,* and *Salvinia auriculata* occur. Emergent species include *Pontederia cordata* and *Eleocharis interstincta.* Submerged species are *Cabomba piauhyensis, Egeria najas,* and *Utricularia* spp. (Abdon *et al.* 1998).

The vegetation on the *baías* (temporary or permanent ponds) includes: *Eichhornia azurea, Eleocharis interstincta, Eleocharis minima, Hydrocleys nymphoides, Nymphaea gardneriana, Papalidium paludivagum, Pontederia cordata, Pontederia lanceolata, Salvinia auriculata,* and *Scirpus cubensis* (Abdon *et al.* 1998). The seasonally flooded grasslands are covered by *Eichhornia, Nymphaea, Reussia, Pontederia, Scleria, Eleocharis, Thalia, Axonopus, Oryza, Nymphoides,* and *Luziola* (Alho *et al.* 1998).

In or near flooded areas the *"espinheiral"* or *"macegal"* occurs, a formation characterized by spiny and creeping vegetation such as *Byttneria filipes, Bauhinia bauhinioides, Cissus spinosa, Ipomoea carnea, Polygonum* spp., and *Thalia geniculata.*

Gallery-forest and forest habitats

These habitats form a line of forest along rivers or other types of drainage. The strips along riverbanks are irregular in shape. These forests are dense reaching 20 to 25 m in height, with the following species: *Ficus* spp., *Tabebuia heptaphylla, Inga* spp., *Triplaris surinamensis, Guazuma tomentosa, Bactris glaucescens, Erythroxylum* sp., and *Scheelea phalerata.* Some semi-deciduous forests have as representative species *Tabebuia roseo-alba, T. impetiginosa,* and *Scheelea phalerata.* The mixed forest presents *Tabebuia aurea, Copernicia alba, Myracrodon urundeuva, Anadenanthera colubrina, Tabebuia nodosa, Ficus* spp., *Guazuma tomentosa,* and *Scheelea phalerata.*

The forest habitats can be subdivided into the following units:

1. *Deciduous forest.* The trees lose most of their leaves during the dry season. This forest is about 20 m high. The most-common species are: *Sebastiania brasiliensis, Ceiba boliviana, Ficus calyptroceras, Aspidosperma pyrulifolium, Urera baccifera, Allophylus edulis, Sapium glandelatum,* and others; in total about 20 tree species (Bortolotto *et al.* 1996). Salis *et al.* (1996) considered *Protium heptaphyllum* to be the most-important tree.

2. *Semi-deciduous forest.* The trees lose some of their leaves during the dry season. This forest is about 30 m high and there are about 25 tree species. The most importance are: *Anadenanthera colubrina, Acacia paniculata, Acosmium cardenasii, Neca* spp., *Aspidosperma* spp., *Pseudocopaiva chodatiana, Sapindus* spp., and *Casearia gossypiasperma.* The palm *Sheelea phalerata* occurs frequently.

3. *Gallery forest.* This forest follows the river courses, such as the Paraguay. Common tree species are: *Inga vera, Triplaris gardneriana, Ocotea suaveoleus, Crataera tapia, Vochysia divergens, Cecropia pachystachya, Eugenia polystachya, Tabebuia heptaphylla, Myrcia mollis,* and *Albizia polyantha.*

Forest habitats may be dominated by one or a few species, for example: *"cambarazal"* with dominance of *Vochysia divergens* common in the subregions of Poconé and Barão de Melgaço; *"paratudal"* with dominance of *Tabebuia aurea;* and *"carandazal"* with dominance of *Copernicia alba.*

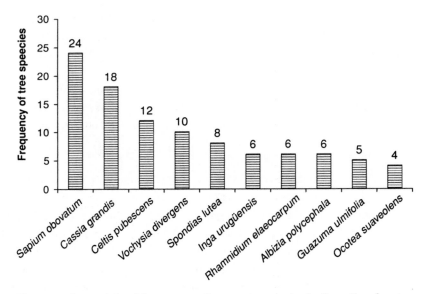

Figure 7.5 Occurrence of the ten most-frequent tree species in the gallery-forest habitat of the Cuiabá River in the Barão de Melgaço subregion surveyed in eight samples (quadrats of 10 m × 10 m for each sample) according to M. Conceição in Alho *et al.* (1998).

The forest along the Cuiabá River inside the Serviço Nacional do Comercio (SESC) Reserve (RPPN-SESC Pantanal: Reserva Particular do Patrimônio Natural) includes *Inga uruguensis, Bergeronia sericea,* and *Combretum* spp. (Alho *et al.* 1998). The mixed forest inside the reserve, along the Riozinho, is dominated by *Vochysia divergens, Ocotea suaveolens, Ocotea velloziana, Tabebuia aurea, Cecropia pachystachya, Cassia grandis, Tabebuia impetiginosa,* and *Mouriri guianensis* (Alho *et al.* 1998).

Other forest habitats surveyed in the SESC Reserve contained the following species: *Hymenaea coubaril, Vitex cymosa, Enterolobium contortisiliquum, Scheelea phalerata, Dipteryx alata, Spondias lutea, Dilodendron bipinnatum, Casearia decandra, Anadenanthera colubrina, Myracrodrum urundeuva,* and *Cedrella fissilis* (Fig. 7.5). In some other forest habitats *Magonia pubescens, Sterculia apetala,* and *Diptychandra aurantiaca* occur in addition (Alho *et al.* 1998).

Finally, an attempt to identify vegetation cover using analogic data of Landsat-TM was conducted by Abdon *et al.* (1998). Seven habitats were identified in the Nhecolândia subregion: (1) *"cerradão"* (woodland); (2) *"cerrado"* (savanna); (3) *"cerrado aberto"* (open savanna); (4) *"campo com manchas de cerrado"* (grassland with savanna patches); (5) *"campo"* (grassland); (6) *"vazantes com capões de matas"* (drainage-channel grassland with patches of gallery forest; (7) *"vegetação aquática arbustiva"* (aquatic vegetation and shrubs) (Fig. 7.6). The water bodies cover

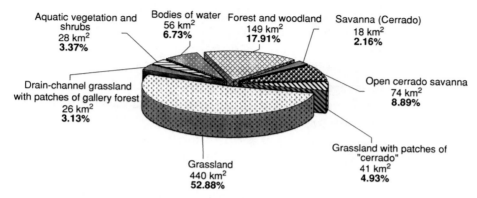

Figure 7.6 Distribution of the major vegetation formations in the Nhecolândia subregion.

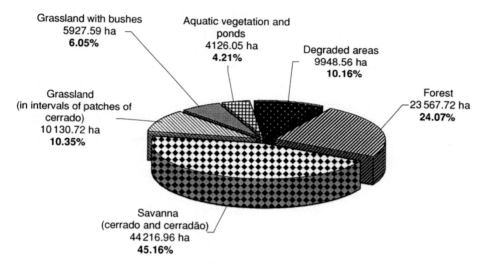

Figure 7.7 Distribution of the major vegetation formations in the Barão de Melgaço subregion.

56 km² – 6.73% of the surveyed area – but may vary greatly according to the season since the survey was conducted during the dry season. Note that open habitats such as different kinds of grasslands and flooded fields are the dominant landscape, making up more than 50% of all types of habitats. A similar survey was conducted for the Barão de Melgaço subregion (Fig. 7.7).

Fauna

The mixture of major vegetation formations that occurs in the Pantanal has resulted in diverse and abundant fauna. The species that are able to exploit a wide range of resources become both widespread and locally abundant. Endemic species are rare in the Pantanal. There are no interspecies differences in the degree of ecological specialization, but the resources used by some species are both more widespread and locally more abundant (or productive) than those used by some other species.

Caimans (*Caiman crocodilus*) are widespread and capybaras (*Hydrochaeris hydrochaeris*) are common throughout the Pantanal. Waterfowl are exceptionally abundant and include 13 species of herons and egret (e.g. *Casmerodius, Egretta,* and *Pilherodius*), 3 stork species (*Mycteria, Ciconia,* and *Jabiru*), 6 ibis and spoonbill species, and 5 species of kingfisher (*Ceryle* and *Chloroceryle*). Parrots are ubiquitous (19 species) and comprise 5 species of macaw, including *Anodorhynchus hyacinthinus*. Rheas (*Rhea americana*) and crested seriemas (*Cariama cristata*) are common.

In addition to the diverse and abundant resident fauna, there are 658 bird species occurring in the floodplain and surrounding area (Brown 1986), of which only 463 species have been recorded in the Pantanal floodplain (Tubelis & Tomas 2002, 2003a, 2003b). The Pantanal receives dozens of migrant species from both the north and the south (e.g. *Pluvialis dominica, Falco peregrinus,* and *Dolychonix orizivorous*) (Sick 1983). The Pantanal is used as a wintering and stopover area for three migratory bird routes: central Brazil, Rio Negro, and Cis-Andean (Sick 1983). Some of the shorebird species breeding in Canada that migrate to the Pantanal are: *Pluvialis dominica, P. squatarola, Bartramia longicauda, Numenius borealis, N. phaeopus, Limosa haemastica, Arenaria interprens, Calidris alba, C. pusilla, C. fuscicollis, C. baiardii, C. melanotos, C. himantopus, Tryngites subruficollis, Tringa melanoleuca,* and *T. flavipes.*

The Pantanal floodplain serves as a breeding ground for many species, usually with a wide geographical distribution, that can use the Pantanal's seasonal resources; this provides exceptional abundance but few species. Through analysis of the avifauna (658 species) and of butterflies (more than 1100 species), Brown (1986) confirmed: the low endemism (somewhat higher at the subspecies level for insects); the predominance of widely distributed organisms, Amazonian species that arrived in the region but did not penetrate the floodplain; and the smaller numbers of species – coming from southeastern Brazil, from the Cerrado biome of central Brazil, and from the Chaco – whose diffusion is also blocked by the Pantanal.

Fish

Out of its 138 183 km^2 the Pantanal is estimated to have an average inundated area of 43 000 km^2, an area that expands during the wet season. About 400 fish species are estimated to live in the region (plateaus and plains). Britiski *et al.* (1999) listed 263 species for the Pantanal. This list does not include species living in the upper-river habitats.

Fish are an important resource, both ecologically and socially. Because of the great variety of feeding and reproductive niches for fish, the Pantanal harbors high species diversity and considerable abundance. Fishing is of fundamental socio-economic importance for local people. In addition, fishing for sport is one of the incentives to bring tourists to the region.

Fish resources in the Pantanal have been classified according to their use as follows:

(a) a fundamental biotic component of the ecosystem, supporting the local biodiversity and being part of it
(b) food for subsistence and income of local people
(c) of interest for sport fishing
(d) a genetic resource
(e) an ornamental resource.

In some places there are conflicts between these uses. The controls and records on fish disembarkation in different ports are incomplete. Some authors (Silva 1986) point out that about 50% of fishing activity in the Pantanal is illegal; that is, fishing during the restricted periods (migration and reproduction) or using prohibited fishing devices.

The most-captured commercial fish species are: "pintado" *Pseudoplatystoma corruscans*, "cachara" *Pseudoplatystoma fasciatum*, "dourado" *Salminus maxillosus*, "pacu" *Piaractus mesopotamicus*, "curimba" *Prochilodus lineatus*, "piranhas" *Serrasalmus spilopleura* and *S. marginatus*, "piavuçu" *Leporinus macrocephalus*, "barbado" *Pinirampus pinirampu*, "jaú" *Paulicea luetkeni*, "bagre" *Pimelodus argenteus*, "cabeçudo" *P. ornatus*, "jurupuca" *Hemisorubim platyrhynchos*, "jurupensem" *Surubim lima*, "pacu-peba" *Mylossoma orbygnyanum*, and "piraputanga" *Brycon microlepis*. Fish farming is a growing activity in the region.

A fish survey carried out on the Miranda River floodplain showed that 101 species were recorded in adjacent flooded areas, illustrating the high diversity of the region (Resende & Palmeira 1996). The fish species composition may change from one wet season to another, depending on the pattern and duration of the flood.

Amphibians and reptiles

Compared with other Brazilian biomes the Pantanal presents a herpetofauna low in diversity but high in abundance. There are around 85 reptile species living on the plains and around 179 species when the Cerrado biome is included. Among amphibians there are around 80 species occurring in the upper Paraguay basin; 35 of these occur on the plains and 45 in the uplands (Alho *et al.* 2002, 2003).

During the rainy season the region presents vigorous populations of amphibians thanks to the expansion of favorable habitats. A study conducted by Christine Strüssmann (see Alho *et al.* 1998) in the subregions of Poconé and Barão de Melgaço shows 30 species of amphibians living in the region; this represents 5% of the total for Brazil.

Many Pantanal species are distributed throughout Brazil: the rococo toad *Bufo paracnemis* and the Chaco frog *Leptodactylus chaquensis*; the dwarf tree frogs *Hyla fuscovaria*, *Hyla acuminata*, and *Hyla raniceps*; the green leaf frog *Scinax acuminatus*; the marbled tree frog *Phrynohyas venulosa*; and the common washroom frog *Scinax nasicus*. The abundant tiny green frog *Lysapus limellus* has semi-aquatic habits, living on floating plants, and eating insects and other invertebrates.

About half of the anuran species in the Pantanal live in trees. Some species, such as the spotted tree frog *Hyla punctata*, show association with permanent bodies of water (rivers and ponds) and others – such as the purple-barred tree frog *Hyla raniceps*, the green leaf frog *Scinax acuminatus*, the yellow-and-black tree frog *Scinax fuscovarius* – tolerate droughts but the populations suddenly grow when flooding comes, usually October to May. Frogs are also more vocal during this period.

The tiny clicking frog *Lysapsus limellus* lives on floating vegetation and also vocalizes by day. Also vocalizing on floating plants are the paradox frog *Pseudis paradoxa* and the speckled-bellied frog *Physalaemus albonotatus*. During the rainy season this frog, *Physalaemus albonotatus*, is one of the most conspicuous and vocal, making a noisy chorus even by day.

Amphibians with terrestrial habits are the leaf toad *Bufo typhonius*; the frogs *Chiasmocleis mehelyi*, *Leptodactylus elenae*, and *Physalaemus cuvieri*; and the arboreal frog *Phrynohyas venulosa*. Another tiny frog living in holes in dead trees in the forest is *Chiasmocleis mehelyi*, a frog which was only recently reported in the Pantanal. Some other species live at the water-line between aquatic and terrestrial habitats – such as *Pseudopaludicola falcipes*, *Leptodactylus fuscus*, *Leptodactylus podicipinus*, *Bufo paracnemis*, *Bufo granulosus*, and *Elachistocleis ovale*. A colorful aposematic species is *Phyllomedusa hypochondrialis*.

The reptiles in the Pantanal are represented by more than 30 species of snake. The yellow anaconda *Eunectes notaeus* is very common on the plains and is small in size compared with the other species, for example the green anaconda *E. murinus* which lives at the edge of the Pantanal and may reach 5 m in length, with some observations reporting a size of 6 to 8 m. Another large snake is the water queen *Hydrodynastes gigas*, which occurs at the borders of gallery forests or patches of savannas looking for toads, their preferred food. Small nocturnal snakes, which prey upon frogs, are *Thamnodynastes strigilis*, *Leptodeira annulata*, and *Liophis poecilogyrus*.

There are four species of poisonous snakes in the Pantanal: the Brazilian lancehead *Bothrops moojeni*, the Neuwid lancehead *B. neuwiedi*, the Neotropical rattlesnake *Crotalus durissus*, and the Pantanal coral snake *Micrurus tricolor*.

The occurrence of species within the subregions of the Pantanal varies according to the composition and distribution of local species, depending on the influence of the nearby biomes such as the Chaco, the Cerrado, and the Amazon. Among the snakes of the northern subregion of Poconé, for example, Strüssmann and Sazima (1993) observed that the most-abundant species were *Eunectes notaeus*, *Helicops leopardinus*, and *Hydrodynastes* cf. *strigilis*. In contrast, the southern subregion of Nhecolândia presented a different species composition with *Leptodeira annulata*, *Liophis typhlus*, and *Lystrophis mattogrossensis*; snakes common throughout the Brazilian Cerrado. The same pattern is observed for amphibians, but with a difference in local abundance which is more noticeable in the Pantanal for these species.

There is one terrestrial turtle, the red-footed tortoise *Geochelone carbonaria*, plus one aquatic species, the large-headed Pantanal swamp turtle *Acanthochelys macrocephala*. The caiman *Caiman crocodilus* is abundant and conspicuous, particularly during the dry season, being one of the symbols of the Pantanal.

Twenty species of lizards are known for the region, all preferring dry habitats except for the Pantanal caiman lizard *Dracaena paraguayensis* which lives in the water. Two lizards species, *Kentropyx viridistriga* and *Mabuya guaporicola*, are able to swim and dive to escape predators. Common geckos, *Phyllopezus policaris* and *Polychrus acutirostris*, exploit the branches of bushes. Three lizards can be easily observed searching for prey on the ground or rapidly escaping from intruders: *Tupinambis merianae*, *Ameiva ameiva*, and *Cnemidophorus ocellifer*. The green iguana *Iguana iguana* is also seen in trees along the rivers or on riverbanks.

Fifty officially authorized caiman ranches in the Pantanal utilize the skin and meat of *Caiman crocodilus yacare*. This farming procedure follows a Government protocol (Portaria 126/90 of IBAMA). Under the ranching schedule the farmer is allowed to collect caiman eggs from the wild to incubate and raise the hatchlings for commercial purposes. The farmer is obliged to protect the habitat and the adult population in a given management area.

Birds

There are 463 bird species recorded for the floodplains alone, 665 species when the uplands are included, and 837 species for the Cerrado biome (Silva 1995; Tubelis & Tomás 2002, 2003a, 2003b). Bird species with aquatic habits are very common and abundant. They include egrets such as species of the genera *Casmerodius*, *Egretta*, *Ardea*, *Tigrisoma*, and *Botaurus*; as well as the wood stork *Mycteria americana*, the maguari stork *Ciconia maguari*, and the jabiru *Jabiru mycteria*. Kingfishers are present with five species of the two genera *Ceryle* and *Choroceryle*. Other aquatic species are the southern screamer *Chauna torquata*, the muscovy duck *Cairina moschata*, the fulvous whistling duck *Dendrocygna bicolor*, the white-faced whistling duck *D. viduata*, the black-bellied whistling duck *D. autumnalis*, and the Brazilian duck *Amazonetta brasilienses*. Among birds of prey are the snail kite *Rosthramus sociabilis*, the black-collared hawk *Busarellus nigricollis*, the great black hawk *Butteogallus urubitinga*, and the crane hawk *Geranospiza caerulescens*. Parrots are abundant. I observed a group of 206 turquoise-fronted parrots *Amazona aestiva* in the SESC Reserve at Barão de Melgaço. There are 19 species of psitasids including the hyacinth macaw *Anodorhynchus hyacinthinus*.

A survey (Marini *et al.* 1994) shows that the subregions of Miranda and Abobral of the Pantanal harbor 191 bird species, distributed within 53 families and 19 orders. Some 43 species (21.9%) out of those 191 annotated species occurring in the region have aquatic habits. The order Passeriformes is represented by a total of 18 families (34%) and 73 species (38%). The non-passerine species are represented by 35 families (66%) and 118 species (61%).

Brown (1986) found that only 1.5% of birds species were endemic. About 60% (382 species) are widespread birds, occurring on both sides of the Pantanal, one-fifth of them aquatic. The bird species, which came from the Amazon region and reached the Pantanal, are mixed forest groups (Dendrocolaptidae, Formicariidae, Tycannidae, Thraupidae, among others). The bird species from the Chaco biome are seed feeders and species from open habitats, such as Furnariidae and Fringillidae.

Common and abundant bird species include species of the genera *Phalocrocorax*, *Ardea*, *Egretta*, *Mycteria*, *Dendrocygna*, *Cairina*, *Cathartes*, *Coragyps*, *Polyborus*, *Rosthramus*, *Columbina*, *Anodorhynchus*, *Ara*, *Piaya*, *Guira*, *Crotophaga*, *Aramus*, *Ceryle*, *Chloroceryle*, *Pteroglossus*, *Ramphastos*, *Agelaius*, *Thraupis*, *Tangara*, *Myospiza*, *Sicalis*, and *Volatinia*. Their abundance is probably due to mobility, body size, ability to exploit the available seasonal resources (Fig. 7.8), homeothermy, longevity, association with the water (86 species), or being generalist predators (397 species – 343 of which are insectivorous). As Fig. 7.8 shows, where loss of habitat occurs, the frugivore bird species would be the first to be impacted, particularly species belonging to the families Cracidae and Trogonidae. The potential loss of species due to habitat disruption is also shown in Fig. 7.9, which examines the substrate used by bird species. It is observed that only 13% of the Pantanal bird species are terrestrial while 15% of the species occasionally occupy that substrate. The loss of forested habitats would harm forest dwellers and benefit species of open habitats such as *Rhea americana*, *Crypturellus parvirostris*, *Rhynchotus rufescens*, *Nothura maculosa*, and *Cariama cristata*.

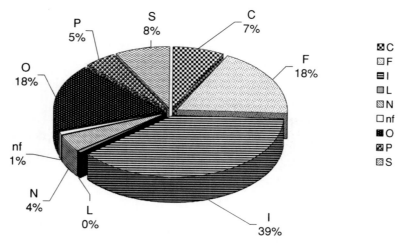

Figure 7.8 Proportions of different types of diet of bird species living in the Pantanal: C, carnivore (prey predominantly on vertebrates); F, frugivore; I, insectivore; L, folivore; N, nectarivore; nf, necrofagous (feeding on dead animals); O, omnivore; P, piscivore; S, granivore (seeds being the major food item).

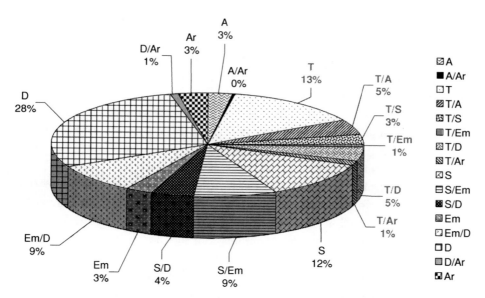

Figure 7.9 Classification of bird species of the Pantanal according to the substrates used: T, terrestrial; S, under-store and medium stratum; D, canopy; A, air and water; Em, emergent wetland; Ar, arboreal. Where two strata are combined, the order does not imply more frequent use of the first stratum.

As well as being great migrants, waterfowl are sizeable birds, congregating at times in wide open spaces and are good indicators of the Pantanal's richness and health. They also form one group of criteria established for the choice of the wetlands to be listed under the provisions of the Ramsar Convention; that is, the "criteria pertaining to the importance of wetlands for waterfowl populations and species."

The Pantanal presents one of the highest concentrations of aquatic bird species known (Stotz *et al.* 1996) with 13 species of herons (genera *Casmerodius*, *Egretta* and *Pilherodius*), storks (*Mycteria* and *Euxenura*), and jabiru (*Jabiru*) in addition to many others.

Mammals

According to the taxonomic compilation conducted by Wilson and Reeder (1993) there are 4629 mammal species world-wide. Brazil harbors 545 mammal species from 11 out of the 27 orders in the class, representing 11.8% of all known species in the world (Fonseca *et al.* 1996). A total of 132 mammal species occur in the Pantanal while in the Cerrado biome there are 195 species. Capybaras (*Hydrochaeris hydrochaeris*) occur throughout the region (Alho *et al.* 2002, 2003).

A survey and trap – mark – recapture survey was conducted at Fazenda Nhumirim (subregion of Nehcolândia) (Alho *et al.* 1988b); two observers on horseback worked for ten days of each month for a year and identified 7 orders, 16 families, 28 genera, and 34 species of mammals. The coati *Nasua nasua* was the most-frequently observed species during the diurnal census. Coatis are diurnal and scansorial, foraging on the ground in open areas during the dry season or arboreally in forest habitats. They are opportunistic feeders eating crabs and other invertebrates such as bugs, termites, and cicadas in grasslands near ponds during the dry season or feeding on fruits in arboreal habitats.

The fox "lobinho" *Cerdocyon thous* was the second most-frequently observed species. This fox ranges through a variety of habitats; from open fields to savanna, woodland, and forest. They are omnivorous, eating fruits and preying on insects, amphibians, reptiles, birds, and mammals. During the dry season they prefer crustaceans such as crabs. The giant anteater *Myrmecophaga tridactyla* is active during the day, being a distinctive animal with its long tail and elongated snout. The giant anteater forages in open areas visiting termite mounds or ant nests where it finds insects by rooting with its nose or by digging with its powerful front claws. In the Pantanal it is quite common to observe young attached to its mother's back. The other observed anteater species, *Tamandua tetradactyla*, is smaller in size. The tail is prehensile since this species has a more-arboreal habit, also feeding on both termites and ants.

The armadillos such as *Euphractus sexcinctus* and *Dasypus novemcinctus* are found in the savannas, forest edges, and adjacent fields; they prefer drier habitats. They are excellent diggers and frequently cause damage in flat areas that local farmers use as runways to land their small airplanes. The giant armadillo *Priodontes maximus* is a rare species but I observed it in the SESC Reserve (subregion of Barão de Melgaço), in 1998, when I was conducting field work for the management plan of the Reserve. The species is mainly nocturnal and fossorial, and is therefore difficult to observe. Its burrows are usually located near termite mounds. Its feeding habit is essentially myrmecophagous.

The howler monkey *Alouatta caraya* is observed in canopies of gallery forests and other forest habitats. They are diurnal and vocal animals occurring in small multi-male groups. They prefer moister forests, principally gallery forest along the rivers. They are easily observed along the major rivers crossing the Pantanal. They are vegetarian, feeding mainly on new sprouts of trees, and so they depend upon the phenological rhythms of the forest.

Deer species observed are the marsh deer *Blastocerus dichotomus*, the pampas deer *Ozotocerus bezoarticus*, and the red brocket *Mazama americana*. Marsh deer prefer more-hydric habitats such as flooded grasslands. The pampas deer or "veado campeiro" inhabits open areas and, in the Pantanal, the stags observed had antlers in velvet between June and August. The red bocket or "veado mateiro" prefer thick forest in moist areas where they mainly feed on fruits.

The order Carnivora is well represented in the Pantanal including species listed as endangered. The maned wolf *Chrysocyon brachyurus* frequents grasslands and scrub habitats. This species prey on small mammals, insects, and birds, and eat large quantities of the fruit "fruta-do-lobo" *Solanum lyocarpum*. The bush dog *Speothos venaticus* also occurs in the Pantanal. The crab-eating raccoon *Procyon cancrivorus* is common in the Pantanal, spending the day sleeping in trees and foraging during the night. The tayra *Eira barbara* is active both during the day and at night; this species ranges from open grasslands to forest habitats. The otter *Lontra longicaudis* is found where ample riparian vegetation is present along rivers and lakes. They have their shelters in burrows at the riverbanks. In the SESC Reserve (subregion of Barão de Melgaço) I observed large groups swimming in the "corixo" (a branch of river) Riozinho. The most-spectacular carnivore inhabiting the Pantnal is the jaguar *Panthera onca*; it is the largest of the American cat species.

Although mammal diversity is similar in the plains and in the upland plateaus covered by cerrado, when the most-observed 15 mammal species are compared between Pantanal and Cerrado, there are remarkable differences in local abundance, expressed as frequency of observations. Capybaras (*Hydrochaeris hydrochaeris*), coatis (*Nasua nasua*), marsh deer (*Blastocerus dichotomus*), fox

(*Cerdocyon thous*), pampas deer (*Ozotoceros bezoarticus*), and other species have distribution in both biomes, Pantanal and Cerrado. However, local abundance differs sharply especially for capybaras, marsh deer, and pampas deer – and even for mammal species officially declared endangered, such as *Myrmecophaga tridactyla*, *Blastocerus dichotomus*, *Priodontes maximus*, *Panthera onca*, and *Pteronura brasiliensis*; all of these species are easily observed in the Pantanal.

In general, most mammal species living in the Pantanal depend on forested or arboreal natural habitats (Alho *et. al.* 2002).

Conservation

Environmental threats

The Pantanal has been impacted by unsustainable socio-economic development practices. The major economic activities are cattle ranching, fishing, agriculture, mining, and tourism. The urbanization of the areas surrounding the plains is causing water pollution by discharges of liquid and solid waste and rubbish; this is the case for the Cuiabá River, which passes through the large city of Cuiabá where it receives untreated sewage discharge.

The implementation of a conservation plan for the Pantanal needs to be enforced since the region regulates water regimes; supports habitats for spectacular flora and fauna; and is a biome of great economic, cultural, scientific, and recreational value. This value is stressed in the Convention on Wetlands of International Importance Especially as Waterfowl Habitat (Ramsar).

Some major conservation problems of the Pantanal floodplain originate on the plateaus. Many farms have been established in the highlands surrounding the Pantanal and much of the natural vegetation (savanna) has been converted to soybean plantations or is used for other activities (Alho *et al.* 1988a, Alho & Martins 1995, Alho & Vieira 1997). These conservation problems include: erosion; compacted soil; pollution, including environmental contaminants; alterations in the water level; damming of rivers; and deposition of sewage and solid waste.

Deforestation, expanding agriculture, illegal fishing and hunting, unplanned tourism, and pollution by pesticides have caused a progressive deterioration of natural habitats. Because of the huge demand for soybean plantations on the upland plateaus surrounding the Pantanal, the application of toxic agricultural chemicals is very common (Alho & Vieira 1997).

A new road system has motivated landowners to subdivide their land into several small lots for "development." This has resulted in altering natural habitats, killing wildlife on the roads, and encouraging illegal fishing and hunting, while producing an abundance of litter including plastic objects. The threats are considered in detail below.

Fire

This is a major threat. Ranchers in the Pantanal set fire to the vegetation during the dry season as a "management" technique to "clean" the vegetation not used by cattle. The fire is initially started in the grassland but due to the open areas, dry vegetation, and wind, the fires often spread to savannas, woodland, and forest. In 1999, fires destroyed enormous areas of grassland and forest in the subregions of Poconé, Barão de Melgaço, Cáceres, and many other regions of the Pantanal, causing considerable harm to the structure and functioning of natural habitats, and to wildlife. In Poconé, along the Transpantaneira road, the fires burned the vegetation for more than 20 days; I saw three wooden bridges transformed to ashes. I also saw wildlife roaming throughout, trying to escape from the fires. In addition to habitat disruption, fire affects slow-moving animals, young, and nests; particularly for species with terrestrial habits. Changes in habitat structure due to frequent fire can be noticed in some places.

Brandão (1996) monitored fire in the Pantanal; he pointed out that 3000 km^2 were affected by fire in the 1991–1992 dry season, when precipitation from January to September was 885 to 866 mm. In drier years such as 1993, with precipitation of 443 mm, the area burned was three times larger. Another problem is that when the flood comes, the ashes may act as a toxic substance and kill fish. Fire is so common during the dry season that the airports of Corumbá and Cuiabá stay closed for landing or take-off for long periods.

Moreover, the fire monitoring program of the Brazilian Government during the period of 1991–1996 suggests that the Pantanal region has had high incidences of fire, especially during the dry season (MMA 1998).

Deforestation

Deforestation to replace savanna habitats and other woodlands with pastures for cattle is increasing. Silva *et al.* (1998b) concluded that 3.9% of the Pantanal (5437.73 km^2 of savanna, woodland, and forest habitats) has been deforested. These authors report that the Poconé subregion alone has an area converted into pasture corresponding to 8% of its total. Considering only the plains, the subregion of Porto Murtinho has had about 20% of its area converted. Other subregions, such as Cáceres and Barão do Melgaço, show less than 2% of lost natural areas. The habitats converted to pasture include *cerradão* (woodland), different kinds of *cerrado* (savannas) and semi-deciduous forest. This is a conservative estimate since Brandão (1996) indicated that many forest habitats have been cleared for pastures and other purposes, contributing to the loss of about 30% of forested area in the Pantanal. Figure 7.10 shows how sensitive the bird species living in the Pantanal are to habitat disturbance such as deforestation.

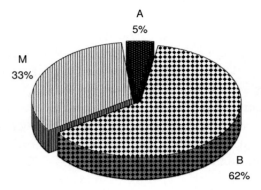

Figure 7.10 Distribution of bird species occurring in the subregions of Poconé and Barão de Melgaço in relation to their sensitivity to habitat disturbances such as deforestation. A, high sensitivity (12 species); M, medium sensitivity (86 species); B, low sensitivity (166 species).

Removal of the forest eliminates food and shelter, especially for forest-dwelling wildlife and epiphytic plants. Deforestation also increases erosion since most elevated areas have sandy soil that is easily blown or washed away by rain.

The flux of water in the Taquari River and Coxim River valleys has been altered by eroded material coming from the highlands (Veneziani *et al.* 1998). This study identifies seven different erosion classes and three accumulation classes in determining the relationship between erosion and other factors such as physical, chemical, and mechanical properties of the lithologic types – including ruptibility–plasticity, water infiltration, runoff, and landslide – complemented with identification of relief type and declivity. The junction of the Taquari River and the Paraguay River is almost completely blocked with sand.

Over the last two decades, a significant increase in annual-culture plantations on the highlands has been observed. Because of the conversion of natural savannas into food-crop plantations, the rainfall on bare soil increases the runoff and production of sediments transported to the plains.

Cattle ranching

"Tucura" is a cattle breed introduced into the region by Europeans over 200 years ago. This and other breeds well adapted to the region have small stature, low reproductive rates, and slow growth. However, they thrive in the flooded conditions while utilizing native forage. The problem is that they can no longer compete commercially with the more-advanced cattle production of the ranches on the plateaus.

Some studies contend that cattle numbers in the Pantanal have reduced from 4.98 million animals in 1970 to 3.53 million in 1980 because pastures for cattle have dwindled, among other factors. The reduction in available pasture areas, according to these studies, has been due to flooding of grassland in lowland areas since 1974. Today the Center for Agricultural Research in the Pantanal (CPAP-EMBRAPA) estimates that there are more than 3 million head of cattle in the region.

Environmental contaminants

The introduction of toxins and other contaminants to the Pantanal is an undesirable trend in habitat quality, since it affects valuable wildlife and fish resources as well as the quality of associated natural resources, including surface and groundwater. The introduction of pollutants to ecosystems results in changes in an interrelated series of variables or processes that can affect the structure and function of the ecosystem in the short or long term.

Alho and Vieira (1997) point out that unregulated gold mining has contaminated Pantanal habitats with mercury. Fish samples showed high percentages of contamination (Cuiabá and Bento Gomes rivers) with mercury beyond the levels allowed by international standards for contamination. Bird species that feed on fish – like the olivaceous cormorant *Phalacrocorax olivaceus*, the limpkin *Aramus guarauna*, and the snail kite *Rosthramus sociabilis* – were also contaminated.

In addition to gold mining, the extraction of iron ore, manganese, and calcium carbonate has been contaminating the water.

Small-scale, low-density cattle ranching was the predominant land-use activity in the Pantanal for centuries. Nowadays it cannot compete financially with large-scale agriculture supported by petroleum-based inputs of agricultural chemicals. As a consequence there has been considerable investment in the improvement of pastures in the floodplain, by converting arboreal natural habitats into pastures, as well as the development of agricultural areas on the highlands. The natural vegetation cover of *cerrado* (savanna) has been removed to provide open space for food crops, mainly soybean. Frequent and uncontrolled use of pesticides and herbicides has occurred. It is difficult to quantify and qualify the use of pesticides and herbicides on the borders of the Pantanal since no information is available. The law says that these products must be registered, but it has been difficult to enforce the law. The soybean producers are forced by commercial circumstances to maximize their production.

Depending on location, the sediments and habitats of the Pantanal have received a wide range of agricultural and domestic waste, much of it is persistent in flooded sediments and may accumulate in food chains where it can kill fish and wildlife.

Sewage treatment for the great majority of the municipalities surrounding the Pantanal is practically non-existent. The waste goes directly into the water courses.

According to the Agência Municipal de Serviços de Saneamento da Cidade de Cuiabá (Cuiabá Municipal Agency for Water and Sewage), on some days the water collected from points of the Cuiabá and Coxipó rivers – depending on the location of the water treatment station – shows levels of fecal coliforms that may reach nearly 40 000 per 100 ml of water. The federal CONAMA (Conselho Nacional do Meio Ambiente [National Council for the Environment]) recommends a maximum acceptable level of 20 000 fecal coliforms per 100 ml of water. However, in general the level of contamination is lower. On March 15, 2000 the treatment station at Parque Cuiabá collected water containing 8000 total fecal coliforms per 100 ml and the treatment station at Porto collected water containing 5120 total fecal coliforms per 100 ml. The city of Cuiabá has seven water treatment stations at different locations. The Cuiabá River is one of the major tributaries of the Paraguay River, in the Pantanal region. According to the same source, about 80% of the water collected in the city returns to the river in the form of sewage. It has been estimated that only about 10% of the city sewage receives treatment before draining into the river. This shows that the city of Cuiabá has a considerable negative impact on the water quality draining into the Pantanal. The same trend can be observed in other cities near or inside the Pantanal area, such as Corumbá, Cáceres, Barão de Melgaço, and many others.

Another problem is the disposal of litter into the river by the city's inhabitants. Usually the location chosen as a final destination for solid waste is close to roads, rivers, or streams. The NGO ADERCO (Associação de Defesa do Rio Coxipó [Association for the Defense of the Coxipó River]) reports that in 1997 on the occasion of the campaign SOS Rio Cuiabá, 50 tons of litter were collected from the river. About 2000 school students and their families implemented the campaign. The majority of the litter found in the river is from poor districts where public litter collection is non-existent. ADERCO concluded that about 90% of the litter in the river came from the cities. Along the rivers – for example the Paraguay and Cuiabá rivers – all houses, ranches, small hotels, and many "*pesqueiros*" (fishing places for tourists) have no sewage treatment and rarely have organized garbage collection.

Alterations in the level and quality of water and river damming in the highlands have also contributed to the adverse impact on the plains. Recently (1999–2000) a dam for hydroelectrical power (210 MW) was built at Manso River, an important tributary of the Cuiabá River. The Manso basin represents an area (9365 km^2) that covers 40% of the Cuiabá River basin (22 226 km^2) down to the city of Cuiabá. The reservoir formed by the Manso dam is about 400 km^2. The Manso basin provides around 70% of the water of the Cuiabá River at the point nearest the city of Cuiabá, just before draining into the Pantanal (SONDOTÉCNICA 1999).

Infrastructure and unplanned human occupation

Two major, large-scale projects are underway in the Pantanal: the Bolivia–Brazil pipeline for natural gas, which crosses the floodplain and has already become a reality; and the controversial Paraguay–Paraná waterway. To take advantage of the natural gas it is intended to develop the petrochemical center in Corumbá, at the margins of the Paraguay River.

In 1991, Argentina, Brazil, Paraguay, and Uruguay formed MERCOSUL (in Spanish "MERCOSUR"), the Southern Cone Common Market of South America, which was later joined by other countries. Because the Paraguay–Paraná river system flows south through Brazil – and with Bolivia, Paraguay, Argentina, and Uruguay also draining the Plata basin – the waterway has a high strategic and symbolic value for the integration of these countries.

In fact, means of transportation is a key factor for the integration of MERCOSUL. Although the system is already navigable, there are sectors where and times when navigation upstream is difficult for small vessels and impossible for large ones due to the occurrence of sandbanks and rocky outcrops. In order to allow navigation for large cargo convoys from Buenos Aires (Argentina) up to Cáceres (Brazil) it would be necessary to dredge a uniformly deep and wide riverbed within the section of the Paraguay River, particularly between Corumbá and Cáceres, just in the Pantanal area. As said before, the river passes through the wetland in this sector. Although the project was considered to be both physically and economically feasible, it was strongly contested by environmentalists because of the obvious negative impact on the Pantanal ecosystem. Since various studies (WWF 1999) objected to the project, the Brazilian Government officially gave up constructing the *hydrovia*. However, large cargo convoys continue to navigate through the rivers in the Pantanal and, because of their length, these vessels touch and damage the riverbanks, in addition to causing other damage such as oil spills and waste.

Some official and private roads constructed in the Pantanal dam the waters and so block the normal flow. There are significant data showing the impact of traffic on roads crossing areas of rich and abundant wildlife. One study conducted by Fisher (1997) points out the dramatic impact of road killings on several species of wildlife along the road BR-262, crossing the Pantanal from Campo

Grande to Corumbá in the state of Mato Grosso do Sul. From May, 1966 to November, 1997, this author registered 1402 animals killed by cars – including birds, reptiles, amphibians, and mammals belonging to a total of 84 species. Among those species, 6 were officially declared endangered, such as the marsh deer *Blastocerus dichotomus*, the maned wolf *Chrysocyon brachyurus*, two wild cats (*Felis pardalis* and *Panthera onca*), the otter *Lontra longicaudis*, and the giant anteater *Myrmecophaga tridactyla*. The study showed a rate of road death of up to 105 kills per month, 3 per day along that road. The average number of vehicles running on that road is 1800 per day.

International literature points out that, depending on the alterations that the road makes to the natural environment, these roads may function as barriers for the wildlife (Barrientos 1993, Drews, 1995, Reijnen & Foppen 1995). In some cases the roads function as a place of attraction for the animals, especially during the flooding season. In fact, on some roads crossing the Pantanal it is common to see animals resting on the roads, mainly capybaras. Another problem is that in some places the road crosses a gallery forest that goes along the river, which is usually a corridor for medium and large mammals. This interruption in the gallery forest forces animals to cross the road. The road going from Santo Antônio de Leverger to Barão de Melgaço, in the state of Mato Grosso, interrupted some drainage channels; this compromised fish migration from river to flooded grounds and vice versa.

The road system is expanding throughout the Pantanal, mainly in the category of parkway. The Transpantaneira road, for example, which has existed since 1970 as a non-paved road, is going to be improved so that it becomes a parkway.

Unregulated tourism

Tourism, if well planned and regulated, provides an excellent alternative economy for the region. There is a booming tourist trade in the Pantanal; unfortunately most of this tourism is predatory. Tour groups may invade areas that should be preserved (e.g. waterfowl nesting grounds or rookeries); sport-fishing groups may over-fish and generally spread litter – particularly in illegal camp sites in gallery forest, where these fishermen leave signs of their predatory presence. Numerous tourist hotel boats navigating throughout the Pantanal do not treat waste and spread solid waste on their way.

The high season for sport fishing is in July, September, and October; large numbers of fishermen – and the containers to keep their fish in – gather in the fishing hotels, riverside camps, and boat hotels. They come mainly from São Paulo state.

Most of the boat or bus tours that come to the Pantanal do little or nothing to teach visitors about the ecology and conservation of the region.

Too-few protected areas

The area is still far away from the planned objective to have 10% of its territory protected. Two major federal protected are as have been established: the Pantanal National Park, with 135 000 ha, and the Taiamã Reserve, with 11 200 ha. Others protected areas are private reserves, for example: the Ecological Station of SESC, at the subregion of Barão de Melgaço; and Acurizal, Penha, and Dorochê at the vicinities of the National Park. Some protected areas are located in the uplands such as the Chapada dos Guimarães and Serra da Bodoquena (IBAMA 2004).

Threatened species are those officially recognized as endangered, threatened, or otherwise at risk, through criteria established by the Brazilian Institute of Environment (IBAMA 2004) or by the international policy of the World Conservation Union (IUCN Red List).

The criteria used to establish listed species takes into consideration the geographic range of the taxa and estimates concerning population size and decline, especially resulting from the degradation or loss of habitat. As emphasized before, the number of endemic species is very low in the Pantanal. Thus, the presence of an important number of listed species in the region is due to the relatively well-preserved and productive Pantanal natural habitats in relation to other geographic ranges where the same species occur.

Many officially threatened and endangered species can be observed ranging free in the Pantanal. Large mammals such as the jaguar *Panthera onca*, marsh deer *Blastocerus dichotomus*, giant anteater *Myrmecophaga tridactyla*, giant armadillo *Priodontes maximus*, and maned wolf *Chrysocyon brachyurus* – among others – are present in natural habitats. Other mammal species listed are: bush dog *Speothos venaticus*; wild cats such as ocelot *Leopardus pardalis*, oncilla *L. tigrinus*, margay *L. wiedii*, wildcat *Oncifelis colocolo*, puma *Puma concolor*; pampas deer *Ozotoceros bezoarticus*, and otters (*Lontra longicaudis* and *Pteronura brasiliensis*).

Among bird species the following are listed and occur in the region: fasciated tiger heron (*Tigrisoma fasciatum*), black-and-white hawk eagle (*Spizastur melanoleucus*), harpy eagle (*Harpia harpyja*), chestnut-bellied guan (*Penelope ochrogaster*), hyacinth macaw (*Anodorhynchus hyacinthinus*), sharp-tailed tyrant (*Culicivora caudacuta*), and great-billed seed finch (*Oryzoborus maximiliani*).

There are no listed species of amphibians and reptiles occurring in the region.

Human migration, urbanization, lack of education, and environmental consciousness

The human population living in the upper Paraguay basin is estimated to be low, about 2 million people, 83% of them living in urban areas and 17%

in rural areas. The rural human densities are between 4 and 5 people per km^2, which is equivalent to one family per 100 ha. There are places where the density is one family per 1500 ha. The level of formal education of the population is very low and so it is difficult to introduce and reinforce environmental consciousness.

The major economic activity in terms of land occupation is cattle ranching. Official studies (demographic statistics from the Brazilian Institute of Geography and Statistics – IBGE 2001) identify 26% of the pastures as natural grasslands and 39% as cultivated pastures. The major crops are corn and soybean, according to IBGE statistics of 2001. The forest lands are at a critical level in some basins, such as the São Lourenço (with only 17% of forested habitats remaining) and the Paraguay basin (with 25%) – percentages considered low in view of the characteristics of these regions.

The percentage of homes which receive treated water averages 83%. The situation of treated sewage is more critical; 85% of the municipalities in the sub-basin of Taquari rely on rudimentary domestic devices (75% at Miranda, 73% at Apa, and 37% at Cuiabá). Many homes receive no treatment at all (Acorizal 36%, Barão de Melgaço 35%, Jangada 43%, Nossa Senhora do Livramento 42%, Paraguay basin 30%, and so on).

The official activities of existing registered enterprises (detected by the IBGE census) are: 20 establishments dealing with fishing; 187 associated with mining, and 2329 involved with lodgings and restaurants. However, there are plenty of unregistered activities that go undetected by the official census.

Critical problems related to human occupation

Biodiversity loss

The loss and modification of natural habitats due to deforestation or conversion of savanna into pastures has been significant in the Pantanal (Alho *et al.* 1988a; Silva *et al.* 1998b).

As the natural habitats are dependent on the flooding pattern, modifications in hydrology or the flow of the waters – due to local and upland deforestation and inappropriate land use – affect habitat quality.

Commercial and sport fishing has become so intense that these activites are out of the control of the environmental agencies, with consequent negative impacts on fish stocks and natural habitats. The same trend is observed with illegal hunting activities. New roads and other access routes have recently been opened, facilitating human activities in previously well-preserved wild lands.

Many large ranches have been subdivided into small plots, modifying the original arrangement of extensive cattle raising. New and improved roads contribute to the subdivision of large pieces of land into small lots.

As pointed out throughout this chapter, the Pantanal supports a magnificent biodiversity and some officially listed species that are threatened by extinction. Therefore, one challenge is to respond positively to increasing threats to biodiversity by means of effective conservation actions. The species of Special Concern for conservation are good indicators of the vital ecological status of the entire ecosystem.

Brazilian environmental legislation is considered up-to-date and very good, but the problem is its actual enforcement.

Soil degradation

Over the last 30 years a series of trends has changed land use in the Pantanal. The expansion of agriculture – especially the large-scale production of cash crops such as soybeans, predominantly on the plateaus and with drastic conversion of the original *cerrado* vegetation into soybean fields – has started soil erosion and severe sedimentation from tilled land, resulting in damming of rivers. The crops receive heavy applications of agricultural chemicals, which drain into upstream tributaries that feed the Pantanal. Excessive silting up and erosion of riverbeds caused by adjacent deforestation in elevated areas is affecting water drainage. The erosion resulting from these activities is evident in the case of the Taquari River.

On the plains, traditional cattle ranching is facing difficulties in competing economically with the modern and more-productive cattle management of the plateaus. Intensive cattle management needs to convert *cerrado* savanna and forest into pasture. Cattle affect the vegetation through selective grazing and the damage they cause to the open savanna and the forest understory. Their selective feeding modifies the vegetation cover by seed dispersal and by increasing invasive plants. The dry-season practice of burning grasses to promote new growth has a detrimental effect on soil.

The use of pesticides, herbicides, and other toxic substances modifies the soil. In addition, the construction of illegal or unauthorized buildings on the riverbanks for sport fishing has contributed to deforestation and soil degradation.

Gold mining and other mining activities were carried out intensively for 20 years (although they have decreased during the last 10 years) with consequent soil movement and release of contaminants, especially mercury.

The impact of cattle ranching on soil degradation has not been satisfactorily calculated, especially taking into account the introduction of African forage species and compacting of the soil.

Water pollution and conflicts surrounding its use

The following activities have been identified as responsible for water pollution on the floodplains: mining, urban liquid and solid waste including untreated sewage, unregulated tourism and related unauthorized buildings on the river banks, toxic products used in agriculture, and debris from industrial plants. Turbidity is one measure that responds rapidly to water pollution.

The excessive and uncontrolled growth of the cities surrounding the Pantanal – such as Cuiabá, Corumbá, Miranda, Cáceres, Poconé, and many others – has led to the disposal of sewage and urban garbage, including solid waste, into rivers, with consequent marked water contamination.

ANA (Brazilian National Water Agency) is tackling some of the problems in the public use of water through participatory management. Another issue to be dealt with is the training of local personnel in integrated basin management, so that they are qualified to deal with the use of water for mining, agriculture and irrigation, tourism, and so on. The major conflict is the use of water in the uplands versus flooding in the floodplains (agriculture, hydroelectric dams, pollution, etc.).

Social and economic losses

Over-fishing is responsible for economic and social losses in the upper Paraguay basin. When fish availability is reduced, river fishermen may move to urban centers in search of jobs.

Unregulated tourist activities may also cause economic and social losses because they impinge on a range of issues: from water contamination by solid and liquid waste, to the erosion of river banks due to inadequate utilization of fluvial navigation, and the reduced interest of other visitors.

Uncontrolled fire is another element of economic and social loss since it damages landscape, soil, water, and biodiversity.

Uncontrolled flooding with reduction of productive areas, as is seen in the Taquari subregion, may also cause economic and social losses. The same problem may occur with the productivity of the floodplains being reduced due to permanent flooding caused by human disturbance.

It is fundamental to develop a reliable forecasting system to deal with severe floods and with the drought that contributes to uncontrolled wildfire, in order to prevent economic, social, and biological losses. For floods, some attempts have been made (Adamoli 1996) and for wild fire the federal program PREVFOGO (National Program to Prevent and Combat Wild Fires) is in action in cooperation with state governments. In addition, ANA (Brazilian National Water Agency) is setting up an observatory to collect data on floods along the Paraguay River, which is designed to contribute to flood control.

Biodiversity loss, soil depletion, and urban impact on the rivers cause economic and social losses, since they generate critical problems that are costly to reverse. It also takes a very long time to try to restore natural conditions.

Fragility of social organization

The fragile institutional basis, the need for management policies, and the lack of skilled personnel are identified as important elements contributing to environmental degradation. Thus, three elements need to be strengthened to improve participatory management: (1) the knowledge of the decision makers involved in managing the Pantanal's hydrological resources; (2) the skill of the stakeholders in participating; (3) the motivation of the local residents to participate in social decisions. A recent federal law on hydrological resources (Law 9433/1977) encourages participatory management through specific committees. However, its full implementation requires motivation, knowledge, and skilful personnel.

For some regions these committees are already at work, implementing the recommendations of the Law, as in the cases of the Miranda and Apa rivers. In these cases, a diagnosis of hydrological resources was drawn up and a proposal for integrated basin management has been presented (CIDEMA 2002).

Priorities for action

Major projects and studies

The PCBAP (Plan for Conservation of the Upper Paraguay Basin), carried out by the Brazilian Ministry of Environment (MMA), was concluded in 1997, and was created to deal with organized regional economic development – under a conservation framework of natural resources, incentives for production, and respect to local cultural traditions and knowledge – aiming toward sustainable use of the Pantanal and its surrounding uplands. The guidelines of the PCBAP deal with a large spectrum of problems (physical characteristics, biotic components, hydrology, climatic parameters, socio-economic structure, and economic development) to suggest a comprehensive checklist of actions.

Pantanal Program

The Brazilian Ministry of the Environment (MMA) is presently implementing the most-ambitious project for the region: the Program for Sustainable Development of the Pantanal or the Pantanal Program. It has received a loan of US$165 million from the Inter American Bank for Development to implement sustainable development in the Pantanal through the *"Programa Pantanal"* (Contract 1290-BR) in the states with territories in the Pantanal: Mato Grosso and Mato Grosso do Sul. The total amount of financial resources reaches US$400 million (implementation from 2002 to 2006).

The Program goals are to accomplish brown, blue, and green agendas. The brown agenda deals with pollution problems, mainly water pollution and especially urban sewage discharge. The blue agenda deals with actions to improve water quality and its public use. This activity involves the participation of the Brazilian National Water Agency (ANA). The green agenda leads to conservation and sustainable use of biodiversity by strengthening protected areas, mainly by the construction of parkway roads throughout the Pantanal.

At the time of writing, this project is at the stage of preliminary studies for implementation.

Pantanal and Upper Paraguay Basin Project

This is a project on Practices in Integrated Management of the Hydrographic Basin of the Pantanal and Upper Paraguay Basin carried out by ANA (Brazilian National Water Agency) with the support of GEF (Global Environmental Facility), UNEP (United Nations Environmental Program) and AOS (American Organization States); it has resources of around US$9 million. Its objective is to implement some recommendations made by PCBAP by supporting subprojects on the following components: water quality, conservation, land degradation, stakeholder participation, and institutional structure; all of these components contribute to an integrated management program for the basin. This is an ongoing project programmed to finish by the end of 2004 (ANA 2004).

Research, experiments, and studies on cattle ranching, agriculture, flora, and fauna performed by CPAP-EMBRAPA

The Center for Agriculture and Livestock Research of the Pantanal (CPAP) belonging to the Brazilian Enterprise for Agricultural Research (EMBRAPA), located in Corumbá, has carried out influential studies on the Pantanal including in the areas of wildlife and fishing.

Pantanal Ecology Project

This is a project named *Ecologia do Gran Pantanal* carried out at the Federal University of Mato Grosso in cooperation with the German Max-Planck-Institut für Limnologie with support of CNPq (Brazilian Council for Scientific Research). The main emphasis is on studies in limnology, but other focuses have also been selected, principally for the post-graduate theses of German and Brazilian students. This program has been running since 1991, and has published a considerable amount of literature.

Environmental studies on the Manso region

The upland of Chapada dos Guimarães was the focus of 21 studies on environmental issues (climate, minerals, hydrology, erosion, water quality, flora, fauna including fish, and others) in order to construct the hydroelectric dam and plant at Manso. The local wildlife there is some of the best known in the region, as much field work has been carried out there and then published (Alho *et al.* 2000, 2003).

Priority Actions for Conserving Cerrado and Pantanal Biodiversity

This study, concluded in 1999, was an initiative of the Brazilian Ministry of Environment in cooperation with other participants (institutions and researchers). The result was the *Ações Prioritárias para a Conservação da Biodiversidade do Cerrado e Pantanal* (Priority Actions for Conserving Cerrado and Pantanal Biodiversity). It identifies critical priority areas for conservation through the establishment of protected areas as well as corridors linking existing or potential reserves.

The study concludes that the conservation strategy for the Pantanal should consider the region as a whole, connecting all subregions and different ecosystems. The protected areas should be representative of each subregion as well as considering the role of the region as a corridor for the dispersion of species and integration of the adjacent biomes.

There are three categories of priority: level 1 includes core areas where establishment of conservation units is recommended; level 2 includes areas where development should pay attention to deforestation, erosion, and pollution; priority level 3 involves remaining areas where sustainable development should be carried out.

The corridors for conservation are identified in north–south and east–west directions. Going along the Paraguay River from north to south to the Apa River, near the city of Porto Murtinho, the region includes the protected area of the Biological Reserve Serra das Araras (on the highlands) linking it with the Taimã Ecological Station, the National Park of the Pantanal (on the plains), and the private reserves (RPPN Doroche and Penha) near the Amolar highlands. In the same region there are two priority areas for conservation: Urucum and Nabileque; both are near the Paraguayan Chaco, with drier vegetation formations.

From east to west, the areas include the region of the Cuiabá, São Lourenço, and Piquiri rivers. The corridor links the Chapada dos Guimarães (highlands) to a private reserve (SESC Pantanal) and the Indian Bororo Reserve (plains). In the region of the Piquiri River protected areas are suggested for the northern part of the Paiaguás subregion. The median axis connects the Pantanal with the highlands of the state of Goiás, specifically with Emas National Park (Cerrado biome). In this region the headwaters of the Taquari, Jauru, Coxim, and Verde rivers are located; these exert a strong influence on the Pantanal, being responsible for the characteristics of the subregions of Nhecolândia and Paiaguás. The expansion of Emas National Park (outside the Pantanal) and the protection of the upper Taquari River (highlands) are proposed.

In summary, this important document (BDT 1999) emphasizes priority actions for conservation of the biodiversity of the Pantanal – integrated with the Cerrado biome – based on six major topics: (1) *change of focus*, with the explicit inclusion of biodiversity conservation (genetic resources, species, and ecosystems) in all planing documents; (2) *ecological corridors and regional protection*, with joint efforts of local and federal governments in order to implement the identified corridors and to promote economically sustainable activities; (3) *lobby for integrated policies*, with the participation of local and federal-government agencies to implement policies on environment, land use, agriculture, energy, water, education, and health care; (4) *legislation*, with efforts to enforce the existing legislation, believing that this procedure must protect nature; (5) *implementation of conservation units*, with regularization of land ownership and incentives for creation of private reserves; and (6) *research on inventory, monitoring, and conservation of biodiversity*, with the creation of integrated information on scientific data as well as incentives for new studies.

Guidelines for conservation and sustainable use of the Pantanal

Through a document published in 1999, the Brazilian Ministry of Environment (Portaria 298, MMA) established a multi-disciplinary and inter-institutional task force (starting in February 2000) to work for one year to produce guidelines for conservation and sustainable use of the Pantanal's biodiversity. The task force's mission was to bring together a group of specialists – with representatives from academia, research institutions, NGOs, government agencies, and others – to set priority policies for conservation and sustainable use of the Pantanal. The goal of that steering committee was to establish a national conservation program linked to the need for social, cultural, and economic development of the region (Table 7.1).

Research, studies, and theses produced by local universities and international NGOs

Local universities in both states, Mato Grosso and Mato Grosso do Sul, have been active in producing studies on the Pantanal; mainly research performed by professors, and theses and dissertations produced by the postgraduate programs. In addition to the scientific output of the federal universities, private

Table 7.1 *Priority themes and guidelines for conservation established by a multi-disciplinary and inter-institutional committee working under the leadership of the Brazilian Ministry of the Environment.*

Environmental issues

Land use, soil conservation, and management

1. Promote agricultural practices for soil use that avoid loss of soil, including erosion.
2. Promote economic activities related to the objectives of the protected areas' buffer zones and experimental projects for extractive reserves.

Water resources

1. Develop mandatory requirements for studies on the environmental impact of large development projects such as waterways.
2. Secure the control of environmental contaminants including pesticides according to international protocols.
3. Enforce the existing legislation on water resources including their springs.
4. Consider the hydrological basin and microbasin as a conservation unit or ecosystem.
5. Implement the effective participation of the Basin Committees in order to enforce legislation.
6. Promote the conservation of wetlands that fit into the concept of the Ramsar Convention.

Air pollution and climatic change

1. Establish shared management between government agencies and the public to control wildfire.
2. Conduct technical training, environmental education, and campaigns to prevent and combat wildfire.
3. Carry out environmental restoration in degraded areas to improve carbon absorption (carbon sequestration), among other benefits.

Biodiversity: conservation, research, and sustainable use

1. Promote the expansion of protected areas, ideally to reach 10% of the region as intended by the government (40% of indirect-use conservation units and 60% of direct use).
2. Secure land ownership in protected areas, the development of their management plan and its effective implementation, including the necessary staff.
3. Target priority incentives for the creation of private reserves (RPPN).
4. Promote incentives for the implementation of ecological sales taxes (ICMS Ecológico).
5. Undertake the administration of bioregional areas including the concept of ecoregions and biosphere reserves.
6. Carry out experimental pilot projects for sustainable use in direct-use protected areas.
7. Provide incentives for the creation of *ex-situ* reserves.
8. Provide incentives for sustainable use of biological resources including wildlife.
9. Promote the certification of products from sustainable-use programs.

Scientific and technological issues

Research and technology

1. Support shared participation between government and the private sector, aiming at the achievement of innovative technologies.

(cont.)

Table 7.1 (*cont.*)

2. Promote basic and applied research for the sustainable use of resources and technological practices for sustainable development.

Institutional issues

Institutional strength and shared management

1. Integrate information and actions of institutions engaged in conservation of the region.
2. Promote governmental policies to implement organizational strength including infrastructure, personnel, programs, and dissemination of results.

Legal and economic instruments

1. Integrate sectoral policies in order to promote regional conservation and development.
2. Create incentives for shared environmental management at all levels.
3. Promote law enforcement.
4. Implement ecological–economic zoning.

Social–cultural issues

Land use, territorial expansion with new agricultural frontiers

1. Produce guidelines for implementing ecological–economic zoning through shared participation and development indicators for sustainability.

Urban and metropolitan expansions

1. Develop means to control urban migration.

Poverty and life quality

1. Develop programs to support health and education for better quality of life.

Cultural diversity and traditions

1. Recognize the value of ethno-cultural diversity and traditional knowledge for conservation and sustainable use of resources.

Communication and environmental education

1. Plan, regulate, and implement programs on environmental education to diffuse and consolidate the education process of local people and to disseminate the information through modern means of communication.

Economic issues

Mineral exploitation

1. Conduct sustainable mining.
2. Create environmental certification for mining.
3. Integrate the processes of authorization, law enforcement, and control of mining.

Ecobusiness and sustainable tourism

1. Develop incentives for sustainable use of biodiversity.
2. Develop incentives for sustainable tourism.

Infrastructure

Harmonize planning and implementation of infrastructure, mainly for transport and energy, with recommendations for ecological–economic zoning as well as undertaking reliable studies on environmental impacts for each case.

institutions like UNIDERP (the University for the Development of the State and the Region of the Pantanal) in the city of Campo Grande, maintain research stations in the Pantanal.

International NGOs such as the World Wide Fund for Nature (WWF), Conservation International (CI), and The Nature Conservancy (TNC) have played an important role in studies on biodiversity, the impact of the Paraná–Paraguay waterway, management of protected areas, public policies, and other issues.

Publications

There are important introductory publications on the Pantanal. (1) Implementation of a Strategic Action Plan for the Integrated Management of the Pantanal and Upper Paraguay River Basin Following up the Upper Paraguay River Basin Conservation Plan (PCBAP 1997, ANA 2004), including studies on physical, biotic, and socio-economic aspects. (2) the *Anais do Simpósio sobre Recursos Naturais e Sócio-econômicos do Pantanal*, published by CPAP-EMBRAPA – the first one in 1984, the second in 1996, and the third in 2002 – also including physical, biotic, and socio-economic studies. (3) A list of plants collected in the region and published as the field guide *Plantas do Pantanal* (Pott & Pott 1994). (4) A series of papers published in a special edition of the Brazilian journal of agricultural research: *Pesquisa Agropecuária Brasíleira*, **33** (número especial), 1998; mainly articles on remote sensing applied to studies of the Pantanal. (5) An article on environmental contaminants (Alho & Vieira 1997). These publications provide a reliable perspective on the region, including trends and actions for the future.

Protected areas

In Brazil there are two major kinds of officially recognized protected areas or conservation units: (1) reserves for direct use such as Extractive Reserves, National forests, etc.; and (2) reserves for indirect use, where the exploitation of natural resources is forbidden, such as National Parks, Biological Reserves and Ecological Reserves. The problem is that many protected areas are precariously implemented, abandoned without law enforcement, and are, therefore, vulnerable to human activities.

In the Pantanal there are three federal conservation units: the Pantanal National Park (135 000 ha), the Taiamã Ecological Reserve (11 200 ha), and one indigenous reserve – comprising 1.3% of the regional territory. In the uplands there are: the National Park of Chapada dos Guimarães (33 000 ha) and National Park of Serra da Bodoquena (76 481 ha). The state-protected areas are: in Mato Grosso, APA das Cabeceiras do rio Cuiabá and APA da Chapada dos Guimarães; in Mato Grosso do Sul, Parque Estadual das Nascentes do Rio Taquari and Parque Estadual da Serra de Sonora (see IBAMA 2004). The Pantanal Program plans to implement the following parkways as especial protected areas for tourist interest: in Mato Grosso, Estrada Parque Santo Antonio do Leverger-Porto de Fora and Estrada Parque Transpantaneira; in Mato Grosso do Sul, MS 184 and MS 228. The most-important private reserve in the Pantanal is the Estância Ecológica SESC Pantanal, a large strip of land between the Cuiabá and São Lourenço rivers, in the subregion of Barão de Melgaço, covering 100 000 ha.

New protected areas have been proposed, such as the linkage of the National Park of Serra da Bodoquena (in the state of Mato Grosso do Sul) to proposed protected areas (such as the State Park of Nabileque and the State Park of Rio Apa), and the existing nearby private reserves (Acurizal, Dorochê, and Penha – managed by ECOTRÓPICA). This large area could then connect to the National Park Pantanal Matogrossense. Another suggestion is the National Park of Paraguaizinho being linked to the existing Ecological Station of Taiamã. This proposed area would link the National Park of Pantanal Matogrossense, the SESC Taiamã private reserve, and the Ecotrópica and the Serra das Araras private reserves.

The Brazilian Federal Government has made a commitment to protect 10% of the territory. The new proposed areas would be a way of accomplishing that commitment. In practice there is an enormous gap between the need for protecting and the actual implementation of the protected areas. A large percentage of Brazil's officially declared protected areas exist only on paper, the so-called "paper parks." The degree of vulnerability of the paper park depends upon the degree of implementation the protected area has experienced.

Valuing the Pantanal's natural resources

There are at least two ways of recognizing the value of the Pantanal: one is expressed by its residents through traditional cattle ranching and fishing; the second is its clear recognition by outsiders who go to the region to appreciate its beautiful landscape and animals, and to enjoy fishing. This second value already has an international significance.

In order to conserve the region, however, there is another important value which is not yet clear to most people. This almost-hidden value deals with ecosystems, which means it is about the functions upon which we depend for life support, habitat maintenance, livelihood, and lifestyle. A scientific approach to this issue is fundamental if we are to address conservation and sustainable development in a way that provides a wide range of benefits to society.

The functional approach focuses on ecosystems, and thus has a technical side. As it encompasses a broad range of environmental factors, its consideration is also fundamental in analyzing benefits derived from the ecosystems. These benefits may be expressed in terms of practices such as traditional cattle ranching, agriculture, fishing, tourism, and any other activity planned to be sustainable.

The ecosystem value of the Pantanal may or may not be quantified. When a tourist travels along the Transpantaneira road, destined to become a parkway, the waterfowl he observes may be described in terms of numbers and given a value. It may also be possible to measure the economic benefits from ecological tourism associated with the concentrations of these bird species. In the following discussion, the concept of value will be emphasized (Bond *et al.* 1992).

The understanding of the concept of value to most people comes from *use* value, either by consumption – such as subsistence sport, or commercial fishing – or by uses that can be termed non-consumer, such as bird watching, water quality, etc. There are also more-intangible functions or values such as *existing* value and *choice* value.

The concept of choice value is related to the fact that the user of services provided by the Pantanal is presently uncertain whether he will be a user in the future. The existing value is based on the fact that individuals may suffer economic losses from the development of the Pantanal even if the individual is not a current user and will not be a future user. The concept is based on altruism, the desire to preserve the Pantanal for future use by others. Thus, it involves empathy towards nature.

The importance of valuing natural resources is relevant as the Pantanal continues to degraded and its natural resources are continually being reduced.

The present focus on economic development is mainly based on economic values. This can be seen in the deforestation of uplands to expand grain monoculture and create pastures for cattle ranching, without considering the value of hydrology for the floodplains. It is now clear that other values must be considered such as: the sustainability of wildlife (mainly waterfowl), fish production, storage and slow release of large quantities of water, erosion protection, aesthetic protection, and tourism and recreation.

While some resources or benefits are easily measurable – such as cattle production, jobs for fishermen, and tourism – others are more difficult to measure, such as ecosystem functions like the hydrological pattern, nutrient cycling, and habitat maintenance. For most people, these values may have a remote or abstract meaning, since they may not contribute to products that clearly have a market value in society – such as fish, cattle, visitors, etc.

It is essential to stress that the Pantanal has different values which vary in type, magnitude, and time scale.

Ecosystem functions and their values relate to the capacity of the Pantanal to regulate and maintain essential ecological processes and biodiversity support systems. An example, as described earlier in this chapter, is hydrology; this is critical to the maintenance of the habitats and their associated biodiversity. This element is closely related to the aesthetic and recreational potential for the tourist industry, and many other socio-economic factors. This element is also crucial for a complex web of energy transfers, including those between flora and fauna. The Pantanal supports a variety of birds with large concentrations of waterfowl, fish, mammals (some on the endangered-species list). The major symbols or icons of the Pantanal, as expressed in photographs and other illustrations, are wildlife species, which attract visitors, photographers, and hikers.

In conclusion, the ecosystem value is based on the maintenance of biodiversity, habitat seasonal productivity, maintenance of nutrient cycle and food chains, providing a habitat for migrant species, providing a nursery habitat, and biomass storage. These values can also be redirected to other socio-cultural values such as recreation and tourism; aesthetics; ethical, spiritual or traditional, cultural and artistic inspiration; educational and scientific information; and importance for future generations.

The application of some concepts of decision making in conservation is important for the conservation of the Pantanal. One of these concepts is the opportunity cost. It is the benefit that someone loses when the decision is made to protect the Pantanal from some deleterious damage. For example, in the case of a rancher planning to convert a wooded savanna area into pasture for livestock, the opportunity cost of conservation is the net benefits of pasture implantation (production of meat and other products) forfeited by choosing to protect natural habitats in the floodplains. The opportunity costs of development are the net benefits of conservation (in terms of scenic value, recreation, water quality, etc.) forfeited by choosing to transform this natural landscape into pasture.

A framework of economic valuation is a valid technique for environmental evaluation. There are developmentally sound ways to evaluate environmental amenities and other goods that are not necessarily bought and sold on the market. It is possible to give a value to biodiversity losses, habitat degradation, and changes in ecosystem diversity as a result of environmental disruptions caused by human activities.

Sustainable resources

As mentioned above, sustainable use of resources in the Pantanal may rely on: traditional cattle raising, fishing (sport and commercial), and ecotourism. A good example of how these elements may be viewed in practice is offered in the subregions of Barão de Melgaço–Poconé. SESC (Association of Commercial Partners) is an entity that brings together members who work in business in Brazil, such as in stores and others businesses. SESC bought ranches in the Pantanal, created a 90 000-ha private reserve in the area and built a hotel for the recreation of its associates from all over Brazil, so they could enjoy nature in the Pantanal. Many other small rural hotels called *"pousadas"* are also flourishing in the region. There have been efforts to create new protected areas and implement those officially created through the *Projeto Pantanal.*

Although tourism is increasing in the Pantanal, the industry needs improvement to achieve a better balance between recreation and conservation. Much current tourism in the region has a destructive effect on nature. When understood, sustainable tourism may be a positive force to protect nature. Also, when ecotourism is truly understood and implemented, the motivation for maintenance of the natural environment and natural attractions is evident. In addition, the activity can provide unique opportunities to raise environmental awareness and so aid nature conservation. An example of tourism in the Pantanal usually promoted as ecotourism is sport fishing, mainly the annual fishing contest of Cáceres. Unfortunately the majority of these activities are predatory, with harmful effects on fish species as well as on nature. To mitigate such impacts tourism should be carried out following a detailed plan; monitored to make sure its objectives are being accomplished, and implemented in a way that is environmentally sustainable, socially beneficial, and economically viable.

Tourism can also promote cultural and historical traditions, such as cattle ranching in the Pantanal, and so enhance nature conservation. The Pantanal is a living classroom for those who enjoy recreation and appreciate nature. Contact with nature can teach basic ecological ideas, such as energy flow, nutrient cycling, food chains, conservation of nature including threatened species, carrying capacity, etc. Environmental education or nature consciousness is one relevant theme. Recreational experiences, associated with the opportunity for a change in attitudes towards nature conservation, are remarkable stimuli for visitors. The abundant life forms evoke curiosity and increase motivation to protect nature.

Finally, the new large-scale projects, such as the *Projeto Pantanal* designed to implement sustainable use of resources in the region, have to emphasize two points: (1) recognition that the region is an important ecosystem for maintaining hydrogeological conditions that support natural habitats and their biodiversity; and (2) that well-planned tourism, fishing, and other traditional land uses – including sustainable use of wildlife – should provide opportunities to achieve sustainable use of these resources with environmental, social, and economic benefits.

The complex beauty and environmental intricacy associated with the nuances of a fragile and threatened ecosystem mean that the Pantanal's ecological, cultural, and aesthetic qualities deserve urgent conservation policies. Those who have worked in this vast wetland undeniably feel a profound sense of challenge, in terms of both knowledge and conservation: knowledge to develop a better understanding of its ecological complexities and conservation of its mystical beauty and vibrant nature.

Acknowledgements

CNPq (Brazilian National Research Council) funded this study. This paper is a product of research conducted in the Pantanal for more than one decade. I gratefully acknowledge the invitation of Lauchlan Fraser (Canada Research Chair in Community and Ecosystem Ecology, Thompson Rivers University, British, Columbia, Canada) and Paul Keddy (Schlieder Endowed Chair, Southeastern Louisiana University, Louisiana, USA) to attend the Millennium Wetland Conference, Symposium on the World's Largest Wetlands, August 6–12, 2000, Québec city, Québec Canada). I thank James Dietz (Conservation Biology Program, University of Maryland), Susan Catherine Casement, and my wife Celina Alho for their valuable comments and careful revision of the manuscript. I also thank Luís Augusto S. Vasconcellos and Maurício Schneider for their assistance on graphs and other illustrations.

References

Abdon, M. M., Silva, J. S. V., Pott, V. J., Pott, A., and Silva, M. P. (1998). Utilização de dados analógicos do Landsat-TM na discriminação da vegetação de Parte da sub-região da Nhecolândia no Pantanal. *Pesquisa Agropecuária Brasileira*, **33** (número especial), 1799–813.

Adamoli, J. (1996). Previsão de médio prazo dos níveis do rio Paraguai em Ladário, MS. In *Anais do II simpósio sobre recursos naturais e sócio-econômicos do Pantanal*. Corumbá, MS: CPAP-EMBRAPA and UFMS, pp. 59–72.

Alho, C. J. R. and Martins, E. S. (1995). De grão em grão o cerrado perde espaço. In *Cerrado: impactos do processo de ocupação*. Brasília, Brazil: WWF.

Alho, C. J. R. and Vieira, L. M. (1997). Fish and wildlife resources in the Pantanal wetlands of Brazil and potential disturbances from the release of environmental contaminants. *Environmental Toxicology and Chemistry*, **16**(1), 71–4.

Alho, C. J. R., Conceição, P. N., Strussman, C., Vasconcellos, L. A. S., and Schneider, M. (1998). *Plano de Manejo da RPPN SESC-Pantanal*. Brasília, Brazil: FUNATURA.

Alho, C. J. R., Lacher, T. E., Jr, and Gonçalves, H. C. (1988a). Environmental degradation in the Pantanal ecosystem of Brazil. *Bioscience*, **38**(3), 164–71.

Alho, C. J. R., Lacher, T. E., Jr, Campos, Z. M. S., and Gonçalves, H. C. (1988b). Mamíferos da Fazenda Nhumirim, sub-região de Nhecolândia, Pantanal do Mato Grosso do Sul: levantamento preliminar de espécies. *Revista Brasilaira de Biologia*, **48**(2), 213–25.

Alho, C. J. R., Campos, Z. M. S., and Gonçalves, H. C. (1989). Ecology, social behavior, and management of the capybara (*Hydrochaeris hydrochaeris*) in the Pantanal of

Brazil. In *Advances in Neotropical Mammalogy*, eds. K. H. Redford and J. F. Eisenberg. Gainesville, FL: Sandhill Crane Press, pp. 163–94.

Alho, C. J. R., Conceição, P. N., Constantino, R. *et al.* (2000). *Fauna silvestre da região do Rio Manso, MT.* Brasília, Brazil: Edições IBAMA.

Alho, C. J. R., Strüssmann, C. E., and Vasconcellos, L. A. S. (2002). *Indicadores da magnitude da diversidade e abundância de vertebrados silvestres do Pantanal num mosaico de hábitats sazonais.* Published in digital format. Corumbá, MS: EMBRAPA.

Alho, C. J. R., Strüssmann, C., Volpe, M. *et al.* (2003). *Conservação da Biodiversidade da Bacia do Alto Paraguai Editura UNIDERP*, Campo Grande, MS.

Almeida, N. N. (1998). Estrutura e dinâmica de uma comunidade de plântulas em uma floresta sazonalmente inundável no Pantanal de Poconé, MT. M.Sc. thesis, Universidade Federal de Mato Grosso, Instituto de Biociências, Cuiabá, Brazil.

ANA (National Water Agency – Brazil) (2004). Integrated Management of the Pantanal and Upper Paraguay River Basin (GEF Pantanal/Alto Paraguay Project). http://www.ana.gov.br/gcfap

Antas, P. T. Z. (1992). Projeto Tuiuiú. Relatório consolidado das atividades de 1992. Brasília, Brazil: CEMAVE, IBAMA (unpublished report).

Antas, P. T. Z. and Nascimento, I. L. S. (1996). *Tuiuiú: sob os céus do Pantanal.* Brasília, Brazil: SEMAVE and Monsanto.

Barrientos, L. M. (1993). Mortalidad de vertebrados em la red viaria española: millones de animales mueren atropellados cada año em las carreteras españolas. *Quercus*, **83**, 13–25.

BDT (Base de Dado Tropical) (1999). Priority actions for conserving Cerrado and Pantanal biodiversity. http://www.bdt.fat.org.br/workshop/cerrado/br

Bond, W. K., Cox, K. W., Heberlein, T. *et al.* (1992). *Wetland Evaluation Guide.* Ottawa, Canada: North American Wetlands Conservation Council.

Bortolloto, I. M., Damasceno, G. A., Jr., and Isqierdo, S. W. G. (1996). Caracterização das unidades fitosifisonômicas da bacia da Lagoa Negra em Ladário, MS. In *Anais do II simpósio sobre recursos naturais e sócio-econômicos do Pantanal.* Corumbá, MS.: CPAP-EMBRAPA and UFMS, pp. 283–9.

Brandão, G. (1996). Uso de levantamento aéreo para estudo de distribuição e abundância de grandes vertebrados no Pantanal Mato-Grossense. Unpublished Ph.D. thesis, INPA-Universidade Federal do Amazonas, Manaus, Brazil.

Britiski, M. A., Silimon, K. Z., and Balzac, S. L. (1999). *Peixes do Pantanal. Manual de identificação.* Corumbá, MS: EMBRAPA-CPAP.

Brown, K. S., Jr. (1986). Zoogeografia da região do Pantanal Matogrossense. In *Simpósio sobre recursos naturais e sócio-econômicos do Pantanal.* Brasília, Brazil: EMBRAPA, DTC, pp. 137–78.

Cadavid-Garcia, E. A. and Castro, L. H. R. (1986). Análise da freqüência de chuva no Pantanal Mato-Grossense. *Pesquisa Agropecuária Brasileira*, **21**(9), 909–25.

Carvalho, N. O. (1984). Hidrologia da bacia do Alto Paraguai. In *Anais do I simpósio sobre recursos naturais e sócio-Econômicos do Pantanal.* Brasília, Brazil: EMBRAPA, pp. 43–9.

CIDEMA (Consórcio Internacional para o Desenvolvimento Integrado das Bacias dos Rios Miranda e Apa) (2002). Consolidação do Consórcio Internacional (CIDEMA) como organismo da bacia e seu fortalecimento para a participação na gestão hidrográfica do rio Miranda. Campo Grande, MS: CIDEMA (unpublished report).

Cunha, C. N. (1998). Comunidades arbustivo-arbóreas de capão e de diques marginais no Pantanal de Poconé-MT: caracterização e análise de gradiente. Unpublished Ph.D. thesis, Universidade Federal de São Carlos, Brazil.

Cunha, C. N. and Junk, W. J. (2000). Distribution of woody plant communities along the flood gradient in the Pantanal of Poconé, Mato Grosso, Brazil. In *The Millenium Wetland Event, August 6–12, 2000, Quebec, Canada.*

Drews, G. (1995). Road kills of animals by public traffic in Mikumi National Park, Tanzania, with notes on baboon mortality. *African Journal of Ecology*, **33**(2), 89–100.

EDIBAP (Estudo de Desenvolvimento Integrado da Bacia do Alto Paraguai) (1979). *Relatório da primeira fase: descrição física e recursos naturais.* Superintendência do Desenvolvimento da Região Centro-Oeste 3. Brasília, Brazil: Superintedência.

Fernandes, E., Lucati, H. L., Capellari, B. C., and Queiroz Neto, J. P. (1996). Modelo digital para tratamento de cartas topográficas do Pantanal da Nhecolândia. In *Anais do II simpósio sobre recursos naturais e sócio-econômicos do Pantanal.* Corumbá, MS: CPAP-EMBRAPA and UFMS, pp. 159–66.

Ferreira, A. R. (2000). A influência do pulso de inundação na produção de frutos de *Bactris glaucescens*. Drude, no município de Barão de Melgaço, Pantanal mato-grossense, Mato Grosso, Brazil. Unpublished M.Sc. thesis, Universidade Federal do Mato Grosso, Instituto de Biociências, Cuiabá, Brazil.

Fisher, W. A. (1997). Efeitos da BR-262 na mortalidade de vertebrados silvestres: síntese naturalística para a conservação da região do Pantanal, MS. M.Sc. thesis, Universidade Federal de Mato Grosso do Sul, Campo Grande, MS.

Florenzano, T. G. (1998). Imagens TM-Landsat e HRV-Spot na elaboração de cartas geomorfológicas de uma região do rio Taquari, MS. *Pesquisa, Agropecuária Brasileira*, **33** (número especial), 1721–7.

Fonseca, G. A. B., Hermann, G., Leite, Y. L. R., and Mittermeier, R. A. (1996). *Lista anotada dos mamíferos Brasileiros.* Occasional Papers in Conservation Biology, Conservation International. Occasional Paper 3. Washington, DC: Conservation International.

Franco, M. S. M. and Pinheiro, R. (1982). Geomorfologia. In *Brasil, Ministério das Minas e Energia. Departamento Nacional de Produção Mineral. Projeto RADAMBRASIL.* Folha SE. 21 Corumbá and SE 20. Levantamento de Recursos Naturais 27, pp. 161–224.

Guedes, N. M. R. (1993). Reproductive biology of the *Anodorhynchus hyacinthinus* in the Pantanal – MS, Brazil. Unpublished M.Sc. thesis, Universidade São Paulo, ESALQ, Piracicaba, SP.

Hamilton, S. K., Sippel, S. J., and Melack, J. M. (1995). Oxygen depletion and carbon dioxide and methane production in waters of the Pantanal wetland of Brazil. *Biogeochemistry*, **30**, 115–41.

(1996). Inundation patterns in the Pantanal wetland of South America determined from passive microwave remote sensing. *Archiv für Hydrobiologie*, **137**, 1–23.

Hamilton, S. K., Sippel, S. J., Calheiros, D. F., and Melack, J. M. (1997). An anoxic event and other biogeochemical effects of the Pantanal wetland on the Paraguay river. *Limnology and Oceanography*, **42**(2), 257–72.

Hamilton, S. K., Souza, O. C., and Coutinho, M. E. (1998). Dynamics of floodplain inundation in the alluvial fan of the Taquari River (Pantanal, Brazil). *Verhandlungen der Internationale Vereinigung Fur Theoretische und Angewandte Limnologie*, **26**, 916–22.

Hardoim, E. L. and Heckman, C. W. (1996). The seasonal succession of biotic communities in wetlands of the tropical wet-and-dry climatic zone: IV. The free-living Sarcodines and Ciliates of the Pantanal of Mato Grosso, Brazil. *Internationale Revue gesamten Hydrobiologie*, **81**(3), 367–84.

Heckman, C. W. (1994). The seasonal succession of biotic communities in wetlands of the tropical wet-and-dry climatic zone: I. Physical and chemical causes and biological effects in the Pantanal of Mato Grosso, Brazil. *Internationale Revue gesamten Hydrobiologie*, **79**(3), 397–421.

(1996). Geographical and climatic factors as determinants of the biotic differences between the Northern and Southern parts of the Pantanal mato-grossense. In *Anais do II Simpósio sobre recursos naturais e sócio-econômicos do Pantanal*. Corumbá, MS: CPAP-EMBRAPA and UFMS, pp. 167–75.

(1997). Ecosystems dynamics in the Pantanal of Mato Grosso, Brazil. *Verhandlungen der Internationale Vereinigung für Theoretische und Angewandte Limnologie*, **26**, 1343–7.

Hernandez Filho, P., Ponzoni, F. J., and Pereira, M. N. (1998). Mapeamento da fitofisionomia e do uso da terra de parte da bacia do alto Taquari mediante o uso de imagens TM/Landsat e HRV/Spot. *Pesquisa Agropecuária Brasileira*, **33** (número especial), 1755–62.

IBAMA (Brazilian Institute for the Environment and Renewable Resources) (2004). Conservations Units; Official List of Threatened Species. http://www.gov.br

IBGE (Instituto Brasilairo de Geografia e Estatistica) (2001). *Ministério do Planejamento, Orçamento e Gestão*.

Junk, W. J. (1992). Wetlands of tropical South America. In *Wetlands of the World: Inventory, Ecology, and Management*, eds. D. Wigham, D. Dykyjova, and S. Heiny. Dordrecht, the Netherlands: Junk, pp. 679–739.

Keast, A. and Morton, E. (eds.) (1980). *Migrant Birds in the Neotropics. Ecology, Behavior, Distribution and Conservation*. Washington, DC: Smithsonian Institution.

Klammer, G. (1982). The paleodesert of the Pantanal of Mato Grosso and the Pleistocene climatic history of the central Brazilian tropics. *Zeitschrift Fur Geomorphologie*, **26**, 393–416.

Kretzchmar, A. U., Ferreira, S. A., Hardoim, E. L., and Heckman, C. W. (1993). Peak growth of the *Asplanchna sieboldi* (Leydig 1854). Rotifer aggregation in relation to the seasonal wet-and-dry cycle in the Pantanal, Mato Grosso, Brazil. In *Wetlands* and *Ecotones: Studies on Land–Water interactions,* eds. B. Gopal, A. Hillbricht-Ilkowska, and R. G. Wetzel. New Delhi, India: National Institute of Ecology, pp. 293–301.

Lacher, T. E., Jr. and Alho, C. J. R. (1989). Microhabitat use among small mammals in the Brazilian Pantanal. *Journal of Mammology,* **70**(2), 396–401.

Lacher, T. E., Jr., Alho, C. J. R., and Campos, Z. M. S. (1986). *Densidades y preferencias de microhábitats de los mamíferos en la Hacienda Nhumirim, sub-región Nhecolândia, Pantanal de Mato Grosso del Sur. Ciencia Interamericana, OEA,* **26**(1–2), 30–8.

Mares, M. A. and Ernest, K. A. (1994). Population and community ecology of small mammals in a gallery forest of central Brazil. *Journal of Mammalogy,* **76**(3), 750–68.

Marini, A. C., Marques, E. J., Vetanabaro, M, Souza, L. O., and Froehlichi, O. (1994). Levantamento preliminar da fauna da sub-região Miranda/Abobral-Pantanal MS. Campo Grande, MS: Universidade Fedderal de Mato Grosso do Sul, Centro de Ciências Biológicas e da Saúde, Departamento de Biologia (unpublished report).

Mittermeyer, R. A., Gil, P. R. P., and Mittermeyer, C. G. (1977). *Megadiversity: Earth's Biologically Wealthiest Nations.* Mexico: CEMEX, Agrupación Sierra Madre.

MMA (Ministério do Meio Ambiente) (1998). *Dos Recursos Hídricos e da Amazônia Legal. Primeiro Relatório Nacional para a Convenção da Diversidade Biológica.*

Nordemann, D. J. R. (1998). Periodicidades, tendências e previsão a partir da análise espectral dinâmica da série dos níveis do rio Paraguai, em Ladário (1900–1995). *Pesquisa Agropecuária Brasileira,* **33** (número especial), 1787–90.

Oliveira, D. M. M. (1997). Sucesso reprodutivo e conservação de tuiuiú *Jabiru mycteria* (Aves: Cinoniidae) no Pantanal de Poconé, Mato Grosso. Unpublished M.Sc. thesis, Universidade Federal de Mato Grosso, Cuiabá, Brazil.

PCBAP (Plano de Conservação da Bacia do Alto Paraguai) (1997). Vol. 1, *Metodologia do plano de conservação para a bacia do alto Paraguai.* Vol. 2, *Diagnóstico ambiental da bacia do alto Paraguai.* Ch. 1, Meio físico; Ch. 2, Hidrossedimentologia; Ch. 3, Meio biótico; Ch. 4, Sócio-economia de Mato Grosso; Ch. 5, Sócio-economia de Mato Grosso do Sul; Ch. 6, Aspectos jurídicos e institucionais de Mato Grosso; Ch. 7, Aspectos jurídicos e institucionais de Mato Grosso do Sul. Vol. 3, *Análise integrada e prognóstico da bacia do alto paraguai.* Programa Nacional do Meio Ambiente, Ministério do Meio Ambiente.

Pott, A. and Adamoli, J. (1996). Unidades de vegetação do Pantanal dos Paiaguás. In *Anais do II simpósio sobre recursos naturais e sócio-econômicos do Pantanal.* Corumbá, MS: CPAP-EMBRAPA and UFMS, pp. 183–202.

Pott, A. and Pott, V. J. (1994). *Plantas do Pantanal.* Corumbá, MS: CPAP-EMBRAPA.

Pott, V. J., Cervi, A. C., Bueno, N. C., and Pott, A. (1996). Dinâmica da vegetação aquática de uma lagoa permanente da Fazenda Nhumirim, Pantanal da Nhecolândia, MS. In *Anais do II simpósio sobre recursos naturais e sócio-econômicos do Pantanal.* Corumbá, MS: CPAP-EMBRAPA and UFMS, pp. 227–35.

Prado, A. L., Heckman, C. W., and Martins, F. R. (1994). The seasonal succession of biotic communities in wetlands of the tropical wet-and-dry climatic zone: II.

The aquatic macrophyte vegetation in the Pantanal of Mato Grosso, Brazil. *Internationale Revue gesamten Hydrobiologie*, **79**(4), 569–89.

Prance, G. T. & Schaller, G. B. (1982). Preliminary study of some vegetation types of the Pantanal, Mato Grosso, Brazil. *Brittonia*, **34**(2), 228–51.

PRODEAGRO (1997). *Projeto de desenvolvimento agroambiental do estado de Mato Grosso.* Governo do Estado de Mato Grosso. Cuiabá. Paper in digital format (CD). Cuiba, Brazil: Meio Biótico.

Reijnen, R. and Foppen, R. (1995). The effects of car traffic on breeding bird populations in woodland. IV. Influence of population size on the reduction of density close to a highway. *Journal of Applied Ecology*, **32**(3), 481–91.

Resende, E. K. and Palmeira, S. S. (1996). Estrutura e dinâmica das comunidades de peixes da planície inundável do rio Miranda, Pantanal de Mato Grosso do Sul. In *Anais do II simpósio sobre recursos naturais e sócio-econômicos do Pantanal.* Corumbá, MS: CPAP-EMBRAPA and UFMS, pp. 249–81.

Sá, L. D. A., Sambatti, S. B. M., and Galvaoão, G. P. (1998). Ondeleta de morlet aplicada ao estudo da variabilidade do nível do rio Paraguay em Ladário, MS. *Pesquisa Agropecuária Brasileira*, **33** (número especial), 1775–85.

Salis, S. M., Pott, V. J., and Pott, A. (1996). Fitossociologia de formações arbóreas da bacia do Alto Paraguai, Brazil. In *Anais do II simpósio sobre recursos naturais e sócio-econômicos do Pantanal.* Corumbá, MS: CPAP-EMBRAPA and UFMS, pp. 357–74.

Schaller, G. B. and Crawshaw, P. G. Jr. (1980). Movement patterns of jaguar. *Biotropica*, **12**, 161–8.

Schaller, G. B. and Vasconcellos, J. (1978a). Jaguar predation on capybara. *Zeitschrift fur Saugetierkunde*, **43**, 296–301.

(1978b). A marsh deer census in Brazil. *Oryx*, **14**, 345–51.

Schessl, M. (1997). Flora und vegetation des nördlichen Pantanal von Mato Grosso, Brasilien. Unpublished Ph.D. thesis, University Ulm, Martina-Galunder-Verlag, Wiehl, Germany.

Shimabukuro, Y. E., Novo, E. M., and Ponsoni, F. J. (1998). Índice de vegetação e modelo linear de mistura espectral no monitoramento da região do Pantanal. *Pesquisa Agropecuária Brasileira*, **33** (número especial), 1729–37.

Sick, H. (1983). *Migrações de aves na América do sul continental.* Publicação Técnica 2. Brasília, Brazil: CEMAVE.

Silva, C. J. and Esteves, F. A. (1993). Biomass of three macrophytes in the Pantanal of Mato Grosso, Brazil. *International Journal of Ecology and Environmental Sciences*, **19**, 11–23.

(1995). Dinâmica das características limnológicas das baías Porto de Fora e Acurizal (Pantanal de Mato Grosso) em função da variação do nível da água. *Oecologia Brasiliensis*, **1**, 47–60.

Silva, J. M. C. (1995). Birds of the cerrado region, South America. *Steenstrupia*, **21**, 69–92.

Silva, J. S. V. (1991). Aplicações de técnicas de sensoriamento remoto e sistema de informação geográficas na avaliação da dinâmica de inundação no Pantanal. Unpublished M.Sc. thesis, INPE, São Jos.

Silva, J. S. V. and Abdon, M. M. (1998). Delimitação do Pantanal Brasileiro e suas sub-regiões. *Pesquisa Agropecuária Brasileira*, **33** (número especial), 1703–11.

Silva, J. S. V., Abdon, M. M., Book, A., and Silva, M. P. (1998a). Fisionomias dominantes em parte das sub-regiões do Nabileque e Miranda, sul do Pantanal. *Pesquisa Agropecuária Brasileira*, **33** (número especial), 1713–19.

Silva, J. S. V., Abdon, M. M., Silva, M. P., and Romero, H. R. (1998b). Levantamento do desmatamento no Pantanal Brasileiro até 1990/91. *Pesquisa Agropecuária Brasileira*, **33** (número especial), 1739–45.

Silva, M. V. (1986). *Mitos e verdades sobre a pesca no Pantanal sul-matogrossense, Fipan, MS*. Campo Grande.

SONDOTÉCNICA (1999). Programa 5: Monitoramento Hidrológico. Procedimentos para determinação das vazões a serem restituídas durante o enchimento. Culabá, Brazil: APM-Manso and FURNAS – Centrais Elétricas (unpublished report).

Stotz, D. F., Fitzpatrick, J. W., Parker, T., III, and Moskovits, D. K. (1996). *Neotropical Birds: Ecology and Conservation*. Chicago, IL: University of Chicago Press.

Strüssmann, C. and Sazima, I. (1993). The snake assemblage of the Pantanal at Pocone, Western Brazil: faunal composition and ecological summary. *Studies on Neotropical Fauna and Environment*, **28**(3), 157–68.

Tomás, W. (1993). Status and ecology of a marsh deer (*Blastocerus dichotomus*) population in southern Pantanal, Brazil. Brasília, Brazil: WWF (unpublished report).

Tubelis, D. P. and Tomás, W. M. (2002). *Caracterização da avifauna da planície do Pantanal. Indicadores da magnitude da diversidade e abundância de vertebrados silvestres do Pantanal num mosaico de hábitats sazonais*. Published in digital format. Corumbá, MS: CPAP-EMBRAPA.

Tubelis, D. P. & Tomas, W. M. (2003a). Bird species of the Pantanal wetland, Brazil. *Ararajuba*, **11**(1), 5–37.

Tubelis, D. P. & Tomas, W. M. (2003b). The contributions of museum collections and of records not involving collections of the knowledge of the bird species composition of the Pantanal, Brazil. *Ararajuba*, **11**(2), 55–62.

UNESCO (United National Educational, Scientific, and Cultural Organization) (2004). World Heritage List: Pantanal Conservation Area. http://whc.unesco.org

Veneziani, P., Santos, A R., Crepani, E., Anjos, C. E., and Okida, R. (1998). Mapa de classes de erodibilidade de parte da região do Rio Taquari baseado em imagens TM-LANDSAT. *Pesquisa Agropecuária Brasileira*, **33** (número especial), 1747–54.

Vinson, M. R. and Hawkins, C. P. (1998). Biodiversity of stream insects: variation at local, basin and regional scales. *Annual Review of Entomology*, **43**, 271–93.

Wantzen, K. M. and Junk, W. J. (2000). The importance of stream–wetland systems for biodiversity: a tropical perspective. In *Biodiversity in Wetlands: Assessment, Function and Conservation*, eds. B. Gopal, W. J. Junk, and J. A. Davis. Leiden, the Netherlands: Backhuys Bublishers, pp. 11–34.

Wantzen, K. M., Butakka, C. M., Tietböhl, R. S., and Paula, A. M. de. (2000). Benthic invertebrates in the Pantanal wetland: a review. In *Anais do III simpósio sobre recursos naturais e sócio-econômicos do Pantanal: Os desafios do novo milênio*, dezembro 27–30, 2000. Resumo 342. Corumbá, MS: CPAP-EMBRAPA.

Wilson, D. E. and Reeder, D. M. (eds.) (1993). *Mammal Species of the World: a Taxonomic and Geographic Reference*, 2nd edn. Washington, D.C.: Smithsonian Institution.

WWF (WWF Canada) (1999). *A Review of the Hydrovia Paraguay–Paraná Official Studies*. Full report and executive summary. Toronto, Canada: WWF.

8

The Mississippi River alluvial plain

G. P. SHAFFER
Southeastern Louisiana University

J. G. GOSSELINK
Louisiana State University

S. S. HOEPPNER
Southeastern Louisiana University

Introduction

The Mississippi River is the third-largest river in the world. It is the longest and largest river in North America, ranking third in length and watershed area and seventh in discharge among the world's largest rivers (Wiener *et al.* 1998). The river derives its name from the Ojibwa (Chippewa) Indian language, in which Mississippi means "great river" or "gathering of waters" – an appropriate name for a river that has a watershed that contains parts of 31 states in the United States and 2 Canadian provinces (Fig. 8.1). With its average discharge of about 15 400 m^3 s^{-1} (Gosselink *et al.* 1998), the Mississippi River accounts for roughly 90% of the freshwater inflow into the Gulf of Mexico (Dinnel & Wiseman 1986, National Oceanic and Atmospheric Administration 1987). Along with this water, it also delivers approximately 210 to 240 billion kg of sediments to its delta and into the Gulf of Mexico each year (Milliman & Meade 1983, Gosselink *et al.* 1998). The river can be divided into four major zones. The headwaters begin at Lake Itasca, downstream from the St. Anthony Falls in Minneapolis, Minnesota. The next section, often referred to as the "upper Mississippi River," extends from the mouth of the Missouri River near St. Louis to the mouth of the Ohio River. The relatively narrow bands of batture lands (the floodplains contiguous with the river) along these two sections are highly populated and have been

The World's Largest Wetlands: Ecology and Conservation, eds. L. H. Fraser and P. A. Keddy.
Published by Cambridge University Press. © Cambridge University Press 2005.

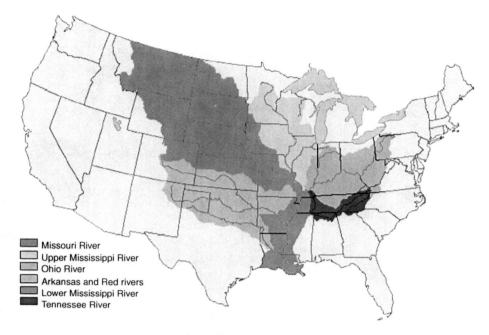

Figure 8.1 The watershed of the Mississippi River drains approximately 41% of the landmass of the United States or about one-eighth of the North American continent into the Gulf of Mexico (redrawn from Weiner *et al.* 1995).

isolated from the river for over a century. These upper reaches of the river have been impounded since the construction of 29 navigation dams with locks in the early 1930s. Most of the wetlands associated with the Mississippi River are located along the lower two sections, which define the Mississippi River alluvial plain (MSRAP) and delta.

The MSRAP originates at the confluence of the Mississippi and Ohio rivers at Cairo, Illinois, and extends for more than 1000 km through parts of Missouri, Kentucky, Tennessee, Arkansas, Mississippi, and Louisiana to the Gulf of Mexico (Fig. 8.2) (Llewellyn *et al.* 1996). It is made up of two main intergrading zones, which are characterized to a large extent by different flora, fauna, and ecological driving forces. The upper reaches of the MSRAP act mostly as a forested riverine corridor that funnels runoff water from 4.76 million km², or approximately 41% of the land mass of the United States, into the Gulf of Mexico (Rabalais *et al.* 1994, Coleman *et al.* 1998, Gosselink *et al.* 1998). The Mississippi River deltaic plain is the receiving end of this corridor. It is a broad depositional zone where the river's water, nutrients, toxins, and sediments mix with the tidal water of the Gulf of Mexico to form an extensive, flat marsh interface

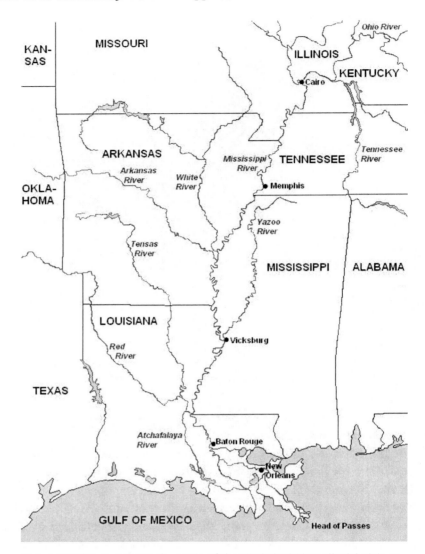

Figure 8.2 This map shows the origin of the Mississippi River alluvial plain at the confluence of the Ohio and Mississippi rivers, as well as some of the major tributaries that join the Mississippi River in its more than 1000-km journey to the Gulf of Mexico (redrawn from Wiener *et al.* 1995).

between ocean and upland, grading from fresh at its inland edge to saline at the ocean. From Cairo, Illinois to the Gulf of Mexico these floodplains cover an area of 21 million ha (Wiener *et al.* 1998). Due to the vast differences in the ecological driving forces, we will discuss the alluvial and deltaic plains as separate sections.

Characterization

Alluvial plain

The present surface of the alluvial plains of the Mississippi River valley is characterized and shaped by the meandering, silt-laden Mississippi River and its southerly flowing tributaries including the Black, Tensas, Yazoo, Big Sunflower, White, and St. Francis rivers (Fig. 8.2). It is an area of broad, gently sloping floodplains and low terraces on unconsolidated alluvial material that contains many sloughs and oxbow lakes. The relief of the alluvial valley has generally less than 15 m of vertical change, although terraces and natural levees may rise several meters above the adjacent bottomlands (Wiener *et al.* 1998). Historically, this zone was almost entirely populated by hardwood forests and forested swamps (Abernethy & Turner 1987, Llewellyn *et al.* 1996, Hunter & Faulkner 2001).

Originally, the MSRAP was dominated by mesic riparian ecosystems, commonly called "bottomland hardwood forests," which are one of the dominant types of riparian ecosystems in the southeastern United States (Fig. 8.3). Bottomland hardwoods can be characterized as forested habitats that are periodically inundated or saturated by surface water or groundwater during the growing season. At these times, the soils within the root zone are hydric and may become anaerobic for variable periods of time. The prevalent woody plant species associated with bottomland hardwood forests, therefore, are species that have demonstrated the ability to survive, mature, and reproduce under these challenging conditions due to a variety of morphological and/or physiological adaptations (Mitsch & Gosselink 2000).

In particular, the soils of a bottomland hardwood forest are more hydric than those of a terrestrial forest and less hydric than those of a swamp. Most of the extensive forests of the Mississippi River floodplain are characterized as zones of deposition. These river systems are dominated by spring floods and late-summer flow minima. Typical water budgets show that river-water throughput is far more important than other water sources and sinks in the riparian zone (Mitsch & Gosselink 2000).

Vegetation

The vegetation of southeastern riparian ecosystems is dominated by diverse trees that are adapted to the hydrological conditions on the floodplain. The plant communities change distinctly along the hydrological gradient that is the result of the river's variable flooding regime (Fig. 8.4). The lowest parts of the bottomland are nearly always flooded and consist of bald cypress–tupelogum (*Taxodium distichum–Nyssa aquatica*) swamps. At slightly higher elevations, the soils

Figure 8.3 Bottomland hardwood forests, marked in black, constitute one of the dominant riparian ecosystems in the southeastern United States. The great majority of these wetland forests are found in the MSRAP (after Putnam *et al.* 1960).

are only semi-permanently inundated and support an association of black willow (*Salix nigra*), silver maple (*Acer saccharinum*), and sometimes cottonwood (*Populus deltoides*) in the pioneer stage. A more-common association in this zone includes overcup oak (*Quercus iyrata*) and water hickory (*Carya aquatica*), which often occur in relatively small depressions on floodplains. Furthermore, green ash (*Fraxinus pennsylvanica*), red maple (*Acer rubrum*), and river birch (*Betula nigra*) can be found in this zone. New point bars that form in the river channel are often colonized by monospecific stands of either black willow, silver maple, river birch, or cottonwood.

Higher still on the bottomland floodplain, in areas flooded or saturated for one to two months during the growing season, an even wider array of hardwood trees is found. Common species in this zone include laurel oak (*Quercus obtusa*), green ash (*Fraxinus pennsylvanica*), American elm (*Ulmus americana*), and sweet-gum (*Liquidambar styraciflua*) – as well as sugarberry (*Celtis laevigata*), red maple (*Acer rubrum* var. *drummondii*), willow oak (*Quercus phellos*), and sycamore (*Platanus*

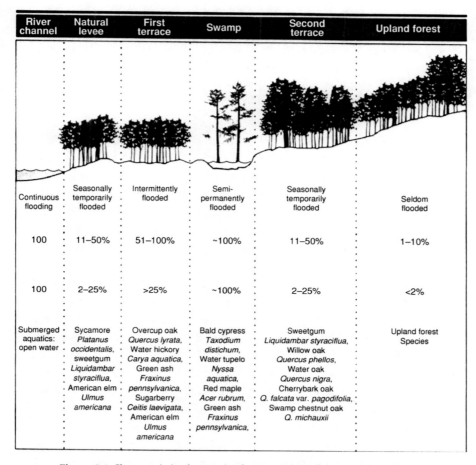

River channel	Natural levee	First terrace	Swamp	Second terrace	Upland forest
Continuous flooding	Seasonally temporarily flooded	Intermittently flooded	Semi-permanently flooded	Seasonally temporarily flooded	Seldom flooded
100	11–50%	51–100%	~100%	11–50%	1–10%
100	2–25%	>25%	~100%	2–25%	<2%
Submerged aquatics: open water	Sycamore *Platanus occidentalis,* sweetgum *Liquidambar styraciflua,* American elm *Ulmus americana*	Overcup oak *Quercus lyrata,* Water hickory *Carya aquatica,* Green ash *Fraxinus pennsylvanica,* Sugarberry *Ceitis laevigata,* American elm *Ulmus americana*	Bald cypress *Taxodium distichum,* Water tupelo *Nyssa aquatica,* Red maple *Acer rubrum,* Green ash *Fraxinus pennsylvanica,*	Sweetgum *Liquidambar styraciflua,* Willow oak *Quercus phellos,* Water oak *Quercus nigra,* Cherrybark oak *Q. falcata* var. *pagodifolia,* Swamp chestnut oak *Q. michauxii*	Upland forest Species

Figure 8.4 Characteristic changes in the vegetation of southeastern US bottomland hardwood forests in response to floodplain topography, flood frequency, and flood duration (after Wharton *et al.* 1982, Clark & Benforado 1981).

occidentalis). Pioneer communities in this zone can consist of monotypic stands of river birch or cottonwood.

Temporarily or infrequently flooded terraces at the highest elevations of the floodplain (Fig. 8.4) are flooded for less than a week to about a month during each growing season. Several oak species that are tolerant of occasionally wet soils appear here. These include swamp chestnut oak (*Quercus michauxii*), cherry-bark oak (*Quercus falcata* var. *pagodifolia*), and water oak (*Quercus nigra*). Hickories (*Carya* spp.) are often present in this zone in association with the oaks. Two pines, spruce pine (*Pinus glabra*) and loblolly pine (*Pinus toeda*), occur at the edges of this zone in many bottomlands of the Mississippi River alluvial plain. Dominant shrub species in these forested wetlands include dwarf palmetto (*Sabal minor*), buttonbush (*Cephalanthus occidentalis*), wax myrtle (*Myrica cerifera*), eastern baccharis (*Baccharis halimifolia*), marsh elder (*Iva frutescens*), two-wing silverbell (*Halesia diptera*), and swamp privet (*Forestiera acuminata*). There are also 25 to 100 species of herbaceous plants that have adapted to the infrequently flooded conditions of this elevation zone.

Fauna

River floodplain systems are particularly productive and provide high-quality habitat for a wide variety of vertebrates. Over 240 fish species, 45 species of reptiles and amphibians, and 37 species of mussels depend on the river and floodplain system of the MSRAP for breeding habitat and resources (Weitzell *et al.* 2003). Furthermore, 50 species of mammals and about 60% of all bird species in the contiguous United States currently use the Mississippi River, and its tributaries and their floodplains (Fremling *et al.* 1989, Sparks 1992, Weitzell *et al.* 2003).

Birds. As with the flora, the fauna typical of the Mississippi River floodplain forests is diverse and well adapted to the widely variable environmental conditions as well as the corresponding vegetative conditions. Millions of migratory birds use the MSRAP as a migration corridor each year. Eighty-five percent of land birds in eastern North America (200 of 236 species) can be found in the MSRAP at some stage of their life cycle (Smith *et al.* 1993). Waterfowl are the most-prominent and economically important group of migratory and resident birds in this region (Wiener *et al.* 1998). The resident avifauna of these forested wetlands can be characterized by the presence and relative abundance of several wading and/or water birds – such as the great blue herons (*Ardea herodias*), wood ducks (*Aix sponsa*), and lesser scaups (*Aythya affinis*) – as well as by barred owls (*Strix varia*), red-headed woodpeckers (*Melanerpes erythrocephalus*), red-bellied woodpeckers (*M. carolinus*), pileated woodpeckers (*Dryocopus pileatus*), downy woodpeckers (*Picoides pubescens*), common grackles (*Quiscalus quiscula*), blue jays (*Cyanocitta cristata*), prothonotary warblers (*Protonotaria citrea*), acadian flycatchers (*Empidonax virescens*), red-winged blackbirds (*Agelaius phoeniceus*), swamp sparrows (*Melospiza georgiana*), and, further south, northern parulas (*Parula americana*) (Burdick *et al.* 1989, North American Breeding Bird Survey 2002). Furthermore, the upper Mississippi River is a major migration route and wintering area for bald eagles (*Haliaeetus leucocephalus*) (Wiener *et al.* 1998). Among the less-frequently spotted birds that are relatively abundant in these wetlands in comparison to their overall distribution are green-backed herons (*Butorides striatus*) and winter wrens (*Troglodytes troglodytes*). According to national breeding-bird surveys (North American Breeding Bird Survey 2002), most of these birds also have particularly abundant nest sites in the MSRAP compared with elsewhere in the United States; even relatively uncommon birds, such as the Mississippi Kite

Figure 8.5 The largest reptile in North America, the American alligator, occurs abundantly in the forested wetlands of the MSRAP.

(*Ictinia mississippiensis*) and Swainson's warbler (*Limnothlypis swainsonii*) frequently breed here.

Mammals. The MSRAP also supports many mammal species that are of economic, ecological, and/or of aesthetic interest. Of particular economic interest are the mink (*Mustela vison*), muskrat (*Ondatra zibethicus*), and nutria (*Myocaster coypus*) populations for fur-trapping; as well as the eastern gray squirrel (*Sciurus carolinensis*), the swamp rabbit (*Sylvilagus aquaticus*), and white-tailed deer (*Odocoileus virginianus*) populations for hunting. Other mammals typically occurring include the river otter (*Lutra canadensis*), raccoon (*Procyon lotor*), hispid cotton rat (*Sygmodon hispidus*), rice rat (*Oryzomys palustrus*), white-footed mouse (*Peromyscus leucopus*), beaver (*Castor canadensis*), and, further south, the armadillo (*Dasypus novemcinctus*) (Wiener *et al.* 1998).

Amphibians and reptiles. Only one of the many amphibians that inhabit the Mississippi River wetlands is extensively hunted: the bullfrog. Other commercially important reptiles include the American alligator (Fig. 8.5), common snapping turtle, alligator snapping turtle, smooth softshell, and spiny softshell. Furthermore, one may commonly encounter such variably picturesque species of snakes and other reptiles as are listed in Gosselink *et al.* (1998). Several species of map turtles inhabit the more strictly riverine portions of this highly variable wetland ecosystem, including the common map turtle, the false map turtle, and the Mississippi map turtle. Even the more-terrestrial timber rattlesnakes are closely associated with the bottomland hardwood forests of the MSRAP throughout their distribution in the Mississippi River valley. However, they commonly

Table 8.1 *Some of the characteristic birds and mammals of the Mississippi River alluvial and deltaic plains.*

Common name	Scientific name	MSRAP	Deltaic plain
Birds			
American white pelican	*Pelecanus erythrorhynchos*		+
Anhinga	*Anhinga anhinga*	+	+
Black-bellied plover	*Pluvialis squatarola*		+
Black skimmer	*Rhynchops niger*		+
Black-necked stilt	*Himantopus mexicanus*		+
Common snipe	*Gallinago gallinago*		+
Eastern brown pelican	*Pelecanus occidentalis*		+
Forster's tern	*Sterna forsteri*		+
Great blue heron	*Ardea herodias*	+	+
Green-backed heron	*Butorides striatus*	+	+
Killdeer	*Charadrius vociferus*	+	+
Little blue heron	*Egretta caerulea*		+
Pied-billed grebe	*Podilymbus podiceps*	+	+
Sandwich tern	*Sterna sandvicensis*		+
Snowy egret	*Egretta thula*		+
Tricolored heron	*Egretta tricolor*		+
White ibis	*Eudocimus albus*		+
White-faced ibis	*Plegadis chihi*		+
Willet	*Catoptrophorus semipalmatus*		+
Yellow-crowned night heron	*Nyctanassa violacea*	+	+
American coot	*Fulica americana*	+	+
Lesser scaup	*Aythya affinis*	+	+
Wood duck	*Aix sponsa*	+	+
Bald eagle	*Haliaeetus leucocephalus*	+	+
Barred owl	*Strix varia*	+	+
Mississippi kite	*Ictinia mississippiensis*	+	+
Red-shouldered hawk	*Buteo lineatus*	+	+
Red-tailed hawk	*Buteo jamaicensis*	+	+
American woodcock	*Scolopax minor*	+	+
Clapper rail	*Rallus longirostris*		+
Common moorhen	*Gallinula chloropus*		+
King rail	*Rallus elegans*	+	+
Purple gallinule	*Poryphyrula martinica*		+
Sora	*Porzana carolina*		+
Downy woodpecker	*Picoides pubescens*	+	
Pileated woodpecker	*Dryocopus pileatus*	+	
Red-bellied woodpecker	*Melanerpes carolinus*	+	+
Acadian flycatcher	*Empidonax virescens*	+	

Table 8.1 (*cont.*)

Common name	Scientific name	MSRAP	Deltaic plain
Birds			
Blue jay	*Cyanocitta cristata*	+	
Boat-tailed grackle	*Quiscalus major*		+
Common grackle	*Quiscalus quiscula*	+	+
Marsh wren	*Cistothorus palustris*	+	+
Northern parula	*Parula americana*	+	+
Prothonotary warbler	*Protonotaria citrea*	+	+
Purple martin	*Progne subis*		+
Red-winged blackbird	*Agelaius phoeniceus*	+	+
Swainson's warbler	*Limnothlypis swainsonii*	+	+
Swamp sparrow	*Melospiza georgiana*	+	
Winter wren	*Troglodytes troglodytes*	+	+
Mammals			
Armadillo	*Dasypus novemcinctus*		+
Beaver	*Castor canadensis*	+	
Cotton mouse	*Peromyscus gossypinus*		+
Eastern gray squirrel	*Sciurus carolinensis*	+	+
Hispid cotton rat	*Sygmodon hispidus*		+
Mink	*Mustela vison*	+	+
Muskrat	*Ondatra zibethicus*	+	+
Northern river otter	*Lutra canadensis*	+	+
Nutria	*Myocaster coypus*		+
Raccoon	*Procyon lotor*	+	+
Rice rat	*Oryzomys palustrus*	+	+
Swamp rabbit	*Sylvilagus aquaticus*	+	+
White-footed mouse	*Peromyscus leucopus*	+	
White-tailed deer	*Odocoileus virginianus*	+	+

only occur in the blufflands immediately adjacent to the river in the northern portions of their range in Minnesota, Wisconsin, and Iowa.

Endangered species. Many endangered, threatened, and rare taxa in the United States depend on wetlands; 50% of the 188 animal species federally designated in these categories in 1988 were associated with wetlands (Gosselink *et al.* 1998). The most prominent of these include the Louisiana black bear (*Ursus americanus luteolus*), the red wolf (*Canis rufus*) – which has been declared extinct in the wild – and the Florida panther (*Felis concolor*), which is locally extinct in the MSRAP (Fig. 8.6). Among birds, the ivory-billed woodpecker (*Campephilus principalis*) and Bachman's warbler (*Vermivora bachmanii*) are also locally extinct or near extinction (Table 8.2). Additional threatened and endangered animal species that

Figure 8.6 The Florida panther, red wolf, and Louisiana black bear are just three of the endangered species that depend on the wetlands of the MSRAP. Of these, the Florida panther is considered "locally extinct," the red wolf as "extinct in the wild," and the black bear is considered "severely threatened in its range."

depend on the Mississippi and/or its associated wetlands are listed in Table 8.2. Of the 2500 plants still in need of protection in 1988, about 700 were associated with wetlands (Niering 1988). In terms of restoration efforts, the threatened Louisiana black bear is particularly interesting because its scarcity and extensive range (<40 000 ha) make it a "shepherd" protected species of critical importance in management plans.

Deltaic plain

The Mississippi River deltaic marshes are blessed with a subtropical climate, full sunlight, abundant rainfall (about 150 cm per year), and the enormous flow of fresh water delivered by the Mississippi River. As the river approaches the Gulf of Mexico, the riverbed becomes broad and deep. At Head-of-Passes, Louisiana the river splits like the toes of a bird's foot into several outlet channels, called "passes," which then deliver the water to the Gulf of Mexico. On the low sedimentary platform of the continental shelf the river has thus formed the modern Balize Delta, one of two active deltas in the vast Mississippi River deltaic plain. The deltaic plain in its entirety extends southward from the head of the Atchafalaya River south to the Gulf of Mexico, and laterally from the Mississippi border to Galveston, Texas. The deltaic plain includes: the river delta proper, built over the past 8000 years by Mississippi River sediment discharged into shallow coastal waters (Russell *et al.* 1936, Frazier 1967, Coleman *et al.* 1998); and the Chenier Plain, built indirectly by the Mississippi River mud stream discharged to the Gulf and carried westward by the prevailing coastal currents (van Lopik 1955, van Heerden 1983, Wells & Roberts 1980, Kemp 1986). Therefore, the entire coast of Louisiana was built, directly or indirectly, by the Mississippi River. Most of the deltaic wetlands are marshes interspersed with swamps and bottomland hardwood forests at their upland edges. Only the coastal cheniers of the Chenier

Table 8.2 *Plant and animal species listed as endangered or threatened in Louisiana.*

Common name	Scientific name	Federal status	State status	Habitat
Plants				
American chaffseed	*Schwalbea americana*	E	–	Longleaf pine savanna
Earthfruit	*Geocarpon minimum*	T	–	Saline prairie
Louisiana quillwort	*Isoetes louisianensis*	E	–	Blackwater streams on sand and gravel beach bars
Invertebrates				
American burying beetle	*Nicrophorus americanus*	E	E	
Fat pocketbook	*Potamilus capax*	E	–	
Inflated heelsplitter	*Potamilus inflatus*	T	T	Sandy or silty rivers
Louisiana pearlshell	*Margaritifera hembeli*	T	E	Small sandy streams
Pink mucket	*Lampsilis abrupta*	E	–	
Amphibians				
Mississippi gopher frog	*Rana sevosa*	T	–	Uplands
Fish				
Pallid sturgeon	*Scaphirhynchus albus*	E	E	Main channels of Mississipi and Atchafalaya rivers
Gulf sturgeon	*Acipenser oxyrhynchus desotoi*	T	T	Coastal waters, big rivers (breeding)
Reptiles				
Green sea turtle	*Chelonia mydas*	T/E	T	Estuaries, SAVs, sandy beaches
Hawksbill sea turtle	*Eretmochelys imbricata*	E	E	Estuaries, SAVs, sandy beaches
Kemp's ridley sea turtle	*Lepidochelys kempii*	E	E	Estuaries, SAVs, sandy beaches
Leatherback sea turtle	*Dermochelys coriacea*	E	E	Sandy beaches for nesting
Loggerhead sea turtle	*Caretta caretta*	T	T	Estuaries, SAVs, sandy beaches
Gopher tortoise	*Gopherus polyphemus*	T	T	Uplands
Ringed sawback turtle	*Graptemys oculifera*	T	T	Clean rivers (Pearl River)
Birds				
Brown pelican	*Pelecanus occidentalis*	E	E	Barrier islands (nests), marshes

(cont.)

Table 8.2 (*cont.*)

Common name	Scientific name	Federal status	State status	Habitat
Bald eagle	*Haliaeetus leucocephalus*	T	E	Swamp snags
Peregrine falcon	*Falco peregrinus*	T/E	T/E	Coastal marsh and lakes
Attwater's greater prairie chicken[a]	*Tympanuchus cupido attwateri*	E	E	
Whooping crane[a]	*Grus americana*	E	E	Coastal prairie
Eskimo curlew[a]	*Numenius borealis*	E	E	
Piping plover	*Charadrius melodus*	T/E	T/E	Beaches and mudflats (uncommon in Louisiana)
Interior least tern	*Sterna antillarum athalassos*	E	E	Riverine sand bars
Ivory-billed woodpecker[a]	*Campephilus principalis*	E	E	Bottomland hardwood forests, upland forests
Red-cockaded woodpecker	*Picoides borealis*	E	E	Longleaf pine forests, upland forests
Bachman's warbler[a]	*Vermivora bachmanii*	E	E	Bottomland hardwood forest, swamp
Mammals				
Manatee	*Trichechus manatus*	E	E	Coastal waters, bays, rivers
Blue whale	*Balaenoptera musculus*	E	E	Coastal waters
Finback whale	*Balaenoptera physalus*	E	E	Coastal waters
Sei whale	*Balaenoptera borealis*	E	E	Coastal waters
Sperm whale	*Physeter macrocephalus*	E	E	Coastal waters
Red wolf[a]	*Canis rufus*	E	—	
Black bear	*Ursus americanus luteolus*	T	T	Bottomland hardwood forest, swamp
Florida panther[a]	*Felis concolor coryi*	E	E	

—, Unlisted.

[a] Extinct or nearly extinct in Louisiana.

SAV, submerged aquatic vegetation.

Adapted from the Louisiana Natural Heritage Program website (http://www.wlf.state.la.us/apps/netgear/pagel.asp).

Plain and the reworked beach headlands east of Bayou Lafourche support the last remaining coastal forest on the Mississippi River delta plain. This coastal forest is dying as the cheniers, on which it is growing, subside. The slow death of this coastal forest is attested by the silhouettes of dead trees along its lower edges. Aside from this minor occurrence of a coastal forest, the forested wetlands of the Mississippi River deltaic wetlands can be characterized similarly to those from the alluvial plain and thus will not be characterized further in this section.

The deltaic plain of the Mississippi River was formed by the deposition of river-borne sediments as the river emptied into the shallow coastal waters of the Gulf of Mexico. About 18 000 years ago, at the height of the last glaciation, the oceans were about 120 m below their present levels (Coleman *et al.* 1998). As the climate warmed, sedimentation could not keep up with the pace of rising sea levels and a shallow submerged platform was built out into the Gulf of Mexico (Gosselink 1984). In the past 5000 to 6000 years, the river has been building a series of emergent delta lobes on this platform, forming the present coastline as we know it. Figure 8.7 illustrates the major Mississippi River delta lobes that were deposited during this period (Fisk & McFarlan 1955, Frazier 1967). Each of these delta lobes had a typical cycle of growth, abandonment, and destruction (Fig. 8.8) (Scruton 1960). When the river switches its course and debauches into a new shallow-water area, there is first a period of subaqueous sediment deposition, followed by a period of rapid growth of exposed islands that merge into a delta lobe. This initial phase of delta growth is currently occurring in the Atchafalaya Basin (Shlemon 1975, van Heerden & Roberts 1988, Roberts 1998). During the growth period the delta is overwhelmingly riverine and the mineral-sediment load is high. As a result, the newly emerging sediments are mineral and the first marshes to appear have fresh water. As the delta grows, the freshwater marshes expand. This expansion is not uniform; growth occurs by the development of a series of smaller subdeltas, each with its own 50- to 100-year cycle of growth and abandonment (Coleman & Gagliano 1964). As the entire delta lobe expands, the surface slope decreases and becomes less efficient at carrying water and sediments. Finally, the river diverts to another, more-efficient channel to the Gulf. At present, the most-efficient route to the Gulf is via the Atchafalaya River, but a man-made control structure at Old River forces 70% of the flow to remain in the old main channel and prevents the river from abandoning the Balize Delta. The process of delta abandonment can be seen in various stages from the oldest Sale–Cypremort complex to the most recently abandoned Plaquemine Delta (Fig. 8.8). During the course of abandonment, the periphery of the deltas becomes increasingly saline. Here, the vegetation changes to salt marsh, and tides supply the energy for sediment movement and deposition. Because the mineral-sediment supply of the river is decreasing and can no longer keep up with the subsidence of the lobe, the marshes of the delta begin to submerge and degrade (Scruton 1960, Frazier 1967). Further marsh development and maintenance, especially at the inner (riverine) end of the delta lobe, is increasingly controlled by the growth of the marsh vegetation, which forms peat (Fisk 1958).

Superimposed on the 1000-year deltaic cycle are many processes of shorter duration. An example of these processes can be seen in the active delta of

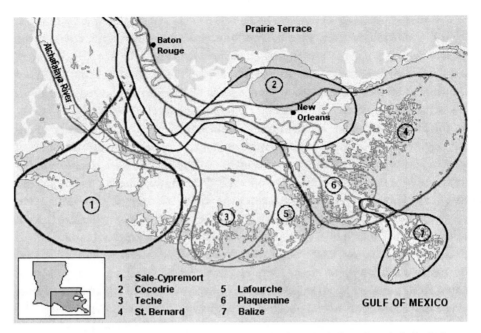

Figure 8.7 In the 5000 to 6000 years since the last glaciation, the Mississippi River has built seven major deltas in the shallow coastal waters of the Gulf of Mexico. The modern Balize Delta (7) is the most recent of these (redrawn from Wiener *et al.* 1995).

the present Mississippi River. Here, in the small Cubits Gap subdelta, the whole cycle of growth, abandonment, and destruction has been traced over the past 100 years (Fig. 8.9): from the formation of a crevasse in the Mississippi River in 1862, through a period of growth, to the beginning of abandonment in 1922, and advanced stages of decay by 1971 (Wells *et al.* 1982, Gosselink *et al.* 1998). Thus, geological processes may make major changes in the physiography of an estuary within the lifetime of an individual. For example, in the abandonment and destructional phases of a delta lobe one may watch, over a number of years and in a specific location: the decrease in freshwater influence, the gradual closing of some natural channels and increase in the size of others, increases in salinity associated with increased tidal influence, and marsh degradation resulting from a loss of sediments and a change in hydrology.

Vegetation

Two primary environmental factors control the distribution of plant species throughout the coastal wetlands: salinity and elevation. The observable broad vegetation bands, caused by the fresh water to salt water gradient from upstream to down-estuary, reflect primarily salinity differences. Elevation

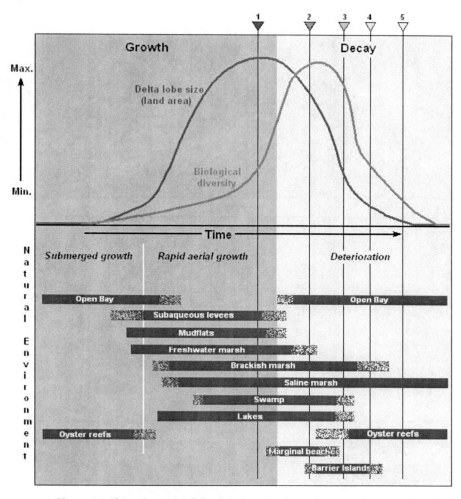

Figure 8.8 This schematic of the deltaic cycle shows the natural progression of wetland creation and deterioration that occurs with each delta switching. All but one of the deltas associated with the Mississippi River are in the destructional phase of this cycle and even this delta, the Balize Delta, is in the last stages of its growth (redrawn from Wiener *et al.* 1995).

is an important secondary species determinant adjacent to the larger coastal streams, where slightly elevated natural levees allow less-flood-tolerant species to grow.

The Mississippi River delta estuarine complex contains the largest salt-marsh area and the second-largest freshwater-marsh area in the continental United States, representing about 40% of the coastal marshes in the continental United States (LCWCRTF–WCRA 1998). However, there have been few detailed

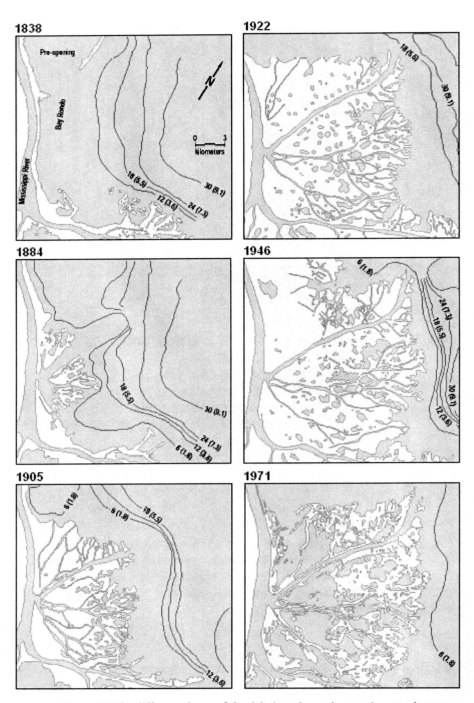

Figure 8.9 The different phases of the deltaic cycle can be seen in a much more rapid progression in the small subdeltas that form periodically from crevasse splays in the river channel of the Mississippi River. In this panel, the deltaic cycle of the Cubits Gap subdelta is traced from its creation in 1862 to its advanced stages of deterioration in 1971 (redrawn from Wiener *et al.* 1995).

descriptions of the diverse plant communities that occur in this large expanse of wetlands. Penfound and Hathaway (1938) provided the earliest descriptions of the plant community types found in the Mississippi River delta. Their efforts were followed by O'Neil (1949), who published the first map of major vegetation associations for coastal Louisiana as part of an inventory of muskrat habitat.

A thorough vegetation survey was completed by Chabreck *et al.* (1968), who surveyed approximately 5000 vegetation stations throughout coastal Louisiana. Chabreck and his colleagues (Chabreck *et al.* 1968, Chabreck & Linscombe 1978, 1988) delineated and mapped four vegetation zones (fresh, intermediate, brackish, and saline) mainly, on the basis of Penfound and Hathaway's (1938) descriptions of the major vegetation types of the Mississippi River delta (Fig. 8.10). The most-recent description of the major habitats within coastal Louisiana was completed by Visser *et al.* (1998). This vegetation survey refines Chabreck's classification into several smaller, distinct vegetation associations (Visser *et al.* 1998). Plant-species richness markedly increases from salt marshes to fresh marshes (O'Neil 1949, Chabreck 1972, White 1983, Sasser *et al.* 1994, Visser *et al.* 1998). The salt marshes (>15 p.p.t. salinity) tend to be dominated by smooth cordgrass (*Spartina alterniflora*) and salt grass (*Distichlis spicata*), as well as small pockets of black mangrove forest (*Avicennia germinans*). Brackish marshes (5 to 15 p.p.t.) can be characterized by the occurrence of wiregrass (*Spartina patens*), smooth cordgrass, black needle rush (*Juncus roemerianus*), three-cornered grass (*Schoenoplectus americanus*), and leafy three-cornered grass (*Bolboschoenus robustus*). The next broad band of vegetation is intermediate marsh with salinities ranging from 0 to 5 p.p.t., which is typified by Jamaican sawgrass (*Cladium jamaicense*), roseaucane (*Phragmites australis*), cattail (*Typha* spp.), giant bullwhip (*Schoenoplectus californicus*), wiregrass, three-cornered grass, leafy three-square (*Scirpus maritimus*), and big cordgrass (*Spartina cynosuroides*). The last marsh zone before reaching forested wetlands is the fresh marsh with salinities of less than 1 p.p.t. This zone has several diverse associations dominated by either maidencane (*Panicum hemitomon*), bulltongue (*Sagittaria lancifolia*), cutgrass (*Zizaniopsis miliacea*), smartweed (*Polygonum* spp.), arrow arum (*Peltandra virginica*), cattail, roseaucane, or Jamaican sawgrass; there are also common occurrences of spikerush (*Eleocharis* spp.), wild rice (*Zizania aquatica*), alligatorweed (*Alternanthera philoxeroides*), bullrush (*Scirpus americanus*), asters (*Aster* spp.), scratchy grass (*Leersia oryzoides*), Walter's millet (*Echinochloa walterii*), and several sedge species. Active deltas – such as the Atchafalaya delta – are mostly dominated by the colonizing species arrowhead (*Sagittaria lancifolia*) and duckpotato (*Sagittaria platyphylla*), and contain mixtures of the above (mostly freshwater) species.

A particularly interesting type of marsh in the Mississippi River delta complex is the floating marsh (Sasser 1994). Floating marshes occur predominantly in the

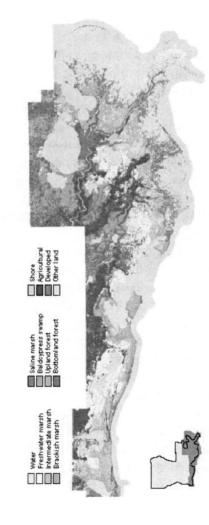

Figure 8.10 This map illustrates the major vegetation zones of the deltaic wetlands of coastal Louisiana. Vegetation changes generally follow both salinity as well as elevation gradients.

freshwater zone of the coast, although some intermediate and even a few brackish marshes do float. Floating marshes are most-commonly dominated by maidencane, bulltongue, scratchy grass, and spike rush. They apparently develop in quiet freshwater environments, where organic-matter production – in the absence of mineral-sediment inputs – makes the marsh mat buoyant. As the underlying mineral substrate subsides, the buoyancy of the mat eventually leads to its separation from the substrate, and it subsequently floats on the water surface. Sasser *et al.* (1994) estimated that about 70% of the freshwater marshes in the Barataria–Terrebonne estuary (Fig. 8.10) are floating, a total of about 116 000 ha.

The Gulf of Mexico is also rimmed with beaches and a low-dune/swale habitat that supports plant species adapted to drier and harsher conditions. Although these habitats tend to be much smaller than the marsh and wetland forest habitats and are generally confined to the Gulf-shore and barrier-island beaches, they contain a variety of distinct communities separated through strong gradients in salinity and flooding. The plant community is generally similar to that on the south-Atlantic coast and the rest of the Gulf coast (Barbour *et al.* 1987, Visser & Peterson 1995). The sandy beach front, which is regularly inundated and reworked by tides, is largely non-vegetated with only sporadic occurrences of sea rocket (*Cakile fusiformis*) and sea purslane (*Sesuvium portulacustrum*). Moving up in elevation into the foredune and dune habitats, only occasional salt-water sprays reach the vegetation. However, non-vegetated dune sands shift in the constant coastal breezes and frequent storms, providing a different challenge to establishing vegetation. Bitter panicum (*Panicum amarum*) and sea oats (*Oniola paniculata*) dominate this region with occasional occurrences of wiregrass (*Spartina patens*) and morning glory (*Ipomoea* spp.) in the mix. They help to stabilize the shifting dune face. This community is then interspersed with seaside goldenrod (*Solidago sempervirens*) and beach tea (*Croton punctatus*) in the relative wind shade of the rear dune. As the elevation decreases again towards the bayside of a barrier island or behind beach dunes, the community shifts to include more wiregrass, as well as a shrubby combination of baccharis (*Baccharis halimifolia*), wax myrtle (*Myrica cerifera*), and marsh elder (*Iva frutescens*) slightly above the average high-tide line. The shallow, even lower elevation zone right above the high-tide line on this gently sloped side of the dune, which is called the "swale," frequently has soil salinities of more than 40 and up to 80 p.p.t. where the standing salt water of the rare inundation events evaporates. In this hostile environment for plant growth, only the most-halophytic, succulent plants such as saltwort (*Batus maritima*) and glasswort (*Salicornia* spp.) can survive. As elevations drop below normal high-tide levels again, the more-common plant communities of wiregrass-dominated high marshes and smooth cordgrass – or mangrove-dominated low marshes or

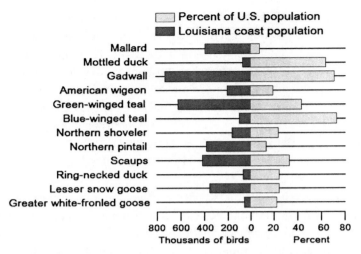

Figure 8.11 The wetlands of coastal Louisiana support an enormous number of waterfowl. This graph shows the individual numbers of the predominant waterfowl species in coastal Louisiana (1969–94 mean) as well as the mean percentage proportion of the US wintering population that is represented by the Louisiana coastal population (after Michot 1994).

wetland forests – emerge once more (Barbour *et al.* 1987, Gunter 1967; Kessel & Reed 1995, Visser & Peterson 1995).

Fauna

Birds. Of the 400 species of birds that are known to occur in Louisiana, most inhabit the coastal zone, while more than half of all (approximately 160 species) confirmed breeding birds in Louisiana breed in the MSRAP or the deltaic wetlands (Gosselink *et al.* 1998, North American Breeding Bird Survey 2002). Many of the migratory birds that use the alluvial plain as their migratory flyway use the deltaic wetlands as major staging grounds before crossing the Gulf of Mexico or flying around it. The remaining migrants overwinter in Louisiana, such as the black-bellied plover (*Pluvialis squatarola*) and the bald eagle. The migratory birds that continue onwards include 180 species of passerines, and a few species of cuckoos and goatsuckers (Gosselink *et al.* 1998). In particular, the coastal wetlands provide important habitat for numerous species of waterfowl, which provide a substantial commercial resource for the recreational-hunting industry valued to exceed US$10 million in Louisiana alone (Fig. 8.11) (LCWCRTF 1993). Non-waterfowl game species include the American coot (*Fulica americana*), clapper rail (*Rallus longirostris*), king rail (*Rallus elegans*), sora (*Porzana carolina*), common moorhen (*Gallinula chloropus*), purple gallinule (*Poryphyrula martinica*), American

Figure 8.12 The brown pelican, once threatened to near-extinction through exposure to polychloronated biphenyls (PCBs), is making a good recovery in the coastal wetlands of Louisiana.

woodcock (*Scolopax minor*), and common snipe (*Gallinago gallinago*) (Michot 1984).

There are also hundreds of non-game species that inhabit the coastal marshes. Some of the most-prominent wading and water birds in this region are the American white pelican (*Pelecanus erythrorhynchos*), brown pelican (*Pelecanus occidentalis*, Fig. 8.12), anhinga (*Anhinga anhinga*), snowy egret (*Egretta thula*), little blue heron (*Egretta caerulea*), tricolored heron (*Egretta tricolor*), green-backed heron (*Butorides striatus*), yellow-crowned night heron (*Nyctanassa violacea*), white ibis (*Eudocimus albus*), pied-billed grebe (*Podilymbus podiceps*), killdeer (*Charadrius vociferus*), willet (*Catoptrophorus semipalmatus*), and black-necked stilt (*Himantopus mexicanus*) (Lowery 1974, North American Breeding Bird Survey 2002). Other non-game birds include the red-tailed hawk (*Buteo jamaicensis*), red-shouldered hawk (*Buteo lineatus*), barred owl, purple martin (*Progne subis*), red-winged blackbird, common grackle, boat-tailed grackle (*Quiscalus major*), marsh wren (*Cistothorus palustris*), and swamp sparrow. There are also various sandpipers, gulls, and terns (Lowery 1974, North American Breeding Bird Survey 2002). More than 90 species of birds nest in the deltaic wetlands, including 28 species of seabirds and wading birds that have established nesting colonies in the Louisiana coastal zone (Portnoy 1977, Keller *et al.* 1984). In a more-recent survey of the Louisiana nesting colonies, only 12 of these species were confirmed (Visser & Peterson 1998). For some of these species, Louisiana provides the most-important breeding area, accounting for as much as 44% to 77% (44% for the black skimmer *Rynchops niger*, 52% for

Forster's tern *Sterna forsteri*, and 77% for the sandwich tern *Sterna sandvicensis*) of their total US breeding populations (Keller *et al.* 1984).

Mammals. Of the 58 species of land mammals that occur in Louisiana, many inhabit the deltaic coastal marshes, swamps, and bottomland hardwood forests. Generally, these are the same as those that are found in the MSRAP, although the wetlands of the deltaic plain can also have an impact on the lives of dolphins and manatees that frequently enter the estuaries (Gosselink *et al.* 1998).

Amphibians and reptiles. Again, the amphibians and reptiles commonly found on the deltaic plain of the Mississippi River are largely the same as those that are found in the MSRAP. Common sightings in the coastal marshes include green water snakes (*Nerodia cyclopion*), banded water snakes (*Nerodia fasciata*), speckled kingsnakes (*Lampropeltis getula*), and the green tree frog (*Hyla cinerea*) as well as many others. In addition, the gulf salt snake (*Nerodia clarkii clarkii*) and diamond-back terrapin (*Malaclemys terrapin*), are generally confined to brackish to saline marshes (Michot 1984) and have special tolerances of the saline conditions found in these environments. The only amphibian of interest to hunters besides the omnipresent bullfrog is the pig frog (*Rana grylio*). Both the bullfrog and the pig frog are freshwater species.

Fish and crustaceans. Although most fish and crustaceans are not necessarily associated with wetlands, nearly all commercial species rely on coastal wetlands for parts or all of their life cycles (Gunter 1967, Herke & Rogers 1989). Examples of important species that use the coastal wetlands as nursery grounds or primary habitat are brown shrimp (*Penaeus aztecus*), white shrimp (*Penaeus setiferus*), eastern oysters (*Crassostrea virginica*), blue crabs (*Callinectes sapidus*), blue catfish (*Ictalurus furcatus*), gulf menhaden (*Brevoortia patronus*), Atlantic croaker (*Micropogonias undulatus*), red drum (*Sciaenops ocellatus*), and speckled trout (*Cynoscion nebulosus*) (Gosselink *et al.* 1998). The dependence of these species on wetlands is important to consider, given that they comprise approximately 30% of the US commercial seafood harvest (US Department of Commerce 1986). In 2002, the Louisiana coastal fisheries alone accounted for 26.7% of the harvest of the US commercial fisheries and 12.1% of the fin-fish recreational harvest in 2001 in the coterminous United States (NMFS 2002).

Endangered species. In addition to the endangered species listed in the MSRAP characterization, there are several other endangered or threatened birds and reptiles that use or depend on the coastal wetlands of the Mississippi delta. These include the eastern brown pelican, piping plover, interior least tern, bald eagle, and American peregrine falcon, as well as several species of turtles that use sandy beaches for nesting (The Louisiana Natural Heritage Program 2002). Several of the species that are still listed as endangered within the United States have already become locally extinct in Louisiana.

Present status

Alluvial plain

Over the past 100 years, the bottomland hardwood forests of the MSRAP have been logged for their timber (Fig. 8.13) (Llewellyn *et al.* 1996), while the drainage of large portions of the floodplains has resulted in additional land-clearing for agricultural purposes. As a result of these changes, much of the original forested wetlands have disappeared. Weitzell *et al.* (2003) estimated that before European settlement the MSRAP supported about 9.7 million ha of riparian forests; about 1.87 million ha remained in 1991 (Fig. 8.13), which indicates a loss of approximately 80% of the original forested area (Llewellyn *et al.* 1996, Weitzell *et al.* 2003). Most of this remaining habitat is found in the wettest backswamp sections of the Yazoo River in Mississippi, the Cache, Bayou deView, and White rivers in Arkansas, and the Tensas and Atchafalaya river systems in Louisiana (Weitzell *et al.* 2003). Moreover, the loss of riparian wetlands has been accompanied by fragmentation: whereas single forest blocks used to cover hundreds of thousands of hectares, there now remain only isolated fragments, most less than 100 ha in size and surrounded by agricultural fields (Gosselink *et al.* 1990). A recent forest fragmentation analysis revealed that the MSRAP forests now exist as 35 000 discrete blocks, 1 ha in size or larger (Mueller *et al.* 1999). To date, the Tensas Basin in northeastern Louisiana is the most-extensively studied individual watershed. At the turn of the twentieth century, over 90% of the Tensas Basin was comprised of wetland forests. Then, starting in the early 1900s and lasting until the late 1970s, the bottomland hardwood forests in this area were clear cut and converted to agricultural land uses at a rate of approximately 10 000 ha per year, as shown in Fig. 8.14 (Gosselink *et al.* 1990, Shaffer *et al.* 1992). Logging activities have been limited since the 1980s and a few attempts have been made to allow some agricultural forests to revert back to wetland forests. It is particularly noteworthy, however, that the majority of the continued logging activities resulted in further fragmentation of the remaining large tracts of forest, whereas most of the forest gains were small, isolated patches (Gosselink *et al.* 1990).

The decline in forest habitat in the alluvial plain was accompanied by the highest percentage decline of high-conservation-priority bird species and the second-highest percentage decline of all bird species in the 24 physiographical regions of the southeastern United States (Hunter 1993). In the Tensas Basin, a survey analysis of breeding-bird species decline also indicated that three to four birds species went locally extinct every decade (Burdick *et al.* 1989); a trend that still continues to this day throughout the MSRAP. Further analysis of these data show that there is a significant relationship between the decreases in forest area

Figure 8.13 This map shows the remaining bottomland hardwood forests of the MSRAP following extensive logging activities in the river basin since 1882 (after Lewellyn *et al.* 1996).

and the observed decreases in forest-bird abundance and densities (Burdick *et al.* 1989).

Although the lower Mississippi River has not been dammed, it has been impacted by several major hydrological alterations. As early as 1879, the Mississippi River Commission was formed in order to control flooding in the MSRAP. Massive flood-control projects were initiated following the flood of 1927 (MacDonald *et al.* 1979). Virtually all the major tributaries of the Mississippi

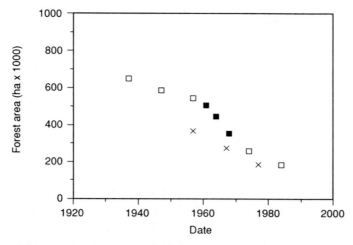

Figure 8.14 Areal changes in bottomland hardwood forests of seven parishes in the Tensas Basin, Louisiana since 1935. Symbols refer to the following sources of data: □, Earles (1975) and May and Bertelson (1986); ■, Yancy (1970); ×, MacDonald *et al.* (1979).

River were dammed in the 1950s and 1960s, and the present sediment load of the river is only about 20% of its historic load (Kessel & Reed 1995). Channels have been created in the river and its length has been shortened by 230 km, while its surrounding floodplain wetlands have been reduced by approximately 90% in area through the construction of about 2700 km of levees on both sides of the river (Wiener *et al.* 1998). Overall, more than 7500 km of levees were built along the Mississippi River and its tributaries (Galloway 1980). Further dikes and revetments used to control the flood waters of the river prevent it from creating new habitats, a natural process that is necessary to replace the floodplain and oxbow-lake habitats that rapidly fill with sediment once they become separated from the river (Gagliano & Howard 1984, Cooper & McHenry 1989). The straightening of the river has also greatly decreased local ponding and increased runoff efficiency, greatly exacerbating the effects of both droughts and floods. This has been shown to occur in the Tensas Basin, where major hydrological alterations of its three major streams since 1935 resulted in a much-greater variability of discharge and duration of flood waters, causing much-shorter and more-sporadic bottomland forest flooding than in the past (Gosselink *et al.* 1990).

Water quality is highly degraded in essentially all of the streams and rivers of the Tensas Basin (Gosselink *et al.* 1990), indicative of conditions throughout the MSRAP (Mitsch *et al.* 2001). For example, phosphorous concentrations exceeded the US Environmental Protection Agency's water-quality standard of 0.1 mg l^{-1} in 96% of the samples taken from the three streams during the 1980s. Omernik (1977), in a national study, showed that a stream's phosphorous levels usually exceeded 0.1 mg l^{-1} when more than 50% of its watershed is disturbed. Thus, the elevated phosphorous concentrations in the Tensas Basin are not surprising, because approximately 85% of the watershed had already been cleared at that time. These increases in phosphorous and turbidity are primarily attributable to the hydrological alterations (e.g. runoff and stream modifications) in the Tensas Basin (Gosselink *et al.* 1990) and are representative of the hydrological changes of the MSRAP as a whole.

Deltaic plain

The coastal zone of Louisiana contains about 25% of US wetlands and about 41% of US coastal wetlands, which makes it one of the Earth's largest and richest estuarine areas. Historically the deltaic plain reached a maximum of about 19 400 km^2 (8200 km^2 contributed by the Atchafalaya delta complex was also included in the area given for alluvial bottomland forest). Unfortunately, during the 1980s and 1990s these wetlands were being lost to open water or non-wetland habitats, because of natural and human causes, at a rate of about 65 to 91 km^2 per year (Barras *et al.* 1994). Wetland loss rates were even higher in the 1960s and 1970s (Britsch & Dunbar 1993, Johnston *et al.* 1995). The specific causes of these losses are hotly debated (Turner 1997, 2001, Day *et al.* 2000, 2001, Gosselink 2001). As much as 12% of this wetland loss can be attributed to direct removal by canal dredging and associated spoil-bank construction (Fig. 8.15) (Britsch & Dunbar 1993). A further 32% of this wetland loss is a direct result of altered hydrology, sediment starvation because of upstream dams and river leveeing, and substrate collapse due to oil and gas extraction. The remaining 56% of wetland loss in the deltaic plain is attributable to natural processes (Penland *et al.* 1996). This alarming rate of wetland loss is further exacerbated by predicted increases in eustatic sea-level rise, currently estimated to be about 1 to 2 mm per year (Gornitz *et al.* 1982, Peltier & Tushingham 1989), which may constitute a rise in sea level of 30 cm or more by the mid twenty-first century (Hoffman *et al.* 1983, Kerr 1989); this is in addition to the accompanying increase in frequency and magnitude of severe-weather events predicted by general circulation modeling (Trenberth 1999). The effects of global climate change and sea-level rise have the most-acute impact on deltaic wetlands, as these wetlands – along with other areas of coastal wetlands – experience regional subsidence (Fig. 8.16) in addition to eustatic sea-level rise. The sum of these two processes (subsidence and eustatic rise) result in a relative sea-level rise in coastal Louisiana of approximately 1 cm per year (Penland *et al.* 1996).

At present, aside from the active delta at the mouth of the Mississippi River and a small delta emerging in Atchafalaya Bay, the major delta lobes of

Figure 8.15 The hydrological disturbance resulting from the dredging of oil-field canals and construction of their associated levees is one of the contributing causes of the rapid wetland loss in coastal Louisiana (Photo: National Wetlands Research Center, US Geological Survey, Lafayette, Louisiana).

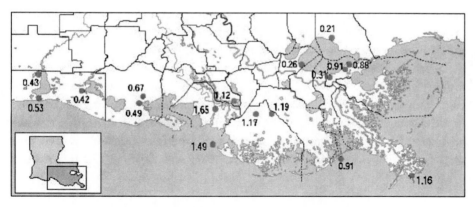

Figure 8.16 Wetland subsidence rates in coastal Louisiana range from 0.21 to more than 1.65 cm per year, without taking eustatic sea-level rise into account (redrawn from Wiener *et al.* 1995).

the river are all in the destructional phase. The time span that governs the deltaic cycle from the construction of a river delta (1000 years) to its eventual abandonment and slow deterioration (about 3000 to 4000 years), has accelerated considerably in the Mississippi River deltaic plain as a result of human intervention in the natural deltaic processes (Coleman *et al.* 1998). Historically, the sediments and accompanying fresh water delivered by the river built the extensive wetlands as the active channel of the river moved east and west across the coast (Fig. 8.7). The annual spring floods, overflowing the river's natural levees, nourished and sustained the wetlands in older delta lobes. Today, with 70% of the river's flow confined to a single leveed channel, these nutrients and sediments are shunted offshore into the deep waters of the Gulf of Mexico. The resulting sediment and nutrient starvation of the estuarine wetlands has greatly accelerated deltaic deterioration (Pezeshki & DeLaune 1995). Approximately 0.95 million tons of nitrate – the vast majority of which originates in the northern states of Iowa, Illinois, Indiana, Minnesota, and Ohio – are discharged annually from the Mississippi River basin; this may produce over 20 million tons of organic carbon annually in the Gulf (Goolsby 2000). This organic carbon annually triggers the development of a hypoxic zone as large as 20 000 km^2 (Fig. 8.17) (Rabalais et al. 1994, 1996). For hypoxia to develop, the water column in the Gulf must be stratified and organic matter must be present to deplete oxygen; two conditions that are easily met by the buoyant and eutrophic fresh water that the Mississippi delivers to the Gulf. A 2.6-fold increase in the mean nitrate concentration in the main stem of the Mississippi River has occurred over the last century, while concentration increases in the tributaries may be even more extreme (Goolsby 2000). The principal sources of nitrogen inputs to the Mississippi basin are mineralization of soil organic matter, commercial fertilizer, legumes, animal manure, atmospheric deposition, and matter from municipal/industrial point sources. Of these sources, only fertilizer inputs have increased dramatically (6-fold) since the 1950s (Fig. 8.18) and account for approximately 60% of the nitrate delivered to the Gulf. Goolsby et al. (1999) found that 11% of the total nitrogen flux to the Gulf (1.57 million tons) was from municipal and industrial point sources, while up to 17% can be attributed to animal manure. Aside from the deleterious effects of this eutrophic water on coastal fisheries through hypoxia, the increased nutrient loadings may also trigger toxic algal blooms (Rabalais et al. 1996) and drastically degrade water quality.

Restoration challenges

As a whole, the indices addressed in the previous sections paint a dismal picture of ecosystem function in the Mississippi River alluvial plain and delta. Forested wetlands have been reduced by nearly 80%, the hydrology of the Mississippi River and local streams and rivers has been severely altered, water quality is poor, wetland subsidence rates are strikingly high, and biota are on the decline. Fortunately, however, several programs are underway to

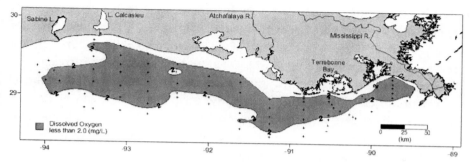

Figure 8.17 Eutrophication of the Mississippi River causes the creation of a hypoxic zone as large as 20 000 km² along the coast of Louisiana (after Goolsby 2000).

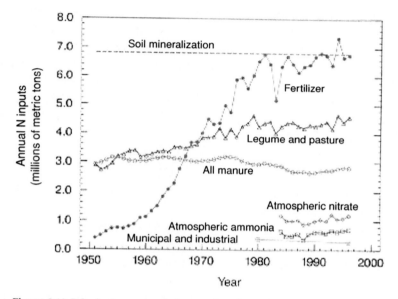

Figure 8.18 Principal sources of nitrogen inputs (in millions of tons) into the Mississippi River and eventually the Gulf of Mexico since 1950. Note that, of the sources identified, fertilizer inputs increased by a factor of six, while most other sources remained relatively stable, albeit high (after Goolsby 2000).

restore the Mississippi River alluvial plain and delta as a network of functioning ecosystems.

Alluvial plain

The dominant strategy in the alluvial plain involves the reforestation of key patches of marginal agricultural land. From both farming and reforestation perspectives, the most cost-effective land to convert from agriculture to wetland forest is what is called "marginal agricultural land." Marginal agricultural lands are fields prone to regular periods of flooding; they generally flood too frequently to be profitable. These areas, because of their wetland soil characteristics, are ideal for colonization by and establishment of wetland plant species; streams and riverbanks are also ideally suited to reforestation. With minimal infringement to agricultural crops, replanting a 50-m-wide strip along the edges of streams and rivers will improve water quality measurably (Lowrance *et al*. 1984), increase the total area and primary and secondary productivity of forested wetlands, and serve as habitat corridors for a variety of wetland fauna.

Over the last decade, The Nature Conservancy has spearheaded a long-term partnership dedicated to creating and implementing a viable, cooperative, landscape-level restoration project that encompasses the entire MSRAP. Important phases of the process were: (1) development of an extensive network of partners – including state and federal agencies, private landowners, conservation groups, academicians, and other interested citizens; (2) development of a geographic information system (GIS) for the entire extent of the system; (3) identification and discussion of sites that will presumably conserve or restore all elements of biodiversity in the MSRAP; (4) prioritization of sites that constitute a cohesive network of restored habitat; (5) the implementation of the restoration plan; and (6) the initiation of ecological research, inventory, and monitoring programs that will improve the quality and comprehensiveness of the restoration program in the future (Weitzell *et al*. 2003). The Nature Conservancy's plan aims to consider both the ecology and the economy of the region and to work directly with the local communities.

The first and foremost priority of The Nature Conservancy's restoration plan is to preserve all existing large (>4000 ha) forested wetland patches and to reforest their edges to increase their sizes. Then, as further forested corridors are established through reforestation to connect these larger forest patches, The Nature Conservancy is planning to draw up a number of target habitat sizes of continuous wetland forests that are needed to preserve target species of conservation concern. Long-term viability is achieved by conserving or restoring those ecosystem functions necessary to ensure the indefinite maintenance of a self-sustaining population of a selected target species. In some areas it has been shown that a minimum of 2800 ha of forest interior is required to sustain viable populations of a local suite of Neotropical migratory bird species (Robbins *et al*. 1989). Including a buffer of 500 m surrounding the forest interior yields a minimum patch size of 4000 ha (Llewellyn *et al*. 1996). Conservation targets include: 10 types of upland and wetland ecosystems; 3 migratory-bird guilds; 1 wide-ranging mammal (the black bear); 5 aquatic systems at the landscape scale (40 000 ha); 63 plant-community types at the intermediate scale (8000 ha);

and 43 individual species at the smallest scale (4000 ha), 8 of which are federally listed as endangered or threatened (Weitzell *et al.* 2003). The plan shown here (Fig. 8.19) focuses on the restoration goals for the three Neotropical migrant bird species which have been selected to represent the three migratory-bird guilds, namely Bachman's warbler (*Vermivora bachmanii*; requiring 4000 ha of interior forest for successful breeding habitat), the Cerulean warbler (*Dendroica cerulea*; requiring 8000 ha of interior forest), and the swallowtail kite (*Elanoides forficatus*; requiring 40 000 ha of interior forest). The logic for prioritizing the reforestation areas involves the consideration of: (1) the total area of the patch in question; (2) the percentage forest of that patch; (3) the position of the patch relative to other forested areas and the condition of the surrounding land; (4) whether the patch is within an area that can be restored based on geological and soil conditions; (5) the general condition of the vegetation with regards to past, present, and future management; and (6) the degree of the effect of hydrological alteration on vegetation and ecosystem function (Weitzell *et al.* 2003). Some alluvial forest community types targeted for restoration have sufficient upland characteristics to be of great agricultural value and are thus unlikely to be restored in great amounts. Using this prioritization technique, 54 sites or about 3.6 million ha are targeted for restoration within the next century (Weitzell *et al.* 2003). Twenty three of these sites have been deemed critical and are targeted for restoration within the next decade.

Using incentive-based federal programs – such as the Wetlands Reserve Program (a government-supported program in the United States that offers Landowners the opportunity to protect, restore, and enhance wetlands on their property) – landowners, conservation agencies, and organizations have already initiated these reforestation efforts in the three-state area of Louisiana, Arkansas, and Mississippi. Over the last decade over 200 000 ha of marginal agricultural lands have thus been converted back to floodplain forest and natural hydrological conditions have been restored to most. On one 2000-ha restoration site in the midwestern side of the Tensas Basin, 15 000 kg of acorns and over 500 000 oak seedlings have been planted. Although this site does not yet give a clear appearance of a restored forest, the groundwork has been laid: the hydrology has been restored and the long-lived forest species have been established. The idea is that additional wind-, water-, and animal-dispersed plant species will colonize these newly restored sites, establish on their own, and then attract the fauna typical of these habitats.

Deltaic plain

Nowhere on the planet Earth is wetland loss to open water higher than in coastal Louisiana. This situation has been recognized by federal and state

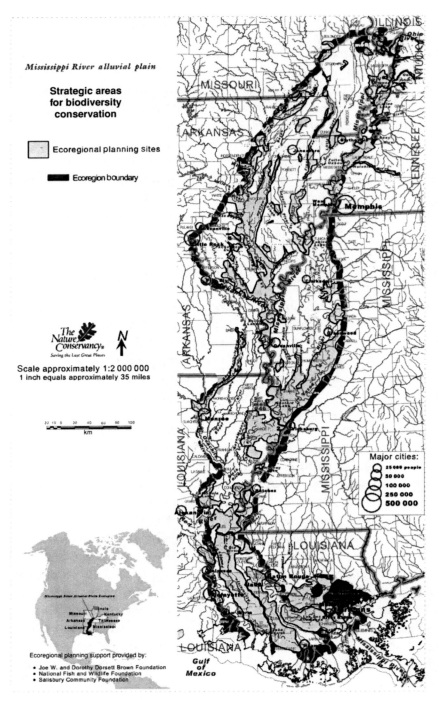

Figure 8.19 The restoration plan of The Nature Conservancy focuses on the restoration goals for the three Neotropical migrant bird species, namely Bachman's warbler (requiring 4000 ha of interior forest), the Cerulean warbler (requiring 8000 ha of interior forest), and the swallowtail kite (requiring 40 000 ha of interior forest) (redrawn from Weitzell *et al.* 2003).

agencies as a problem of immediate national concern and has led to the passing of the Coastal Wetlands Planning, Protection, and Restoration Act (CWPPRA,
1990, Public Law 101-646) that provides funding to support remediation and
restoration projects intended to slow or reverse coastal wetland loss. CWPPRA
has resulted in the coordinated effort among five federal agencies, the state of
Louisiana, local government, private interests, and the academic and conservation community. One of the most-promising restoration techniques investigated
appears to be the construction of controlled and/or uncontrolled river diversions, a technique that would restore the natural flow of sediments, nutrients,
and fresh water into degrading swamps and marshes to slow or halt the process
of deterioration (Coleman *et al.* 1998, Day *et al.* 2000). Because pulsing events
of nutrient and sediment supply to wetlands from river floods or storm events
have been found to be essential to the stability of coastal wetlands and the ability of these wetlands to offset relative sea-level rise (RSLR), future management
and restoration plans must reincorporate these pulsing energies into deltaic
functioning (Day *et al.* 1995, Odum *et al.* 1995). Currently, Louisiana has six operational freshwater diversions and several more are in various stages of planning,
evaluation, or construction (Day *et al.* 1999). Water-quality data from the Caernarvon diversion (Louisiana's first experimental diversion) into Breton Sound show
that the receiving wetlands experienced decreases in salinity and show a nearly
complete assimilation of nutrients and sediments (Lane *et al.* 1999). These conditions have increased plant productivity and vertical accretion to compensate
for RSLR and the rapid loss of wetlands in this estuary. To date, approximately
550 ha of wetlands have been created.

Besides freshwater diversions, other coast-wide common strategies include
the beneficial use of dredged material from maintenance operations, dedicated
dredging, shoreline protection, hydrological restoration, barrier-island restoration, and terracing (Table 8.3) (LCWCRTF and WCRA 1998).

In many cases, herbivore control – especially of the introduced rodent,
nutria – and vegetative plantings are used to supplement these strategies
(LCWCRTF 1997; LCWCRTF–WCRA 1998). In 2003, US$0.2 million were allocated
from CWPPRA, expressly to be used as an incentive to reduce nutria populations;
these rodents have been responsible for massive habitat destruction, through
"eat-outs" since their introduction in 1938 (Mitsch & Gosselink 2000). Other, relatively small-scale and low-cost, wetland restoration projects considered to be
very cost-effective include backfilling of man-made canals, restoration of abandoned agricultural lands, construction of small crevasses near the river mouth,
and spoil-bank management (Turner 1999).

Since 1990, approximately 70 projects have been proposed for potential funding each year. In an attempt to fund the most-cost-effective projects, each project

Table 8.3 *Description of the major types of wetland creation, restoration, and protection projects funded under CWPPRA in coastal areas of the Mississippi River deltaic plain.*

Project type	Description
Barrier-island restoration	Barrier-island restoration projects involve dredging coarse sand from shallow waters of the Gulf to rebuild the eroding islands. In addition, hard structures are often installed to protect islands from the erosive forces of the Gulf. Sand fences and vegetative plantings are also used to stabilize and rebuild sand dunes.
Dedicated dredging	Through dedicated dredging, new marshes are created from shallow-water areas at elevations that select for wetland vegetation. These projects often arise from the need to conduct maintenance dredging of navigation and access channels. However, in many cases, such as in "terracing" projects, shallow-water lake edges are deepened to create a network of islets at marsh elevation, or to re-establish wetlands that have eroded to shallow water.
Freshwater diversion	Freshwater diversions involve routing water from the upper layers of the Mississippi River – using siphons, gates, or culverts – into deteriorated marshes and swamps that were historically periodically connected to the river. River waters offer nutrients, sediments, and fresh water to revitalize wetlands and greatly increase primary and secondary production.
Marsh management	Marsh management entails altering hydrological conditions, generally with weirs, and historically was used to enhance waterfowl and fur-bearer habitat. More recently such efforts have been deemed "hydrological restoration" projects and aim to restore human-altered wetland landscapes to historic conditions by prohibiting salt-water intrusion and increasing throughput in impounded areas.
Crevasse splays	Crevasse splays involve making cuts into levees of the Mississippi River near its mouth so that sediment-laden waters flow into shallow-water areas. Eventually these areas accrete to subaerial mudflats (Fig. 8.9) that succeed to subdelta wetlands, often dominated by *Sagittaria latifolia* and *S. platyphylla*.
Shoreline protection	Shoreline-protection projects include myriad techniques designed to decrease shoreline erosion. Structures include rock berms, earthen levees, and Christmas-tree fences. In addition, segmented breakwaters are often built in near-shore open water to decrease wave energy and promote sediment deposition.
Vegetative plantings and herbivore control	Vegetative plantings are often used in conjunction with the above techniques that do not utilize the Mississippi River. Most commonly, smooth cordgrass (*Spartina alterniflora*) is planted in brackish and saline wetlands, whereas California bullwhip (*Scirpus californicus*) or giant cutgrass (*Zizaniopsis miliacea*) are planted in intermediate and fresh marshes; bald cypress (*Taxodium distichum*) is planted in swamps. Nutria-exclusion devices and/or trapping efforts are commonly necessary to control this pesky, introduced rodent.

is evaluated through a process called the "Wetland Value Assessment." One state and five federal agencies collaborate with a team of coastal scientists to quantify the potential benefits of each project over a 20-year period by comparing scenarios of the future with and without project implementation. This process is used to narrow the list of projects down to generally four or five that can be funded. To date, about US$500 million have been appropriated for wetland restoration projects in coastal Louisiana, which means that each year US$40 to 50 million are made available (at 75% federal funding). Currently, 39 CWPPRA projects and 9 state-funded projects have been implemented and are undergoing evaluation (LCWCRTF 1997). Although the anticipated wetland acreage created, restored, or protected is 1800 km^2 during the next 20 years, the anticipated loss during that same time period is approximately 10 600 km^2 (LCWCRTF 1997). Obviously, these efforts are only a first measure necessary to attain a sustainable coastal wetland ecosystem. To achieve substantial reductions in coastal land loss, this restoration process needs to integrate an adaptive management approach, in which existing projects are evaluated for their actual and sustainable benefits to guide further project implementations. In many cases, an integrated approach using a combination of several different restoration techniques may be appropriate to restore a larger wetland area. Modeling studies by Costanza et al. (1990) have shown that iterative simulations of combinations of restoration techniques are essential to understanding the cumulative impact of this approach, because the impacts of individual techniques are not necessarily additive in nature. The most-recent restoration effort involves the collaboration of a large team of researchers, as well as scientists from several state and federal government agencies, to assemble a US$14 billion, comprehensive restoration plan for the Louisiana coastal wetlands. This effort combines the best techniques available in desktop and computer simulation modeling, using 38 000 1-km^2 cells of the Louisiana coastal wetlands, to evaluate the potential benefits of 32 alternative restoration scenarios on the Louisiana coast (LCA 2003).

Although these restoration efforts are already extremely encouraging in targeting the conservation of biodiversity in the MSRAP, other important ecological issues such as water quality and hydrology need to be addressed, using methodologies developed by researchers world-wide. Some techniques to improve water quality include; (1) the establishment of riparian buffer zones to control non-point-source pollution; (2) tertiary treatment of point-source pollution through constructed wetlands; (3) improved agricultural techniques that result in reduced fertilizer application; (4) a reduction of atmospheric pollutants; and (5) river diversions into deltaic wetlands (Mitsch & Gosselink 2000, Mitsch et al. 2001). Major hydrological restoration techniques should seek to reintroduce river meandering by reconnecting historic oxbow lakes or constructing new meanders, minimizing the number of dams modulating river discharge, and using set-back levees to encourage flood-water storage in streamside wetlands (Dahm 1995, Moustafa 1999, Mitsch & Gosselink 2000).

Only through integrated, landscape-scale efforts – such as the Louisiana Coastal Area (LCA) Restoration Study and the large-scale MSRAP restoration plan spearheaded by The Nature Conservancy – can the vast expanses of the Mississippi River alluvial and deltaic plains be restored and sustained as a network of functional ecosystems.

References

Abernethy, Y. and Turner, R. E. (1987). US forested wetlands: 1940–1980. *Bioscience*, **37**, 721–7.

Barbour, M. G., Rejmanek, R., Johnson, A. F., and Pavlik, B. M. (1987). Beach vegetation and plant distribution pattern along the northern Gulf of Mexico. *Phytocoenologia*, **15**, 210–23.

Barras, J. A., Bourgeois, P. E., and Handley, L. R. (1994). *Land Loss in Coastal Louisiana, 1956–1990*. National Biological Survey, National Wetlands Research Center Open File Report 94-01.

Britsch, L. D. and Dunbar, J. B. (1993). Land loss rates: Louisiana Coastal Plain. *Journal of Coastal Research*, **9**, 324–38.

Burdick, D. M., Cushman, D., Hamilton, R., and Gosselink, J. G. (1989). Faunal changes due to bottomland hardwood forest loss in the Tensas watershed, Louisiana. *Conservation Biology*, **3**, 282–92.

Chabreck, R. H. (1972). *Vegetation, Water and Soil Characteristics of the Louisiana Coastal Region*. Louisiana State University, Agricultural Experiment Station Technical Bulletin 664. Baton Rouge, LA: Louisiana State University.

Chabreck, R. H. and Linscombe, R. G. (1978). *Vegetative Type Map of the Louisiana Coastal Marshes*. New Orleans, LA: Louisiana Department of Wildlife and Fisheries.

(1988). *Louisiana Coastal Marsh Vegetative Type Map 1988*. Baton Rouge, LA: Louisiana Department of Wildlife and Fisheries.

Chabreck, R. H., Joanen, T., and Palmisano, A. (1968). *Vegetative Type Map of the Louisiana Coastal Marshes*. New Orleans, LA: Louisiana Wildlife and Fisheries Commission.

Clark, J. R. and Benforado, J. (eds.) (1981). *Wetlands of Bottomland Hardwood Forests*. Amsterdam, the Netherlands: Elsevier.

Coleman, J. M. and Gagliano, S. M. (1964). Cyclic sedimentation in the Mississippi River Deltaic Plain. *Transactions of the Gulf Coast Association of Geological Societies*, **14**, 67–80.

Coleman, J. M., Roberts, H. H., and Stone, G. W. (1998). Mississippi River Delta: an overview. *Journal of Coastal Research*, **14**(3), 698–716.

Cooper, C. M. and McHenry, J. R. (1989). Sediment accumulation and its effects on a Mississippi River oxbow lake. *Environmental Geology and Water Sciences*, **13**, 33–7.

Costanza, R., Sklar, F. H., and White, M. L. (1990). Modeling coastal landscape dynamics. *Bioscience*, **40**, 91–107.

CWPPRA (Coastal Wetlands Planning, Protection, and Restoration Act) (1990). Public Law 101-646.

Dahm, C. N. (ed.) (1995). Kissimmee River restoration. *Restoration Ecology* (Special issue), **3**, 145–283.

Day, J. W., Jr., Pont, D., Hensel, P. F., and Ibañez, C. (1995). Impacts of sea-level rise on deltas in the Gulf of Mexico and the Mediterranean: the importance of pulsing events to sustainability. *Estuaries*, **18**(4), 636–47.

Day, J. W., Jr., Rybcyk, J., Scarton, F. *et al.* (1999). Soil accretion dynamics, sea-level rise and the survival of wetlands in Venice Lagoon: a field and modeling approach. *Estuaries, Coastal and Shelf Science*, **49**, 607–28.

Day, J. W., Jr., Shaffer, G. P., Britsch, L. D. *et al.* (2000). Pattern and process of land loss in the Mississippi Delta: a spatial and temporal analysis of wetland habitat change. *Estuaries*, **23**, 425–38.

Day, J. W., Jr., Shaffer, G. P., Reed, D. J. *et al.* (2001). Patterns and processes of wetland loss in Coastal Louisiana are complex: a reply to R. E. Turner. 2001. Estimating the indirect effects of hydrological change on wetland loss: if the Earth is curved, then how would we know it? *Estuaries*, **24**, 647–51.

Dinnel, S. P. and Wiseman, W. J., Jr. (1986). Freshwater on the Louisiana shelf. *Continental Shelf Research*, **6**, 765–84.

Earles, J. M. (1975). *Forest Statistics for Louisiana Parishes*. US Department of Agriculture Forest Service, Southern Forest Experiment Station, Forest Service Research Bulletin SO-52.

Fisk, H. N. (1958). Recent Mississippi River sedimentation and peat accumulation. In *Quatrieme congres pour l'avancement des etudes de stratigraphic et de géologie du Carbonifère, septembre 15–20, 1958, Heerlen, the Netherlands*. Compte rendu, 3. vols. Heerler, the Netherlands: Geology Bureau, pp. 187–99.

Fisk, H. N. and McFarlan, E., Jr. (1955). *Late Quaternary Deltaic Deposits of the Mississippi River. Crust of the Earth*. Geological Society of America Special Paper 62, pp. 279–302.

Frazier, D. E. (1967). Recent deltaic deposits of the Mississippi River, their development and chronology. *Transactions of the Gulf Coast Association of Geological Societies*, **17**, 287–315.

Fremling, C. R., Rasmussen, J. L., Sparks, R. E. *et al.* (1989). Mississippi River fisheries: a case history. In *Proceedings of the International Large River Symposium*, ed. D. P. Dodge. Canadian Special Publication of Fisheries and Aquatic Science 106.

Gagliano, S. M. and Howard, P. C. (1984). The neck cut-off oxbow lake cycle along the Lower Mississippi River. In *River Meandering*, ed. C. M. Elliot. New York: American Society of Civil Engineers, pp. 147–58.

Galloway, G. E., Jr. (1980). *Ex-post Evaluation of Regional Water Resources Development: the Case of the Yazoo-MS Delta*. US Army Corps of Engineers Institute for Water Resources, Report IWR-80-D-1.

Goolsby, D. A. (2000). Mississippi Basin nitrogen flux believed to be cause of Gulf hypoxia. *Eos*, **81**, 321–27.

Goolsby, D. A., Battaglin, W. A., Lawrance, G. B. *et al.* (1999). *Flux and Sources of Nutrients in the Mississippi–Atchafalaya River Basin: Topic 3 Report for the Integrated Assessment on Hypoxia in the Gulf of Mexico.* NOAA, Coastal Ocean Program, Decision Analysis Series 17. Silver Spring, MD: NOAA, Coastal Ocean Office.

Gornitz, V., Lebedeff, S., and Hansen, J. (1982). Global sea level trend in the past century. *Science*, **215**, 1611–14.

Gosselink, J. G. (1984). *The Ecology of Delta Marshes of Coastal Louisiana: a Community Profile.* US Fish and Wildlife Service, Biological Service Program, FWS/OBS-84/09.

(2001). Comments on "Wetland loss in the Northern Gulf of Mexico: multiple working hypotheses." by R. E. Turner (1997). [*Estuaries*, **20**(1), 1–13]. *Estuaries*, **24**(4), 636–8.

Gosselink, J. G., Shaffer, G. P., Lee, L. C. *et al.* (1990). Landscape conservation in a forested wetland watershed: can we manage cumulative impacts? *Bioscience*, **40**(8), 588–601.

Gosselink, J. G., Coleman, J. M., and Stewart, R. E., Jr. (1998). Coastal Louisiana. In *Status and Trends of the Nation's Biological Resources*, vol. 1, eds. M. J. Mac, P. A. Opler, C. E. Puckett Haecker, and P. D. Doran. Reston, VA: US Department of the Interior, US Geological Survey, pp. 385–436.

Gunter, G. (1967). Some relationships of estuaries to the fisheries of the Gulf of Mexico. In *Estuaries*, ed. G. H. Lauff. AAAS Publication 83, pp. 621–38. San Francisco, CA: American Association for the Advancement of Science.

Herke, W. H. and Rogers, B. D. (1989). Threats to coastal fisheries. In *Marsh Management in Coastal Louisiana: Effects and Issues. Proceedings of a Symposium.* Washington, DC: US Fish and Wildlife Service. Baton Rouge, LA: Louisiana Department of Natural Resources, pp. 196–212.

Hoffman, J. S., Keyes, D., and Titus, J. G. (1983). *Projecting Future Sea Level Rise. Methodology, Estimates to the Year 2100, and Research Needs.* United States Environmental Protection Agency Report, EPA 230-09-007.

Hunter, W. C., Carter, M. F., Pashley, D. N., and Barker, K. (1993). Partners in flight species prioritization scheme. In *Status and Management of Neotropical Migratory Birds*, eds. D. M. Finch and P. W. Stangel. USDA Forest Service General Technical Report RM-229, pp. 109–19.

Hunter, R. G. and Faulkner, S. P. (2001). Denitrification potentials in restored and natural bottomland hardwood wetlands. *Soil Science Society of America Journal*, **65**, 1865–72.

Johnston, J. B., Watzin, M. C., Barras, J. A., and Handley, L. R. (1995). Gulf of Mexico coastal wetlands: case studies of loss trends. In *Our Living Resources: a Report to the Nation on the Distribution, Abundance, and Health of US Plants, Animals, and Ecosystems*, eds. E. T. LaRoe, G. S. Farris, C. E. Puckett, P. D. Doran, and M. J. Mac. Washington, DC: US Department of the Interior, National Biological Service, pp. 269–72.

Keller, C. E., Spendelow, J. A., and Greer, R. D. (1984). *Atlas of Wading Bird and Seabird Nesting Colonies in Coastal Louisiana, Mississippi, and Alabama: 1983.* US Fish and Wildlife Service FWS/OBS-82/13.

Kemp, G. P. (1986). Mud deposition at the shoreface: wave and sediment dynamics on the Chenier Plain of Louisiana. Ph.D. dissertation, Louisiana State University, Baton Rouge, LA.

Kerr, R. A. (1989). Bringing down the sea level rise. *Science*, **246**, 1563.

Kessel, R. and Reed, D. J. (1995). Status and trends in Mississippi River sediment regime and its role in Louisiana wetland development. In *Status and Historical Trends of Hydrological Modification, Reduction in Sediment Availability, and Habitat Loss/Modification in the Barataria and Terrebonne Estuarine System*, ed. D. F. Reed. BTNEP Publication 20. Thibodaux, LA: Barataria-Terrebonne National Estuary Program.

Lane, R. R., Day, J. W., and Thibodeaux, B. (1999). Water quality analysis of a freshwater diversion at Caernarvon, Louisiana. *Estuaries*, **22**, 327–36.

LCA (Louisiana Coastal Area) Restoration Study (2003). *Science Workshop for the Louisiana Coastal Area (LCA) Restoration Study, April 23–24, 2003, New Orleans, LA*. Baton Rouge, LA: Louisiana Department of Natural Resources.

LCWCRTF (Louisiana Coastal Wetland Conservation and Restoration Task Force) (1993). *Louisiana Coastal Wetlands Restoration Plan*. Coastal Wetlands Planning Protection and Restoration Act. New Orleans, LA: US Army Corps of Engineers.

  (1997). 1997 Evaluation Report. S. Underwood, D. Meffert, B. Good, L. Bahr, B. Ethridge, M. Floyd, S. Green, R. Hartman, R. Paille, D. Reed, and J. Johnston. Baton Rouge, LA: Louisiana Department of Natural Resources, Coastal Restoration Division.

LCWCRTF–WCRA (Louisiana Coastal Wetlands Conservation and Restoration Task Force and Wetlands Conservation and Restoration Authority) (1998). *Coast 2050: Toward a Sustainable Coastal Louisiana*. Baton Rouge, LA: Louisiana Department of Natural Resources.

Llewellyn, D. W., Shaffer, G. P., Craig, N. J. *et al.* (1996). A decision-support system for prioritizing restoration sites on the Mississippi River Alluvial Plain. *Conservation Biology*, **10**(5), 1446–55.

Louisiana Natural Heritage Program (2002). Species listed as threatened (T) and endangered (E) in Louisiana. Louisiana Natural Heritage Program, Department of Wildlife and Fisheries, Baton Rouge, LA. http://www.wlf.state.la.us/apps/netgear/page1.asp.

Lowery, G. H., Jr. (1974). *Louisiana Birds*, 3rd edn. Baton Rouge, LA: Louisiana State University Press.

Lowrance, R., Todd, R., Fail, J., Jr. *et al.* (1984). Riparian forests as nutrient filters in agricultural watersheds. *Bioscience*, **34**, 374–7.

MacDonald, P. O., Frayer, W. E., and Clauser, J. K. (1979). *Documentation, Chronology, and Future Projections of Bottomland Hardwood Habitat Loss in the Lower Mississippi Alluvial Plan*. Vicksburg, MS: US Department of Internal Fisheries and Wildlife Service.

May, D. M. and Bertelson, D. F. (1986). *Forest Statistics for Louisiana Parishes*. US Department of Agriculture Forest Service, Southern Forest Experiment Station, Forest Service Research Bulletin SO-115.

Michot, T. C. (1984). *Louisiana Coastal Area Study: Interim Report on Land Loss and Marsh Creation*. Lafayette, LA: US Fish and Wildlife Service, Ecological Services.

Milliman, J. D. and Meade, R. H. (1983). World-wide delivery of sediment to the ocean. *Journal of Geology*, **91**, 1–21.

Mitsch, W. J. and Gosselink, J. G. (2000). *Wetlands*, 3rd edn. New York: John Wiley.

Mitsch, W. J., Day, J. W., Jr., Gilliam, J. W. *et al.* (2001). Reducing the nitrogen loading to the Gulf of Mexico from the Mississippi River Basin: strategies to counter a persistent ecological problem. *Bioscience*, **51**(5), 373–88.

Moustafa, M. Z. (1999). Nutrient retention dynamics of the Everglades nutrient removal project. *Wetlands*, **19**, 689–704.

NMFS (National Marine Fisheries Service) (2002). *Fisheries of the United States, 2001*. National Oceanographic and Atmospheric Administration National Marine Fisheries Service, Office of Science and Technology, Fisheries Statistics and Economics Division.

NOAA (National Oceanographic and Atmospheric Administration) (1987). *National Estuarine Inventory. Data Atlas*. Rockville, MD: National Oceanographic and Atmospheric Administration.

Niering, W. A. (1988). Endangered, threatened, and rare wetland plants and animals of the Continental United States. In *The Ecology and Management of Wetlands*, vol. 1, *Ecology of Wetlands*, eds. D. D. Hook, W. H. McKee, Jr., H. K. Smith *et al.* Portland, OR: Timber Press, pp. 227–38.

North American Breeding Bird Survey (2002). National Wildlife Research Centre, Canadian Wildlife Service, Canada and Patuxent Wildlife Research Center, US Geological Survey, Laurel, MD. http://www.mp2-pwrc.usgs.gov/bbs.

Odum, W. E., Odum, E. P., and Odum, H. T. (1995). Nature's pulsing paradigm. *Estuaries*, **18**, 547–55.

Omernik, J. M. (1977). *Nonpoint Source–Stream Nutrient Level Relationships: a Nationwide Study*. US Environmental Protection Agency, EPA-600/3/77–105.

O'Neil, T. (1949). *The Muskrat in the Louisiana Coastal Marshes: a Study of the Ecological, Geological, Biological, Tidal, and Climatic factors Governing the Production and Management of the Muskrat Industry in Louisiana*. New Orleans, LA: Louisiana Department of Wild Life and Fisheries.

Peltier, W. R. and Tushingham, A. M. (1989). Global sea level rise and the Greenhouse effect: might they be related? *Science*, **244**, 800–10.

Penfound, W. T. and Hathaway, E. S. (1938). Plant communities in the marshlands of Southeastern Louisiana. *Ecological Monographs*, **8**, 1–56.

Penland, S., Mendelssohn, I., Wayne, L., and Britsch, D. (1996). *Natural and Human Causes of Coastal Land Loss in Louisiana: Workshop Summary*. Baton Rouge, LA: Coastal Studies Institute, Wetland Biogeochemistry Institute, Louisiana State University.

Pezeshki, S. R. and DeLaune, R. D. (1995). Coastal changes and wetland losses in the Mississippi River deltaic plain, USA. In *Proceedings of the International Conference "Coastal Change 95" Bordomer-IOC, Bordeaux*, pp. 415–26.

Portnoy, J. W. (1977). *Nesting Colonies of Seabirds and Wading Birds: Coastal Louisiana, Mississippi, and Alabama*. US Fish and Wildlife Service FWS/OBS-77/07.

Putnam, J. A., Furnival, G. M., and McKnight, J. S. (1960). *Management and Inventory of Southern Hardwoods*. USDA Agricultural Handbook 181. Washington, DC: US Department of Agriculture.

Rabalais, N. N., Wiseman, W. J. J., and Turner, R. E. (1994). Comparison of continuous records of near-bottom dissolved oxygen from the hypoxia zone along the Louisiana coast. *Estuaries*, **17**, 850–61.

Rabalais, N. N., Turner, R. E., Justic, D. *et al.* (1996). Nutrient changes in the Mississippi River and system responses on the adjacent continental shelf. *Estuaries*, **19**(2b), 386–407.

Robbins, C. S., Dawson, D. K., and Dowell, B. A. (1989). *Habitat Area Requirements of Breeding Forest Birds of the Middle Atlantic States*. Wildlife Monographs 103. Bethesda, MD: The Wildlife Society.

Roberts, H. H. (1998). Delta switching: early responses to the Atchafalaya River diversion. *Journal of Coastal Research*, **14**(3), 882–99.

Russell, R. J., Howe, H. V., McGuirt, J. H. *et al.* (1936). *Lower Mississippi Delta: Reports on the Geology of Plaquemines and St. Bernard Parishes*. Louisiana Geological Survey, Geological Bulletin 13. New Orleans, LA: Louisiana Department of Conservation.

Sasser, C. E. (1994). *Vegetation Dynamics in Relation to Nutrients in Floating Marshes in Louisiana, USA*. Baton Rouge, LA: Center for Coastal, Energy, and Environmental Resources, Louisiana State University.

Sasser, C. E., Swenson, E. M., Evers, D. E. *et al.* (1994). *Floating Marshes in the Barataria and Terrebonne Basins, Louisiana*. Report LSU-CEI-94-02. Baton Rouge, LA: Louisiana State University, Coastal Ecology Institute. Prepared for the US Environmental Protection Agency.

Scruton, P. C. (1960). Delta building and the deltaic sequence. *Recent Sediments, Northwest Gulf of Mexico*, eds. F. P. Shepard, F. B. Phleger, and T. H. van Andel. Tulsa, OK: American Association of Petroleum Geologists, pp. 82–102.

Shaffer, G. P., Burdick, D. M., Gosselink, J. G., and Lee, L. C. (1992). A cumulative impact management plan for a forested wetland watershed in the Mississippi River Floodplain. *Wetlands Ecology and Management*, **1**(3), 199–210.

Shlemon, R. J. (1975). Subaqueous delta formation: Atchafalaya Bay, Louisiana. In *Deltas, Models for Exploration*, ed. M. L. Broussard. Houston, TX: Houston Geological Society, pp. 209–21.

Smith, W. P., Twedt, D. J., Wiedenfeld, D. A. *et al.* (1993). *Point Counts of Birds in Bottomland Hardwood Forests of the Mississippi Alluvial Valley: Duration, Minimum Sample Size, and Points Versus Visits*. Southern Forest Experimental Station Research Paper SO-274. New Orleans, LA: US Department of Agriculture Forestry Service.

Sparks, R. E. (1992). Can we change the future by predicting it? In *Proceedings of the 48th Annual Meeting of the Upper Mississippi River Conservation Committee (UMRCC), March 10–12, 1992, Red Wing, MN*. In *Restoring the Big River*, eds. A. R. Robinson and Marks (1994). Izaak Walton League. Natural Resources Defense Council.

Turner, R. E. (1997). Wetland loss in the Northern Gulf of Mexico: multiple working hypotheses. *Estuaries*, **20**, 1–13.

(1999). Low-cost wetland restoration and creation projects for Coastal Louisiana. In *Recent Research in Coastal Louisiana: Natural System Function and Response to Human Influence*, eds. L. P. Rozas, J. A. Nyman, C. E. Proffitt *et al*. Louisiana Sea Grant College Program. Baton Rouge, LA: Louisiana State University, pp. 229–37.

(2001). Estimating the indirect effects of hydrological change on wetland loss: if the Earth is curved, then how would we know it? *Estuaries*, **24**(4), 639–46.

Trenberth, K. E. (1999). The climate system and climate change. *Current Topics in Wetland Biogeochemistry*, **3**, 4–15.

US Department of Commerce (1986). *Fisheries of the United States, 1985*. Current Fisheries Statistics. National Marine Fisheries Service Report 8380.

van Heerden, I. L. (1983). Sediment responses during flood and non-flood conditions, New Atchafalaya Delta, Louisiana. M.Sc. thesis, Louisiana State University, Baton Rouge, LA.

van Heerden, I. L. and Roberts, H. H. (1988). Facies development of Atchafalaya Delta, Louisiana: a modern bayhead delta. *American Association of Petroleum Geologists Bulletin*, **72**(4), 439–53.

van Lopik, J. R. (1955). *Recent Geology and Geomorphic History of Central Coastal Louisiana*. Coastal Studies Institute Technical Report 7. Baton Rouge, LA: Louisiana State University.

Visser, J. M. and Peterson, G. W. (1995). *Vegetation Survey of Raccoon Island: Before and After Restoration*. Baton Rouge, LA: Louisiana State University Prepared for LA Department of Wildlife and Fisheries.

(1999). *Survey of Louisiana Seabird Colonies to Enhance Oil Spill Response*. Louisiana Applied and Educational Oil Spill Research and Development Program, OSRADP Technical Report Series 98-012.

Visser, J. M., Sasser, C. E., Chabreck, R. H., and Linscombe, R. G. (1998). Marsh vegetation types of the Mississippi River Deltaic Plain. *Estuaries*, **21**, 818–28.

Weitzell, R. E., Khoury, M. L., Gagnon, P. *et al.* (2003). *Conservation Priorities for Freshwater Biodiversity in the Upper Mississippi River Basin*. Baton Rouge, LA: NatureServe and The Nature Conservancy.

Wells, J. T. and Roberts, H. H. (1980). Fluid mud dynamics and shoreline stabilization: Louisiana Chenier Plain. In *Proceedings of the 17th International Coastal Engineering Conference (ASCE), March, 1990, Sydney, Australia*. New York: ASCE, pp. 1382–1401.

Wells, J. T., Chinburg, S. J., and Coleman, J. M. (1982). *Development of the Atchafalaya River Deltas: Generic Analysis*. Baton Rouge, LA: Louisiana State University, Coastal Studies Institute, Center for Wetland Resources. Prepared for US Army Corps of Engineers.

Wharton, C. H., Kitchens, W. M., Pendleton, E. C., and Sipe, T. W. (1982). *The Ecology of Bottomland Hardwood Swamps of the Southeast: a Community Profile*. US Fish and Wildlife Service, FWS/OSB-81/37.

White, D. A. (1983). Vascular plant community development on mudflats in the Mississippi River delta, Louisiana, USA. *Aquatic Botany*, **45**, 171–94.

Wiener, J. G., Fremling, C. R., Korschgen, C. E. *et al.* (1995). Mississippi River. In *Status and Trends of the Nation's Biological Resources*. Washington, DC: US Geological Survey.

Wiener, J. G., Fremling, C. R., Korschgen, C. E. *et al.* (1998). Mississippi River. In *Status and Trends of the Nation's Biological Resources*, vol. 1, eds. M. J. Mac, P. A. Opler, C. E. Puckett Haecker, and P. D. Doran. Reston, VA: US Department of the Interior, US Geological Survey, pp. 351–84.

Yancy, R. K. (1970). Our vanishing hardwoods. *Louisiana Conservationist*, **23**, 26–31.

9

The Lake Chad basin

J. LEMOALLE
IRD

Introduction

The total area of wetlands in Africa has been estimated at 300 000 to 345 000 km^2 (Balek 1977, Howard-Williams & Thompson 1985); while the World Resources Institute (2000) gives a somewhat overestimated value of more than 1 100 000 km^2. Large wetlands are situated along the equator in the humid Congo–Zaire basin with 130 000 km^2 of permanent or seasonally inundated forests and a number of large shallow lakes (Compère & Symoens 1987). These water bodies characterize a region with a humid climate and result from a fairly high and continuous direct rainfall. Wetland systems and floodplains may also be found in a semi-arid climate. In the West African Sahel, the semi-arid region south of the Sahara desert, the main wetland systems are those of the Chad basin and the Inner Delta of the River Niger in Mali (Fig. 9.1). They are fed mainly by streams originating in more-humid tropical regions that have a pronounced seasonality.

In a semi-arid climate, water is the limiting factor for the development of vegetation and the associated trophic webs. Wetlands or floodplains are thus a singularity in the landscape within an arid region: they are areas where water is much-less limiting than in the surroundings. The vegetation that may develop depends on the seasonality, duration, and depth of the inundation.

A number of classifications have been proposed for floodplains and wetlands. In these, the role of the hydrological cycle is often put forward together with the duration of the inundation, the connectivity with the river, and the relative variation of the inundated area during the yearly cycle (Junk 1982, Junk & Weber

The World's Largest Wetlands: Ecology and Conservation, eds. L. H. Fraser and P. A. Keddy.
Published by Cambridge University Press. © Cambridge University Press 2005.

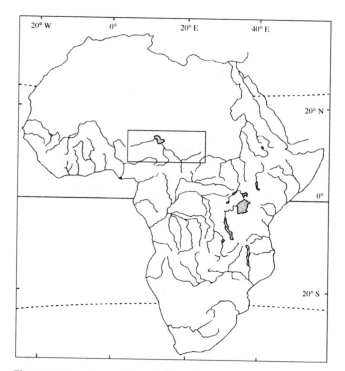

Figure 9.1 Location of Lake Chad and its main tributaries in Africa.

1996). The ratio of permanently flooded area to seasonally flooded area is an ecologically significant variable. On one extreme, the Sudd (Nile basin), the Okavango (Botswana), and the inundated forest in the western part of the Congo–Zaire basin have a permanent-to-seasonal ratio of 0.6:1. These are extensive permanent marshes of seasonally variable area. At the other extreme, the floodplains of the rivers Niger and Senegal had a ratio of 1:6 before the construction of dams which regulated their course (Talling & Lemoalle 1998).

Much-smaller values of this ratio apply to the 90 000 km^2 of riverine floodplains of the Chad basin. These systems are practically devoid of water during the dry season, and are characterized by a short growing season. The aquatic phase of the cycle starts again at the beginning of the rain/flood season of the following year.

Although a number of smaller regions may be submersed, the main floodplains of the Chad basin may be subdivided as follows (Fig. 9.2):

1.   In the southeast of the basin, the extensive but poorly known Salamat floodplains (50 000 km^2) border the tributaries of the upper River Chari: Bahr Salamat, Bahr Keita, and Bahr Aouk. These rivers have their origin

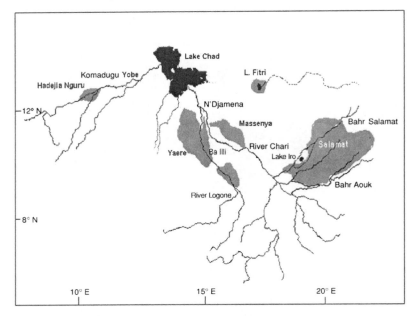

Figure 9.2 The main rivers and wetlands of the Chad basin.

in the Darfour mountains in Sudan. Part of the course of Bahr Aouk forms the border between Chad and the Central African Republic. Lake Iro (10° 10′ N, 19° 23′ E, 95 km²) is a permanent circular lake with a large belt of riparian macrophytes. It is fed by Bahr Salamat and direct rainfall. The seasonal water-level variation is about 2 m.

2. The Yaere (approximately 10° 50′ to 12° 30′ N and 14° 00′ to 15° 20′ E) on the left bank of the River Logone, north of the town of Bongor, includes part of the National Park of Waza in Cameroon. Its area is about 8000 km². At the end of the flood, part of the water of the Yaere flows toward Lake Chad through the El Beïd (or Ebeji) River.

3. The floodplain of Ba Illi, facing the Yaere on the right bank of the River Logone, between the Chari and the Logone (4000 km²), is fed by outflows of both the Chari and the Logone, with a number of tributaries in which the flow direction depends on the relative level of the main rivers. Some levees have been constructed on the two banks of the River Logone to control the flooding of the area.

4. The floodplain of Massenya (10° 30′ to 11° 30′ N and 16° 00′ to 17° 00′ E) is fed by the Bahr Erguig, a side arm of the River Chari. The lower end of Bahr Erguig drains some water back to the River Chari. The maximum inundated surface area is about 7000 km².

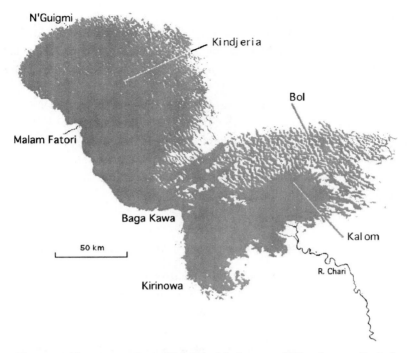

Figure 9.3 The water surface of Lake Chad in January, 1973, a few months before its transition to "small" Lake Chad. Mosaic of Landsat data from Lemoalle (1978). The main gauge stations are indicated.

5. The Hadejia–Nguru wetlands (centred on 12° 35′ N and 10° 30′ E) in northern Nigeria, functions as an inner delta (2000 km²) of the rivers Hadejia, Kafin Hausa, and Jama'are which join to form the Komadugu Yobe (or Yobe River), the outlet of the floodplain at Gashua. The Yobe River flows into the northern basin of Lake Chad at Yau/Boso, some 250 km downstream of Gashua.

Lake Chad was considered as a large shallow lake until 1973, with 18 000 to 20 000 km² of open waters (Fig. 9.3). It has been regarded as a seasonal wetland since 1976, after the onset of the present dry climatic phase which started in 1973 in the African Sahel: the inundated areas have seasonally varied between 4000 and 9000 km² in the southern basin of the lake and between 50 and 7000 km² in its northern basin. For the whole lake, the ratio of permanently flooded area to maximum seasonally inundated area has varied between 1:3 and 1:4, resulting in a dense and relatively more stable macrophytic vegetation than in the riverine floodplains.

Another wetland system exists in Chad, but does not contribute to the main basin: the endoreic Lake Fitri, maximum surface area usually 800 km^2, with its main inflow the seasonal River Batha. It is a reduced model of Lake Chad, with similar seasonal and inter-annual variations in surface area, and similar biota (Lemoalle 1987).

As in other regions of the world, the permanent marshes of Lake Chad, Lake Fitri, and Lake Iro host macrophytic associations that are different from, and much-more dense than, the temporary riverine floodplains. However, in both types of systems, the ecological processes which regulate the water quality and the interactions between the biological communities are similar in nature, although they may differ in their intensity.

Key introductory papers published on the Chad wetlands system

Within the framework of the Scientific Committee on Problems of the Environment (SCOPE), a group of scientists joined in 1982 to share their experience and knowledge of the shallow water bodies of Africa. Two books on the *"African Wetlands and Shallow Water Bodies"* have resulted from their meetings: one gathering the references to date (Davies & Gasse 1988) and the other giving a summary of the knowledge of the main wetlands and shallow lakes of Africa (Burgis & Symoens 1987); this latter volume contains a useful synopsis on the floodplains of the Chad basin and on Lake Chad itself.

A more-extensive synopsis of the scientific studies on Lake Chad, with a focus on its biological structure and food-web, was published in 1983 (Carmouze et al. 1983). The hydrology of the lake has been presented in a more-recent book (Olivry et al. 1996). Compared with the lake, the riverine floodplains have been much-less studied – especially the Salamat floodplains. The importance of the Hadejia–Nguru wetland for the waterfowl has drawn the attention of the IUCN (the World Conservation Union) when dams have been constructed in the upper basin of the wetland. An analysis of some aspects of its ecology and a proposal for management plans have been presented by Hollis et al. (1993). As part of the Extreme North Province in Cameroon, many aspects of the Yaere have been described in an atlas of this province (Seignobos and Iyébi-Mandjek 2000).

Hydrological cycles in the Chad basin wetlands

The extension of the floodplains in the Chad basin results from the combination of the seasonality of the rainy season and a very flat landscape. For instance, the mean slope of the lower 700 km of River Chari is only 0.1 m km^{-1}.

Table 9.1 *Mean annual budget of two riverine floodplains in the Chari–Logone system (from Gac 1980).*

	Input	Output	Budget
Yaere			
Rain − evaporation (km^3)	8.5	10.55	
Suspended solids (× 10^3 t)	897	27	−870
Dissolved substances (× 10^3 t)	185	151	−34
Surface water (km^3)	1.7	0.8	−0.9
Massenya			
Rain − evaporation (km^3)	11.55	12.45	
Suspended solids (× 10^3 t)	257	16	−241
Dissolved substances (× 10^3 t)	104	101	−3
Surface water (km^3)	3.2	1.15	−2.05

The rains are brought by the displacement of the intertropical convergence zone (ITCZ), which moves northward over the active part of the basin from February to August at a mean speed of 200 km per month. The rains occur earlier than the river flood in the floodplains of the lower basin. They usually contribute to the beginning of the growing season of the vegetation and to the inundation of the lower depressions, while the overspill from the rivers starts later. In the Yaere (11° to 12° N), the two successive events occur, respectively, in June to July and in late August or September. During October and November, the water flows back to the River Logone and to Lake Chad via the El Beïd. In December, the surface water is restricted to a small number of isolated pools; very few of these pools hold water until the next rainy season, except when they have been artificially deepened.

Tentative estimates have been made of the water volume, and the dissolved and particulate solids budgets of some floodplains of the Chad Basin. Examples are given in Table 9.1 for the Yaere and Massenya floodplains. Even though the duration of inundation does not exceed six months, the losses of water through evaporation exceed the direct rainfall input. As a result, the surface outflow is smaller than the inflow. Preliminary results of a recent UNESCO programme indicate that the floodplain does not contribute significantly to the recharge of the water table (B. Mpondo, personal communication 2000). The floodplains may thus be considered as sinks in the regional water budget.

Lake Chad lies in an endoreic basin: there is no surface outflow; river and rain inputs are compensated mainly by evaporation, by some seepage (between 5% and 10%), and by area changes according to both seasonal and interannual variations in inputs (Carmouze *et al.* 1983).

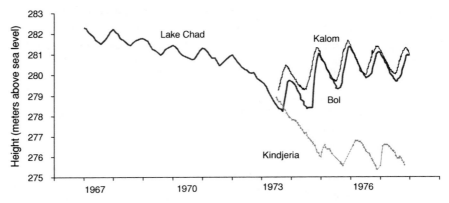

Figure 9.4 The change in the water level of Lake Chad from 1966 to 1979, as a result of the Sahelian drought. In 1973, the lake was split into separate water bodies, and the Bol gauge became indicative of only part of the eastern archipelago and of the open water in the southern basin. In the "small" Chad state, the northern basin of the lake is separated from the main inflow by the Grande Barrière ("Great Barrier"). It is fed by direct rain, some inflows from the Yobe River, and overspills over the Grande Barrière when the Chari inputs are sufficient. The "small" Chad was still prevailing in 2004. See Fig. 9.3 for the locations of the gauge stations.

The interannual variability

During the last century, the African Sahel experienced some climatic variations with some drought periods resulting from a shorter displacement of the seasonal northward migration of the intertropical convergence zone. Relatively short drought periods have occurred from 1904 to 1915 and around 1940, with low inflows to Lake Chad and a marked reduction of its surface area. Another drought period started at the beginning of the 1970s and was still prevailing in 2004. The whole rainfall distribution has shifted southward by some 150 km (a loss of 150 mm over most of the basin) with impacts on the hydrology of the rivers, the floodplains, and Lake Chad (Fig. 9.4). It is thus very important to state to which period a description of the aquatic system applies.

The mean annual rainfall on Lake Chad has been estimated as 329 mm per year for the period 1950–71, and only 207 mm in 1972–89 (Olivry *et al.* 1996). In the southern floodplains of the Chari–Logone basin (Salamat), the annual rainfall has decreased by 150 mm from a long-term mean of 1037 mm per year (1921–2000) (L'Hôte *et al.* 2002).

Most of the observations on the floodplains were made before the present drought period. For Lake Chad, the observations cover both humid and dry periods during the transition from a "normal" to the present "small" Lake Chad.

Table 9.2 *Influence of the water level during the River Logone peak flood (Bongor gauge) on the hydrology of its floodplain (the Yaere on the left bank and the Chari–Logone plain on the right bank) (from Lemoalle 1979a).*

	Water level at peak flood at Bongor (m at gauge)	Peak water level of the Yaere outflow (m at Tilde gauge)	Total inundated area (km²)
1972–3	3.50	0.95	1 777
1975–6	4.25	4.20	11 600

The duration and extent of the inundation of a riverine floodplain depends upon the river flood. The water spills over the lower sills in the natural levees along the river when the river level or the discharge has attained some characteristic threshold value. For instance, the occasionally outflowing branch Bahr Erguig starts feeding the Massenya floodplain when the River Chari reaches 3.5 m on the gauge in Miltou, a nearby upstream locality. This has happened only twice during the last 25 years, because of low river discharge, and the inundation of the floodplain has been limited to small ponds.

The extent of the inundation of the Yaere depends mainly on the flood of the River Logone. In Table 9.2 values for the dry year 1972–3 have been compared with a normal year such as 1975–6: a minimum of 3.5 m at the Bongor gauge (discharge of 1200 m^3 s^{-1}) is needed to initiate the main flood in the Yaere.

Since 1973 and the onset of a dry climatic sequence in the African Sahel, river floods have been much lower, with a mean annual discharge from the River Chari to Lake Chad as follows (data from Direction des Ressources en Eau et de la Météorologie, DREM, Chad):

- period 1960–9,   41.0 km^3;
- period 1970–9,   31.1 km^3;
- period 1980–9,   16.6 km^3;
- period 1990–9,   20.4 km^3.

According to the decrease in water inflows, the area of Lake Chad has changed considerably, from a "normal" to a "small" Lake Chad. "Normal" here refers to a state when there was only one single body of water covering about 18 000 to 20 000 km^2, while "small" applies to several water bodies separated by shoals covered with a dense vegetation through which the water overflows occasionally during the lake flood. The pictures provided by the US Geological Survey (USGS 2001) are clear examples of the observed changes. They also illustrate the

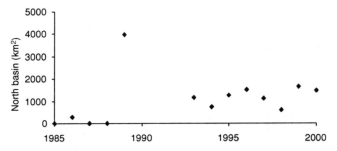

Figure 9.5 Maximum annual open-water extent in the northern basin of Lake Chad. The area is measured from Meteosat data, using the reflectance of open water as a reference, the large inundated marshes covered with vegetation are not included (updated from Lemoalle 1991).

inundation–submersion cycle of a system of sand dunes (erg) which form the northeast coast of the lake. As the water level decreases, new dune summits appear and form new islands; when the summits are about 0.5 m below the surface, reeds develop and form patches of vegetation which are locally called "reed islands."

One of the main shoals between isolated water bodies of the lake is the Grande Barrière. It separates the southern basin of the lake, fed directly by the River Chari inflows, and the northern basin which receives a small contribution from the Yobe River (mean of 430 Mm^3 per year between 1980 and 2000) and the over-spill of the southern-basin when the River Chari flood is sufficient. The extent of the yearly inundation in the northern basin of Lake Chad usually occurs in January. It has been monitored from daily Meteosat data, using the reflectance of the southern-basin open water as a reference (Lemoalle 1991, Olivry et al. 1996) (Fig. 9.5).

The Hadejia–Nguru wetlands are situated between the cities of Hadejia, Katagum, Gashua, and Nguru in the northeast of Nigeria. The annual wet-season flooding was over 2000 km^2 in the 1960s and around 1500 km^2 in the 1970s. Between 1964 and 1987 observed flood extents ranged from 50 to 3265 km^2. Subsequently dams have been constructed in the upper basin of the Yobe River. Estimations have shown that full implementation of all the schemes planned would cause flooding to be less than 375 km^2 for 60% of the time and ground-water storage would fall by over 5500 Mm^3. Alternative water-management plans have been proposed to provide artificial floods and to enable satisfactory distri-bution of water between formal irrigation, small-scale irrigators, the wetlands, and downstream users. This regime would provide assured flooding, of around 1000 km^2 each year, and a reduced loss of groundwater storage (Thompson & Hollis 1995).

Recently, weed development (*Typha*) and blockages on the Hadejia River have been attributed to increased dry-season flows (from 4% to 32% of the annual flow) after the completion of the Hadejia Barrage. These blockages contribute to the inundation of the floodplain during the rainy season (Goes 2001).

Geochemical processes

The overspill from the river toward the floodplain occurs only when a given water level has been attained. This occurs usually when the concentration of suspended solids is high (up to $900\,mg\,l^{-1}$ in the River Logone). The major sedimentation of particles in the floodplain is clearly related to the suspended-solids concentration of the Chari and Logone rivers when overspills occur, with mean concentrations of 200 to $300\,mg\,l^{-1}$ (Gac 1980). A resulting apparent paradox is that a larger quantity of sediments is brought to the lake during years with a low flood (no overspill to the floodplain) than during wet years (Lemoalle 1974). During the recession of the river level, very clear water flows from the floodplains back to the river, with a suspended-solids concentration often less than $10\,mg\,l^{-1}$.

Analyses of the major dissolved substances have shown a slight loss in the floodplains, as a result of interactions between the dissolved material, clay, and living or dead organic matter particles during evaporation in the floodplain (Table 9.1). Silica, calcium, and magnesium were found to be partly retained in the floodplain.

The impact of the formation of a dense macrophytic vegetation on the ionic contents of the water has been observed in Lake Chad at Bol, a station where the water chemistry has been monitored weekly over three successive years. Before the macrophyte establishment (in 1973), the water evaporation during the dry season led to an increase in conductivity and sodium and potassium concentrations, while calcium and magnesium partly precipitated. In the middle of 1973, a very-low water level was attained, and the first rains promoted an extensive germination of seeds buried in the sediment. In 1974 and 1975 the water circulated through a dense vegetation consisting mainly of *Cyperus papyrus*, *Typha australis*, and *Aeschynomene elaphroxylon*. In the presence of macrophytes, the potassium concentration was lowered (potassium was absorbed by the macrophytes which contained about 2.2% potassium dry weight), but the relative composition of the other ions remained similar to that of the River Chari which feeds 95% of the surface input to the lake (Table 9.3).

Before the macrophyte establishment, calcium and magnesium were mainly involved in chemical equilibria with precipitation of carbonates, adsorption on suspended clay particles, and possible neoformation of clay (Carmouze 1983).

Table 9.3 *Relative cationic composition of the lake water at Bol before and after the development of macrophytes (dry season, conductivity 400 µS cm⁻¹), of the River Chari water (annual mean), and of the aquatic macrophytes. Ca, Mg, Na, and K are given as a percentage of total cation mass per liter (from Lemoalle 2002).*

	Ca (%)	Mg (%)	Na (%)	K (%)
Lake at Bol on May 22, 1973	16.9	19.4	47.8	16.0
Lake at Bol on June 20, 1974	39.0	34.9	22.9	3.2
Macrophytes	20.2	12.4	3.3	64.0
River Chari annual mean	39.3	36.9	14.8	9.1

In the presence of macrophytes, an increased CO_2 partial pressure ($10^{-2.4}$ atm) was attributed to the decomposition of the organic matter associated with the macrophytes. It prevented the precipitation of calcium and magnesium carbonates, while sorption equilibria were limited by a reduced fetch and low sediment resuspension.

Flora and fauna

The vegetation

Riverine floodplains

The distribution of the macrophytic vegetation of a floodplain depends upon three main variables: the soil quality, and the depth and the duration of the inundation. The data presented below are from Fotius (2000) and Gaston (1996). They indicate three main types of vegetation in the Yaere depending on the inundation cycle (Fig. 9.6).

Grass savanna is found on areas of deep water and long duration of inundation with *Vossia cuspidata* and *Echinochloa stagnina* along the longer-lasting channels. Other species colonizing these areas are *Echinochloa obtusiflora*, *Sorghum lanceolatum*, or *Panicum anabaptistum*. *Hyparrhenia rufa* is found in areas of moderate depth and long inundation duration, but with a variety of ecotypes.

Shrub savanna (moderate inundation duration and depth) contains woody species tolerant of some flooding such as: *Pseudocedrela kotschyi*, *Mitragyna inermis*, *Piliostigma thonningii*, and *P. reticulata*; and some *Acacia* species, *A. seyal*, *A. sieberiana*, and *A. ataxacantha*. The grass species include those found in the grass savanna as well as *Echinochloa colona*, *Panicum maximum* and *P. anabaptistum*, *Pennisetum pedicellatum*, and *Eriochloa fatmensis*.

Thorny shrub steppes withstanding only short flooding are characterized by several species of *Acacia* – *A. seyal*, *A. nilotica*, and *A. campylacanta* – and grasses

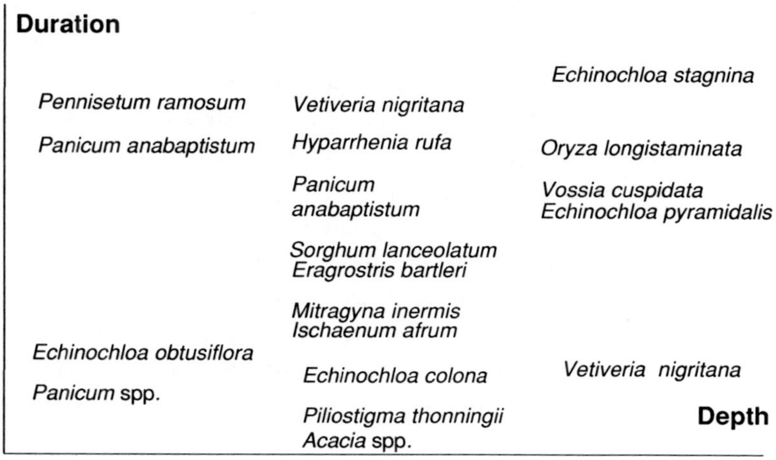

Duration

		Echinochloa stagnina
Pennisetum ramosum	*Vetiveria nigritana*	
Panicum anabaptistum	*Hyparrhenia rufa*	*Oryza longistaminata*
	Panicum anabaptistum	*Vossia cuspidata* *Echinochloa pyramidalis*
	Sorghum lanceolatum *Eragrostris bartleri*	
	Mitragyna inermis *Ischaenum afrum*	
Echinochloa obtusiflora	*Echinochloa colona*	*Vetiveria nigritana*
Panicum spp.	*Piliostigma thonningii* *Acacia* spp.	**Depth**

Figure 9.6 Schematic distribution of the main macrophytes in the floodplain, according to depth and to duration of the flood. The three main groups have been determined according to the depth axis.

such as *Sorghum aethiopicum, S. lanceolatum, Panicum laetum, Eriochloa fatmensis,* and *Echinochloa obtusiflora.*

The small quasi-permanent ponds are most-often devoid of macrophytes, but some of them have *Nymphea, Utricularia,* and sometimes *Polygonum.*

Lake Chad

Descriptions of the macrophyte vegetation have been published by Léonard (1969) for the "normal," pre-1973, Lake Chad; and by Fotius (1974, 2000) for the transition to, and stabilization of, the "small" Lake Chad. A summary of these data has been given by Iltis and Lemoalle (1983).

Observations during the "normal" Lake Chad indicated a south–north gradient with the progressive disappearance of *Cyperus papyrus* and an increase in the density of *Typha australis* associated with a progressive increase in water conductivity. Rooted and floating vegetation was found mainly along the shores on the flat and clayey shores in the south, and on the sandy and steeper dune flanks in the northeast archipelago. The species were common to the Sahel and West African water bodies: *Jussiaea repens, Polygonum senegalense, Cyperus maculatus, C. bulbosus, C. articulatus,* and *Typha domingensis.* Floating euhydrophytes were mainly represented by *Pistia stratiotes* and *Salvinia molesta.* Until now, *Eichhornia crassipes* has not been recorded. Compared with helophytes, submersed plants covered smaller areas; the main species were *Potamogeton schweinfurthii, Vallisneria spiralis,* and *Ceratophyllum demersum.*

Reed islands, common in the southern basin, were mainly colonized by *Phragmites australis*, *Cyperus papyrus*, and *Vossia cuspidata*. They became more numerous during the transition to "small" Lake Chad in 1973–4.

The lake shores were then covered with the woody species *Mimosa pigra*, *Sesbania* spp., and the tall leguminous *Aeschynomene elaphroxylon*. The seeds of this plant can stand several years in the sediment under water. They germinate only when the sediment is exundated. The plant grows very quickly and may reach 7 to 8 m in less than a year. The vascular trunk, up to 0.3 m in diameter, is made of a very light wood that is used as floats by the people inhabiting the islands.

Prosopis sp., an invading exotic tree, has developed on large areas of the northern basin of the lake during the years 1980–90. The species cannot withstand long inundation. After 1999, when the flooding of this basin became longer and deeper, many of the trees died.

Biomass estimates of the above-ground aquatic vegetation have been given at the end of the "normal" Lake Chad in 1970: for a vegetated surface area of 2400 km^2, the biomass was 7 210 000 t dry weight, with a density of 3 kg m^{-2} for *Cyperus papyrus* and *Phragmites* stands (Carmouze et al. 1978).

Microalgae have been surveyed, both qualitatively and quantitatively, in Lake Chad and in the lower River Chari: about 1300 species and infraspecific taxa were collected, in which diatoms and desmids were the most numerous. Cyanophyceae were the main contributors to the biomass (Compère & Iltis 1983). During the transition period to the "small" Lake Chad, some isolated pools behaved as evaporation pans, with a sharp increase in their morphoedaphic index (increasing conductivity and decreasing depth). The phytoplankton concentration followed closely the morphoedaphic index and reached high values, in the range 500 to 2000 mg Chl m^{-3} (where "Chl" is chlorophyll) (Lemoalle 1983).

The aquatic fauna

Extensive studies on the taxonomy, distribution, and productivity of the zooplankton and of the benthic organisms (oligochaetes, molluscs, and insects) have been conducted from 1966 to 1975 in Lake Chad, but not in the riverine floodplains (Lévêque et al. 1983). They indicated a rich bottom fauna, with a biomass dominated by molluscs, benefiting from organic detritus and favorable oxygenation near the water–sediment interface. Fewer data are available for the "small" Lake Chad period and its extensive cover of macrophytes (Lévêque & Saint-Jean 1983).

The zooplankton of the "normal" Lake Chad was diverse – when compared with other African lakes – with nine abundant species, of which seven were simultaneously present and abundant throughout the year (three cladocera, one calanoid, and three cyclopoids). During the beginning of the "small" Lake Chad period, modifications in species composition were observed, with a great increase in rotifer numbers, the development of some cyclopoids – particularly *Thermocyclops neglectus* – and the regression of cladocera other than *Moina* and *Diaphanosoma* (Saint-Jean 1983).

The Chad basin shares a number of fish species in common with the neighbouring Niger, Congo–Zaïre, and Nile basins. There are no endemic fish species in the Chad basin, and, within this basin, no species is restricted to the lake itself. This last observation may be related to the long-term instability of the lake, with possible periods of quasi-total dryness. A total of 128 species from 25 families have been described which belong to the Nilo-Soudanian province (Lévêque & Paugy 1999).

Many of the fish migrate for reproduction, either within the lake or within the river basin, or from the lake to the river system. When dealing with fish ecology, Lake Chad with the lower reaches of the River Chari and its floodplains on the one hand, and the Komadugu Yobe up to its floodplain on the other hand, may be regarded as ecological units. A typical behavior, which would equally apply to a number of other species, may be described for *Alestes baremoze* (a zooplanktivorous Characidae), a major component of the fisheries' catches in the pre-drought period. The adults migrate from the lake upstream at the beginning of the rainy season; some spawn in the river, close to the floodplain inflows, others penetrate into the floodplain to spawn. The juveniles grow for three to four months in the floodplains where they benefit from the epibionts associated with the macrophytes and also from a low pressure from predators. They return to the lake either by the main river or by the El Beïd, a direct outflow of the Yaere to the lake.

Many young fishes were caught over this period by traditional fisheries, but adults also formed an important part of the catches during their upstream migration. The adult fish have become less important since 1975 and the advent of the dry period, except in the years immediately after rather high floods of the Chari and Logone rivers (e.g. 1989 or 1998). This has been interpreted as a restoration of the population, even with the modest size of the breeding stock, when good conditions for the development of the juveniles are provided by a large and lengthy inundation of the floodplains.

It has been observed that the juvenile fish usually return to the main water body in a given order, according to the outflow from the floodplain (Fig. 9.7). More generally, the relationship described for other floodplain systems by Welcomme (1979) also applies to the fisheries of the Yaere and the

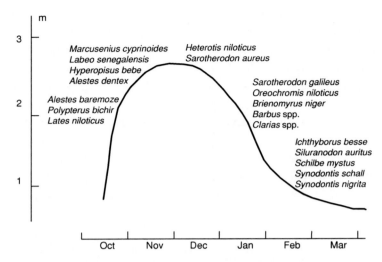

Figure 9.7 Groups of migratory fish species observed at Daga, a station on the El Beïd outlet from the Yaere, as a function of time and water level (solid line) (from Bénech & Quensière 1983).

Chari–Logone floodplain: the fish catch is a function of the extent/duration of the inundation (see Fig. 9.8 below).

Other floodplains also contribute as fish habitats and breeding areas: integrated management, including fisheries management and breeding stock conservation in the Hadejia–Nguru wetlands on the Komadugu Yobe, has recently been studied (Hollis *et al.* 1993). The aquatic ecology of the floodplains of the middle (Massenya, Chari–Logone floodplains) and upper Chari basin (Salamat) remains poorly, if at all, documented. The Salamat floodplain has been considered as the main supplier of dried fish to the Central African Republic.

Communities distribution and environmental conditions

In Lake Chad, variations in time and space of environmental conditions may be considered as primary factors influencing the distribution of the aquatic flora and fauna. Let us first consider spatial distribution.

Spatial distribution

During the "normal" Lake Chad, some variation in the distribution of some organisms was observed and was related to the water conductivity, which increased through evaporation as a function of the distance from the River Chari delta. Characteristic values were about $80 \, \mu S \, cm^{-1}$ near the delta and

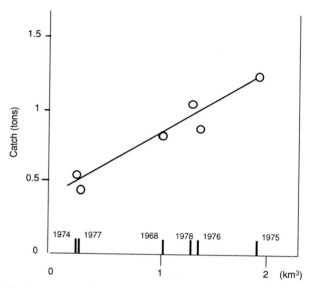

Figure 9.8 Relationship between fish catch at Daga, on the main outflow of the Yaere, and the floodplain hydrology (from Bénech & Quensière 1983).

$1200\,\mu S\,cm^{-1}$ along the north shore of the northern basin of the lake. The correlated biological changes included the following groups:

1. As stated above, some macrophytes common in the southern basin (low conductivity), such as *Cyperus papyrus*, were absent from the northern basin. The limit was about 300 to $500\,\mu S\,cm^{-1}$ and could not be attributed to any other environmental factor.

2. The quality of the sediment was clearly an important variable for the distribution of the zoobenthos in the lake. However, in stations with similar sediments, some benthic organisms were nevertheless absent from the northern basin. These include oligochaetes (Alluroididae replaced by Tubificidae on clay sediments) and molluscs (*Cleopatra bulinoides, Bellamya unicolor,* or *Melania tuberculata*). Benthic molluscs were totally absent in stations of the northern basin where the conductivity reached $750\,\mu S\,cm^{-1}$, whereas pulmonate molluscs were present. Besides the influence of conductivity, the possibility of a lack of recolonization after dry episodes may also be invoked here.

3. The distribution of some species of chironomid larvae was also related to the water quality: some of them preferred high conductivities – such as *Chironomus calipterus* and *Dicrotendipes polosimanus* – while others were more abundant in stations with a low water conductivity, e.g. *Chironomus pulcher, C. acuminatus,* and *Dicrotendipes peryngeyanus* (Lévêque *et al.* 1983).

4. Some fish species were also absent from the northern half of the north-ern basin, the more-saline region of the lake, but were present almost everywhere in the basin. They included *Schilbe uranoscopus*, *Brachysynodon-tis batensoda*, and several species of Mormyridae such as *Pollimyrus isidori* or *Hyperopisus bebe*. The absence of the mormyrids may be explained by their use of electric signals to investigate their environment and to communicate. When the water conductivity increases, the field of their electric signal is modified and becomes less useful because of a much-reduced range.

Changes in distribution with time

A major factor of change in habitat has been the transition from the previous "normal" lake with large open-water areas to the "small" lake with extensive permanent or seasonal marshes. Some processes involved during the transition will be dealt with further in this chapter. What is described in this section is the differences in the composition of the fish community, and of the fish catch resulting from the changes in the lake habitats (Table 9.4).

Intensive sampling has been operated with beach seine (1971–2) and gillnets in the archipelago of the southern basin (Bol region) from April, 1971 to March, 1977 (Bénech & Quensière 1983). In the Bol region, the environment changed from a "normal" lake with some aquatic vegetation fringing the islands in 1971–2 to a generalized marsh with small areas of open deep water from 1974 to the present time. As a result of changes in the local habitat and maybe also, for some species, in the accessibility of the floodplains, about 22 species disappeared from the experimental catch in the Bol region while a few others appeared for the first time. Five of the new or remaining species had accessory respiratory organs, a favorable attribute for living in the marshes.

New fishing techniques have been adapted to the marsh environment, and have resulted in an increase in the production of catfish (*Clarias* spp.) and tilapias (*Oreochromis*, *Sarotherodon*, and *Tilapia sensu stricto*) in the more-permanent south-ern basin as well as in the northern basin which has been functioning as a seasonal floodplain over recent times.

The water-related fauna

Although most terrestrial animals are dependent on surface water for their survival, we shall here restrict our scope to those that spend most of their time in marshes or wetlands. Chardonnet and Lamarque (1996) have given a general overview of the wildlife in the Lake Chad Conventional Basin, which is partly used here.

Table 9.4 *Changes in the fish communities around Bol in the archipelago of the southern basin of Lake Chad.*

Fish species	1971–2	1976–7
Mormyrus rume[a]	+	
Mormyrops anguilloides	+	
Hyppopotamyrus pictus	++	
Bagrus bajad	+	
Chrysichthys auratus	+	
Labeo coubie	+	
Brycinus macrolepidotus	+	
Hydrocynus brevis[a]	+	
Hydrocynus forskalii	+	
Citharinus citharus[a]	+	
Hemisynodontis membranaceus[a]	+	
Lates niloticus	+	
Hyperopisus bebe[a]	+	
Marcusenius cyprinoides[a]	+	
Petrocephalus bane[a]	+	
Pollimyrus isidori[a]	+	
Labeo senegalensis[a]	+	
Schilbe mystus[a]	+	
Synodontis clarias	+	
Polypterus bichir[b]	+	
Polypterus endlicheri[b]	+	
Auchenoglanis spp.	+	
Schilbe uranoscopus[a]	+	(+)
Brachysynodontis batensoda[a]	+	(+)
Synodontis frontosus	+	(+)
Synodontis schall[a]	+	+
Alestes dentex[a]	+	+
Alestes baremoze[a]	+	+
Brycinus nurse	+	+
Distichodus rostratus[b]	+	+
Gymnarchus niloticus[b]	+	+
Clarias spp.[b]	+	+
Tilapia zillii	+	+
Sarotherodon galileus	+	+
Oreochromis niloticus	+	+
Oreochromis aureus	+	+
Polypterus senegalus[b]	(+)	+
Schilbe intermedius	(+)	+
Heterotis niloticus[b]	(+)	+
Brienomyrus niger[b]	(+)	+
Siluranodon auritus		+

[a] Fish usually migrating in the River Chari lower basin.

[b] Fish species with accessory respiratory organs.

Fish that were rare or present for only part of the time periods are indicated with parentheses. Simplified from Bénech and Quensière (1983).

The hippopotamus (*Hippopotamus amphibius*) is a common resident of the lower River Chari and of Lake Chad. It spends the daytime in the water and feeds on grasses at night. During the drought, with the disappearance of both aquatic and terrestrial vegetation, there has been a strong mortality of the species as the Lake level receded. The animals lost much weight and energy, and many died in the mud of isolated pools of the lake or were killed for their meat. A rather-large group survived in the River Chari delta.

Two African otter species may be observed in Lake Chad: the spotted-necked otter *Lutra maculicollis*, which is registered in the IUCN *Red List of Threatened Species*; and the larger African clawless otter *Aonyx capensis*, with a body of over 60 to 100 cm long. Both are considered as competitors by fishermen.

Among the antelopes, the sitatunga (*Tragelaphus spekei*) is probably the most water dependent. It lives in the permanent marshes of the southern shore of Lake Chad and may swim across some distances between islands in the archipelago. Its status is at present not precisely known (rare or endangered). A variety of other antelopes spend a large part of the year in the floodplains, to graze upon the annual or perennial grasses, but their presence here is more related to the available fodder than to the aquatic system itself: the Buffon's kob (*Kobus kob kob*), the Defassa waterbuck (*Kobus ellipsiprymnus*), the Bohor reedbuck (*Redunca redunca*) or the Central African korrigum *(Damaliscus lunatus)* may be seen in abundance, especially in national parks, but to a lesser extent than 50 years ago.

The crocodile (*Crocodylus niloticus*) is legally protected and the trade of its skin is forbidden. It is present in small numbers in the rivers and in Lake Chad, but it is reported to have disappeared from Lake Fitri after heavy commercial shooting some 50 years ago. The Nile monitor (*Varanus niloticus*) has benefited from the development of the marshes of the "small" Lake Chad and is quite commonly seen. This is in contrast to the rarely observed aquatic terrapins from the lower River Chari and Lake Chad, *Pelomedusa subrufa* and *Pelosius subniger*.

A great number of migratory and sedentary species of birds are found in the Lake Chad basin. We shall here rely mainly on Dejoux (1983) for Lake Chad and on Chardonnet and Lamarque (1996) for the whole basin, considering only those birds which are dependent on wetlands.

Endemic bird species are rare and the recently described river prinia (*Prinia fluviatilis*) is already considered to be endangered.

The Chad basin wetlands are a main feature for migratory palaearctic and Afrotropical birds. They are situated on the Mediterranean route with El Kala (Algeria) and Ichkeul (Tunisia) wetlands as the first African stations on the way from Europe to the African coast between Ghana and Angola. Some 70 species make stopovers each year, including numerous garganey (*Anas querquedula*), pin-tail (*A. acuta*), and the ruff (*Philomachus pugnax*). Other numerically important species include grey heron (*Ardea cinera*) and purple heron (*A. purpurea*), large flocks of crested cranes (*Regulorum gibbericeps*), the black-winged stilt (*Himantopus himantopus*) and the glossy ibis. The white stork (*Ciconia ciconia*) breeds in Europe but winters in great numbers in the Chad basin, where it feeds on locusts and is then much less dependent on water than when in Europe.

The distribution of the waterfowl depends on the availability of water, food, and shelter; it may change from one wetland to another, from year to year or within one season. The permanent shallow Maga Lake, the man-made reservoir upstream of rice fields in the Yaere, attracts great numbers of Afrotropical water birds (90 000 have been counted) such as the white-faced tree duck (*Dendrocygna viduata*), the spur-winged goose (*Plectropterus gambiensis*), or the knob-nosed goose (*Sarkidiornis melanotos*).

Pelicans (*Pelecanus onocrolatus*) and shags (*Phalacrocorax africanus*) may be seen in large numbers in the Chari delta and on the southern basin of Lake Chad. Caspian and gull-billed terns (*Sterna tschegrava* and *S. nilotica*) are mainly fish eaters while the whiskered and white-winged black terns (*S. hybrida* and *S. leucoptera*) have a mixed diet of fish and insects. The large emergence of chironomids or mayflies often leads to considerable aggregations of white-winged black terns. The lily trotter and the lesser lily trotter (*Actophilornis africana* and *Microparra capensis*) live near stands of submersed plants such as *Potamogeton* and also feed on aquatic insects and larvae.

Some important ecological processes

Time-related processes

In the riverine floodplains of the Chad basin, an important ecological determinant is obviously the succession in time of a number of events. The first rains may be considered as the trigger. They usually start a little earlier in the floodplains than over the lake. They allow for the germination of seeds and the start of the vegetative period for perennials in the floodplain and give a signal to the maturing fish in the lake and in the main riverbed. The young plants (*Echinochloa*) have to be able to grow sufficiently before the inundation to avoid complete submersion, and the fish have to spawn when the inflow into the floodplain allows for the dispersal of eggs, larvae, or juveniles.

Rains on the upper reaches of the basin generate the river flood. They occur some time before the first rainfall on the lake, which is taken as the signal for fish migration. However, the success of the fish reproduction depends on the synchronicity of the presence of mature fish and of a sufficient river water level at the main connections of the floodplain with the river. As all the fish do not migrate at exactly the same moment, all of them do not reach the floodplain entrance at the best moment for the success of their reproduction. The between-year variability of the time sequence of rain and flood ensures that different species may be the most successful at reproducing in different years; this is favorable for the conservation of biodiversity. In addition, the proper biological rhythm may also interfere: the spawning of some species such as *Brycinus leuciscus* is clearly related to the lunar cycle, which may not coincide with the inflow to the floodplain (Bénech 2002).

The same interannual variability in the rainfall and river discharge also has a qualitative and quantitative influence on the fish community. In a wet year, a high flood discharge has several positive impacts:

- a long inflow of river water to the floodplain increases the likelihood of the juveniles having access to the plain.
- the plain is inundated for a longer period, and the young fish may benefit longer from the shelter and access to more food.

On the negative side, in a dry year the few species normally surviving during the dry season – in the ponds remaining in the plain – may become dried out before the reproduction.

A relationship between fish catch and the extent (or duration) of the inundation of riverine tropical floodplains has been proposed by Welcomme (1979). This relationship applies to the Yaere; especially if the group of *Oreochromis–Sarotherodon*, which belong to the sedentary fraction of the El Beïd river community, is excluded (Fig. 9.7).

The match between hydrological and biological events, as described for the fish, is also important for other components of the floodplain such as the migratory birds nesting in the trees of the floodplain that prey on the juvenile fish to feed their youngsters. The same applies to the domestic or wild herbivorous fauna that breed at the beginning of the rainy season and graze first upon rain-fed grasses and later on the vegetation of the floodplain: the longer the inundation, the longer the availability of fodder (and water) from the lowest areas; this is necessary for the growth of the young animals and their survival until the next rainy season.

Trends and reversibility

Periods of dry climate and low river discharge have an obvious impact on the extent of the floodplains, and thus on their vegetation and their ecological functioning. Reduced extent of flooding may also result from water diversion for other uses. It has been observed in the past that the interannual variability is a component of the long-term functioning of the floodplains. The question then arises as to the reversibility of a multi-year drought such as the one observed in the African Sahel. What would happen if the "normal" hydrological cycle was re-established? A small set of observations on the Yaere and on the fisheries indicate that some reversibility is possible, but the critical values for some variables are as yet undefined.

The Yaere has been affected both by the drought and by the construction of the Maga Dam which blocked part of the inflow to the floodplain. The Waza Logone Project was set up by IUCN to restore some flooding by opening the Maga Dam and other dams along the River Logone (Braund 2000). The experiment was performed from 1994 to 1997 with variable water inputs. It has been reported that an increase of the inflow from the river proved favorable for some fishing activities, and the 300 km² increase in the inundated surface area has allowed the regrowth of the perennials grazed during the dry season by the cattle and the large wild mammals of the Waza National Park. It is, however, difficult to estimate the time elapsed since the previous inundation of the observed area, and thus the maximum sustainable duration of the absence of inundation.

Since 1976, relatively high river floods (within the drought period) and extensive inundation of the Chari–Logone floodplains have occurred in 1978, 1988, 1998, 1999, and 2001. Observations from fisheries in the year following these floods have indicated a significant increase in the catch of one-year-old migratory fish species with high fecundity, such as *Alestes baremoze*. Here also, the minimum breeding stock has until now been preserved, despite heavy fishing pressure with fine-meshed nets. This positive reaction is probably due to the complementarities between the habitats – floodplain, Lake Chad, and the lower River Chari.

Further upstream in the River Chari – and especially in the River Logone and River Yobe where water uptake for irrigation during the dry season strongly decreases the available space for fish, and increases its catchability – the question of the conservation of a minimal breeding stock should be considered.

Some fish of the floodplains may be considered as sedentary: the black fish, as opposed to the migratory white fish (Welcomme 1979). Before the onset of the rains, these sedentary fish survive in the water or in the mud of the remaining pools and are adapted to low concentrations of dissolved oxygen. They usually breed at the beginning of the rainy season. Some may also survive without water, by encysting in a cocoon in dry mud (*Protopterus annectens*) or by laying diapausing eggs that hatch at the beginning of the next rainy season (*Nothobranchus*). In traditional fisheries of floodplain ponds – a social and localized exploitation of a common resource – some management of the breeding stock has been maintained through accepted regulations, allowing for the survival of some fish through the dry season. Such a protection is especially useful in dry years when the environmental conditions in the pools worsen because of the relatively short duration of the previous inundation. With an increased local population, and the drought-driven migration of new ethnic groups toward water, the traditional regulations are sometimes overcome. The combination of natural and human pressures may then threaten the sustainability of the fishery.

Depth-related processes

The period of the progressive recession of the water level in Lake Chad was the occasion to monitor environmental changes in the lake until the emergence of large surface areas of sediment which split the formerly single lake into several independent water bodies. Changes in some environmental variables (water transparency and conductivity), and in some biological components (chlorophyll concentration, and fish mass mortalities) are summarized here.

Rather strong winds occur on Lake Chad, with a mean annual wind speed greater than $5\,\mathrm{m\,s^{-1}}$ in the morning, between 0600 h and midday. This wind and a rather-long fetch explain the low water transparency as a result of the stirring of the bottom sediments. With decreasing depth, the sediment became progressively more exposed to turbulence and the transparency decreased steadily in the different regions of the lake:

- from 1.2 m in October, 1964 to 0.1 m in July, 1973 in Bol, in the southern basin of the lake,
- from 0.8 m in December, 1967 to less than 0.1 m in July, 1975 in Kindjeria, in the northern basin (Fig. 9.9, from Lemoalle 1979b).

Apart from a progressive decrease in transparency, the increased sensitivity of the lake bottom to wind-induced turbulence first appeared in the rainy season of 1972, when mass fish mortalities occurred after short violent storms, strong sediment resuspension, and a resulting partial anoxia ($0.5\,\mathrm{mg\,O_2\,l^{-1}}$); a phenomenon that had not occurred in previous years but which happened on different occasions in 1973 and 1974 (Bénech et al. 1976). Progressive changes were also observed in the benthic-mollusc community during the recession of the water level, especially in the regions of soft sediment. These changes were attributed to the same increased bottom turbulence (Lévêque et al. 1983).

The decrease in transparency was initially a result of an increase in bottom turbulence and suspended sediment but the phytoplankton played an increasing part in the light attenuation. The phytoplankton concentration increased from 10–20 mg Chl m^{-3} in 1967 to 250 mg m^{-3} in Bol in September, 1973 and 2500 mg m^{-3} in Kindjeria during August, 1974. These high concentrations were

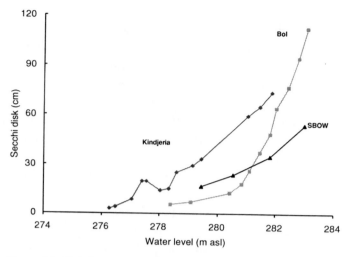

Figure 9.9 The changes in water transparency as a function of water level (meters above sea level) in three regions of Lake Chad during a period of progressive level recession: Bol (1964–73), Kindjeria (1967–75), and the southern basin open water (SBOW) near Kalom (1964–76) (from Lemoalle 1979b).

measured in isolated ponds that had been subjected to strong evaporation with resulting high conductivity. With low inflows to the lake, the decrease in water level was caused by an excess of evaporation compared with the inputs and resulted in a relative increase of the water conductivity. In these environments, the phytoplankton concentration increased as a direct function of the morphoedaphic index (water conductivity: mean depth), from the "normal" Lake Chad of c. 20 000 km² to small ponds less than 1 ha in surface area.

While the phytoplankton, with a short response time, have apparently coped with the environmental changes, the belts of rooted macrophytes along the shores could not follow the rapid level recession and most of them disappeared in 1973. A new community developed with the germination of seeds in the exposed sediments at the beginning of the rainy season, and continued its expansion in the following years when the water level was partly re-established (Fotius & Lemoalle 1976, Iltis & Lemoalle 1983).

Conservation

Threats and priorities for conservation

The availability of water is an obvious limiting resource for the development of part of the Lake Chad basin, where the variability of rainfall does not allow for food security from rain-fed agriculture for an increasing population.

Withdrawal of surface water for irrigation may change the hydrological cycle of riverine floodplains and of Lake Chad. The increased population also means increased demand for the use of the natural resources of the floodplains – such as for fisheries, cattle breeding, or recession cultivation. The threat here is from two directions: from changes in hydrology and from overexploitation.

The implementation of development schemes should take into account the resources provided by the wetlands and their possible alteration. Recent experience shows that this is not always the case: the Waza Logone Project for the Yaere, and the IUCN Project for the Conservation of the Hadejia–Nguru Wetlands, were set up after the construction of dams upstream of the floodplains. Both projects proposed corrective measures to preserve part of the benefits provided by naturally functioning wetland systems (GEPIS 2000). A recent United Nations Development Programme project for the integrated water-resources management planning in Chad has included the wetlands as a major component of the environmental resource.

Good knowledge of the hydrology, ecology, and also of the human use of the wetlands is a prerequisite for proper management of the water resource on a basin-wide scale. In the Chad basin, shared by five countries, the Lake Chad Basin Commission is a useful tool for a concerted approach, but the basic and/or updated data are often lacking to provide details of:

- the relationship between rainfall, river flood, and the extension of the inundation in the floodplain (especially for the Salamat floodplain);
- the updated hydraulic characteristics of the sills between riverbed and floodplain;
- the importance of the water-table recharge by the Chari–Logone floodplains;
- the sensitivity of the hydrology of flat regions to small modifications of their topography: the construction of permanent roads has had a large impact on the water flow in floodplains; this is particularly the case in the Yaere with the roads from Kousseri to Mora in Cameroon, and to Maiduguri in Nigeria;
- the role of the floodplains as flood reservoirs in preventing inundation of large cities such as N'Djamena and Kousseri at the confluence of rivers Chari and Logone.

On the other hand the same basic data are also needed to evaluate which measures are needed for a sustainable conservation and use of the wetlands and their biota. The concept of Critical Natural Capital has been put forward by the European Union to include both the needs for conservation and the benefits provided by natural ecosystems including wetlands (IFEN 2001). This concept – which may also prove useful in the Chad basin – requires local, national, and international appreciation of a wetland, including biodiversity conservation.

Fish diversity and fisheries

Dry and wet periods have occurred in the geological past and have contributed to the present composition of the fish community. The selection has been such that Lake Chad may be considered as a fluctuating extension of the habitat, which is colonized by the riverine fish community when circumstances are favorable. The lake is a useful and usually long-lasting feeding ground that contributes to the size of the fish community, but it is not necessary for its diversity. As a result, only one fish species has been described as endemic to the lake: *Brycinus nurse dageti* (formerly *Alestes dageti*), which may also be considered as a lacustrine dwarf form of *B. nurse*. It seems that this fish has not been observed since the transition to the "small" Lake Chad, when its usual habitat – submerged macrophyte stands – was temporarily but completely destroyed during the level recession in 1973.

If the fish community is primarily riverine, then care should be taken to preserve the fish stock and the river environment. Intensive fishing and disregard of mesh-size regulations may lead toward an overexploitation of the fish stock. This overexploitation is presently not substantiated by the available biological data.

The river habitat is important, especially during low water in dry years. A reduced flow of water during the warm season may restrict oxygen availability; however, fishing pressure on a vulnerable fish stock is the main danger, especially if pesticides or other chemicals are used. Agreements have been signed by Cameroon and Chad to limit irrigation intakes from their common border, the lower River Logone, during the low-flow period. However, in dry years, the resultant flow may still be insufficient for the sustainability of the fish stock and its diversity.

Protected areas

Some protected areas in the Lake Chad basin include the following wetlands:

1. In Chad, the Lake Fitri Reserve, a Ramsar site of 1950 km^2 including the lake and its wetlands, where agreements between the local people allow for integrated use of the natural resources by fisheries, recession agriculture, and cattle breeding.
2. In Cameroon, the Waza National Park (1700 km^2), a Biosphere Reserve since 1979. Included in the Yaere, the Park attracts international tourists

with its rich savanna fauna. The Kalamaloue National Park (45 km^2) is situated a few kilometers north of Waza and includes a side arm of the River Chari.

3. In Nigeria, the Chad Basin National Park, divided into three different and rather-distant settings. Two of them may be considered as seasonal wetlands. The Chingurmi–Duguma is situated in the Logone plain on the west of the Yaere and of Waza National Park. It is partly flooded by rains and by some overflows of the Yaere. The Badde–Nguru wetlands include part of the Hadejia–Nguru wetlands.

It has been proposed that corridors should be created between three national parks: Waza and Kalamaloue in Cameroon and Chigurmi–Duguma in Nigeria. According to the availability of fodder and of water, elephants and ungulates migrate between these parks and become vulnerable to shooting and poaching.

Another proposal, presently under discussion, is the creation of a protected area in Lake Chad itself. The first phase has been a memorandum of cooperation between the bureau of the convention on wetlands (Ramsar) and the Lake Chad Basin Commission, and was published in 2002. Some of the countries which share the lake have designated their parts of Lake Chad as Ramsar sites.

The drought in the African Sahel, which started with the low rainfall of 1972 and 1973, has pushed populations toward those areas where water allowed for cattle breeding and cultivation. When arriving at the shores of Lake Chad, some peasants turned to fishing. The result of these migrations toward all the wetlands of the basin has been an increased pressure on the natural resources, and a transition from traditional management to more-unregulated practices. The impact of this situation on the ecosystems has not been evaluated, partly because quantitative long-term observations are lacking, and partly because of the co-occurrence of the drought and of the new human settlements. Increased fishing activity on juvenile fish, increased disturbance and shooting of waterfowl and mammals, and reduction of the habitat may progressively put some components of the natural system in danger.

The present status of the antelope sitatunga, for example, is not known. The marshes of the southern shore of Lake Chad, its former habitat, are now grazed by numerous cattle or are used for recession agriculture.

Priorities for action

In the context of necessary development and intensification in the use of natural resources, including water and wetlands, a basin-wide integrated approach is essential. For the Chad basin, this is often an international approach, due to the transboundary nature of the water resource.

Wetlands can be taken into account only if sufficient knowledge is available about their functioning (hydrological and ecological) and about the benefits they provide to society (local and international). At present, the necessary basic data should be updated. Surveys on the functioning of the main wetlands, including the present use of their resources by man, are a priority. They should provide information on the issues and relationships listed above, and probably others that are more specific to each wetland. They will form the basis for the planning of a sustainable development, taking into account the diversity of interacting actual or potential uses.

The reasons why such surveys have not been developed recently may be economic (lack of local capacity, and long duration and high cost for still-poor countries) or political (other more-urgent priorities exist). If it appears that the conservation of some floodplains or wetlands of the Chad basin is an international concern, these surveys should be financed by bilateral or international funding. The reclamation of a number of wetlands is underway in developed countries (e.g. Everglades in Florida, USA; the French national program for wetlands) and is a clear illustration that the conservation of wetlands may be a good investment for the long term.

References

Balek, J. (1977). *Hydrology and Water Resources in Tropical Africa*. Amsterdam, the Netherlands: Elsevier.

Bénech, V. (2002). Les migrations latérales des poissons dans le delta intérieur du Niger. *Gestion intégrée des ressources naturelles des zones inondables tropicales*, ed. D. Orange. Paris: IRD, pp. 329–42.

Bénech, V. & Quensière, J. (1983). Migrations de poissons vers le lac Tchad à la décrue de la plaine inondée du Nord-Cameroun. III: Variations annuelles en fonction de l'hydrologie. *Revue d'Hydrobiologie Tropicale*, **16**, 287–316.

Bénech, V., Lemoalle, J., and Quensière, J. (1976). Mortalités de poissons et conditions de milieu dans le lac Tchad au cours d'une période de sècheresse. *Cahiers ORSTOM, série Hydrobiologie* **10**, 119–30.

Braund, R. (2000). Restauration de la plaine Waza Logone. In *Plaines d'inondation sahéliennes, enjeux et perspectives*. Actes de la conférence régionale. Ouagadougou, Burkino Faso: IUCN, Bureau régional pour l'Afrique de l'Ouest, pp. 49–63.

Burgis, M. and Symoens, J.-J. (1987). *African Wetlands and Shallow Water Bodies*. Directory. Paris: ORSTOM.

Carmouze, J. P. (1983). Hydrochemical regulation of the lake. In *Lake Chad*, eds. J. P. Carmouze, J. R. Durand, and C. Lévêque. Monographiae Biologicae 53. The Hague, the Netherlands: Junk, pp. 95–123.

Carmouze, J. P., Fotius, G., and Lévêque, C. (1978). Influence qualitative des macrophytes sur la régulation géochimique du lac Tchad. *Cahiers ORSTOM, Série Hydrobiologie*, **12**, 63–5.

Carmouze, J. P., Durand, J. R., and Lévêque C. (eds.) (1983). *Lake Chad. Ecology and Productivity of a Shallow Tropical Ecosystem.* Monographiae Biologicae 53. The Hague, the Netherlands: Junk.

Chardonnet, P. and Lamarque, F. (1996). Wildlife in the Lake Chad basin. In *Livestock Atlas of the Lake Chad Basin*, ed. I. de Zborowski. The Hague, the Netherlands: CTA. Paris: CIRAD, pp. 109–24.

Compère, P. and Iltis, A. (1983). The phytoplankton. In *Lake Chad*, eds. J. P. Carmouze, J. R. Durand, and C. Lévêque. Monographiae Biologicae 53. The Hague, the Netherlands: Junk, pp. 145–97.

Compère, P. and Symoens, J. J. (1987). Bassin du Zaïre. In *African Wetlands and Shallow Water Bodies. Directory*, eds. M. Burgis and J.-J. Symoens. Paris: ORSTOM, pp. 401–56.

Davies, B. and Gasse, F. (1988). *African Wetlands and Shallow Water Bodies. Bibliography.* Paris: ORSTOM.

Dejoux, C. (1983). The impact of birds on the lacustrine ecosystem. In *Lake Chad*, eds. J. P. Carmouze, J. R. Durand, and C. Lévêque. Monographiae Biologicae 53. The Hague, the Netherlands: Junk, pp. 519–25.

Fotius, G. (1974). *Problèmes posés par l'évolution de la végétation liée à la baisse du Lac Tchad.* N'Djaména: ORSTOM.

  (2000). Phytogéographie. In *Atlas de la Province Extrême Nord Cameroun*, eds. C. Seignobos and O. Iyébi-Mandjek. Paris: IRD, pp. 30–7.

Fotius, G. and Lemoalle, J. (1976). *Reconnaissance de la végétation du lac Tchad entre janvier 1974 et juin 1976.* N'Djaména: ORSTOM.

Gac, J. Y. (1980). *Géochimie du bassin du lac Tchad: bilan de l'altération de l'érosion et de la sédimentation.* Paris: ORSTOM.

Gaston, A. (1996). La végétation pastorale du bassin du Lac Tchad. In *Atlas d'élevage du bassin du Lac Tchad*, ed. I. de Zborowski. Montpellier, France: CIRAD. Wageningen, the Netherlands: CTA, pp. 39–56.

GEPIS (Groupe d'Experts sur les Plaines d'Inondation Sahéliennes) (2000). *Vers une gestion durable des plaines d'inondation sahéliennes.* Gland, Switzerland; Cambridge, UK: IUCN.

Goes, B. J. M. (2001). *Effects of Damming the Hadejia River in Semiarid Northern Nigeria: Lessons Learnt for the Future.* IAHS Publication 268; pp. 73–80.

Hollis, G. E., Adams, W. M., and Aminu-Kano, M. (1993). *The Hadejia–Nguru Wetlands: Environment, Economy and Sustainable Development of a Sahelian Floodplain Wetland.* Gland, Switzerland; Cambridge, UK: IUCN.

Howard-Williams, C. and Thompson, K. (1985). The conservation and management of African wetlands. In *The Ecology and Management of African Wetland Vegetation*, ed. P. Denny. The Hague, the Netherlands: Junk.

IFEN (Institut Français de l'Environnement) (2001). *Développement durable et capital naturel critique.* Etudes et Travaux 32. Orléans, France: IFEN.

Iltis, A. and Lemoalle, J. (1983). The aquatic vegetation of Lake Chad. In *Lake Chad*, eds. J. P. Carmouze, J. R. Durand, and C. Lévêque. Monographiae Biologicae 53. The Hague, the Netherlands: Junk, pp. 125–44.

Junk, W. J. (1982). Amazonian floodplains: their ecology, present and potential use. *Revue Hydrobiologie Tropicale*, **15**, 285–302.

Junk, W. J. and Weber, G. E. (1996). Amazonian floodplains: a limnological perspective. *Verhandlungen Internationale Vereinigung fuer Theoretische und Angewandte Limnologie*, **26**, 149–57.

Lemoalle, J. (1974). Bilan des apports en fer au lac Tchad (1970–73). *Cahiers ORSTOM, Série Hydrobiologie*, **8**, 35–41.

  (1978). Application des images Landsat à la courbe bathymétrique du lac Tchad. *Cahiers ORSTOM, Série Hydrobiologie*, **12**, 83–7.

  (1979a). *Etude des potentialités du bassin conventionnel du Lac Tchad: utilisation de la télédétection pour l'évaluation des surfaces inondées*. Paris: ORSTOM.

  (1979b). *Biomasse et production phytoplanctoniques du lac Tchad (1968–1976). Relations avec les conditions du milieu*. Paris: ORSTOM.

  (1983). Phytoplankton production. In *Lake Chad*, eds. J. P. Carmouze, J. R. Durand, and C. Lévêque. Monographiae. Biologicae 53. The Hague, the Netherlands: Junk, pp. 357–84.

  (1987). Lac Fitri. In *African Wetlands and Shallow Water Bodies. Directory*, eds. M. Burgis and J. J. Symoens. Paris: ORSTOM, pp. 275–7.

  (1991). *The Hydrology of Lake Chad During a Drought Period (1973–1989)*. FAO Fisheries Reports 445, pp. 54–61.

  (2002). Aspects de la production et du fonctionnement écologique des zones humides tropicales: l'exemple du bassin tchadien. In *Gestion intégrée des ressources naturelles des zones inondables tropicales* ed. D. Orange. Paris: IRD, pp. 303–14.

Léonard, J. (1969). Aperçu sur la végétation aquatique. In *Monographie du Lac Tchad*. Fort Lamy, Chad: ORSTOM.

Lévêque, C. and Paugy, D. (1999). Peuplements des cours d'eau et des biotopes associés. In *Les poissons des eaux continentales africaines. Diversité, écologie, utilisation par l'homme*, eds. C. Lévêque and D. Paugy. Paris: IRD, pp. 283–94.

Lévêque, C. and Saint-Jean, L. (1983). Secondary production (zooplankton and zoobenthos). In *Lake Chad*, eds. J. P. Carmouze, J. R. Durand, and C. Lévêque. Monographiae Biologicae 53. The Hague, the Netherlands: Junk, pp. 385–424.

Lévêque, C., Dejoux, C., and Lauzanne, L. (1983). The benthic fauna: ecology, biomass and communities. In *Lake Chad*, eds. J. P. Carmouze, J. R. Durand, and C. Lévêque. Monographiae Biologicae 53. The Hague, the Netherlands: Junk, pp. 233–72.

L'Hôte, Y., Mahé, G., Somé, B., and Triboulet, J.-P. (2002). Analysis of a Sahelian annual rainfall index from 1896 to 2000; the drought continues. *Hydrological Science Journal*, **47**, 563–72.

Olivry, J. C., Chouret, A., Vuillaume, G., Lemoalle, J., and Bricquet, J. P. (1996). *Hydrologie du Lac Tchad*. Paris: ORSTOM.

Saint-Jean, L. (1983). The zooplankton. In *Lake Chad* eds. J. P. Carmouze, J. R. Durand, and C. Lévêque. Monographiae Biologicae, 53. The Hague, the Netherlands: Junk, pp. 199–232.

Seignobos, C. and Iyébi-Mandjek, O. (eds.) (2000). *Atlas de la Province Extrême Nord Cameroun*. Paris: IRD.

Talling, J. F. and Lemoalle, J. (1998). *Ecological Dynamics of Tropical Inland Waters*. Cambridge, UK: Cambridge University Press.

Thompson, J. R. and Hollis, G. E. (1995). Hydrological modelling and the sustainable development of the Hadejia–Nguru Wetlands, Nigeria. *Hydrological Science Journal*, **40**, 97–116.

US Geological Survey (2001). http://edcwww.cr.usgs.gov/earthshots/slow/LakeChad/LakeChad

Welcomme, R. L. (1979). *Fisheries Ecology of Floodplain Rivers*. London; New York: Longman.

World Resources Institute (2000). *World Resources 2000–2001. People and Ecosystems*. Washington, DC: World Resources Institute (http://www.wri.org).

10

The River Nile basin

I. SPRINGUEL
South Valley University

O. ALI
University of Khartoum

Introduction

The River Nile is one of the largest rivers in Africa and is the longest river in the world, flowing 6825 km from southeast Africa to the north of Africa – its latitude extending from 4° S to 31° N (Fig. 10.1). Its basin embraces many climates from extreme arid – with annual rainfall of less than 1 mm in the Nubian part of Egypt and Sudan – to 1500 mm on the Ethiopian plateau, and as much as 1800 mm in the mountains of Rwanda and Burundi. Two primary factors govern the present extent of the vegetation along the Nile, namely the climate and the hydrographic network. However, the aquatic and riparian vegetation of the Nile basin is not greatly affected by local climatic changes, the swamp conditions existing whenever the land is either permanently under water or subjected to seasonal flooding.

Although the downstream part of the Nile crosses an extremely arid region without any significant water gains, Täckholm (1976) describes the Egyptian landscape of the Nile valley in the ancient past: "during the Neolithic and also the Pharaonic times [it] had the character of the Sudd region of the present Sudan, a river with marshy shores where huge papyrus thickets offered a splendid abode for hippopotami and crocodiles, for birds and other animals." Her description was based on plant remains found in Pharaonic tombs, ancient drawings, and records written on papyrus.

However, with Egypt's increasing population and growing demand for food, all the land of the Nile valley – which once was covered by flourishing riverine

The World's Largest Wetlands: Ecology and Conservation, eds. L. H. Fraser and P. A. Keddy.
Published by Cambridge University Press. © Cambridge University Press 2005.

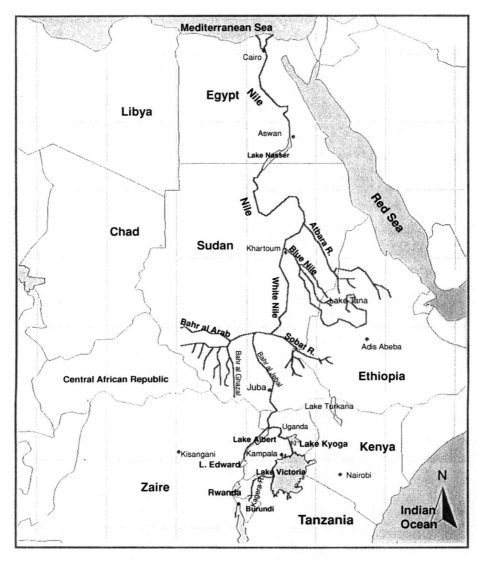

Figure 10.1 Nile basin with locations of described wetlands.

vegetation – has been converted to cultivated fields. Urbanization has led to the construction of large settlements on fertile lands of the Nile valley. Complete control of the river flow by a series of major barrages, the latest of which is the Aswan High Dam, has caused the disappearance of the fringe swamps that once bordered the Nile. The only remains of riverine wetlands still can be seen on the First Cataract Islands at Aswan and in the lakes of the river's delta.

Further south of the town of Aswan, the huge man-made reservoir (Aswan High Dam Lake) flooded the whole Nubian Nile valley and deeply penetrated inside the desert. Immediately before the reservoir filled, a few aquatic plants were seen in the shallow waters of the River Nile (El Hadidi 1976) in Nubia, but earlier travelers had not observed reeds and swamps on the Nile banks (Rzoska 1976a). The raised terraces of the Nubian valley were cultivated, mainly with date palms, and human settlements were located on the edge of the desert to escape the seasonal river flood. With the establishment of the lake, the wetlands bordering the shores of the lake have provided habitats for rich fauna – particularly birds, insects, and reptiles (White 1988).

Almost 85% of the Nile flow into the lake is water of the Blue Nile, the River Atbara, and the River Sobat; these three rivers drain the Ethiopian Highlands, and are characterized by their torrent nature and violent floods from August to October. The Nile is also renowned for its significant seasonal and annual fluctuations in water flow in different years and periods. However, the small amount of water provided by the White Nile is distributed relatively uniformly through the year and is more reliable. Growing water demand resulting from population increases in Egypt and the Sudan, naturally focuses attention on the potential of the huge swamps of the Sudd region in southern Sudan, where more than half the water from equatorial sources is lost by evapotranspiration. In connection with the present and proposed projects for control of the River Nile flow, and their effects on the environment, among the most-important research work undertaken is that of the Jonglei Investigation Team which was published by the Sudan Government in five volumes entitled *Equatorial Nile Project*, hereinafter referred to as ENP (1954).

This chapter does not aim to summarize previous publications but rather it emphasizes both the diversity and the common features of selected wetland areas of the Nile basin; these areas face similar environmental problems caused by the impact of human societies on the river hydrology. The water of the Nile is a limited resource and is in high demand, hence the desire by humans to control the river.

The wetlands selected for discussion are the huge swamps of the Sudd region, the floodlands of Aswan High Dam Lake which are in the pioneer stage of wetlands formation, relict riparian vegetation on the First Cataract Islands in Aswan, and the swamps of Lake Burullus in the Nile Delta.

The Wetlands of the upper stretches of the Nile in the Sudan

The huge area of swamp and marshland of the southern Sudan known as "the Sudd" (from the Arabic "*sudd*" meaning blockage) is a massive "blockage"

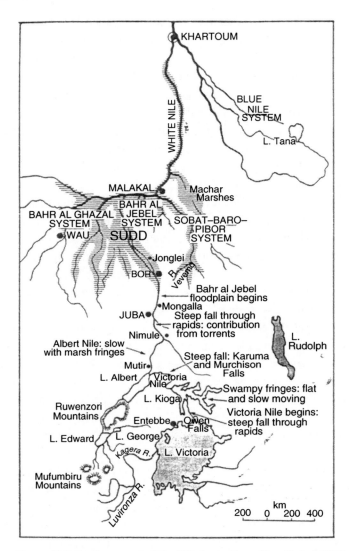

Figure 10.2 Southern part of the Nile basin (from Howell *et al.* 1988).

of vegetation that chokes the water channels of main rivers (Fig. 10.2). The Sudd lies between 5° and 9° 30′ N and between 30° and 32° E.

The climate of the southern region of the Sudan is that of tropical summer rainfall in which rainfall is associated with the passage of the intertropical convergence zone (ITCZ). The climate is characterized by diurnal and annual temperature fluctuations. Rainfall is strongly seasonal; it varies from just over 1300 mm at the southern end (latitude 4° N) of the floodplain area – with the

Table 10.1 *The areas of the "big five" African wetlands.*

Wetland complex	Seasonal swamp (km²)	Permanent swamp (km²)
Bangweulu	8 500	2 500
Okavongo	12 000	3 000
Chad	13 800	2 400
Upemba	8 500	4 500
Upper Nile	80 000	8 000 (19 200)[a]

Source: Denny (1985).

[a] Data from Howel *et al.* (1988).

heaviest rainfall between April and October – to slightly less than 400 mm at the northern end (about latitude 13° N) where rain only occurs during a shorter season (ENP 1954).

Table 10.1 reflects two features highlighting the uniqueness of the Upper Nile wetlands: the disproportionately large seasonal floodplain and the fact that the area of permanent swamp is larger than the largest seasonal swamp in the whole of Africa. The area of permanent Sudd swamp has increased from 6700 km² in 1952 to 19 200 km² in 1980 (Howell *et al.* 1988).

In addition to the Sudd, which comprises the swamps of Bahr al-Jebel, two other important wetlands are found in the Sudan: the Machar Marshes and the Bahr al-Ghazal Swamps. The first is a triangle of swampy country north of the River Sobat and east of the White Nile, it takes its name from the Khor Machar, a water course that enters the area from the Baro River near Lokau on the borders of the Sudan and Ethiopia. The marshes and permanent swamps are fed not only by local precipitation, but also by a large number of other sources such as the Daga and Yabous rivers and numerous small torrents rising in the Ethiopian foothills over a south–north distance of about 200 km. The area also receives spill water through various channels from the Sobat – when in flood – into what can be described as the southern Machar Marshes (ENP 1954). Although there are at times measurable discharges into the White Nile from two outlets (Khors Adar and Wol rivers), the amount has been relatively small. The area of seasonally flooded marshland and some swamp is estimated at not less than 6500 km² (Howell *et al.* 1988).

The other wetland in the upper reaches of the Nile is the Bahr al-Ghazal Swamp, which is fed by local precipitation and numerous rivers and their tributaries rising from the Sudan–Zaire watershed. Large amounts of water flow into this region; the combined annual mean discharge of the main Bahr al-Ghazal tributaries is approximately 13.5 km³. However, most of this water never reaches the Nile, being taken up by evaporation and transpiration in the seasonally inundated floodplains and permanent swamps in which many of these rivulets terminate.

Considering all the Upper Nile wetlands in the Sudan, Beadle (1974) and Rzoska (1974) claimed that these swamps occupy an area of 92 000 km^2 including floodplain; of this, 40 000 km^2 can be considered as permanent swamp, thus qualifying as being the most-extensive swamp in the world.

Environmental characteristics of the Bahr al-Jebel Swamps

Topography

Given the seasonal pattern of inflow and its long-term variations, the passage of water through the Sudd depends on topographical factors. The area within which the river is incised is an even plain sloping gently north or slightly east of north. At Nimule the Albert Nile, emerging from Lake Albert in Uganda, is renamed Bahr al-Jebel. North of Juba, the Bahr al-Jebel runs in an incised trough, bound by scarps (with a rise of a few metres) which mark the limit of the woodland on either side. These scarps decrease in height from south to north and extend just north of Bor on the east bank and almost to Shambe on the west.

Between Juba and Bor, Bahr al-Jebel wanders in one or more channels from one side of the restraining trough to the other, and divides the floodplain into a series of isolated basins or islands. Between Bor and Jonglei the river flows within a shallow trough about 15 km wide, which, in the southern part, is sufficiently well defined for there to be little lateral spillage from it.

At Bor, the Bahr al-Jebel forms the main channel and abuts on the east bank of the trough. To the west lies the more-complex channel of the Aliab. This is joined, north of Lake Fajarial, by an outflow from the Bahr al-Jebel to form what was, before the 1960s, the main navigation channel. This flows northwards, close to the west bank of the trough, and does not rejoin the new navigation channel until Lake Shambe. The new navigation channel, sometimes called the Bahr al-Jadid ("new river"), follows a fairly central course through the swamps. Four major, eastward outflows from it form the Atem system, which flows through and past a series of lakes and rejoins the Bar al-Jadid at Jonglei. Between the four channels there are many lakes, some forming interconnecting series.

Between Jonglei and Lake Shambe, the main channel and lake complex continue to remain within a band about 15 km wide, but are no longer confined within a trough on the eastern side. Consequently there is extensive eastward spillage, causing large areas of seasonally flooded grassland and permanent swamp.

In the Shambe–Adok reach, the Sudd attains its greatest width – with vast, largely inaccessible swamps, and fewer lakes and side channels than further south. The Bahr al-Jadid and the Bahr al-Jebel recombine at the outflow from Lake Shambe, and with little water following the eastern courses of the Awai and southern Zeraf, the Bahr al-Jebel carries a high proportion of the total flow. South of Adok, a number of small channels flow westward out of the Bahr al-Jebel. There are fewer lakes in this section; most of them are within meanders, close to, but isolated from, the river.

The last section of the Sudd swamp is the Adok-Malakal. The Bahr al-Jebel and the Bahr al-Zeraf are here separated by 50 to 60 km of swamp and seasonally flooded grassland. Lakes are very few, and virtually none are connected to the river. The Bahr al-Ghazal enters from the west, through the very shallow Lake No, but contributes little to the flow. Here the river becomes the Bahr al-Abiad (the white river), and turns, starting to flow from west to the east with a number of elongated lakes parallel to its course. Three major affluents join the White Nile from the south: the swift-flowing Bahr al-Zeraf, the sluggish Khor Atar, and the seasonally swiftly flowing River Sobat. The Sobat shows huge seasonal variations that affect the main river to the north of the confluence, and also hold back the flow of the White Nile upstream.

Hydrology

About half the discharge of the White Nile comes from Bahr al-Jebel through the Sudd swamps and the other half from the River Sobat. The average annual discharge of Bahr al-Jebel is 29.13×10^9 m^3 measured at Mongalla, 128 km south of Bor at the head of the Sudd swamps. Below Mongalla the river channel gradually loses its trough, and when it reaches Bor the channel trough cannot hold discharge greater than 65×10^6 m^3 and any excess flood discharge is laterally spilled on both sides of the channel. North of Bor the effective carrying capacity of the river channel is reduced to only 30×10^6 m^3 per day, leading to the excess flooding and huge permanent swamps of the Sudd. Consequently, out of the normal annual yield of the river of 29.13×10^9 m^3 at Mongalla, the river emerges with a yield of only 14.7×10^9 m^3, having lost 50% in its passage through the Sudd.

The discharge of Bahr al-Jebel, unlike other tributaries of the Nile system, varies little throughout the year due to the regulating effect of the swamps of the Sudd. When a rise occurs upstream, most of it will be spilled over the banks to be absorbed into the swamps, and very little or no effect of the rise will be felt downstream. Conversely, when the river falls there is a tendency for the swamps and side channels to drain back into the main stream. However, there was a large increase in the discharge of Bahr al-Jebel between 1960 and

Table 10.2 *Mean annual discharges of eastern water systems (Bahr al-Jebel swamps) (Howell* et al. *1988).*

Period	At Mongalla (km³)	At tail of swamps (km³)	% loss
1905–60	26.8	14.2	47.0
1905–80	33.0	16.1	51.2
1961–80	50.3	21.4	57.5

1980 (Table 10.2), which was linked to the floods of the early 1960s and the subsequent increased discharged volumes from Lake Victoria northwards (Howell *et al.* 1988) .

Biodiversity of the Sudd region

Phytoplankton and zooplankton

The growth of phytoplankton in the Sudd is limited due to the combined effect of the strong current and high turbidity of the waters of the main river channels (Howell *et al.* 1988). The diatom *Melosira granulata* dominates the sparse community in the dry season, but it is replaced by the blue green alga *Lyngbya limnetica* during the wet season. Lakes and pools support a richer algal flora that include *Padaina* spp., *Eudorina* spp., desmids, and filamentous and blue-green algae. Some of the temporal pools last for 200 days and when the water-soluble salts become concentrated by evaporation and water enriched by organic matter (from cattle and bird droppings), they support a rich flora of Euglenophytes (*Euglena, Phacus,* and *Trachelomonas*) and dinoflagellates (*Peridinium*). In Lake No the major components of the phytoplankton include *Lyngbya limnetica, Melosira granulata,* and *Anabaena flos-aquae.* Desmids, in particular, have been recorded in abundance in one place only in the entire Nile basin, that is Lake Ambadi in Bahr al-Ghazal. The samples collected in 1955 (Gronblad *et al.* 1958) revealed 21 new species, 32 varieties, and 7 formae. Two of these new discoveries acquired new nomenclature (*nomen nudum*). These algal groups are all desmids. A diverse phytoplankton community is also present. Another group of algae, which included two new species, was found to be epiphytic on the submerged *Ceratophyllum demersum*; for detailed study refer to Gronblad *et al.* (1958).

In backwaters and lakes of the Sudd, cladocerans, rotifers, and copepods are reported; while in the seasonal floodplain dense communities of ciliates, testate amoebae, rotifers, and crustaceans are formed (Baily 1991). The data on the invertebrates of Lake No and Lake Ambadi are attributed to Green (1987). In Lake No some of the crustaceans and rotifers were listed as zooplankers while the bottom fauna was reported to be dominated by oligochaetes and chironmid larvae. Green (1987) also encountered ostracods of the genus *Darwinula*, balacarid mites of the genus *Limnohalacarus*, as well as the bright-red Odonata *Crocothemie erythrema*. The microinvertebrate fauna of Lake Ambadi is sparse and diverse with 32 species of testate rhizopods, 26 species of rotifers, and over 20 species of microcrustacea. Numerous oligochaetes, snails, dragonflies, and caenid mayflies have been found (Green 1987).

Flora and vegetation

Despite the fact that written records of the vegetation of southern Sudan date back to the beginning of the last century (Garstin 1904, Brown 1905), there is still no complete record of the aquatic plants of the region. Attempts to list and categorize the hydrophytes of the Sudd region are attributed to Ali (1977, 1999), Denny (1984), and Howell *et al.* (1988). From the above-mentioned studies, the following features have been recognized:

- two phenotypes (pteridophytes and angiosperms) are represented but not the gymnosperms;
- the aquatic macrophytes have a wide spectrum of life and growth forms;
- vegetation exhibits a distinct zonation (Denny 1984).

Around 13 monocotyledonous and 9 dicotyledonous plant families were encountered in the Sudd region. With regard to richness and endemism, Howell *et al.* (1988) claim that the floodplain vegetation is poor in species, only 350 species having been definitely identified. They attribute this paucity to the fact that the area has low habitat diversity and is devoid of a harsh environmental extremes such as drought, floods, and fires. Another speculation is that the whole region is young in geological terms, so that there has been insufficient time for a rich flora to develop (Howell *et al.* 1988). In support of this theory, there is only one endemic plant, namely the remarkable swamp grass *Suddia sagitifolia* that was discovered in 1979 as a new genus (Renvoize *et al.* 1984).

In general, the swamps comprise two main formations: the "*toich*," a common Nilotic word meaning the floodplain seasonally inundated from the rivers and tributaries; and the "*sudd*," the permanent swamp, which is almost always under water or waterlogged. There are different definitions of "*sudd*" swamps, and in the present work we refer to Drar (1951) who identified the Sudd as a "blockage;" this includes all plant communities, not only floating mats as described by Thompson (1985), but also the associated rooted plants. The vegetation of the Sudd region has been described by many authors in relation to the water-storage projects which began in the last century (Chipp 1930, Migahid 1947, Andrews 1948, the Jonglei Investigation Team [ENP 1954], Rzoska 1976a, 1976b, 1976c, and Howell *et al.* 1988).

Table 10.3 *Occurrence of common species of Sudd-region swamps in relation to the water regime. The depth of water where these species were recorded and the duration of the flood are obtained from tables representing the situation in different swamp regions and published by the Equatorial Nile Project (ENP 1954).*

Species	Depth (cm)		Flood duration (days)	
	Minimum	Maximum	Minimum	Maximum
Cyperus papyrus	30	450	175	365
Vossia cuspidata	10	450	60	365
Echinochloa stagnina	67	340	20	365
Oryza barthii	0	197	30	365
Echinochloa pyramidalis	0	340	0	365
Phragmites (communis) australis	10	246	7	293

Permanent swamps are dominated by *Cyperus papyrus* (ENP 1954). There are many associated climbers such as *Luffa cylindrica*, *Vigna luteola*, *Cissus ibuensis*, and *Ipomoea cairica*; *Vossia cuspidata* can form pure populations that fringe the papyrus, being rooted to the bank and sending out shoots several meters long, which float on the water and send up leaves of 90 to 120 cm in length (Hurst 1952). Within the swamps there are a large number of lakes that support communities of both floating and submerged hydrophytes. *Pistia stratiodes* grows near the fringe of the papyrus, often in association with *Ipomoea aquatica* and submerged *Ceratophyllum demersum*. A new invader, *Eichhornia crassipes*, was first recorded in Sudan near the town of Bor in 1957 (Gay 1958). Rzoska (1976a, 1976c) reported the appearance of *Eichhornia* in the Sudd region in the 1957–58 period and described this event: "In August 1958, plants appeared near the Gebel Aulia Dam; in October 1958, the whole river from Juba to the Dam over a distance of 1800 km was infested. In January 1960 and December 1961 . . . over a stretch of about 1600 km of the White Nile from Kosti to Juba . . . was occupied by floating mats." Since that invasion, the swamps have become a "perennial" centre of *Eichhornia crassipes* infestation.

The main constituents of all riverain grassland are *Echinochloa* species (*E. stagnina* and *E. pyramidalis*) as well as *Oryza barthii* and *Vossia cuspidata*. In the 1940s, *Typha* grew in small, pure isolated populations in the riverain swamp pasture (ENP 1954). *Phragmites australis* is more-or-less limited to termite hills and alluvial banks.

Both the depth and the duration of flooding are primary factors controlling the distribution of plants over flood areas. Table 10.3 gives the range of distribution of species at the minimum and maximum limits of the flood.

Phragmites australis, E. pyramidalis, and *Oryza* spp. are unable to float on the rising flood water and, most probably, they could not tolerate complete inundation. Consequently distribution along the floodplain is limited by the depth of flood water since these species are unable to tolerate a site where the depth of the water exceeds the normal height for the species (ENP 1954).

Cyperus papyrus, Vossia cuspidata, and *E. stagnina* are not limited by the depth of the water to the same extent, because their buoyant rhizomes enable the plants to float on the rising flood waters, thereby ensuring that the upright shoots are not completely submerged (ENP 1954).

In relation to soil compactness, the longer the flood duration, the greater the penetrability of the soil. Areas with less soil compactness (longer inundation) are more suitable for *Cyperus papyrus, Vossia cuspidata,* and *E. stagnina.* Plants with tough root development such as *Phragmites communis, E. pyramidalis* and *Oryza* spp., are able to overcome the greater soil resistance met in the more-compacted part of the floodplain (ENP 1954).

Another important factor determining the nature of the environment is the velocity of the water current, especially along the main Nile and its principal tributaries. Plants with buoyant rhizomes limit themselves to sheltered areas where the current velocity is slow (Hurst 1952, Migahid 1952, ENP 1954).

Fauna

Zoobenthos. The descriptions of zoobenthos are based on Bailey (1991). River and lake bottoms of the Sudd region have an impoverished zoobenthic fauna of oligochaetes, chironomids, and bivalves. In contrast, submerged and fringing vegetation contains diverse communities contributing to a complex food-web in which odonatans, ephemeropterans, snails, and the shrimps *Caridina nilotica* and *Macrobrachium niloticus,* play significant roles. Interstitial swamp water supports air-breathing and oxygen-thrift insects and molluscs, and large aestivating snails occur in the seasonal floodplain in the dry period. Bailey (1991) revealed that more than 70 species of coleopterans, over 60 species of mosquitoes, and over 24 species of dragonflies are represented in the highest number of species taxa recorded.

Fish. Lakes, khors, and water channels provide the greatest variety of fish in the wetlands of southern Sudan. Bailey (1991) summarized the earlier studies (Sandon 1950, Bailey 1987) on the fish species of Sudd wetlands; about a hundred species have been recorded including 31 siluroids, 16 characoids, 14 cyprinoids, 11 mormyrids, 8 cichlids, and 7 cyprinodontids. He stated that: "Those fishes which inhabit the swamp or emerge, often in large numbers, on to the seasonal floodplain, are mostly known or reputed air-breathers, for example *Protopterus, Polypterus, Heterotis, Gymnarchus, Xenomystus, Clarias* and *Channa,* or are adapted in some other way to oxygen-deficient water, for example small mormyrids, cyprinodonts and tilapias." Sixteen fish species were associated with papyrus and *Typha*, 22 species were recorded on seasonally river flooded grass-lands. However the majority of the Sudd fish spawn on the permanent system. *Protopterus, Polypterus, Heterotis*, and *Gymnarchus* nest in the permanent and sea-sonal swamps, while clariid catfish and many of the accompanying small species are intent on spawning amongst the grassland invaders (Bailey 1987). The Sudd region, which has been protected from heavy fishing pressure because of the war conditions, is presently regarded as the replenisher of fish stocks for the Jebel Aulia reservoir (Beshir 2000). In Lake No a wide selection of nilotic fish have been found. However, the fish of Lake Ambadi have not been studied (Green 1987).

Amphibians and reptiles. Only a few studies have been undertaken on amphib-ians and reptiles of Sudan, and the Sudd region in particular. Hussein (1976) affirmed that it is difficult to provide realistic numbers for species present but he believes that in Sudan the fauna is more rich than in Egypt where 93 species of amphibians and reptiles were recorded. However, snakes are better studied than other reptiles: 44 species were recorded. According to Hussein (1976), this improved recording is attributed to the attention that the Sudan government agencies have given to snakes, as a result of their value for medicinal purposes. Quoting Bailey (1987): "At least nine species of frogs and toads are known in the Sudd. Crocodiles have reportedly declined but the monitor lizard, *Varanus niloticus*, and two terrapin species are common in the swamp and floodplain."

Birds. These are among the most-prominent inhabitants of the Sudd region; the majority are associated with the floodplains, which are regarded as having the richest avifauna of any African wetland (Bailey 1987). The position of the Sudd on the major migratory route from Europe and Asia to Africa provides an ideal habitat for palaearctic migrants as well as intra-African migrants (Howell *et al.* 1988). An extensive list of the birds of the Upper Nile was documented by Macleay (1959) where 142 species were observed during a fortnight's expedition. However within the Sudd, in the Jonglei Canal area alone, Howell *et al.* (1988) recorded 270 bird species in period between 1979 and 1982 and mention that another 200 species could occur in this area, making a total of 470 species. A peculiar feature of the area is the enormous population size of water birds which also varies according to the seasons. For example, the population of glossy ibis in the early dry season reached 1 695 240 individuals, the cattle egret population in the mid wet season was population 172 359 individuals and 344 487 openbill storks were recorded in the late dry season (Howell *et al.* 1988). The region is also an important wintering ground for migrants from the palaearctic regions – such as the garganey duck, yellow wagtail, red-throated pipit, and sand martin. The shoebill, or the whale-headed stork (*Balaeniceps rex* Gould), is the most-important species in the swamps. The world population of this species is confined to the

Sudd (Beshir 2000). The sacred ibis, once abundant in the Egyptian Nile valley and well documented in Pharaoh art and hieroglyphs, has found its refuge in the Sudd wetlands.

Bailey (1987) categorized the birds of the Sudd according to their feeding habits: about 20 species, mainly ducks and geese, feed on submerged vegetation in shallow water; 100 species, including storks, ibises, waders, lily-trotters, rails, and wagtails feed on the ground; in the air, swifts, swallows, and pratincoles feed on aquatic or emergent invertebrates; 40 species – including grebes, cormorants, pelicans, herons, storks, fish eagles, terns, and kingfishers – are known to catch and eat fish and amphibians.

Mammals. The Sudd is rich in mammals in terms of both numbers and diversity. The substantial seasonal variations of Sudd wetlands affect the behaviour of most large-mammal species, which are obligated to be seasonal migrants either to escape the flooding in the wet season or to seek the only remaining water supply in the dry period (Howell *et al.* 1988). The main year-round inhabitants of the Sudd are hippopotamus, buffalo, Sitatunga antelope, and Nile lechwe; the Sudd supports a high proportion of the world's population of the Nile lechwe. Other important animals feeding or periodically visiting the wetlands especially during the dry seasons are: tiang, Mongalla gazelle, reedbuck, roan antelope, bushbuck, white-eared kob, waterbuck, giraffe, oribi, elephant, and Grant's zebra. Of these, tiang are the most abundant of the wild herbivores in the Jonglei area. The carnivore population includes jackal, genet, wild cats, civet, white-tailed mongoose, spotted hyena, lion, and a very small population of leopard (Mageed 1985, Bailey 1987, 1991, Howell *et al.* 1988). *Hippopotamus amphibius* was seen in both Lake No and Lake Ambadi (Green 1987).

Importance and use of southern-Sudan wetlands

The wetlands of the southern Sudan are a very-important complex of ecosystems. They have economic, cultural, and historical importance. The role these formations have played and will play is two-sided. On the credit side, they have:

(a) attracted and protected a wide variety of wildlife;
(b) provided cottage-building material, grazing, and useful plant products;
(c) supplied feeding, breeding, and refuge areas for fish of commercial importance;
(d) stored water and kept rivers flowing during dry seasons;
(e) played a significant role in mineral cycling and regulation of the nutrient regime;
(f) increased rainfall which is linked with increased rates of evapotranspiration;

(g)   provided cultural values;

(h)   provided research sites and opportunities.

In addition, they are regarded as a rich gene reserve and represent a potential source of food and fiber.

On the debit side, they have:

(a)   interfered with water flow and drainage;

(b)   favored and spread water-related diseases;

(c)   lost water by evaporation and by seepage;

(d)   impeded navigation;

(e)   delayed the discovery of the Nile source;

(f)   restricted fishing;

(g)   inflicted a financial burden due to weed-control programs.

They could also cause pollution as a result of chemical weed control.

Threats and pressures

Projects for water conservation in the Sudd region

The growing demands for water caused by population increases in Egypt and the Sudan have focused attention on enhancing water resources, particularly by reducing the water losses from evaporation and transpiration in the Sudd region and neighbouring wetlands. One important project in this area is the Jonglei Canal scheme, which would increase the water available at Aswan (Egypt). The Jonglei Canal (Stage I), with a total length of 360 km, would circumvent the Sudd region from Bor on the Bahr al-Jebel to the junction of the River Sobat with the White Nile (Howell & Lock 1994, Said 1993). The digging of the Jonglei Canal began in June, 1978 but was halted in November, 1983 after 240 km had been built, because of civil war in the Sudan (Said 1993, FAO 1997).

A large-scale drainage scheme to tap the waters of the western Ghazal swamps is included in the master plan for Egyptian Nile water. The plan broadly involves a northbound canal harnessing the Jur, Pongo, Bahr al-Arab, and Bahr al-Ghazal rivers at a point near Lake No; the canal would be about 425 km long.

To overcome the problems of seasonal fluctuations and hence the water lost by spill, another canal (of some 225 km) known as the "direct line," and passing from Lake No to Melut, would be included in the scheme. The gross benefit of water saved is estimated at 5.1 km^3. This plan is accompanied by another to tap the more-southerly rivers with a canal of about 300 km long, which would probably link with the head of the Jonglei Canal and carry the water downstream by this route (Howell & Lock 1994).

The civil war

The civil war in the south of Sudan lasted from 1956 to 1972, and then broke out again in 1983 and still continues (the GOS signed a peace agreement with the Sudanese Popular Liberation Movement on January 9, 2005 to end the civil strife). There has been no study on the effect of the war on the wetland ecosystem of the southern Sudan. Nevertheless, one could envisage certain scenarios. The cutting of woody forests that is inevitable as a direct action in war or as a secondary activity by the army troops, could lead to significant soil erosion. This would increase sedimentation of the water bodies, especially the lentic ones, and might cause a shift in the aquatic communities at the expense of floating and submerged species. Burning and cutting of *Papyrus*, *Phragmites*, and *Typha* for access could adversely affect these species and those associated with them: i.e. climbers and twiners. Chemicals and explosives could also burn, disrupt, and pollute plant communities. The adverse impacts on wildlife cannot be overemphasized.

Oil exploration

New potential threats to the wetlands of the Nile system in the Sudan are activities pertaining to the exploration for new oil-rich sites and the extraction, transportation, and exportation of oil. With such activities now approaching Bahr al-Ghazal, not only is the biodiversity of the wildlife, aquatic macrophytes, and woody forests under threat, but even the hydrology of this intricate ecosystem might change.

Conservation and sustainable use

Howard-Williams and Thompson (1985) described the four small game reserves in the Sudd region: Zerat, Fanikang Islands, Shambe, and Rodigeru, with total areas of 92 000 and 10 000 km^2 for wet and dry seasons, respectively. The conservation status of these game reserves is uncertain. Despite its rich biodiversity, the wetlands of the Sudd region have no real protection status because the civil war since 1983 has prevented any steps forward in this direction.

The need to conserve and sustainably use these habitats and their communities cannot be overemphasized. However, much work needs to be done. There is a need for well-equipped colleges and university departments staffed by qualified aquatic scientists; this is crucial and a prerequisite for any conservation and utilization policies. There is a need to survey, identify, and document all the aquatic biota of the southern Sudan. The case of *Suddia sagitifolia* highlights such a need. It is most important that biologists receive the necessary support to investigate the real potential of the wetland ecosystem; management may then be based on the fullest information.

As Mitchell *et al.* (1985) state, "exploitation need not be the antithesis of conservation," the best policy to manage the wetlands of the southern Sudan should be based on a three-pillar strategy: conserve, co-use, and control (Ali 1999). All these measures should be linked to the aspirations of the inhabitants of the local areas. Thus, it is highly desirable to involve members of local communities affected by development decisions. Indigenous knowledge is of paramount importance for the future potential use of aquatic plants, especially for medicinal purposes. However, prior to all the above measures and recommendations, the civil strife in southern Sudan has to be halted. Once that has been achieved, plans to study, document, and conserve these wetlands should be formulated – adopting a multi-disciplinary approach that envisages the region as one ecosystem. These suggestions are highlights of a project coined "The Sudd Initiative"; this project is being drafted by O. Ali, to be submitted – via the Institute of Environmental Studies at the University of Khartoum, and the Higher Council for Environment and Natural Resources – to international donors and research institutes.

Aswan High Dam Lake (Lake Nasser and Lake Nubia)

Environmental characteristics

The Aswan High Dam Lake is a huge man-made reservoir extending about 500 km upstream from the Aswan High Dam between the latitudes 23° 58' and 20° 27' N, and between longitudes 30° 35' and 33° 15' E (Fig. 10.3). On completion of the construction of the High Dam in the 1970s, the lake covered the entire Nubian Nile valley in Egypt and Sudan, and deeply penetrated into the surrounding desert through wadis (dry desert riverbeds). The Aswan High Dam Lake is the combined name for the entire reservoir, the part of reservoir within Egypt being named Lake Nasser while the Sudanese part is referred to as Lake Nubia.

The climate is extremely arid (annual precipitation 4 mm and evaporation around 3000 mm per year; Entz 1976) with hot summers (temperatures above +40 °C) and mild winters (temperatures from +10 to +20 °C) but occasionally temperatures below zero have been recorded. The area is in the transition zone between the tropical climate with summer rain and the Mediterranean climate with winter rain. Occasionally, very-sporadic rains can fall in any season, but mainly fall in autumn.

The lake is 495.8 km long (at above 180 m sea level) and narrow in shape with an undulating shoreline determined by the surrounding topography. The

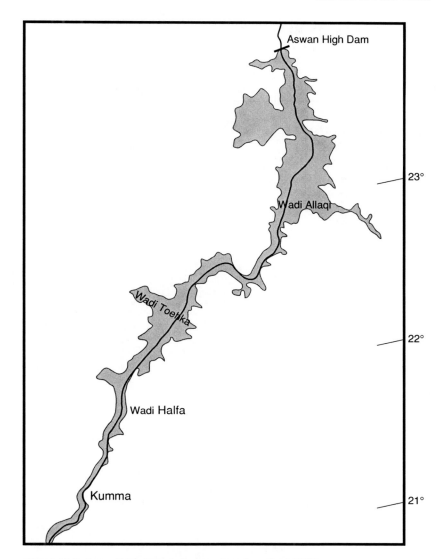

Figure 10.3 Aswan High Dam Lake (map based on Said 1993).

morphological parameters of the lake are given in Table 10.4. In the reservoir itself, about 26% of the capacity is dead storage. About 11% of reservoir water is lost by evaporation annually (White 1988).

The mean annual storage of silt in the reservoir has been estimated to be 110 million tons. Almost all the silt brought by the River Nile is deposited within Lake Nubia and only the fine silt enters Lake Nasser. About 134 million tons of silt is deposited annually within the Sudan, most of it being deposited south of Halfa, where a new delta is in formation (E. S. El-Zain, personal communication 2001).

Table 10.4 *Morphological data of the Aswan High Dam Lake (Entz 1976).*

Water level	160 m above sea level	180 m above sea level
Length (km)	430.0	495.8
Surface area (km^2)	3057.0	6216.0
Volume (km^3)	65.9	156.9
Shoreline (km)	6027.0	9250.0
Mean width (km)	7.1	12.5
Mean depth (m)	21.6	25.2
Maximum depth (m)	110.0	130.0

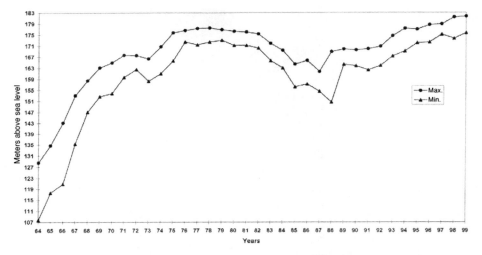

Figure 10.4 Maximum and minimum water level in Lake Nasser.

Variations in the size and shape of the lake are affected by the annual inflow – which depends on the upstream Nile flood – and outflow according to the yearly policy for the release of water from the dam.

Since the formation of the lake, the water level has increased and decreased, not only seasonally with the rise and fall of the flood, but varying enormously in extent over periods of years (Fig. 10.4). A yearly fluctuation in water level by as much as 30 m has been recorded, which may lead to considerable changes in the lake's surface area.

The physical, chemical, and biological characters of the lake are very diverse in time and space. It is mainly lacustrine, except in its southern part which has riverine characteristics. Based on a classification of the reservoir by fish and benthic production, given by Bishai *et al.* (2000), the shallow khors of the lake are eutrophic while the main channel is less productive, ranging from mesotrophic to oligotrophic.

Biodiversity

Vegetation

The fluctuation of the lake's water level has led, during recess, to periodic exposure of large areas, where a wetland ecosystem prevails. In particular, large wetlands have formed in the deltaic mouths of dry wadis where they join the lake. One such wetland at the mouth of Wadi Allaqi has been under observation since 1981; that is, from the beginning of the formation of floodplain vegetation. Here, the seasonal wetlands were formed on land that was extremely arid desert prior to the lake formation. The pioneer plants that colonized the exposed land were numerous seedlings of *Tamarix nilotica*, *Glinus lotoides*, and *Heliotropium supinun*.

From the start of the lake's formation until the present, there have been very few records on the floating hydrophytes such as *Potamogeton nodosus*, but not those hydrophytes that could cause permanent swamp formation. Among the submerged euhydrophytes in shallow water, the most common are *Najas* spp., *Ceratophyllum demersum*, *Vallisneria spiralis*, and *Potamogeton crispus*. Denny (1985) mentioned that the occurrence of *Ceratophyllum* would appear to be a feature of most African man-made lakes during their stabilization. The vegetation pattern of the floodplain is organized into zones according to the water availability and flooding periods. Growth of the annuals (*Glinus lotoides* and *Heliotropium supinun*), grasses (*Cynodon dactylon*), and sedges (*Crypsis schoenoides*, *Cyperus michelianus* subs. *pygmaeus*, and *Fimbristylis bisumbellata*) is restricted to the short period following inundation. Dense growth of *Tamarix nilotica* forms almost a monospecies zone with the height of shrubs reaching 7 to 8 m. *Pulicaria crispa* forms the transition (ecotone) zone with desert land.

The vegetation dynamic is one of the most-peculiar features of this wetland. The changes in vegetation distribution can be accounted for in terms of the relationship between the lake level and the consequent pattern of overspill (Fig. 10.5). The floodplain that is bordered by the annual minimum and maximum water-level fluctuation is the wetland dominated by *Tamarix* and *Glinus* – and closer to water by the short grasses and sedges (*Fimbristylis bisumbellata*, *Crypsis schoenoides*, and *Eragrostis* spp.). During periods of rising water in the lake, this zone is covered by water. When the level falls the dense growth of *Tamarix* is established on the exposed areas covered by a thick layer of silt deposit. *Tamarix* is flourishing after ten years without inundation. *Pulicaria crispa* forms dense growth in the

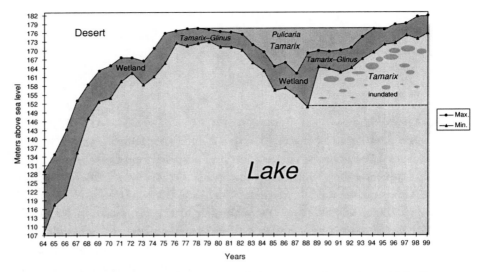

Figure 10.5 Dynamics of wetland in relation to water fluctuations of Lake Nasser since the beginning of lake formation in 1964. The area between the annual absolute minimum and maximum water level (the lake shore) is dominated by a *Tamarix–Glinus* community. Areas inundated at high flood and exposed for a number of years are dominated by *Pulicaria crispa* and *Tamarix nilotica* communities. Lands inundated over the last decade are dominated by *Tamarix* and aquatic weeds.

transition zone with surrounding desert. As the water rises the *Tamarix*, which is partly covered by water, still flourishes and continues to grow.

An answer to the question of why *Tamarix* took over from other wetland plants could help to predict the vegetation dynamic and establish management programs for sustainable development of the area around the lake and protection of the lake itself, taking into consideration its unique value as the main water source for Egypt. At present, it is only possible to put forward some hypotheses that are related to plant characteristics and the environment.

Tamarix colonized the exposed land because the seeds were present in the desert soil prior to inundation, and/or seeds were brought by water. *Tamarix* tolerates a wide ecological amplitude; it can survive and even grow vigorously after more than 15 years without inundation, as well as withstanding complete inundation for a few years. Once it has colonized the area, *Tamarix* becomes a strong edificator in plant communities by changing the environment, particularly by increasing the soil salinity of the upper layer through salt recycling (Springuel 1994) and preventing the invasion of new species.

In addition, the unstable water regime of the lake, with large annual and year-to-year water fluctuations, prevents the establishment of wetland grasses that are characteristic of the Upper Nile swamps. The actual depth and duration of flooding for six common grasses of the Sudd region are summarized in Table 10.3. As mentioned above, the distribution of *Oryza*, *Echinochloa pyramidalis*, and *Phragmites* along the floodplain is limited by the depth of flood water; as they are firmly anchored to the ground, these species could not tolerate complete submersion (ENP 1954). As the annual flood of the lake may exceed 4 m and can be above 10 m at high flood, it is unlikely that these species could invade the lake shores in the present situation. On the other hand, the plants that possess buoyant rhizomes (*Cyperus papyrus*, *Vossia* spp., and *Echinochloa stagnina*) and hence are able to float on the rising flood water, are relatively unaffected by the depth of water. However, the high year-to-year fluctuations of the lake's water level will probably prevent their establishment.

Phytoplankton

With the formation of the lake, the phytoplankton communities quickly established with very-diverse species. A total of 135 phytoplankton species, belonging to five classes (Chlorophyceae, Cyanophyceae, Bacillariophyceae, Dinophyceae, and only one species of Euglenophyceae), were recorded in the lake by different investigators in the period from 1981 to 1993 (Bishai *et al.* 2000). The composition of the phytoplankton communities varied in time and space. Shallow water in numerous khors sustained higher densities of phytoplankton than in the main stream, and the southern part of the lake is more productive than its northern part; however, during the flood, the phytoplankton pushed forward to the north. Water blooms caused by flourishing Cyanophyceae species have occasionally occurred in the southern part of the lake; however, recently the bloom spread throughout the length of the lake (Bishai *et al.* 2000).

Fauna

Zooplankton. The zooplankton of Lake Nasser have attracted the attention of many investigators in light of their importance in the aquatic food chain and hence fish production. Bishai *et al.* (2000) summarized the findings of many authors writing on relevant subjects. They concluded that the lake is rich in zooplankton with a total of 79 species belonging to four major groups: Protozoa, Platyhelminthes, Rotifera, and Arthropoda. Rotifera had the largest number of species (48), which could be ascribed to the alkaline water in the lake. Species density and diversity show spatial, horizontal, and seasonal variations. The southern part of the lake is richer in zooplankton than its northern part, while the shallow waters of numerous khors are more species rich in standing crops of zooplankton than the deep water in the main channel. The higher densities of zooplankton were observed in the upper water layers.

Bottom fauna (zoobenthos). The zoobenthos in Lake Nasser have been recorded by different authors and are summarized by Bishai *et al.* (2000). They comprise 59 species belonging to five major groups: Cnidaria, Bryozoa, Arthropoda, Annelida, and Mollusca. Among those, Arthropoda comprised the highest number of species (33). Annelids and insects are the most-abundant groups of benthos comprising 38.7% and 31.9%, respectively, of all benthos. Molluscs represented the higher biomass (above 40%) of all benthos on the west and east sides of the lake. Of all the benthos species, the three above-mentioned groups are most important as food for fish. The bottom fauna had a higher density and biomass in the knors than in the main body of the lake.

Fish. Lake Nasser is one of the most-important national sources of fish production, contributing from 10% to 15% to the total production of the inland fisheries in Egypt. More than 57 species of fish belonging to 16 families were recorded in Lake Nasser during the first few years after its establishment. The most-abundant species in open water were *Alestes* spp., *Hydrocynus forskalii*, and *Schilbe niloticus* while *Sarotherodon galilaeus*, *Oreochromis niloticus*, *Brycinus nurse*, and *Lates niloticus* were abundant in inshore water (Latif 1974). Fish species occupied different ecological niches in relation to their behavioural characteristics. According to their feeding behaviour they were subdivided into: periphyton–plankton feeders; zooplankton–insect feeders; omnivores; and carnivore (Latif *et al.* 1979).

The fish-species diversity of the lake has decreased over the last two decades. Bishai *et al.* (2000) gave an account of 23 fish species recently recorded in the lake. The lake fisheries depend on 15 fish species, of which only two species – *Sarotherodon galilaeus* and *Oreochromis niloticus*, both periphyton–plankton feeders – comprise 90% to 95% of the total fish catch in the lake. *Tilapia* spp. inhabit the shallow waters of the khors and show similar swamping behavior by building nests in flood areas. Two peaks of flooding in March to May and August to September (Bishai *et al.* 2000) are close to the annual minimum water level in the lake which extends from May to August. In Bishai *et al.* (2000), the direct relationship between fish production and water-level fluctuation has been demonstrated by different authors.

Birds. The Aswan High Dam Lake, the huge water body in the heart of the great Sahara desert, has become increasingly important as a wintering area for migratory palaearctic water birds. The number of bird species seen on the lake has continuously increased. Meininger and Mullie (1981) recorded 19 species of water birds. During the 1989–90 winters, Atta *et al.* (1994) identified 47 bird species from the shores of the lake alone. Baha El-Din (1999) estimated that there were about 200 000 water birds wintering in the entire lake in February 1995; this places the lake's wetlands on the list of Egypt's most-important bird areas. Among the most-abundant birds were: black-necked grebe, white pelican, tufted duck, northern pochard, northern shoveler, wigeon, and black-headed gull. During the summer, significant numbers of yellow-billed stork and pink-backed pelican were seen on the lake.

With an increasing population of water birds, the fisheries authorities of the lake are concerned about the birds' impact on fish production. Sharing the same feeding habitats, the birds may affect the fish population by competing for food as well as by direct fish consumption. Mekkawy (1998) listed 17 bird species feeding on fish and provided estimates of fish requirements. Among those, the lesser pied kingfisher (*Ceryle rudis rudis*) heads the list by consuming 365.5 tons of fish annually in the lake. Tharwat (1998) reported 19 fish-eating birds from the lake. Among these are pink-backed pelican and white pelican, which can consume 776 and 1201 g of fish per day, respectively. For example, both of these pelican species consumed, in one year, about 580 642 kg of fish from Lake Edward (Din & Eltringham 1972). Taking into consideration the large number of white pelicans wintering on the lake (around 1157 individuals counted by Baha El-Din 1999), the worries of the lake's fisheries authorities are not unfounded. The impact of birds on physicochemical and biological water parameters (e.g. pH, conductivity, biological oxygen demand, organic matter, nitrogen, phosphorus, coliform bacteria, and plankton) has been recorded by different authors (Bishai *et al.* 2000).

Reptiles. The lake shores and its floodplain have provided new opportunities for reptiles to inhabit these areas. Only a few large reptile species have been recorded. Among these is the Nile crocodile, which was once common through-out the Nile valley but at present only successfully inhabits the lake shores; however, its population is continuously increasing. Other reptiles recorded on the lake shores are the Nile monitor and the Nile soft-shelled turtle.

Development projects

One of the largest projects on the lake (the national Toshka Project) is the construction of a canal which will withdraw water from the lake for reclamation of 500 000 feddans (*c.* 200 000 ha) of desert land on the west side of the lake (SEDP 1998). Water withdrawn by the canal could reduce the lake's surface area, especially in years of low flood. Depending on the management practices used to operate the canal, the reduction in peak flows that can be expected could be beneficial for the development of wetland on the lake shores.

Conservation status

The lake wetlands in the delta of Wadi Allaqi are part of the Wadi Allaqi Biosphere Reserve (UNESCO MAB Programme: United Nations Educational, Scien-tific, and Cultural Organization–Man and the Biosphere Programme), which has had protected status since 1989. The wetlands of the Biosphere Reserve represent the buffer zone where research work is conducted and the local semi-nomadic population can exploit the rich natural resources of the area, which prior to lake formation was extreme arid desert. The creation of Lake Nasser offered new ecological niches for birds, particularly for the locally breeding population of the Egyptian goose. On the other hand, the fulvous babbler disappeared from the Nile valley after its breeding grounds were permanently flooded by the lake (Goodman & Meininger 1989).

One winter visitor of the lake, the ferruginous duck, is on the list of Globally Threatened Bird Species. Large numbers (more than 1% of the biogeographic population) of white pelican winter on the lake; this is also an endangered species (Goodman & Meininger 1989, Baha El-Din 1999).

Regarding the country's important birds, the African skimmer and African pied wagtail breed on the lake's wetland but not in other areas in Egypt (Baha El-Din 1999). In addition, the lake shores are the only habitat for the Nile crocodile in Egypt.

The First Cataract Islands

Environmental conditions

Downstream of the Aswan High Dam, the wetlands on the shores of the First Cataract Islands in Aswan (Fig. 10.6) are the only remains of swamps and natural floodplain vegetation, while north of Aswan every piece of land in the Egyptian Nile valley is now cultivated. The climate is extreme arid, typical of the Nubian Nile valley and similar to the Aswan High Dam Lake described above. The First Cataract has a drop of 15 m in a length of 15 km (Willcocks 1904). The soft material (silt and sand) brought by water was deposited behind the rocks and fertile soil formed. The Nile water rapids (or "cataracts") control the formation of wetlands that are restricted to protected sites in the islands' bays and between islands when the water flow is slowed down. Before the construction of the High Dam, all of the islands were covered by water during high flood (Table 10.5) and water stored in the deposits supported the rich plant growth. Following the construction of the Aswan High Dam (after 1970 in Table 10.5), the regular flood ceased and water flow was controlled by the dam according to agricultural needs.

Biodiversity

Vegetation

The remains of semi-natural vegetation on the First Cataract Islands at Aswan are the relict of a Nile valley gallery forest formed by *Acacia* trees.

Table 10.5 *Absolute minimum and maximum river levels in Aswan in some selected years before (1960) and after (1970) construction of Aswan High Dam (data from the Ministry of Irrigation, Aswan).*

Years	Month	Absolute minimum (mASL)	Month	Absolute maximum (mASL)
1940	July	96	January	121
1950	August	98	January	121
1960	July	95	January	121
1970	January	101	October	112
1975	February	107	June	109
1980	August	105	August	109
1985	September	104	January	110

River levels are given in meters above sea level (mASL).

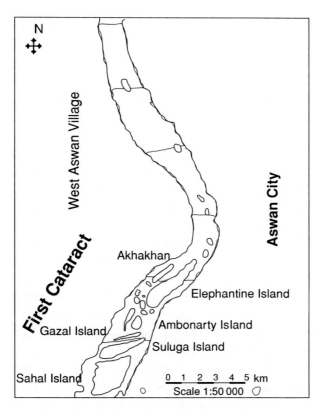

Figure 10.6 First Cataract Islands in Aswan.

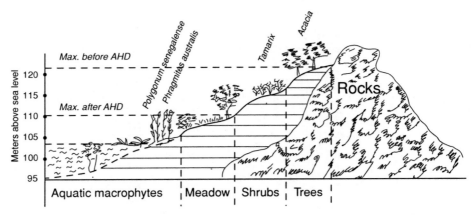

Figure 10.7 Zonation of vegetation on the First Cataract Islands in relation to water-level fluctuation of the River Nile, before and after construction of the Aswan High Dam (AHD).

Springuel (1981) recognized three vegetation types according to the time of formation and the position in the relief (Fig. 10.7).

Xeromesophytic forest. This occupies the highest (from 7 to 10 m above river water level) and presumably the oldest silt terraces of the islands. It comprises communities dominated by *Acacia* species (*Acacia nilotica*, *A. seyal*, and *A. raddiana*) and *Faidherbia albida*. *Ziziphus spina-christi* is often associated with acacias. The woody twiner, *Leptadenia arborea*, densely covers trees and when it cannot find support it spreads on the ground. *Acacias* have grown so densely that they are difficult to pass through. The ground under the trees is covered by litter from fallen *Acacia* leaves and is completely devoid of herbs. Small fragments of *Acacia laeta* communities are recorded in one location only; an area close to the shore, which is inundated during the high flood. It should be mentioned that different *Acacia* species occupy different positions in the relief according their water requirements and ability to withstand inundation. Of the mentioned species, *Acacia seyal* has a lower position on the silt terrace compared with *Acacia raddiana* – which is drought resistant and a typical element of desert wadis.

Xerohalophytic shrubs. These occupy slightly elevated ground, which could be the old levee, where *Tamarix nilotica* shrub is dominant. Usually *Tamarix* forms a monospecies stand because of its salt-recycling effect on the soil, as described above. However, the ecological succession of these sites result in *Acacia* replacing *Tamarix* to form a mixed stand of *Tamarix* and *Acacia* in the late seral stages. *Leptadenia arborea* and grass *Imperata cylindrica* are common associates.

Hydromesophytic meadow and swamps. These have a lower, regularly inundated position in the relief. Low grass and sedge communities are dominated by

Cynodon dactylon, Panicum repens, Cyperus rotundus, and *Fimbristylis bisumbellata*. Plants start to grow as soon as land is exposed to the air and vegetation lasts while available water is held in the soil. Individual trees of *Acacia seyal* and *A. nilotica* are also present. The shallow levees are covered by bushes of *Mimosa pigra, Acacia seyal, Conyza dioscorides, Sesbania sesban*, and *Oxystelma alpini*.

The undulating shorelines of the islands – with numerous lagoons – support fragments of permanent swamps, dominated by *Polygonum senegalense* whose dense rhizomes form almost-floating mats. Close to the shores, *Phragmites australis* grows in pure stands. The height of reeds can reach up to 5 m. *Typha domingensis* is less common, forming mixed stands with *Cyperus alopecuroides* and *C. longus*.

Submerged macrophytes. Shallow water in the lee of the islands, where the water current slows down, provides habitats for populations of submerged macrophytes dominated by *Ceratophyllum demersum, Potamogeton crispus*, and *Najas* spp. Other species that have recently invaded these communities are *Potamogeton perfoliatus* and *Myriophyllum spicatum*. Since 1986, small patches of *Eichhornia crassipes* have occasionally been seen near the west banks of the Nile in Aswan, but its distribution seems not to have increased.

A similar vegetation pattern of river floodplain was described by Springuel (1990b) along a narrow strip of the Nubian Nile Valley. Small patches of non-cultivated floodplain became almost extinct due to the conversion of agricultural lands after construction of the High Dam. Before the construction of the High Dam, only a few hydrophytes occurred along the edge of the river because the annual flood removed plants and cleaned Nile banks and channels. There is strong evidence for an increasing diversity and abundance of freshwater macrophytes in the Upper Nile valley (Springuel & Murphy 1991). The regulation of river-water flow allowed aquatic plants to be established along the Nile banks and caused the formation of numerous islands in its channel (Springuel 1990a).

Fauna

Not much can be said about mammals in the Nile Valley in Upper Egypt. Every piece of fertile soil is under cultivation and small non-cultivated islands do not support populations of mammals. Only rock drawings in surrounding wadis provide records of rich wildlife in the past (Fig. 10.8). However the remains of non-cultivated pieces of floodplain, with their diverse habitats, are still important for Nile wildlife. The Upper Nile valley, with its numerous islands and fragments of wetlands, is among the most-important bird areas of Egypt (Baha El-Din 1999). The First Cataract Islands are likely to be of importance for resident and visiting water birds (herons, ducks, waders, and terns) and other migrants during the migration seasons. A total of at least 100 bird species, both migratory

Figure 10.8 Carved relief in the tomb-chapel of the mastaba of Ti at Saqqara (from Houlihan 1995).

and resident, are recorded in the protected area (Aswan Governorate 1993). In the winter season, Sorensen *et al.* (1994) observed 25 bird species on the Nile in Aswan, among which the black-headed gull (*Larus ridibundus*) and the cattle Egret (*Bubulcus ibis*) had the largest population sizes. In the autumn (October to November, 2001) Dick Hoek (personal communication 2002), observed 60 bird species on the First Cataract Islands and another 31 bird species in the Aswan region. Among the recorded species, at least 35 are typical reed and water birds. The large populations of wetland birds, those with populations of over 100, are represented by little egret (*Egretta garzetta*), cattle egret (*Bubulcus ibis*), Egyptian goose (*Alopochen aegyptiacus*), and common moorhen (*Gallinula chloropus*). Small flocks (around 20 individuals) of greater flamingo (*Phoenicopterus ruber*) have been seen on the Nile in Aswan since 1995. H. Hasib (personal communication 2002) provided a list of 84 bird species seen on the First Cataract Islands in different seasons. Sorensen *et al.* (1994) and Dick Hoek (personal communication 2001) observed colonies of breeding birds (little egret, squacco heron, black-crowned night heron [on *Acacia* trees], night heron, and striated heron) in marshy habitats on the Nile at Aswan and on the First Cataract Islands.

Conservation status

The Aswan High Dam regulates the flow of the Nile waters, preventing further inundation of the islands. This has encouraged urbanization of the area: building permanent settlements and hotels for the tourist industry. Only two of the First Cataract Islands have been granted conservation status and have been protected by Egyptian law since 1986.

The total area of the protected islands is about 40 ha. It has strict protection and only small groups of visitors are allowed, mainly bird-watchers. The current program includes the reintroduction of threatened plant species, particularly papyrus and lotus that previously were a component of the wetland ecosystem. Of the five *Acacia* species that occur here, two (*A. laeta and A. seyal*) – as well as *Faidherbia albida* – are very rarely present elsewhere in Egypt. The ferruginous duck *Aythya nyroca*, recorded by Dick Hoek (personal communication 2001) on the First Cataract Islands in 2001, is on the list of Globally Threatened Bird Species (Baha El-Din 1999).

The Nile Delta wetlands

Environmental characteristics

The Nile approaches the Mediterranean Sea at a latitude of 31° 26′ N and has a typical Mediterranean climate with winter rain (average of 180 mm) and average temperatures of 26.6 °C in summer and 15 °C in winter. The Nile Delta supports the northern remains of the Nile wetlands. In the past, eight distributaries formed the delta which created a complex network of river arms, islands, natural levees, alluvial flats, and backswamps. Between 7000 BC and 4000 BC when the Mediterranean Sea rose 20 m to its present level, the northern third of the Delta was reduced to a vast tract of swamps and lagoons (Butzer 1976) (Fig. 10.9). In the late Predynastic and early Dynastic period the seasonally

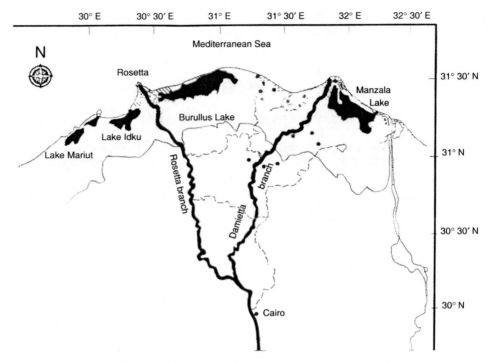

Figure 10.9 Changes in the Nile wetlands. Light-shaded areas indicate the maximum extent of the Delta's lagoons and marshland in Dynastic times (based on Butzer 1976). Dark-shaded areas showed the present size of the Delta's lakes (based on Serag 2000).

inundated river plains supported a considerable and diversified fauna and the Delta backswamps were called the "bird tank of pleasure" and the "papyrus lands." Papyrus and lotus were the most-characteristic plants of these marshy, game-rich depressions (Butzer 1976, Goodman & Meininger 1989). This is supported by pollen spectra from a deep coring below the marshes near the Rossetta branch, with an abundance of *Phragmites*, *Cyperus papyrus*, *Typha*, *Riccia*, and lotus (Saad & Sami 1967).

At present, the only two remaining natural branches are Rossetta on the western boundary and Damietta on the eastern boundary of the classical triangular-shaped delta, which covers about 22 000 km^2 of the most fertile and most densely populated land in Egypt (Fig. 10.9). The northern delta lakes support the remains of the wetlands that widely covered the Nile Delta in the past. The wetlands of Lake Burullus, which is less polluted than other delta lakes were described by Goodman and Meininger (1989) as the "most virginal community of the Delta."

Lake Burullus is located in the central part of the northern section of the Nile Delta and is connected to the sea through a 50-m-wide outlet on its eastern side. The catchment area of the Burullus wetlands covers about 74.3% of the Nile Delta region. The lake is shallow (from 0.42 to 2.07 m), about 65 km in length, and varies in width from 6 to 16 km. About 50 to 75 small islands are scattered in the lake (Khedr & Lovett-Doust 2000, Med Wet Coast 2002, EL-Shinnawy 2003). In spite of the saline sea water on its eastern side, the water is almost fresh on the western side of the lake. Up to the seventh century the lake was traversed by the now-defunct Sebennetic branch of the Nile (Montasir 1937). At present, the lake receives Nile water mainly through drainage canals (79%) which discharge an annual water volume of about 3.7 to 3.9 km^3 (El-Shinnawy 2003). Agricultural drainage enriched the lake water with nutrients and silt eroded from the surrounding cultivated lands. It is habitat to a total of 779 species, 9 of which are endemic and 20 of which are threatened (Med Wet Coast 2002).

Biodiversity

Flora and vegetation

The flora of Lake Burullus comprises 196 plant species including 11 hydrophytes and 1 species of water fern (*Azolla filiculoides*). Most typical of the wetlands are communities of *Phragmites australis–Arthrocnemum macrostachyum*. The lake shores are occupied by *Juncus acutus–Phragmites australis*, *Sarcocornia fruticosa–Arthrocnemum macrostachyum*, and *Phragmites australis–Typha domingensis* communities. *Arthrocnemum macrostachyum–Juncus acutus*, *Halocnemum strobilaceum–Polypogon monspeliensis*, and *Suaeda vera–Inula crithmoides* communities are most common on the islets and along the drains; while *Phragmites australis–Suaeda pruinosa* are restricted to the drains.

The southern shore of the lake is bordered by an extensive fringe of reed swamps, which currently cover over 25% of the lake area (ARE–UNEP 2002). Plant communities are represented by *Phragmites australis* on the lake shores, *Phragmites australis–Potamogeton pectinatus* and *Potamogeton pectinatus–Eichhornia crassipes* in open water, and small patches of *Typha domingensis–Ceratophyllum demersum* along the shores of islets. Among the common species forming the swamps, *Phragmites australis* and *Typha domingensis* are rooted on the lake bottom, *Eichhornia crassipes* forms floating mats while *Potamogeton pectinatus* and *Ceratophyllum demersum* are submerged hydrophytes. Other associated plant species are *Cyperus alopecuroides*, *Echinochloa stagnina*, *Lemna perpusila*, *Ludwigia stolonifera*, *Wolffia hyalina*, and *Potamogeton crispus* (Med Wet Coast 2002, ARE–UNEP 2002).

Phytoplankton. The phytoplankton of the Lake is rich in species, represented mainly by three classes (Bacillariophyceae, 108 species; Chlorophyceae,

52 species; and Cyanophyceae, 31 species) most of which are fresh- to brackish-water forms (ARE–UNEP 2002).

Fauna

Zooplankton. The Lake Burullus water and bottom fauna are represented by three groups of zooplankton: Rotifera, Copepoda, and Cladocera; with a total of 48 species, all of freshwater origin. Most species are rare and only eight species dominate the zooplankton communities (ARE–UNEP 2002). El Shabrawy (2002) estimated the standing crop of zooplankton to be 666 576 individuals per milliliter with the Rotifera group contributing 66.3% to the total amount.

Fish. The large biomass and high diversity of plankton, bottom fauna, and macrophytes provide excellent feeding ground for consumers – particularly fish and birds. The fish population of the lake is composed of 25 species occupying different ecological niches according to their habitat requirements and behavior. The majority are freshwater fish (15 species); 4 species of marine fish temporarily invade the lake according to the hydrological regime, i.e. when its level is low and sea water enters the lake; the other 6 fish species migrate to the sea for spawning. Five main species of freshwater fish are economically important: *Oreochromis niloticus, O. aureus, Sarotherodon galilaeus, Tilapia zillii* (30% of tilapia catch), and *Clarias gariepinus.*

Birds. The Lake Burullus wetland is one of the internationally important sites for wintering birds (Sorensen *et al.* 1994). A list of 90 bird species recorded on the lake was provided in the Management Plan for Burullus Lake (ARE–UNEP 2002), of which 35 species are breeding on the lake (Baha El-Din 1999). Atta *et al.* (1994) counted a total of 100 010 individual waterfowl on the lake in the 1989–90 winter. The largest populations included: wigeon, northern shoveler, ferruginous duck, northern pochard, European coot, and redshank. It seems that the numbers of wintering birds varies considerably from year to year; a 10-fold difference in the number of some birds has been reported by different investigators (Baha El-Din 1999, Atta *et al.* 1994). However, even the total of 100 010 birds, which is believed to be an underestimate, would considerably affect the water quality of the lake by increasing the pH, conductivity, biological oxygen demand, organic matter, nitrogen, and phosphorus. There is no doubt that such large concentration of birds influence the fish population by sharing the food resources and consuming fish.

Reptiles and amphibians. A total of 22 species of reptiles and amphibians have been recorded in Lake Burullus and surrounding areas. Among the most interesting are the Nile valley toad (*Bufo kassasii*) which is endemic to Egypt, the loggerhead turtle (*Caretta caretta*) which breeds locally, and the green turtle (*Chelonia mydas*) (ARE–UNEP 2002).

Conservation status

With Egypt's increasing population and growing demand for food, most of the wetlands of the Nile Delta have been converted to cultivated fields. Complete control of the river flow by a series of major barrages, the latest of which is the Aswan High Dam, have altered the old basin irrigation system to a permanent one, and reclamation of wetlands has caused the further disappearance of the swamps that once flourished in the Nile Delta. The alarming situation of dramatically shrinking Mediterranean wetlands, including the Nile Delta, has caused international concern over the fate of the migratory birds that are wintering on these lands. Wetlands, with their ability to buffer the drainage to the Mediterranean Sea, are also of major concern to countries that share the Mediterranean basin. Biodiversity decline is not only of concern to environmentalists, but is also important to the national economy, in particular fish production. Protection of wetlands has become an important component of the Egyptian Environmental Affairs Agency and the lake was declared a protected area by Egyptian law in 1998. The lake has been designated as an Important Bird Area (IBA) by Bird Life International and it is one of two Ramsar sites in the country. Two bird species inhabiting Burullus Lake, namely the lesser kestrel (*Falco naumanni naumanni*) and the ferrugineous duck, and two turtles – the loggerhead turtle (*Caretta caretta*) and the green turtle – (*Chelonia mydas*) are in the IUCN *Red List of Threatened Animals* (IUCN 2000 and 2002). Vulnerable ferrugineous duck wintering on the lake comprise one of the largest populations on the eastern Mediterranean coast.

Because of the importance of its wetlands, Lake Burullus was selected in 1999 by the Med West Coast (Project for Conservation of Wetlands and Coastal Ecosystems in the Mediterranean Region) as one of three sites on the Egyptian coast for the GEF Project "Conservation of Wetlands and Coastal Ecosystems in the Mediterranean Region," implemented by the Arab Republic of Egypt and the United Nations Environmental Programme to develop the management plan and an infrastructure for the protected area.

Environmental problems of wetlands

The wetlands of the Nile basin are very diverse in various respects: e.g. age, size, shape, ecology, biology, habitats, and species composition; as well as in conservation status. The selected wetlands discussed above represent the diverse

Table 10.6 *The Bahr al-Jebel floodplain (Bor to Malakal)*
(source: Howell et al. *1988, Tables 1.2 and 5.2).*

	1952	1980	Increase
Permanent swamp	2 700	16 200	13 500
Seasonally river-flooded grassland	10 400	13 600	3 200
Total	13 100	29 800	16 700

Areas are given in km^2.

systems: large old lake transformed to swamp; the pioneer stage of wetland formation on the man-made lake; fragments of floodplain wetlands on the river islands; and delta wetlands that are spread within the River Nile along a wet-tropic to extreme-arid climate continuum.

Despite being different in most of the environmental parameters, all of the described wetlands are united by the fact that water flow, both in and out, is controlled by hydrology and water regimes rather than by climatic conditions.

For thousands of years, the wetlands of the southern Sudan have enjoyed stable conditions, with no significant anthropogenic interference. It is worth mentioning that the term "stable" here has a special context. As described by Odum (1967), and cited in Denny (1984), wetlands are described as being "pulse-stable" ecosystems. This means that their stability relies on alternating "pulses" of environmental conditions (in this case wet and dry phases). The communities of pulse-stable systems are characteristically very resilient to change. However, certain events, both natural and man-made, have affected the flora of the wetlands of the southern Sudan. One significant effect has been attributed to the hydrological regime of the Nile system in the Sudd area.

A change in the river hydrology – by both natural and anthropogenic factors – could alter the dynamics of the ecosystems, with all the associated ecological feedback, and could have beneficial or adverse consequences for humans. Among the most-important parameters affecting the wetlands are hydrology and water chemistry, and their interaction with the biological organisms; in particular the primary producers.

Hydrology and area changes

The main environmental problems facing the Nile wetlands are associated with the river regime, with its great variations that cause at their extremes either flood or drought. One of the well-known examples is the great variation of the wetland areas of the Sudd region.

Bailey (1991) gives similar figures for 1952, but in 1980 he estimated the area of permanent swamps to be 16 500 km^2 and seasonal swamps to be 15 000 km^2, giving total areas of 31 500 km^2.

Between 1952 and 1980 there was a large increase in the swamp area caused by the heavy rainfall in the East African catchment, the rise in water levels in Lake Victoria, and the sustained discharge into the Sudd resulting in heavier floods. The permanent swamps were heavily affected, compared with those of the seasonally river-flooded wetlands. Changes in the gross area of the swamps influenced the composition of the plant communities and distribution of plant species. *Vossia cuspidata*, *Phragmites*, and *Cyperus papyrus* have spread upstream and along the banks. On the other hand, *Echinochloa pyramidalis* has become confined to the higher ground near the river. This is the case in Aliab above Bor, but could be taken as a model of the dynamic state of the Sudd. An enormous expansion of *Typha* was observed in 1980 (Howell *et al.* 1988) in comparison with the small areas of pure stands recorded by the Jonglei Investigation Team (ENP 1954). However, no evidence was provided for any increase in populations of *Vossia* and papyrus but both plants changed their distributions by moving southward (Howell *et al.* 1988). The hydrological pattern and the distribution of the plants species have in turn had their effect on land use. Grazing sites and cattle camps have had to be shifted to higher grounds. Wildlife diversity and distribution have also been affected. Floodplain species of buffalo and tiang are reported to be edged out by the increased flooding and changed vegetation. Those who could thrive, such as the hippopotamus and elephant, have increased the size of their populations (Howell *et al.* 1988). Thus, there is a clear dynamic interaction between upstream hydrology (lake levels), local topography, pattern of flooding, vegetation, and land use.

With the construction of the bypass canals, it is expected that areas of the swamps will shrink considerably, because of the reduction in discharge through the natural river channels; there will be a reduction in the river spill and therefore a reduction in the areas that are seasonally flooded and permanently flooded. It is expected that the permanent swamps will be affected to a greater extent than the seasonally flooded lands. The available data on the effect of the Jonglei Canal on the Bahr al-Jebel swamps (Howell *et al.* 1988) indicate that permanent swamps will decrease in area by between 32% and 43% depending on the operating regime of the canal. The grasslands will decrease in area by between 10% and 32%, and the zones occupied by *Oryza longistaminata* and *Echinochloa pyramidalis* will decrease in area, and also move closer to the main river. In the permanent swamps, *Vossia* and papyrus will retreat downstream and the width of the belt that they form alongside the river will decline. A substantial reduction may also be expected in the zone occupied by *Typha*. A fall in the river level will cause a marked decline in the river-derived water level in these swamps remote from the river.

The quantity of water flowing out of the Sudd area of the Nile is about half the quantity of that flowing into it. As a result of the planned Jonglei Canal (Stage I), the benefit downstream will be additional water: 4.7 km^3 at Malakal and 3.8 km^3 at Aswan, having allowed for transmission and in-channel losses. Under the Nile Water Agreement of 1959, this additional water would be divided equally between Egypt and the Sudan (Howell & Lock 1994), yielding an additional 1.9 km^3 for Egypt. At present, additional water is stored in the reservoir of the Aswan High Dam where the development of wetlands on its shores is controlled by vertical and horizontal movements of water levels. However, the operation of the Toshka Canal, which is now being constructed, will withdraw approximately 5 km^3 from the Aswan High Dam reservoir (about 10% of the water that is provided for the whole of Egypt) for the irrigation of newly cultivated lands (SEDP 1998, Wichelns 2002). It is expected that when the canal is fully operational, there will be a decrease in water-level fluctuations in the lake; this will favor the invasion of hydrophytes and lead vegetation to the new dynamic stage.

The water regime downstream of Aswan is completely controlled by the operation of the High Dam. Differences between absolute maximum and minimum river water levels decreased from above 20 m (before the dam) to less than 10 m in the Nile at Aswan after the dam construction. A decrease in water turbidity and reduced water-level fluctuations favors wetland vegetation. Intensive invasion of submerged hydrophytes in Upper Egypt Nile was observed after the dam construction (Springuel & Murphy 1991). Fringes of wetlands along the First Cataract Islands enlarged and reeds (mainly *Phragmites australis*) replaced the floating mats of *Polygonum senegalense* that dominated the wetlands in 1970 (Springuel 1981). The better water transparency may have improved feeding conditions for several piscivorous birds such as pied kingfisher and little egret in Upper Egypt. Species dwelling in reedbeds, such as the purple gallinule and clamorous reed warbler, have recently established themselves along the whole length of the Nile below the dam (Goodman & Meininger 1989).

Moving to the north, there are very few small fragments of Nile wetlands in Upper Egypt while all the Nile valley lands are under cultivation. Land reclamation affects remaining oases of wetlands in the delta lakes. Despite slight differences in the figures from different publications (Meininger & Mullie 1981, Sorensen *et al.* 1994, ARE–UNEP 2002, Med Wet Coast 2002), all have agreed that Lake Burullus (referring to open water) has shrunk considerably, by 49% in the period from 1801 (1092 km^2) to 1913 (556 km^2) and by about 62% by the year 2002 (410 km^2). However, the wetlands, both the salt marshes and swamps, increased in size from 312 km^2 in 1962 to 776 km^2 in 1997, most probably as a result of increased drainage water from reclaimed lands in surrounding areas (Abdel-Rahman & Sadek 1995, El-Bayomi 1999). El-Shinnawy (2003) pointed out that one-third of the annual drainage water discharges to the Mediterranean Sea through Lake Burullus. Without winter closure, the water level of the lake is always above sea level with small water-level fluctuations from 28 to 61 cm above sea level that create the most-favorable conditions for wetland vegetation. However, during the two-week period for maintenance of the irrigation canals in the winter the water level of the lake drops 26 cm below sea level, which allows the intrusion of approximately 100 million m^3 of sea water to move into the lake; thus restricting the growth of freshwater hydrophytes.

Increased coastal erosion combined with the almost-complete cessation of Nile-sediment discharge into the Mediterranean Sea (SAP BIO Project 2002) are among the most-harmful effects of the dam on the delta wetlands, which simply could disappear under rising sea levels.

Water chemistry

Although Denny (1985) has raised a very scintillating question by wondering whether wetlands are Gaia's kidneys, it is apparent that swamps modify the chemistry of the water flowing through them, but do not necessarily purify the water. Thompson (1976) stated that the elements such as chloride, sodium, and magnesium appear to pass through papyrus unaffected. However, he referred to Bishai (1962) who reported the depletion of the chloride load of the Nile as it passed through the Sudan swamps. Studies on the quality of water samples taken from Bahr al-Gebel at Bor, and at the tail of the swamps on the White Nile at Malakal, showed that the changes that had occurred were fairly complex. Quoting Howell et al. (1988): "A reduction in turbidity is accompanied by an increase in the level of alkalinity and silica, a shift in the balance of dissolved nitrogen from the oxidised nitrate to the reduced ammonium ions, an increase in carbon dioxide, and a drop in river-borne algae as evidenced by reduced chlorophyll values."

The quality of water passing through the swamps can be better understood in relation to the dynamics of the plant communities. Thompson (1976) pointed out that a papyrus swamp could be regarded as a *nutrient sieve*. During the dry season it tends to store chemicals and during the wet period to release them, some to a greater extent than others. When the Jonglei Canal is built, much of the area occupied by papyrus will dry out and the effect of burning will play a crucial role in the enrichment of water with nutrients. Because swamps provide important pasture for the animal husbandry of Nilotic tribes living in the Sudd region, a large part of swamp vegetation is burnt each year.

The complete burning of papyrus and its rhizomes is accompanied by the release of large quantities of nutrients, particularly phosphorus. It is possible to envisage a situation in which large areas of papyrus swamp dry out as a result of the opening of the canal, combining perhaps with low flood. If all of the dry material is burnt, it would release large quantities of nutrients into the river system. While it is likely that much of these would quickly be absorbed by the remaining swamp plants it is possible that it could provoke a dramatic flush of growth of *Eichhornia*, and probably of phytoplankton in those lakes receiving water from the river. (Howell *et al.* 1988)

The canal would also carry the sediments, which at present are filtered out by the swamps, to a lower level (Thompson 1976); these sediments, together with enriched water, would flow into the Aswan High Dam Reservoir (Lake Nasser and Lake Nubia) where they might create favorable conditions for weed invasion. It may be noted that at its present stage this lake has alkaline water (pH about 8; Entz 1976; Murphy *et al.* 1990) and high nutrient availablility (Murphy *et al.* 1990), which is not surprising considering the high evaporation rate of about 11% of water lost annually through evaporation. There are notable differences in water characteristics between the southern and northern sections of the lake; decreases in phosphates, chlorides, sodium, potassium, silicon, and turbidity – and an increase in sulphur – have been observed in the northern part of the lake.

In spite of most limnological attributes showing good water quality there are some symptoms that could lead to ecological problems. In the period from 1987 to 1992 particularly, water bloom caused by overgrowth of Cyanophycian species occurred eight times in six years in the southern part of the lake. At present, water bloom occurs recurrently all-year round in different parts of the lake (Bishai *et al.* 2000). Another alarming fact is the greater than 1000-fold increase in bacteria counts in the last two decades. In 1982, fish mortality was reported in the Sudanese section of the lake. Investigations ascribed the phenomenon to a bloom of *Ciratium hirundinella*, a temperate dinoflagellate not previously reported in Africa or in any other man-made reservoir (El Moghraby *et al.* 1986). Intensive pesticide application in irrigation schemes in central Sudan seems to have con- taminated the fish in Lake Nubia. In a study conducted in 1981, tissues of all 18 tested Kass fishes (*Hydrocynus forskalii*) were found to contain dichlorodiphenyl- trichloroethane (DDT). Accordingly, this predator fish was recommended as an indicator fish for monitoring pesticide pollution in the Nile (El Zorgani *et al.* 1979).

The historical control of water hyacinth using chemicals such as 2,4-D (2, 4-dichlorophenoxy acetic acid) could have posed a threat to non-target, floating-type species such as *Pistia*, *Lemna*, *Wolffia*, and *Spirodella*. Other floating macrophytes, such as *Nymphaea* and *Limnophyton*, could also be under threat.

Just north of the dam, in the vicinity of the First Cataract Islands, the quality of water is good with low salt content and without pollution symptoms: almost neutral pH 7, conductivity of around 360 μS cm^{-1}, and total dissolved solids of 250 mg l^{-1} (Ali *et al.* 1999). However, just 2 km downstream, water begins to be polluted with the discharge of untreated industrial, agricultural, and municipal sewage into the Nile; there are also about 200 pleasure boats/floating hotels contributing to pollution of the Nile in Upper Egypt. The most-polluted spots on the Nile are characterized by the absence of submerged macrophytes.

Nile water approaches the delta lakes through agricultural drainage canals that receive surplus water from irrigation. Despite keeping a balance between the fresh and saline characteristics of the lake, the drainage water is heavily polluted thus making the water brackish rather than fresh.

Biodiversity loss

Kassas (1972) stated: "A natural river seems wasteful and awesome; its challenge has throughout history urged in man the will to control." With the progress of technology humans have succeeded in fully controlling the great river in its downstream part traversing Egypt. With the construction of the barrages across the river, water-storage reservoirs, and irrigation schemes the wetlands had been altered into cultivated fields. The habitat loss has led to the elimination of characteristic swamp species, among which the classical examples are the disappearance of the papyrus, lotus, and sacred ibis – the symbols of Pharaoh Egypt. The sacred ibis was regarded as the God of wisdom and learning, patron of the scribal profession, and Lord of the moon. It is well documented in many Pharaoh arts but has not been seen in Egypt since November 1891 (Houlihan 1995). Täckholm and Drar (1950) believed that papyrus was once widespread in Egypt during Pharaoh times and the memory of it remains in numerous ancient signs. They regarded its disappearance from Egypt as being largely due to siltation, drainage, and intensive cultivation along the banks of the Nile. The demand for papyrus products has also resulted in its large-scale cultivation in the past. The plant was doomed, however, once linen was substituted for papyrus in the tenth century. Untended stands of semi-domesticated papyrus were overtaken by aggressive competition from the native perennial hydrophytes (*Phragmites australis* and *Vossia cuspidata*), by reclamation for agriculture, and by the drying out of wetlands when some Delta tributaries ceased to flow. After

1812, *Cyperus papyrus* was considered extinct. However, in 1968 this plant was rediscovered in Wadi el-Natrun, where a small thicket had survived as a relict of an ancient backswamp (El Hadidi 1971, Boulos 1985); it was also found recently by Serag (2000) in the Nile Delta at the Damietta Branch. It is worth mentioning here that in 1960, the Egyptian scientist Hassan Ragab reintroduced papyrus to Egypt from the Sudd region and planted extensive areas on the Nile islands in the Giza district. He became a very successful businessman by establishing a flourishing papyrus industry for tourists and producing more than 10 million sheets of papyrus (Zahran & Willis 2003).

We can argue with Thompson (1985) who wrote that papyrus swamps are more typical of stable hydrological regimes than any other reedswamp type and are rare in wetlands with seasonal amplitudes greater than 2.5 m. As shown above, the maximum depth of water supporting the growth of *Cyperus papyrus* in the Sudd region was reported to be 4.5 m and the plant also formed floating mats; hence, it should be less affected by high flood than rooted hydrophytes. It is doubtful that, as suggested by Thompson (1985), papyrus became extinct in Egypt and northern Sudan because of the increasing amplitude of the lower Nile.

What will be the fate of the papyrus in the Sudd swamps in connection with the building of canals and land reclamation? Most probably *Typha*, whose fast expansion has recently been observed, will replace it. The rhizomes of *Typha* are generally buried in mud, and are not burnt even if the swamp dries out entirely; however, the rhizomes of papyrus often form a floating mat that, if completely dry, can burn. Also *Typha* swamps are normally associated with sites of internal drainage, with alkaline water and with more dissolved material than in the more-acidic waters occupied by papyrus (Howard-Williams & Walker 1974). According to data in Thompson (1985), papyrus swamps are usually about pH 6.5 and can tolerate a wide range of pH values (pH 4 to 8) but not saline conditions; in contrast, for *Typha*, the water pH ranged from 7 to 11 and in the Nile Delta, the water supporting *Typha* showed alkaline reactions and high concentrations of phosphate (Khedr & El-Khabery 2000).

Although the construction of the Jonglei Canal was halted in 1983 because of the civil war (only 86 km of the 360 km remain to be excavated), once completed the canal would definitely have an impact on the migratory species such as tiang, white-eared kob, and zebra. Consequently, the migratory species would be under stress and many of them might die. Unconfirmed reports indicated that substantial numbers have already died by jumping into the completed part of the canal while attempting to cross to the other side via the steep banks.

Another threat to biodiversity is the invasion of exotic plants. The case of *Eichhornia crassipes* could be the most-remarkable unintentional human impact on the environment in the Nile system in the Sudan (Ali 1991). *Eichhornia* has largely replaced the water lettuce (*Pistia stratiotes*), which was formerly abundant in Sudanese swamps (Migahid 1947) but now survives only in rain pools and a few swamp channels (Howell *et al.* 1988). Up until 1957, this species was the largest free-floating macrophyte in the Nile system in the Sudan. In 1957, the exotic water hyacinth (*Eichhornia crassipes*) reached the southern Sudan (Gay 1958) and has since spread, largely replacing the once-abundant water lettuce. The growth forms of the two species account adequately for the replacement. *Pistia stratoites* has no leaf-stalkes and so cannot raise its leaves in crowded conditions. *Eichhornia crassipes*, on the other hand, can develop long leaf-stalks in crowded conditions and can shade out *P. stratoites*. Bailey and Litterick (1993) stated that the hyacinth appears to have replaced the niches formerly provided by the water lettuce for aquatic invertebrates in the Sudd. *P. stratoites* persists in temporary pools, where it seeds freely and thus survives the dry season. It is also found within swamps, in sites remote from the river. The case of the water lettuce could be repeated and other native species could be threatened if alien species are introduced, accidentally or intentionally.

Another remarkable example of biodiversity loss linked with the construction of dams occurred after the impoundment of el Roseiris Dam in 1966. The heavy deposition of silt within the dam basin has led to the wiping out of the entire population of the gigantic bivalve (mussel) *Etheria elliptica* (Hammerton 1972).

References

Abdel-Rahman, S. I. and Sadek, S. A. (1995). *The Application of Multi-Spectral Remote Sensing to the Assessment of North Nile Delta, Egypt.* Academy of Scientific Research and Technology. Cairo, Egypt: National Information and Documentation Centre.

Ali, O. M. (1977). *Hydrophytic Plants from the Southern Stretches of the White Nile.* Report of the Jonglei Canal Project Mission (unpublished report). Aquatic Biological Consulting Services and UNESCO.

(1991). An ecological assessment of the Nile system in the Sudan over the last thirty years. *Nile Geographer*, **1**, 1–9.

(1999). Biodiversity of aquatic plants in the southern Sudan. In *Workshop of "Strategy and National Action Plan for Biodiversity" (IUCN and HCENR)* (unpublished report).

Ali, M. M., Springuel, I., and Yacoub, H. A. (1999). Submerged plants as bioindicators for aquatic habitat quality in the river Nile. *Journal of Union of Arab Biologist Cairo. Cytogenetics, Ecology and Flora*, **9**(B), 403–18.

Andrews, F. W. (1948). The vegetation of the Sudan. In *Agriculture in the Sudan*, ed. J. D. Tothill. Oxford: Oxford University Press, pp. 32–61.

ARE–UNEP (Arab Republic of Egypt–United Nations Environment Programme) (2002). *Management Plan for Burullus Protected Area*. GEF Med Wet Coast. Project number EGY/97/G33/A/1G/99. ARE and UNEP.

Aswan Governorate and ARE (1993). *Environmental Profile and Action Plan of Aswan Governorate*. Aswan Governorate and Arab Republic of Egypt.

Atta, G. A. M., Baptist, H. J. M., Meininger, P. L. *et al.* (1994). Counts of waterbirds in Egypt, winter 1989/90. In *Ornithological Studies in Egyptian Wetlands 1989/90*, eds. P. L. Meininger and G. A. M. Atta. FORE report 94-01, WIWO report 40.

Baha El-Din, S. M. (1999). *Directory of Important Bird Areas in Egypt*. Cairo, Egypt: Palm Press.

Bailey, R. G. (1987). The Sudd. In *African Wetlands and Shallow Water Bodies. Directory*, eds. M. J. Burgis and J. J. Symoens. Paris: ORSTOM.

(1991). The Sudd. *Biologist*, 38(5), 171–6.

Bailey, R. G. and Litterick, M. R. (1993). The macroinvertebrate fauna of water hyacinth fringes in the Sudd swamps (River Nile, southern Sudan). *Hydrobiologia*, **250**, 97–103.

Beadle, L. C. (1974), 1981. *The Inland Waters of Tropical Africa. An Introduction to Tropical Limnology*, 2nd edn. London: Longmans.

Beshir, M. (ed.) (2000). *Sudan Country Study on Biodiversity*. HCENR, IUCN, UNDP, CBD. Khartoum, Sudan: Silver Star Press.

Bishai, H. M. (1962). The water characteristics of the Nile in the Sudan. *Hydrobiologia*, **19**, 357–82.

Bishai, H. M., Abdel-Malek, S. A., and Khalid, M. T. (2000). *Lake Nasser*. Publication of National Biodiversity Unit 11. Cairo, Egypt: Egyptian Environmental Affairs Agency.

Boulos, L. (1985), The arid eastern and south-eastern Mediterranean region. In *Plant Conservation in the Mediterranean Area*, ed. C. Gomez-Campo. Dordrecht, the Netherlands: Junk, pp. 123–40.

Brown, A. F. (1905). Some notes on the *Sudd* formation of the Upper Nile. *Botanical Journal of the Linnean Society*, **37**, 51–8.

Butzer, K. W. (1976). *Early Hydraulic Civilization in Egypt*. Chicago, IL and London: University of Chicago Press.

Chipp, T. F. (1930). Forests and plants of the Anglo-Egyptian Sudan. *Geography Journal*, **75**, 123–43.

Denny, P. (1984). Permanent swamp vegetation of the Upper Nile. *Hydrobiologia*, **110**, 79–90.

(1985). Submerged and floating-leaved aquatic macrophytes. In *The Ecology and Management of African Wetlands Vegetation*, ed. P. Denny. The Hague, the Netherlands: Junk.

Din, N. A. and Eltringham, S. K. (1972). Ecological separation between white and pinkbacked pelicans in the Ruwenzori National Park, Uganda. *Ibis*, **116**, 28–42.

Drar, M. (1951). The problem of the Sudd in relation to stabilizing and smothering plants. *Botaniska Notiser*, **1**, 33–46.

El Bayomi, M. G. (1999). *Lake Burullus, a Geo-morphological Study*. Ph.D. thesis, Helwan University, Egypt.

El Hadidi, M. N. (1971). Distribution of *Cyperus papyrus* L. and *Nymphaea lotus* L. in inland waters of Egypt. *Mitteilungen der Botanischen Staatssammlung Munchen*, **10**, 470–75.

(1976). Riverain flora of Nubia. In *The Nile, Biology of an Ancient River*, ed. J. Rzoska. The Hague, the Netherlands: Junk.

El Moghraby, A., El Seed, M. T., Sinada, F., and Ali, O. M. (1986). Recent ecological changes in the Nile System in the Sudan. *GeoJournal*, **13**(1), 417–9.

El Shabrawy, G. M. (2002). *Ecological Survey of Burullus Nature Protectorate: Zooplankton Conservation of Wetland and Coastal Ecosystem in the Mediterranean Region*. Final Report. Cairo, Egypt: Nature Conservation Sector, Egyptian Environmental Affairs Agency.

El-Shinnawy, I. A. (2003). Water budget estimate for environmental management at Al-Burullus Lake, Egypt.
http://www.eeaa.gov.eg/english/main/Env2003/Day3/Protectorates/shinaay.ecri.pdf.

El Zorgani, G. A., Abdalla, A. M., and Ali, M. E. T. (1979). Residues of organochlorine insecticides in fishes in Lake Nubia. *Environmental Contamination Toxicology*, **22**(1&2), 44–8.

ENP (Equatorial Nile Project) (1954). *Equatorial Nile Project. Its Effects in the Anglo-Egyptian Sudan*. The Report of the Jonglei Investigation Team, vols. I–V. Khartoum, Sudan Government.

Entz, B. (1976). Lake Nasser and Lake Nubia. In *The Nile, Biology of an Ancient River*, ed. J. Rzoska. The Hague, the Netherlands: Junk, pp. 271–98.

FAO (Food and Agriculture Organization) (1997). *Irrigation Potential in Africa: a Basin Approach*. FAO Land and Water Development Division, FAO Land and Water Bulletin 4.

Garstin, W. (1904). Report upon the basin of the Upper Nile. *Parliamentary Accounts and Papers*, **111**, 315–785.

Gay, P. A. (1958). *Eichhornia crassipes* in the Nile of the Sudan. *Nature*, **182**, 538–9.

Goodman, S. M. and Meininger, P. L. (1989). *The Birds of Egypt*. Oxford: Oxford University Press.

Green, J. (1987). Lakes No and Ambadi. In *African Wetlands and Shallow Water Bodies. Directory*, eds. M. J. Burgis and J. J. Symoens. Paris: ORSTOM.

Gronblad, R., Prowse, G. A., and Scott, A. M. (1958). Sudanese desmids. *Acta Botanica Fennica*, **58**, 3–82.

Hammerton, D. (1972). The Nile River: a case history. In *River Ecology and Man*, eds. R. T. Oglesby, C. A. Carison, and J. A. McCann. London: Academic Press.

Houlihan, P. F. (1995). *The Animal World of the Pharaohs*. Cairo, Egypt: American University in Cairo Press.

Howell, P. and Lock, M. (1994). The control of the swamps of the southern Sudan: drainage schemes, local effects and environmental constrains on remedial development. In *The Nile: Sharing a Scarce Resource*, eds. P. Howell and J. A. Allan. Cambridge, UK: Cambridge University Press.

Howell, P., Lock, M., and Cobb, S. (1988). *The Jonglei Canal: Impact and Opportunity*. Cambridge, UK: Cambridge University Press.

Howard-Williams, C. and Thompson, K. (1985). The conservation and management of African wetlands. In *The Ecology and Management of African Wetland Vegetation*, ed. P. Denny. Dordrecht, the Netherlands: Junk.

Howard-Williams, C. and Walker, B. H. (1974). The vegetation of a tropical African lake: classification and ordination of the vegetation of lake Chilwa (Malawi). *Journal of Ecology*, **62**, 831–54.

Hurst, H. E. (1952). *The Nile: a General Account of the River and the Utilization of its Water*. London: Constable Publishers.

Hussein, F. (1976). Amphibia and reptiles. In *The Nile, Biology of an Ancient River*, ed. J. Rzoska. The Hague, the Netherlands: Junk.

IUCN (2000 and 2002). *Red List of Threatened Animals*. Gland, Switzerland and Cambridge, UK: IUCN.

Kassas, M. (1972). Ecological consequences of water development projects. In *The Environmental Future*, ed. N. Polunin. London: Macmillan.

Khedr, A. A. and El-Khabery, E. M. (2000). An ecological study on *Typha domingensis* (Pers.) Poir Ex Steud in the Nile Delta. In *Proceedings of First International Conference on Biological Sciences, Tanta University, Egypt*, vol. 1, pp. 242–55.

Khedr, A. A. and Lovett-Doust, J. (2000). Determination of floristic diversity and vegetation composition on the islands of Burollos Lake, Egypt. *Applied Vegetation Science*, 3, 147–56.

Latif, A. F. A. (1974). *Fisheries of Lake Nasser*. Aswan: Aswan Regional Planning, Lake Nasser Development Center.

Latif, A. F. A., El-Etreby, S. G., Abdel-Azim, M. E., and Shereie, H. S. A. (1979). *Reservoir Fishes and Fishery Resources*. Report on River Nile and Lake Nasser Project. Cairo, Egypt: Academy of Scientific Research and Technology.

Macleay, K. N. G. (1959). *Observations on Birds of the Nile Valley*. Sixth Annual Report of the Hydrobiological Research Unit, University of Khartoum, pp. 12–18.

Mageed, Y. A. (1985). The Jonglei Canal: a conservation project of the Nile. In *Large-Scale Water Transfers: Emerging Environmental and Social Experiences*, eds. G. N. Golubev and A. K. Biswas. Oxford, UK: UNEP, Tycooly Publishing.

Med Wet Coast (Project for Conservation of Wetlands and Coastal Ecosystems in the Mediterranean Region) (2002). *Zero Issue 2002*.

Meininger, P. L. and Mullie, W. C. (1981). *The Significance of Egyptian Wetlands for Wintering Waterbirds*. New York: Holy Land Conservation Fund.

Mekkawy, I. A. A. (1998). Fish stock assessment of Lake Nasser fisheries, Egypt, with emphasis on the fisheries of *Oreochromis niloticus* and *Sarotherodon galilaeus*. *Journal of the Egyptian, German Society of Zoology*, **25**(B), 283–404.

Migahid, A. M. (1947). An ecological study of the "Sudd" swamps of the Upper Nile. *Proceedings of the Egyptian Academy of Sciences*, 3, 57–86.

  (1952), *Velocity of Water Current and its Relation to Swamp Vegetation in the Sudd Region of the Upper Nile*. Cairo, Egypt: Fouad I University Press.

Mitchell, D. M., Denny, P., and Howard-Williams, C. (1985). African wetland vegetation: concluding perspective. In *The Ecology and Management of African Wetland Vegetation*, ed. P. Denny. Dordrecht, the Netherlands: Junk.

Montasir, A. H. (1937). On the ecology of Lake Manzala. *Bulletin of The Faculty of Science, Cairo: University*, **12**, 1–50.

Mubarak, M. O., Bari, E. A., Wickens, G. E., and Williams, M. A. J. (1982). The vegetation of the central Sudan. In *A Land Between Two Niles*, ed. M. A. J. Williams and D. A. A. Adamson. Rotterdam; the Netherlands: Balkema.

Murphy, K. J., Rorslett, B., and Springuel, I. (1990). Strategy analyses of submerged lake macrophytes communities: an international example. *Aquatic Botany*, **36**, 303–23.

Odum, E. P. (1967). The strategy of ecosystem development. *Science*, **164**, 262–70.

Renvoize, S. A., Lock, J. M., and Denny, P. (1984). A remarkable new grass genus from the southern Sudan. *Kew Bulletin*, **39**(3), 455–61.

Rzoska, J. (1974). The Upper Nile Swamps: a tropical wet-land study. *Freshwater Biology*, **4**, 1–30.

  (1976a). River and Nile Valley before man's interference. In *The Nile, Biology of an Ancient River*, ed. J. Rzoska. The Hague, the Netherlands: Junk.

  (1976b). Descent to the Sudan Plains. In *The Nile, Biology of an Ancient River*, ed. J. Rzoska. The Hague, the Netherlands: Junk, pp. 197–214.

  (1976c). The invasion of *Eichhornia crassipes* in the Sudanese White Nile. In *The Nile, Biology of an Ancient River*, ed. J. Rzoska. The Hague, the Netherlands: Junk, pp. 315–20.

Saad, S. I. and Sami, S. (1967). Studies of pollen and spores content of Nile Delta deposits (Berrenbal region). *Pollen Spores*, **9**, 467–502.

Said, R. (1993). *The River Nile*. London: Pergamon Press.

Sandon (1950). In Bailey, R. G. (1987). 5.1 The Sudd. In *African Wetlands and Shallow Water Bodies. Directory*, eds. M. J. Burgis and J. J. Symoens. Paris, ORSTOM.

SAP BIO Project (2002). *Strategic Action Plan for the Conservation of Biodiversity in the Mediterranean Region*. National Report of Egypt.

SEDP (Southern Egypt Development Project) (1998). Arab Republic of Egypt. Ministry of Public Works and Water Resources National Water Research Center.

Serag, M. S. (2000). The rediscovery of the papyrus (*Cyperus papyrus* L.) on the bank of Damietta Branch, Nile Delta, Egypt. *Taeckholmia*, **20**(2), 195–8.

Sorensen, U. G., Meininger, P. L., Petersen, I. K., and Atta, G. A. M. (1994). Environmental status of Egyptian wetlands, with special reference to birds. In *Ornithological Studies in Egyptian Wetlands 1989/90*, eds. P. L. Meininger and G. A. M. Atta. FORE report 94-01; WIWO report 40. Vlissingen, the Netherlands: Zeist.

Springuel, I. (1981). Studies on Natural Vegetation of the Islands of the First Cataract. Ph.D. thesis, Assiut University, Assiut, Egypt.

  (1990a). Riverain vegetation in the Nile valley in Upper Egypt. *Journal of Vegetation Science*, **1**, 595–8.

  (1990b). Plant successions on recently-formed Nile islands in Nubia, Egypt. In *Proceedings of the Second National Conference on Environmental Studies and Research*. Cairo, Egypt: Institute of Environmental Studies and Research, pp. 113–30.

  (1994). Riparian vegetation in the hyper-arid area in upper Egypt, Lake Nasser area, and its sustainable development. In *Proceedings of the International Workshop* on *The Ecology and Management of Aquatic–Terrestrial Ecotones*. Seattle, WA: University of Washington, pp. 107–19.

Springuel, I. and Murphy, K. (1991). Euhydrophyte communities of the River Nile and its impoundment in Egyptian Nubia. *Hydrobiologia*, **218**, 35–47.

Täckholm, V. (1976). Ancient Egypt, landscape, flora and agriculture. In *The Nile, Biology of an Ancient River*, ed. J. Rzoska. The Hague, the Netherlands: Junk.

Täckholm, V. and Drar, M. (1950). *Flora of Egypt*, vol. II. Cairo, Egypt: Fouad I University Press.

Tharwat, A. A. (1998). Fish eating birds in Lake Nasser. *ICLARM Symposium on Ecological Basis and Management Policy for Sustainable Fish Production in Lake Nasser, June 20–23, 1998, Aswan, Egypt*. Aswan, Egypt: High Dam Lake Development Authority.

Thompson, K. (1976). Swamp development in the head waters of the white Nile. In *The Nile, Biology of an Ancient River*, ed. J. Rzoska. The Hague, the Netherlands: Junk.

   (1985). Emergent plants of permanent and seasonally-flooded wetlands. In *The Ecology and Management of African Wetlands Vegetation*, ed. P. Denny. The Hague, the Netherlands: Junk.

White, G. F. (1988). The environmental effects of the High Dam at Aswan. *Environment*, **30**(7), 5–40.

Wichelns, D. (2002). Economic analysis of water allocation policies regarding Nile River water in Egypt. *Agricultural Water Management*, **52**, 155–75.

Willcocks, W. (1904). *The Nile in 1904*. London, New York: E & FN Spon.

Zahran, M. A. and Willis, A. J. (2003). *Plant Life in the River Nile in Egypt*. Riyadh, Sand: Arabia: Mars Publishing House.

11

The prairie potholes of North America

A. G. VAN DER VALK
Iowa State University

Introduction

Prairie potholes or sloughs are small, shallow, palustrine wetlands, common in north-Central North America, with vegetation that is usually herbaceous (Fig. 11.1). In the Aspen Parkland in Canada, which is the transition zone between the prairies and the boreal forest, aspen (*Populus* spp.), willows (*Salix* spp.), and other tree species are often found around the periphery of potholes. The suppression of fire has resulted in tree and shrub invasion of prairie-pothole basins throughout much of the region. Their primary sources of water are precipitation and groundwater. Most do not have surface inflows or outflows, except during exceptionally wet years when they fill up and surface-water flows temporarily connect them. In most years, water leaves prairie potholes primarily by evapotranspiration and groundwater recharge. During droughts, there is often no standing water in them at all. Their catchments are typically very small and this, combined with significant changes in seasonal and annual precipitation, results in rapid and large changes in water levels within and among years. These water-level changes can result in changes in the species composition and ecosystem functions of these wetlands from year to year, especially in deeper potholes. In other words, prairie potholes are very dynamic, shallow depressional wetlands in which plant and animal populations are constantly adjusting their distribution and population size to changing water levels. Although no single prairie pothole would ever qualify as one of the world's largest wetlands, collectively they are one of the largest and most-important wetland complexes on the planet.

The World's Largest Wetlands: Ecology and Conservation, eds. L. H. Fraser and P. A. Keddy.
Published by Cambridge University Press. © Cambridge University Press 2005.

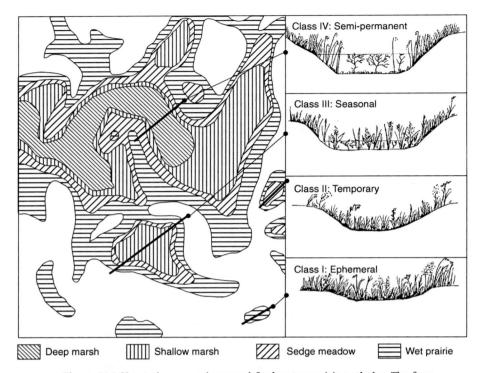

Figure 11.1 Vegetation zones in several freshwater prairie potholes. The four transects illustrate the vegetation zones found in ephemeral, temporary, seasonal, and semi-permanent prairie potholes. From Galatowitsch and van der Valk (1994). See also Fig. 11.5.

The literature on prairie potholes is extensive. Fortunately, there have been a number of monographs and reports that have reviewed and summarized much of this literature. The most important of these are *Northern Prairie Wetlands* (van der Valk 1989), *Prairie Basin Wetlands of the Dakotas: a Community Profile* (Kantrud *et al.* 1989), *Restoring Prairie Wetlands* (Galatowitsch & van der Valk 1994), a special issue of *Great Plains Research* (vol. 6, Spring 1996), and *Prairie Wetland Ecology* (Murkin *et al.* 2000a). The chapter on "Wetlands of the prairies of Canada" (Adams 1988) in *Wetlands of Canada* provides a good overview of the ecology of prairie potholes in Canada. Information on the soils of prairie potholes can be found in Richardson *et al.* (1994). *Wetlands of the American Midwest* (Prince 1997), although it covers much more than the prairie-pothole region, provides a good overview of the history of agricultural drainage of wetlands and how this drainage was organized. This chapter is not intended to be an exhaustive review of the literature on prairie potholes. It does attempt, however, to provide an overview of the ecology of these wetlands and to be a gateway to the rich and extensive literature on them.

In this chapter, the origin and hydrology of prairie potholes will first be considered followed by their classification, vegetation (composition, primary production, and mineral cycling), and use by waterfowl. Their conservation and restoration are also briefly reviewed. Because cyclical changes in water levels and the changes in the flora and fauna that they induce are a defining characteristic of prairie potholes, these cyclical changes will be emphasized.

Geology and climate

As its name implies, the boundaries of the prairie-pothole region (Fig. 11.2) are defined by both its vegetation and geology. The southern boundary of the Wisconsin glacial advance is also the southern boundary of the prairie-pothole region. Those sections of Wisconsin glacial deposits that were historically covered with grasslands (prairies) and forest–grassland transitions (parklands as they are called in Canada) constitute the prairie-pothole region. This region is estimated to cover about 700 000 km^2 (Kantrud et al. 1989). It runs from central Iowa through western Minnesota and eastern South and North Dakota and across the southern portions of the Western Canadian provinces of Manitoba, Saskatchewan, and Alberta (Fig. 11.2).

A complex landscape of moraines, glacial meltwater channels, outwash plains, and lacustrine plains was created by the retreat of Wisconsin-age glaciers. For the most part, this new landscape was poorly drained and was covered with numerous shallow depressions. The size, maximum depth, shape, and connectivity of these shallow depressions were highly variable and were a function of the type of glacial deposit in which they were located (Adams 1988, Winter 1989, LaBaugh et al. 1998). Potholes are most abundant in areas of end and stagnation moraines (up to 90 potholes per km^2) where the relief can be steep. Their densities are much lower in areas of hummocky ground moraine (c. 10 to 20 km^{-2}), and outwash plains (c. 5 km^{-2}). Regardless of local topography, most potholes are small and typically less then 1 ha.

In the Canadian portion of the region, there are estimated to be between 4 and 10 million potholes (Adams 1988). In North and South Dakota, there were estimated to be about 2.3 million in the 1960s (Kantrud et al. 1989). Because so many had been drained before counts were attempted and many potholes contain no water in dry years and were ignored in some surveys, both the number of prairie-potholes prior to European settlement, i.e. drainage, and the current number are unknown. Assuming 18 potholes per km^2, as is the case in Canada (Adams 1988), the total number of prairie potholes prior to European settlement

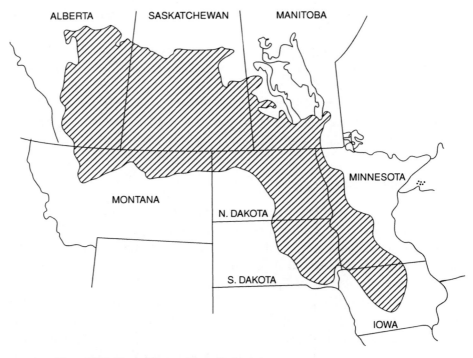

Figure 11.2 Map of the prairie-pothole region.

would have been around 12.6 million. Assuming the average pothole was about 0.5 ha or 0.005 km², which is the case in North and South Dakota (Kantrud *et al.* 1989), prairie potholes covered approximately 63 000 km². Collectively prairie potholes represented a significant portion of the total inland wetland area of the United States and Canada.

The entire prairie-pothole region has a continental climate. Maximum summer temperatures can reach over 40 °C over most of the region, but are more typically in the 20 to 30 °C range. Winter minimum temperatures can drop to −40 °C, but in January are normally in the −5 to −20 °C range. Most prairie potholes are frozen for about half the year. Annual precipitation varies from over 800 mm per year in the southeastern part of the region to less than 350 mm per year in the northwestern part. Because of the region's relatively dry climate and hot summers, annual evapotranspiration normally exceeds total annual precipitation (Winter 1989). For many potholes, snow trapped by standing litter plays an important part in their annual hydrological budgets. Annual precipitation, however, can vary significantly from year to year with periods of drought alternating with periods of above-normal precipitation. For example, for

Milford, Iowa between 1951 and 2000, annual total precipitation ranged from a low of 254 mm in 1957 to 1196 mm in 1993, a difference of 942 mm, with a mean over this period of 725 mm. Because of the small size of pothole catchments, changes in an annual precipitation can result in significant changes in water levels from year to year (van der Camp & Hayashi 1998). These changes in water levels can have a profound effect on the species composition, species distribution, and ecological functions of potholes.

Hydrology

Prairie potholes are depressional wetlands in a geologically new landscape that is in the early stages of developing an integrated surface drainage system (LaBaugh et al. 1998). Potholes are not yet a part of this developing drainage system and only infrequently have a stream channel either entering or leaving them. Although they are often viewed as being isolated basins, this is not actually true. During wet years, prairie potholes can overflow and become connected to each other. In effect this is the beginning of the development of an integrated drainage system that will eventually eliminate these wetlands as this landscape ages. They are also usually connected to adjacent potholes through groundwater flows, especially in areas with some relief (see Winter 1989). Depending on their position in the landscape, and regional and local groundwater flow patterns, prairie potholes can be groundwater discharge areas, groundwater recharge areas, or groundwater flow-through wetlands (Winter 1989, LaBaugh et al. 1998, Rosenberry & Winter 1997, Winter & Rosenberry 1998). Although water levels in all prairie potholes are affected by changes in annual precipitation to some extent, potholes with significant groundwater inputs will rarely go completely dry.

Because the entire prairie-pothole region has a climate in which precipitation varies seasonally and interannually, the water levels in prairie potholes are constantly changing (Fig. 11.3). Due to a combination of spring runoff and rain, water levels are highest in the spring and then decline slowly during the summer. Years of above-normal total annual precipitation are often followed by below-normal years. These cyclical changes in annual precipitation, "wet–dry" or "habitat" cycles, are about 10 to 15 years in duration (van der Valk & Davis 1978a, Kantrud et al. 1989).

Prior to European settlement, groundwater tables in the region were often close to the surface, especially in the southern part of the region (Prince 1997). This had an adverse effect on crop growth because the saturated zone just below the surface of the soil was anaerobic and crop roots would not grow in it.

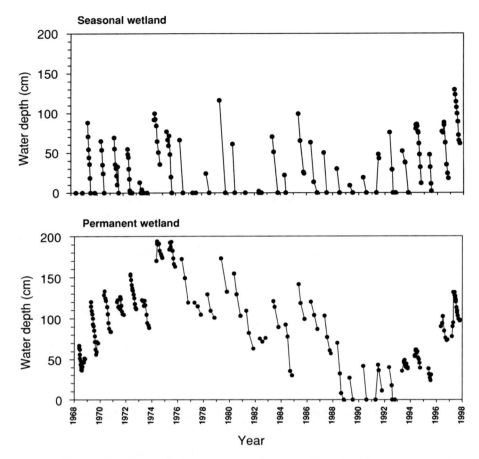

Figure 11.3 Water level changes in a small, seasonal (S109) and large, permanent (S50) prairie pothole at the St. Denis National Wildlife Refuge, Saskatchewan, Canada. The gaps in the records indicate periods when these wetlands were frozen and no data were collected. Adapted from van der Camp and Hayashi (1998).

The presence of potholes also made it difficult to move equipment around a farm and limited the size of some types of equipment, e.g. plows. Potholes were drained almost exclusively to create more farmland or to improve the field layout of existing farms. Drainage required the establishment of drainage networks, either using surface channels (northern parts of the region) or drainage tiles (southern parts) to create a man-made network that joined these wetlands to the existing natural drainage networks. Prince (1977) provides a detailed description of the legal organization, methodology, and extent of drainage in the entire American Midwest, which includes the American portion of the prairie-pothole region.

Classification

Stewart and Kantrud (1971) working in North Dakota devised a scheme for classifying prairie potholes that is based on the type of wetland vegetation found in the deepest portions of their basins (Fig. 11.4). They recognized five types of prairie potholes: Class 1, ephemeral ponds (with wet prairie in deepest areas); Class II, temporary ponds (wet meadow); Class III, seasonal ponds (shallow marsh); Class IV, semi-permanent ponds (deep marsh); Class V, permanent ponds (submersed aquatics). (The Class-I wetland type of Stewart and Kantrud [1971] is no longer considered a wetland, but a type of wet prairie.) The number of vegetation zones in a basin depends on its maximum water depth (Figs. 11.1 and 11.4). prairie potholes also differ in water chemistry (saline versus brackish water) with saline potholes most common in the Canadian Prairie Provinces. Although the Stewart and Kantrud (1971) classification of prairie potholes has now been supplanted by newer American (Cowardin *et al.* 1979) and Canadian (National Wetlands Working Group 1988) national wetland classification systems, it, nevertheless, remains a regionally useful system.

As noted, the maximum water depth in a basin is the single-most-important feature of potholes (Stewart & Kantrud 1971). The deepest potholes, i.e. Class V (Fig. 11.4), have four different types of wetland vegetation or zones. Starting in the deepest part of the basin, these four zones are described below.

1. *Open-water zone.* This is the deepest zone and it is permanently flooded. Submerged vascular aquatic plants are the dominant species, e.g. species of *Potamogeton, Najas, Myriophyllum, Utricularia, Ceratophyllum,* etc.
2. *Deep-marsh zone.* This zone is semi-permanently flooded and only goes dry during drought years. The vegetation is dominated by tall emergents, e.g. typically species of *Typha* and *Scirpus*, with an understory of submerged aquatic and small free-floating species (e.g. *Lemna, Spirodella,* and *Ricciocarpus*).
3. *Shallow-marsh zone.* This zone is only seasonally flooded, typically in the spring. The vegetation tends to be dominated by tall grasses and sedges (*Carex* spp.) with a sprinkling of forbs.
4. *Wet-meadow zone.* This zone is only temporarily flooded for a few weeks in the early spring. The vegetation is dominated by a mix of medium-height grasses, sedges, and rushes (*Juncus* spp.), and many species of forbs. Trees and shrubs may also be found in this zone and may be the dominant species in some potholes.

Potholes from classes IV, III and II (Fig. 11.4) have three, two and one wetland vegetation zones, respectively. The boundaries between adjacent zones are sometimes

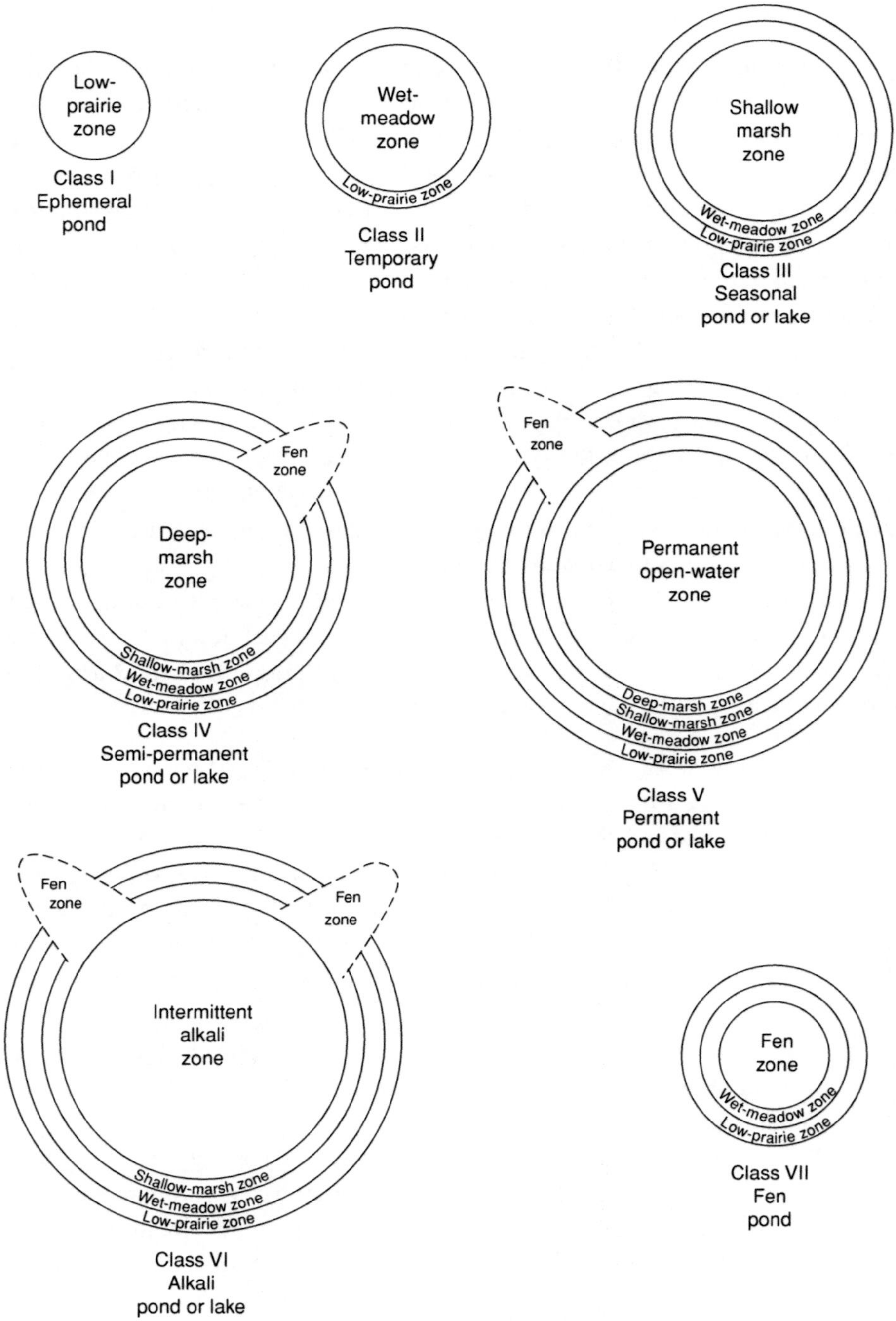

Figure 11.4 Classification of prairie potholes of Stewart and Kantrud (1971).

difficult to delineate and normal zonation patterns can be replaced by a variety of atypical patterns caused by the deletions of one or more zones, doubling of zones, or inversions of zones due to water-level fluctuation patterns. Atypical zonation patterns can often be used to reconstruct the recent hydrology of a prairie pothole (Kantrud *et al.* 1989).

Vegetation

Changes in water levels caused by changes in total annual precipitation have a major impact on plant and animal populations in the deeper prairie potholes, i.e. classes IV and V (Fig. 11.4). Among the first researchers to recognize that changes in these wetlands were cyclical were Weller and Spatcher (1965). They outlined a five-stage habitat cycle: dry marsh (drawdown), dense marsh (several years after reflooding), hemi-marsh (50% emergent, 50% open water), open marsh (more than 50% open water), and open-water marsh (emergents largely or completely eliminated). The open-water marsh persists until the next drought, which lowers water levels and eventually exposes the marsh sediments. This marks the start of the next dry-marsh stage. Weller and Spatcher (1965) also noted that water-level changes and herbivory by muskrats, which contributed to the elimination of emergent vegetation during high-water years, caused these cycles. They also documented the impact of water-level and vegetation changes on bird usage of prairie potholes. These cyclical changes in prairie potholes came to be known as "habitat" or "wet–dry" cycles.

Subsequent studies by van der Valk and Davis (1976, 1978a), Pederson (1981), Pederson and van der Valk (1985), and Poiani and Johnson (1989) established the central role of seed banks (viable seed in the sediments) in these wetlands for the persistence of plant species from one cycle to the next and for the ability of the vegetation in these wetlands to adjust quickly to different water depths during the cycle. They emphasized the importance of drawdowns, the dry-marsh stage, in the habitat cycle for the re-establishment of emergent species and for mudflat annuals, a group of species that are only found in these wetlands during drawdowns. Figure 11.5, which is taken from van der Valk and Davis (1978a), outlines the vegetation cycle as it was understood in the late 1970s. They simplified the cycle proposed by Weller and Spatcher (1965) by combining the hemi-marsh and open-marsh stages, during both of which emergent vegetation is declining. The four stages in the van der Valk and Davis vegetation cycle are the dry marsh, regenerating marsh (≡ dense marsh), degenerating marsh (≡ hemi-marsh and open marsh), and lake marsh (≡ open-water marsh).

The classic habitat cycle as described above is mainly a feature of the deeper and larger prairie potholes, i.e. classes IV and V, in which a significant range of

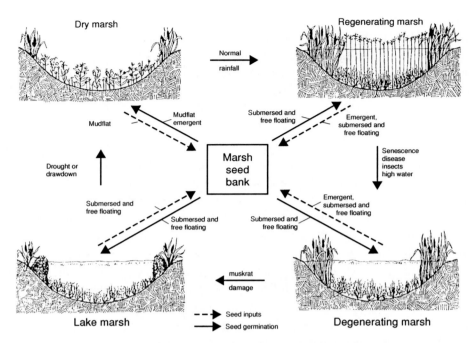

Figure 11.5 Idealized habitat cycle in a semi-permanent prairie pothole (van der Valk & Davis 1978a). See also Fig. 11.1.

water levels (*c.* 1.5 to 2 m) can occur. Only in deep potholes can water levels in wet years become deep enough, for long enough, to eliminate emergent plant species. Habitat cycles also occur in shallower potholes, but they do not produce such marked changes in the composition and distribution of vegetation. Their impact is primarily on understory plant species and the fauna.

The cyclical changes in the vegetation in potholes are a type of succession, herein defined as a change in the floristic composition of the vegetation in an area from one year to another (van der Valk 1981, 1982, 1985, 1987). According to this definition, succession occurs whenever a new species becomes established or a species is extirpated. Several models of succession in potholes have been proposed. The earliest was the critical life-history model of van der Valk (1981). This qualitative model uses expected or effective life span, propagule longevity, and propagule establishment requirements of plant species to predict the species composition of a wetland during various stages of a habitat cycle. Poiani and Johnson (1993) developed a computer simulation model in which a vegetation submodel that determines the responses of six classes of prairie-wetland species to water-level changes is linked to a hydrology submodel that estimates water depths from precipitation and evapotranspiration data.

Water depth is usually the most-important determinant of the position of plant species along elevation gradients in freshwater wetlands (Shay & Shay 1986, van der Valk & Welling 1988). In order to develop spatially explicit models at the species level, a model was needed that incorporated the water-depth tolerances of each species. Unfortunately, with a few exceptions (e.g. Squires & van der Valk 1992), there is little experimental data on the water-depth tolerances of most species in northern prairie wetlands. Nevertheless, two such models of the responses of emergent species to water-level changes have been developed for the Delta Marsh [located on the south shore of Lake Manitoba (98° 23' W, 50° 11' N)]. De Swart et al. (1994) developed a series of logistic regression models to predict the distribution of dominant emergent species after changes in water levels. Seabloom et al. (2001) developed a cellular automaton model in which adult and seed distributions, and a set of rule-based functions, determine the fate of each emergent species and the annual guild within each cell of a grid covering the wetland. Seabloom et al. (2001) have evaluated the strengths and weaknesses of these two models. The models of Poiani and Johnson (1993), De Swart et al. (1994), and Seabloom et al. (2001), although they are pioneering efforts, have demonstrated that it is possible to develop models that can reliably predict changes in the composition and distribution of vegetation in prairie wetlands during habitat cycles.

Primary production and mineral cycling

The cyclical changes in the vegetation during a habitat cycle significantly alter the primary production, secondary production, and mineral cycling in prairie potholes (van der Valk & Davis 1978b, 1980, van der Valk 1994, Murkin et al. 2000a, 2000b, van der Valk & Murkin 2001). These functional changes over an entire cycle have never been measured in a prairie pothole, although some data on production and mineral cycling are available (van der Valk & Davis 1978b, 1980, Davis & van der Valk 1978a, 1978b, 1978c). They were quantified for an experimentally induced habitat cycle that was carried out over a ten-year period in the Delta Marsh (Murkin et al. 2000a). Although the Delta Marsh is a lacustrine marsh, it is in the prairie-pothole region and, prior to the establishment of water-control structures to control flooding, it underwent the same kinds of water-level fluctuations as permanently flooded prairie potholes (Batt 2000). From the primary production data from the Delta Marsh, it is possible to estimate the relative magnitude of the changes in standing biomass, nitrogen, and phosphorus during a cycle (Kadlec et al. 2000, Murkin et al. 2000b, van der Valk 2000, van der Valk et al. 2000). The Delta Marsh is at the northeastern edge of the prairie-pothole region. Consequently, the primary production in this wetland is lower than in potholes further south.

Dry marsh

During the dry-marsh stage, when this wetland was drawn down for two years, total macrophyte biomass was about $440\,g\,m^{-2}$ of which $365\,g\,m^{-2}$ was above ground. Annual species made up 50% or more of the total biomass. Newly recruited *Phragmites australis* and *Scirpus lacustris* contributed most of the rest of this biomass. Mean below-ground biomass was around $75\,g\,m^{-2}$ or 17% of the total.

Regenerating marsh

During the regenerating stage, mean total biomass reached a maximum of $475\,g\,m^{-2}$. Above-ground biomass ($220\,g\,m^{-2}$) was actually lower than during the dry-marsh stage and the main contributors to it were emergents and submersed aquatics. The increase in total biomass was due primarily to increases in the below-ground biomass of emergent species. Mean below-ground biomass was $255\,g\,m^{-2}$ or 54% of the total. The main change in primary production with the reflooding of the wetland was a 3-fold increase in the amount of below-ground biomass as the dominant species switched from annuals and emergent seedlings to fully grown emergents.

Degenerating marsh

Mean total biomass declined ($380\,g\,m^{-2}$) during the degenerating-marsh stage due to the localized or complete extirpation of emergent species (especially *Scolochloa festucacea* and *Scirpus lacustris*). Above-ground biomass declined to $155\,g\,m^{-2}$ and below-ground biomass to $225\,g\,m^{-2}$. Algal production, however, increased during this stage. The emergent species that continued to grow during this stage continued to increase their below-ground biomass.

Open marsh

During the open-marsh stage, when water levels were over 1 m above the long-term mean water level, the emergent vegetation was mostly extirpated and was replaced by submerged aquatics and metaphyton. Although there was little above-ground emergent biomass during the first and second years of deep flooding, below-ground biomass persisted at high levels until the fall of the second year of deep flooding. After two years of open water, total biomass was at the lowest level found, $85\,g\,m^{-2}$ – of which $60\,g\,m^{-2}$ or 70% was above ground. Algal production, however, is highest during this stage.

Over the entire simulated wet–dry cycle, above-ground biomass did not vary as much as previously estimated by van der Valk and Davis (1978b); it varied about 6-fold, not the 20-fold predicted.

Table 11.1 *Estimated mass of N (kg ha⁻¹) in the major pools during the growing season in the four stages of an idealized wet–dry cycle.*

	Stage			
Pool	Dry	Regenerating	Degenerating	Lake
Macrophytes				
Above ground	73	44	31	12
Below ground	15	51	45	5
Total	88	95	76	17
Algae	–	5	14	12–15[a]
Invertebrates	–	2	1	0.6–3
Surface water				
Inorganic	–	1	1	0.8–2
Organic	–	17	22	10–30
Pore water				
Inorganic	–	11	18	6–23
Organic	–	29	32	26–30
Total	88	160	164	73–120

[a] Low estimate from reference cells; high estimate from second year of deep flooding.

These changes in biomass during a habitat cycle resulted in major changes in the size of nutrient-storage compartments (water, plants, litter, invertebrates, vertebrates, etc.) and movements of nutrients among these compartments, i.e. in nutrient cycles (Tables 11.1 and 11.2). Other than the soils, the largest compartment for both nitrogen and phosphorus during most of a habitat cycle is the vegetation, except in the lake stage when the surface-water compartment may be larger. Although there are changes in the size of algal, invertebrate, and vertebrate compartments during the cycle, they are minor when compared with the changes in the vegetation. In short, it is changes in the size of the macrophyte compartment and fluxes into and out of this compartment that drive mineral cycling in prairie potholes (Murkin et al. 2000b).

Waterfowl

The prairie-pothole region is one of the major waterfowl-breeding areas in North America (Batt et al. 1989). It is also a major migration corridor in the fall and spring for ducks, geese, and other birds. Because most potholes are isolated from lakes and streams in the region, go dry periodically, and are largely

Table 11.2 *Estimated mass of P (kg ha⁻¹) in the major pools during the growing season in the four stages of an idealized wet–dry cycle.*

| | Stage | | | |
Pool	Dry	Regenerating	Degenerating	Lake
Macrophytes				
Above ground	27	7	5	2
Below ground	2	5	5	0.5
Total	29	12	10	2.5
Algae	–	1.5	1.8	1.6–2.2[a]
Invertebrates	–	0.2	0.1	0.1–0.3
Surface water				
Inorganic	–	0.3	0.4	0.8–1.5
Organic	–	0.3	0.4	0.3–0.7
Pore water				
Inorganic	–	2.6	3.3	1.6–5.3
Organic	–	0.7	0.8	0.5–1.0
Total	29	17	17	7–13

[a] Low estimate from reference cells; high estimate from second year of deep flooding.

anaerobic in areas covered with emergent vegetation (Rose & Crumpton 1996), they usually do not contain fish – except possibly a couple of species of minnows that can tolerate low oxygen levels (Peterka 1989). The absence of fish makes all of the invertebrate production in these wetlands available to waterfowl. This is especially important early in the breeding season when female ducks require large amounts of protein in their diets while laying eggs (Swanson & Duebbert 1989, Alisauskas & Ankney 1992, Krapu & Reinecke 1992). The lack of fish in prairie-pothole food chains is a major reason why they are such a productive waterfowl-breeding habitat. The prairie region produces about 50% of the game ducks (Smith 1995), but makes up only 10% of the remaining waterfowl-breeding habitat in North America. The absence of fish also makes potholes a productive breeding habitat for amphibians. In potholes with fish, amphibian eggs and larvae become prey items for many fish species. When potholes have been connected to large lakes, as has happened in the Iowa Great Lakes region, amphibian populations in these formerly isolated potholes have declined significantly (Lannoo 1996).

Twelve of the thirty-four species of North American ducks are common breeders in the region. The prairie-pothole region alone has about 60% of the breeding population of seven species (mallard, gadwall, blue-winged teal, northern

Table 11.3 *Size of total duck breeding population in the prairie-pothole region and numbers of potholes with water in May, 1986–95. Adapted from Smith (1995).*

| Year | Number of breeding ducks | Number of potholes with water | | |
		Total	United States	Canada
1986	18 429 000	5 760 000	1 735 000	4 025 000
1987	16 521 000	3 872 000	1 348 000	2 524 000
1988	13 515 000	2 901 000	791 000	2 110 000
1989	12 725 000	2 983 000	1 290 000	1 693 000
1990	13 399 000	3 508 000	691 000	2 817 000
1991	11 944 000	3 200 000	706 000	2 494 000
1992	14 256 000	3 609 000	825 000	2 784 000
1993	12 180 000	3 611 000	1 350 000	2 261 000
1994	18 997 000	5 985 000	2 216 000	3 769 000
1995	21 892 000	6 336 000	2 443 000	3 893 000
Mean	15 385 800	4 176 500	1 339 500	2 837 000

shoveler, northern pintail, redhead, and canvasback) in most years (Smith 1995). The number and distribution of ducks in the region each year depends on water conditions (Batt *et al.* 1989). Population sizes and reproductive success of these ducks are positively correlated with the number of potholes holding water in May and July (Johnson & Grier 1988, Batt *et al.* 1989). During drought years, many ducks move to other parts of the continent, e.g. to the boreal-forest or tundra regions (Johnson & Grier 1988). Northern pintail and blue-winged teal are more affected by droughts because they tend to use temporary and seasonal wetlands, whereas canvasbacks and lesser scaup – which use deeper, semi-permanent, and permanent wetlands – are less likely to be displaced, except during severe drought. Reproductive success is generally reduced during droughts because of lower nesting success and lower survival rates of ducklings. For example, from 1986 to 1995, spring water conditions in the prairie-pothole region, as measured by the number of potholes with water, ranged from: good in 1986 (more than 5 million potholes with water); to very poor during 1988–93 (3.6 million or less), a prolonged drought period; to excellent by 1994–95 (Table 11.3). During this decade, the mean number of breeding ducks was 15 385 000 (Table 11.3), 16% lower than the long-term average (1955–95) of 18 166 000. The number of breeding ducks was lowest (11 944 00 in 1991) during the 1988–93 drought. With the end of the drought in 1994–5, breeding-duck populations increased rapidly and were estimated to be 21 892 000 by spring 1995, which is higher than the long-term average. Drought during 1988–93 reduced the amount of wetland habitat available to breeding waterfowl. This reduced waterfowl population sizes because of the displacement of ducks, particularly pintails and mallards, to other regions. The rebound of duck species populations in 1994–5 was due to the refilling of the potholes.

Regionally, the effects of droughts on breeding-duck population sizes are highly species specific (Table 11.4). Lesser-scaup populations were halved by the drought in 1989 versus 1986, but had returned to pre-drought levels in 1995. Mallard, northern-shoveler, and blue-winged-teal populations (Table 11.4) were low during the drought years (1988–93) and increased in the wet years (1994–5). Gadwall numbers dropped only slightly below their long-term average during 1987–8 and in 1995 gadwall numbers were twice their long-term average. Gadwall are more-closely associated with the prairie-pothole region than other ducks, with more than 90% of the US gadwall population normally found in the region. Pintails had record lows during the drought years and showed a doubling of the populations from 1993 to 1994. Redhead, canvasback, wigeon, and green-winged-teal populations declined to some extent during the drought compared with other species, but did increase in 1994 – and especially 1995 – to population sizes larger than their long-term means.

Waterfowl and habitat cycles

Changes in water levels result in changes in vegetation cover and structure, and in type of food available within a wetland; these changes in turn affect the number and kinds of birds found in a wetland at any given time in a habitat cycle (Weller 1994, Murkin & Caldwell 2000). Collectively, these changes in bird use during the habitat cycle in a given wetland produce the overall changes in waterfowl populations that occur over the entire region. Weller and Spatcher (1965) documented changes in bird use during habitat cycles and the Delta Marsh experimental study documented similar changes as well as changes in plant cover and food sources on which the birds rely (Murkin *et al.* 1997, Murkin & Caldwell 2000).

Dry marsh

The vegetation during the dry-marsh stage is a combination of annuals and newly established emergent species. Initially this vegetation may have little cover value because it is too sparse and low. Exposed mudflats are common at the beginning of the dry-marsh stage and areas of mudflats may remain during the entire stage in some cases. These mudflats are ideal feeding places for many shorebirds. They feed on the invertebrates and seeds in the mudflats. As the soil dries out and the vegetation becomes denser and taller, many

Table 11.4 Breeding populations (in thousands) of ten duck species in the prairie-pothole region in 1986–95 (Smith 1995).

Species						Year						
	1986	1987	1988	1989	1990	1991	1992	1993	1994	1995	TYM	LTM
Mallard	3900	3678	2726	2957	2800	2863	3326	3188	4516	5352	3531	4678
Blue-winged teal	3892	2800	2761	2438	2318	3113	3572	2409	4199	4847	3235	3594
Gadwall	1463	1244	1237	1301	1458	1443	1916	1636	2201	2734	1663	1293
Northern pintail	1655	1398	674	1002	966	524	905	1075	2066	1805	1207	3112
American wigeon	544	440	440	398	508	510	685	504	763	852	564	1021
Northern shoveler	1609	1349	930	930	1080	1078	1195	1290	2187	2177	1382	1444
Lesser scaup	1311	856	1023	621	741	822	919	738	1020	1253	930	1107
Redhead	509	479	398	458	416	349	498	403	581	855	495	512
Green-winged teal	297	307	345	309	356	331	403	281	574	686	389	530
Canvasback	285	309	240	201	238	247	215	210	293	491	273	329

TYM, ten-year mean; LTM, long-term mean (1955–95).

terrestrial and semi-terrestrial invertebrates become more common. This in turn attracts upland birds such as bobolinks (*Dolichonyx oryzivorus*), meadowlarks (*Sturnela neglecta*), and mourning doves (*Zenaida macroura*). Many small mammals may also become established during the dry-marsh stage, including deer mice (*Peromyscus maniculatus*). During the dry-marsh stage, some dabbling ducks may nest in the wetland if there is permanent water nearby and some upland bird species may rest the taller patches of vegetation. Most of the species that are typically found in prairie potholes are absent during the dry-marsh stage and are replaced by an assemblage of terrestrial species. The longer this stage lasts, the more terrestrial this assemblage becomes.

Regenerating marsh

The reflooding of the wetland makes it suitable habitat again for wetland invertebrate and vertebrate species. Aquatic invertebrates in the soil, on plants, and in the water column quickly return. Algal populations often flourish and can become very abundant, especially the metaphyton. The spread of emergents during this stage can result in very-dense vegetation over all or most of the wetland, depending on water levels. Submerged aquatic macrophytes are often common during the first year or two before being shaded out by emergents. Wetlands during the regenerating stage are re-colonized by breeding waterfowl and other water birds, e.g. rails and coots, as both suitable food and cover are again available for them. Marsh wrens and blackbirds, which nest in emergents, also return and muskrats become re-established.

Degenerating marsh

The decline in emergent species marks the onset of the degenerating marsh. This decline is due to high water levels, or muskrat feeding and lodge building, or some combination of these. The early stage of the degenerating marsh, when there is a mix of open water and emergent vegetation, is the most-favorable stage for the majority of animal species in prairie potholes, especially birds. Submerged aquatic vegetation dominates the open-water areas. Invertebrate populations shift from those characteristic of temporary water to those found in permanent water (e.g. amphipods and chironimids). Diving ducks become more common during this stage. Muskrats may also become very abundant in this stage, and their activities may greatly accelerate the rate of loss of emergent species.

Lake marsh

With the continued decline of emergent populations, a point is reached where these species are reduced to a thin fringe around the edge of the wetlands.

The wetland now resembles a pond or lake. The invertebrate fauna in this stage is dominated by benthic species, and there is little cover or shelter because of the absence of emergents. Submerged aquatics and planktonic algae are the dominant plants. Fish may also become established or become more abundant if already present. Overall, food sources for most birds are limited. Only birds that use open water, e.g. diving ducks, are found during this stage. Other common wetland species, e.g. dabbling ducks, no longer use the wetland except as a stopover during migration. Some relict populations of rails, coots, and blackbirds may remain in the emergent fringe along the edge.

Potholes as nutrient sinks

As with many other kinds of wetlands (Kadlec & Knight 1996), prairie potholes can remove nutrients from the water that enters them (Neely & Baker 1989, Crumpton & Goldsborough 1998). Consequently, potholes can reduce non-point-source pollution from farmland, which is the major source of nutrients entering lakes and streams in the prairie-pothole region (van der Valk & Jolly 1992). Because so many prairie potholes have been drained, the restoration of prairie potholes is often proposed as a cheap and efficient way to treat runoff in agricultural watersheds (Galatowitsch & van der Valk 1994).

Published data on the fate of inorganic nitrogen and phosphorus in agricultural runoff entering prairie potholes is still limited, especially for natural wetlands. The best long-term data set comes from Eagle Lake, Iowa. This wetland receives most of its surface inputs through two large drainage ditches at the south end and its only surface outflow is over a low dam at the north end (Davis et al. 1981). As the data from this study indicate (Table 11.5), Eagle Lake was a perfect nutrient sink for nitrogen (both nitrate and ammonia) and phosphate for three out of four years. The main reason for this was that this wetland had no outflows for three years. However, during the fourth year the flow in drainage tiles increased significantly and nutrient inputs also increased as the drought ended and there were outflows from the wetland. Nevertheless, Eagle Lake remained a nutrient sink in year four, and its nutrient removal efficiency was about 80% for ammonia, 85% for nitrate, and 20% for phosphate. However, as with most wetlands, when soluble organics are considered the situation is very different. For example in 1979 when there was an outflow from Eagle Lake, inputs of soluble carbon were about $300 \, kg \, ha^{-1}$ while outputs were $516 \, kg \, ha^{-1}$. Eagle Lake was acting as a source for dissolved organic compounds.

Eagle Lake and subsequent studies (Crumpton & Goldsborough 1998) have demonstrated that prairie potholes are good sinks for inorganic nitrogen

Table 11.5 *Inputs and outputs of water (mm) and nutrients (kg ha⁻¹) for Eagle Lake, Iowa. Adapted from Davis et al. (1981).*

	1976	1977	1978	1979
Water				
Precipitation	575	963	709	944
Surface inflows	33	36	163	1620
Total inputs	608	999	872	2564
Surface outflow	0	0	0	1758
Ammonia				
Precipitation	4.0	6.7	5.0	6.6
Surface inflows	0.1	0.5	0.8	2.5
Total inputs	4.1	7.2	5.8	9.1
Surface outflow	0	0	0	2.0
Nitrate				
Precipitation	4.1	6.8	5.0	6.7
Surface inflows	7.1	3.7	25.4	202.8
Total inputs	11.2	10.5	30.4	209.5
Surface outflow	0	0	0	29.8
Phosphate				
Precipitation	0.20	0.33	0.24	0.32
Surface inflows	0.05	0.18	0.75	3.20
Total inputs	0.25	0.51	0.99	3.52
Surface outflow	0	0	0	2.81

compounds, but not necessarily ideal sinks for inorganic phosphorus. Since nitrate is the major nutrient in the runoff from farmland in much of the region (Neely & Baker 1989), existing potholes – and restored and created potholes – have the potential to reduce non-point-source pollution problems in the region.

Conservation

Fortunately, the prairie-pothole region is not experiencing rapid population growth or development. In fact, the number of people living in many rural parts of the region is declining. Consequently, development pressure on prairie potholes is not as intense as it is for many other kinds of wetlands around the United States and the rest of the world. The main threat to prairie potholes remains agricultural drainage. In the United States, such drainage has mostly ceased for several reasons. These include: the end of federal subsidies for drainage; the judicial ruling that these wetlands are protected under the Clean Water Act; and the Swampbuster provision of the 1985 Food Security Act. The latter prevents farmers from obtaining a variety of government farm subsidies if they drain wetlands on their property. The use of prairie potholes by migratory waterfowl provided a legal rationale, the Migratory Bird Rule, used to justify the protection of isolated wetlands – i.e. wetlands not contiguous with or adjacent to navigable water – by the Clean Water Act under Section 404. Most prairie potholes are not associated with navigable waters (van der Valk & Pederson 2003). In 2002, the US Supreme Court's decision in the case of the Solid Waste Agency of Northern Cook County versus US Army Corps of Engineers, the "SWANCC decision," invalidated the use of the Migratory Bird Rule. The SWANCC decision could result in a significant reduction in the legal protection of prairie potholes from drainage (van der Valk & Pederson 2003). Although Swampbuster will continue to prevent the drainage of potholes in the United States in the short term, the removal of most potholes from protection under the Clean Water Act will make it easier to provide exemptions to and to repeal Swampbuster.

Because the prairie-pothole region has long been recognized as a major breeding area for waterfowl, there has been a significant movement to protect potholes from drainage since the 1930s. Ducks Unlimited has been the most visible and effective private organization working to protect wetlands in the United States and Canada, and the US Fish and Wildlife Service and Canadian Wildlife Service – and their state and provincial counterparts – have been the most visible and effective government entities. Initially, the main efforts of these organizations were to preserve existing potholes through establishing wildlife refuges and Waterfowl Protection Areas (WPAs). "Duck Stamps" issued by various government agencies funded the acquisition of pothole areas to protect them from drainage. Hunters were required to buy these stamps before they could legally hunt waterfowl.

In 1986, Canada, the United States, and Mexico adopted the North American Waterfowl Management Plan. This major new international initiative brought together a consortium of private organizations and government agencies with the primary goal of conserving wetlands and increasing waterfowl and other wetland bird populations. The North American Waterfowl Management Plan resulted in the formation of a number of "joint ventures," one of which is the Prairie Pothole Joint Venture that has been operating since 1987. Through a variety of cooperating organizations (federal agencies, state and provincial agencies, and Ducks Unlimited) and federal and state conservation and farm programs, including various US Department of Agriculture land set-aside programs, the Prairie Pothole Joint Venture has worked to protect and increase wetland acreage by buying land, by conservation easements, and by restoring wetlands on private land. The Prairie Pothole Joint Venture has well-defined habitat objectives (hectares of land to be protected, restored, or enhanced) as well as waterfowl-population objectives (number of breeding and migrating ducks and a target recruitment rate).

Restoration

The restoration of prairie potholes in the United States has increased dramatically because agricultural land set-aside programs either allowed farmland in the prairie-pothole region to be restored to wetlands or, more recently, required that the farmland be restored to wetlands. Galatowitsch and van der Valk (1994) have reviewed the techniques used to restore prairie potholes. Gray et al. (1999) have reviewed restorations in the Canadian part of the region. Over the last 15 years or so, thousands, perhaps tens of thousands, of prairie potholes have been restored. Wetland restorations typically have three stages: environmental restoration, vegetation restoration, and ecosystem restoration. Environmental restoration involves restoring the hydrology to something like pre-drainage conditions. Vegetation restoration involves re-establishing the indigenous species that were formerly found in the wetland. Ecosystem restoration involves restoring the functional attributes of the wetland such as its primary production, food chains, and mineral cycles. Most wetland restorations assume that this last stage will occur automatically and stop with the establishment of suitable vegetation.

Unfortunately prairie-pothole restoration usually stops at the environmental-restoration stage. Restoring the hydrology in drained prairie potholes is done by disrupting drainage-tile lines or filling in drainage ditches (Galatowitsch & van der Valk 1994). Although environmental restoration is simple in theory, it can be much more complex in reality. Wetlands to be restored today are often connected by tile lines or ditches to an organized drainage network. By law, the drainage of land upstream from a restored wetland cannot be adversely affected by its restoration. This may require some elaborate and expensive re-engineering of the existing networks, including routing new tile lines or ditches around the restored wetland. Drained wetlands today are often bordered or bisected by roads, railway tracks, gas pipelines, and a variety of utility right-of-ways (phone, electric, water, sewage, etc.) These generally have to be protected from re-flooding; this often requires building dams to protect some areas in the wetland basin from flooding. Former wetlands that straddle property boundaries can be particularly challenging to restore if one landowner is not willing to cooperate.

Prairie-pothole restorations are not unique in stopping after the environmental-restoration stage. Other wetland restorations also stop at this stage, e.g. the Kissimmee River restoration in South Florida. For the Kissimmee River restoration, however, there was good evidence prior to the restoration that a combination of propagules in the seed bank and of propagules that would quickly reach the site would result in the re-establishment of pre-drainage vegetation (Toth *et al.* 1995, Wetzel *et al.* 2001). All the available evidence, however, suggested that this would not be the case for prairie potholes. Restored potholes are mostly isolated from remaining extant wetlands, and they do not have seed banks that contain propagules of many native wetland species (Wienhold & van der Valk 1989). Consequently, the vegetation in restored prairie potholes is often very depauperate and dominated by a small number of weedy species (Galatowitsch & van der Valk 1995). The two seed-dispersal mechanisms that can still transport seeds from natural to restored wetlands are waterfowl (Mueller & van der Valk 2002) and wind. Dispersal by waterfowl for plant species other than submerged aquatics seems to occur very slowly. When waterfowl-dispersed species finally reach a restored wetland, they may not be able to become established because wind-dispersed weedy species, e.g. cattails, may already dominate the restored basin.

As noted previously, there are different kinds of prairie potholes that are distinguished primarily by their maximum depth. To date, the restoration of prairie potholes, however, has not resulted in the restoration of all types of prairie potholes in proportion to their former abundance on the landscape (Galatowitch & van der Valk 1995). Instead, mostly semi-permanent and permanent wetlands are being restored. Even basins that were historically temporary and seasonal wetlands are being restored to semi-permanent and permanent wetlands by building a dam across the lowest point of the basin to increase its effective depth. Galatowitsch *et al.* (1998) have suggested that future prairie restorations be planned at the landscape level, not the individual-basin level as is currently the case, and that restoring the pre-drainage landscape should become the goal of these coordinated restorations.

In summary, a significant number of prairie potholes over much of the region, especially in the United States, have been restored and more will continue to be restored in the near future. However, much could be done to improve the quality of these restorations by paying more attention to the establishment of suitable vegetation and by restoring all types of prairie portholes, not just the deeper ones.

Threats

Attempts to preserve existing prairie potholes and to restore drained prairie potholes are undermined to some extent by three problems: (1) invasion by weedy species; (2) altered regional and hydrology; and (3) environmental degradation due to nutrient and sediment inputs. Galatowitsch *et al.* (1999) have reviewed the literature on invasive species in freshwater wetlands, including prairie potholes. Three invasive emergent species can be major problems in the region: *lythrum salicaria*, *Typha glauca*, and *Phalaris arundinaceae*. Eurasian water milfoil (*Myriophyllum spicatum*) has also recently invaded the eastern part of the region and threatens to become a problem in deeper permanently flooded potholes. All of these species tend to outcompete other species in prairie potholes and all are very difficult to eradicate (Wetzel & van der Valk 1998). Not only have invasive plants become established in the region, but so have invasive animal species. Among the problem animal species in the region are: the bullfrog, which has negatively affected indigenous amphibian species in the southern prairie-pothole region (Lannoo *et al.* 1994, Lannoo 1996); and the European carp, whose spawning in some larger potholes results in the destruction of submerged vegetation.

Many potholes have been destroyed by agricultural drainage. The best data on losses are for the American portion of the region (Dahl 1990). The highest losses (*c.* 90%) occurred in Iowa at the southern end of the region with less-severe losses in North (*c.* 50%) and South (*c.* 35%) Dakota. Drainage in some areas, especially the southern part of the prairie-pothole region had resulted in regional lowering of the groundwater table. This in turn has altered the hydrology of the remaining wetlands. There are no studies that have documented the effects of groundwater lowering on the flora, fauna, or functions of prairie potholes. Even changes in upland land use can alter the hydrology of potholes by altering water yield from their catchments (Euliss & Mushet 1996).

The conversion of most of the uplands around prairie potholes to crop fields or pastures has significantly degraded the quality of water entering these wetlands. In tile-drained sections of the region, the remaining potholes receive water with much-higher nutrient levels than prior to European settlement of the region (Neely & Baker 1989). In the surface-drained sections, increased sediment loading can be an even more severe problem for benthic invertebrates, algae, and submersed aquatic plants (Martin & Hartman 1987, Gleason & Euliss 1998, Euliss & Mushet 1999).

The changes caused by environmental degradation in prairie potholes are hard to document because there are so few studies of the wetlands of the region prior to the onset of agricultural drainage, and today agriculture is so widespread in the region that there is not a pothole that is not directly or indirectly affected by it. The available evidence suggests, not surprisingly, that prairie potholes have lost many species in the last 100 years. For example in northwest Iowa, Galatowitsch and van der Valk (1995) examined species lists from pristine prairie potholes, i.e. wetlands sampled prior to agricultural disturbance, and contemporary lists from extant potholes surrounded by agricultural land. The number of plant species in potholes in the 1990s was roughly half of that found at the time of European settlement (Galatowitsch & van der Valk 1995). Although the prairie-pothole region does not have any species unique to this region, the drainage of so many of the potholes and the degradation of the remaining potholes has resulted in many plant and animal species in various states and provinces in the region becoming locally rare, threatened, endangered, or even extirpated (Lammers & van der Valk 1977, 1978, Dinsmore 1994, Bultena *et al.* 1996, Lannoo 1996).

Priorities for action

Although there are existing programs such as the North American Waterfowl Management Plan that will help to ensure the conservation and even restoration of prairie potholes, additional efforts are needed to prevent their loss to agricultural drainage in Canada and even in the United States because of the SWANCC decision. The most-pervasive and most-insidious threat to prairie potholes is poor water quality (in terms of sediment, nutrients, and pesticides). Although government agencies have made considerable efforts to reduce nutrient inputs into lakes and streams in order to protect them from degradation, there has been almost no effort to protect wetlands from such inputs. Ironically, the reputation that wetlands have developed as sinks for nutrients has misled many regulators and policy makers into thinking that wetlands are not degraded by such inputs, but this is not the case. As with lakes, which are also good nutrient sinks, wetlands are significantly degraded by such inputs through the loss of species and increased susceptibility to invasion and spread of weedy species. Wetland degradation due to inputs of agricultural runoff has been well documented for some wetlands, such as the Everglades (Davis 1994); but, as noted, degradation has been little studied in prairie potholes. One of the major changes seen as a result of increases in nutrient inputs from agricultural runoff in the Everglades was the displacement of indigenous species by invasive species. Invasive species are also widespread in the prairie-pothole region and they deserve more attention than they have received. Historical data suggest that species diversity in prairie potholes is declining, in part because of invasive species like hybrid cattail *Typha glauca*. This species continues to spread westward in the region and is currently taking over the Delta Marsh (Shay *et al.* 1999). To date very little effort has been made to control invasive species in prairie potholes. This is in large part due to the fact that most of the potholes are on private lands and private landowners have no incentives to protect their wetlands. The key to preserving the wetlands of the prairie-pothole region is convincing private landowners to protect them and to improve their management.

References

Adams, G. D. (1988). Wetlands of the prairies of Canada. In *Wetlands of Canada*, National Wetlands Working Group, Environment Canada, Ecological Land Classification Series 24. Ottawa, Canada: Environment Canada. Montreal, Canada: Polyscience Publications Inc., pp. 155–98.

Alisauskas, R. T. and Ankney, C. D. (1992). The cost of egg laying and its relationship to nutrient reserves in waterfowl. *Ecology and Management of Breeding Waterfowl*, eds. B. D. J. Batt, A. D. Afton, M. G. Anderson *et al.* Minneapolis, MN: University of Minnesota Press, pp. 30–61.

Batt, B. D. J. (2000). The Delta Marsh. In H. R. Murkin., A. G. van der Valk, and W. R. Clark. (eds.) *Prairie Wetland Ecology: the Contribution of the Marsh Ecology Research Program*, eds. H. R. Murkin, A. G. van der Valk, and W. R. Clark. Ames, IA: Iowa State University Press, pp. 17–33.

Batt, B. D. J., Anderson, M. G., Anderson, C. D., and Caldwell, F. D. (1989). The use of prairie potholes by North American ducks. In *Northern Prairie Wetlands*, ed. A. G. van der Valk. Ames, IA: Iowa State University Press.

Bultena, G. L., Duffy, M. D., Jungst, S. E. *et al.* (1996). Effects of agricultural development on biodiversity: lessons from Iowa. In *Biodiversity and Agricultural Intensification: Partners for Development and Conservation*, eds. J. S. Srivastava, N. J. H. Smith, and D. A. Forno. Washington, DC: The World Bank, pp. 80–94.

Cowardin, L. M, Carter, V., Golet, F. C., and LaRoe, E. T. (1979). *Classification of Wetlands and Deepwater Habitats of the United States*. US Fish and Wildlife Service, FWS/OBS-79/31.

Crumpton, W. G. and Goldsborough, L. G. (1998). Nitrogen transformation and fate in prairie wetlands. *Great Plains Science*, **8**, 57–72.

Dahl, T. E. (1990). *Wetlands Losses in the United States 1780's to 1980's*. Washington, DC: US Department of the Interior, Fish and Wildlife Service.

Davis, C. B. and van der Valk, A. G. (1978a). Litter decomposition in prairie glacial marshes. In Simpson (eds.). *Freshwater Wetlands*, eds. R. E. Good, D. F. Whigham, and R. L. Simpson. New York: Academic Press, pp. 99–113.

  (1978b). The decomposition of standing and submerged litter of *Typha glauca* and *Scirpus fluviatilis*. *Canadian Journal of Botany*, **56**, 662–75.

  (1978c). Mineral release from the litter of *Bidens cernua* L., a mudflat annual at Eagle Lake, Iowa. *Verhandlungen Internationale Vereinigung Limnologiae*, **20**, 452–7.

Davis, C. B., Baker, J. L., van der Valk, A. G., and Beer, C. E. (1981). Prairie pothole marshes as traps for nitrogen and phosphorous in agricultural runoff. *Selected Proceedings of the Midwest Conference on Wetland Values and Management, July 17–19, 1981, St. Paul, MN*. Navarre, MN: Freshwater Society, pp. 153–63.

Davis, S. M. (1994). Phosphorus inputs and vegetation sensitivity in the Everglades. In *Everglades: The System and Its Restoration*, eds. S. M. Davis and J. C. Ogden. Boca Raton, FL: St. Lucie Press, pp. 357–8.

de Swart, E. O. A. M., van der Valk, A. G., Koehler, K. J., and Barendregt, A. (1994). Experimental evaluation of realized niche models for predicting responses of plant species to a change in environmental conditions. *Journal of Vegetation Science*, **5**, 541–52.

Dinsmore, J. J. (1994). *A Country So Full of Game: the Story of Wildlife in Iowa*. Iowa City, IA: University of Iowa Press.

Euliss, N. H., Jr. and Mushet, D. M. (1996). Water-level fluctuation in wetlands as a function of landscape condition in the prairie-pothole region. *Wetlands*, **16**, 587–93.

(1999). Influence of agriculture on aquatic invertebrate communities of temporary wetlands in the prairie-pothole region of North Dakota, USA. *Wetlands*, **19**, 578–83.

Galatowitsch, S. M. and van der Valk, A. G. (1994). *Restoring Prairie Wetlands: an Ecological Approach*. Ames, IA: Iowa State University Press.

(1995). Natural revegetation during restoration of wetlands in the southern prairie-pothole region of North America. In *Restoration of Temperate Wetlands*, eds. B. D. Wheeler, S. S. Shaw, W. J. Fojt, and R. A. Robertson. Chichester, UK: John Wiley, pp. 129–42.

Galatowitsch, S. M., van der Valk, A. G., and Budelsky, R. A. (1998). Decision-making for prairie wetland restorations. *Great Plains Research*, **8**, 137–55.

Galatowitsch, S. M., Anderson, N. O., and Ascher, P. D. (1999). Invasiveness in wetland plants in temperate North America. *Wetlands*, **19**, 733–55.

Gleason, R. A. and Euliss, N. H., Jr. (1998). Sedimentation of prairie wetlands. *Great Plains Research*, **8**, 97–112.

Gray, B. T., Coley, R. W., MacFarlane, R. J. *et al.* (1999). Restoration of prairie wetlands to enhance bird habitat: a Ducks Unlimited Canada perspective. In *Aquatic Restoration in Canada*, eds. T. Murphy and M. Munawar. Leiden, the Netherlands: Backhuys, pp. 171–94.

Johnson, D. H. and Grier, J. W. (1988). *Determinants of Breeding Distributions of Ducks*. Wildlife Monographs 100. Jamestown, MD: Northern, Prairie Wildlife Research Center.

Kadlec, R. H. and Knight, R. L. (1996). *Treatment Wetlands*. Boca Raton, FL: Lewis.

Kadlec, J. A., Murkin, H. R. and van der Valk, A. G. (2000). The baseline and deep flooding years. In *Prairie Wetland Ecology: the Contributions of the Marsh Ecology Research Program*. Ames, IA, eds. H. R. Murkin, A. G. van der Valk and W. R. Clark. Iowa State University Press, pp. 55–74.

Kantrud, H. A., Krapu, G. L., and Swanson, G. A. (1989). *Prairie Basin Wetlands of the Dakotas: a Community Profile*. US Fish and Wildlife Service, Biological Report 85.

Krapu, G. L. and Reinecke, K. J. (1992). Foraging ecology and nutrition. In *Ecology and Management of Breeding Waterfowl*, eds. B. D. J. Batt, A. D. Afton, M. G. Anderson *et al.* Minneapolis, MN: University of Minnesota Press, pp. 1–29.

LaBaugh, J. W., Winter, T. C., and Rosenberry, D. O. (1998). Hydrological functions of prairie wetlands. *Great Plains Research*, **8**, 17–37.

Lammers, T. G. and van der Valk, A. G. (1977). A checklist of the aquatic and wetland vascular plants of Iowa. I. Ferns, fern allies, and dicotelydons. *Proceedings of the Iowa Academy of Science*, **84**, 41–88.

(1978). A checklist of the aquatic and wetland plants of Iowa. II. Monocotyledons, plus a summary of the geographic and habitat distribution of all aquatic and wetland species in Iowa. *Proceedings of the Iowa Academy of Science*, **85**, 121–63.

Lannoo, M. J. (1996). *Okoboji Wetlands: a Lesson in Natural History*. Iowa City, IA: University of Iowa Press.

Lannoo, M. J., Lang, K., Waltz, T., and Phillips, G. S. (1994). An altered amphibian assemblage: Dickinson County, Iowa, 70 years after Frank Blanchards's survey. *American Midland Naturalist*, **131**, 311–19.

Martin, D. B. and Hartman, W. A. (1987). The effect of cultivation on sediment composition and deposition in prairie-pothole wetlands. *Water, Air, and Soil Pollution*, **34**, 45–53.

Mueller, M. H. and van der Valk, A. G. (2002). The potential role of ducks in wetland seed dispersal. *Wetlands*, **22**, 170–8.

Murkin, H. R. and Caldwell, P. J. (2000). Avian use of prairie wetlands. In *Prairie Wetland Ecology: the Contributions of the Marsh Ecology Research Program*, eds. H. R. Murkin, A. G. van der Valk, and W. R. Clark. Ames, IA: Iowa State University Press, pp. 249–86.

Murkin, H. R., Murkin, E. J., and Ball, J. P. (1997). Avian habitat selection and prairie wetland dynamics. *Ecological Applications*, **7**, 1144–59.

Murkin, H. R., van der Valk, A. G., and Clark, W. R. (eds.) (2000a). *Prairie Wetland Ecology: the Contributions of the Marsh Ecology Research Program*. Ames, IA: Iowa State University Press.

Murkin, H. R., van der Valk, A. G., and Kadlec, J. A. (2000b). Nutrient budgets and the wet–dry cycle of prairie wetlands. In *Prairie Wetland Ecology: the Contributions of the Marsh Ecology Research Program*, eds. H. R. Murkin, A. G. van der Valk, and W. R. Clark. Ames, IA: Iowa State University Press, pp. 99–121.

National Wetlands Working Group (1988). *Wetlands of Canada*. Environment Canada, Ecological Land Classification Series 24. Ottawa, Canada: Environment Canada. Montreal, Canada: Polyscience Publications Inc.

Neely, R. K. and Baker, J. L. (1989). Nitrogen and phosphorus dynamics and the fate of agricultural runoff. In *Northern Prairie Wetlands*, ed. A. G. van der Valk. Ames, IA: Iowa State University Press, pp. 92–131.

Pederson, R. L. (1981). Seed bank characteristics of the Delta Marsh, Manitoba, Canada. In *Selected Proceedings of the Midwest Conference on Wetland Values and Management*, ed. B. Richardson. Navarre, MN: Freshwater Society, pp. 61–9.

Pederson, R. L. and van der Valk, A. G. (1985). Vegetation change and seed banks in marshes: ecological and management implications. *Transactions of the North American Wildlife and Natural Resources Conference*, **49**, 271–80.

Peterka, J. J. (1989). Fishes in northern prairie wetlands. In *Northern Prairie Wetlands*, ed. A. G. van der Valk. Ames, IA: Iowa State University Press, pp. 302–15.

Poiani, K. A. and Johnson, W. C. (1989). Effect of hydroperiod on seed-bank composition in semipermanent prairie wetlands. *Canadian Journal of Botany*, **67**, 856–64.

(1993). A spatial simulation model of hydrology and vegetation dynamics in semi-permanent prairie wetlands. *Ecological Applications*, **3**, 279–93.

Prince, H. (1997). *Wetlands of the American Midwest: a Historical Geography of Changing Attitudes*. Chicago, IL: University of Chicago Press.

Richardson, J. L., Arndt, J. L., and Freeland, J. (1994). Wetland soils of the prairie potholes. *Advances in Agronomy*, **52**, 121–71.

Rose, C. and Crumpton, W. G. (1996). Effects of emergent macrophytes on dissolved oxygen dynamics in a prairie pothole wetland. *Wetlands*, **16**, 495–502.

Rosenberry, D. O and Winter, T. C. (1997). Dynamics of water-table fluctuations in an upland between two prairie-pothole wetlands in North Dakota. *Journal of Hydrology*, **191**, 266–89.

Seabloom, E. W., Moloney, K. A., and van der Valk, A. G. (2001). Constraints on the establishment of plants along a fluctuating water-depth gradient. *Ecology*, **82**, 2216–32.

Shay, J. M. and Shay, C. T. (1986). Prairie marshes in western Canada, with specific reference to the ecology of five emergent macrophytes. *Canadian Journal of Botany*, **64**, 443–54.

Shay, J. M., de Geus, P. M., and Kapinga, M. R. M. (1999). Changes in shoreline vegetation over a 50-year period in the Delta Marsh, Manitoba in response to water levels. *Wetlands*, **19**, 413–25.

Smith, G. W. (1995). *A Critical Review of Aerial and Ground Surveys of Breeding Waterfowl in North America*. National Biological Service Biological Science Report 5.

Squires, L. and van der Valk, A. G. (1992). Water-depth tolerances of the dominant emergent macrophytes of the Delta Marsh, Manitoba. *Canadian Journal of Botany*, **70**, 1860–7.

Stewart, R. E. and Kantrud, H. A. (1971). *Classification of Natural Ponds in the Glaciated Prairie Region*. US Fish and Wildlife Service Resource Publication 92.

Swanson, G. A. and Duebbert, H. F. (1989). Wetland habitats of waterfowl in the prairie-pothole region. In *Northern Prairie Wetlands*, ed. A. G. van der Valk. Ames, IA: Iowa State University Press, pp. 204–67.

Toth, L. A., Arrington, D. A., Brady, M. A., and Muszick, D. A. (1995). Conceptual evaluation of factors potentially affecting restoration of habitat structure within the channelized Kissimmee River ecosystem. *Restoration Ecology*, **3**, 160–80.

van der Camp, G. and Hayashi, M. (1998). The groundwater recharge functions of prairie wetlands. *Great Plains Research*, **8**, 39–56.

van der Valk, A. G. (1981). Succession in wetlands: a Gleasonian approach. *Ecology*, **62**, 688–96.

(1982). Succession in temperate North American wetlands. In *Wetlands: Ecology and Management*, eds. B. Gopal, R. E. Turner, R. G. Wetzel, and D. F. Whigham. Jaipur, India: International Scientific Publications, pp. 169–79.

(1985). Vegetation dynamics of prairie glacial marshes. In *Population Structure of Vegetation*, ed. J. White. The Hague, the Netherlands: Junk, pp. 293–312.

(1987). Vegetation dynamics of freshwater wetlands: a selective review of the literature. *Archiv für Hydrobiologie Beiheft Ergebnisse der Limnologie*, **27**, 27–39.

(1989). *Northern Prairie Wetlands*. Ames, IA: Iowa State University Press.

(1994). Effects of prolonged flooding on the distribution and biomass of emergent species along a freshwater wetland coenocline. *Vegetatio*, **110**, 185–96.

(2000). Vegetation dynamics and models. In *Prairie Wetland Ecology: the Contributions of the Marsh Ecology Research Program*, eds. H. R. Murkin, A. G. van der Valk, and W. R. Clark. Ames, IA: Iowa State University Press, pp. 125–61.

van der Valk, A. G. and Davis, C. B. (1976). Seed banks of prairie glacial marshes. *Canadian Journal of Botany*, **54**, 1832–8.

(1978a). The role of the seed bank in the vegetation dynamics of prairie glacial marshes. *Ecology*, **59**, 322–35.

(1978b). Primary production of prairie glacial marshes. In *Freshwater Marshes*, eds. R. E. Good, D. F. Whigham, and R. L. Simpson. New York: Academic Press, pp. 21–37.

(1980). The impact of a natural drawdown on the growth of four emergent species in a prairie glacial marsh. *Aquatic Botany*, **9**, 301–22.

van der Valk, A. G. and Jolly, R. W. (1992). Recommendations for research to develop guidelines for the use of wetlands to control rural NPS pollution. *Ecological Engineering*, **1**, 115–34.

van der Valk, A. G. and Murkin, H. R. (2001). Changes in nutrient pools during an experimentally simulated wet-dry cycle in the Delta Marsh, Manitoba, Canada. *Verhandlungen Internationale Vereinigung Limnologiae*, **27**, 3444–51.

van der Valk, A. G. and Pederson, R. L. (2003). The SWANCC decision and its implications for prairie potholes. *Wetlands*, **23**, 590–6.

van der Valk, A. G. and Welling, C. H. (1988). The development of zonation in freshwater wetlands: an experimental approach. In *Diversity and Pattern in Plant Communities*, eds. H. J. During, M. J. A. Werger, and J. H. Willems. The Hague, the Netherlands: SPB Academic Publishing, pp. 145–58.

van der Valk, A. G., Murkin, H. R., and Kadlec, J. A. (2000). The drawdown and reflooding years. In *Prairie Wetland Ecology: the Contributions of the Marsh Ecology Research Program*, eds. H. R. Murkin, A. G. van der Valk, and W. R. Clark. Ames, IA: Iowa State University Press, pp. 75–97.

Weller, M. W. (1994). *Freshwater Marshes*, 3rd edn. Minneapolis, MN: University of Minnesota Press.

Weller, M. W. and Spatcher, C. S. (1965). *Role of Habitat in the Distribution and Abundance of Marsh Birds*. Special Report 43, Ames, IA: Iowa Agriculture and Home Economics Experiment Station.

Wetzel, P. R. and van der Valk, A. G. (1998). Effects of nutrient and soil moisture on competition between *Carex stricta*, *Phalaris arundinacea*, and *Typha latifolia*. *Plant Ecology*, **138**, 179–90.

Wetzel, P. R., van der Valk, A. G., and Toth, L. A. (2001). Restoration of wetland vegetation on the Kissimmee River floodplain: potential role of seed banks. *Wetlands*, **21**, 189–98.

Wienhold, C. E. and van der Valk, A. G. (1989). The impact of duration of drainage on the seed banks of northern prairie wetlands. *Canadian Journal of Botany*, **67**, 1878–84.

Winter, T. C. (1989). Hydrological studies of wetlands in the northern prairie. In *Northern Prairie Wetlands*, ed. A. G. van der Valk. Ames, IA: Iowa State University Press, pp. 16–54.

Winter, T. C. and Rosenberry, D. O. (1998). Hydrology of prairie-pothole wetlands during drought and deluge: a 17-year study of the Cottonwood Lake wetland complex in North Dakota in the perspective of longer term measured and proxy hydrological records. *Climatic Change*, **40**, 189–209.

12

The Magellanic moorland

M. T. K. ARROYO
Universidad de Chile

P. PLISCOFF
Universidad de Chile

M. MIHOC
Universidad de Concepción

M. ARROYO-KALIN
University of Cambridge

Introduction

Globally, wetlands cover an estimated 7 to 8 million km^2 (Mitsch *et al.* 1994). These azonal ecosystems are widely and disjunctively spread throughout all major biomes of the Earth, following no evident pattern. Under the guise of wetlands fall a wide variety of ecosystems, ranging from open water bodies to peatlands. A comprehensive global strategy for the conservation of wetlands, thus requires recognition of the huge diversity of wetlands, and intimate knowledge of local environmental conditions and the biota of each wetland area and surrounding vegetation types. Because major wetland areas occur at many latitudes and are embedded in many different terrestrial ecosystems, it stands to reason that the sum total of wetland biodiversity could turn out to be quite high on a global scale in comparison with land area occupied by wetlands.

The southwestern border of southern South America is characterized by cool and windy summers, with recorded annual average precipitation reaching as high as 7 m on one offshore island. This area (and others further to the north) was heavily glaciated in the Pleistocene, and today consists of a highly dissected, rugged landscape interrupted by two major icefields (Southern Patagonian and North Patagonian) and numerous fjords. Corresponding closely in its distribution to this heavily glaciated land area is found a major area of cool temperate wetlands (Fig. 12.1). This peat-forming complex, widely separated geographically from other cool temperate wetland areas in the southern hemisphere, and known as the Magellanic tundra or moorland complex (Pisano 1977,

The World's Largest Wetlands: Ecology and Conservation, eds. L. H. Fraser and P. A. Keddy.
Published by Cambridge University Press. © Cambridge University Press 2005.

1981, Moore 1979), contains four major subtypes (Fig. 12.2). Under present-day climatic conditions the wetland complex is distributed in a continuous fashion from the extreme southern part of the continent to around 43° S in the Region XI of Chile and from sea level to above treeline (Pisano 1983). Outlying areas of peatlands appear northward on the island of Chiloé (Ruthsatz & Villagrán 1991), and at several locations further north in the Coast Range to around 38° S (Looser 1952, Ramírez 1968) as well as inland along the Andes to around 40° S (Fig. 12.1). A few additional *Sphagnum* patches are found in the mediterranean area in central Chile as far north as 31° S where they are associated with disjunct forest islands considered to be postglacial relicts (Hauser 1996). Although the wetland zone is concentrated west of the main Andean cordillera, significant extensions of *Sphagnum* bogs can be found in Tierra del Fuego to the east of the Andean divide (Arroyo *et al.* 1996a) where they extend to the extreme southeastern tip of the island. With the exception of those peatlands occurring east of the Andes on the extreme tip of the Argentine sector of Tierra del Fuego, the vast majority of southern South American temperate peatlands are located in what is Chilean territory.

Cool temperate South American wetlands have received limited attention in the wetland literature (e.g. Moore 1979, Pisano 1983). Although mapped in Mitsch's (1994) global overview of wetlands, such peatlands were not described in the text. In an effort to ameliorate this situation, in this chapter we: (1) outline the present-day distribution of peatlands in southern South America, drawing on information deriving from a recent land survey in Chile (CCB 1999); (2) describe the various peatland subtypes; and; (3) provide a first estimate and phytogeographic analysis of native vascular plant biodiversity for the entire peatland complex. The level of wetland protection, and threats and opportunities are then discussed as elements for developing an integral strategy for peatland conservation in southern South America.

Extent of southern South American peatlands

A recent Geographic Information System survey (CCB 1999) of the major vegetation types in Chile allows the first fairly accurate estimate of the extent of southern South American peatlands. Based on information for regions VIII to XII of Chile, wetlands, without distinction as to kind, occupy 4.36 million ha, with the vast majority (4.25 million ha) located in the southernmost XI and XII political regions (44° to 55° S). Although there are no published figures with regard to different wetland types, it can safely be assumed that the great majority of wetlands at these latitudes correspond to peatlands of the typical

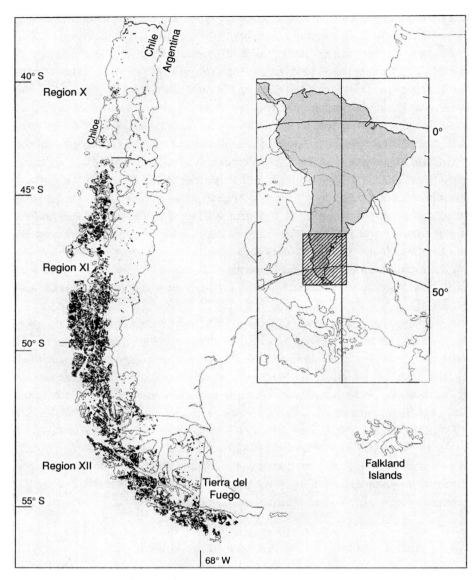

Figure 12.1 Distribution of wetlands in southwestern southern South America. The wetland category corresponds principally to peatlands (see explanation in text). Original data from CCB (1999). The map of South America superimposed on an inverted North America shows relative land areas at equivalent latitudes in the two hemispheres.

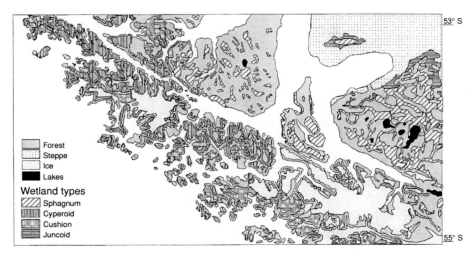

Figure 12.2 Distribution of four peatland types across the east–west rainfall gradient in South America. Modified after Pisano (1977).

Magellanic tundra (or moorland) complex. In regions IX and VIII (where wetlands are insignificant on a regional scale: a total of 34 000 ha) the broad wetland category includes some high-elevation Andean bogs of an entirely different nature as well as marshes and swamp forest (neither of which will be considered here). Taking the latter into account, and accommodating for a small area of peatlands in Argentine Tierra del Fuego, as a conservative estimate, the Magellanic tundra complex covers around 4.4 million ha, an area equivalent to 1.7% of boreal peatlands (based on a total boreal-peatlands area of 260×10^6 ha; Apps *et al.* 1993). The proportion of total land area occupied by wetlands increases markedly with increasing latitude, reaching 23.5% in the southernmost Region XII of Chile (Fig. 12.3). Although the total area is small on a global scale, southern South American peatlands make up 25.5% of the combined area of forests and peatlands, whereas boreal peatlands represent only 17% of the northern forest–peatland complex (Apps *et al.* 1993). The relative importance of peatlands versus forest, moreover, increases dramatically with increasing latitude in southern South America, to the extent that the former come to occupy a greater amount of the land area than forests south of 49° S (Region XII) (Fig. 12.3). Thus peatlands are salient ecosystems in southern South America.

Characteristics of the peatland complex

Southern South American peatlands are strongly embedded within the southern temperate forest matrix (Fig. 12.2). This being so, it should be

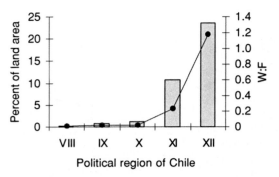

Figure 12.3 The percentage of total land area covered in wetlands in five political regions of Chile (bars), and the ratio of wetlands to native forest (W:F) for those regions (line). The wetland category corresponds principally to peatlands (see explanation in text). See Fig. 12.1 for latitudinal limits of political regions.

self-evident that peatlands and forests are intimately connected at the level of ecosystem processes. Peatlands, for example (particularly, *Sphagnum*-dominated peat bogs in the drier and windy eastern part of the wetland zone – see below), can play a vital role in maintaining the water balance in forests. Wetlands develop where local drainage conditions impede the growth of forest (mostly *Nothofagus* dominated): or in areas where temperature and frost conditions may be amenable to forest development, but exposure to wind is not. Soils are generally nutrient deficient and poor in bases (Ruthsatz & Villagrán 1991). Bog development is enhanced throughout the peatland zone by impermeable igneous rock (Andean diorite) and metamorphic schists (Precambrian and/or Paleozoic) which engender poor drainage and extensive paludification. From south to north, wetlands of the Magellanic moorland complex penetrate the "boreal" temperate rain forest and perhumid evergreen rainforest zones (Arroyo *et al.* 1996a), where they can be found interfingering with evergreen Magellanic rain forest dominated by *Nothofagus betuloides*, *N. dombeyi*, and *Fitzroya cupressoides*. To the east, peatlands penetrate into the deciduous temperate forest zone dominated by *Nothofagus pumilio* and *N. antarctica*. The peatlands find their greatest development in areas of oceanic climate where the mean temperature of the warmest month is low (7.5 to 9.0 °C; Tuhkanen *et al.* 1990) and frosts are rare – reflecting the range of forest types in which they are embedded; however, southern South American peatlands can be found over an amazingly wide precipitation range, varying from as little as 500 mm on the eastern border of the *Sphagnum*-dominated peat bog zone in Tierra del Fuego (Arroyo *et al.* 1996a), to over 4000 mm at coastal locations on the southwestern continental margin (di Castri & Hajek 1976), and as much as 7330 mm on the island of Guarello just off the mainland at 50° S. Indeed, as better knowledge has arisen of the distribution of *Sphagnum* peat bogs in Tierra del Fuego and cushion bogs in Chiloé, it has become evident that peatland development is not excluded under mildly continental climates. The extensive *Sphagnum* bogs in central Tierra del Fuego may be found under a mean summer temperature of 10 °C, a coldest-month temperature below zero, and the presence of frost – as deduced from the climatic zones defined by Tuhkanen *et al.* (1990) for Tierra del Fuego. On the island of Chiloé, upland cushion and cyperoid bogs are sporadically subjected to frost throughout the entire year (Ruthsatz & Villagrán 1991).

Pisano (1983) recognized four main peatland subtypes in the wetland complex. These subtypes develop under different rainfall, drainage, and wind regimes; and vary in their physiognomy, dominant plant species, and abundance of *Sphagnum*. The distribution of the four subtypes over an east–west gradient is illustrated in Fig. 12.2. Under a regime of 500 to 1500 mm precipitation, corresponding to the drier eastern part of the wetland zone (Pisano 1977, Arroyo *et al.* 1996a), rain-fed, ombrotrophic raised and blanket bogs are the norm. Raised and blanket bogs are found predominantly in the deciduous-forest zone and on the deciduous-forest–evergreen-rain-forest ecotone to the west. Such bogs, dominated by *Sphagnum*, are found mostly at higher latitudes and lower elevations, and stand out on the landscape because their intense brick-red colour contrasts against the surrounding green forest matrix. Their greatest development is seen in the central and southern parts of Tierra del Fuego. In strongly water-logged areas, *Sphagnum*-dominated bogs give way to juncoid bogs dominated by *Marsippospermum grandiflorum* overtopping a dense and continuous understorey of *Sphagnum*. At the drier end of the rainfall gradient, the typical *Sphagnum* and juncoid bogs are associated with increasing cover of *Empetrum rubrum*; at the wetter end, stunted individuals of the small gymnosperm, *Pilgerodendron uviferum*, are typical. Development of swampy conditions at the bog edge in both *Sphagnum*-dominated and juncoid bogs is generally associated with a band of stunted individuals of *Nothofagus antarctica*. Raised bogs tend to be sharply differentiated from the surrounding forest matrix and are associated with extensive peat development (Hauser 1996).

In areas of intermediate rainfall (1000 to 2000 mm) to the west and north of the *Sphagnum* bog zone, the typical bog is the non-raised cyperoid type (also referred to as "graminoid bog" as a result of the plant form of *Schoenus antarcticus*; Pisano 1983). Cyperoid bogs are dominated by *Schoenus antarcticus*, with the presence of typical species such as: *Carpha alpina*, *Schoenus andinus*, and *Rostkovia magellanica*; a number of grass species; and stunted individuals of a few shrubs and *Nothofagus antarctica*. Physiognomically flatter, such bogs contain variable amounts of *Sphagnum* and other mosses which form a basal stratum. This bog type varies enormously in size from hundreds of hectares to local patches of a few square meters within forests. The dominant species may penetrate the forest understorey along swampy streamsides and be found in forest hollows. Cyperoid bogs are associated with shallower peat development, in comparison with *Sphagnum* bogs, and deep soils that are rich in humified organic matter. Forest islands or isolated individuals of *Nothofagus antarctica*, *N. betuloides*, *N. nitida*, and *Pilgerodendron uviferum* are commonplace such that the ecotone of the forest tends to be more gradual.

Along the extremely exposed and wet western border of the wetland zone, cyperoid bog gives way to non-raised cushion bog (Pisano 1977, 1981), also known as "Magellanic moorland" *sensu stricto* (Godley 1960, Moore 1983). Dominant cushion species include *Donatia fascicularis*, *Bolax caespitosa*, *Astelia pumila*, *Oreobolus obtusangulus*, *Caltha dioneifolia*, and *Drapetes muscosa*. Such bogs may entirely lack *Sphagnum*, or may contain only limited amounts in an understorey position. Cushion bog also typically contains several species of sedges, dwarf-shrubs, and stunted individuals of *Nothofagus antarctica* and *N. betuloides*. Cushion bog appears again at higher elevations close to the treeline on the eastern side of the Andes in Tierra del Fuego. On account of the harsher environmental conditions, the ecotone between cushion bog and forest tends to be more abrupt than in the case of cyperoid bogs.

Biodiversity in southern South American peatlands

Biodiversity is generally measured at the ecosystem and species levels. More-sophisticated currencies of biodiversity attempt to incorporate phylogenetic content and even genes. Knowledge of the biodiversity in peatlands of southern South America is still woefully patchy even at the most-basic levels. While the main peatlands subtypes have been described, their distribution – other than in the extreme south of the continent – is poorly known. The latter is perhaps not surprising given that huge areas of the vast, highly dissected wetland zone are accessible only by way of the sea, determining that much of the zone still remains unexplored. Many basic questions remain to be answered. For example, where does the northern limit of *Sphagnum*-dominated wetlands lie? It is well known that the diversity of peatland subtypes is higher at the southern than at the northern extreme of the wetland complex. However, huge knowledge gaps remain in between. As in other poorly explored parts of the world, knowledge at the species level varies enormously among the taxonomic groups. Best known are the vascular plants and the dominant mosses, which will

Table 12.1 *Native mammals and birds found in* Sphagnum-*dominated peatlands in Tierra del Fuego, southern South America. Sources: Schlatter* et al. *(1995), Willson* et al. *(1995), Arroyo* et al. *(1996a).*

Mammals
 Hippocamelus bisulcus
 Lama guanicoe

Birds
 Chloephaga picta
 Chloephaga polycephala
 Elaenia albiceps
 Falco peregrinus
 Falco sparverius
 Gallinago paraguaiae
 Geranoetus melanoleucus
 Lessonia rufa
 Muscisaxicola macloviana
 Podiceps occipitalis
 Polyborus plancus
 Pygochelidon cyanoleuca
 Pyrope pyrope
 Rallus sanguinolentus
 Rollandia rolland
 Tachycineta leucopyga
 Vultur gryphus

be referred to extensively here. Information on mammals and birds is limited (Table 12.1). Even for vascular plants, present knowledge is only sufficient to evaluate diversity on a broad, regional scale. Still less is known about the ecological dynamics of peatlands. For example, practically nothing is known about successional processes in southern temperate peatlands, not to mention functional biodiversity.

The four major peatland types, while physiognomically different, intergrade floristically. Based on a survey of the published literature and examination of herbarium records carried out by us, the total vascular plant flora – considering all peatland subtypes – numbers around 277 species contained in 134 genera (Table 12.2). This number can be expected to increase as more sites are studied. The dominant vascular plant species (although different in each of the peatland subtypes) tend to be invariant for each subtype throughout the entire latitudinal range of the wetlands. Many species listed as occurring in the

Table 12.2 *Genera of vascular plants in southern South American temperate peatlands.*

FE	Genus	Family	N	FE	Genus	Family	N
ST	*Abrotanella*	Asteraceae	4	C	*Isoetes*	Isoetaceae	1
ST	*Acaena*	Rosaceae	5	T	*Isolepis*	Cyperaceae	2
W	*Agrostis*	Poaceae	7	C	*Juncus*	Juncaceae	8
T	*Alopecurus*	Poaceae	1	W	*Lagenophora*	Asteraceae	1
SA	*Amomyrtus*	Myrtaceae	1	SA	*Lebetanthus*	Epacridaceae	1
W	*Anagallis*	Primulaceae	1	SA	*Lepidothamnus*	Cupressaceae	1
T	*Apium*	Apiaceae	1	ST	*Leptinella*	Asteraceae	1
T	*Armeria*	Plumbaginaceae	1	ST	*Lilaeopsis*	Apiaceae	1
C	*Asplenium*	Aspleniaceae	1	T	*Litorella*	Plantaginaceae	1
ST	*Astelia*	Liliaceae	1	ST	*Lomatia*	Proteaceae	1
T	*Aster*	Asteraceae	1	C	*Luzula*	Juncaceae	4
SA	*Asteranthera*	Gesneriaceae	1	ST	*Luzuriaga*	Philesiaceae	2
SA	*Azorella*	Apiaceae	5	W	*Lycopodium*	Lycopodiaceae	4
T	*Baccharis*	Asteraceae	2	SA	*Macrachaenium*	Asteraceae	1
W	*Berberis*	Berberidaceae	4	ST	*Marsippospermum*	Juncaceae	1
C	*Blechnum*	Blechnaceae	3	SA	*Misodendrum*	Misodendraceae	2
SA	*Bolax*	Apiaceae	2	T	*Montia*	Portulacaceae	1
W	*Botrychium*	Opioglossaceae	1	SA	*Myoschilos*	Santalaceae	1
T	*Bromus*	Poaceae	1	SA	*Myrceugenia*	Myrtaceae	1
W	*Callitriche*	Callitrichaceae	1	C	*Myriophyllum*	Haloragaceae	1
T	*Caltha*	Ranunculaceae	3	SA	*Myrteola*	Myrtaceae	1
W	*Cardamine*	Brassicaceae	1	SA	*Nanodea*	Santalaceae	1
C	*Carex*	Cyperaceae	24	W	*Nertera*	Rubiaceae	1
ST	*Carpha*	Cyperaceae	1	ST	*Nothofagus*	Fagaceae	5

Zone	Genus	Family	No.
W	*Cerastium*	Caryophyllaceae	1
SA	*Chiliotrichum*	Asteraceae	1
SA	*Chloraea*	Orchidaceae	2
SA	*Chusquea*	Poaceae	2
ST	*Colobanthus*	Caryophyllaceae	2
ST	*Cortaderia*	Poaceae	1
T	*Deschampsia*	Poaceae	5
SA	*Desfontainia*	Desfontainiaceae	1
ST	*Deyeuxia*	Poaceae	3
ST	*Donatia*	Donatiaceae	1
SA	*Drapetes*	Thymelaeaceae	1
SA	*Drimys*	Winteraceae	1
C	*Drosera*	Droseraceae	1
C	*Eleocharis*	Cyperaceae	3
SA	*Embothrium*	Proteaceae	1
T	*Empetrum*	Empetraceae	1
T	*Epilobium*	Onagraceae	2
W	*Equisetum*	Equisetaceae	1
C	*Erigeron*	Asteraceae	2
SA	*Escallonia*	Saxifragaceae	3
W	*Euphrasia*	Scrophulariaceae	2
W	*Festuca*	Poaceae	6
SA	*Fitzroya*	Cupressaceae	1
T	*Fragaria*	Rosaceae	1
ST	*Gaimardia*	Centrolepidaceae	1
C	*Galium*	Rubiaceae	3
SA	*Olsynium*	Iridaceae	1
ST	*Oreobolus*	Cyperaceae	1
SA	*Ortachne*	Poaceae	1
ST	*Ourisia*	Scrophulariaceae	2
SA	*Ovidia*	Thymelaeaceae	1
C	*Oxalis*	Oxalidaceae	2
SA	*Perezia*	Asteraceae	3
SA	*Philesia*	Philesiaceae	1
ST	*Phyllachne*	Stylidiaceae	1
SA	*Pilgerodendron*	Cupressaceae	1
W	*Pinguicula*	Lentibulariaceae	2
C	*Plantago*	Plantaginaceae	1
T	*Poa*	Poaceae	8
T	*Polypogon*	Poaceae	1
C	*Polystichum*	Dryopteridaceae	1
C	*Potamogeton*	Potamogetonaceae	1
W	*Pratia*	Campanulaceae	2
W	*Primula*	Primulaceae	1
ST	*Pseudopanax*	Araliaceae	1
T	*Puccinellia*	Poaceae	1
T	*Ranunculus*	Ranunculaceae	8
ST	*Rostkovia*	Juncaceae	1
C	*Rubus*	Rosaceae	1
T	*Rumex*	Polygonaceae	1
SA	*Saxegothaea*	Podocarpaceae	1
T	*Saxifraga*	Saxifragaceae	1

(cont.)

Table 12.2 (cont.)

FE	Genus	Family	N	FE	Genus	Family	N
SA	*Gamochaeta*	Asteraceae	1	W	*Schizaea*	Schizaeaceae	1
W	*Gaultheria*	Ericaceae	6	ST	*Schizeilema*	Apiaceae	1
T	*Gentiana*	Gentianaceae	1	C	*Schoenoplectus*	Juncaceae	2
SA	*Gentianella*	Gentianaceae	1	W	*Schoenus*	Cyperaceae	3
T	*Geum*	Rosaceae	2	C	*Senecio*	Asteraceae	5
W	*Gleichenia*	Gleicheniaceae	3	SA	*Serpyllopsis*	Hymenophyllaceae	1
SA	*Greigia*	Bromeliaceae	1	SA	*Sisyrinchium*	Iridaceae	1
W	*Gunnera*	Gunneraceae	2	SA	*Tapeinia*	Iridaceae	1
SA	*Hamadryas*	Rosaceae	1	T	*Taraxacum*	Asteraceae	1
ST	*Hebe*	Scrophulariaceae	1	SA	*Tepualia*	Myrtaceae	1
T	*Hierochloe*	Poaceae	2	SA	*Tetroncium*	Juncaginaceae	1
C	*Hippuris*	Hippuridaceae	1	T	*Thlaspi*	Brassicaceae	1
T	*Hordeum*	Poaceae	2	SA	*Tribeles*	Saxifragaceae	1
W	*Huperzia*	Fagaceae	1	C	*Triglochin*	Juncaginaceae	1
W	*Hymenophyllum*	Hymenophyllaceae	6	T	*Trisetum*	Poaceae	4
T	*Hypochaeris*	Asteraceae	2	ST	*Uncinia*	Cyperaceae	3
SA	*Iocenes*	Asteraceae	1	T	*Viola*	Violaceae	3

FE, floristic element; C, cosmopolitan; T, temperate; ST, southern temperate; SA, South American; W, widely distributed; N, number of species in genus in peatlands.

peatlands are found there only occasionally, being more typical of the forest and alpine habitats. A recent checklist of Chilean mosses provided by He (1998), cites 15 species and 3 varieties of *Sphagnum*; however, it is unclear as to how many of these species occur in peatlands. Included is *Sphagnum magellanicum* Brid., a widespread species in boreal peatlands, and a dominant species in *Sphagnum* bogs in southern South America. There are many other bryophytes, but taxonomic uncertainties do not allow reliable figures for these groups at this point in time. Better knowledge of bryophytes is highly desirable for assessing wetland biodiversity in southern South America. He (1998) shows that moss diversity increases with latitude in Chile. He lists 450 species of mosses for the Region XII of Chile, and similarly high numbers for the regions XI and X; with these kinds of figures, a large number of moss species can be expected for peatlands. Baseline studies at two locations in Tierra del Fuego indicate that *Sphagnum* bogs contain a very-rich lichen flora varying in composition from the edges of bogs to their centers (Arroyo *et al.* 1996a). Species of the following genera of lichens (including important nitrogen fixers) may be associated with peat bogs in Tierra del Fuego: *Caldia, Caldonia, Cladina, Clasia, Coleocaulon, Coelopogon, Endocaena, Hypogymnia, Icmadophila, Lecidea, Leptogium, Micrea, Ochrolechia, Peltigera, Polycladium, Pseudocyphellaria, Psoroma, Rhizocarpon, Siphula, Siphulastrum, Sphaerophorus, Sticta,* and *Usnea* (Galloway 1995). In order to evaluate the biodiversity of peatlands, it becomes interesting to compare species richness with that of other ecosystems. It comes as a surprise that, in terms of numbers of species, the peatland vascular flora is 63% of the size of the rain-forest flora (comprising 443 species of vascular plants, Arroyo *et al.* 1996b).

For native animals, peat bogs are the homes or feeding sites of several species of birds, including two species of wild geese. "Guanaco" (*Lama guanicoe*) and the rare *Hippocamelus bisulcus* ("huemul"), two large mammals, may be found browsing in peat bogs. The "huemul" is Chile's national symbol.

In Table 12.2 the 134 plant genera occurring in peatlands have been classified into major floristic elements. Carrying out this exercise is, of course, fraught with pitfalls as all genera do not fall neatly into the categories used. Nevertheless, this kind of analysis is useful in order to understand the origin and phylogenetic diversity contained in the peatland flora. Examination of Table 12.2 and Fig. 12.4 shows that southern South American peatlands have provided an important point of convergence for a diverse cadre of vascular plant genera. As noted by earlier workers (Godley 1960, Moore 1979, Pisano 1983), and confirmed in the more-comprehensive survey carried out here, the peatland flora contains a high proportion of southern-temperate elements (Table 12.2 and Fig. 12.4). Here are found many physiognomic dominants. Typical south-temperate elements include *Astelia* (Bromeliaceae), *Donatia* (Donatiaceae),

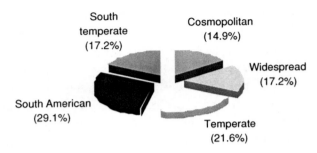

Figure 12.4 Floristic elements and their percentage contribution in the 134 genera of vascular plants found in cool temperate peatlands in southern South America.

Gaimardia (Centrolepidaceae), *Marsippospermum* (Juncaceae), *Oreobolus* (Cyperaceae), and *Phyllachne* (Stylidiaceae). Species from these genera moreover, are practically restricted to the wetland habitat. The peatlands also contain a significant contribution of species belonging to plant genera endemic to (mostly southern) South America – e.g. *Azorella, Bolax* (Apiaceae), *Drapetes* (Thymelaeaceae), *Lepidothamnus* (Cupressaceae), *Nanodea* (Santalaceae), *Tapeinia* (Iridaceae), and *Tetroncium* (Juncaginaceae). Although rarely dominant, a significant number of the taxa belonging here are in practice restricted to the wetland habitat (e.g. *Lepidothamnus, Nanodea, Tapeinia,* and *Tetroncium*). As occurs in boreal peatlands, the cosmopolitan and widespread element is also well represented, as are genera of wide temperate distribution in the northern and southern hemispheres (Table 12.2 and Fig. 12.4).

An exceptional number of the southern-temperate elements in the peatlands are represented by one or a few species in southern South America (Table 12.2) (e.g. *Astelia, Carpha, Donatia, Oreobolus, Phyllachne, Drapetes, Lebetanthus, Myrteola, Nanodea, Tetroncium* and *Tribeles*). This last feature, interestingly, is also characteristic of the southern South American rain-forest flora where, moreover, there are many monotypic endemic genera (Arroyo *et al.* 1996b). The more speciose genera in the wetland flora (reaching an extreme in *Carex* with 24 species), in contrast, tend to derive from the cosmopolitan and widespread elements; however, species belonging to these last floristic elements are rarely dominant and many have only been reported for a few localities. A comparison of the peatland subtypes reveals an interesting pattern. The southern-temperate element seems to be most-strongly represented in the cushion-bog subtype. The foregoing tendencies could indicate that the South American peatland complex is ancient, dating to the time when South America, Antarctica, New Zealand, and Australia made up a single land mass. Such a complex would have been present on Antarctica presumably in the Eocene–Miocene interval, with strong representation of the cushion-bog form. Subsequent to the break-up of the continents, the wetlands probably diversified ecologically and became enriched with additional South American elements, as well as with additional widespread and cosmopolitan elements to those perhaps already present earlier on, leading to the interesting generic mix seen today. Viewed in this light, the wetlands not only play an important role in protecting local southern South American biodiversity, but also biodiversity that is unique to southern-hemisphere lands. Needless to say, this hypothesis needs to be rigorously tested. Emerging evidence from phylogenetic (mostly molecular) studies indicates that some generic-level present-day disjunctions between southern South America and the Australasian–Pacific area can be fairly certainly ascribed to past continental connections (e.g., Mitchell & Wagstaff 2000, Renner *et al.* 2000, Swenson *et al.* 2001). However, in many cases long-distance dispersal seemed to be the more-parsimonious conclusion (Wagstaff *et al.* 2000, Winkworth *et al.* 2002). Phylogenetic information for southern South American wetland genera is still sparse. In *Phyllachne*, the New Zealand species could equally have evolved from a Tasmanian or South American lineage (Wagstaff & Wege 2002), but the timing and mode of the disjunction is not clear. For *Oreobolus*, Seberg (1988) admits that it is not easy to interpret results. In any event, the advent of molecular systematics and the molecular clock open a new and largely unexplored window for understanding wetland biodiversity. The extent to which wetland taxa have dispersed over major geographical areas versus traveling by now-separated lands is an essential question. Knowing which wetland taxa have good dispersability and are open to repeated recolonization events, and which are not, should be a factor that is taken into account when ranking the ecological vulnerability of wetlands.

Conservation

The necessarily strong focus on saving threatened temperate forests in southern South America at the present time tends to overshadow the conservation needs of other equally important ecosystems. Fortunately, by international standards, a high proportion of continental Chile is protected (19%; Arroyo & Cavieres 1997) and wetlands have fared relatively well. The recent vegetation survey (CCB 1999) shows that wetlands in general (including high-Andean wetlands and other types) enjoy a high degree of protection, with an outstanding 77% of all wetlands being contained in the State Protected Area System (comprising National Parks, National Reserves, and National Monuments). Considering southern South American wetlands separately, this figure increases to 79%. For peatlands outside Chilean territory, Parque Nacional Tierra del Fuego (63 000 ha) in southeastern Tierra del Fuego is important. The proportion of wetland area

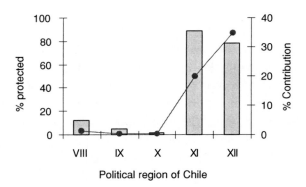

Figure 12.5 Percentage of wetlands protected in the Chilean State Protected Area System (SNASPE) for different political regions (bars) and the percentage contribution of wetlands in protected areas (line) for those regions. The wetland category corresponds principally to peatlands (see explanation in text). See Fig. 12.1 for latitudinal limits of political regions.

protected is especially high in regions XI and XII of Chile (Fig. 12.5), although the smaller outlying areas to the north (regions VIII, IX, and X) are poorly protected. Moreover, wetlands constitute a significant proportion of protected land per se in regions XI and XII (Fig. 12.5). At first sight, these figures appear to paint a positive scenario for peatland conservation in southern South America. However, this conclusion fades when the four wetland types are considered individually. As can be deduced from the location of protected areas in Muñoz-Schick *et al.* (1996), practically all of the protected areas in Chile found within the wetland zone in southern South America are located on the extreme western edge of the continent. While this location greatly favors cushion bog – and to a lesser extent cyperoid bogs – *Sphagnum* and juncoid bogs are poorly protected, perhaps as low as to the level of 10%. The largest extension of state-protected *Sphagnum*-dominated bogs in all of southern South America is probably to be found in Parque Nacional Tierra del Fuego on the southwestern tip of Argentina. Thus there is a major imbalance in the protection of different peatland subtypes. Recognition of this last situation is critical for developing future conservation strategies for southern South American peatlands. At the same time, it seems imperative to conserve more of the disjunct northern outlying areas of peatlands.

Further consideration reveals that many of the protected areas in the wetland complex fall into the category of National Reserves. In Chile, such reserves were originally set aside as frontier parks, probably more with the aim of saving land for future development schemes than for the protection of biodiversity and ecosystems per se (Armesto *et al.* 1998). Although the Chilean government does not allow extractive activities (timber harvest, etc.) in far-southern National Reserves, some reserves have recently been opened up for the development of ecotourism by the private sector, with its own inherent set of dangers when such fragile ecosystems as wetlands are concerned. The very-dynamic scene regarding development within state-protected areas in Chile makes it essential to establish clear guidelines for the conservation of peatlands and other ecosystems contained therein.

Threats and opportunities

The threats to the integrity of southern-temperate South American wetlands are: (1) timber harvesting in native forests; (2) introduced beaver; (3) exotic species; and (4) peat exploitation.

Timber harvesting in native forests

Huge tracts of native forest in the forest–wetland complex in southern South America are privately owned. Management plans exist for sustainable harvesting of one tree, *Nothofagus pumilio*, and harvesting is occurring at several locations on the island of Tierra del Fuego where *Sphagnum*-dominated bogs are most abundant. The rain forests on the Coast Range to the north, with embedded disjunct areas of peatlands, are also under threat. One major timber company in Tierra del Fuego (see Arroyo 1997), the owner of around 270 000 ha of land, has responded to the urging of Chilean scientists and has taken several measures to protect the borders of *Sphagnum* bogs, voluntarily placing around 6000 ha of peatlands under permanent protection. However, over time the removal of huge tracts of forest, no matter how careful the harvesting method, is likely to affect the delicate ecology of the fragile southern peatlands. These far-southern forested lands and their globally unique embedded wetland should be conserved.

Introduced beaver

In 1946, 26 pairs of the North American beaver (*Castor canadensis*) were released in Tierra del Fuego (Lizarralde 1993). The absence of natural predators lead to their rapid spread throughout the main and close offshore islands, leading to what could turn out to be one the greatest ecological disasters on Earth. Less than 40 years after the date of their introduction, Sielfeld and Venegas (1980) estimated 4.2 to 6.5 individuals per km^2 for Navarino Island, with peatlands being the favored habitat of beaver. Today, beaver dams and the associated effects of beavers are found from the steppe border up into the alpine region, with practically every watershed affected. Beaver damage has lead to increased paludism in existing bogs and in forested areas, with resultant invasion of

Sphagnum into previously forested areas following the death of trees. Simultaneously, the centers of existing bog are being subjected to major flooding. It is too early to predict the overall affect of beaver on wetland biodiversity and abundance. However, it is likely that the continued action of beavers will lead to local floristic impoverishment in flooded *Sphagnum* bogs. Out of defeat, local officials generally consider that the beaver problem in Tierra del Fuego is unmanageable. Fortunately, there appear to be no substantiated reports of beavers colonizing areas north of the Straits of Magellan at this stage.

Exotic species

Among the wetland subtypes, raised *Sphagnum*-dominated bogs seem to be most prone to invasion by exotic plant species. Fortunately, at this stage, the number of exotic species reported in peatlands is still relatively low (18), of which >50% are grasses. However, more introduced species are likely to arrive, especially in central Tierra del Fuego. Over the past 15 years, the island has seen an exponential increase in the number of *Lama guanicoe* ("guanaco") as a result of the latter's status as a protected animal (see Arroyo *et al.* 1996a) and lack of natural predators. Overpopulation has driven animals out of their preferred natural habitat, the Patagonia steppe (where exotic species abound; Moore 1983), into the forest habitat and other adjacent vegetation types in search of alternative resources, with the resultant establishment of exotic species along well-trampled trails in the bogs. Roads associated with timber-harvesting operations are providing additional conduits for the entrance of invasive species into peatlands. Developing a good and acceptable management plan for "guanaco" and strict specifications for road building would go a long way toward ameliorating these problem.

Peat exploitation

Under Chilean law, peat per se comes under the Mining Code, and like any mineral is considered to belong to the state, regardless of who the owner of the land may be. The right to exploit peat is granted by the court, which in turn sets the price of a patent to be paid annually to the state. Promulgation of the environmental law in Chile in the mid 1990s ushered in a potentially more-positive scenario for controlling the mining of peat. As pointed out by Hauser (1996), in that peat extraction corresponds to a mining activity, and all mining activities come under the jurisdiction of the Chilean Environmental Law, anybody wishing to exploit peat is now obliged to undertake an environmental impact study. Lappalainen (1996) estimates that 1 400 000 ha of bogs in regions XI and XII of Chile (*c.* 33% of total wetlands) are potentially expoitable for peat and/or surface *Sphagnum*. Hauser (1996) estimates the energy content of ground peat with 30% humidity at $3.24\,GJ\,m^{-3}$, for a total reserve of $15\,400 \times 10^6\ m^3$. In 1996, according to Hauser (1996), peat was being exploited commercially by private companies only at two locations in the extreme south of Chile, with concessions granted for a total of 140 ha. The extracted peat is transported some 2500 km north to central Chile for use in the fruit, horticulture, and mushroom industries. Fortunately, neither at this time, nor to any extent in the past, has peat been mined commercially for use as a fuel, as has occurred in boreal peatlands. In a relative sense, it can be said that southern peatlands are in remarkably better shape than their northern-hemisphere counterparts. However, under present economic pressures in Chile and Argentina, anything could happen.

Concluding remarks

Southern South American peatlands, occupying some 4.4 million ha, constitute an island of southern-temperate and South American biodiversity distantly placed from northern peatlands and from other southern-temperate wetlands in New Zealand and Tasmania. Such peatlands can be a dominant feature of the southern South American landscape to the extent of occupying more land than forests at the extreme southern latitudes. Their interesting floristic mix of putatively ancient and more recently dispersed elements could hold many secrets regarding how wetlands are created and how they are maintained over geological time. The peatlands – thanks largely to their inaccessibility – seem not to have been exploited for fuel or peat to any extent and, except for extensive introduced-beaver activity on the island of Tierra del Fuego, are presently fairly well conserved. These wetlands definitely deserve attention from the international scientific and conservation communities.

In that southern South American peatlands and forests are intricately connected at the ecosystem level, the fate of peatlands will largely determine the future of southern South American temperate forests, and vice versa. It thus becomes imperative to develop an integral strategy to protect southern-temperate peatlands and forests. While overall protection of the wetland complex is good, and exploitation of peatlands is still moderate, major imbalances among peatland subtypes in the protected-area system make it clear that *Sphagnum*-dominated bogs, located principally in Tierra de Fuego, are at the highest risk. This risk is real, given that huge tracts of *Sphagnum*-dominated peatlands in southern South America presently lie in the hands of forestry companies. What can, and what will be done about this situation, however, is far from clear. With 50% of the land area in the Magellanic region of Chile (where most

Sphagnum-dominated peatlands lie) already contained in the State Protected Area System, it seems unlikely that the government of Chile will devote more land to conservation. It is less probable that conservationists would accept a swap of conserved forest lands for wetlands, no matter how desirable the latter. All other things being equal, in the absence of some sort of concerted international effort, it seems that conservation efforts by the private sector constitute the only real possibility for conserving the extraordinary *Sphagnum*-dominated peatlands.

Undoubtedly, carbon credit schemes, as espoused in the Kyoto Protocol, offer a potential mechanism for achieving adequate conservation of *Sphagnum*-dominated peatlands on private lands. Peat bogs represent huge stores of organic carbon, whose release through burning or draining is well known to contribute to global warming (Gorham 1991). Peat depths in southern South American bogs are variable. Palynological studies report peat depths in the range of 1 to 5.5 m (Auer 1958, Heusser 1993). However, deeper excavations in some peat bogs in the Magallanic region have revealed two separate peat layers: one composed of typical red *Sphagnum* peat of 1 to 1.8 m, and a second layer of 6 to 7 m of compact black peat with a high organic component (Hauser 1996). One detailed study suggests that the upper 50 cm of cushion-bog peat in Chiloé contains an average of around 37% carbon (dry weight) (Ruthsatz & Villagrán 1991). One large forestry company in Tierra del Fuego has already gone through the process of attaining international certification to sell carbon credits. This, and other similar initiatives, unfortunately, are on standby due to the intransient position of the United States regarding the Kyoto Protocol.

The makings of any explicit integral strategy for saving cool, southern-temperate South American wetlands should involve the participation of all stakeholders, including the private land owner. This strategy should take into account non-ecological values of peatlands as well as their biological, ecological, and landscape values. As in the northern hemisphere (French 2002), southern-temperate wetlands may in the long-run turn out to have untold archeological value due to extremely good preservation of organic evidence. The importance of such remains cannot be overemphasized: the archeological site of Monte Verde (Dillehay 1989, 1997), in Region X of southern Chile, was preserved as a result of the formation of peat over a Late Pleistocene settlement on the margin of a small creek; the water-saturated deposits afforded excellent preservation for organic remains, enabling researchers the rare chance to identify and characterize plant species used in the inhabitants' diet, as well as aspects of their wood technology. Monte Verde is the earliest archeological site in South America that is unanimously accepted by the scientific community, and has debunked long-held views about the initial peopling of the Americas (Meltzer *et al.* 1997). Palynological work suggests that outlying peatlands in the northern part of the wetland zone are remnants of a peatland area that expanded greatly during the cold–wet cycles of the Pleistocene (Villagrán 1988). In particular, the far-southern lands of South America are the home of several indigenous tribes (Selk'nam, Ala-calufes, and Yamañas). These hunter–gatherers occupied different environments, including steppe, forest–wetland boundaries, and coastal zones. Preserving peat-lands, should thus be a high priority for both Argentina and Chile.

Acknowledgements

This work was supported by a grant from the Chilean Millennium Sci-entific Initiative (ICM) and various FONDECYT-Chile grants to M T K A over the years. Information on the flora of the *Sphagnum*-dominated peatlands of Tierra del Fuego was obtained under the auspices of the Río Cóndor Project Scien-tific Commission. We thank Nicolas Garcia for providing additional last-minute florististic data from the poorly studied peat bogs of Region IX of Chile.

References

Apps, M. J., Kurz, W. A., Luxmoore, R. J. *et al.* (1993). Boreal forest and tundra. *Water, Air and Soil Pollution*, **70**, 39–53.

Armesto, J. J., Rozzi, R., Smith-Ramírez, C., and Arroyo, M. T. K. (1998). Conservation targets in South American temperate forests. *Science*, **282**, 1271–2.

Arroyo, M. T. K. (1997). Sustainable forestry and biodiversity conservation in the Río Cóndor Project. In *Nature and Human Society. The Quest for a Sustainable World*, ed. P. H. Raven. Washington, DC: US National Academy of Sciences Press, pp. 530–42.

Arroyo, M. T. K. and Cavieres, L. (1997). The mediterranean-type climate flora of Central Chile: what do we know and how can we assure its protection. *Noticiero de Biología*, **5**(2), 48–56.

Arroyo, M. T. K., Donoso, C., Murúa, R. *et al.* (1996a). *Toward an Ecologically Sustainable Forestry Project. Concepts, Analysis and Recommendations. Protecting Biodiversity and Ecosystem Processes in the Río Cóndor Project – Tierra del Fuego*. Departmento de Investigación y Desarrollo, University of Chile.

Arroyo, M. T. K., Riveros, M., Peñaloza, A., Cavieres, L., and Faggi, A. M. (1996b). Phytogeographic relationships and regional richness patterns of the cool temperate rainforest flora of southern South America. In *High-Latitude Rainforests and Associated Ecosystems of the West Coasts of the Americas. Climate, Hydrology, Ecology and Conservation*, eds. R. G. Lawford, P. B. Alaback, and E. Fuentes. New York: Springer Verlag, pp. 134–72.

Auer, V. (1958). *Wissenschaftliche Ergebnisse der Finnischen Expeditionen nach Patagonien 1937–38 und der Finnisch-Argentinischen Expeditionen 1947–53*. Helsinki, Finland: Annales Academiae Scientiarum Fennicae.

CCB (CONAF–CONAMA–BIRF): Corporación National Forestal–Comisión Nacional del Medio Ambiente–Banco International de Reconstrucción y Fomento) (1999).

Catastro y Evaluación de Recursos Vegetacionales Nativos de Chile, 14 vol. Santiago de Chile: CONAF and CONAMA.

di Castri, F. and Hajek, E. R. (1976). *Bioclimatología de Chile*. Dirección de Investigación, Vicerectoría Académica, Universidad Católica de Chile, Santiago.

Dillehay, T. (1989). *Monte Verde: a Late Pleistocene Settlement in Chile*, vol. 1, *Palaeoenvironment and Site Context*. Washington, DC: Smithsonian Institution Press.

(1997). *Monte Verde: a Late Pleistocene Settlement in Chile*, vol. 2, *The Archeological Context and Interpretation*. Washington, DC: Smithsonian Institution Press.

French, C. A. I. (2002). *Geoarchaeology in Action: Studies in Soil Micromorphology and Landscape Evolution*. London: Routledge.

Galloway, D. (1995). *Liquenes*. Report made to the Río Cóndor Scientific Commission, Santiago, Chile.

Godley, E. J. (1960). The botany of southern Chile in relation to New Zealand and the subantarctic. *Proceedings of the Royal Society of London*, **152**, 457–72.

Gorham, E. (1991). Northern peatlands: role in the carbon cycle and probable responses to global warming. *Ecological Applications*, **1**(2), 182–95.

Hauser, A. (1996). Los depósitos de turba en Chile y sus perspectivas de utilización. *Revista Geológica de Chile*, **23**(2), 217–29.

He, Si. (1998). A checklist of the mosses of Chile. *Journal of Hattori Botanical Laboratory*, **85**, 103–89.

Heusser, C. J. (1993). Late quaternary forest-steppe contact zone, Isla Grande de Tierra del Fuego, subantarctic South America. *Quaternary Science Review*, **12**, 169–77.

Lappalainen, E. (1996). *Global Peat Resources*. UNESCO Geological Survey of Finland. Finland: International Peat Society.

Lizarralde, M. S. (1993). Current status of introduced beaver (*Castor canadensis*) populations in Tierra del Fuego, Argentina. *Ambio*, **22**(6), 351–8.

Looser, G. (1952). *Donatia fascicularis* en la Cordillera de Nahuelbuta. *Revista Universitaria (Universidad Católica de Chile)*, **37**, 7–9.

Meltzer, D. J., Grayson, D. K., Ardila, G. *et al.* (1997). On the Pleistocene antiquity of Monte Verde, southern Chile. *American Antiquity*, **62**, 659–63.

Mitchell, A. D. and Wagstaff, S. J. (2000). Phylogeny and biogeography of the Chilean *Pseudopanax laetevirens*. *New Zealand Journal of Botany*, **38**, 404–14.

Mitsch, W. J., Mitsch, R. H., and Turner, R. E. (1994). Wetlands of the Old and New Worlds: ecology and management. In *Global Wetlands: Old World and New*, ed. W. J. Mitsch. Amsterdam, the Netherlands: Elsevier Science, pp. 3–56.

Moore, D. M. (1979). Southern oceanic wet-healthland (including Magellanic moorland). In *Ecosystems of the World*, vol. 9A, ed. R. I. Specht and D. W. Goodhall. Amsterdam, the Netherlands: Elsevier Science.

(1983). *The Flora of Tierra del Fuego*. Oswestry, UK: Anthony Nelson.

Muñoz-Schick, M., Nuñez, H., and Yánez, J. (1996). *Libro Rojo de los Sitios Prioritarios para la Conservación de la Diversidad Biológica en Chile*. Santiago, Chile: Ministerio de Agricultura, CONAF.

Pisano, E. (1977). Fitogeográfia de Fuego-Patagonia chilena. I. Comunidades vegetales entre las latitudes 52 y 56°S. *Anales del Instituto de la Patagonia (Chile)*, **8**, 121–250.

(1981). Bosquejo fitogeográfico de Fuego-Patagonia. *Anales del Instituto de la Patagonia (Chile)*, **12**, 159–71.

(1983). The Magellanic tundra complex. In *Ecosystems of the World*, vol. 4B, *Mires: Swamp, Bog, Fen and Moor*, ed. A. P. J. Gore. Amsterdam, the Netherlands: Elsevier Science, pp. 295–329.

Ramírez, C. (1968). Die vegetation der Moore der Cordillera Pelada (Chile). *Berichte Oberhessischen Gesellschaft für Natur und Heilkunde, Naturwissenschaftliche Abteilung*, **36**, 95–101.

Renner, S. S., Murray, D., and Foreman, D. (2000). Timing transantarctic junctions in the Atherospermataceae (Laurales): evidence from coding and noncoding chloroplast sequences. *Systematic Biology*, **49**(3), 579–91.

Ruthsatz, B. and Villagrán, C. (1991). Vegetation pattern and soil nutrients of a Magellanic moorland on the Cordillera de Piuchué, Chiloé Island, Chile. *Revista Chilena de Historia Natural*, **64**, 461–78.

Schlatter, R., Venegas, C. and Torres-Mura, J. C. (1995). *Ornitología*. Report made to the Río Cóndor Scientific Commission, Santiago, Chile.

Seberg, O. (1988). Taxonomy, phylogeny, and biogeography of the genus *Oreobolus* R. Br. (Cyperaceae), with comments on the biogeography of the South Pacific continents. *Botanical Journal of the Linnean Society*, **96**, 119–95.

Sielfeld, K. and Venegas, C. (1980). Poblamiento e impacto ambiental de *Castor canadensis* Kuhl, en Isla Navarino, Chile. *Anales del Instituto de la Patagonia (Chile)*, **11**, 247–57.

Swenson, U., Backlund, A., McLoughlin, S., and Hill, R. S. (2001). *Nothofagus* biogeography revisited with special emphasis on the enigmatic distribution of subgenus *Brassospora* in New Caledonia. *Cladistics*, **17**, 28–47.

Tuhkanen, S., Kuokka, I., Hyvonen, J., Stenroos, S., and Nicmels, J. (1990). Tierra del Fuego as a target for biogeographical research past and present. *Anales del Instituto de la Patagonia (Chile)*, **19**(2), 1–107.

Villagrán, C. (1988). Expansion of Magellanic moorland during the late Pleistocene: palynological evidence from northern Isla de Chiloé, Chile. *Quaternary Research*, **29**, 294–306.

Wagstaff, S. J. and Wege, J. (2002). Patterns of diversification in New Zealand Stylidiaceae. *American Journal of Botany*, **89**, 865–74.

Wagstaff, S. J., Martinsson, K., and Swenson, U. (2000). Divergence estimates of *Tetrachondra hamiltonii* and *T. patagonica* (Tetrachondraceae) and their implications for austral biogeography. *New Zealand Journal of Botany*, **38**, 595–606.

Willson, M., Sabag, C., and Traveset, A. (1995). *Interacciones planta-animal*. Report made to the Río Cóndor Scientific Commission, Santiago, Chile.

Winkworth, R. C., Wagstaff, S., Glenny, D., and Lockhart, P. J. (2002). Plant dispersal N.E.W.S. from New Zealand. *Trends in Ecology and Evolution*, **17**, 514–20.

13

The future of large wetlands: a global perspective

L. H. FRASER
Thompson Rivers University

P. A. KEDDY
Southeastern Louisiana University

Introduction

It is a difficult task to write the concluding chapter of *The World's Largest Wetlands* because one could imagine two quite different audiences drawn to this book. Some will know a great deal about wetland science and will probably use the book for the many examples and descriptions of large wetland systems offered. Others may be encountering the science of wetland ecology for the first time, and perhaps may not have the academic resources readily at hand to interpret the content, or to draw common parallels between the large wetland systems. In reviewing these chapters and considering the two audiences, we constructed four themes that are shared across chapters: (1) threats to wetlands; (2) efforts to save wetlands; (3) wetlands, water, and humans; and (4) moving toward conservation. For somebody already well-versed some, or even all, of this summary may not be needed; but for others it will be a helpful capstone to the discussion of large wetland systems. Keep in mind that there are other wetlands books with much more detail that the reader should go to for a more-thorough reference.

The estimated annual value of wetlands, based on ecosystem services and natural capital, is US$12 790 trillion (Constanza *et al.* 1997); this accounts for over one-third of the total value for the world. Much of the value associated with wetlands is related to the role they play in the hydrological cycle (e.g.

The World's Largest Wetlands: Ecology and Conservation, eds. L. H. Fraser and P. A. Keddy.
Published by Cambridge University Press. © Cambridge University Press 2005.

water storage and water quality). Fresh water is a limited resource and yet the rate of human acquisition of fresh water is rising with the increase in human population (Fraser *et al.* 2003). We present here an overview of global wetland loss and future threats, wetland conservation efforts, and the inherent values and benefits of large wetland systems.

An area is a wetland if there are three of the following major components: flooding, hydrology, hydrarch soils, and water-tolerant vegetation. The variation that occurs within each of these three factors results in a wide range of possible wetland types. The four major types of wetland are marsh, fen, bog, and swamp. On a general level, wetlands are controlled by only a few major factors: hydrology, fertility, disturbance, competition, grazing, and burial (Keddy 2000). However, each wetland type functions very differently as a result of variation in biomass, diversity, and species composition – particularly within their biogeochemical pathways (Mitsch & Gosselink 2000). The large wetlands and wetland complexes featured in this book represent, either collectively or individually, all four of the major wetland types. Some of the large wetland complexes are dominated by just one major wetland type; for example, the Siberian wetlands (Chapter 2) and the Magellanic moorland complex (Chapter 12) are mainly peatlands, prairie potholes (Chapter 11) are predominantly freshwater marshes, and the majority of the Mississippi floodplain (Chapter 8) is a bottomland hardwood forest. Others, like the Mackenzie River basin (Chapter 6), contain a mosaic of different wetland types. With all of the variation found among wetlands how is it possible, then, to make general management recommendations on wetlands, and large wetland systems in particular? First, it is necessary to focus on the shared characteristics. Next, management goals must be clearly defined.

The universal common denominator of all wetlands is the occurrence of water. Wetlands are a unique ecosystem because of their spatial location between aquatic and terrestrial zones. Due to their location, wetlands form an important component of the hydrological cycle. Most surface water originating from terrestrial systems must pass through wetlands in order to reach its oceanic outlet. Many of these waters contain an array of dissolved mineral nutrients. For this reason, some wetland types (e.g. temperate salt marshes) are the most highly productive ecosystems in the world (Kaswadji *et al.* 1990). The high productivity results in a rich diversity of life forms, which is why wetlands have been referred to as "biological supermarkets" (Mitsch & Gosselink 1993). Wetlands receive and collect many different dissolved compounds. The combination of the chemical properties of the water molecule, the biogeochemistry of wetlands, and the high level of productivity found in wetlands mean that wetlands are capable of transforming and reducing these compounds. For this reason, wetlands have also been referred to as "the kidneys of the landscape." Not only do wetlands act as transformers and reducers of dissolved compounds, but they also receive air-borne compounds. Large northern peatlands are important in the global carbon cycle because they have the capacity to fix and retain large carbon supplies (Clymo *et al.* 1998), thereby potentially reducing the rate of global increase in carbon dioxide resulting from the burning of fossil fuels. Wetlands also serve an important social and historical role in society. The major societies of civilization have developed on or beside wetlands because many wetlands provide in abundance the necessary products that sustain life, food, and water (de Villiers 1999).

Despite the growing understanding and appreciation of the importance of wetlands, wetland loss is very high. More than half of the world's original wetland area has been lost (Dugan 1993, Moser *et al.* 1996). The purpose of this chapter is to: (1) present the general factors that threaten the health and existence of wetlands around the world; (2) review the international efforts to save wetland areas, with specific reference to the Ramsar Convention; and (3) present some of the common values of large wetlands, including (a) economic value, (b) influence on global climate change, and (c) water purification.

Threats to wetlands

Direct effects: loss of area

Total global wetland area is difficult to estimate because of inadequate data, inconsistencies in defining a wetland, and the fluctuating nature of wetland habitat due to seasonal water-level changes. Matthews and Fung (1987) calculated that global wetland area was ∼5.3 million km^2 from the integration of three independent global, digital sources: (1) vegetation; (2) soil properties; and (3) fractional inundation. Darras *et al.* (1999) estimate global wetland area at somewhere between 5 and 9 million km^2. More-recent figures estimate global wetland area between 12.76 and 12.79 million km^2, well in excess of estimates given above (Finlayson & Davidson 1999; Table 13.1). The wide differences in areal estimates reduces the confidence in their value. Clearly, better and more-consistent measures are required for accurate and much-needed measurements.

It has taken humans approximately 100 years to reduce global wetland area by 50% (Dugan 1993, Moser *et al.* 1996). The major cause of wetland loss is the conversion of wetlands through draining or filling for human settlements, agriculture, and silviculture (Dahl 2000). In the United States, 53% of all historical wetlands in the lower 48 states have been destroyed by anthropogenic causes (Dahl 1990). Sixty percent of the wetlands in Europe have been lost to agricultural development (WRI 2000). Rice cultivation in Asia accounts for the greatest

Table 13.1 *Wetland area by major region*
(from Finlayson & Davidson 1999).

Region	Area (million km^2)
Africa	1.213 22–1.246 86
Asia	2.042 45
Eastern Europe	2.292 17
Neotropics	4.149 17
North America	2.415 74
Oceania	0.357 5
Western Europe	0.288 22
Total	12.758 47–12.792 11

wetland losses in the central plains of India, and in large areas of Thailand, Vietnam, and China (Moser *et al.* 1996). In addition to wetland losses from draining and filling, damming for hydroelectric power can result in large wetland losses. While some wetland area is lost upstream of dams through the construction of reservoirs, much wetland area is lost downstream due to changes in water-level fluctuations. Figure 13.1 demonstrates how by changing the amplitude of water levels, marshes and wet meadows can be eliminated from the landscape. Dam construction over the past 50 years has been rampant. At the beginning of the 1950s, there were approximately 5000 dams over 15 m high world-wide; by 1999 there were over 45 000 (WCD 2000). Three of the soon-to-be largest dams in the world are currently under construction (Table 13.2).

Despite efforts to conserve and restore wetlands, the rate of wetland loss in the United States continues to exceed wetland gain (Dahl 2000), and this trend is probably similar at the global level (see Finlayson & Davidson 1999). Future threats to the remaining wetland area include agriculture, urban sprawl, damming, and sea-level rise as a result of global climate change. The Hadley Centre for Climate Prediction and Research (Exeter, UK) estimates a loss of at least 40% to 50% of the world's remaining coastal wetlands by 2080 due to a predicted 1-m rise in sea levels (Hinrichsen 2000). Of course, loss of overall wetland area is not the only concern; wetlands are also at risk in terms of their general degradation (i.e. the loss of ecosystem integrity).

Indirect effects: changes in composition

In addition to outright loss, wetland composition can be changed and function can be reduced by indirect effects including eutrophication and non-native-species invasions (Keddy 1983). Consider as an example the effects of eutrophication. Figure 13.2 shows the number of plant species and the number

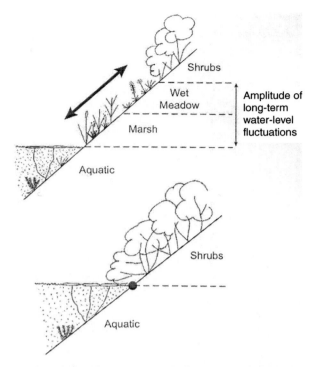

Figure 13.1 Stablizing water levels through dam construction compresses wetlands from four zones (top) to two zones (bottom) (from Keddy 1991).

of rare plant species in relation to biomass (a surrogate for productivity) of shoreline wetlands. The diversity of plant species is highest at intermediate levels of biomass and the number of rare species is greatest on the sites with the lowest levels of biomass. Eutrophication will reduce the length of this gradient and slowly cause more areas of shoreline to converge on the high-biomass vegetation type, thereby reducing the occurrence of rare species. To compound the problem, a few large and fast-growing species (e.g. *Typha* spp., *Phalaris* spp.) usually prosper in the fertile wetlands. Different species and community types can occur at the less-fertile sites depending on the particular constraints. Shallowly sloping sands may develop fens, gravel shorelines may have isoëtid plants, wet prairies may occur where fire or water-level fluctuations kill woody plants, panne vegetation may develop between sand dunes (over a fragile crust of alkaline sand with a high water table), and so on. The benign ends of many gradients are similar enough that we can describe them as a "core" habitat that can be dominated by the same species. At the peripheral end of each axis, however, species with specific adaptations to particular sources of adversity occur. This pattern is termed "centrifugal organization" (Fig. 13.3). Many peripheral habitats radiate outwards from the single, central core habitat.

Table 13.2 *The 25 largest dams in the world (data from US Department of the Interior, Bureau of Reclamation and World Commission on Dams).*

Dam	Location	Volume (thousands)		Year completed
		Cubic meters	Cubic yards	
Syncrude Tailings	Canada	540 000	706 320	UC
Chapetón	Argentina	296 200	311 539	UC
Pati	Argentina	238 180	274 026	UC
New Cornelia Tailings	United States	209 500	274 026	1973
Tarbela	Pakistan	121 720	159 210	1976
Kambaratinsk	Kyrgyzstan	112 200	146 758	UC
Fort Peck	United States	96 049	125 628	1940
Lower Usuma	Nigeria	93 000	121 644	1990
Cipasang	Indonesia	90 000	117 720	UC
Atatürk	Turkey	84 500	110 522	1990
Yacyretá-Apipe	Paraguay–Argentina	81 000	105 944	1998
Guri (Raul Leoni)	Venezuela	78 000	102 014	1986
Rogun	Tajikistan	75 500	98 750	1985
Oahe	United States	70 339	92 000	1963
Mangla	Pakistan	65 651	85 872	1967
Gardiner	Canada	65 440	85 592	1968
Afsluitdijk	Netherlands	63 400	82 927	1932
Oroville	United States	59 639	78 008	1968
San Luis	United States	59 405	77 700	1967
Nurek	Tajikistan	58 000	75 861	1980
Garrison	United States	50 843	66 500	1956
Cochiti	United States	48 052	62 850	1975
Tabka (Thawra)	Syria	46 000	60 168	1976
Bennett W. A. C.	Canada	43 733	57 201	1967
Tucuruí	Brazil	43 000	56 242	1984

UC, under construction in 2004; W. A. C., William Andrew Cecil.

With eutrophication, excess nutrients allow tall, fast-growing plants to dominate increasingly large areas of landscape, and often these plants are non-native invasives (Grime *et al.* 1997). Recent work by Woo and Zedler (2002) reveal that experimental nutrient addition alone can cause a shift from a native sedge meadow toward dominance by the invasive *Typha* × *glauca* in as little as one year. In northeastern North America, *Typha* dominates the core region. In

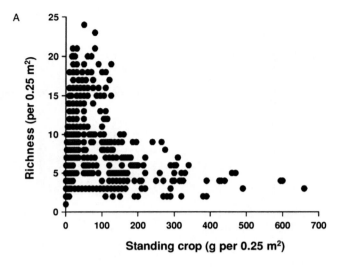

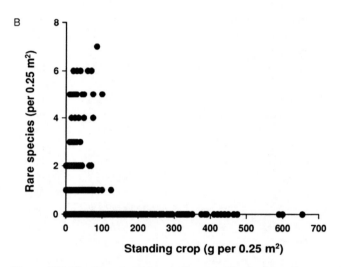

Figure 13.2 Plant species richness along gradients of standing crop for
(A) 401 0.25-m² quadrats in eastern North America and (B) the same quadrats,
but with nationally rare species only (from Moore *et al.* 1989).

other climatic regions, herbaceous perennials in the genera *Papyrus*, *Phragmites*,
Phalaris, and *Calamagrostis* may play a similar role.

Efforts to save wetlands

There are many local and regional organizations established to conserve
wetland habitat, but these are mainly found in the developed world. National

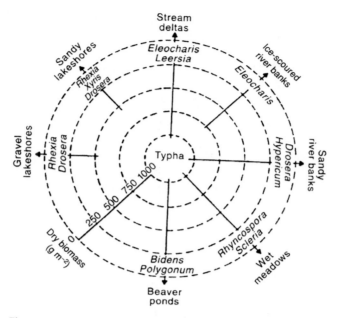

Figure 13.3 When many gradients radiate outward from a shared core habitat, the pattern is termed "centrifugal organization" (Wisheu & Keddy 1992).

and, particularly, international organizations are less common. At the national level, the current federal policy of the United States is to protect remaining wetlands and replace habitats destroyed by development (Votteler & Muir 1996). For example, the 1977 Clean Water Act, the "Swampbuster" provisions of the 1985 Food Security Act, the "no net loss" policy formulated in 1998, and the Wetlands Reserve Program (WRP) have protected or restored many remaining wetlands. Common techniques used in constructing or restoring wetlands include grading and excavation to create the necessary topography, installation of dams and stop-log structures to control hydrology, stocking desired plants and animals, and controlling pests and invasive plants with insecticides and herbicides (Hammer 1996).

Although constructed and restored wetlands are being used to mitigate for the loss of existing habitats, these "man-made" wetlands often lack ecological functions provided by natural habitats (Kentula 1996, Zedler 1993). For example, a study of 168 mitigation wetlands in the US Midwest and Florida found that only 15% were fully successful (Gallihugh & Rogner 1998). Efforts to improve the success of wetland construction projects are hampered by a lack of understanding of factors that determine plant and animal community structure. This has resulted in an increased interest in understanding ecological processes in these habitats, including factors that impact the biota and affect its distribution.

Table 13.3 *The top ten countries with the most Ramsar sites and the largest cumulative areas of Ramsar sites (Frazier 1999).*

	Number of sites	Total area (1 000 000 ha)
Countries with the most Ramsar sites		
United Kingdom	119	513 585
Australia	49	5 099 180
Italy	46	56 950
Ireland	45	66 994
Denmark	38	2 283 013
Spain	38	158 216
Canada	36	13 050 975
Russian Federation	35	10 323 767
Germany	31	672 852
Sweden	30	382 750
Countries with the most Ramsar area		
Canada	36	13 050 975
Russian Federation	35	10 323 767
Botswana	1	6 864 000
Australia	49	5 099 180
Brazil	5	4 536 623
Peru	7	2 932 059
Denmark	38	2 283 013
Islamic Republic of Iran	18	1 357 150
Mauritania	2	1 188 600
United States	17	1 172 633

The most-comprehensive international organization working to save and protect wetlands is known as the Ramsar Convention on Wetlands. It is involved in implementing the Convention on Wetlands of International Importance Especially as Waterfowl Habitat. Eighteen nations met on February 2, 1971 in Ramsar, Iran to sign this international treaty which provides for legislation to conserve wetlands of international importance. The selection of Ramsar sites is to be based on "international significance in terms of ecology, botany, zoology, limnology, or hydrology" (Frazier 1999). By 1999, the Ramsar Convention had grown to include 114 nations, with over 1000 Ramsar sites covering approximately 0.7 million km^2 (Frazier 1999). Table 13.3 lists the dominant signatories of the Convention, with their numbers and total areas of Ramsar sites.

Wetlands, water, and humans

All ecosystems on Earth have intrinsic value, but historically the important functional role of wetlands has been ignored. In fact, wetlands have been considered more of a hindrance than a system with any beneficial properties. It is mainly for this reason that half of the world's wetlands have been lost in recent times. It is now broadly recognized that wetlands are extremely important systems. Below, we illustrate these values with an emphasis on the increased values inherent to large wetland systems. We discuss: (1) the economic value of wetlands, (2) the influence on global climate change, and (3) water purification.

Economic value

The Earth's ecosystems provide the goods and services essential for human welfare. Therefore, it can be argued that ecosystems represent a real and measurable value. Traditionally, ecological concerns have been considered a financial burden on economic development. However, Constanza *et al.* (1997) measured the value of the services that ecosystems provide to the world economy.

Seventeen ecosystem services and functions were reviewed and valued by Constanza *et al.* (1997), ranging from landscape-level geophysical services (e.g. gas regulation and climate regulation) to ecosystem-level biogeochemical services (e.g. nutrient cycling and waste treatment), to community-level ecological services (e.g. pollination and biological control), to population-level ecological services (e.g. genetic resources), and finally to human societal services (e.g. recreation and cultural). The total value of all biomes on Earth was calculated at US$33.268 trillion; approximately 1.8 times greater than the global gross national product of US$18 trillion per year. This establishes in general the great value that ecosystems provide. Interestingly, the total value of wetlands, including both fresh and salt water, was US$8.816 trillion. Therefore, according to the services and functions determined by Constanza *et al.* (1997), wetlands account for 26.5% of the total value of the world's ecosystems, even though wetlands cover only 1.5% of the planet's surface! The issue of valuation, argues Constanza *et al.* (1997), is inseparable from the decisions that need to be made regarding ecological systems (but see Kelman 1981).

Influence on global climate change

Forecast changes in climate are expected to significantly change the temperature and length of growing seasons on Earth, and thereby modify the distributions of plant and animal species (Prentice *et al.* 1992, Woodward *et al.*

1995). Large wetlands may moderate such changes in global climate in at least three ways. Peatlands are a major sink of atmospheric carbon, and probably reduced the rate of increase in atmospheric carbon dioxide levels from fossil-fuel emissions. In addition, wetlands may alter albedo and store latent heat. We will discuss these in turn.

Peatlands are large deposits of organic carbon (Clymo 1970, Clymo & Reddaway 1971) distributed mainly in the northern Hemisphere in cold climates. Although plant growth rates are low, decomposition rates are lower still. Decomposition is reduced by three factors: (1) high and constant water levels at or near the soil surface, (2) low temperatures, and (3) low pH. Since the last deglaciation, peatlands have sequestered nearly as much carbon (400 to 500 Pg) as currently occurs in the atmosphere (Clymo et al. 1998) and it is likely that there is still a net accumulation of organic carbon in peatlands (Belyea & Clymo 2001). Should the area of peatlands be reduced in the future, the rates of carbon removal from the atmosphere would decline. Furthermore, microbial decomposition of existing peat could release stored carbon dioxide to the atmosphere.

Large wetlands may also influence global changes in temperature through modifying albedo, which is a measure of the proportion of the incoming short-wave radiation that is absorbed by the Earth. Ecosystems may themselves affect climate (Chase et al. 2000, Foley et al. 2003). Wigley and Raper (2001) forecast that global average temperatures will rise 4 to 7 °C over the coming century. Foley et al. (2003) suggest, for example, that the northward migration of the boreal forest into the arctic tundra could cause a decline in albedo at these latitudes, leading the Earth to warm more than predicted by other models (Foley et al. 2003).

The capacity of water to store latent heat may also have global implications. We can speculate that the loss of wetlands may have affected global temperatures through the redistribution of large water bodies and the loss of lag effects in the hydrological cycle (Chase et al. 2000). Water has a high specific heat (specific heat being the energy required to warm 1 g of a substance by 1 °C), which means that the temperature of water will change relatively slowly for a given energy input. Larger water bodies (and, possibly, larger wetlands) have smaller temperature fluctuations. This property of water can directly affect air temperature by moderating extremes in adjoining terrestrial areas. Large-scale loss of wetlands could therefore exacerbate the effects of global warming, particularly at local scales.

Water purification

Freshwater wetlands are sinks for chemicals, effectively buffering other ecosystems against contamination by removing toxins from effluents and reducing excessive concentrations of nitrogen and phosphorus (Kadlec & Knight 1996, Mitsch & Gosselink 2000). There may be a critical link between water supply, water quality, and wetland loss. The Postel, Daily, and Ehrlich (PDE) model (Postel *et al.* 1996) was designed to address the current and future issue of the human appropriation of freshwater from 1990 to 2025, in relation to projections of population growth and dam construction. As the global population continues to grow, it will be increasingly difficult – across all regions – to meet per-capita water demands beyond 2025 (Fig. 13.4A). In 1990, humans used 54% of runoff that is geographically and temporally accessible (AR). Despite modest increases in AR, by 2025 over 70% of runoff will be utilized; and, the model does not even include per capita increases in human water use!

Fraser *et al.* (2003) recalculated the PDE model with a conservative per-capita increase of 1.125% (see Postel 1992). When per-capita increases in water use are included in the PDE model (all other parameters being equal), human appropriation of AR is 99% of accessible AR by 2025, an increase of 27% (Fraser *et al.* 2003). Not only does this have obvious and direct effects on freshwater availability for human use, the aquatic environment is threatened because of dam construction, river diversions, heavy pollution loads, and other habitat changes (Gleick 2000).

The two major differences between the PDE model and the Fraser *et al.* (2003) global freshwater-treatment-wetland model are: (1) calculation of annual per-capita increases in human water use; and (2) incorporation of constructed wetlands to treat wastewater. The global treatment-wetland model assumes linear functions for population growth and dam construction, including a 1.125% annual per-capita increase in water use, which is consistent with established trends (Postel 1992).

Through the construction of wetlands, the need for the dilution factor (which serves as a proxy for in-stream uses) within the PDE model is negated. The wetlands themselves, as well as the treated effluent from the wetlands, can serve the in-stream uses. The withdrawal values estimated by PDE were applied to the global treatment-wetland model, and then an approximate percentage of wastewater effluent from the three withdrawal classes (agriculture, industry, and municipalities) that produce effluent was determined (Table 13.4).

Evapotranspiration losses were judged to be 15% of the calculated wastewater volume during treatment. A linear increase in the construction of treatment wetlands was projected, up to 100% implementation by 2025 (Fraser *et al.* 2003). With an increase in treatment wetlands, there is a subsequent linear reduction in the need for in-stream uses because the constructed wetlands serve that purpose, which results in a reduction in the human appropriation of AR. In addition, treatment returns – through "clean" effluent produced by agricultural,

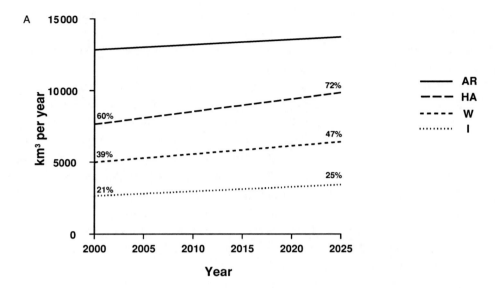

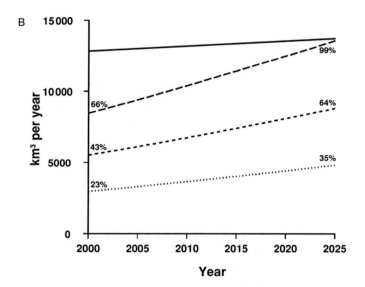

Figure 13.4 Change in human appropriation of accessible runoff over time as a function of population growth under three model conditions: (A) PDE assumptions (Postel *et al.* 1996); (B) PDE assumptions plus per capita increase in freshwater use; (C) global treatment-wetlands model (see text for explanation). AR, accessible runoff; HA, human appropriation of accessible runoff; W, withdrawals; I, in-stream uses; R, freshwater returns.

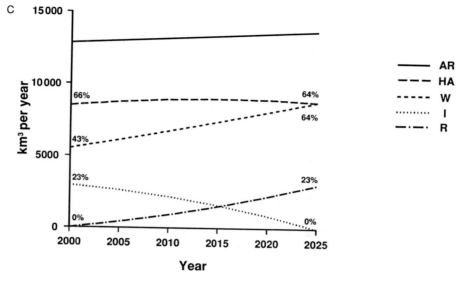

Figure 13.4 (*cont.*)

industrial, and municipal withdrawals – were calculated as a potential re-usable source of fresh water for future withdrawals.

The global treatment-wetland model clearly demonstrates the potential benefits of treatment wetlands for human freshwater use and availability (Fig. 13.4C). The most-significant result is the reduction in the overall percentage of the human appropriation of accessible runoff, from 66% in 2000, to 64% in 2025. The reason for this reduction is the transfer of fresh water – used for instream uses – to the construction of treatment wetlands, resulting in instream uses appropriating 0% of human appropriation of accessible runoff by 2025.

In addition, up to 23% (2131 km^3 per year) of treatment returns – through effluent produced by agricultural, industrial, and municipal withdrawals – can potentially be re-used for withdrawals (at least for most agricultural, in-stream, and non-potable uses). Within this model, these treatment-wetland returns have not been calculated into the human appropriation of annual runoff. If humans appropriated all the treatment-wetland returns, these returns could substitute for the human appropriation of annual runoff, thereby further reducing the human appropriation of annual runoff to 42%.

How much wetland area is required to treat all the waste water produced by 2025? First, it was estimated that 2507 km^3 per year of waste water is produced (Fraser *et al.* 2003). Since it is not reasonable to expect that treatment wetlands can be 100% effective 100% of the time (e.g. due to seasonality and maintenance) treatment wetlands were calculated to not be in use for 90 days during the year.

Table 13.4 *Amount of freshwater use within the three separate withdrawal classes producing wastewater, for the years 2000 and 2025.*

Withdrawal classes	Use[a] (km³ per year)		Percentage of use producing wastewater (%)	Amount of use producing wastewater (km³ per year)		Percentage of wastewater receiving conventional primary and secondary treatment[b] (%)	Adjusted amount of use producing wastewater after conventional treatment (km³ per year)	
	2000	2025	2000–2025	2000	2025	2000–2025	2000	2025
Agriculture	3617	5826	25[b]	904	1457	0	904	1457
Industry	1225	1972	85[c]	1041	1676	50	521	838
Municipalities	377	607	70[d]	264	425	50	132	212
Total	5219	8405	Not applicable	2209	3558	Not applicable	1557	2507

[a] Based on projected levels from Postel et al. (1996).

[b] From Postel et al. (1996).

[c] From Metcalf & Eddy Inc. (1979).

[d] From Metcalf & Eddy Inc. (1979) and Novotny (1989).

Table 13.5 *Area of treatment wetlands needed to treat total amount of waste water produced, c. 2025.*

Waste water (km^3 per year)	2507
Waste water (cm^3 per day)	6.86×10^{15}
Wetland hectares required to treat waste water	17 111 400
Wetland square kilometers required to treat waste water	171 114
Number of 45-ha treatment wetlands required	380 253
Number of 45-ha treatment wetlands required to treat New York City	1238

Based on the standard wetland loading rate of 5 cm per day (Mitsch & Gosselink 2000), Fraser *et al.* (2003) estimate the required treatment-wetland area to be 171 114 km^2 (Table 13.5). To calculate this, the total number of wetland areas required to treat a constant loading rate of 5 cm per day (137 286 km^2) was determined plus the extra wastewater flow generated from "off-season" production (33 828 km^2), which assumes that the "off-season" flow is stored and then evenly applied at a constant rate throughout the treatment period (i.e. 275.25 days).

To put this size into perspective, the current global wetland area, from coastal swamps to inland floodplains, has been estimated to be between 5 and 12.79 million km^2 (Darras *et al.* 1999, Finlayson & Davidson 1999). Considering that over half of the world's wetlands have been lost in the last 100 years (Dugan 1993, Moser *et al.* 1996) the total area of treatment wetland needed is perhaps not an unreasonable goal.

Obviously, the construction of all the wetlands that would be needed to treat globally produced waste water is not realistically feasible due to a number of factors – including economics, current land cover, and basic logistics (i.e. construction of wetlands would be required beside every source of polluted runoff on the planet). Nevertheless, the model highlights the potential importance of wetlands to the global freshwater supply (Fig. 13.5). Fresh water is a limited resource, and increases in human population are quickly exhausting available annual runoff.

Towards conservation

Wetlands are complex and dynamic ecosystems, and each of the large wetlands described in this book has different species compositions, different ecological processes, and different controlling factors. Is there one scientific framework that can provide assistance in understanding these patterns, and simultaneously guide restoration? We suggest that one such framework is provided

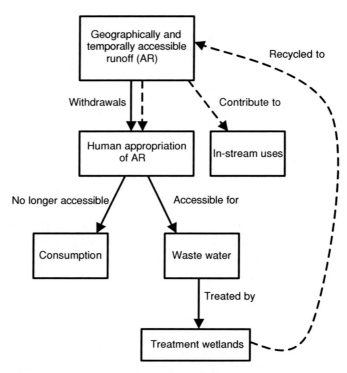

Figure 13.5 Conceptual flow chart illustrating human appropriation and re-use of fresh water according to the model described in the text. Solid lines refer to non-treated fresh water; dashed lines are treated, recycled, and generally non-potable fresh water.

by assembly rules, the trait and filter view of ecological communities (Keddy 1992, 2000). Diamond (1975) coined the term "assembly rules" to describe the ecological rules that predict how communities are formed from a pool of species that can potentially colonize a habitat, although similar ideas were offered by Muller-Dombois and Ellenberg (1974). Figure 13.6 shows how knowledge of the species pool, species' traits and environmental filters can be used to predict the resulting ecological community. In the case of northern salt marshes, for example, flooding eliminates terrestrial plants, salinity eliminates freshwater plants, and frost eliminates woody plants such as mangroves, the result being herbaceous salt marsh. Constructing assembly rules for a habitat requires knowledge about three sets of data: the local species pool, their traits, and the environmental filters that occur in the habitat (Keddy 1992, 1999, Weiher & Keddy 1995). Water level and soil fertility are the two key abiotic factors that determine the distributions of many plants and invertebrates (Batzer & Resh 1991, Cody 1991, Corti *et al.* 1997, Gleason 1939, Peckarsky & Dodson 1980, Keddy & Fraser 2000).

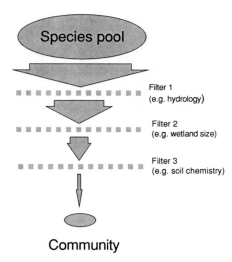

Figure 13.6 Conceptual diagram of how assembly rules predict the species composition of a community. In this example, three filters are identified (hydrology, wetland size, and soil chemistry). The width of the arrow represents the number of species. Species in the species pool that have the necessary traits to resist the environmental filters will colonize the habitat and make up the community found in the habitat. The filters, the resulting community assemblage, or the presence/absence of particular species can be used as habitat *indicators*.

In some cases, it is convenient to group species into functional groups or guilds based upon their ecomorphological traits (e.g. Grime 1977, Cummins & Klug 1979, Pianka 1980, Severinghaus 1981, Simberloff and Dayan 1991, Boutin & Keddy 1993, Wilson & Roxburgh 1994, Westoby *et al.* 2002). There is still much to be done to develop predictive assembly rules for wetland habitats, but much of the needed work requires knowledge of the traits of wetland organisms and the key factors controlling their occurrence.

In any attempt to conserve or restore wetlands, we also need one or more measures of success. That is, we need sets of indicators or gauges to judge whether a particular restoration effort, or a national conservation program, is producing the desired results. This is sometimes known as "adaptive management" (Holling 1978).

Ward's (1966) concept of Earth as a spaceship is well-accepted, but we now realize that it is a spaceship without an instrument panel. Because of this, we have no way to judge our ship's current ecological course, and no way to determine whether decisions on the bridge are leading to changes in course. No matter which political parties seize control of the bridge, this technical task must be completed. The search for gauges to insert in the instrument panel has been loosely directed by terms such as "environmental indicators" and "ecological integrity" (Woodley *et al.* 1993).

A world-wide monitoring system is needed. Two specific decisions must be made: (1) what gauges do we need, and (2) what are the danger zones for each of them? For each large wetland, and for each wetland type (i.e. fen, bog, marsh, swamp), we need a set of essential characteristics that can be monitored to inform us about the ecological state of the system. Choosing these characteristics is difficult (Keddy *et al.* 1993) because we still lack quantitative scientific models of ecosystems in general, or wetlands in particular, that tell us which characteristics are most important in maintaining function, sustaining productivity, and predicting future behavior.

Conclusion

Although wetlands now cover under 2% of the surface of the Earth, they are critical for the functioning of the biosphere (Constanza *et al.* 1997, Keddy 2000, Mitsch and Gosselink 2000). Half of the world's wetlands have been lost over the past century, and while there are ongoing efforts to conserve and restore these valuable habitats, there is still a global net loss. The exponential growth of human populations is likely to accelerate the direct and indirect impacts of humans on wetlands. This book has brought together a global team of experts to assess and prioritize the world's largest wetlands. Now that we know where they are, and the risks that face them, co-ordinated action is possible. We hope that in the short term this book will inspire and guide protection efforts, and that in the long term it will inspire and guide restoration.

References

Batzer, D. P. and Resh, V. H. (1991). Trophic interactions among a beetle predator, a chironomid grazer, and periphyton in a seasonal wetland. *Oikos*, **60**, 251–7.

Belyea, L. R. and Clymo, R. S. (2001). Feedback control of the rate of peat formation. *Proceedings of the Royal Society of London B*, **268**, 1315–21.

Boutin, C. and Keddy, P. A. (1993). A functional classification of wetland plants. *Journal of Vegetation Science*, **4**, 591–600.

Chase, T. N., Pielke, R. A., Sr., Kittel, T. G. F., Nemani, R. R., and Running, S. W. (2000). Simulated impacts of historical land cover changes on global climate in northern winter. *Climate Dynamics*, **16**, 93–105.

Clymo, R. S. (1970). The growth of *Sphagnum*: methods of measurement. *Journal of Ecology*, **58**, 13–49.

Clymo, R. S. and Reddaway, E. J. F. (1971). Productivity of Sphagnum (bog-moss) and peat accumulation. *Hidrobiologia (Bucharest)*, **12**, 181–92.

Clymo, R. S., Tutunen, J., and Tolonen, K., (1998). Carbon accumulation in peatland. *Oikos*, **81**, 368–88.

Cody, M. L. (1991). Niche theory and plant growth form. *Vegetatio*, **97**, 39–55.

Constanza, R., d'Arge, R., and de Groot, R. *et al.* (1997). The value of the world's ecosystem services and natural capital. *Nature*, **387**, 253–260.

Corti D., Kohler, S. L., and Sparks, R. E. (1997). Effects of hydroperiod and predation on a Mississippi River floodplain invertebrate community. *Oecologia*, **109**, 154–65.

Cummins, K. W. and Klug, M. J. (1979). Feeding ecology of stream invertebrates. *Annual Review of Ecology and Systematics*, **10**, 147–72.

Dahl, T. E. (1990). *Wetlands Losses in the United States, 1780s to 1980s*. Washington, DC: US Department the Interior, Fish and Wildlife Service.

Dahl, T. E. (2000). *Status and Trends of Wetlands in the Conterminous United States 1986–1997*. US Department of the Interior, Fish and Wildlife Service.

Darras, S., Michou, M., and Sarrat, C. (1999). *IGBP-DIS Wetland Data Initiative: A First Step Towards Identifying a Global Delineation of Wetlands*. IGB-DIS Working Paper 19. Toulouse, France: International Geosphere–Biosphere Programme: Data and Information System.

de Villiers, M. (1999). *Water*. Toronto, Canada: Stoddart Publishing Co.

Diamond, J. A. (1975). Assembly of species communities. In *Ecology and Evolution of Communities*, eds. M. L. Cody and J. M. Diamond. Cambridge, MA: Belnap Press, pp. 342–445.

Dugan, P. (1993). *Wetlands in Danger*. London: Michael Beasley, Reed International.

Finlayson, C. M. and Davidson, N. C. (1999). *Global Review of Wetland Resources and Priorities for Wetland Inventory*. Ramsar Bureau Contract 56. Gland, Switzerland: Ramsar Convention Bureau.

Foley, J. A., Costa, M. H., Delire, C., Ramankutty, N., and Snyder, P. (2003). Green surprise? How terrestrial ecosystems could affect earth's climate. *Frontiers in Ecology and the Environment*, **1**, 38–44.

Fraser, L. H., Bradford, M. E., and Steer, D. N. (2003). Human appropriation and treatment of fresh water: a global hydrology model incorporating treatment wetlands. *International Journal of Environment and Sustainable Development*, **2**, 174–83.

Frazier, S. (1999). *Ramsar Sites Overview*. Wageningen, the Netherlands: Wetlands International.

Gallihugh, J. L. and Rogner, J. D. (1998). *Wetland Mitigation and 404 Permit Compliance Study*, vol. 1. Burlington, IL: US Fish and Wildlife Service, Region III. Chicago, IL: US Environmental Protection Agency, Region V.

Gleason, H. A. (1939). The individualistic concept of the plant association. *American Midland Naturalist*, **21**, 92–110.

Gleick, P. H. (2000). *The World's Water 2000–2001: The Biennial Report on Freshwater Resources*. Washington, DC: Island Press.

Grime, J. P. (1977). Evidence for the existence of three primary strategies in plants and its relevance to ecological and evolutionary theory. *American Naturalist*, **111**, 1169–94.

Grime, J. P., Thompson, K., and Hodgson, J. G. (1997). Integrated screening validates primary axes of specialization in plants. *Oikos*, **79**, 259–81.

Hammer, D. A. (1996). *Creating Freshwater Wetlands*, 2nd edn. Boca Raton, FL: CRC Press.

Hinrichsen, D. (2000). *The Oceans are Coming Ashore*. Washington, DC: World Watch.

Holling, C. S. (ed.) (1978). *Adaptive Environmental Assessment and Management*. Chichester, UK: John Wiley.

Kadlec, R. and Knight, R. (1996). *Treatment Wetlands*. Boca Raton, FL: Lewis Publishers.

Kaswadji, R. F., Gosselink, J. G., and Turner, R. E. (1990). Estimation of primary production using five different methods in a *Spartina alterniflora* salt marsh. *Wetlands Ecology and Management*, **1**, 57–64.

Keddy, P. A. (1983). Freshwater wetlands human-induced changes: indirect effects must also be considered. *Environmental Management*, **4**, 299–302.

(1991). Biological monitoring and ecological prediction: from nature reserve management to national state of environment indicators. In *Biological Monitoring for Conservation*, ed. F. B. Goldsmith, London: Chapman and Hall.

(1992). Assembly and response rules: two goals for predictive community ecology. *Journal of Vegetation Science*, **3**, 157–64.

(1999). Wetland restoration: the potential for assembly rules in the service of conservation. *Wetlands*, **19**, 716–32.

(2000). *Wetland Ecology: Principles and Conservation*. Cambridge, UK: Cambridge University Press.

Keddy, P. and Fraser, L. H. (2000). Four general principles for the management and conservation of wetlands in large lakes: the role of water levels, nutrients, competitive hierarchies and centrifugal organization. *Lakes and Reservoirs: Research and Management*, **5**, 177–85.

Keddy, P. A., Lee, H. T., and Wisheu, I. C. (1993). Choosing indicators of ecosystem integrity: wetlands as a model system. In *Ecological Integrity and the Management of Ecosystems*, eds. S. Woodley, J. Kay, and G. Francis. Ottawa, Canada: St. Lucie Press.

Kelman, K. (1981). *Cost Benefit Analysis: an Ethical Critique*. Regulation (Jan.–Feb.). Washington, DC: American Enterprise Institute for Public Policy Research.

Kentula, M. E. (1996). Wetland restoration and creation. In *National Water Summary on Wetland Resources*, J. D. Fretwell, J. S. Williams, and P. J. Redman. US Geological Survey Water-Supply Paper 2425, pp. 87–92.

Matthews, E. and Fung, I. (1987). Methane emissions from natural wetlands: global distribution, area, and environmental characteristics of sources. *Global Biogeochemical Cycles*, **1**, 61–86

Metcalf & Eddy Inc. (1979). *Wastewater Engineering: Treatment Disposal Reuse*, revised by G. Tchobanoglous. New York: McGraw-Hill.

Mitsch, W. J. and Gosselink, J. G. (1993). *Wetlands*, 2nd edn. New York: John Wiley.
(2000). *Wetlands*, 3rd edn. New York: John Wiley.

Moore, D. R. J., Keddy, P. A., Gaudet, C. L., and Wisheu, I. C. (1989). Conservation of wetlands: do infertile wetlands deserve a higher priority? *Biological Conservation*, **47**, 203–17.

Moser, M., Prentice, C., and Frazier, S. (1996). A global overview of wetland loss and degradation. In *Proceedings of the Sixth Meeting of the Conference of Contracting Parties of the Ramsar Convention*, vol. 10, *March 19–27, 1996, Brisbane, Australia*. Gland, Switzerland: Ramsar Convention Bureau.

Mueller-Dombois, D. and Ellenberg, H. (1974). *Aims and Methods of Vegetation Ecology.* New York: John Wiley.

Novotny, V. (1989). *Karl Imhoff's Handbook of Urban Drainage and Wastewater Disposal.* New York: John Wiley.

Peckarsky, B. L. and Dodson, S. I. (1980). An experimental analysis of biological factors contributing to stream community structure. *Ecology*, **61**, 1283–90.

Pianka, E. R. (1980). Guild structure in desert lizards. *Oikos*, **35**, 194–201.

Population Reference Bureau (1994). Washington, DC: Population Reference Bureau.

Postel, S. (1992). *Last Oasis: Facing Water Scarcity.* New York: Norton.

Postel, S. L., Daily, G. C., and Ehrlich, P. R. (1996). Human appropriation of renewable fresh water. *Science*, **271**, 785–8.

Prentice, I. C., Cramer, W., Harrison, S. P. *et al.* (1992). A global biome model based on plant physiology and dominance, soil properties and climate. *Journal of Biogeography*, **19**, 117–34.

Severinghaus, W. D. (1981). Guild theory development as a mechanism for assessing environmental impact. *Environmental Management*, **5**, 187–90.

Simberloff, D. and Dayan, T. (1991). The guild concept and the structure of ecological communities. *Annual Review of Ecology and Systematics*, **22**, 115–43.

US Department of the Interior, Bureau of Reclamation. http://www.usbr.gov/dataweb/dams/index.html (accessed February, 2005).

Votteler, T. H. and Muir, T. A. (1996). Wetland protection legislation. In: *National Water Summary on Wetland Resources*, eds. J. D. Fretwell, J. S. Williams, and P. J. Redman. US Geological Survey Water-Supply Paper 2425, pp. 49–56.

Ward, B. (1966). *Spaceship Earth.* New York: Columbia University Press.

WCD (World Commission on Dams) (2000). *Dams and Development: a New Framework for Decision-Making.* The Report of the World Commission on Dams. London: Earthscan Publications Ltd.

Weiher, E. and Keddy, P. A. (1995). The assembly of experimental wetland plant communities. *Oikos*, **73**, 323–35.

Westoby, M. D., Falster, S., Moles, A. T., Vesk, P. A., and Wright, I. J. (2002). Plant ecological strategies: some leading dimensions of variation between species. *Annual Review of Ecology and Systematics*, **33**, 125–59.

Wigley, T. M. L. and Raper, S. C. B. (2001). Interpretation of high projections for global-mean warming. *Science*, **293**, 451–4.

Wilson, H. M. and Roxsburgh, S. H. (1994). A demonstration of guild based assembly rules for a plant community, and determination of intrinsic guilds. *Oikos*, **69**, 267–76.

Wisheu, I. C. and Keddy, P. A. (1992). Competition and centrifugal organization of plant communities: theory and tests. *Journal of Vegetation Science*, **3**, 147–56.

Woo, I. and Zedler, J. B. (2002). Can nutrients alone shift a sedge meadow towards dominance by the invasive *Typha* × *glauca*? *Wetlands*, **22**, 509–21.

Woodley, S., Kay, J., and Francis, G. (1993). *Ecological Integrity and the Management of Ecosystems*. Ottawa, Canada: St. Lucie Press.

Woodward, F. I., Smith, T. M., and Emanuel, W. R. (1995). A global land primary productivity and phytogeography model. *Global Biogeochemical Cycles*, **9**, 471–90.

World Commission on Dams.
    http://www.dams.org/kbase/survey/ (accessed February, 2005).

World Health Organization (WHO) and UNICEF. (2000). Global Water Supply and Sanitation Assessment 2000 Report.

WRI (World Resources Institute) (2000). *World Resources 2000–01*. Washington, DC: WRI.

Index

Franklin Pierce University

00180351

DATE DUE

GAYLORD   PRINTED IN U.S.A.

LaVergne, TN USA
29 October 2009

162372LV00003B/1/P

9 780521 111362